# A Certain Arrogance

# A CERTAIN ARROGANCE

❖

U.S. Intelligence's Manipulation of Religious Groups
and Individuals in Two World Wars and the Cold War,
and the Sacrificing of Lee Harvey Oswald

## George Michael Evica

To order additional copies of this book, contact:
Xlibris Corporation
1-888-795-4274
www.Xlibris.com
Orders@Xlibris.com
20082

# CONTENTS

# Reading Guidelines, Thanks, And Dedication

The Epilogue may be the most useful place to begin this study of the abuse of religious individuals and groups by U.S. intelligence through two World Wars and the Cold War and the sacrificing of Lee Harvey Oswald. The endnotes for the prologue, the eight essays, and the epilogue are organic constituents of the book's argument and are extended analyses and documentation of the book's central thesis: see, for example, the endnotes' review of the families of Ruth and Michael Paine and their major U.S. government and intelligence connections. I strongly recommend the reader review each section's endnotes after having read that particular section. The endnotes exhibit obvious and, I hope, useful repetitions of citations (instead of the usual Latin abbreviations); occasionally a single "Same" is given as a citation.

I thank: Ernest Cassara, former officer of Albert Schweitzer College; Professor Emeritus Paul Lacey; the clergy of all denominations who have given witness to the abuses of U.S. intelligence and who requested anonymity; the West Hartford Main Library and its departments of Reference and Interlibrary Loan; the University of Hartford Library and its departments of Reference and Interlibrary Loan; Tom Jones and Deborah Conway of JFKLANCER; the Rev. Leon Hopper, former director of Liberal Religious Youth; the Unitarian/Universalist Association in Boston; the Unitarian Service Committee in Cambridge, Massachusetts; Frances O'Donnell, Archivist of the Andover-Harvard Theological Library, Harvard Divinity School; Ghanda Di Figlia, now at Harvard University, for her research, writing, and irreplaceable help; Alycia Brierley Evica for her patience and faith; and Charles Robert Drago for his wit, intelligence, and enduring friendship.

With love and great respect, this work is dedicated to the life and memory of

Mary Ferrell

i

# Introduction

## To Withdraw From the Tumult of Cemeteries
## by Charles R. Drago

*Human kind*
*Cannot bear very much reality.*
T.S. Eliot, "Burnt Norton," Four Quartets

Let me be clear from the outset: *A Certain Arrogance* is no more "about" the assassination of John F. Kennedy than cancer surgery is "about" the tumor.

George Michael Evica, one of the preeminent prosectors of the malignant growth that disfigured the American body politic on November 22, 1963, for decades has focused his intellect and intuition on the search for a cure for the underlying disease. In the course of forty years of research, analysis, writing, broadcasting, and teaching, he has followed its devastating metastasis from the vital organs of government to the extremities of business, culture, and religion. All the while he has cut away necrotic tissue and struggled valiantly, in the company of a surgical team as distinguished as it is obscure, to keep the patient alive.

Professor Evica, author of *And We Are All Mortal: New Evidence And Analysis In* The *Assassination Of John F. Kennedy,* published in 1975 by the University of Hartford, can be numbered among the most honored of the so-called second generation of Kennedy assassination researchers. Their labors to refine, reinforce, and draw attention to the discoveries of their predecessors validate this direct statement of fact: Anyone with reasonable access to the evidence in the homicide of John F. Kennedy who does not conclude that the act was the consequence of a criminal conspiracy is cognitively impaired and/or complicit in the crime.

Conspiracy in the Kennedy killing is as well-established an historical truth as is the Holocaust. Further, those in a position to know this truth who nonetheless choose to deny it in service to the darkest political and cultural agendas are morally akin to Holocaust deniers.

*A Certain Arrogance* stands as Professor Evica's response to the unavoidable question: How do we define and effect justice in the wake of the world-historic tragedy in Dallas? Clearly he understands that, at this late date, being content merely to identify and, if possible, prosecute the conspiracy's facilitators and mechanics would amount to hollow acts of vengeance. Cleaning and closing the wound while leaving the disease to spread is simply not an option.

With the nobility of knowledge comes obligation: How to utilize all that has been learned to heal and immunize the long-suffering victims of the malady of which the assassination of John F. Kennedy is but the most widely appreciated and putrescent manifestation?

The method by which Professor Evica honors his *noblesse oblige* is hardly novel. Like many other researchers, he has chosen to explore an aspect of the complex life of the lead character in the assassination drama, Lee Harvey Oswald. To carry the cancer metaphor forward: Think of the accused killer as a tumor cell whose sojourn through the host organism in theory can be traced back to its source.

Oswald's movements, however, are not easily discerned. False trails and feints abound. Promising clues have been obscured by a host of ham-handed interlopers and sinister obfuscators.

Rather than traverse well-worn pathways, Professor Evica has chosen to follow one of the few remaining under-examined passages of an otherwise over-mapped life. His uniquely painstaking investigation of Oswald's involvement with Albert Schweitzer College (hereinafter ASC), including the processes and implications of his application, acceptance, and nonattendance, has led both to major discoveries and to significant refinements of previously developed hypotheses.

In the former category our attention is drawn to what Professor Evica terms "one of U.S. intelligence's last important secrets". the involvement by the Central Intelligence Agency and psychological operations (psyops) in student and youth organizations—especially those with religious affiliations.

The U. S. government's faith-based initiatives, it seems, did not originate with George W. Bush's alleged administration.

As he meticulously follows Oswald's ASC paper trail, the author is led not toward the Swiss campus, but rather into brick walls and empty rooms. A prime example: Oswald applied to the college on March 19, 1959. Less than two months later, when the pastor of the First Unitarian Church of Providence, Rhode Island submitted to Switzerland a list of American student applicants, Oswald' s name was included.

Today that document, a critically important piece of evidence in the investigation of the crime of the century, does not exist in any official repository—even though a copy, or perhaps even the original, was in the Providence ASC file seized by the FBI after the assassination. This troubling absence, within a broader context fully substantiated in *A Certain Arrogance,* inevitably leads the author to conclude that Oswald's application to ASC is "a still-protected American intelligence operation."

I do not wish to spoil the bittersweet joy of discovery to be experienced as you accompany Professor Evica on his journey through unknown territory. Yet the methodology and ultimate value of *A Certain Arrogance* as a "whodunit" (as opposed to the "howdunit" nature of the overwhelming majority of JFK assassination-related volumes) must be fully appreciated. To discover the identities of Oswald 's early manipulators is to be drawn into the core of the disease in all of its terrible scope. And so, thanks to the Evica investigation of the ASC episode, we are left with a preliminary, shattering conclusion regarding the "who" we seek.

> "Whoever directed the Oswald [assassination] Game was thoroughly knowledgeable about both the OSS 's and CIA's counterintelligence manipulation of Quakers, Unitarians, Lutherans, Dutch Reformed clerics and World Council of Churches officials as intelligence and espionage contacts, assets, and informants."

From the mountains and snowfields and quaint villages of Switzerland, Professor Evica escorts us through a darker, more mysterious inner landscape. Examination of what he neatly summarizes as "U.S. covert intelligence operating under humanitarian cover" leads to a confrontation with psychological operations—*psyops* and its *propaganda, disinjormation,* and *morale operations* alter egos.

Professor Evica was the first to understand the Kennedy assassination and other intelligence operations as theatrical productions, replete with all the essential elements of drama—including shameless manipulation of audiences' minds and emotions. Within these pages he further supports and refines this hypothesis.

> "Psychological manipulation of individuals and groups, whatever the procedure may have been called in the 18th and 19 centuries, drew upon discoveries in anatomy, mesmerism, hypnotism, counseling, studies in hysteria, rhetorical theory, psychoanalysis, advertising, behavior modification, and psychiatry. In the same periods, the literary forms of irony, satire, and comedy and the less reputable verbal arts of slander, libel, and manufactured lies were applied."

Before we are tempted to argue that the realities of war often require an honorable combatant to assume, for a limited period and with noble intent, the darker strategies of an evil foe, Professor Evica reminds us that, "Most of these genres and strategies were enlisted in the service of social class and political power." He then identifies the likely director of the aforereferenced Oswald Game.

Prepare to make the acquaintance of C. D. Jackson, "the psyops expert who organized and ran General Dwight David Eisenhower's Psychological Warfare Division at SHAEF . . . an official of the Office of War Information . . . [and] a veteran of the North African campaign."

Jackson's career and impact upon 20th century American history, heretofore marginally understood at best (he is widely known to be the Time-Life editor who purchased the Zapruder film), are major focuses of *A Certain Arrogance.* Nowhere is both the validity of Albert Einstein's observation that "the distinction between past, present and future is only a stubbornly persistent illusion," and the contemporary relevance of Professor Evica's discoveries more clearly underscored than in the author's exposition of the Jackson *oeuvre.* In particular we are drawn to the discussion of how mass media early on was identified as a key weapon in the mind control arsenal.

In a 1946 letter to Jackson, General Robert McClure, at one time Eisenhower's chief of intelligence for the European theater, boasts to his civilian psyops counterpart of the scope of their manipulation.

> "We now control 37 newspapers, 6 radio stations, 314 theaters, 642 movies, 101 magazines, 237 book publishers, 7,384 book dealers and printers, and conduct about 15 public opinion surveys a month, as well as publish one newspaper with 1,500,000 circulation . . . run the AP of Germany, and operate 20 library centers."

Fairness and balance, it seems, did not originate with the Fox Network's alleged news division.

Haunting the pages of *A Certain Arrogance,* in the company of the shades of John F. Kennedy and Lee Harvey Oswald, is a realization so menacing in its assault on convention as to provoke a reflexive shielding of our eyes from its searing light. Yet the author cannot spare us the psychic pain that is the unavoidable byproduct of his scholarship, insofar as such suffering remains the *sine qua non* for the eradication of our common malady and the return to robust good health.

Orbiting low around the core of the disease, Professor Evica has discovered "a treasonous cabal of hard-line American and Soviet intelligence agents whose masters were above Cold War differences."

Accordingly, we are left with no choice but to embrace a new paradigm of world power.

Professor Evica reveals the universally accepted vertical, East v. West Cold War confrontation to have been a sophistic construct*, illusory in its advertised *raison d'etre*, all too real in its bloody consequences—created by the powerful yet outnumbered manipulators of perception to protect what they recognized as an all too fragile reality. The true division of power, he teaches us, then as now is drawn on a horizontal axis.

Envision the earth so bifurcated, with the line drawn not at the equator, but rather at the Arctic Circle. Above the line are the powerful few, the "haves;" below the line, in vastly superior numbers, are the powerless, the "have-nots."

Can we bear so much reality?

While contemplating the moral implications of Professor Evica' s research, I was reminded of how Francis Ford Coppola struggled to find the right thematic hook on which to hang the plot of "The Godfather, Part Ill." It is said that he considered and ultimately rejected the Kennedy assassination as the most cinematically viable expression of systemic evil in full flower. Instead—perhaps wisely, perhaps not he opted to dramatize the Vatican Bank scandal.

Upon initial examination, the conjoined stories of the looting of the *Banco Ambrosiano,* the perfidy of Roberto Calvi and P2, the death of John Paul I, and the corruption of the Roman Catholic Church at its highest levels present as the cellular components of yet another tumor, the most horrific manifestation imaginable of the disease being probed by Professor Evica. We are incredulous. We are outraged.

Then reason returns.

The manipulation of religious institutions by elements of the deep political structure for unholy purposes should provoke neither surprise nor anger. Religion is politics by other means. The assault on Albert Schweitzer, however, is another story.

"The ethical spirit . . . must be awakened anew," Dr. Schweitzer instructed at the height of the Cold War. The defiling of the name and the perversion of the mission of that saintly man no doubt provoked sweet satisfaction within the breasts of those for whom a worldview informed by ethics was anathema.

So what of justice? Have we any reason to expect the guilty to be punished, the disease to be eradicated? The novelist Jim Harrison:

---

\*    Updated for contemporary use; see "clash of cultures," "terrorists v. free peoples," *et al.*

"People finally don't have much affection for questions, especially one so leprous as the apparent lack of a fair system of rewards and punishments on earth . . . We would like to think that the whole starry universe would curdle . . . the conjunctions of Orion twisted askew, the arms of the Southern Cross drooping. Of course not: immutable is immutable and everyone in his own private manner dashes his brains against the longsuffering question that is so luminously obvious. Even gods aren't exempt: note Jesus' howl of despair as he stepped rather tentatively into eternity."

It is for us to deliver justice and heal ourselves, to muster the courage to ask questions and the strength to endure answers.

Within the pages of *A Certain Arrogance,* George Michael Evica leads by example.

# Prologue

## "This Dirty Rumor"[1]

The Warren Commission's first executive session was quickly followed by (at least) two later sessions concerned with a threatening "dirty rumor": that Lee Harvey Oswald had been a paid asset, an "informer," in fact, for the FBI. Afterward, having once been burned dealing with this topic, the Commission (or at least its chair Chief Justice Earl Warren) clearly intended to avoid any future backdraft as the Commission faced four months of testimony often touching on that same "dirty rumor."

The fifth volume[2] of the Warren Commission's twenty-six volumes of support materials is central to the topic of Oswald's possible participation in U.S. intelligence activities, containing a surprisingly rich collection of relevant testimony. In Washington, Dallas, and elsewhere, from May 6th, 1964, through September 6th, 1964, the Commission listened to representatives of the FBI, including J. Edgar Hoover; the U.S. Army (on wound ballistics); the CIA, including its Director and its Deputy Director for Plans; Texas law enforcement officers on the state, county, and city levels; the U.S. State Department, including the Secretary of State; the Secret Service, including its Chief, James J. Rowley; and the Treasury Department, including Treasury Secretary C. Douglas Dillon. The Commission also took testimony from Mark Lane, asked by Oswald's mother to represent the accused assassin; from the President of the United States, Lyndon Baines Johnson and his wife; and from several prominent residents of Dallas, including Marina Oswald and Jack Ruby.

### The Belmont Ploy

First on this distinguished list of witnesses was Alan Belmont Assistant Director of the FBI, who testified in Washington on May 6th, 1964.[3]

After some preliminary questions and comments, Commission member Allan Dulles began the more serious inquiry, asking Belmont about Teletype operations connecting FBI offices; Dulles' specific example was, appropriately for an Oswald focus, the link between the New Orleans and Dallas Bureau offices.[4]

Commission member John J. McCloy, also adopting an Oswald focus, asked about U.S. "defections" to the Soviet Union.[5] Both McCloy and Dulles questioned whether the so-called Oswald file had been "closed" or "open."[6] Within a half-hour of Alan Belmont being sworn in, two Commission members (for whatever their reasons) had begun to explore important issues in the Oswald "dirty rumor" story.

Samuel A. Stern, Warren Commission staff assistant counsel, referred to an April 6th, 1964, FBI letter prepared and reviewed by Belmont (signed by FBI Director Hoover) and sent to J. Lee Rankin, Chief Counsel of the Warren Commission.[7] Though its contents were not given at that moment in Belmont's testimony, the letter did indeed summarize (according to Belmont) the FBI's relationship with Lee Harvey Oswald.[8] The letter, dated May 4th, 1964, reportedly answered "a number of questions which the Commission posed to the FBI."[9] The communication, a response to a meeting on May 4th, 1964, between Warren Commission staff members and Belmont, briefly described 69 items contained in the FBI's Oswald file.[10] Earlier, the Warren Commission had written a letter to the FBI (dated March 26th, 1964) inquiring about the FBI's knowledge of Lee Harvey Oswald before November 22nd, 1963; the Bureau's replies to the Commission's thirty questions posed by the Commission's staff were delivered in an FBI letter (dated April 6th, 1964) with a separate cover letter signed by Director Hoover. Many of the Warren Commission's questions asked for information bearing directly on the Oswald-as-agent question.[11]

Earlier in the session, Commission staff assistant counsel Stern had established the Commission's primary focus: Lee Harvey Oswald. Belmont had commented: "As the individual in charge of all investigative operations, [I am responsible for] the Lee Harvey Oswald investigation . . . , the same as any other investigative case in the Bureau."[12]

Stern soon arrived at the hearing's crucial point: Belmont's "examination of the investigation . . . of the nature of the FBI interest in Oswald."[13] Clearly, Stern wished to explore through Belmont the key issue of Oswald's rumored intelligence links. But Warren interrupted Stern twice[14], obviously attempting to shut off Stern early in the session.[15] In this exchange (and later exchanges involving Warren's own Chief Counsel Rankin), the Warren Commission counsel (Rankin and Stern) and Earl Warren were demonstrating quite different agendas relative to Lee Harvey Oswald and U.S. intelligence.

But despite Warren's objections, Stern persisted in exploring the Oswald-as-agent theme, querying Belmont about both the FBI's domestic intelligence and identification divisions, including questions concerning defection, Oswald's Marine fingerprints, Oswald's correspondence, and the Albert Schweitzer College puzzle.[16] Clearly, Stern was intent on examining the topic of false identity, a critical counterintelligence area of great interest to both the CIA and the FBI. Stern elicited from Belmont that the FBI had "set up" certain "connections with the State Department passport file" on Oswald's (undefined) "activities" and on Oswald's "dealing with the [U.S.] Embassy in Moscow"[17], but neither Stern nor any Commission member (nor, later, any Commission counsel) apparently pursued that crucial topic.

Belmont asserted that the FBI had no interest in Oswald when the Marine defector returned from the Soviet Union[18]; according to Belmont, Oswald was "not known" to be connected to FBI "sources" in New Orleans.[19]

Despite Warren's interruptions and objections, Stern (on behalf of Rankin and his Commission counsel and staff) had at least been able to begin exploring hints of Oswald's possible American intelligence connections.

## The FBI "HQ" Oswald File

Stern then introduced the Belmont summary of the "HQ" FBI on Oswald, its cover letter to Rankin dated May 4th, 1964, entered into the Commission's evidence as CE 834.[20] Stern established that Belmont, as he sat before the Commission, at that moment was in possession of Oswald's actual FBI file.[21]

Stern asked Belmont about "materials in that [Oswald] file . . . for security reasons you would prefer not to disclose . . . ."[22] Belmont responded by defining the file's "security" materials: "The file contains the identity of some of our informants in subversive movements." Commissioners Warren, McCloy, and Dulles and counsels Stern and Rankin (at least) must have understood the FBI's "informants in subversive movements"[23] in the so-called Oswald file had to include informants in New Orleans and (possibly) Dallas who had operated as double agents inside pro-Castro organizations and whose identities might have led directly to evidence establishing Oswald as a U.S. intelligence agent or asset. Stern therefore cautioned Belmont: "I think that is enough, Mr. Belmont, on that."[24]

But it was not "enough" for Commissioner McCloy[25], whose query of Belmont elicited a response from Warren who attempted to cut off any further questioning of Belmont on security "matters" in the FBI's Oswald file.[26] Though he complimented Warren on his security-conscious behavior, Belmont indicated that J. Edgar Hoover had insisted Belmont be of "utmost help" to the Commission.[27]

Belmont's testimony strongly suggested that 1. the FBI (through Belmont) and Chief Justice Earl Warren had earlier scripted the FBI's offer of the so-called Oswald file to the Warren Commission so that Warren could reject it on "security" grounds, but that 2. Commission Counsels Stern and Rankin, unaware of this FBI-Warren accommodation, were working against Warren in order to accept the FBI's seeming offer of the file.

After Stern elicited from Belmont that the FBI file was "available to the Commission"[28], Warren countered by establishing the "security matter" involving identified FBI informers was contained in the allegedly complete file before them.[29] Belmont verified that fact: "This file is as it is maintained at the Bureau with all information in it."[30] Justice Warren responded: "With ALL information in it?"[31] Belmont answered: "Yes sir; THIS [the file either in Belmont's hands or on the table in front of him] is the actual file."[32] Warren commented: "I see."[33]

Chief Counsel Rankin intervened, asking Belmont if he would indeed leave that actual file in the Commission's possession so "any of the Commissioners [could] . . . examine it personally."[34]

Obviously, Rankin intended to secure the purported entire FBI Oswald dossier for his Commission staff.

Belmont agreed to leave the file.[35]

But Warren immediately interrupted with a confused statement about non-existent "conditions" and not wanting "information that involves our security."[36] How the identity of FBI informants in New Orleans or Dallas might compromise the security of the United States ("our security") was never made clear.

Warren then pushed his argument further, rejecting the possession (and therefore the assumed use) of ANY sensitive intelligence documents[37], opting for Belmont's vocal testimony alone. Rejecting a reportedly full intelligence file (on the accused assassin) and relying solely on the sworn statements of an intelligence officer therefore helped establish the Warren Commission's antipathy toward ANY documentation of Oswald's suspected intelligence links.

Warren concluded his argument with a muddled statement in favor of "open" discussion as opposed to reading and talking about sensitive documents "in privacy."[38]

Rankin was now apparently willing to give up almost all of his ground if only to be allowed to examine the FBI file; he promised that "the [Commission] staff will not examine it,"[39] a statement quite obviously directed at Warren rather than Belmont. But Warren countered that to read the FBI file was "one thing" (whatever that meant), but for him, asking Belmont questions about his summary of the Oswald FBI file was quite enough.[40] Finally, Warren defined his bottom-line position: "I really would prefer not to have a secret file . . . that contains [security] matters of that kind in our possession."[41]

Why had no one suggested a "sanitized" file?

## The "Dirty Rumor"

Rankin now had little leverage except to air the vexing "dirty rumor" directly, a topic he strongly hinted at in his final major argument for accepting the FBI's offer of the "HQ" Oswald file. Though his impromptu statement was garbled, Rankin obviously wanted the FBI Oswald file available so that the Warren Commission could, as he said, "be satisfied that nothing was withheld for it [the Commission] in regard to this particular question[: the 'dirty rumor']. That was the purpose of the inquiry."[42] Rankin's two phrases, "this particular question" and "the purpose of the inquiry," clearly pointed to the Commission's continuing problem: the "rumor" of Oswald's Bureau link.

Allan Dulles accepted Warren's lead, but McCloy, apparently looking directly at a copy of the actual FBI file, interfered, indicating that Belmont's "summary" was disturbingly not "a complete description" of the file's contents as McCloy examined it.[43]

Warren again tried to head off objections[44], but Rankin counterattacked, articulating the Warren Commission's strongest argument for independent analysis of intelligence files, concluding: "we did want the [Warren Commission] record in such condition that the Commission could say in its report, 'We have seen everything that they have.' I think [this file] . . . is important to the case."[45]

Indeed, Commissioner McCloy remained dubious, suggesting that the Commission might miss "the full impact of all the narrative" in the file's Bureau reports on Oswald.[46] Both Belmont and Warren then argued with McCloy, telling him that the Commission already had possession of the particular FBI reports to which he referred.[47] But why not let McCloy look at the reports, wherever they were? What difference did some duplication make? This Belmont/Warren response to McCloy was additional evidence of an earlier agreement by Belmont and Warren to script the Belmont offer of the "HQ" file that would be followed by Warren's rejection of the file.

Warren was, in fact, blocking any curious Commissioner from reading through actual files and documents, whether those materials were in the possession of the Commission's staff or not. For Warren, the question seemed to be: Where would it all end?

Rankin still persisted, trying to emphasize his (and Stern's) argument: that the Warren Commission would be in possession of "everything . . . the FBI had [on Oswald] . . . : this is their total file . . . so that . . . nothing [would be] withheld from you as far as the FBI is concerned. That is . . . what we [the staff counsel] are trying to develop this morning . . . ."[48] Obviously the staff understood: if the so-called Oswald HQ file was rejected, the Commission could never assert that "nothing" had been "withheld."

Former CIA Director Allan Dulles again supported Warren, speaking to a separate issue involving the staff, allowing Warren to close with his argument against sharing files with non-government investigators: "the same people who would demand that we see everything of this kind would also demand that they be entitled to see it, and [because] it is security matters [,] we can't let them see it. It has to go back to the FBI without their [those demanding people's] scrutiny."[49] Warren's warning concerning people who would argue for openness in the JFK assassination inquiry was clearly anticipatory.

But Commissioner McCloy still persisted in opposing Warren, apparently examining Belmont's file summary on telegrams from "the Embassy" and "Mexico," key issues relevant to both the so-called Second Oswald mystery and CIA manipulation of the "Oswald" in Mexico story.[50] Warren, however, triumphed, and Stern and Warren finally moved to admit only the Belmont file "summary"[51] into the official record.[52] For one last time, Warren emphasized his point with Belmont: "There are no security matter[s] in this [Belmont summary]?[53]

Belmont then continued his testimony, asserting that Oswald was neither an agent of nor an informant for the FBI[54], speaking at length but to no productive purpose about the FBI, the Secret Service, cooperation, and presidential security; about Ruby and Communism; and, at least for the FBI, about minor matters.[55]

On behalf of the Warren Commission, its Chairperson Chief Justice Earl Warren had successfully refused accepting the alleged FBI file on Lee Harvey Oswald, ultimately relying on the unsupported statements of US intelligence officers that Lee Harvey Oswald was not an agent or asset of the American intelligence community. Later, circumstantial evidence and some of the CIA's Oswald files would be made available to the House Select Committee on Assassinations, strongly supporting the argument Oswald may either have thought he was a US intelligence agent or had been, indeed, an agent or asset of any of several US intelligence services.

Ably assisted by Alan Belmont, Assistant Director of the FBI, Chief Justice Earl Warren, the head of President Johnson's assassination commission, had successfully refused the so-called "Headquarters" file of the Federal Bureau of Investigation on Lee Harvey Oswald. Though transparently a ploy, the offer of the file raised significant issues, especially as Belmont's testimony is closely examined. For the Warren Commission, John McCloy seemed genuinely interested in exploring the "dirty rumor"; Stern and Rankin, representing the Commission's staff, were obviously dedicated to opening up the topic; and Allan Dulles made some shuffling noises with his Agency shoes but then supported Warren's rejection of the Bureau file

## Was the FBI Monitoring Oswald's Mail?

Standing against Belmont's testimony were two major questions that were, in fact, one, since they related directly to the "dirty rumor": was the FBI monitoring Oswald's mail and, if so, did the Bureau then know that a mail-order rifle was being delivered to Oswald's post office box? After four years of research and analysis, my conclusions still remain: the FBI was indeed opening Oswald's first-class mail, and the Bureau was indeed aware that the Carcano was arriving in his mail. But those conclusions also pointed directly to the FBI itself manipulating the mails (and Oswald) in a pre-assassination spy game. If so, then Sylvia Meagher's conclusion was correct: the FBI had prior knowledge of the mail-order weapon, most probably because the FBI itself had effected both its purchase and its delivery to the post office box of Lee Harvey Oswald, the FBI's asset.

## Was Albert Schweitzer College the Key?

The Albert Schweitzer College "puzzle" was the other most important area Belmont had spoken to briefly. If Oswald had been an asset or agent of some U.S. intelligence agency, even if he had only been manipulated by that agency, then the weird "Oswald Misses All His College Classes" Comedy Hour winding up in Moscow would make some sense, especially after Oswald became the object of an FBI False Identity/Illegals investigation.

If Chief Justice Warren had accepted the FBI "HQ" file on Oswald from Belmont (as it was apparently being offered to him), the exposure of the Bureau's mail intercept program directed at Oswald and his tragi-comic Albert Schweitzer College documents story could have delivered the investigation of the death of John F. Kennedy to the truth.

# Essay One

# Lee Harvey Oswald: Missing From Switzerland

It was February, 1960.

The FBI agent[1] stared at the woman sitting before him. Just a moment before, her hands were crossed[2], their palms upward.[3] Now they were flying. Finally they alighted on her lap, palms facing upward again. She examined them, as she were reading some arcane communication in their lines and grooves.[4]

She thought he had said his name was "Fannan."[5]

The translucent skin of her round and almost unlined face[6] flushed briefly. Her correspondence with the Soviet Union was stacked on the small table next to her: the first, the returned $20 money order with her son's scribbled, hasty note rejecting the order as useless; the second, returned unopened, its $20 bill still inside; the third, again returned and unopened, its Foreign Money Transfer for $25 inside.[7]

The agent carefully surveyed her corseted, rectangular body[8] for some sign of stress. Her graying hair, almost white[9], had somehow begun to lift slightly, as if disturbed by a breeze blowing through her Fort Worth home.

For such a stout lady, she seemed formed of very small bones.[10]

"You understand, don't you?" she asked him.

He was passive. The Bureau had already intercepted her mail to the Soviet Union.[11] Her foreign money transfer to Lee had been taken seriously by the Bureau's New York field office.[12]

"Lee ending up in Russia, my letter unopened and returned. And you know, he took his birth certificate with him."[13]

The agent stiffened. He was about to blurt out a question, then he caught himself, relaxed, and remained silent.

"My son has . . . completely disappeared. His brother Robert hasn't heard from him since the middle of December.[14] I haven't heard from him since early January.[15] He's just . . . gone."

The agent knew she was Lee's one living parent.[16] He spoke carefully.

"It doesn't look good, ma'm. It looks like your son doesn't WANT to be found."[17]

"Please help me," she implored.[18]

He smiled.

"Of course. I'd say you ought to write directly to the Secretary of State, you know, at the State Department in Washington? And to Sam Rayburn and Jim Wright, your representatives? Ask all of them to assist you in any way possible."[19]

Her hands fluttered again, then dropped to her lap.

He was pleased with his improvisation. It would seem helpful, but he hoped it would be a major deflection that kept Lee's mother and the Washington bureaucracy busy for a long time.[20]

"I will, I will," she promised.

Long after the agent left, the light fading in Marguerite's clear Texas sky, she sat and brooded over the mail she'd sent to her son at his Metropole Hotel address in Moscow. Now he was living somewhere else in that vast and distant Soviet Union, refusing to make contact.

All the envelopes had been addressed to him in her careful, left-handed script.

She loved her strange and wonderful Lee, though she often did not understand him. And she had begun to entertain a disturbing possibility: that her young son was some sort of secret agent for the American government.[21]

## Missing From Albert Schweitzer College

Mrs. Oswald had waited. Now it was April, 1960. She thought Lee was supposed to have gone to that oddly-named college in Switzerland for its Fall, 1959, session.[22] But two months after her FBI visitor had been so helpful, after weeks and weeks of frustrating correspondence, Marguerite Oswald received some very bad news. Lee, who according to the letter was expected at the Swiss Albert Schweitzer College[23] for the Spring Trimester, had neither made an appearance nor informed the college he would not be attending.[24]

Her precious letters were scattered at her feet. The college correspondence slipped from her fingers to the floor, joining them. Her son, Lee Harvey Oswald, was missing from Switzerland.

According to one knowledgeable CIA source, "Mail from Soviet agents in the United States would not have been sent directly to Moscow . . ."[25] but through "neutral countries such as Switzerland . . . ."[26] The same procedure would have been followed for clandestine mail from Moscow that was ultimately destined for the States. During the Cold War, Switzerland had been a postal transit for major espionage message exchanges, but its use by American intelligence had dated back to the first World War.

Switzerland as the most strategic "neutral" country fulfilled its valuable mail drop function through World War II, when espionage chief Allen Dulles, then the director of the Office of Strategic Services in Bern, Switzerland[27], controlled an intelligence network inside the country of Swiss civilians, Swiss military personnel, and American, British, and German agents, including doubled operatives out of Nazi intelligence.[28] From his Swiss base, Allan Dulles operated a European-wide spy network in Switzerland, France, Germany, Hungary, Italy, and Yugoslavia.[29]

Switzerland, covert operations, and mail intercepts were all significant elements of Lee Harvey Oswald's paper trail, a trail made up almost entirely of his postal correspondence that was carefully monitored by American intelligence, including Oswald's letters to the American Embassy in Moscow and to his family in the United States. Soviet intelligence also monitored that paper trail when Oswald was in the Soviet Union and, later, when he communicated with individuals in the Soviet Union after he returned to the United States.[30]

## Oswald's Defective Marine Documents

Oswald's Swiss connection became of intense interest to the FBI, specifically embodied in the suspicions of both Alan Belmont, the Bureau's number three officer, and the FBI's Director himself, J. Edgar Hoover.

That interest began when active Marine Lee Harvey Oswald applied for his passport on September 4th, 1959 (and received it on September 10th, 1959, out of Los Angeles).[31] Though Oswald would later reportedly have possession of his birth certificate while in the Soviet Union, and though a birth certificate was the usual identification in applying for a passport, Oswald submitted a Department of Defense Identification Card.[32]

But except for several crucial and undeniable reasons, Lee Harvey Oswald should never have had a DOD ID card on September 4th, 1959. On September 11th, possibly, but NOT on September 4th, 1959.

The Department of Defense card was allegedly found in a wallet reportedly belonging to Oswald just after his arrest at the Texas Theatre on November 22nd, 1963.[33] The card clearly signaled to those who understood it that the bearer had some official connection to American intelligence,[34] and the Marine Corps admitted that it had issued that identity card to Lee Harvey Oswald before he was separated from the Corps.[35] But the practice of issuing that type of card to Marine reservists ended officially as of July, 1959.[36] According to a Marine Corps public affairs officer, Oswald was probably issued the card because he was about to fill a civilian position overseas needing a military identification card.[37]

Was Oswald scheduled to begin a new non-military job that would take him to Europe as an asset (or agent) of the CIA or as a civilian employee of the Office of Naval Intelligence?

A helpful Marine Corps public affairs officer did not explain how on September 4th, 1959, in Santa Ana, California, Oswald apparently had in his possession an "MCR/INACTIVE I.D. CARD #N4,271,617" that was "SUBMITTED" to the Clerk of the Superior Court, L.B. Wallace, as identification in Oswald's passport application when, officially, Oswald would not have been issued that card until September 11th, 1959, the day he was "released from Active Duty and Transferred to the Marine Corps Reserve (Inactive) . . . ."[38]

Did someone other than Oswald have possession of that card before he did?

And whose photo was on the DOD card? Its image was exactly the same as the one on the "fake" Selective Service card clumsily made out to "Hidell" and reportedly found in Oswald's post-assassination wallet.[39] That card called attention to itself rather blatantly, since its erasures were clearly visible. Besides, a Selective Service card did not have or even need a photo.

But the photo problem did not end there. The picture in question was a Warren Commission document (buried though it was) without either its DOD I.D. card or "Hidell" Selective Service card contexts. According to the FBI, the picture was "taken in Minsk,"[40] a photo on an American military identification card issued BEFORE Oswald went to the Soviet Union that was identical to a fake Selective Service card photo "taken in Minsk" after Oswald defected to the Soviet Union.

The actual card was not viewable at the National Archives: Sue McDonough in the Archives' Civil Reference Branch[41] reported the FBI had effectively destroyed the card through "extensive chemical forensic testing."[42]

The Oswald postal problem again presented itself. On the readable copy of the DOD card in the Dallas Police evidence files,[43] one postmark (and possibly two postmarks) could be read. The clearest postal stamp was October 23rd, 1963, but the card had 'officially' expired as of December 7th, 1962.[44] On the 'reverse' side of the card were the following instructions: "If found, drop in any mail box," and then, directed to any responsible postal employee, "Return to Department of Defense, Washington 25, D.C."[45] Was there any possible way to gain some sort of meaning from this postal noise?

The DOD card existed in someone's possession in Santa Ana, California, when it was used to obtain Oswald's passport in September, 1959. No official and verified record of that card then apparently existed until it was reportedly found on November 22nd, 1963, in a wallet allegedly the property of Lee Harvey Oswald.

But someone did have possession of that card after September, 1959, and either 'lost' the card sometime before October 23rd, 1963, or retained the card until October 23rd, 1963. Who possessed the card at that moment then made it part of the records of the American postal system no later than October 23rd, 1963, when it was delivered to the Department of Defense in Washington, D.C. Between October 23rd, 1963, and November 22nd, 1963, the card was apparently transferred from Washington, D.C. presumably to Lee Harvey Oswald (wherever he was), who then placed it in a wallet that was later reportedly discovered on his person in Dallas, Texas, on November 22nd, 1963.

But the card might have made one last but important appearance prior to November 22, 1963. Between August 21 and September 17, 1963, a "Navy ID" card was reportedly used for identification in Clinton, LA, during the CORE voter registration drive by someone who said he was Oswald (possibly Oswald himself) that might have been identical to Lee's Department of Defense card.[46]

Even if we assume that Oswald retained possession of the DOD card until October 23rd, 1963, when he either lost the card (that was subsequently mailed to the Department of Defense) or he himself dropped it into a mail box (for some still-to-be-discovered reason), how did Oswald regain possession of the card so that it made an appearance in his confiscated wallet on November 22nd, 1963?

Or did someone at the Department of Defense have possession of the card and assisted in having it placed in Oswald's wallet on November 22nd, 1963?

In fact, after its use in obtaining Oswald's 1959 passport, the DOD identification card had no other reported and verified function except to link Oswald to "Hidell" and the rifle reportedly discovered at the Texas School Book Depository.

The original DD Form 1173, "Uniformed Services and Identification and Privilege Card,"[47] had at the very least a strained reality. Oswald submitted his passport application on September 4th, 1959. His I.D. card (on its 'reverse' side) established it had been issued on September 11th, 1959, issued eight days after it had ALREADY been used as identification in Oswald's passport application[48] on the exact day Oswald had been placed on inactive status in the Corps. On that same day, September 11th, Oswald signed a statement pledging he would not "in any manner" give information that would negatively effect the national security of the United States "which I gained during my employment . . ." by the US Marine Corps.[49]

Could the Oswald DOD card have been issued to (inactive status Marine) Lee Harvey Oswald in, for example, the Soviet Union by American intelligence at the United States Embassy in Moscow?

Though an attractive alternative to entropy, the latter possibility is not available. The Department of Defense I.D. card was reportedly signed in Santa Ana, California by Marine 1st Lt. A.G. Ayers, Jr.,[50] who was responsible for developing Oswald's transfer to inactive status on September 11, 1959.[51] According to the available Marine record, Oswald became an inactive Marine reservist "by reason of hardship"; further, the Oswald I.D. card was issued according to standing Marine Corps procedures.[52]

But how did Marine Lt. Ayers sign both Oswald's I.D. card and Oswald's "Separation Section" document[53] and not immediately perceive the contradictions between Oswald's Marine hardship argument and his passport educational/tourist travel statements? For one important reason: Marine Officer Ayers did NOT sign the "Separation Section" document attached to Oswald's passport application.[54]

According to the Warren Commission's records, a Marine First Sergeant Stout actually signed for Ayers.[55] But this "Sergeant Stout" was, in fact, a paper fiction[56], a non-existent Marine sergeant who had signed for an apparently absent officer Ayers.

Oswald did have a close Marine buddy named Zack Stout; they had served together in Japan and the Philippines in 1957 and 1958.[57] But Stout did NOT serve with Oswald at El Toro in 1959, when the separation document was signed by the fictional Sergeant Stout.[58]

Combining an earlier real Marine "Stout" with a later fictional Marine "Stout" only added one more bizarre element to Oswald's paper trail.

And these major contradictions between Oswald's "separation" date and authorizing signature, his DOD I.D. card, and his passport application were apparently ignored both by American intelligence in 1959 and 1960 and, later, by the Warren Commission.

## Oswald's Strange Passport Application

How Oswald obtained his passport was suspicious enough. But the contents of the passport application itself were suspect. Oswald listed (given here in alphabetical order) Cuba, the Dominican Republic, England, Finland (specifically Turku, Finland), France, Germany, "Russia," and Switzerland as countries he intended to visit.[59] "Turku" referred to the University of Turku, which for some time had not been in the city of Turku but in Helsinki. The mistaken site of the university was still another instance of a series of repeated errors, of names, dates, places, and people in the Oswald paper record.

An itinerary so ambitious for someone with so few resources should have raised at least some American intelligence eyebrows. How could Oswald pay for such a tour? Was he being financed? If so, by whom? Was his trip an intelligence action? If so, it would not matter to the State Department, the FBI, the CIA, or the National Security Agency that a domestic-based counterintelligence operation (possibly run by the Office of Naval Intelligence) was involved. If the action was apparently secret, the excluded agencies would feel an immediate and fiercely territorial interest. And that interest would have been catalyzed by Oswald's passport application.

The list of countries Oswald was to visit was itself provocative. It included two nations in the troubled Caribbean, where reactionary repression and progressive revolution were vying for power, especially in Cuba; the usual culture stops in Europe, but oddly enough no visit to Italy; Finland, the "gateway" to the Soviet Union; and "Russia."[60]

No stop in Italy would be a variation on the detective theme of the non-barking dog; the CIA's James Jesus Angleton, a veteran of the OSS's Italian escapades in World War II, would have been immediately alert to Italy's absence. Unless, of course, Angleton had been responsible for sending Oswald into Europe in the first place as an espionage "dangle" (as several researchers have suggested), hoping Soviet intelligence would take the bait.

Finland and the Soviet Union were possibly the most provocative, the latter called in Oswald's trip list "Russia," a country name almost always preceded by the word "Communist."

But Oswald had named Switzerland and the Swiss Albert Schweitzer College, hand-printed on Oswald's passport application as "thE CollEGE of A. SchwETZER, CHUR SwiTZerlAnd," where "CHUR" represented either "Chur" or "Churwalden" (or both) in his travel destinations.

Finally, Oswald had also listed his intention to study at the University of Turku in (Helsinki) Finland.

According to his application to the Swiss college reportedly sent March 19th, 1959, he intended to study in Switzerland from April 12th, 1960, to June 27th, 1960[61], the college's so-called "third" term in its "trimester" schedule.[62] His passport, however, listed "4 months" as his total length of stay outside the United States[63], enough time, but only enough, to attend the college's FALL trimester. Attending the college's third trimester meant he would be in Europe for nine months rather than his listed four. But what about all those other listed stops?

Was any evidence found that clearly indicated Oswald would be attending the Fall trimester rather than the later and last trimester? In 1995, the Assassination Records Review Board was able to effect the release of a set of documents sent by the FBI Legat at the American Embassy in Paris to Bureau Director J. Edgar Hoover. Among those papers was an October 12, 1960, memorandum stating that Oswald indicated, reportedly from Moscow, he would be attending the Fall trimester, 1959, NOT the third and last trimester[64], according to the Swiss Federal Police.[65]

But this Swiss Federal Police report, summarized in the first of four communications from the Legat to Director J. Edgar Hoover, was subsequently contradicted (without explanation) by the fourth and last Legat communication to Hoover, suspiciously anticipating the Warren Commission's conclusions about Oswald's Albert Schweitzer College intentions.

The Warren Report, basing its conclusion on Oswald's official college application sent from Santa Ana, California, had indeed stated Oswald expected to attend the college's third trimester. But Oswald's preparations for exiting the Marines and obtaining a passport all support the Swiss Federal Police's first conclusion: that Oswald was targeting the Fall trimester at Albert Schweitzer College (not the last).

Since Oswald had obligated active duty in the Marine Corps until December 7th, 1959[66], he could not have made it to Europe and to Albert Schweitzer College for the Fall, 1959, trimester unless he exited the Corps no later than the middle of September, 1959. And that was exactly the outcome of Oswald's hardship/early discharge plan inaugurated in August, 1959, including what could only have been a faked workplace "accident" suffered by his mother, falsely documented by her doctor and other witnesses, and Lee's argument to the Corps that he was the sole support of his disabled parent who now needed him as quickly as possible in Fort Worth, Texas.

But the deception also had to rely on the Marine Corps itself. Why the Corps? Because no one at El Toro seemed the least bit disturbed that while still an active Marine, Oswald had applied for a passport for almost immediate travel to both the Caribbean and Europe. Certainly not 1st Lt. A.G. Ayers, Jr., who apparently allowed someone (who did not exist) to sign Oswald's Marine Corps "Separation Section" document on September 4th, 1959 (five days before Oswald applied for his passport), a document certifying Oswald was "scheduled to be released from Active Duty and Transferred to the Marine Corps Reserve (Inactive) on 11 September 1959."[67]

In fact, the Marine "Separation Section" document itself had been attached to Oswald's passport application and stamped (upside down):

Received
Department of State

1959 SEP 9 AM 9 54

PASSPORT OFFICE
LOS ANGELES[68]

Oswald received his passport on September 10th, 1959[69], while still on active duty in the Marine Corps, an unusual accommodation made by both the Corps and the State Department's Passport Office for a Private First Class with (to be charitable) an undistinguished service record.

In four days, on September 14th, 1959, Oswald was home in Fort Worth, visiting his 'disabled' mother. On September 19th he was in New Orleans, booking ship passage to Le Havre, France, and posting his breakaway letter to his mother.[70]

So much for Marguerite Oswald's hardship situation and needing her son as her sole support.

## The "Red Marine," Oswald's Monitored Mail, and Albert Schweitzer College

In March, 1959, when he reportedly applied to the Swiss college to attend the third trimester in 1960, Oswald was, of course, still a Marine on active duty. Regardless of his blemished military record, earlier he had been involved in a number of key Marine operations in the Pacific area; later he had been a player in the U-2 spy plane story. And his outspoken support of the Soviet Union during his military duty was in evidence so obvious Oswald could have been called the "Red Marine."[71] Ominously, he had received mail that provoked curiosity and comment: a newspaper, for example, printed in suspicious 'Russian.'[72] But the publication was more than likely a "White Russian" paper, as anti-Stalinist as another of his important postal communications: a subscription to The Worker, "the organ of the Socialist Worker's Party."[73]

Regardless of the shocked mailroom Marines who had to deliver Oswald's "leftist" postal arrivals[74], his mail was, in fact, anti-Stalinist, and therefore ought to have been of interest to (if not directed by) American intelligence.

Received wisdom on the Red Marine Oswald, generated by a series of reliable researchers on Oswald, has been accepted and passed on, an image seldom challenged. Therefore, a contrary image based on primary evidence is significant: U.S. Marines Nelson Delgado, Daniel Powers, Donald Peter Camarata, Peter Francis Connor, Allen D. Graf, John Rene Heindel, Mack Osborne, and Richard Dennis Call all gave sworn testimony in Warren Commission affidavits they never perceived Oswald to be either Socialist or Communist.[75]

Marine Kerry Thornley was heard by the Warren Commission directly: Thornley maintained Oswald had shown a propensity for Marxism[76], but the radical orientation Thornley allegedly witnessed was supported by Oswald's reputed Marine mail, and only by that mail.

Throughout his Marine career, Oswald maintained an active postal life.[77] With the mail he reportedly received while still in the Corps, he would certainly have come to the attention of the Office of Naval Intelligence, especially when he planned an extensive tour of Europe (both Western and Eastern) and Cuba. But no military postal intercept records of Lee Harvey Oswald are available: could any relevant Marine Corps mail documents have been destroyed?[78]

The FBI, the Office of Naval Intelligence, the CIA, the Warren Commission, the House Select Committee on Assassinations, and the Assassination Records Review Board all should have asked a series of obvious questions. How did Lee Harvey Oswald, an active Marine, discover the Swiss college? Where was Oswald's initial letter of inquiry he obviously had to have posted from Santa Ana, California (while still at his Marine base) to Albert Schweitzer College in Switzerland? Was he, in fact, directed to query a domestic address for the college? Why was neither a catalogue nor any other Albert Schweitzer College curriculum information available in any of the JFK assassination records on the college? Where was, for example, the "brochure . . . from this [Swiss] college, dated 1960 . . ."[79] and apparently received through the U.S. mail by Lee's mother, who (at least at one time) had it in her possession? And where were Oswald's three character references (at least one from a chaplain, pastor, or priest)?

In 1975, missing evidence on Lee Harvey Oswald and Albert Schweitzer College concerned Paul L. Hoch, the most cautious of scholarly JFK assassination researchers.[80] In one concentrated page, Hoch pointed to the obvious need to explore both FBI and CIA knowledge of Oswald's relationship to the college. Hoch pointed out that "Oswald had . . . been accepted by that school, despite the apparent absence of the proper references and background."[81] Hoch also questioned why no interagency communication (that is, between the FBI and the Central Intelligence Agency) on Oswald's non-appearance at Albert Schweitzer College was "in the CIA file on Oswald, CD 692."[82] Hoch further identified the central issue, and until now it has not been explored: "The CIA, the FBI and the ONI [Office of Naval Intelligence] should . . . be asked if there was any intelligence interest in [Albert] Schweitzer College, or any direct or indirect [U.S.] government support. That [support] might explain Oswald's peculiar contacts with the College."[83]

Assume that Oswald did indeed discover, somehow, the Swiss educational institution; he would then have (at least normally) written the college in order to receive the application materials that are now part of the Warren Commission's records.[84] But that necessary initial Oswald letter of inquiry does NOT exist in the public record. And it is also apparently NOT among the documents the Swiss Federal Police reportedly received from the college and delivered to the FBI during an inquiry run by the Swiss Police for the Bureau.[85]

Did Oswald's letter of inquiry ever exist? Or did Oswald receive the necessary information about the tiny, almost-unknown Swiss college from someone other than an official of that educational institution? Were the college's application forms, reportedly filled out by Oswald himself, also supplied to him by a domestic source? Did the Central Intelligence Agency or the Office of Naval Intelligence prompt Oswald to apply while he was still a Marine? If so, why? At least one program run by the Office of Naval Intelligence recruiting soon-to-be discharged Navy and Marine servicemen instructed the volunteers to defect to the Soviet Union as double agents for U.S. military intelligence: was it the recruitment vehicle for Lee Harvey Oswald?[86] Certainly several U.S. "dangle" operations of defectors who were, in fact, double agents were in progress during the Cold War.

The Albert Schweitzer College information and registration forms supplied to Oswald could then have been part of that "dangle" program.

Since Oswald's non-appearance at Albert Schweitzer College provoked a major international search first called for by his mother and then by the suspicious FBI, these questions may go to the heart of Oswald's alleged defection to the Soviet Union.

But they may also go to the heart of nothingness.

Whatever American intelligence's reportedly thin information about Albert Schweitzer College, the Warren Commission was concerned about the institution, but that presidential body operated without a clue. The interrogation of Oswald witnesses by the Commission's staff elicited nothing substantial about the college[87], and the Warren Commission did nothing to explore the topic.

## More Oswald Travel Document Fictions

Oswald left for Fort Worth after his Marine discharge, arriving there on September 14th, 1959.[88] He then communicated a series of provocative half-truths, beginning by telling his mother he was in pursuit of ship-board employment and that he might go into the "import-export business."[89] If, however, Mrs. Oswald's memory of her son's passport stamped "IMPORT-EXPORT"[90] is correct, he had already (however improbably) had his passport so designated.[91] Oswald had also reportedly visited his brother Robert in Fort Worth; Lee's brother wrote in his own book of recollections that Lee "planned to go to New Orleans and work for an export firm . . . ."[92]

Promising his mother to make "big money," Oswald left for New Orleans[93], but not before he "had registered his dependency discharge and entry into the Marine Reserve at the Fort Worth Selective Service Board . . ."[94] leaving behind one more entity, the Selective Service Administration, that would be officially interested in his ever-changing postal address.

In New Orleans, he established still another traceable paper link, visiting a New Orleans travel agency, Travel Consultants, Inc.[95], where he filed a "Passenger

Immigration Questionnaire" and booked his passage on a freighter from New Orleans to Le Havre, France.[96] That immigration form allowed Oswald to continue to register his series of half-truths, listing his occupation as "shipping export agent,"[97] a variant of his passport 'occupation.' But he also recorded he would be staying in Europe for only TWO months[98], to complete a planned 'pleasure trip.'[99]

The immigration document obviously contradicted his passport application anticipating an extensive continental tour AND studies at two European higher-education institutions. Further, Oswald's passport had listed "4 months" as the length of his stay[100], but it was a time period almost as unrealistic as the New Orleans immigration document's listing of TWO months. Unless, of course, it implicitly referred to his attendance at ASC during the FALL trimester.

Further, the handwritten "4 months" notation on Oswald's passport application differed significantly from Oswald's vagrant handwriting, although that variance may simply have meant that Oswald inadvertently left it blank, and a helpful clerk filled in the information after asking Oswald: "How long will you be staying?"

But that benign version would not explain Oswald's unrealistic response, except as still another a-logical element in the a-logical traveling universe of Lee Harvey Oswald.

Oswald sailed from Le Havre on October 8th to England, arriving on October 9th.[101] On board the English-bound ship Oswald told his cabin companion, according to the Warren Report, "he intended to travel in Europe and possibly to attend school in Sweden or Switzerland if he had sufficient funds."[102] Oswald had indeed reportedly touched down in Sweden (after entering Finland) apparently at either the American or Soviet Embassy[103], then returned to Finland. But with his two other shipboard passengers, Oswald was reportedly more focused: according to the Warren Report, "he told them he planned to study in Switzerland . . . ."[104]

After Le Havre (October 8th, 1959), Oswald entered England on October 9th.[105] In Southhampton, reporting to "English customs officials," Oswald told them he intended staying in England for one week,[106] after which he would report to "a school in Switzerland,"[107] obviously referring to Albert Schweitzer College.

But, again, Oswald contradicted his own stated plans. He left for Finland (with or without a stop in Sweden), crossed the Finnish border into the Soviet Union, and arrived in Moscow on October 16th, 1959.[108] Oswald's mode of transportation to Finland, his swiftly gaining a Soviet visa, and his crossing into the Soviet Union all were questionable and suspicious, apparently intended to call maximum attention to the defecting college-bound tourist.[109]

But if he hurried, Oswald could still contact Albert Schweitzer College from the Soviet Union, informing the Swiss school that, though he would be a bit late for the Fall trimester that was just opening, he would be on his way immediately.

A rather long way around? Not for Oswald. According to the Swiss Federal Police (who ultimately reported to the FBI on Oswald), he indeed "had announced his planned attendance . . . for the course beginning in the Fall of 1959." [110] Oswald, according to the Swiss Police, "had originally written a letter from Moscow indicating his intention to study . . . at the College."[111]

He, of course, never arrived. The Swiss Police, apparently feeling they might have had been investigating the wrong Fall term (1959), checked registration for the Fall term of 1960, but found "no record of a person possibly identical with the subject [Oswald] . . . registered for the courses beginning October 2[, 1960]."[112]

## Oswald and Patrice Lumumba Friendship University

While he resided in the Soviet Union, Oswald reportedly communicated with Patrice Lumumba Friendship University in Moscow, a Soviet institution of higher learning. His letter of application to the school has not been found in any American public record. But he did receive a Soviet rejection dated May 3rd, 1961; the school only accepted students from countries in the Third World.[113]

Did the Soviets have an espionage goal for their university?

In 1960, Nikita Khrushchev announced Patrice Lumumba University had been established to reach the intellectually gifted of Asia, Africa, and Latin America[114] with a special mission: "To educate students from underdeveloped countries so they [could] . . . return to their homelands to become the nucleus for pro-Soviet activities."[115] The KGB[116] actively participated in the university's origins: its "first vice rector . . . Pavl Erzin, [was] a major general of the KGB."[117] Faculty members were also drawn from the KGB[118], and students were reportedly accepted to Lumumba University "primarily on the basis of their potential usefulness to the KGB."[119] The Soviet institution focused in particular on Mexico and other Latin countries, including Cuba, during the 1960s.[120]

According to author Gordon Thomas, the CIA was aware that Lumumba University was a center for psychological warfare, a training ground for behavior modification techniques and for "mind control" experiments.[121]

Oswald's reported approach to Lumumba University, with the institution's concentration on Hispanic America, left a clear trail of Red pebbles back to the American defector's alleged Communist/Cuban interests. And, though Oswald never officially attended Lumumba, he allegedly made an appearance there, or at least among its students, a record apparently available to American counterintelligence. According to Edward Epstein, Oswald was reportedly "friendly with several foreign students [attending Lumumba], including Mary Louise Patterson, the daughter of William L. Patterson . . . [who was] then serving on the executive committee of the [American] Communist Party . . . and the wife of Roberto Camacho, one of the Cuban leaders then being trained in Moscow."[122] Epstein's key contacts were William Sullivan of the FBI and James Angleton of the CIA, both senior counterespionage officers, and Epstein gave a bizarre but telling source for the identity of the students Oswald reportedly contacted: "The information concerning Oswald's association with this [Lumumba] group [of students] comes from a conversation [held] among leaders of the Fair Play for Cuba Committee [FPCC] on a Cuban plane in 1964 . . . [, a conversation] electronically intercepted by the CIA."[123]

One of the FPCC people on that flight had to have been a CIA asset, wired by the Agency.

Epstein added still more privileged CIA information: "A few weeks after Oswald [who was, of course, in the Soviet Union] decided to return to the United States, he received a letter from [Patrice Lumumba] . . . university signed by 'Voloshin.'"[124] This reported letter, here to Oswald, is absent from the public record, and it cannot be the May 3rd, 1961, letter of rejection sent to him from the "University of the Friendship of Nations named for Patrice Lumumba": the letter was signed "P. Chikarev" (given in Cyrillic type), though the handwritten signature was "illegible." [125] Epstein revealed "Pavel T. Voloshin . . . was . . . an administrator at Patrice Lumumba University, . . . [but he also had been] a KGB officer accompanying . . . . Russian dancers to Los Angeles in 1959 . . . about the same time Oswald was making weekend trips . . . [to Los Angeles] to get his passport . . . for his trip to Moscow, according to the CIA."[126] Epstein's "according to the CIA" suggested new and provocative information whose source was obviously Agency counterintelligence. But why would Oswald make two (or more) "weekend" visits to Los Angeles for "his trip to Moscow"? Why not visit Los Angeles for his stated passport application trip to Switzerland? Why more than one trip to Los Angeles?

## What was Nelson Delgado's Function?

The Oswald/Delgado story can be followed in Warren Commission materials, but Edward Epstein's spin on the story has an important Agency counterintelligence perspective. In the summer of 1959, Oswald reportedly began to involve Corporal Nelson Delgado, his Quonset-hut cubicle partner, in his sometimes strange adventures.[127] A Puerto Rican, Delgado was allegedly interested in Fidel Castro and his Cuban revolution as reportedly was Oswald.[128] In 1975, the Warren Commission's CIA liaison had submitted a memo to the Rockefeller Commission (reviewing the JFK assassination) that was, in fact, a continuing part of the Agency's Delgado spin, calling attention to the Corporal's "credibility."[129] What the CIA never commented on (at least to the Warren Commission) was a series of coincidences, beginning with Oswald and Delgado both interested in Castro and the Cuban revolution, an interest oddly expanded by the Warren Commission's CIA source. The Agency officer had commented to the Rockefeller Commission, just enough to scare off any snooping investigators, that "Delgado's testimony says a lot more of possible [intelligence] operational significance than . . . the Warren Report . . . ."[130]

That intelligence "operational significance" included a shadowy, overcoated visitor to Oswald before he left the Corps; Oswald's reported communications with the "Cuban Consulate" in Los Angeles; and Oswald's duffle bag stuffed with apparent intelligence photos, all operationally significant actions that James Angleton, the CIA's counterintelligence chief, reported to Edward Epstein. According to Epstein (channeling Angleton), Delgado reportedly suggested that Oswald contact the "Cuban Embassy" in L.A.; Delgado was the source of the story about the mysterious trip the two Marines took to Mexico; and Delgado reported, again according to Epstein, that Oswald went to Los Angeles (with Delgado) on several weekends so Oswald could visit the "Cuban Consulate."[131]

But the Warren Commission's record gave a conflicting image of Nelson Delgado. According to his recorded testimony, he was treated by his FBI interrogators as if he were a suspected hostile spy, badgered, intimidated, and lied about by the Bureau.[132] Most importantly, Delgado denied under oath he had accompanied Oswald on his alleged L.A. excursions.[133]

Why was Delgado treated so badly by the FBI? Rather than being just Oswald's Marine buddy, was Nelson Delgado, in fact, an Office of Naval Intelligence or CIA plant? Did Agency counterintelligence chief James Angleton, Epstein's CIA contact, know that? Angleton, using Delgado as his hook, clearly suggested to Epstein that Oswald in 1959 was holding a series of weekend meetings with a KGB officer in Los Angeles ("Voloshin") with whom Oswald would later make contact in Moscow, apparently about Patrice Lumumba University.

But, then, what was Mary Louise Patterson, an American student, doing at Lumumba University, the Soviet institution that had rejected Lee Harvey Oswald's application from Moscow, since the university only accepted students from the Third World?

## Oswald and the First Unitarian Church of Los Angeles

Lee Harvey Oswald's higher education aspirations both in the Soviet Union and Switzerland had Fair Play For Cuba Committee connections, the former in Moscow, the latter in Los Angeles.

Oswald's trips to Los Angeles (beyond the intention of obtaining a passport) may have been the only way he received information about Unitarian-supported Albert Schweitzer College. Unitarian minister Stephen Fritchman[134] had inspired his First Unitarian Church of Los Angeles to become a leading anti-war religious center in the United States. The distinguished U.S. scientist Linus Pauling and his wife, Ava Helen, were among Fritchman's secular parishioners.[135]

Concluding that the atomic bomb was fully capable of destroying all of humanity, Pauling had become a pacifist, joining his wife as an anti-war, civil-rights, and anti-racist activist. The Paulings enlisted on the side of peace. Establishing an ethical bond with Albert Einstein, Pauling openly rejected atmospheric weapons tests and the development of the so-called hydrogen bomb.

Pauling's public appearances, petitions, and personal protests energized the FBI: the Bureau's files on the distinguished U.S. scientist filled with reports of his arguments for unionization and "world government,"[136] and Pauling became the target of both U.S. intelligence and a Red-hunting Congressional investigating committee.

The Unitarians of Los Angeles and Pasadena rallied in support of the Pauling couple, who gave anti-war speeches at several of the area's Unitarian churches. A thousand supporters crowded into Stephen Fritchman's First Unitarian Church of Los Angeles on April 15, 1954, to hear Pauling denounce the Bikini atomic bomb test and its immense and deadly fallout. Pauling and his wife became members of Stephen Fritchman's congregation, despite Pauling having no interest "in the mystical aspects of religion."[137] Pauling commented: "My wife and I joined . . . because [Fritchman's church] . . . accepts as members people who believe in trying to make the world a better place."[138]

In 1958, when Lee Harvey Oswald was preparing to leave the Marines and travel to Europe, Linus Pauling authored a passionate attack on the hydrogen bomb and its chief Cold War enthusiast, Edward Teller. In that same year, the Soviets called for an immediate halt to atomic weapons testing while Pauling brought suit against the Eisenhower administration for what he characterized as its flagrant assault on the "people's right to life through the release of radiation into the atmosphere."[139]

In 1958 and 1959, Lee Harvey Oswald, either alone or reportedly with his Marine buddy Nelson Delgado, visited Los Angeles. Kerry Thornley, another of Oswald's Marine friends, stated in his Warren Commission testimony that "[I] knew Oswald [at the same time] . . . I had been going to the First Unitarian Church in Los Angeles."[140] Thornley testified to the Commission that Fritchman's L.A. congregation was "a group of quite far left people politically."[141]

Were there actual links between Kerry Thornley, Lee Harvey Oswald, Los Angeles, and Stephen Fritchman's "far left" First Unitarian Church? Apparently the FBI thought so; after the JFK assassination, a Bureau agent, interrogating Kerry Thornley, asked him "what Oswald's connection with the First Unitarian Church was[,] and I [Thornley] explained to him that there was none."[142]

But Pastor Stephen Fritchman of the First Unitarian Church of L.A. was a sufficient part of the Oswald story to be represented in the NARA JFK Assassination files by a sixty-page FBI report (including one newspaper article, a photo, a "motion picture" film, and a Fritchman sermon).[143]

The FBI's and the Warren Commission's curiosity about an Oswald/First Unitarian Church/Thornley link most probably indicated both the Bureau and the Commission were interested in Oswald's unexplained ability to obtain information concerning the Unitarian-sponsored Albert Schweitzer College.

Did Kerry Thornley know about a possible Oswald tie to Fritchman's progressive parish? And did Thornley, the eccentric former Marine, withhold relevant facts about Oswald from the JFK assassination investigation?[144] Oswald's mysterious source of information about Albert Schweitzer College could be explained by Thornley's attendance at Fritchman's First Unitarian Church in Los Angeles: given Fritchman's progressive political and theological background, the pastor may well have possessed sufficient information about the college (circulated by the Unitarians) and copies of the requisite college registration forms.[145] When Oswald visited L.A., he could have picked up the college materials directly at the church. Or his Marine friend Thornley, who admitted attending the L.A. Unitarian church, could have picked them up and passed them on to Oswald.

## Oswald, the Fair Play for Cuba Committee, the Unitarian Connection, and V.T. Lee

In the summer of 1963, Lee Harvey Oswald, arrested in a New Orleans street for disruptive political activity, was interviewed by New Orleans police intelligence officer Francis L. Martello. Volunteering information about his one-person New Orleans branch of the Fair Play For Cuba Committee (hastily established and then hastily abandoned by him), Oswald was asked by Martello how he got connected to the FPCC; Oswald replied that "he became interested in that committee in Los Angeles . . . in 1958 while in the U.S. Marine Corps."[146]

The recorded 1958 date was, of course, eighteen months too early for the origin of the Fair Play For Cuba Committee: the national FPCC was established on April 6th, 1960. But Oswald had indicated he was visiting Los Angeles in 1958 when the same (apparently) pro-Castro people who organized the FPCC's Los Angeles branch were in attendance at the progressive and radical Unitarian meetings in Los Angeles in 1958, including those held at Stephen Fritchman's First Unitarian Church.

The reticulate complexity of the Oswald story is apparent with Lee Harvey Oswald's uncalled-for offer of FPCC information to New Orleans police officer Martello. Oswald had begun his correspondence with the N.Y. FPCC office sometime between August 4th and October 8th, 1962.[147] V. T. Lee, actually Army veteran Vincent Tappin[148], had been an early Castro supporter, a frequent visitor to Cuba, and the chief of the FPCC's Tampa branch until he fled to New York after he had been "hounded" (according to Lee) by the FBI.[149] V. T. Lee became the FPCC's chairperson in New York[150], apparently arriving in time to receive Lee Harvey Oswald's letter.

After the autumn of 1962, no official postal record exists of a link between Lee Harvey Oswald and V.T. Lee until April 16th, 1963. But just two weeks earlier, a remarkable reticulation occurred: on April 4th and 5th, on a major speaking tour, V. T. Lee visited Los Angeles. The FPCC activist held a press conference, spoke at the Young Socialist Alliance of UCLA, and, most importantly, was the sponsored presentation guest of Stephen Fritchman, pastor of the First Unitarian Church of Los Angeles.[151] "Reverend Fritchman was an FPCC sympathizer, . . . the public radical spokesman for the L.A. area with validity, because he was a minister."[152]

From Dallas, Lee Harvey Oswald began corresponding regularly with V.T. Lee in New York, twelve days after V. T. Lee appeared at Fritchman's First Unitarian Church; at the same time, the FBI "intensified its probe" of V.T. Lee and the FPCC.[153] The

Bureau's New York field office, utilizing its postal intercept machinery, maintained its awareness of Oswald in touch with V.T. Lee and the FPCC.[154] When Oswald moved to New Orleans, he continued his postal connection to the FPCC, and again his correspondence was intercepted by the Bureau.[155]

Richard Case Nagell,[156] a reputed U.S. intelligence officer, reportedly discovered at least one anti-JFK assassination plot that intended to use Lee Harvey Oswald as its primary patsy. Whether any of Nagell's assertions concerning assassination planning, the CIA, the KGB, and Organized Crime have probity[157], among Nagell's recorded counterintelligence responsibilities were the Fair Play For Cuba Committee; the Los Angeles progressive and radical community; Stephen Fritchman[158], pastor of the First Unitarian Church of Los Angeles[159] and sponsor of the FPCC's V.T. Lee and Linus Pauling; Kerry Thornley; and Lee Harvey Oswald[160], all of whom were carefully recorded in Nagell's investigative notebook.[161]

Oswald had a propensity for association (at a very low degree of separation) with anti-nuclear activists in the 1950s, including U.S. intelligence targets Stephen Fritchman and Linus Pauling.

## Oswald, Patrice Lumumba University, and Congo Uranium

Oswald's application to Patrice Lumumba University, reportedly made from Moscow, concerned the Warren Commission's staff: as American intelligence well knew, Lumumba University, though it was interested in educating its students, was also determined to propagandize them, hoping to recruit them as KGB assets or agents.[162]

But Lumumba University did not exist in 1959 when Oswald identified Albert Schweitzer College and the University of Turku as his two overseas academic choices. His reported application to Lumumba from Moscow was, therefore, completely opportunistic, either devised by Oswald himself (a highly unlikely scenario) or by Soviet or American espionage entities or some combination of the two.[163]

Why would Oswald apply to Lumumba University? Oswald's application to the Soviet institution fit perfectly with his earlier registration with Albert Schweitzer College.

In 1958 and 1959, a highly visible and articulate Patrice Lumumba[164] demonstrated he was the outstanding spokesperson for Congolese political and economic freedom. His radical flamboyance (without evidence, he was accused of being a Communist[165]) was calculated to capture the attention of the thousands of abused and dispossessed Congolese, many of whom were seriously crippled by the terrible conditions in the Congolese mines and the regular practice of brutal whippings. Lumumba's mercurial outspokenness disturbed one official U.S. observer: "[Lumumba is] a spellbinding orator with the ability to stir masses of people to action . . . ."[166] That "action," of course, threatened Congolese stability and, therefore, Western profits.[167]

Patrice Lumumba was the first democratically elected prime minister the country ever had.[168] "His speeches set off immediate alarm signals in Western capitals. Belgian,

British, and American corporations . . . had vast investments in the Congo, . . . rich in copper, cobalt, diamonds, gold, tin, manganese, and zinc[—and, of course, uranium]."[169] The corporations and the governments supporting them rightly feared Lumumba's political charisma: he clearly signaled that all of the African "continent must . . . cease to be an economic colony of Europe."[170]

The Soviet Union had established Patrice Lumumba University in February, 1960, honoring the Congolese independence leader who was the Congo's first elected prime minister.[171]

Three months later, on June 30th, 1960, Oswald was in Moscow, and the Congo became officially independent of Belgium. Almost immediately, the Congo went into chaotic spasms. Katanga province withdrew from the Congo, taking with it the region's mineral riches.[172] Both the United States and the United Nations "refused to supply [Lumumba] . . . with transport for his troops to put down the secession in Katanga province, [so] Lumumba turned to the Soviet Union for aid . . . ."[173] Ten Iluyshin troop transports landed at Leopoldville on August 26th, 1960, with 100 Soviet technicians.[174]

Belgium, Great Britain, and the United States took immediate notice and targeted Lumumba for elimination. In August, 1960, the Congo station of the Central Intelligence Agency sent a cable to Washington: "Embassy and [CIA] station [both] believe Congo [is] experiencing classic communist effort [to] takeover [the] government."[175] Agency Director Dulles noted that a "communist takeover of the Congo [would have] . . . disastrous consequences . . . for the interests of the free world . . . ."[176] Dulles' references to "consequences" included, of course, an independent Congo (whether sympathetic to the Soviets or not) in control of its own highly valuable mineral resources.[177]

Unfortunately for the West, Lumumba could not be bought. Though the CIA had regularly bribed Congolese politicians[178], Patrice Lumumba was judged to be incorruptible. The colonial powers began their major anti-Lumumba move. Allen Dulles, long-time Sullivan and Cromwell partner and CIA spymaster, met with key members of President Eisenhower's political and military intelligence staff and accepted "getting rid of Lumumba" as a viable next action.[179] Dulles approved a $100,000 program whose goal was the elimination of Lumumba and his government, to be replaced by a "pro-western group."[180] Following intelligence, foreign affairs, and military analyses on the Congo submitted to Eisenhower, the president ordered the assassination of Lumumba, and the CIA began its attack[181]; in September and October, 1960, British and Belgian assassination plots against the Congolese prime minister were initiated, and these American, British, and Belgian operations became, finally, a single anti-Lumumba conspiracy.

On January 17th, 1961, Patrice Lumumba was assassinated. Within a week, on January 22nd, 1961, John F. Kennedy was inaugurated, succeeding the president who had ordered Lumumba's murder. Four months later, on May 3rd, 1961, Lee Harvey Oswald was officially rejected by Patrice Lumumba University.

## Why Had an Opportunistic Oswald/Lumumba Connection Been Established?

Beginning in 1885, King Leopold of Belgium, literally the single owner of the Congo, was directly responsible for no fewer than five million Congolese dying inside his highly profitable system of forced labor. The Congo's mineral richness was then, as always, the spur.[182] In 1913, both cobalt and uranium were reportedly discovered.[183] But in August, 1915, Robert Rich Sharp found the Shinkolobwe uranium deposit in the Katanga province of the Congo that gave an astonishing yield of 68% of uranium, the richest discovery in the history of mining.[184] And it was all on the earth's surface[185]: a minimum of work would yield an enormous profit.

In the 1940s, the Congo's splendid uranium resources were crucial both to Belgium, the major uranium exporter to the U.S., and to the United States, the world's major nuclear weapons builder. On March 27th, 1944, for $375,000,000, Belgium sold to the United States and England the absolute right of future (so-called "prior") purchase for all uranium deposits in the Congo.[186] British, American, and Belgian interests in Congolese uranium had been fused, the interests of the same three imperial powers that conspired against Patrice Lumumba.

The United States dropped atomic bombs on Hiroshima and Nagasaki fueled by Belgian Congo uranium[187]; thereafter, America "rewarded Belgium with its own [home] nuclear centre."[188] The Belgians had became an atomic power. "In 1958, when Brussels thought it would hold onto its [Congo] colony for many years, Belgium built the Kinshasa [nuclear] reactor, the first in Africa."[189] The Kinshasa TRIGA reactor was "a part of President Eisenhower's Atoms for Peace Program."[190]

In 1960, one year after Oswald applied to Albert Schweitzer College, Belgium gave the Congo its reported independence, an act clearly intended to initiate the major political instability that followed. The Congolese army, trained and dominated by the Belgians, "mutinied"[191]; the province of Katanga, key to the West's mineral and pitchblende future, announced it had separated from the Congo.[192] The leader of the secession, Moise Tshombe, received his instructions from the government of Belgium. Katanga was ready to deal with the anti-Lumumba West to control both the Congo and its precious uranium.[193]

With Africa threatened by instability and the Congo's uranium at issue, President Dwight David Eisenhower ordered Lumumba's assassination[194], and Belgium[195] and Great Britain cooperated.[196] The alliance that had bought and sold the Congo's uranium power and wealth in 1944 moved against Lumumba.

Suppression of the Congolese working population had always been a primary Belgian and Western corporate consideration, and that work force in 1960 was on the edge of political and economic rebellion.[197] Patrice Lumumba was perceived to be unable to contain that roiling mass[198], and so Great Britain, Belgium, and the United States sanctioned the Lumumba assassination contract.[199]

Patrice Lumumba was murdered, and the CIA's candidate Moise Tshombe[200] helped block any progressive transformation of the Congo threatening the country's uranium ore destined for the West and its atomic weapons.

From Moscow, Lee Harvey Oswald had applied to a Soviet university with significant KGB intelligence connections and Cuban/Communist links, dedicated to a charismatic African leader who opposed the West's control of the Congo's uranium marked for America's nuclear arsenal in its defense against Communism.

And though Oswald's reported approach to Lumumba University was opportunistic, that action dovetailed perfectly with his earlier application to Albert Schweitzer College. In fact, Patrice Lumumba University and Albert Schweitzer College had shared a significant political context, just as Lumumba and Schweitzer themselves were, from the Eisenhower administration's point of view, politically (and negatively) linked.[201]

Asking many questions about Oswald's projected higher education at the Swiss college, Writer Dennis Bartholomew made as much sense as he could of the Oswald/Albert Schweitzer College postal maze.[202] But Oswald's trip preparation, the trip itself, and all the Albert Schweitzer College stories lacked sense except as provocative signs pointing to a highly-suspicious American espionage operation involving Oswald (or an Oswald substitute), the Soviet Union, and Switzerland in a perfect postal intelligence triangle.

## Oswald's Suspect College Documents Record

This dark corner of the JFK assassination closet included "illegals" (espionage agents with false identities), "mail drops," and, in the manipulation of Lee Harvey Oswald, a possible collaboration between Soviet and U.S. intelligence.[203]

The Albert Schweitzer College documents and letters in the Warren Report and in the Warren Commission Hearings volumes are in an illogical order, exhibit suspicious gaps, have strange entries, and are missing crucial information.[204] Bluntly, all the Albert Schweitzer College documents accessed by the Warren Commission in its post-assassination investigation are irrational and suspect[205], strongly suggesting they were elements in a major American intelligence operation.

How aware was the Warren Commission of this possible espionage action? After the assassination of John F. Kennedy, the fictionalized Oswald had to be dealt with or be hidden in plain sight. He was visible in his series of half-truths concerning his trip to Europe (and the Caribbean), all apparently intended to maximize suspicion concerning his journey. The key falsehood was his proposed study in Switzerland: the Albert Schweitzer College application form Oswald submitted was itself a fiction.[206]

While still in the Marines, Lee Harvey Oswald reportedly told Warren Commission witness Richard Dennis Call (who had served with Oswald in the Corps) that he had received a "scholarship" to attend Albert Schweitzer College.[207] Was Oswald attempting to conceal he could not personally afford to go to the college? Was Oswald indeed the recipient of a "scholarship," an academic benefit for which he apparently never applied?

Or was this reported "scholarship" still one more element in a series of deliberately questionable items of information? The Warren Commission's materials, the National Archives documents, the later Assassination Records Review Board discoveries, and the American Friends of Albert Schweitzer College files at Harvard Divinity School Library do not yield a single document referring to a "scholarship" for any prospective American student to the college in the late 1950s.

However, financial support for a scholarship to Albert Schweitzer College for students from the so-called "iron curtain countries" had been proposed and explored by the college's officers.[208] Further, the Central Intelligence Agency had funded support for American youth, including students, to attend educational and cultural events in Europe from 1959 through 1962.[209]

According to his mother, Oswald was planning to "attend the short summer course[210] of the University of Turku, [in] Turku, Finland."[211] Of course, the University of Turku was no longer in the city of Turku: it had long since returned to Helsinki. Oswald had made the mistake, if indeed it was a mistake, on his Albert Schweitzer College application[212], and his mother (apparently) had quoted his Albert Schweitzer College application exactly, but mistakenly assigned the "summer course" statement to Turku.[213] But from where had Mrs. Oswald gotten that exact phrase? Had Oswald's (long form) application gone from the college to Texas Representative Jim Wright and then to Mrs. Oswald? Had Mrs. Oswald then given the document to the Warren Commission staff? Almost certainly Albert Schweitzer College Secretary Erika Weibel sent the college's Oswald file to Jim Wright, who in turn gave that file to the Warren Commission. Where, indeed, did Mrs. Oswald get that exact set of words?

And where did Oswald get ANY information about the University of Turku in Helsinki?

And wasn't Helsinki a known center of both American and Soviet espionage activity?[214]

Albert Schweitzer College (in Switzerland), the University of Turku (in Finland), Patrice Lumumba University (in the Soviet Union): the three were a combination of higher education and sensitive intelligence sites obviously intended to alert any counterespionage analyst.[215]

## Oswald an FBI False Identity Case, the Bureau's Mail Intercepts, and the Illegals

In the first week of November, 1959, following Oswald's announcement of his Soviet defection, the former Marine's FBI security file was opened.[216] In itself, this file was important, but a related FBI action, largely overlooked, spoke directly to the "imposter" Oswald issue that would fuel the Bureau's inquiry: "A stop was placed in the files of the Identification Division of the FBI on November 10, 1959, . . . to alert us in the event . . . [Oswald] returned under a different identity and his fingerprints were received."[217]

Though garbled by typical BureauSpeak, the issue was clearly the FBI's concern for false identity. Either Oswald would return as someone else, or someone else would return as Oswald. But a third possibility was aired: "to evaluate him as a security risk in the event he returned [that is, Oswald as Oswald], in view of the possibility of his recruitment by the Soviet intelligence services."[218]

Lee's second-last letter to his brother Robert on November 8th, 1959, covered Oswald's alleged interest in acquiring Soviet citizenship and living in the Soviet Union, his condemnation of the Unites States, and his intention to accept no further telephone calls.[219] Beyond the newspaper stories of Oswald's so-called defection, that letter was probably the catalyst for the Bureau's identification stop.

Months before Lee's mother was urged to contact the American Secretary of State by Bureau Agent "Fannan," Lee's brother Robert had wired Secretary of State Christian Herter, but he received no response.[220] "Fannan" could have known about Robert Oswald's State Department query and, in effect, indicated in his interview with Mrs. Oswald in February, 1960, that the communication line between the Oswald family and the State Department was now open.

Robert Oswald sent another letter to Lee[221], and Lee's response, a long, well-written, and positive communication[222] of November 26th, 1959[223], certainly confirmed to both American and Soviet intelligence interceptors[224] that this defecting Marxist Marine reservist was serious about his new loyalties. No intervening Robert Oswald letter to Lee has been found in the public record, but Lee's last letter to Robert on December 17th, 1959, helped to establish his Soviet silence.[225] No one but Lee's mother would hear from Oswald for twenty months, and then it would only be a short and questionable note.

Marguerite Oswald sent her son a $20 check on December 18th, 1959, to his Moscow hotel; it was returned, presumably by Lee who asked for cash.[226] On January 5th, 1960, she sent him a $20 bill.[227] But the apparently unopened envelope was returned on February 25th, 1960[228]. Finally, Mrs. Oswald sent Lee a "Foreign Money transfer" for "$25.00."[229] Sometimes accuracy only compounds confusion: the Warren Report stated that Lee's mother "sent him a money order for about $25.00."[230] If we ignore that a "money order" is not the same as a bank's money transfer from one country to another, we can accept that the prevailing exchange rate between American and Soviet currency would make the "money" transfer "about $25." But sometimes accuracy, I repeat, only compounds confusion.

Mrs. Oswald had asked that an official receipt be returned to her bank. The bank never received the confirmation[231], so she assumed (correctly) that the transfer either had not been received or had been rejected.

According to former Navy intelligence officer/historian John Newman, the Bureau never explained how it had acquired its information on Mrs. Oswald's attempted money transfer.[232] But the buried record of the Warren Commission proved that the FBI monitored that most important transaction[233] and probably all three attempts by Marguerite Oswald to send her son money. In fact, Marguerite Oswald's mailings to Lee in the Soviet Union and the FBI's responses to those mailings (in the form of official Bureau memoranda) established a significant pattern of relationships, strongly suggesting constant Bureau postal monitoring.[234]

Robert Oswald's letter of December 17th was followed immediately by Mrs. Oswald's December 18th mailing of the $20 check. Either Lee or someone else in the Soviet Union returned the check that was then received by Mrs. Oswald on January 5th, 1960, with Lee's scribbled request for cash. On January 18th, 1960, the first in a series of Bureau memos was generated directly related to the Oswald family's postal traffic between Texas and the Soviet Union.[235] But the initiating FBI field office was neither Fort Worth nor Dallas; it was the New York field office, the Bureau site responsible for the FBI's Soviet mail interception program.[236] That program, called Z Coverage, was one of several FBI mail intercept operations.[237]

From 1940 through 1966, the Bureau ran its Z Coverage postal program against Soviet espionage "mail drops," monitoring and opening first-class mail between the United States and the Soviet Union; Z Coverage tracked suspected and actual espionage illegals with false identities based on borrowed or stolen legitimate American birth certificates and passports.[238] In 1958, FBI Counterintelligence (run by the Bureau's William Sullivan and Sam Papich) shared mail drop/illegals/false identity information with the CIA's Counterintelligence chief James Angleton.[239] HT/LINGUAL, the Agency's own mail interception program, was functioning in New York at the same time[240], and the CIA would certainly have had an intense interest in mail going to a former Marine who had defected to the Soviet Union.

It is as if Lee Harvey Oswald's defection following his non-appearance at Albert Schweitzer College was timed to intersect with the establishment of the combined FBI/CIA counterintelligence program on false identity, postal interceptions, and illegals.

Significantly, within that new joint enterprise, the FBI sent Oswald material to the CIA in 1960, but the January 18th memo was withheld from the Agency.[241]

Mrs. Oswald posted a $20 bill to Lee on January 5th, 1960. The letter was returned, apparently unopened, on February 25th, 1960.[242] On January 22nd, 1960, Mrs. Oswald sent Lee a $25 Foreign Money transfer purchased at her First National Bank in Fort Worth, Texas.[243] Three days later, the FBI knew of the transaction: "We determined on January 25, 1960, that Mrs. Marguerite Oswald had transmitted the sum of $25 to 'Lee Harvey Oswald' . . . ."[244]

Four days later, on January 29th, the Bureau's New York field office sent a memorandum to Washington[245], obviously responding to the FBI's New York postal intercept of Mrs. Oswald's attempted foreign money transfer. This memo was also not shared with the CIA.[246] Another FBI memo, again from the New York field office, was sent to Bureau headquarters on February 2nd, 1960.[247] This last memo probably confirmed that Mrs. Oswald's bank had not received a receipt of the attempted transfer delivery to Lee Harvey Oswald in the Soviet Union. Again, this memo was not shared with the CIA.[248]

The three memos of January 11th, January 29th, and February 2nd were all cited in a February 26th, 1960, memorandum from the FBI's New York field office.[249] The memo, 32 pages long, has remained a classified U.S. intelligence document except for its first and last pages.[250] But the last page offered more evidence of the FBI's covert information techniques, citing "receipts and disbursements . . . in . . . bank accounts"[251] held to be "strictly confidential" and attributed to a source whose identity was to be kept secret.[252] That source was undoubtedly a cooperating New York postal inspector (or an FBI agent working alongside that postal inspector).

The FBI's New York field office had intercepted Mrs. Oswald's Foreign Money Transfer, traced it to her bank, and then shared that information with the FBI's Washington headquarters. In New York, the memo was placed in Oswald's counterintelligence file[253] for obvious reasons. In Washington, however, it became part of Oswald's DOMESTIC security file.[254] This difference in filing procedures only made sense if the responsible FBI headquarters officer who filed the memo viewed Oswald's reported overseas disappearance as a False Identity case, if and when someone showed up in the United States claiming to be Lee Harvey Oswald, legitimate passport and valid birth certificate in hand.

A False Identity case.

The February 26th, 1960, memorandum, citing the series of memoranda not given to the CIA, was also not shared with the Agency. But later, it was also withheld from the Warren Commission[255], since it would have confirmed two disturbing facts someone on the Commission staff certainly might have suspected: that the FBI had been intercepting Oswald mail as early as 1959 (and no later than the first two months of 1960) and that the Bureau was taking quite seriously the possibility that a 'false identity' Oswald was already in the Soviet Union. The FBI's responses to Mrs. Oswald's correspondence would continue.

Somewhere inside this Bureau monitoring of the Oswald mail came the visit of alleged FBI agent "Fannan" from the Fort Worth field office to Marguerite Oswald.[256] And after that interview, Mrs. Oswald's inquiries to her Texas representatives and Secretary of State Herter followed on March 7th, 1960.[257]

If FBI agent "Fannan" anticipated a bureaucratic bottleneck would be initiated when Mrs. Oswald followed his suggestion to request help from Secretary of State Christian Herter, the resulting postal exchange was, in fact, a classic study in frustration by government. The correspondence between Marguerite Oswald and the State Department began March 7th, 1960, and ended June 7th, 1962: two years and three months of futile mail exchange.[258] Once, very early in the interchange, a curious topic entered: on July 16th, 1960, Mrs. Oswald asked in what city, state, and on what date her son received his passport. The answer was, of course, September 10, 1959, in Los Angeles.[259]

Some odd things were happening at the State Department, and again the flow of American mail was central. Texas Representative Jim Wright had written to the State Department, and after the Department received Mrs. Oswald's letter, Washington wrote to the American Embassy in Moscow; attached to its Oswald query were the letters of both Marguerite Oswald and Representative Jim Wright. The State Department responded to Representative Wright, but it virtually ignored Lee's mother.[260] Further, the Oswald's State file now resided in the Department's "passport office"[261], suggesting that State was also aware of the false identity Oswald potential. Most tellingly, The Department of State's Passport Office was run by two paranoid anti-Communists: Ms. Frances Knight and her key assistant, "the legendary red-hunter Otto Otepka."[262] How did Oswald's suspicious application earlier get past both Knight and Otepka? Or did it?

This passport office file ought to have existed when Oswald applied for a new passport in 1962 while still in the Soviet Union. Yet, despite Oswald's record, including an internationally reported defection, he received his new passport quickly and without a hitch.[263] The Warren Commission, except for one of its members, was "highly suspicious"[264]. That one Commissioner was former CIA Director Allen Dulles, who was obvious in his deflection of the Commission's passport discussion, asserting that neither the State Department nor its Passport Office was aware of Oswald's defection.[265] Dulles, who most certainly knew better, told his Commission associates (rather disjointedly): "I don't think the State Department or in . . . Passport . . . there was no record."[266] He was immediately corrected by one of his fellow Commissioners: "The State Department knew he was a defector. They arranged for him to come back."[267]

The Commission, however, was easily diverted; its Oswald passport exploration ended quickly.

But when it was happening, something was special about Oswald's defection and disappearance, and the entire Oswald case was to be handled in a special way[268], though not necessarily with efficiency. The American Embassy in Moscow recommended a plan that had been successful in the past. The inquiring mother (Mrs. Oswald) would write a letter to her son (Lee Harvey) and that correspondence would then be forwarded to the Soviet Foreign Embassy by the American Embassy in Moscow.[269] The Embassy felt certain the Soviets would supply a current postal address for Oswald.[270] Delaying its decision for almost two months, the State Department in Washington finally vetoed the Embassy plan.[271] One year later, when Oswald's mother flew to Washington and confronted the State Department, it did agree to try the earlier rejected plan.[272] It was, however, a superfluous agreement: by March 22, 1961, State had written to Mrs. Oswald that her son wanted to come home.[273]

But in March, 1960, Mrs. Oswald had heard nothing from either the Soviet Union or the State Department until March 30th, 1960, when she received a cool, wordy postal assurance that the American Embassy in Moscow had been asked to "obtain a report" about Lee's "present welfare"[274] and communicate to him his mother's "continuing desire to help him." Was this Foreign Service message to Mrs. Oswald in some kind of obscure code? Or did it suggest that the State Department and, in particular, its Passport Office did not WANT to find Lee Harvey Oswald?

## The Strange Albert Schweitzer College Mailings

Then the letter from Albert Schweitzer College arrived: it should have been part of a series of rational exchanges through the mail between a prospective student and his future educational institution. It only initiated more postal confusion.

What was the actual set of mail exchanges on Albert Schweitzer College, and in particular what was strange about the letter from Albert Schweitzer College to then Marine Lee Harvey Oswald?

Sometime before March 4th, 1959, Oswald (while still in the Corps) or someone in his name apparently made an inquiry about Albert Schweitzer College seeking information and/or requesting application materials. No official record of such an inquiry has ever been found. I have been informed by an extremely reliable source, however, that Oswald reportedly wrote a letter of inquiry to the "Chairman of the American Admissions Committee" of Albert Schweitzer College[275] in Providence, Rhode Island, in 1959.[276] But if the person posting the letter of inquiry was Oswald, from where did he get the "American Admissions Committee" address and the name of its chief officer in Providence?

Before March 4th, 1959, Oswald (or someone who had used Oswald's name) was sent or given an application form for Albert Schweitzer College.[277] But this document was apparently the short form for the "Summer Study courses" at the college.[278] Only twelve lines long, the document was quite different from the Albert Schweitzer College trimester application.[279] The period of study in which Oswald had apparently expressed an interest was NOT a "Summer Study" course but the third regular session of the college's trimester school year, from April 12th, 1960 to June 27th, 1960, but entered on the short "Summer Study courses" application.[280] Oswald was later informed by the College, in a letter dated March 27, 1959, that he had used the wrong application form.[281]

The Summer application form as it appears in the Warren Commission documents is one-half of an 8 1/2 by 11 sheet of paper[282], duplicated for distribution.[283] The Warren Commission neglected to point out that it was, in fact, the bottom half of a full sheet, the top half of which gave a listing of the Summer, 1960, courses for the 1959-1960 Albert Schweitzer College "year." Oswald by direction, on his own, or someone in his name had possession of information both about the college's regular trimester program (for the third of which Oswald reportedly registered) and the distributed short summer session form.

Sometime before March 4th, 1959, Oswald (or someone using Oswald's name) completed that short (and incorrect) application form.[284] On this form, Oswald (or someone) wrote: "Please inform me of the amount of the deposit . . . ."[285] This application was then mailed to Albert Schweitzer College in Switzerland. The major problem with this document was that the handwritten application date read March 19th, 1959.[286] The longer and correct application form listed a handwritten date of March 4th, 1959, but that date could not have been correct, since it meant the correct

FORM was received and returned by Oswald BEFORE he sent the incorrect form to the college.

Since Albert Schweitzer College wrote Oswald it had received his incorrect application form no later than March 28th, 1959, the college could not have sent out the longer, correct form to him any earlier than March 28th, 1959.

Still, Oswald MAY have written an incorrect date on one or both of the applications.

In a letter dated March 28th, 1959, Erika Weibel, the Secretary of Albert Schweitzer College, wrote Oswald at his Marine Corps address.[287] She reported that the college had received his first application but the (short summer) form he had sent was incorrect.[288] The "proper forms," she wrote, were being sent to him: that is, TWO copies of the "proper" form, one to be completed and sent to Providence, the other to be completed and sent to Switzerland, were reportedly mailed to Oswald by Erika Weibel.[289]

Assuming that Oswald completed both copies of the correct application form, one would have been sent to Albert Schweitzer College[290], the other to Providence, Rhode Island.[291] Indeed, one copy was apparently mailed to Albert Schweitzer College.[292] The other copy was supposed to have been mailed to the college's "Chairman of the American Admissions Committee"[293], Dr. Robert H. Schacht[294], who was at the time pastor of the Unitarian Church, Providence, Rhode Island, where Dr. Schacht received mail at 1 Benevolent Street[295], the Parish House of the Church.[296]

But unless Oswald's Benevolent Street file is retrieved from the FBI[297], no evidence is presently available that Dr. Schacht ever received the required application form from Oswald, or for that matter any other Oswald material, including Oswald's three required "References."

That missing Benevolent Street file might contain Schacht's attempts to contact Oswald's two personal "References" and/or the required "Minister who knows you."[298] But those attempts would of course have failed or faked responses would have been submitted to the College, to Dr. Schacht, or both, because the two personal references and the ministerial reference (apparently supplied by Oswald) were twisted truths: though reality-linked, they were only partly true.[299] Oswald's college application listed his personal references as "Mr. A. Botelho," a U.S. Marine with the "MCAF, MACS-9 Santa Anna, Calif." and "Mr. R. Calore," a U.S. Marine at the same 'location.'[300] The apparent misspelling "Santa Anna" for Santa Ana, California, was consistent with misspellings in other Oswald Albert Schweitzer College records. Two Marines, James A. Botelho[301] (not "A. Botelho") and Anthony Calore[302] (not "R. Calore"), were in the same military group as Oswald in El Toro, California; both knew Oswald, but neither of the two could be called a friend of Oswald close enough to qualify as a personal reference for Albert Schweitzer College.[303] Further, neither the historic Botelho nor Calore is represented in any JFK/Oswald public record document, though their 'references' (from whatever military or intelligence source) COULD have been in Reverend Robert Schacht's Oswald Benevolent file in Providence, spirited away by FBI agents in December, 1963.

## Oswald's Suspect Albert Schweitzer College References

The Warren Commission's photocopy of the application form reproduced the spaces for the two "References" and "a Minister who knows you,"[304] but its PRINTED transcription of the completed application, much easier to read than the apparently faded original document, omitted (without explanation) both the "Name and Address" slots for the "Minister" reference and Oswald's handwritten entries for the ministerial slots at the bottom of the form.[305] Why? A readable application requiring a clerical reference would have strongly suggested the religious context of the college to which Oswald (or someone in his name) was applying. Since the FBI, the CIA, other investigative agencies, and apparently the Warren Commission and its staff presumably knew about the liberal religious character of Albert Schweitzer College, only those individuals and groups who made post-assassination inquiries (beyond the official government investigation) might miss the required ministerial reference. Oswald's handwritten ministerial reference (given in response to "Name and Address of a Minister who knows you") was "Chaplin [sic] W. Waters, MCAF Chapel, MCAF, Santa Anna [sic], California" (CE 228). Like Oswald's two enlisted Marine references, his ministerial reference was at best half-true. No "W. Waters" counseled the Santa Ana servicemen, but Rev. Howard E. Waters, a Southern Baptist minister stationed at MACAF, Santa Ana, California, from 1947 through 1959 (retiring in June, 1970) was available. I wrote to Rev. H.E. Waters, but he apparently decided not to respond to my queries concerning his Marine service (including his inclusion in CE 228).

Albert Schweitzer College never suggested to Oswald in any surviving correspondence that his acceptance was automatic. In the same paragraph of the letter dated March 28, 1959, from Erika Weibel, Secretary of Albert Schweitzer College, to Oswald[306] that directed him to use the "proper forms" to be mailed to Switzerland and Providence, Weibel wrote: "Upon [your] acceptance, a deposit [from you] . . . is required."[307] Obviously some minimum evaluation process was to take place either in Switzerland, in Providence, or both (if both, more letters were therefore exchanged). According to Weibel, if Oswald were accepted, the college would duly inform him, and Oswald would then acknowledge his acceptance and send a deposit to Switzerland.[308]

Was an evaluation process carried out? Dr. Robert Schachtwas interviewed by the FBI on December 5th, 1963; the Unitarian pastor "recalled Oswald had filled out an application . . . in the spring of 1959 while still in the Marine Corps . . . . Because the Oswald application was approved, I [Dr. Schacht] am sure that he must have given three references[,] and their reports must have appeared satisfactory. But I cannot recall now who they were."[309]

Dr. Schacht's comments have always needed careful consideration. First, Schacht did not cite Oswald's reported letter of inquiry to him; rather, Schacht cited Oswald's March, 1959, ASC application. Did Schacht indeed receive a copy of Oswald's longer, "correct" application form? Second, Schacht stated that Oswald's "application was approved . . . ."[310] From where did Schacht get this information? Did the Swiss office of the college inform him of Oswald's acceptance? Did the FBI tell Schacht that Oswald had been accepted by Albert Schweitzer College? Or did his own Benevolent Street Oswald file contain that evidence? No existing documents support Dr. Schacht's statements.

But any relevant materials present in the Benevolent Street file would have been appropriated by the FBI, evidence apparently still held by the Bureau.

Only after an "acceptance" that obviously would be announced by mail was Oswald "required" to send "a deposit of $25.00" to Switzerland.[311] His registration, short of an actual physical appearance at the college, would then be complete.

Sometime after March 28th, 1959[312], and before June 19th, 1959[313], while still in the Marine Corps, Oswald received a letter of acceptance from ASC, a communication not now in any public record. Why do we know that? Because he could not have anticipated sending his deposit until after he was accepted: "Upon acceptance."[314]

On June 19th, 1959, Oswald wrote to Albert Schweitzer College, apparently citing the college's acceptance of his application and submitting his "required" deposit.[315] Oswald reportedly had written to the college when he enclosed the deposit: "I am very glad to have been accepted for the third term of your college next year."[316] But Oswald also added a curious request: "Any new information on the school or even the students who will attend next year will be appreciated."[317]

Sometime in late June or early July, 1959, Lee Harvey Oswald wrote to his mother that he had been "accepted" by Albert Schweitzer College and that he "had sent a registration fee [to the college]."[318] But that letter also is not in the public record.

Despite the fact that Oswald could not attend Albert Schweitzer College unless he received an early discharge, after his college acceptance letter arrived, Oswald wrote to his brother: "Pretty soon I'll be getting out of the Corps and I know what I want to be and how I'm going to be it . . . ."[319]

In one of those curious knots of events and postal communications in Oswald's life story, Lee's mother had written to him of a long-standing insurance claim she had brought against a Fort Worth store alleging her nose had been injured when a candy jar fell on it; according to Mrs. Oswald, though four doctors found her fit and in good health, she was totally disabled.[320] Lee wrote to his mother in June, 1959, that the Red Cross would be contacting her to validate his argument he had to be discharged from the Marine Crops in order to return home and be her sole support.[321] Had a real investigation of Mrs. Oswald's reportedly disabling injury occurred, the Red Cross would have issued a negative report and Lee's application for an early discharge would most likely have been disallowed.

Oswald filed his documents in July, 1959, with the Red Cross[322], and his mother sent him communications from two of her friends, a lawyer and a doctor, and included her own affidavit.[323] Again, the transparency of Mrs. Oswald's disability would have been recognized had the Marine Corps done any real investigation. Oswald's request for an early discharge based upon a disability claim was filed on August 17th, 1959, and it was approved: on September 3rd, 1959, Oswald was "detached from duty."[324] On September 4th, 1959, Oswald requested a passport that he was granted six days later.

Earlier, on July 10th, 1959, Erika Weibel, the Albert Schweitzer College Secretary, responded to Oswald's (June 19th, 1959) "letter" that most probably acknowledged the college's acceptance of his application, writing to thank him for his June 19th letter with its "enclosed deposit . . . for the third term [that is, the third trimester of the regular Albert Schweitzer College year] . . . ."[325]

Beyond this series of odd, delayed, and (for the historical record) missing postal responses, Albert Schweitzer College now expected Lee Harvey Oswald to attend its up-coming program of instruction.

But on March 22, 1960, Hans Casparis[326], the founder, director, and ultimately the president of Albert Schweitzer College in Switzerland, wrote to Lee Harvey Oswald, apparently assuming that Oswald was still in the Marine Corps, and reportedly changed the college's initial schedule. That letter was finally opened by Lee's mother in Fort Worth, giving Mrs. Oswald some hope that her son was indeed not lost.

## Only for Oswald: The ASC Schedule Change

The letter from Hans Casparis, the Albert Schweitzer College director, was posted to Lee Harvey Oswald at Lee's Marine Corps address, forwarded several times[327], and finally arrived in Marguerite Oswald's mail on April 6th, 1960, just six days before the announced opening date of the regular third term at Albert Schweitzer College.

That Hans Casparis letter has always demanded a careful evaluation.

It was mailed on March 22, 1960[328], to Oswald at his correct Marine address, though the city's name was misspelled: "Santa Anna" instead of "Santa Ana."[329] Oswald himself had twice misspelled the name of the city in his two application forms.[330] However, the heading of the Casparis letter from Albert Schweitzer College was itself incorrect, listing the wrong California city entirely: "Santa Barbara."[331]

The letter was signed by Professor Hans Casparis of Albert Schweitzer College[332], the founder[333] and (at least in 1959-1960) the director[334] of the Swiss institution.

According to Casparis, the college's "first lecture" would be held on April 19th, 1960, rather than April 21st.[335] This change meant that students would have to "arrive either on the evening of Monday, the 18th, or before noon on April 19th,"[336] making it possible to end the term "the weekend of July 2nd, instead of the 6th . . . ."[337]

But this 'change' did NOT match either the information Oswald apparently had available when he applied to the college or the official application form Oswald reportedly mailed (according to the Warren Commission) to the college; Oswald's Spring trimester was to run from April 12th, 1960, to June 27th, 1960[338], the college's listed "third" term[339]. Casparis' Spring trimester was scheduled for April 19th through July 6th, according to Casparis' letter to Oswald (posted to him at his Marine Corps address and eventually opened by Lee's mother).[340] Casparis' change for prospective student Lee Harvey Oswald constituted the THIRD different Spring trimester opening at Albert Schweitzer College, but I have found no record in the available Albert

Schweitzer College documents at Harvard Divinity School Library supporting this schedule modification.

Casparis hoped that Oswald could "fit this change" into his "travel plans,"[341] but the college president assured Oswald that "we" (presumably the college's administration) would understand if he could not, and asked Oswald to "drop us a line so that we know."[342] The casual tone of Casparis' letter to Oswald, reporting a major change in the college's calendar while at least some of the college's estimated forty students were in transit, is disturbing. Even if fewer than fifty students were expected at the college, so odd a schedule change necessitating so many personal itinerary changes should have provoked serious questions about the college's administration.

But did it ever happen?

Dennis Bartholomew (a diligent JFK researcher) succeeded in finding a former Albert Schweitzer College student who had attended the Spring trimester in 1960.[343] That student confirmed Bartholomew's doubt about the Casparis letter, asserting that the delay (reportedly announced to Oswald by the college's founder and director Casparis) never took place.[344] According to this crucial witness, all the registered students for the Spring trimester arrived on time for the college's previously scheduled opening.[345] Further, the student did not recall seeing Lee Harvey Oswald's name on the student roster for that trimester.[346]

Yet I discovered an Albert Schweitzer College document verifying the school was indeed expecting Oswald for the Spring trimester, according to a post-assassination review of the college's Oswald connection that took place in Churwalden.[347]

Still, the March 22, 1960, Casparis letter to Oswald announcing the college's schedule change must have given his mother's spirits a tremendous lift, whatever its oddity, as it came just when she was getting little or no support from her sludgy State Department.

Lee might still be on his way to Switzerland.

The letter's importance, of course, went far beyond the personal: it initiated a series of postings[348] that helped to energize the FBI's Oswald investigation in Switzerland.

## More Strange ASC Mailings

Lee' mother immediately responded to Casparis' letter. Mrs. Oswald's postal answer, written and (probably) mailed on April 6th, 1960, the day she opened the Casparis letter to her son[349], was as odd as Casparis' change of schedule letter.[350]

Mrs. Oswald wrote: "A few months ago he [Lee] wrote me that he was accepted by your college and [he] had sent a registration fee [to you]."[351]

But what could Mrs. Oswald have been thinking when she wrote Professor Casparis that Lee had sent her a letter just a "few months ago"? From July 10th, 1959, to a "few months" prior to April 6th, 1960, was at least EIGHT months: had Mrs. Oswald suddenly lost touch with her timeline?

On July 10th, 1959, the college acknowledged receiving Oswald's deposit[352] in a letter from Lee dated June 19th, 1959.[353] In Lee's letter of June 19th, 1959, he was "very glad" to be accepted, so he had to have received an acceptance letter prior to June 19th, 1959.[354]

Sometime around June 19th, 1959, Oswald must have informed his mother of his acceptance and that he was "looking forward to going there."[355] This missing letter would, of course, have been written to his mother while Oswald was still in the Marine Corps.

Recall that on January 22nd, 1960, Mrs. Oswald had sent Lee a $25.00 Foreign Money Transfer that was returned to her.[356] This transfer was monitored by the New York FBI office.[357] The Bureau memo on that aborted transfer was one of four memos withheld from the CIA, and the cover memo of February 26th, 1960, was withheld from the CIA and later the Warren Commission. The most crucial of the Bureau's counterintelligence responses to Mrs. Oswald's Moscow mailings now occurred. The New York Office requested that Mrs. Oswald be interviewed.[358]

## Oswald's Mother and the FBI's False Identity/Illegals Investigation

But this interview was not an ordinary one. The FBI had most probably been intercepting both Mrs. Oswald's and Robert Oswald's mail. Alan Belmont testified quietly to the Warren Commission that Oswald's "mother had sent . . . $25 to him in Moscow so we [the FBI] went to interview her in April 1960 . . . ."[359] But TWO interviews were scheduled, of course, apparently by Bureau Counterintelligence, originating either with Alan Belmont or William Sullivan in Washington; a March 9th, 1960, instruction memorandum from headquarters was sent to the New York Bureau field office and then relayed to the Bureau's Dallas field office.[360] The New York field office's Oswald file on the projected interviews was designated as a counterintelligence concern.[361] The subsequent FBI file on Oswald covering these interviews was opened "under the Foreign Counterintelligence Matters serial 105, file 976."[362]

The local Bureau was given specific guidelines on how to manage interviewing Marguerite Oswald.[363] Four full paragraphs of this memo remain censored by the FBI[364], but with what is left, the import of the interview and the guidelines governing it are measurable.

John Newman's observation on this Bureau memorandum was off the mark: "The instructions we are able to see appear to be general rules applicable to any interview . . . [in] what was apparently an FBI program for siphoning information from people's bank accounts."[365] The "siphoning" of bank account information was indeed a part of the operation, but it was not its ultimate goal.

Examine each of the uncensored lines in the instruction memo. First: "The Bureau has furnished the following instructions to be observed in this program."[366] The phrase "this program" together with the specific history of Oswald's background, trip to Europe, and his subsequent 'disappearance,' all clearly point to a Bureau counterespionage operation that featured interviewing family members in the United States on material of value sent to family members in the Soviet Union, other Communist countries, or "neutral" countries (for example, Switzerland and Finland).

The rest of what has remained of the memo and the record of the FBI interview gives further evidence supporting this hypothesis.

The Bureau agents were urged to gain the "cooperation" of those interviewed: "the impression should not be created that the Bureau is investigating the persons being interviewed, or that their action is, in itself, derogatory as in regard to their loyalty to the US."[367] The memorandum instructed interviewing agents to cover a specific series of topics[368]: What were the reasons for the funds' transmittal? What was the identity of the purchaser of the transmittal document? What was the "relationship" between the purchaser and the "payee"?[369]

Further, and significantly, the "individuals interviewed" were to be questioned as to whether they had been asked "to furnish items of personal identification to their relatives abroad."[370]

These questions to be asked were not intended to elicit information for the "FBI's bank peeping project"[371]; rather, the other way around. Foreign money transfers, especially to Communist countries or to ostensibly neutral countries such as Switzerland, were investigated as leads in suspected false identity cases: in the FBI's pursuit of espionage "illegals." The opening, doubling and hiding of counterintelligence, internal security, New York, Dallas, and Bureau headquarters files on Lee Harvey Oswald from October, 1959 through no later than May, 1960[372] were all evidence Oswald constituted a major, troubling "illegal" case, THE critical issue for the FBI, serious enough so that the Bureau withheld everything from the Warren Commission except the thinnest version of its fear of an Oswald false identity problem.

But that FBI suspicion was also the basis for withholding both the Bureau's false identity concern AND the evidence for its false identity/"illegal" hypothesis from the CIA.

## The Oswald Challenge Game

Imagine a multi-dimensional game board of intelligence and espionage activities stretching across the Eurasian meta-continent in its developmental mode for over a century or more and being played with greater and greater sophistication by the 1950s. Among the many trained players, pawns, and ambiguous game pieces was Lee Harvey Oswald. Espionage game imagery has had a long and fascinating history, an especially relevant use that of Flora Lewis in her well-written though not necessarily accurate study of Noel Field.[373] Field's stepdaughter specifically rejected the "pawn" designation for her stepfather, insisting he was, in fact, a major piece or player. If so, he apparently was able to transform (or be transformed) from red to black and back to red again: but no current version of chess or any extension has a piece capable of playing for both sides, though it is a fascinating possibility. And Noel Field would certainly qualify. Edward

Epstein adopted the game-playing imagery (possibly influenced by James Angleton), specifically identifying Oswald as a minor piece offered up as a provocative and possibly entrapping sacrifice in his Chapter VIII title: "The Russian Gambit—Accepted."[374] Epstein's Chapter XIII was also called "Oswald's Game." Finally, Jean Davison borrowed Epstein's exact phrase for the title of her own book.

But Oswald was more than either a pawn or game piece, no matter how complex: he himself was the center of "The Oswald Challenge"[375] within the greater espionage contest. Other individuals, real or invented, have been similar in form or function in this larger espionage challenge.[376] The Oswald Challenge was readily apparent in the 1959-1961 period when, almost joyfully, FBI and CIA intelligence and counterintelligence figures (and possibly cooperating or competing KGB and GRU agents) entered, using the 'real' or the fictionalized Oswald (or both) in several espionage and counterintelligence operations. The Soviet Union, Mexico City, and Dallas were three of the most important game board sites. In fact, John Newman caught some of the game-playing nuances when he observed how "Oswald-related information was handled [as] . . . part of an [Angleton/CIA counterintelligence] operation to search out . . . [a] suspected [KGB] mole [in the CIA]." [377]At the same time, Newman concluded that evidence also strongly suggested a second and separate Agency counterintelligence action had made use of Oswald's alleged defection to the Soviet Union.[378] If Newman is correct, Lee's trip to Europe itself would qualify as a separate sub-game, possibly run by the Office of Naval Intelligence, the CIA, or both.

Initially having nothing to do with the JFK assassination but eventually used by the facilitators who ran the Dallas assassination, the Oswald Challenge would account for a number of extraordinary complications and contradictions in the Oswald narrative. While some elements of the CIA and the FBI were complicit in the game, others (who were not players) were concerned.

## The FBI's Stolen Identity Investigation

The Bureau's suspicion that Oswald had become part of, or fallen victim to, a stolen identity operation in the Soviet Union or Switzerland (or both) shaped the FBI's interviews of both Robert Oswald and Lee's mother. And that same suspicion blocked the Bureau from sharing its intercept of Mrs. Oswald's mail material with the CIA and later accounted for the FBI withholding its false identity concerns from the Warren Commission (and thereby protecting the Bureau's massive postal opening program).

When Mrs. Oswald was interviewed on April 28th, 1960, by FBI agent John Fain, she reviewed with him a number of significant topics. She reportedly spoke of her aborted foreign money transfer; gave a short history of the Oswald family; reviewed Lee's Marine Corps experience; told Fain about her letters sent to Texas Representatives Rayburn and Wright and Secretary of State Christian Herter; and she reviewed the Hans Casparis letter from Albert Schweitzer College, that, according to Bureau Agent Fain (from the Dallas Bureau field office) "raised her hopes . . . [Lee] might actually be en route to . . . Switzerland . . . ."[379] Oddly enough, she told the FBI agent she intended to write a letter to the college inquiring whether it had "received any word from Lee."[380] But she had already done so several weeks prior to her FBI interview. Why the (possible) deception? Or did Mrs. Oswald confuse the two ("Fannan" and Fain) interviews? She did indeed write Rayburn, Wright, and Herter AFTER the reported EARLIER "Fannan" interview. The letters were sent out on March 7th, 1960, more than a month BEFORE FBI Special Agent Fain saw her, who then reported on exactly those mailings.[381]

Wouldn't a key event such as a Fort Worth FBI agent responding to your plea for help represent an important precedent for her Dallas Bureau interview? But either Mrs. Oswald withheld information about her earlier FBI "Fannan" interview or, for whatever reason, Fain neglected to report the visit to Mrs. Oswald by the alleged Fort Worth Bureau agent.

But Fain did ask Lee's mother one of the key questions relating to stolen personal identity: did she, he inquired, send "any items of personal identification" to her son?[382] No, Mrs. Oswald had replied, though she reported that Lee had taken his birth certificate with him.[383]

The missing item of personal identification certainly impressed Dallas Agent Fain, precisely because an authentic birth certificate was a key document in a false identity espionage case. His report was reviewed by the Bureau's New York field office[384] whose counterintelligence intercept program—the FBI's "Z Coverage"—was responsible for monitoring all the mail between the United States and the Soviet Union.[385]

Agent John Fain submitted a report on May 12th, 1960, summarizing his interview of Mrs. Oswald, but his 'case title' was "Funds Transmitted to Residents of Russia." [386]The Fain document was an FBI domestic/internal security report (serial 105)[387], and it became "the first external document [on Oswald] circulated within the Soviet Russia Division at the CIA."[388] A Freedom of Information Act (FOIA) search of the remaining Office of Security files might verify that the CIA's Counterintelligence staff, no later than June, 1960, was deeply interested in the Oswald false identity story, especially as it involved Oswald's new passport and his birth certificate.[389]

On May 23rd, 1960, the FBI's New York field office sent an air telegram to Washington headquarters, indicating the Bureau's New York counterespionage program considered that the information Fain gathered in his interview with Mrs. Oswald pointed to a major false identity case. Specifically, the New York field office targeted the evidence of the undelivered letters and the missing birth certificate.[390] The NY field office also recommended to Bureau headquarters "that a copy of [Mrs. Oswald's] . . . interview be furnished to the State Department . . . ."[391] On May 24th, 1960, the Bureau forwarded the Fain report of that interview to the Department of State.[392]

The "Oswald-imposter thesis"[393] had now become a concern of both FBI headquarters and the State Department, though State, of course, had already been alerted to Oswald's apparent disappearance by his mother's letter to Secretary of

State Christian Herter. J. Edgar Hoover wrote an official Bureau letter to the State Department's Office of Security on June 3rd, 1960, warning that an "imposter" might be using Oswald's birth certificate, asking State to supply the FBI with any information it had "concerning subject [Oswald]."[394]

On June 6th, 1960, Lee's mother wrote to Albert Schweitzer College's Professor Hans Casparis; she was replying to Casparis's letter of April 26th, 1960, that was, in turn, a response to her April 6th, 1960, communication to Casparis.[395] But despite Mrs. Oswald's deep concern for her son's suspicious disappearance, she allowed ALL of May, 1960, to slip away before she wrote Casparis at Albert Schweitzer College.[396]

Where was Lee Harvey Oswald? Why had he disappeared?

# Essay Two

# False Identity and the Soviet and American Illegals Programs

The FBI mounted a major investigation, its hunt for Lee Harvey Oswald, missing from Switzerland. Yet despite the seriousness of the Bureau search, the pace of the inquiry run for the FBI and the reports of that search were as slow as all the correspondence concerning the apparently absent Oswald.

The Bureau record of Oswald's whereabouts or that of a false Oswald in Switzerland was heavily censored in available FBI documents before 1995.[1] But over Bureau objections, in December, 1995, the Assassinations Record Review Board managed to flush out five crucial documents that were largely un-redacted.[2] The documents proved that the FBI did much more than send an agent to talk to Oswald's brother and mother.[3]

The FBI apparently felt that Oswald's reported travels, his alleged defection, his non-response to his mother's postings (two of them having been returned to her unopened), and his Albert Schweitzer College application all constituted a major counterintelligence problem.[4]

## The Missing Oswald as an FBI False Identity/Illegals Case

On June 3rd, 1960, FBI Director Hoover had sent out two inquiries on the 'missing' Lee Harvey Oswald: the first went to the Office of Security in the Department of State.[5] The Bureau's false identity thesis was obvious in Hoover's request: "Since there is a possibility that an imposter is using Oswald's birth certificate, any current information the Department of State may have concerning subject [Oswald] will be appreciated." [6]Hoover's memo, withheld from the Warren Commission, was finally released to the National Archives in 1975.[7]

Richard A. Frank, the Department of State's legal liaison with the FBI, speculated that Bureau Director Hoover and his allies in State's Office of Security effected the disappearance of the memorandum.[8] But David Slawson, former Warren Commission counsel, suggested that if the FBI's inquiry had been about "something related to the CIA," the Agency might then have been able to suppress the Hoover memo.[9]

Of course, the CIA's Office of Security could itself have been the clandestine sponsor of Oswald's false identity operation.

Hoover's second communication concerning the 'missing' Oswald went to the Federal Police of Switzerland[10] (SFP), that country's national intelligence agency, through the American Embassy in Paris.[11] Why the State Department offices in Paris rather than Bern? Bypassing the American Foreign Office presence in Bern by the FBI, despite the fact that a Bureau Legat was stationed in Bern, strongly suggested the FBI still considered the Swiss location was OSS/CIA territory, dating back to both World Wars when spymaster Allen Dulles ran American intelligence programs out of Bern.[12] Bern, therefore, would have been suspect in any FBI false identity investigation that might involve CIA agents or assets.

Peter Dale Scott (former Canadian diplomat, retired professor of literature, investigative historian, and poet) in a private conversation with me in November, 2000, found my "Bern bypass" speculation without merit; he asserted the Legat in Paris was responsible for both France and Switzerland, since no American Embassy existed in Bern. But a part of the Albert Schweitzer College story, that it attracted students who were philosophically or politically liberal and therefore suspect (in the overheated anti-Communist atmosphere of Cold War Washington) persuaded me that Bern was indeed bypassed despite an FBI Legat stationed in Bern who had a major role in the Bureau's Swiss adventure.

## False Conspiracy Stories

The afternoon of November 22nd, 1963, before any real evidence in the JFK assassination was thoroughly analyzed or even initially evaluated, "officials in Dallas and elsewhere were suggesting . . . that Oswald was part of a Communist conspiracy, acting on orders out of Havana or Moscow. Worse yet, highly dubious reports, already in U.S. intelligence files, provided some backing for these false conspiracy stories—which soon began to circulate about Jack Ruby as well."[13] Both the FBI and the CIA promoted the Communist plot theory with the Red Marine Oswald as its hitman, what Peter Dale Scott called the "first-phase" explanation of the JFK murder. When the Communist conspiracy charges reached their peak, however, "phase two" kicked in, and both Oswald and Ruby became "lone" killers, with their alleged or actual connections to foreign agents, Organized Crime, and American intelligence suppressed by both the FBI and CIA and, later, the Warren Commission.[14]

Both "phase one" and "phase two" explanations were clearly well-coordinated public relations operations[15] run both inside and outside the government, especially within the CIA and the FBI.[16] Inside American intelligence, the two phases were controlled by Agency and Bureau counterespionage officers James Angleton and William Sullivan[17], who were frequent counterintelligence collaborators.

Bureau chief J. Edgar Hoover had put his "anti-subversive specialists" to work early in the JFK investigation, including William Sullivan and William Branigan: together they were responsible for counterintelligence, espionage, the Socialist Workers' Party, the Fair Play for Cuba Committee, and the FBI's mail intercept program[18] (matched in the Agency by James Angleton and William King Harvey, Jr.), all areas that were and still remain relevant to the Oswald story.

## The Kostikov, Cubela, Oswald Triangulation

"Angleton's pretext for [assuming command of the Agency's JFK inquiry] . . . was a cable from [Mexico City CIA Station Chief] Win Scott, linking [reputed KGB agent Valery] Kostikov [in the Soviet's Mexico City consulate] to the CIA's . . . [Western Hemisphere] agent Rolando Cubela."[19] Meetings between Kostikov and Cubela could indeed have occurred, especially if Kostikov himself was a double agent working for the CIA[20]: in 1963, CIA officers Win Scott and Angleton may have decided to use Kostikov opportunistically to reinforce the reputed link between Oswald (as the designated assassin) and both the Soviet Union and Cuba.

In effect, they would have triangulated Kostikov, Cubela, and Oswald.

Indeed, the CIA in 1963 reportedly had (somehow) listened in to a call from "Oswald" to the Soviet Consulate in Mexico City as the caller made an appointment with "Valery Kostikov," ostensibly a Soviet "consular officer."[21] In turn, the Agency reported the intercepted call to the FBI.[22]

Transmitting privileged CIA information or guarding the CIA's Soviet Consulate secret, Epstein wrote that the FBI "knew through a double agent" that Kostikov was KGB.[23] Epstein's source was, of course, James Angleton; Epstein was covering for the Agency when he stated that Kostikov's "Thirteenth Department of the KGB" was in control of "saboteurs" based in North America.[24] In fact, that department was, more importantly, one of the two Soviet centers of civilian false identities, illegals, and assassination, three areas significant to the reality or fiction of both Lee Harvey Oswald and Rolando Cubela.

J. Edgar Hoover himself had ample reason to suppress the Bureau's knowledge of Kostikov as KGB, specifically in support of the survival of the FBI. Not giving the White House any information from the Bureau's security file on Oswald, including the Kostikov material from the CIA, insured that the FBI would not be accused of an enormous lapse in national security. And the suppression of 1. the alleged "Oswald" and "Kostikov" link and 2. the Oswald, Kostikov, and "Cubella" triangulation may have been precisely the CIA's intention when it sent the Mexico City report to the Bureau.[25]

James Angleton had self-servingly informed Epstein the CIA's "SAS Division," reportedly responsible for handling Rolando Cubela and the Agency's assassination plot against Fidel Castro, had withheld Cubela's operational files from Angleton and his staff. Thereby (according to Angleton), the Kostikov/Cubela association was effectively hidden first from Angleton and then from the Warren Commission for whom Angleton served as CIA liaison.[26]

In fact, long before Mexico City and the JFK assassination, Rolando Cubela had been of intense operational interest to both the FBI and the CIA. Hence, it was extremely unlikely that CIA counterintelligence, the Agency's Office of Security, and Angleton in particular lacked knowledge of Cubela.[27]

The triangulation began with 1. Oswald and Kostikov and 2. Cubela and Kostikov: closing that triangulation would link Oswald to Cubela.

## Rolando Cubela

Rolando Cubela was one of the heroes of the anti-Batista uprising. Reputed to have been directly involved in a revolutionary assassination[28], he was actually part of a group of young Cuban students who fired on Batista police and Army officers leaving the Montmartre night club on October 28th, 1956.[29] An officer's wife was slightly wounded, a military colonel more severely wounded, and Colonel Blanco Rico, the chief of Batista's military intelligence, apparently a deliberate target of the Cubela group, was killed.[30] But Rico was the only ranking Batista police officer who disapproved of torturing suspects and detainees[31], and Fidel Castro publicly condemned the killing; could the shooting that included (if not organized by) Cubela have been a provocation?[32]

Later, Cubela "led the Students' Revolutionary Directorate guerrilla forces in the mountains of central Cuba . . . ."[33] Cubela's patron was the exiled Carlos Prio, whose days in Batista's Cuba were marked by close relations with the casino and narcotics operations of Meyer Lansky and Santo Trafficante.[34] Despite funding the yacht *Granma* used by Castro to open his attack on Batista, Prio and his associates were ultimately unacceptable to Castro.[35] Complicating the relationship between Cubela and Castro was Cubela's reputed need for recognition[36]: Cubela brought his Directorate into Havana and precipitated "a confrontation between Castro and [Cubela's] . . . directorate that nearly led to an armed clash the first week after victory."[37]

Cubela was probably working with (or at least had been approached by) the CIA no later than 1959.[38] Of the U.S. intelligence documents on Cubela (sixty-eight of those documents are specifically CIA) in the JFK Assassination Collection at NARA, the earliest is dated April 28th, 1959: the Agency first approached Cubela when he had been posted to Spain by Castro as Cuba's Military Attaché. Scores of FBI documents on Cubela from 1959 though 1963 clearly indicate that American intelligence was closely tracking Cubela. His CIA operation was called AMLASH, and as an asset of the Agency, Cubela was code-named AMLASH-1.[39] Given Cubela's history of involvement with the CIA that ran through 1966 when Cuban counterintelligence finally arrested and charged him, Cubela may have been an early asset of the CIA dedicated to bringing down Batista.[40] Cubela's role as Prio's agent and an Agency asset would explain Prio's support of Castro, Cubela's continuing contacts and meetings with representatives of the CIA in Europe, and Castro's willingness to allow Cubela to play a doubled (if not tripled) espionage role through 1966. Cubela's early anti-Batista action for the CIA would also explain Cubela's 'trial' in Cuba, his later 'prison' interview, and those agents or assets of the CIA who had previously supported Castro against Batista[41] helping Cubela leave Cuba after his sentence was reportedly commuted by Castro. In fact, Cubela may NEVER have been in a Cuban prison except as he was interviewed by writer Anthony Summers. Peter Dale Scott observed: "After 18 years [reportedly] in prison, Cubela was released, and at last report had moved to Spain. Such a relocation seems difficult without [Central Intelligence] Agency help."[42]

The CIA knew about Cubela (AMLASH-1), of course, at the very moment of the JFK assassination, but chose not to reveal the Agency's covert relation to him, since the whole story of CIA assassination attempts against foreign leaders would have been opened, including the anti-Castro CIA/Organized Crime collaboration linked to the Kennedy killing, at least according to the House Select Committee on Assassinations. Had Cubela testified as late as 1975 to the Senate Intelligence Committee, he would have significantly contradicted the Agency's version of his AMLASH role[43], opening up still more unexplored dimensions of the plots against Castro and the CIA's duplicity.[44]

After Cubela was interviewed by author Anthony Summers (reportedly in a Cuban prison) in 1978, Summers concluded, somewhat awkwardly: "If Cubela's version [of his clandestine relationship to the Agency] is accepted as truthful, [then] several CIA officers are exposed as guilty not only of going along with a plan to kill Castro, without authorization, but of actually inciting Cubela to do it . . . ."[45]

Both the FBI and the CIA had information linking the Cubela/AMLASH plot directly to the 1960-1962 attempts against Castro run by an Agency/Syndicate coalition that included Organized Crime boss Santo Trafficante and corrupt Florida Teamsters, established in testimony from a Cubela associate received by a U.S. Senate subcommittee.[46]

But something more was withheld both in 1963-64 and in 1975. According to Castro biographer and journalist Tad Szulc[47], it was the Second Naval Guerrilla, a smaller but more secret version of the Bay of Pigs invasion. Planned for 1964, it reunited the CIA and its anti-Castro Cuban exiles, with James McCord and E. Howard Hunt as Agency players in the action.[48] Both were psychological warfare and CIA Office of Security operatives.

The invasion was to be energized by the killing of Fidel Castro, a CIA plan prepared in Paris and in Madrid with Rolando Cubela the designated assassin.[49] Cubela's friend and associate, Manuel Artime, a CIA asset, was the leader of the Cuban exiles' second invasion.[50] According to Tad Szulc, Second Naval Guerrilla was not abandoned until 1965[51]; in 1966, Rolando Cubela was arrested in Cuba after Fidel Castro's counterintelligence agents exposed the operation.

### The Oswald/Cubela Intelligence Links

What do these assassination and invasion plans implicating Rolando Cubela have to do with Lee Harvey Oswald?

Cubela, approached by the CIA no later than 1959, was being tracked by FBI Legat communications from 1960 through 1966 originating in Madrid, in Paris, and in Bern,

Switzerland, at the same time Lee Harvey Oswald was being tracked by FBI Paris and Bern Legat communications from 1960 through 1964. Narrowly, in the same time period (1960-1964), in two of the same countries (France and Switzerland), and from the same Bureau Legat agents communicating with FBI Director J. Edgar Hoover, the identical intelligence topics were crossing, linked to either Cubela or Oswald.[52]

From 1959 through 1964, the Central Intelligence Agency was monitoring Rolando Cubela, keeping tabs on the Fair Play for Cuba Committee, meeting with Cubela and planning to kill Fidel Castro, and intercepting Lee Harvey Oswald's mail. At the moment of the JFK assassination and for some time beyond, the CIA was directly involved with Rolando Cubela.

From 1960 through 1964, including Oswald's defection to the Soviet Union and the Bureau's JFK inquiry, the FBI Legat cable traffic from Paris and Bern to Washington, D.C., carried messages about Rolando Cubela and Lee Harvey Oswald, *and both men were suspected by American intelligence of being fake defectors.*

James Angleton had called AMLASH-1 "Cubella" apparently because of a message Angleton received from the chief of the CIA station in Mexico City: according to the message, "Cubella" had been in contact with Valery Kostikov in the Soviet Union's Mexican City Consulate office.[53] But the CIA from Mexico City had also reported that Oswald (or, more likely, a fake Oswald) met with Kostikov. Both the CIA and FBI apparently believed or knew that Kostikov was a KGB agent; therefore, American intelligence was concerned that both Oswald and Cubela had (according to the CIA) a KGB association. Through Kostikov, Cubela and Oswald were linked. *The Kostikov connection was a clear signal that the two (possibly fake) defectors, one American (Oswald), the other Cuban (Cubela), had been involved in a Communist conspiracy directed against John F. Kennedy.*

Only after both Oswald and Ruby[54] became officially lone assassins were the ominous connections between Oswald, Kostikov, and Cubela muted and suppressed.[55]

In 1960, American intelligence concerns about Cubela and Oswald that registered when Oswald turned up "missing" in Switzerland were matched in 1963-1964 when Oswald was charged with the murder of John F. Kennedy.

What should have been a straightforward investigation of that missing Oswald, permanently late for his Albert Schweitzer College classes in 1960, was made darkly dense with American intelligence counterespionage; with FBI and CIA messages from Bern, Paris, Madrid; AMLASH; with the Fair Play for Cuba Committee; and with assassination plots against two heads of state in 1963-1964.

Both the FBI and the CIA withheld that dark density from a series of American presidents—and from the American people—for as long as possible.

The AMLASH/Cubela story has remained heavily censored by both the Agency and the Bureau.[56] The CIA and the FBI had good reason to avoid tangling the Cubela story with Lee Harvey Oswald in 1960 and again in 1963-1964. In 1960, the parallel tracks left by Cubela and Oswald led to Cuba, to liberal/left-wing student overseas meetings and education (Cubela was frequently overseas attending those student conferences as Cuba's representative), to Switzerland, and to the Fair Play For Cuba Committee (in the United States and the Soviet Union). In 1963-1964, the stops on the Cubela/Oswald tracks additionally included Mexico City, the KGB and the CIA, and U.S. assassination plots directed against heads of state.

Rolando Cubela had been a prominent Cuban presence in liberal and radical student meetings and conferences; U.S. intelligence in Switzerland was aware of Cubela's operations; Cubela had been tracked by the CIA (and may even have been an agent of the Agency when he was involved in liberal student groups); and Lee Harvey Oswald had registered at a Swiss liberal college. Later, both Oswald and Cubela were reported to have been in close touch with KGB officer Kostikov in Mexico City.

If American intelligence wanted to pursue the Communist conspiracy hypothesis in 1963-1964, the Oswald/Cubela confluence clearly was available. But after the "phase one"[57] Red assassination plot flurry, the American power structure apparently opted for the lone assassin of "phase two," and the Cubela/Oswald correspondences were indecently buried.

Was Bern, therefore, bypassed because of its association with Dulles/OSS/CIA in the 1960 inquiry regarding Oswald's Albert Schweitzer College's absence? The American intelligence cable traffic record now available from the National Archives strongly suggests so. Beginning in 1959, CIA messages on Cubela (to and from Havana, Madrid, and especially Paris) were extremely heavy.[58] In 1960, only three Bureau queries on Oswald went through Paris; no FBI Oswald traffic went through Bern; and, of twenty Bern Legat messages, only one on Cubela (9/29/62) was sent.[59]

The Bern FBI Legat line was always available, but FBI communications on Switzerland and Oswald in 1960 went through Paris; communications on Oswald through Bern opened up only AFTER the JFK assassination.[60]

Despite Peter Dale Scott's argument to me, Bern was indeed bypassed during the 1960 FBI/Swiss investigation of Lee Harvey Oswald, apparently for significant American intelligence reasons.

## The Swiss Federal Police and Oswald in Switzerland

The slow pace of the urgent hunt for Oswald had become obvious: on June 16th, 1960, ten days after Hoover asked his Bureau agent in the US Embassy in Paris to institute an immediate search for the missing Marine, the Embassy communicated with the Swiss Federal Police.[61] According to the Bureau "Legat" in the Paris Embassy, "pertinent information [on Oswald] was furnished . . . and . . . [the Swiss Federal Police] were requested to conduct [an] investigation . . . ."[62] According to that same memo, the Paris FBI "Legat" was in touch with the Swiss Federal Police no earlier than July 21st, 1960.[63]

Despite the June, 1960, Paris to Bern query (on behalf of the Bureau) and the following July 21st communication, the American Embassy in Paris did not confirm to the FBI that the Bureau had made a request for an investigation on "6/16/60" (that is, June 16th) and "discussed" that request on "7/21/60" (that is, July 21st)[64] until July 27th, in a memo from the Embassy in Paris to FBI Director J. Edgar Hoover.[65]

The FBI's false identity investigation had stalled.

Remarkably, the Swiss allegedly could not FIND Albert Schweitzer College.[66] Reportedly, not until September did they locate the college[67] because, according to the Swiss Federal Police, they "had no official records [of the college] on file . . . ." [68] This response by the SFP, however, is extremely suspect. Students from the United States and Europe had been applying to and attending the college since at least 1955 and had been attending the earlier Hans Casparis meetings in the Klosters since 1950. [69] How could hundreds of prospective students with authentic passports and visas from dozens of U.S. states and other nations leave no traceable records with Swiss immigration, tourism, and education offices?

Further, because of the liberal Protestant[70] founding background of the college together with the freedoms it offered its students, the college had, in fact, been in trouble with the Swiss Federal Police concerning its students' possession and use of recreational drugs.[71] Rev. Richard Boake, First President of the American chapter of the International Association for Religious Freedom, visited Albert Schweitzer College in 1964 and reported "some of the Americans brought in marijuana, and the college was a bit in trouble with the Swiss."[72] Certainly, therefore, the Swiss had records that should have been available to the FBI. But apparently the Federal Police were either ordered to report lack of knowledge about or made their own decision to report ignorance of the college.

The hunt for Lee Harvey Oswald had taken some time and effort: the Swiss Federal Police had conferred with the FBI in July, in August, and in September of 1960, finally locating the school, visiting the campus, and reporting back to the American Embassy in Paris.[73] The embassy, in turn, sent the information to the FBI in Washington.[74]

The September 27th memorandum from Paris to FBI headquarters recorded an apparently major intelligence effort by the Swiss: "considerable investigation had been conducted to locate the Albert Schweitzer College . . . since this college was previously unknown, and there was no official record of its existence in the [Swiss] Federal government records . . . ."[75] ASC was, of course, not "previously unknown" but, in fact, both known and readily accessible, at least since 1955[76], so this Swiss difficulty was suspicious, especially because Lee's mother had already been in touch with Albert Schweitzer College BEFORE the Swiss experienced their alleged problems in finding the college.

## The Four Bureau Memoranda from Paris About Oswald and Albert Schweitzer College

On October 12th, 1960, the Bureau's "Legat, Paris" sent the most relevant of the four memoranda to the "Director, FBI" on the hunt for Oswald in Switzerland from the FBI Legal Attaché in Paris to FBI Headquarters in Washington.[77]

Originally this document was "exempted [censored] by the FBI because it contained [so-called] foreign government information." [78]Apparently reviewed in 1977 and "exempted," then reviewed again in 1992 and "severely redacted,"[79] this "document was released in full" in December, 1995 with three other documents in the 1960 series of memos from the "Legat, Paris" to FBI Headquarters.[80]

It is this memorandum of October 12th, 1960, that is most significant.

The original source of the communication was the Swiss Federal Police submitting an investigative report to the American Embassy, the Bureau's "Legat, Paris," at the request of the FBI. [81]This Swiss report was available on October 1st, 1960.[82] According to the Swiss Federal Police (as reported by the FBI "legal attaché" at the Embassy in Paris):

Excerpt #1:

The investigation at the "Albert Schweitzer College"
located at Churwalden, Switzerland, revealed that
Oswald actually had announced his planned attendance at
this . . . school . . . beginning in the Fall of 1959.

. . . . . . . . . . . . . . . . . . . . . . . . . . . . . . . . . . . . . . . . . . . . . . . . . .

Excerpt #2:

He had originally written a letter from Moscow indicating
his intention to attend there [at Churwalden].

. . . . . . . . . . . . . . . . . . . . . . . . . . . . . . . . . . . . . . . . . . . . . . . . . .

Excerpt #3:

A letter which was addressed to him at this address
[the Moscow address or the ACS address?] by his mother
was returned to her since his whereabouts are unknown to the college.

. . . . . . . . . . . . . . . . . . . . . . . . . . . . . . . . . . . . . . . . . . . . . . . . . .

Excerpt #4:

The Swiss Federal Police advised that it is unlikely that he
[Oswald] would have attended the course [assumed to be the
Fall trimester] under a different name.

. . . . . . . . . . . . . . . . . . . . . . . . . . . . . . . . . . . . . . . . . . . . . . . . . .

Excerpt #5:

At the present time there is no record of a person possibly
identical with the subject [Oswald] who is registered for
the [Fall] courses beginning October 2.

These five passages constitute the most important part of what was communicated by the Swiss Federal Police to the "Legat, Paris" and then from the FBI's Legal Attaché in Paris to FBI Director J. Edgar Hoover.

The memorandum was headed by its "Subject": "LEE HARVEY OSWALD" and "INTERNAL SECURITY-R"—the missing Oswald, a domestic intelligence case relating to the Soviet Union. And the entire communication hummed with ominous false identity signals, most (if not all) of them apparently generated by the FBI's initial questions forwarded to the Swiss Federal Police.

Note that this communication focused entirely on Oswald's presumed anticipated attendance at the Fall trimester of the college. Some source, in Switzerland or the United States, made that presumption.

A quick reading by the FBI's headquarters of the communication could only have established a disturbance that its specific statements further reinforced. Remember the obvious: this Swiss investigation was not being run out of Moscow, Dallas, or Washington, but within Switzerland by the Swiss Federal Police. If distortions or falsehoods entered the Bureau's communication pipeline (and subsequently recorded in this crucial memorandum), that false "noise" was generated in Switzerland by the source (or sources) reporting to the Swiss Federal Police, or the Swiss Federal Police, or the FBI legal attaché reporting to Director J. Edgar Hoover through the State Department's Embassy in Paris. The least likely "noise" generator would be the "Legat, Paris"; the most likely generator would be the Swiss Federal Police's Albert Schweitzer College source.

To suspect the Swiss Federal Police itself would be to assume that either former OSS or acting CIA agents and assets were still in contact with the Swiss Federal Police willing to assist the Agency in striking terror into the FBI's cold, cold hearts.

Excerpt #1: Oswald had reportedly "announced" his imminent attendance at the Fall trimester of Albert Schweitzer College (according to the Swiss). Since the Swiss Federal Police reported this Oswald announcement, the Swiss were most likely relying on a source at the college itself, whether that source was truthful or not. But if it was not a college source, then it was a source (other than the college) that supplied the Swiss with Oswald's Fall trimester intention, whether that information was truthful or not. If it were not truthful, then the College itself supplied the Fall intention story, for whatever its institutional reasons.

It would not take the most sensitive FBI analyst, especially in its Counterintelligence section, to run through these alternatives and conclude that the Bureau's false identity hypothesis was alive and unfortunately well, regardless of the ultimate source of the Fall trimester story.

Excerpt #2: Oswald had reportedly written a letter from Moscow indicating his intention to attend Albert Schweitzer College. This Swiss Federal Police statement followed hard on the Fall trimester statement. Any FBI reader (including both the "Legat, Paris" and Director J. Edgar Hoover) would logically assume the statement meant that Oswald's intention (as it was expressed in the letter from Moscow) was to attend the College in the Fall trimester of 1960. Though the major predication gave redundant information, the modifying phrase "from Moscow" was the crucial new material.

Excerpt #3: The next sentence strongly suggested that the letter was from Oswald in Moscow to his mother in Dallas, but no such letter has been found in the public record. In any event, how would the Swiss Federal Police have known about such a letter? Could the college have informed them? If so, where is that letter now? Even if the Swiss were repeating information received from the FBI in the Bureau's investigative briefing (that the Bureau was aware of a letter from Oswald sent from Moscow to his mother that asserted he would, in fact, attend Albert Schweitzer College), where is that letter now? And what letter was returned to Lee's mother? Was it originally delivered to the College? If so, where is THAT letter? The quirky shifting of tenses and modifying forms here only increases the murkiness of the memo: "A letter . . . was returned to her since his whereabouts are unknown to the college."

Excerpts #4 and #5: the tenses and phrasing in these excerpts are again impossible.

## Oswald Missing In Switzerland: A False Identity Investigation

*But what is absolutely clear is that the Swiss Federal Police had run a False Identity investigation for the FBI. That no Oswald, real or fictional, apparently showed up at Albert Schweitzer College only increased the Bureau's fear that Oswald's passport, birth certificate, and persona were all now inside the Soviet intelligence's False Identity machinery.*

Known, of course, to Soviet intelligence through the Soviet Union's "Passport and Registration Office" was that Lee Harvey Oswald had entered the country carrying other important original documents: interviewed by four unidentified "officials" of the Soviet "Passport" office, Oswald reportedly gave them his original "discharge papers from the Marine Corps."[83] Those Marine Corps documents, had Lee Harvey Oswald not been a blinking counterintelligence "WARNING" sign, were of great value to the Soviet Union's on-going illegals operations.

The four memoranda from the Paris FBI Legat to Bureau HQ were dated July 27th, September 27th, October 12th, and November 3rd, 1960. The fourth and last "Legat" letters to FBI headquarters reporting on the Swiss Federal Police investigation was the strangest. It asserted that the Police had supplied "additional information on 10/24/60."[84] But that Legat statement was simply not true. The memo in fact denied the Legat's earlier October 12th memo without calling any attention to the strange reversal.[85] This fourth memo, in fact, anticipated the conclusions of the later Warren Report on Oswald's Albert Schweitzer College adventure. As Denis Barthelemew observed, the memorandum was apparently "one large quote, as if it were quoting some other [still unavailable] document."[86]

The last two letters from the FBI legal attaché in Paris to the Bureau's Director in Washington, D.C., were in direct contradiction to one another, yet since 1995, when the four memoranda were released by the Assassination Records Review Board (ARRB), largely without redaction, only two national articles (as distinct from Bartholomew's two research articles) touched on some disturbing aspects of the documents. And the FBI was absolutely silent about their puzzling contradictions.

## The Bureau Retreats; State Holds the Line

On February 27th, 1961, J. Edgar Hoover sent a communication to the State Department's Office of Security, announcing the FBI's "search for an Oswald imposter in Europe" was over.[87] But the Passport Office of the State Department was less willing to give up the investigation. One month later, on March 31, 1961, a Passport Office official, Edward J. Hickey, wrote a memorandum to the Department of State's Consular division, directed to John T. White, clearly indicating the Passport Office still felt the false identity issue was very much alive. Hickey pointed to the returned Oswald letters and Hoover's suspicion an imposter might be using Oswald's papers constituted an espionage threat, especially if the suspected imposter gained possession of a "valid passport." Hickey cautioned the consular section to hand over that passport to Oswald only "on a personal basis" and only after the American Embassy in Moscow was "assured, to its complete satisfaction, that he [was] . . . returning to the United States."[88]

Though the "Legat" at the American Embassy in Paris promised FBI headquarters that any "further information received [would] . . . be furnished to the Bureau," [89] no such information officially surfaced that helped to explain Lee Harvey Oswald's questionable Swiss postal contacts.

## The FBI Connection at Albert Schweitzer College

What of the Bern connection? After Texas Representative Jim Wright wrote to Albert Schweitzer College on behalf of Oswald's concerned mother, Erika Weibel (the college's secretary) answered Wright in a letter dated April 8th, 1961.[90] Weibel informed Wright that on behalf of the college she was sending him "the complete file on the [Oswald] matter . . ."[91]: the Weibel documents were not identified. How strange that an educational institution should completely strip its records rather than send copies of the requested material. Or did it, in fact, send the "complete file"? One month after the assassination, J. Edgar Hoover had apparently sent a message to the Bureau's Legat in Bern, Switzerland, inquiring again about Oswald and Albert Schweitzer College. On December 31st, 1963, the Bureau's Bern Legat sent a letter of transmittal[92] together with seven Albert Schweitzer College documents[93] to FBI Director J. Edgar Hoover. According to NARA, the seven Oswald documents were obtained by the FBI from a "confidential" source at Albert Schweitzer College[94], a "confidential" Bureau source at the college whose name was included in the Bern Legat's letter to Hoover but censored for intelligence security purposes.[95]

Why did the FBI have a "confidential" source at the college AFTER the JFK assassination whose identity (known at least to the Bern FBI Legat and FBI Director Hoover) was still being hidden in the late 1990s? Why, if Erika Weibel sent Jim Wright the "complete" Oswald file, were seven Oswald documents still at the college to be shared with the FBI alone? Were those 1963 college documents authentic? Could at least one of the documents "been created . . . to provide more [fabricated] evidence of Oswald's intent to attend the third trimester . . . rather than the Fall trimester as stated in the [crucial] Oct. 1960 memo . . . [?]"[96]

Nothing has ever been clear concerning the origins of the Albert Schweitzer documents (whether originals or copies) in the Warren Commission's possession: Mrs. Oswald, Jim Wright, the Paris FBI Legat, and Erika Weibel all qualify as sources. But possibly the most crucial unexamined source is the Bureau Legat at Bern, who in 1963, just after the murder of John F. Kennedy, was in touch with a most helpful "confidential" FBI connection at Albert Schweitzer College.[97] Who was that Bureau source in Switzerland?

The bizarre record of Oswald's Swiss Looking-Glass trip may have accomplished its actual purpose, since it loaded the FBI's files and those of the CIA, Naval Intelligence, and State's Office of Security with unreliable but suspicious Oswald data.

## A Major Soviet Illegals Operation Suspected

But there was still more to the story of Oswald not arriving at ASC.

Indeed: Switzerland, the site of intelligence and espionage activity from the First World War through the death of John F. Kennedy and beyond[98]; Allen Dulles, the superspymaster of Switzerland and the OSS/CIA use of the Quakers, the Unitarians, the World Council of Churches (and other religious groups) as sources of intelligence and information[99]; the Unitarian Church background of the Albert Schweitzer College in Switzerland[100]; and the entire so-called "illegals" program run by Soviet intelligence. The story of Oswald's trip to Europe, his stated intention to study at Albert Schweitzer College and never arriving there, his defection to the Soviet Union, all pointed to what appeared to be a major Soviet "illegals" operation.

The man who returned from the Soviet Union may have been an intelligence fiction, a "legend," someone other than the historic Lee Harvey Oswald. But, maybe not. What may have really mattered was that American intelligence was now faced with a serious improbability: what seemed to have been a faulty false identity operation had in fact succeeded. Or was made to appear as if it had succeeded.

Threading through this complex story was the curious and suspect postal trail Lee Harvey Oswald had laid down: first in the United States, then in Europe, and then back home in America, a trail remarkably like an intelligence "illegal."

## The Illegals

Why was Lee Harvey Oswald suspected of being an "illegal"?

What, in fact, WAS an "illegal"? To define an "illegal," a "legal" agent, specifically a Soviet KGB "legal" agent, should be defined. The KGB ran its overseas espionage operations "chiefly through an extensive network of agents placed in its embassies, missions and official agencies. These 'legal' KGB operators [had] . . . official cover and often diplomatic immunity."[101]

Soviet "legal" agents could hold high or low rank, anywhere from ambassador to embassy doorman.[102] But the term "legal" applied to a Soviet spy (or any other nation's spy) was and is inaccurate. Though the Soviet intelligence agent maintained an identity as an employee of a legitimate Soviet mission, the spy's assignments were not 'legal,' since by definition the agent was breaking the laws of the targeted nation.[103] To be a "legal" agent therefore meant only to be protected by legal (usually diplomatic) cover.

Actual "Illegals," however, had no such protection and therefore were highly vulnerable espionage assets of Soviet intelligence.[104]

An illegal agent for the Soviets or the so-called "Eastern Bloc" was a spy who had illegally entered the United States equipped with a false identity; he or she was a so-called "legend" living "covertly" in the United States[105] who had "established a life based on a false story"[106] supported by "a completely false background or 'legend,' complete with documentation . . . ."[107] To be an illegal was to be a member of the most elite espionage group in the world: to practice "perhaps the purest form of spying, and probably the most dangerous."[108]

These Soviet agents were specially trained to become "average American citizens, usually very conservative politically and very anticommunist."[109] Since Lee Harvey Oswald was suspected of either participating in the creation of an illegal (that is, a false identity) or being himself an illegal or legend[110], what was American intelligence to make of the man who returned from the Soviet Union as a confirmed anti-Communist and anti-Soviet re-defector who yet acted, at least for a time, as an outspoken supporter of Communist Cuba and Fidel Castro?

The internal CIA conflict over the search for James Angleton's suspected mole was ultimately contained within the Agency's controversy over whether Yuriiy Nosenko was a legitimate defector, and the ultimate CIA take on Lee Harvey Oswald was nested within THAT Nosenko controversy.[111]

## Illegals and Legitimate Identity Documents

A Soviet intelligence illegal did not adopt a fictional persona; rather, he or she would be given the identity of a real person[112] whose birth certificate and passport (and possibly other real papers) made up the documentary foundation and therefore established the "legend" of the new Soviet illegal.[113]

From where did the KGB gain these authentic documents? Some came from American tourists in the Soviet Union[114], from people like Lee Harvey Oswald, for example. But why would the KGB want to capture the identity of a real person for its illegals? Why not just invent an identity?[115] Because, quite simply, a real person had a valid historical record. [116]

Actual identity papers were not easy to acquire. By 1954, Soviet intelligence had drawn up (little-known) plans for "a network of 130 'documentation agents' whose sole responsibility was to obtain birth certificates, passports and other documents to support the illegals' legends."[117] KGB officers who specialized in "illegal documentation" were sent to twenty-two countries to snare the valuable paper.[118] A number of key documentation agents were dispatched to collect birth certificates and passports, in, for example, East and West Germany, France, Mexico, Turkey, and the United States[119]: "Operations officers specializing in illegal documentation were posted to New York . . . [and] Mexico City . . . ."[120]

## Intelligence Operations of Illegals

KGB illegals in the United States used a variety of means to communicate with Moscow, including "ordinary mail,"[121] but their letters were seldom if ever sent directly to the Soviet Union.[122] They were transferred through "cover addresses in Western Europe,"[123] among them addresses in Switzerland. "One FBI mail-intercept program, conducted between the 1940s and 1966 . . . involved intercepting and opening letters going to certain European addresses [including Switzerland] considered 'mail drops' for Soviet intelligence. Bureau sources say that [the] program helped expose several important [Soviet] 'illegals.'"[124]

American citizens who established temporary residence in Switzerland were monitored by American intelligence, especially if they had already come to the attention of, for example, FBI counterespionage; though little known, the FBI actually practiced counterintelligence activity with a physical presence overseas.[125]

As part of a KGB illegals-support operation, American citizens' espionage function was to develop "letter drops" for either themselves or other US-based Soviet agents. Letter drops were "innocent" intermediary addresses for intelligence mail transiting between the United States and the Soviet Union. The FBI may have suspected Albert Schweitzer College was to be developed as, or had already become, an espionage letter drop. The Bureau's suspicion would therefore have seemed to be confirmed when Albert Schweitzer College Director (and Founder) Hans Casparis wrote to Lee Harvey Oswald about the strange switch in term starting dates.

"For the FBI, the [successful] search for an illegal [was] . . . the ultimate goal in counterintelligence."[126] William Sullivan and Sam Papich were the widely-accepted false identity experts for the Bureau (both worked closely with their Agency counterpart, James Angleton), but occasionally a commentator with inside knowledge named a lesser-known FBI expert in false identity. In January, 1963, "Anthony Litrento, a

street-smart agent . . . was the bureau's leading expert on Soviet illegals."[127] But when
Don Moore, the chief of the FBI's counterespionage operations for seventeen years,
wanted to meet with Anatoly Golitsin just after Rudolph Abel (a prime Soviet illegal)
was traded for captured U-2 pilot Gary Powers, Moore asked Sullivan's close associate
Sam Papich (Sullivan's counterespionage link to the CIA's Angleton) to accompany
him to the meeting.[128] Abel was a major figure in the history of Soviet illegal spies. The
CIA, the KGB, and an exchange of letters figured prominently in the trade of Abel
(the Soviet illegal) and Powers (the American spy pilot). In May, 1961, Abel's attorney
James Donovan, with major ties to United States intelligence, received a letter from
Leipzig supposedly written by "Hellen Abel," the "purported" wife of Rudolph Abel;
the convicted spy was at that moment a resident of Atlanta Federal Penitentiary.[129] An
exchange of letters between Donovan and Ms. Abel occurred, resulting in the trade of
Powers for Abel. But neither the New York attorney nor the (possibly fictional) "Hellen
Abel" wrote the letters: the correspondence was manufactured by a collaboration
between the CIA and the KGB.[130]

The Soviet "modern illegal" had only one important category of activity: so-called
wet affairs.[131] Illegals infiltrated the United States primarily "to assist [in] and supervise
assassination and sabotage."[132] Little wonder, then, that the bundle of contradictions
called Lee Harvey Oswald evoked such curiosity and suspicion in both the CIA and the
FBI, why his mail was monitored closely by both agencies, and why, after the murder of
President Kennedy, the CIA's James Angleton insisted he and the FBI's William Sullivan,
both deeply involved in mail interceptions and investigating illegals, should carefully
coordinate their Warren Commission statements made about Oswald, denying he had
been an American spy. In 1963, Sullivan and Angleton had many things to hide from
both the Warren Commission and J. Edgar Hoover. For example, beginning in 1961,
Sullivan and Angleton ran "a highly secret international co-operative known as CAZAB,
[including] . . . selected members of the security and intelligence agencies" of the
British Commonwealth and the United States.[133] CAZAB allowed Angleton and Sullivan
to sidestep Hoover's "malign influence over counter-intelligence liaison . . . ."[134]

What other joint Sullivan/Angleton operations were then ongoing?

After he returned from the Soviet Union, Lee Harvey Oswald seemed to have
an interest in both microdots and cipher templates. KGB illegals used microdot
communication in their letters, specks of film that had to be "optically magnified
many times" in order to be read.[135] And both GRU and KGB illegals used "miniature
cipher pads" as unbreakable code templates to send messages in otherwise innocuous
postal messages.[136]

## Soviet Intelligence Illegals Controls and Oleg Kalugin

Inside the KGB[137], the so-called First Chief (or "Main") Directorate was the
operational home for all counterintelligence operations, especially "wet affairs" that
included assassination and the running of illegals, making the First Directorate the

site of both false identity activity and political murder.[138] Officially designated the Soviet's internal espionage network, it was considered "the keystone of the [Soviet] State Security."[139] When Lee Harvey Oswald was in Moscow, his Intourist guide was most probably an "active KGB" agent of that same First Main/Chief Directorate.[140]

"S," a KGB sub-directorate[141], "handled the recruitment, training, maintenance and support of an astonishing number of illegals around the world." [142]This Illegals Directorate (or Directorate S)[143] had a majority of its teaching faculty who had been either illegals or KGB spies protected by "diplomatic cover." [144] But another KGB sub-directorate of the First Directorate designated "K" and run by Soviet counterintelligence was just as potent.

What Soviet superspy finally took control of "K"?

In 1958[145], fresh from the Soviet Union[146], twenty-three-year-old Oleg D. Kalugin was a Fulbright Scholar at Columbia University.[147] Difficult as it was for Soviet students to study in the United States, Kalugin had accomplished that feat while an "undercover operative" of the KGB. [148]Kalugin apparently enjoyed his espionage days in the United States, working as "a Radio Moscow correspondent at the United Nations"[149] after his Columbia campus experience. "He spied at the United Nations from 1960 to 1964 . . . ."[150]

The rising counterespionage star of the Soviet spy system was a key officer in the KGB's New York operation, and U.S. counterintelligence was more than aware of Kalugin's Manhattan spy activities, targeting him in "several FBI setups"[151]. Kalugin was a major part of the KGB's anti-Castro activity in the city, "involved with some secret operations in New York,"[152] possibly intercepting postal communications. Kalugin described one of his operations as "penetrating anti-Castro Cuban groups"[153], but he did not explain the intent of this curious counterintelligence, since the anti-Castro organizations were already heavily infiltrated by the CIA.

Kalugin's connections to the Kennedy assassination story and to Lee Harvey Oswald are striking: Oleg Nechiporenko, a Soviet Consulate/KGB officer in Mexico City who had met with Lee Harvey Oswald (or, more likely, an Oswald double), worked for Oleg Kalugin (no later than the early 1970s).[154] When the first word spread around the world from Dallas that a former defector to the Soviet Union had reportedly murdered President John F. Kennedy, Kalugin and his KGB crew in New York were immediately commissioned by Moscow to spread the official Soviet word: "Oswald had lived in Minsk, [but] . . . he had never been trusted and was suspected of being a CIA agent . . . ."[155]

The late 1960s saw Kalugin in Washington, D.C., stationed at the Soviet Embassy.[156] Each Soviet Embassy had a top "resident" KGB officer who handled "Line PR (political intelligence)."[157] Oleg Kalugin was the "youthful head of Line PR" who processed an extraordinary stream of apparently disloyal U.S. intelligence agents and government workers willing to supply Kalugin and the KGB with sensitive and classified documents, state secrets, and anything else Kalugin desired, collecting thousands of dollars in grateful payment and living far beyond their federal paycheck means without registering a speck of suspicion inside the American intelligence community.[158]

That uninterest in Kalugin's U.S.-based espionage career was highlighted by his involvement in dubious double-agent activities as well as media and FBI disclosures of his operations with no move made to expel him.[159]

Oleg Kalugin was hailed back to the Soviet Union and was commissioned the youngest KGB general in Soviet history; in Moscow, Kalugin became the chief of the KGB's First/Major Directorate from 1973 to 1980[160], given access to and control of the KGB's illegals and false identities files (the Sub-Directorate "K" secrets).

Kalugin emigrated to the United States in 1995, and became active in research, writing, teaching, and lecturing on espionage and counterintelligence,[161] sometimes in partnership with former CIA agents. On June 26th, 2002, "Oleg D. Kalugin, a retired K.G.B. general . . . was convicted of treason in absentia [in Russia] . . . and sentenced to 15 years in prison for disclosing [Soviet/Russian] state secrets to the United States."[162]

When did Kalugin give up those "state secrets' to American intelligence?

From his 1958 espionage activity at Columbia University, his United Nations intelligence operations, his Washington counterintelligence work, and his Moscow assignment directing the KGB's First Directorate headquarters, Oleg Kalugin was always directly involved both as an agent and an officer in illegals and false identity operations. The KGB's First Directorate and its sub-directorate K (officially taken over by Kalugin when he returned to Moscow in 1972) had been responsible for monitoring Lee Harvey Oswald from his arrival in the Soviet Union in 1959 until he went home to the United States and most certainly after.

Was Oleg Kalugin recruited by the Central Intelligence Agency as early as 1958 over an icy-cold stein of beer at the Lion's Den of Columbia University? And might that early recruitment have accounted for Kalugin's remarkable success in signing up so many U.S. intelligence traitors?

Was Oleg Kalugin, in fact, a long-time member of a KGB/FBI/CIA double-agent operation during the Cold War? Was that why in June, 2002, he was "convicted of treason in absentia . . . for disclosing state secrets to the United States"?[163]

Kalugin was on a first-name basis with the best of Washington's mainstream journalists, people like Walter Lippmann who could request a private meeting with a sitting U.S. president and get it almost immediately.[164] During the Cuban Missile Crisis and JFK's moves toward peaceful reconciliation with both Cuba and the Soviet Union (beginning in the spring of 1963), diplomatic back channels connecting Fidel Castro and John F. Kennedy and between the Soviet hierarchy and JFK were opened. In 1962 and 1963, Robert Kennedy himself was a key figure in those peace-enhancing negotiations. A key communication line may indeed have run between an ostensible KGB operative and JFK's most trusted emissary, his own brother: "One of Kalugin's most important contacts was [in fact] Senator Robert Kennedy who, but for his assassination . . . might have won the 1968 Democratic nomination. Before his death [Robert] Kennedy presented Kalugin with a tie-pin showing the PT-109 torpedo boat . . . his brother [John F. Kennedy] . . . captained during the war."[165]

Was Oleg Kalugin one of those back channel agents linking Moscow and Washington? And did Kalugin betray both the Soviet Union and the United States?

When Kalugin was in Moscow in the 1970s, he reportedly was a part of the successful assassination attempt against Bulgarian dissident Georgi Markov[166], an operation that included an umbrella weapon with a poisoned dart.[167] But Kalugin has denied any direct involvement in the Bulgarian "wet" operation.[168]

Among some of Oleg Kalugin's treasured American memories, might some be about Lee Harvey Oswald, that strange American Marine suspected of being a U.S. intelligence dangle or of being manipulated by a KGB collaborator in an espionage "illegals" or false identity game?

## Soviet GRU Intelligence Controls of Illegals

Most discussions of Soviet espionage illegals have been about KGB "legends." But the military side of the Soviet Union's "legend" program was run initially by GRU (Soviet military) intelligence rather than the KGB.[169] A defecting Marine, for example, especially one who had made contact with the American Embassy in Moscow, would have been of great interest to the GRU's "illegals" operations.

The GRU was technically the Chief Directorate of Intelligence of the General Staff of the Soviet Army.[170] In the 1960s, the GRU had six interior operational "directorates" plus an "information" directorate.[171] Though the 5th Directorate was specifically responsible for "Diversion and Sabotage,"[172] the GRU as a whole conducted "military, political, economic and scientific intelligence"[173] as well as "propaganda activities, acts of provocation, blackmail, terrorism and sabotage."[174] GRU illegals could, therefore, be used in any one of these capacities.

The GRU's 1st Directorate was known as its illegals Directorate, responsible for selecting and training of prospective illegals.[175] Several GRU espionage schools both in and near Moscow prepared illegals for overseas duty[176], and "each [GRU] national or area desk [had] . . . its own group of illegals."[177]

Illegals who were prepared for and then monitored once they were in the United States were especially prized.[178] The crucial difference between the KGB (with its own legion of illegals) and the GRU was the latter's "attention to collecting information on the armed forces and military installations of the Western countries . . . ."[179]

The GRU ran a number of so-called "singles" and "doubles" throughout the United States.[180] A GRU illegals "double" consisted of a man and woman living together as a wedded couple, whether the two were actually married.[181]

Throughout the Cold War years, the GRU (Soviet military intelligence and counterespionage) was subject to being compromised by the West. Penetrated by both British MI-6 and the CIA[182] in the 1970s and deeply troubled by this Western intelligence coup, the GRU was finally placed under the complete control of the KGB.[183]

## Turning Soviet Illegals

Every Western counterintelligence operation was interested in the illegals from the East. Key Soviet illegals in the United States were, in fact, periodically approached by the FBI, turned into double agents, and became players in what has been called " . . . the most dangerous game in the world." [184]Though Nigel West supplied impressive lists of Soviet intelligence defectors, postwar Soviet defectors, Soviet intelligence people who were expelled from the United States, and major American espionage cases, his material was rather obviously after-the-fact venting, and West made no mention of the real intelligence games: American illegal mail openings, the CIA's HT/LINGUAL postal intercept program, William King Harvey, Jr., and the Agency's Office of Security, CIA operations in Berlin, and illegals (listed in his index), mail drops, and dead drops.

Though less often publicized, the CIA also turned Soviet illegals and ran them as double agents.[185] One especially crucial KGB illegal in Helsinki, Finland[186], was turned and run by the CIA[187], then betrayed to the South Africans by none other than James Angleton.[188] In turn, the South Africans gave the Agency's now-turned illegal to the Soviets[189], who then executed him.[190] He was, of course, a loyal double agent of the CIA.

Both Soviet and American counterespionage suspected each other of offering up illegal prizes ("dangles") who were booby traps. A Deputy FBI Counterintelligence Chief summarized several decades of Bureau experience in coping with false identity cases: "That's what the [Soviets] . . . always threw out at you. They'd always dangle something . . . [like] an illegal . . ."[191] who would not be what he or she appeared to be. According to one former Navy Intelligence officer, when Lee Harvey Oswald went to the Soviet Union, he looked like an American "dangle" aimed precisely at the Soviets' defector/false identity/illegals programs[192]; but when he came out of the Soviet Union (according to James Angleton, the CIA's expert on Soviet legends and double agents), Oswald looked like a Soviet-invented "legend."[193]

Overlooked in the sometimes micro-analysis of Lee Harvey Oswald's life was his interview in June, 1962, with FBI agent Fain (who had interviewed Oswald's mother when her son failed to appear at Albert Schweitzer College) and Fain's Bureau partner. Fain submitted his interview report to the FBI's Dallas office, recommended that Oswald be reinterviewed, and urged that the redefector's records at the Immigration and Naturalization Service be examined[194]: Fain's INS suggestion clearly indicated Oswald was still considered an illegal/false identity suspect.

## Allen Dulles and the Illegals/False Identity Programs

False identity/illegal agents were a major part of Allen Dulles' massive spy operations throughout two World Wars and the subsequent 'Cold War.' Dulles was a documented expert on false identity operations; he may, in fact, have invented them, at least for the Allies in World War One. In 1917, after the American entry into the war, the Germans "stepped up their previously successful campaign to insert [illegal] agents into the United States, and . . . specialized in forged or stolen documents to win the needed visas for entry from besieged legations such as the one at Bern."[195] Dulles was at the time the "ad hoc intelligence officer for the U.S. Legation in Switzerland."[196] As the American spymaster in residence, Dulles was ecstatic about his skillful confrontations with suspected German undercover agents.[197] "Close questioning and unmasking of these [false identity] spies became a . . . particular pleasure for Allen [Dulles]."[198]

Dulles later used that same counterespionage expertise in the OSS when he again ran intelligence operations in Switzerland and, later, as the post-war director of the CIA. Though the history of American false identity agents has been a carefully guarded secret, some evidence of the U.S. illegals program (so-called deep-cover activity) has become available, especially for World War Two and after.[199]

But in 1964, the obvious expert available was Allen Dulles.

Why, then, did Dulles have absolutely nothing to say about false identity cases and intelligence illegals when his nearly fifty years of hands-on experience in precisely those two areas was needed by the Warren Commission? The gentleman spy did not need to send a letter of inquiry to the presidential-appointed body: he was already one of its select members. At the moment his fellow Warren Commissioners, worried about possible links between American intelligence and Lee Harvey Oswald, began discussing espionage double agents, Dulles might have said: "I've an idea or two on that topic."

But he was silent.

# Essay Three

# Albert Schweitzer College and Lee Harvey Oswald: New Evidence and Analysis

Albert Schweitzer College, the Swiss college to which Lee Harvey Oswald (accused assassin of John F. Kennedy) applied, was accepted, but never attended, was nurtured by the International Association for Religious Freedom (IARF), a world-wide liberal and progressive religious organization, backed by the IARF's liberal Swiss Protestant wing and, in the United States, energized by the Unitarian Church.[1] In remarks celebrating the history of the IARF, the Reverend Maas ("Max") D. Gaebler identified Albert Schweitzer College as "a project initiated and supported chiefly by our Swiss IARF member group . . . [that] served for several years [through the 1950s] as a magnet for our young people from our [IARF] affiliates in many countries. Its contributions to the experience of many young religious liberals . . . [were] significant."[2] But Gaebler added: "Its subsequent history, however, was complex and unfortunate."[3] He did not elaborate on that "subsequent" period.

Just as the college's later history was unusually darkened following the news of its link to Lee Harvey Oswald, so also its earliest history was, in fact, romanticized. Richard Boeke, first president of the American chapter of the International Association for Religious Freedom (IARF), reviewing the Association's history, called Albert Schweitzer College the "crown jewel" of all the IARF's associate religious centers.[4] According to Boeke, the college had initially been "good for liberal Swiss Protestants."[5] By August, 1958, Albert Schweitzer College was registered as an "associate member" of the International Association of Religious Freedom[6], attaining that distinction just prior to Lee Harvey Oswald's application to the Swiss college.

## The Origins of Albert Schweitzer College

Beginning in 1950, approximately five years before Albert Schweitzer College offered its first full year of courses, Hans Casparis and his English wife Therese held summer conferences in Klosters, Switzerland, anticipating the establishment of the College; Hans and Therese were reportedly "the life and soul of the [summer] gathering[s] . . . ."[7] By 1955, Hans Casparis' Swiss meetings reportedly developed into "an international center for the study of ethics, Christian morals and contemporary social, religious and political developments."[8]

An enthusiastic Unitarian supporter of Albert Schweitzer College[9] summarized its origin: "In the summer of 1950, a group of progressive, international-minded citizens—all Swiss—started the . . . College."[10] But the "College" did not operate on a fulltime basis until 1955: the first years were summer programs of study, group interaction, and fun, followed by summer study courses of greater seriousness.

Though the establishing "Swiss liberals" were identified as "primarily ministers," these internationally-oriented and progressive clerics from Switzerland have not been identified except for Professor Hans Casparis, earlier reported to be "a pastor like most of the founding fathers of Albert Schweitzer College . . . ."[11] These liberal pastors may have been linked to the college's first full-time faculty in 1955 or be identical to that initial college faculty[12], but no documentary evidence presently supports that possibility.

Inspired by Albert Schweitzer, the new college "intended to help young people attain spiritual independence by developing a critical mind combined with clear moral and religious convictions."[13] Even beyond its liberal Protestant genesis, Albert Schweitzer College was declared to be "entirely free from denominational ties," welcoming students "of all faiths or those without [any] religious ties."[14]

## The Missing Albert Schweitzer College Records

How did those diverse students discover the college?

On August 23rd, 2001, I visited the Unitarian/Universalist Association (UUA) headquarters at 25 Beacon Street, Boston. I fully expected to find published advertisements for Casparis' summer programs and later announcements on the development and final establishment of Albert Schweitzer College. The key publication that undoubtedly held this necessary information had to be *The Christian Unitarian Register*, first called the *Christian Register*: the UUA in Boston had a complete set of this important religious publication. I also had a second interest in the *Register*: its radical editor from 1943 through 1947 was Reverend Stephen Fritchman, the outspoken and sometimes volatile writer and preacher. Reportedly prodded by Quaker activist Noel Field, Fritchman had supported the creation of the Unitarian Service Committee[15] during World War II; in the 50s, Fritchman was a politically active Unitarian pastor in Los Angeles whose ministry in those years included an important Lee Harvey Oswald connection.[16]

What I found at the Boston UUA, or rather what I did NOT find, was astonishing. Treated warmly by the staff at the Unitarian/Universalist headquarters (and comfortably cooled by the library's air-conditioning), I carefully checked each glossy page of the monthly *Register* from 1948 through 1959. Through ten years of the publication, neither Casparis' summer programs nor Albert Schweitzer College received a single word of coverage: no announcements, no registration information, no news stories were ever published, despite the *Register* including, each month, a special section called "News of the Unitarian World." How could a college named after Albert Schweitzer, embodying Schweitzer's ideas and principles, and supported by the some of the most prominent Unitarians in the United States (and, indeed, the world) have received absolutely no comment in the *Register*, the publication of record of American Unitarians?

Only in the June, 1959, edition of the *Register* did a short announcement appear at the bottom of a page about "summer study courses," but it was bereft of any real news about the college, giving no hint as to how to get any further information.

This June announcement for summer courses also left little or no time to make arrangements for actual study at the college.

From 1950 through June, 1959, nothing was published in the *Register* about Hans Casparis' Swiss social and cultural summers and nothing about Albert Schweitzer College through its momentous early development.

In October, 1961, another announcement (but a month too late to energize anyone interested in registering) was published: according to the Unitarian *Register*, the college, beginning on September 1st, 1961, would have its first full-time director. This rather naked news story reported that the paid position was made possible by the "financial support" of unidentified "American Unitarians." Since ALL the leading American Unitarians associated with Albert Schweitzer College had published regularly in the *Register*, including Robert Schacht of Providence (with at least three articles), the phrase "American Unitarians" was curious. The *Register* was published by American Unitarians at 25 Beacon Street, Boston, with the American Unitarian Association headquartered there and responsible for the *Register*; and the headquarters was a frequent site of letters exchanged concerning Albert Schweitzer College, written on Unitarian Association correspondence letterhead.

How, then, did prominent American Unitarian Association officers, regular contributors to the Unitarian *Register*, become only unnamed "American Unitarians" in a late Albert Schweitzer College news notice in that same Unitarian *Register*?

There was one possible explanation for the absence of Albert Schweitzer material in the *Register*. I discovered an undated but informative brochure on Albert Schweitzer College in the files located at Harvard Divinity School; an excellent photograph of the Swiss college was identified as appearing in the "January" edition of the "Christian Register." However, the photo simply wasn't in ANY January edition of the *Register*. But in several places in the *Register*'s volumes, I noted that pictures and articles had been carefully but clearly razored out. I reported the thefts to the Association staff. Could someone have reviewed the *Register* sometime before I carried out my own survey and carefully removed everything of importance (except for two minor announcements) about Albert Schweitzer College?

The surviving Albert Schweitzer College records at Harvard Divinity School Library suggest the initial thrust of Hans Casparis' summer idylls and later founding of his college came from the European (specifically Swiss) "side" of the International Association of Religious Freedom. Still, between 1947 and 1950, Hans Casparis had to invent, organize, and sponsor summer programs leading to an international "center" that became, by 1955, Albert Schweitzer College. No matter how 'small' the institution's operations, the college would have been a massive undertaking while Casparis held a fulltime teaching position at a local Churwalden high school.

Was Albert Schweitzer College deliberately fenced off, then, from other Unitarian activity? Were the college's announcements intentionally buried? The *Register* from 1948 through 1962 had dozens of articles and reviews about young Unitarians and liberal religious youth and their programs—groups that were obviously just the kind of students Hans Casparis wanted for his summer and later college exercises. Beyond any select razoring out of materials from the *Register*, why was not a single word published to link those American groups with Albert Schweitzer College?[17] Since still existing liberal religious youth groups that I contacted reported absolutely no records of Albert Schweitzer College, how were American students, in fact, ever recruited and chosen?

Was course and registration information about Casparis' summer programs and, afterwards, the full-year curriculum of Albert Schweitzer College quietly handled by liberal and radical Unitarian pastors, including Stephen Fritchman, to avoid any conservative if not reactionary criticism?

The Swiss educational institution was operated by the Swiss Albert Schweitzer College Association, a non-profit organization with its legal headquarters in eastern Switzerland in the village of Churwalden, the capital of the Grisons region[18]. Supporting the new college was a largely Unitarian group from New York and Boston, the American Friends of Albert Schweitzer College, Inc., a "non-profit membership organization . . . incorporated [in New York] to receive tax deductible contributions from United States citizens and corporations . . . ."[19] But many of the records of the Friends, despite Albert Schweitzer's towering eminence, are no longer available.

Though an extraordinary relation (documented in the fragmentary records of the Harvard Divinity School Library) existed between Albert Schweitzer, the world-famous humanitarian, and the Swiss school named after him dedicated to his spirit and good works, nearly all the historical records of Albert Schweitzer College have been lost or eliminated.

## Liberal Protestant Support for Albert Schweitzer College

Crucial to the college's history are the identities of the liberal American Protestant groups supporting the college. What, for example, were their financial and political connections? The Harvard documents supply some information: "The donations of churches . . . [and] institutions, progressive, liberal, liberal-Christian, and free-thinking groups—mostly . . . in Switzerland, . . . could not balance the [college] budget. A substantial contribution committed for several years [helping to balance the budget] was that of the [American] Unitarian Universalist Association [UUA] in Boston . . . ."[20]

This same Harvard Library document noted that two other "American groups" representing young liberal Protestants were in touch with Albert Schweitzer College and bolstered the school's budget[21]: the Student Religious Liberals and the Liberal Religious Youth[22], organizations attractive to young religious liberals and radicals interested in studying in Europe.

Had these student groups been penetrated by the Central Intelligence Agency, just as dozens of other religious and humanitarian groups routinely co-opted with Agency money?[23] Did CIA funding flow through young people's religious organizations into a communion of "progressive" clergymen (including Hans Casparis) who were Albert Schweitzer College's founders?

As distinct from the many OSS connections to the Unitarian Service Committee and key members of the Friends of Albert Schweitzer College[24], the Liberal Religious Youth (LRY), a function of the American Unitarian Association, had no traceable U.S. intelligence links. Reverend Leon Hopper, with whom I had a productive conversation in Boston in March, 2003, was the LRY's director during the late 50s and early 60s. Earlier, Hans Casparis' elder son John Casparis had informed me that prospective students for Albert Schweitzer College were recruited through his father's international presentations, magazine advertisements, official contacts with "elite" U.S. colleges, and a network of personal contacts.[25] But after several months of careful, close, and persistent searching, I found no such presentations, advertisements, or elite college arrangements ever existed.

In Boston, Leon Hopper was not surprised.

At our meeting, Hopper confirmed that student recruitment for Albert Schweitzer College was almost always through personal contacts. We agreed that Hans Casparis quite likely had a rich fantasy life and that Hans' son John may have believed his father actually publicized the college as young John had been told and as John communicated to me.

Hopper also confirmed that Stephen Fritchman could have been an information source about Albert Schweitzer College that became available at Fritchman's First Unitarian Church of Los Angeles. But Hopper did not think Fritchman received *written* material from Boston about the college.

So only personal contact channels remained.

Finally, Hopper confirmed that his Liberal Religious Youth organization concentrated on the summer sessions of Albert Schweitzer College, reaching prospective students through personal contacts. Someone at El Toro Marine Corps station or in Los Angeles, someone familiar with Albert Schweitzer College's summer session programs, especially as those sessions focused on the young, had supplied Lee Harvey Oswald with an Albert Schweitzer College Summer Session application form.

That still unidentified California-based supplier of Albert Schweitzer College information is the major candidate for American intelligence manipulation of Oswald's registration to the Swiss college.

## ASC's Faculty, Albert Schweitzer, and the Establishing of ASC

Eight faculty members had been listed for the first full year of Albert Schweitzer College courses and lectures, including Hans Casparis, his English wife Therese, and Rev. Dr. Joachim Wolff, an "outstanding young German scholar . . . [who had taken] a firm stand against Nazism, and had to flee to Switzerland . . . ."[26] Both the faculty and the projected courses of study at Albert Schweitzer College strongly supported the progressive direction planned for the new college.

The college reportedly drew its sustenance from a close association with the person of Albert Schweitzer: "The most decisive reason for the College's initial growth was the profound interest taken by Dr. Schweitzer in the new enterprise. It is evidenced by several [personal] letters . . . [Albert Schweitzer] exchanged with . . . Casparis and the other [college] founders."[27] But though a few letters from Schweitzer to Hans Casparis are present in the Harvard files, I found neither Casparis' letters to Schweitzer nor any correspondence between the college's "founders" (other than Casparis) and Albert Schweitzer in the Divinity School Library archives. Not only are the historical records of Albert Schweitzer College itself in danger of disappearing; they have been almost completely lost to the educational, cultural, and memorial sites devoted to Albert Schweitzer.[28]

Though the eminent musician, author, medical doctor, and humanitarian never visited the college dedicated to his life work, Albert Schweitzer kept in touch with the college's progenitor and first director, Hans Casparis. In a rare surviving letter to Casparis dated November 22nd, 1954, Schweitzer expressed his "great pleasure" at the "progress . . . our College in Churwalden has made [in two years] . . . ."[29] Schweitzer restated the college's cultural and moral goals: "The ethical spirit . . . must be awakened anew."[30]

Edward Cahill was a member of the founding "subscribers" of the American "Friends of Albert Schweitzer College" and the Director of the American Unitarian Association's Department of World Churches. On April 27th, 1956, Cahill wrote to Frederick May Eliot, another founding "subscriber" of the "Friends," from Charlotte, North Carolina, using the letterhead of the American Unitarian Association (AUA) headquartered at 25 Beacon Street, Boston, where Eliot received his AUA mail.[31] The subject of the letter was the so-called "iron curtain countries."[32] The FBI and the CIA had been monitoring domestic and international mail from the late 1950s on.[33] To American intelligence from 1955 through 1959, the college named after Albert Schweitzer must have been perceived as a radical hothouse dedicated to nurturing left-wing flora, especially with one prominent college faculty member advertising his anti-fascist credentials. Both the domestic and international correspondence concerning the college (as it was located in Switzerland, in effect a giant espionage letter drop), would have been routinely intercepted by the FBI and CIA. Cahill's letter to Eliot, therefore, must have immediately alerted the Agency and Bureau interceptors.

As the Director of the AUA's Department of World Churches, Cahill had followed his attendance at the department's most recent meeting in April, 1956, initiating a "correspondence with Hans Casparis concerning the possibility of offering a scholarship [to Albert Schweitzer College] for students from iron curtain countries."[34] A certain "Mrs. Robinson"[35] whom Cahill thought was the origin of "this idea" was also contacted by him.[36] Though Cahill had made a copy of his letter to her, that copy does not exist in the Unitarian Albert Schweitzer College files at Harvard Divinity School Library. Cahill had asked Eliot for his "reactions" to extending Albert Schweitzer College's reach to students from the "iron curtain countries," but if the prominent Unitarian had offered such "reactions," the record cannot be found in the Divinity School's files.

Conservatively, the correspondence of Albert Schweitzer College was being monitored by the FBI and the CIA no later than April of 1956[37]: therefore, American intelligence would have been prepared for Lee Harvey Oswald to inquire about that liberal Protestant school: prepared, indeed, even for his non-appearance. The intelligence agencies would have been put on full alert when the obvious and provocative Oswald contradictions were discovered in his passport and college applications.[38]

## Albert Schweitzer, ASC, and U.S. Intelligence

Did American intelligence have what it felt was good reason for closely tracking any international activity involving Albert Schweitzer the man, either as a physical or ethical presence?

In 1959, the same year Lee Harvey Oswald reportedly applied to Hans Casparis' Swiss college, President Dwight David Eisenhower's intelligence analysts had concluded that Albert Schweitzer (Hans Casparis' intellectual and moral inspiration) was, in fact, under the influence of Soviet Communism.[39] Four years earlier, however, Albert Schweitzer had been fifth among the "most admired [persons] . . . in the world [according to a Gallop poll]."[40] By 1956, Schweitzer had advanced to being the fourth "most admired" person in the world[41], and both President Eisenhower and John Foster Dulles lavished high praise on the renowned musician, theologian, and ethicist.[42]

Yet within a few months, American support for Schweitzer was completely reversed: "Secretly convinced that he was an adherent of 'the Communist line,' [Eisenhower and Dulles] . . . severed personal contacts with him . . . [and] ordered [both] his domestic and foreign] activities investigated [and penetrated] by the FBI and the CIA, orchestrated rebuttals to his public statements, and discouraged his travel to the United States."[43]

Why?

On April 23rd, 1957, Schweitzer began broadcasting to the world his "Declaration of Conscience" in opposition to all nuclear weapons.[44] Fifty countries heard his message, and planet-wide opposition to atomic weapons was then registered in, for example, Norway, West Germany, Holland, Sweden, Great Britain, and the Soviet Union.[45] In the United States, Schweitzer was criticized by both the liberal and conservative media (including the New York Times and the New York Daily News), and no American radio station carried his historic statement opposing nuclear weapons.[46]

Key elements of the American government moved against Schweitzer's ethical threat.[47] The Central Intelligence Agency monitored Schweitzer's first class mail and intercepted no fewer than four personal letters he had written to Gunnar Jahn and the director of Radio Oslo, Kaare Fostervoll.[48] The Agency then passed these intercepted communications to the U.S. State Department; in turn, the State Department shared the letters with anti-Schweitzer advocates of nuclear weapons.[49]

Albert Schweitzer was clearly the enemy of American atomic bombs. Schweitzer's moral influence in Africa (and beyond) had not been overlooked: his stand against atomic weapons directly threatened the American-Belgian Congo connection that had supplied uranium for U.S. nuclear ordinance. And just months after Schweitzer's anti-atomic broadcasts, Patrice Lumumba would constitute an even greater threat to that same profitable link.

In 1958, Schweitzer again broadcast his opposition to nuclear arms, and people's movements supporting his stance were organized in Japan, Switzerland, England, New Zealand, and Ireland.[50]

The United States responded. American intelligence and the State Department launched new inquiries into Schweitzer's activities[51]: on May 2nd, 1958, the FBI was commissioned to investigate the Schweitzer Fellowship, "the U.S.-based organization that had raised thousands of dollars to maintain Schweitzer's [own] hospital at Lambarene."[52]

In late May, 1958, the U.S. consul general in the Congo (the source of American atomic-weapons uranium) informed the State Department he would be visiting Schweitzer in June of that year.[53] Despite being given specific warnings about Schweitzer's alleged adherence to the "Communist line" on nuclear testing[54], American Consul General James Green visited the renowned humanitarian and reported on Schweitzer's mental alertness, his eloquence, and his sincerity. Green thought Schweitzer independent of the so-called "Communist line."[55]

But the American government remained unconvinced.

Ironically, though the Eisenhower administration was finally forced to agree with Albert Schweitzer's anti-nuclear position, it never forgave him for his ethical initiative supported world-wide. When Schweitzer turned 84, the United States refused to congratulate him, declining to join in welcoming him to Princeton University. The anti-Schweitzer opposition was led by General Andrew Goodpaster, Eisenhower's key White House staffer and the president's crucial CIA connection; Schweitzer, aware of the American government's hostility, dropped his projected visit.[56]

It was 1959, the year Lee Harvey Oswald reportedly made application to Albert Schweitzer College.

But Oswald had not applied to just any Summer-in-Europe collegiate program; he had registered at a Swiss college developed out of a liberal (often radical) Protestant ethic based on the moral principles of the most prominent international humanist absolutely opposed to nuclear weapons. And, while in the Soviet Union, Oswald had reportedly applied to another academic institution, the Soviets' Patrice Lumumba University, dedicated to still another pariah of Eisenhower and the Dulles brothers.

## Oswald's Higher Education: Albert Schweitzer College and Patrice Lumumba University

What were the crucial links between Oswald's two higher education choices, Albert Schweitzer College and Patrice Lumumba University, and the two men for whom they were named?

Both Albert Schweitzer and Patrice Lumumba were residents of Africa, the site of a major Cold War confrontation between the Soviet Union and the United States: Schweitzer was a resident of Gabon, Lumumba of the neighboring Congo.

Both were African leaders, one ethical, the other political, one white, the other black, but both were people-oriented and action-focused. Lumumba had called for the unity of the Congo and ultimately of all Africa; Schweitzer had called for the unity of all humanity.

Schweitzer had made a public declaration opposing nuclear weapons, a stand supported by hundreds of thousands around the world. Lumumba had advocated the preservation of the Congo's natural resources, including its uranium, opposing the secession of Katanga that contained Africa's first atomic reactor, the result of President Eisenhower's Atoms for Peace Program. Both Albert Schweitzer and Patrice Lumumba were, therefore, major threats to an ongoing anti-Soviet nuclear program that sought total atomic hegemony.[57]

Because of their populist stances signaling serious opposition to the Eisenhower administration's Congo aspirations, Schweitzer and Lumumba were both considered enemies of the United States by the president, by CIA Director Allen Dulles, and by John Foster Dulles (Eisenhower's Secretary of State). The administration assumed both Schweitzer and Lumumba were under Soviet/Communist influence; the two African leaders were therefore designated CIA counterintelligence targets by Agency Director Dulles.

With Oswald's attempted registration at Patrice Lumumba University in Moscow, the defecting American Marine's earlier application to Albert Schweitzer College was given obvious political amplification. The institutions were a complementary pair: the Soviet school with its Third-World, Cuban, left-wing/Communist ambiance, linked closely to the KGB and therefore of great interest to American counterintelligence, especially to James Angleton and the CIA; and the Swiss school with its liberal theological origins, attracting radical youth from around the world, dedicated to bringing together citizens of nations that had fought one another in World War II, located in a country suspected by American counterintelligence (in both the FBI and the CIA) of being an espionage mail-drop center.

To attract maximum U.S. intelligence attention, Lee Harvey Oswald could not have applied to two more troubling educational institutions.

## Expecting Oswald at Albert Schweitzer College

Was Lee Harvey Oswald ever listed as someone expected to come to Albert Schweitzer College? The official student lists for the academic year 1959-1960 (that is, the Fall, 1959, the Winter, 1959-1960, and the Spring, 1960) are missing from the college records at Harvard Divinity School Library. As an applicant, Oswald would have appeared somewhere on those lists. Two existing records, the first list for the "STATUS OF STUDENT APPLICATIONS FOR A.S.C."[58]: "Students accepted for 2nd and 3rd terms '60—and those accepted for academic year—1960-1961"[59] dated June 2nd, 1960[60], and the second list, "STUDENTS ACCEPTED FOR ACADEMIC YEAR 1960-'61"[61] suggest how thorough the college was in its record-keeping. The latter 'final' list of students had been copied and sent to four people: Dr. Dana McLean Greeley, Dr. Ernest Kuebler, the Rev. Edward A. Cahill, and the Rev. Leon Hopper.[62]

This 1960-1961 list of Albert Schweitzer College students may have been left in the Harvard Divinity School records by someone who had sanitized those records as a kind of message to future researchers: "See how disorganized and incomplete these records are?" But two major sets of records were left at Harvard. Beginning in 1957, the "Albert Schweitzer Alumni Association" had privately published and distributed a yearbook and memory record called "DAS DING AN SICH."[63] Two of those publications, for December 1959 and December 1960, No. 3 and No. 5, are in the Albert Schweitzer College records at Harvard. In No. 3, published in December, 1959, the last page was "YEAR COURSE 1958-1959": thirty students were listed[64] for the three terms (the ASC trimester program) in 1958 and 1959. In No. 5[65], published in December of 1960, the last page is "YEAR COURSE 1959-60": thirty-nine students were listed[66] for the three terms (the ASC trimester program) in 1959 and 1960. Some of these students attended only one trimester; some attended two trimesters; and some all three.[67]

The "YEAR COURSE 1958-1959" list was accurate, confirmed to me by one of the students, Bjorn Ahlstedt of Sweden, who posted information for some years about Albert Schweitzer College that included his experiences at the school; he also posted a list of seventeen faculty and students. Ahlstedt identified the students only by their first names: with that information, I was able to identify fifteen. Only two are questionable: "George," whom I am certain was a faculty member, and "Pooh," whom I am certain was a student.[68]

Any record of Lee Harvey Oswald as a prospective student at the college is difficult to find. But as distinct from the curious changes of schedule sent by Hans Casparis to Lee Harvey Oswald, no schedule modification was ever received by student Bjorn Ahlstedt. According to the Swede, Albert Schweitzer College's schedule was NEVER changed. Oswald alone apparently received, or at least was sent, the 'revised' schedule.

Ahlstedt was also aware that Oswald was expected but simply never appeared.

Lee Harvey Oswald's name was absent from the memorial 1959-1960 student list[69] because Oswald never arrived at Albert Schweitzer College and, therefore, never attended any of its three trimesters.

But the name of Lee Harvey Oswald was present on at least one official Albert Schweitzer College document. On January 15th, 1964, the Board of Albert Schweitzer College met in Churwalden, Switzerland.[70] Nine board members and ASC President Hans Casparis attended; also present were College Director Ernest Cassara and College Secretary Erika Weibel, acting as Dr. Cassara's interpreter.[71] President Casparis opened the board meeting, welcoming the college's board members, and proceeded to give his "President's Report."[72]

The first order of business was Lee Harvey Oswald, "the suspected murderer of President John F. Kennedy."[73]

If the strange record of Oswald and Albert Schweitzer College can be trusted at all, the Red Marine applied to the college on March 19th, 1959.[74] Fifty-five days later, Dr. Robert Schacht, the pastor of the First Unitarian Church of Providence, Rhode Island, submitted the names of American students who had applied for admission to Albert Schweitzer College for 1959-1960.[75] According to the college's president, Hans Casparis, "Lee H. Oswald was on the list of students who had applied from America, provided by Dr. Schacht on May 13, 1959."[76]

The Schacht document sent from 1 Benevolent Street, Providence, to Switzerland does not exist in any accessible repository, but a copy—or the original of the document—was most probably in Dr. Schacht's Benevolent Street file on Lee Harvey Oswald appropriated by two FBI agents[77] when they visited the Unitarian pastor in Providence after the JFK assassination.[78]

President Casparis' review for the college's board members and Director Cassara of the events subsequent to Oswald's defection to the Soviet Union closely anticipated the conclusions of the FBI and Warren Commission: "He had applied for the 3rd term, the Spring term 1960. He then failed to appear. In Fall 1960 we received an enquiry[79] from the [Swiss Federal] Police in Graubunden, as to whether or not Lee Oswald had arrived. He had disappeared from the USA."[80]

Casparis reported on Representative Jim Wright's investigation on behalf of Lee's mother and the resulting dispatch of the college's entire Oswald file: "We handed our material over to the Congressman."[81] Though the college's director Cassara was present at the meeting, Casparis did not mention that Cassara, when he was informed of the Oswald file story by the college secretary Erika Weibel, disapproved of releasing the material. Weibel had mailed the file to Wright on April 8th, 1961, so presumably nothing pertaining to Lee Harvey Oswald remained in the college's office in Churwalden: except, of course, the seven documents given to the FBI on December 31st, 1963, just fourteen days before Casparis gave his "President's Report" to the board and to Director Cassara and Erika Weibel.[82] The FBI "source" of the documents had to have been someone with access to Albert Schweitzer College's records, someone who was present at the very moment Casparis was giving his report, someone who was silent about an apparent special relationship between that person and American intelligence on the subject of Lee Harvey Oswald. Only three people qualified: Ernest Cassara, Erika Weibel, and Hans Casparis. For several obvious reasons, Cassara was highly unlikely to have been the college officer who submitted the Oswald documents to the Bureau.

## The FBI Source at Albert Schweitzer College

Therefore, either Hans Casparis or Erika Weibel (or both acting in unison) had to have been the still-protected FBI "source" of the documents surrendered to the Bureau on December 31st, 1963. Though Casparis was no longer a resident of Churwalden, the trip from Flims to the college would have been short and easy, and he would certainly have had access to the college's records. Weibel, of course, was still in residence as the college's secretary.

Casparis reported that, following the JFK assassination, the Swiss Federal Police visited him on Monday, November 25th, 1963; according to Casparis, "We had nothing to hide, as for us the matter was closed."[83] Casparis did not indicate whether the Swiss Federal Police had represented the FBI, but someone between November 22nd, 1963, and December 31st, 1963, in the name of the FBI had contacted the college, resulting in seven Albert Schweitzer College documents directly relating to Oswald being delivered to the Bureau.

Oddly enough, Director Cassara had been visited by a Swiss detective reportedly representing INTERPOL just after the Kennedy assassination[84], but on January 16th, 1964, neither Casparis nor Cassara gave the people attending the college's board meeting this information. Of course, Cassara was listening to Erika Weibel's translation into English of Casparis' report and, therefore, may have been distracted. The Swiss detective reportedly speaking for INTERPOL may, in turn, have represented INTERPOL's inquiry on behalf of the FBI.

Certainly Cassara was dealing with more than enough: the college's environment was threatened by a meat-drying factory; the institution was trying to find a permanent director (Cassara had only agreed to be its interim director for 1963-1964); a new scholarship program was being proposed; communications with the American Friends of Albert Schweitzer College were not at their best[85]; and one of the two most valuable officers of the college had "handed in her resignation"[86] sometime between November 6th, 1963, and January 15th, 1964.[87] Erika Weibel, the polyglot secretary (and treasurer) of Albert Schweitzer College for seven years (and the college officer who had reportedly sent the entire Oswald file to Texas Congressman Jim Wright) was leaving because she saw "in the College no possibility of promotion."[88] Later in the meeting, the "Board conveyed its profound gratitude to Frl. Weibel for her great and extraordinarily valuable service . . . given to the college for the past 7 years."[89] Weibel had joined the college one year before Oswald applied. In Cassara's June, 1964, Interim

Director's Report, Cassara reported that Erika Weibel was leaving at the end of the trimester "for an extended holiday in the United States . . . ."[90]

The 1963 Annual Report of Albert Schweitzer College was issued that same month (June, 1964), but it contained nothing of Lee Harvey Oswald and the two international investigations involving the college.

At the meeting on January 16th, 1964, the Board of Albert Schweitzer College did worry over the 1959 Oswald application. Member Rev. Amman asked: "Should the American Committee [headed by Pastor Robert Schacht of Providence] not have examined Lee Oswald's credentials more thoroughly?"[91] Hindsight often does supply excellent criteria, but Amman's 'question' elicited nothing of productive value. President Casparis did offer an interesting response: "There must have been with him [Oswald] some irregularity of a psychological nature. This [possible irregularity] could not be deduced from the application form."[92]

Apparently Casparis had already presented in private the possibility of a defective application form and its inability to elicit from the college's prospective students their possibly twisted backgrounds, since Interim Director Cassara immediately added: "The application form has since then been revised and extended. Further, we now demand 3-4 references. The applicant is also now required to state whether he has undergone psychiatric treatment, so that probably today a candidate like Lee Oswald would not be considered."[93]

Since no public record was officially available to the officers of Albert Schweitzer College on January 15th, 1964, relative to any "psychiatric treatment" that Lee Harvey Oswald may have previously undergone (in the United States, where no "treatment" record is publicly available), Dr. Cassara's "psychiatric" reference was inoperative.

## Oswald's Mishandled and FBI-Confiscated Albert Schweitzer College Documents

But the sense of Reverend Amman's question still remained: how could Lee Harvey Oswald have been placed on Schacht's anticipated student list with his faked references? Or, to bend the question: were faked Oswald references sent somewhere? And, if so, to whom? Any superficial check of Oswald's Marine references, especially his ministerial reference, would have raised immediate and serious questions about him. But IF the faked references had been sent, had they been sent to Rev. Robert Schacht in Providence? If so, the documents would have been in the Benevolent Street file when the team of appropriating Bureau agents visited Schacht after the assassination.

Confiscating the Benevolent Street file, therefore, would have protected any American intelligence operation that had generated fake Oswald references, whether the visiting Bureau agents were aware of that fraudulent generation or not.

But what if the faked Oswald references had been sent either directly to Albert Schweitzer College or indirectly by Robert Schacht to the Swiss college? Those documents would then have been in Oswald's college file until Erika Weibel sent them to Texas Representative Wright, where they then would have disappeared. Or those fake references were withheld from the mailing delivered to Wright by Weibel (for whatever reason) and then sent as part of the package of seven documents given to the FBI.

But, again, the documents would have disappeared.

Whether the Oswald references were sent to Robert Schacht in Providence or directly to the college in Switzerland, any check of those references (as it has been reported) would have established that the Oswald college application was a fraud.

The absence of those references from the public record exposes the Lee Harvey Oswald application to Albert Schweitzer College as a still-protected American intelligence operation.

## Hans Casparis of Albert Schweitzer College

Was the college's founder, Hans Casparis, part of that operation? Who was Hans Casparis?

From 1950 through 1955, Casparis and his wife were host and hostess to a group of international students recruited out of liberal Protestantism in the United States and Europe, helping to establish Albert Schweitzer College in 1955. In 1959, less than four years later, Lee Harvey Oswald (or someone in his name) applied to and reportedly registered for the Spring Trimester (the third term) of the college, April 12th through June 27th, 1960. Given all the suspicious circumstances surrounding Oswald's application; his defection; the first FBI investigation of Oswald's disappearance; Casparis' communications with Lee Harvey Oswald (apparently unsuccessful) and with Oswald's mother; and the post-assassination inquiries of the FBI and Interpol, Casparis' identity is critical.

Born on September 2nd, 1901[94], Hans Casparis reported in various public and personal venues that between the time he was eighteen (in 1919) and when he was thirty-three (in 1934) he had graduated from three universities (including the University of Chicago), studied at a fourth, was the pastor of a local Swiss church, served in the Swiss armed forces (eventually achieving the rank of Captain), met an English woman in Switzerland and married her in London, and was a full-time teacher in a Churwalden educational institution. His son John Casparis added still more academic achievements to his father's resume.

But the public record does not support Hans Casparis' claims.

The Harvard Divinity School Library documents give more detail about Albert Schweitzer College and its faculty, but those same documents invite serious and troubling questions about Hans Casparis. A four-page informational brochure[95] (its earliest distribution presently unknown) introduced the college's first full-year (probably 1955) faculty: Professor Dr. Victor Maag, Seminardirektor Dr. Conrad Buol, Rev. Dr. Joachim Wolff, Rev. Dr. Werner Niederer, Prof. Dr. Martin Schmid, David E. Clarke, Prof. Hans Casparis, and Casparis' wife, Therese Casparis.[96] Maag, Buol,

Wolff, Niederer, Schmid, and Clarke all were resplendent with degrees: the first five all reportedly held doctorates[97], David Clarke reportedly held both a B.A. and an A.M., and Therese Casparis reportedly held a B.A.[98]

Only Hans Casparis had no specific degrees (clerical or academic) listed, though his remarkable record of studies and teaching was summarized.

First, according to the Albert Schweitzer College brochure, Casparis listed himself as "Lecturer in German and Philosophy at Kantonsschule Chur."[99] In other sources he was identified simply as the equivalent of a high school teacher. Casparis reported he was a Lecturer in Education at the School of European Studies in the University of Zurich[100], but the university informed me that Casparis never lectured there.

Of course, the University of Zurich could have been mistaken.

Dr. Conrad Buol and Dr. Martin Schmid were listed on the Albert Schweitzer College faculty list, as, respectively, the head and the "former rector" of the "Graubunden Teachers Training College"[101], possibly accounting for the sometime-mistaken impression that Hans Casparis was an instructor at that same Training College rather than being a Churwalden high school teacher.

Casparis listed himself as a "Graduate of Basel, Zurich and Chicago Universities [who] . . . also studied at Tubingen."[102] A "graduate," of course, is a holder of a degree or diploma from a granting institution. But Hans Casparis was neither a graduate of the University of Chicago, nor of the University of Basel, nor of the University of Zurich.[103] Hans Casparis held no reported diplomas or degrees from Basel, Zurich, or Chicago.

All three universities, of course, could have been mistaken.

Casparis did reportedly attend the University of Chicago in 1946-1947[104], but he did not receive a degree.[105] He also never attended either the University of Basel or the University of Zurich.[106] But again, the three universities could have been mistaken.

Hans Casparis did attend the University of Tubingen (just after he turned 21) from May 11th, 1922, through March 1st, 1923[107], but he did not receive a degree from Tubingen.[108]

Therefore, according to the official responses to all my inquiries, Hans Casparis did not receive a degree from any academic institution either in Europe or the United States.

## Hans Casparis in the United States: the Chicago Context

But from October 1, 1946, to June 13, 1947, Hans Casparis spent almost nine months in Chicago, the site of a synergy of religious, political, and social action and anti-Communist psyops activity. One man who embodied that synergy was Paul H. Douglas, the famous senator from Illinois.

Paul Douglas[109] was a product of Bowdoin College, Harvard, and Columbia, receiving a Ph.D. from the latter institution in 1920. After teaching at the University of Illinois (1917-1918), Douglas began an extended relationship with the University of Chicago as a professor of economics. That same year, Douglas declared himself a Quaker.

Drawn to the Marxist/Leninist "experiment" in the Soviet Union, Douglas visited Russia in 1927 as a trade union representative, where his first-hand observations led him to reject Marxist economics; he remained, however, a Quaker socialist.

As an early political activist in Illinois moving in several socialist and some Democratic circles, he helped draft 1930s state legislation supporting the elderly, the unemployed, low-cost housing, and affordable utility rates. Paul Douglas eventually transformed from rebel anti-warrior to wartime patriot, joining the Marine Corps as a private in 1942 and returning home from the Pacific a lieutenant colonel, the recipient of a Bronze Star.

Douglas rejoined the faculty of the University of Chicago late in 1946 (exactly when Hans Casparis became a student) and was quickly recognized as a brilliant and inspiring professor who emphasized the ethical link between intention and action. In 1947, Douglas was elected to the presidency of the American Economic Association, achieving the highest professional honor of his career. That same year, with his domestic liberal orientation, Douglas declared himself a committed anti-Communist, ultimately supporting the emerging Cold War operations of the newly-created Central Intelligence Agency.

In 1937, Unitarian James Luther Adams, a Chicago political activist already recognized as an expert in religious social ethics, joined the faculty of the Meadville Theological School, a Unitarian seminary in Chicago. After the Unitarians and Univeralists merged, the seminary became the Meadville/Lombard Theological School. By 1943, Adams was both a professor of the University of Chicago's Federated Theological Faculty and the Meadville/Lombard Theological School. In 1945, James Luther Adams earned a doctorate from the University of Chicago, studying with Paul Douglas, the University's liberal political activist who became a close friend of Adams. In turn, Adams was a tireless worker for the Independent Voters of Illinois (the IVI), a liberal "grassroots" organization that aggressively supported Paul Douglas.

Just as James Luther Adams had become a prominent liberal Unitarian, so also did Paul Douglas, who identified himself in his autobiography as both a Quaker and a Unitarian. Douglas and his wife attended two prominent Unitarian churches, All Souls in Washington, D.C., and Cedar Lane Unitarian Church in Bethesda, Maryland.

Paul Douglas forged a distinguished career as a U.S. senator, supporting John F. Kennedy in his 1960 presidential campaign and championing Medicare, civil rights, and Lyndon Johnson's Great Society program. But Senator Douglas had an intelligence dark side.

Paul Douglas moved from support of the Marshall Plan to enthusiasm for the Truman Doctrine, anti-Soviet military alliances, and, after the onset of the Korean "Conflict," unqualified backing of South Korea. Beyond his domestic liberalism, Douglas had become a true believer in America's Cold War programs.

U.S. covert intelligence, operating under humanitarian cover, expressed interest in Paul Douglas, especially through its Operation Brotherhood, a program that ultimately enlisted Douglas as a member of its national committee.[110] The Operation's reported intention was to bring "medical services to isolated regions [of the world]."[111] But the International Rescue Committee, a long-time ally of and conduit for U.S. covert intelligence, was the sponsor of Douglas' Operation Brotherhood, "a CIA operation from start to finish."[112]

The Agency brought CIA agent Edward Lansdale to Vietnam, reputedly successful "in the Philippines, where, from 1950 through 1953, he had advised the [Filipino] government on a program of psychological warfare . . ."[113]; in Vietnam, he drew heavily on his Filipino "counterinsurgency" plans and personnel.[114] Lansdale's International Rescue Committee/Operation Brotherhood medical program, with Oscar Arellano, Filipino Junior Chamber of Commerce International vice-president for South East Asia fronting for President Magsaysay and his CIA control Ed Lansdale , "proved to be an extremely effective cover for [CIA] intelligence gathering and psychological warfare throughout Southeast Asia."[115] In February, 1955, to give the ostensibly humanitarian project in Vietnam its legitimacy, the International Rescue Committee (as a major ally of the CIA) and the U.S. Junior Chamber of Commerce co-sponsored a fund-raiser for Operation Brotherhood, with Senator Paul Douglas of Illinois signed on as a member of the Operation's national committee.[116]

For fifteen years, Douglas maintained his support of International Rescue Committee/CIA psyops[117] until he finally realized how vulnerable he had become. In 1970, he claimed he had been deceived by the IRC's officers and sponsors[118], but the senator's "long record as a staunch Cold Warrior" negated his "professions of innocence."[119] Whatever Paul Douglas' personal motives, the International Rescue Committee and the CIA had manipulated a prominent Quaker/Unitarian in pursuit of covert psyops goals.

James Luther Adams[120] followed an experiential path not unlike Paul Douglas, moving in radical and progressive circles in Chicago and beyond. After receiving his degree from Harvard Divinity School where he prepared for the Unitarian ministry, Adams served as the pastor of two Unitarians parishes in Massachusetts, earned a master's degree at Harvard in comparative literature, taught at Boston University from 1929 through 1932, and engaged in a number of progressive actions, including his public support of the Pequot textile mills strikers. In 1935, Adams was invited to join the faculty at the Unitarian/Universalist Meadville/Lombard Theological School in Chicago.

Adams accepted the call, but requested a year of "study" in Western Europe before he took up his Unitarian teaching tasks. James Luther Adams then spent an intense and defining year (1935-1936) in Germany closely observing Nazi terrorism. Adams was introduced to the anti-totalitarian actions of "clandestine, church-related resistance groups," the offspring of the liberal Protestants who had collaborated with spymaster Allen Dulles in World War One (and who would be Dulles' OSS allies in World War Two).

James Luther Adams had, in fact, made direct contact with the Underground Church movement in Germany.

In a series of acts strongly resembling intelligence operations, Adams used a "home movie camera" to film prominent anti-Nazi dissenters, including Albert Schweitzer; he also recorded images of "pro-Nazi leaders of the so-called German Christian Church." Because of these "religious" activities, Adams was closely interrogated by the Gestapo and "narrowly avoided imprisonment." Possibly because of this involvement with the Underground Church in Germany, Adams was made the subject of two FBI HQ (headquarters) files, HQ 1050002159 and HQ 1050105508, the initial "105" in both file numbers indicating that the Bureau's interest in Adams was "foreign counterintelligence." And Adams did not escape charges from the paranoid anti-Communist right: Louis Budenz accused him of being an agent of a massive Communist plot to infiltrate and take over American education.[121] From 1943 through 1967, the "Red Squad" of the Chicago Police Department maintained a file on Adams' civil rights activities; and in 1952, an Illinois legislator identified Adams (to the lawmaker's own satisfaction) as one of eleven top "subversives" in Illinois.[122]

Between 1927 and the late 30s, Adams had made a series of extended visits to Europe contacting liberal Protestant theologians and thinkers who were anti-Nazis, including Peter Brunner, Lutheran minister and teacher, a friend of Adams from his Harvard days. Brunner had become a leading figure in the anti-Nazi Confessing Church, a group that a few years later would be called on for covert intelligence by Allen Dulles and the Office of Strategic Services.

Returning to Chicago after 1936, Adams was convinced liberal religious individuals and groups had to oppose "the world's evils, and he stated his convictions loudly and clearly." Adams again visited Germany in 1938 and was involved in underground liberal church activity.

A person of both action and idea, Adams has been recognized by Unitarians and Universalists as their leading theologian of the 20th century, numbered among the best of the century's liberal theological thinkers.

In the 1950s, Adams became a commanding figure in the American Unitarian Association, closely associated with key Unitarians on the Unitarian Service Committee, many of whom worked with the Office of Strategic Services; he was a key figure in the Unitarians' mission to liberal religious youth; he was one of the earliest supporters of Hans Casparis and Casparis' vision of Albert Schweitzer College; and he was the first chairperson of the American Admissions Committee of Albert Schweitzer College.

James Luther Adams was also more than likely the source of Hans Casparis' 1946-1947 scholarship to Meadville/Lombard Theological School and thereafter Hans Casparis' professor when Casparis, the future developer of Albert Schweitzer College, studied at Meadville/Lombard. As one of Casparis' obituaries phrased it, "It was then that the thought ripened in him which would lead him to found the 'Albert Schweitzer College,' that is, an institution in which students from . . . countries that used to be enemies could meet in an international free-religious setting . . . ."[123] Adams closely monitored the college as the chair of its American Admissions Committee and, later, as a key member of the American Friends of Albert Schweitzer College. James Luther Adams was most probably the source of Hans Casparis' dream "that ripened in him" when Casparis studied at Chicago's Meadville/Lombard.

If Lee Harvey Oswald's admission papers to Albert Schweitzer College were sent anywhere besides Churwalden, Switzerland, they would have been sent to the probable mentor of Hans Casparis, James Luther Adams[124], key officer of the American Admissions Committee for Albert Schweitzer College.

## Hans Casparis' ASC Partner and Wife

According to public documents in Switzerland, Hans Casparis married "Maud Therese Callie" in London on July 30, 1934.[125] Maud Callie, Maud Therese Callie, or Therese Callie, reportedly born in London on May 21st, 1909, married Hans Casparis, "Pfarrer, Prof. Kant.schule Chur"[126] on July 30th, 1934.[127]

In her short resume published in the Albert Schweitzer College brochure, faculty member Therese Casparis listed receiving an B.A. in Education from the University of London and studying at both Heidelberg and the Sorbonne. But from 1901 through 1934 (the year she married Hans Casparis), she was reportedly a student at only one of these institutions.[128]

According to Ms. Ali Burdon, Assistant Archivist, University of London Library, who "checked the University of London student card index" from 1900 through 1939[129], Maud Therese Callie was enrolled as a student at University College in October 1928, and passed the examination in the Intermediate Arts in that same year; Callie then studied for "the Honors degree in French, with German as her subsidiary subject. She passed her subsidiary subject examination in German in 1930, and then went on to receive a second class honours degree (in the lower division in French)."[130]

In summary, Maud Therese Callie achieved a second class honours 'degree' in French (lower division) from the University College of London.

Ms. Burdon of the University of London also reported that in October, 1931, Marie Therese Callie "enrolled at the London Day Training College to take a Teacher's Diploma."[131] But Ms. Callie "left during the same academic session . . . without taking an examination [for her Teacher's Diploma]."[132]

Therefore, according to the University of London, Maud Therese Callie did NOT receive a "B.A. in Education from the University of London."[133]

Why did both Hans Casparis and Marie Therese Callie Casparis find it necessary to inflate their academic records for the initial advertisement of the Albert Schweitzer College?

From 1934 through 1948, Therese gave birth to five children, with a break between June 6th, 1937 and November 31st, 1937, and with a second break between February 2nd, 1945, and May 24th, 1948. But Mrs. Casparis did not attend any educational institution during either of those periods.

Hans Casparis was absent from Switzerland, September, 1946, through June, 1947, a registered theology student at the University of Chicago, but, according to the University's response to my inquiry, he did not receive a degree from that institution. The trip to the United States MIGHT have marked the end (or at least suspension) of Casparis' clerical connection, since he obviously could not attend to a parish's daily spiritual and administrative needs while living in Chicago; but he also could not have taught in Switzerland during that period. Yet the Casparis family apparently had sufficient income to support Hans' wife Therese, her four children in Switzerland, and Hans himself studying in Chicago for ten months. According to the public record, Hans did have a scholarship in Chicago, and it is entirely possible that either Maud Therese or Hans (or both) had independent incomes, possibly from inherited family funds or gifts.

On July 30th, 1934, Casparis reportedly married Maud Therese Callie in London; but in that same year he apparently held his Swiss Protestant pastorate AND operated as an on-duty Protestant chaplain to a Swiss Army mountain brigade, where, as a member of that unit, he was reportedly elevated to the rank of Captain.[134]

In 1934, when Hans Casparis and Maud Callie married in London and, afterward, when they left for Switzerland, Maud Therese Callie Casparis had already become who she would be in 1950. So also Hans Casparis, except for his reported ten months of study in Chicago, had already become who he would be in 1950. According to the European and English colleges and universities responding to my inquiries, neither Hans nor Maud Therese graduated from nor received a formal degree from any academic institution of higher learning from 1934 through 1950. Further, no significant breaks occurred in either of their histories to allow for a sustained period of university study.

How then did these two young people (with reportedly inflated academic credentials) live and work in Switzerland, raise five children for fifteen years, and then in 1949-1950 establish an international center in the Klosters dedicated to Albert Schweitzer's moral and ethical values that attracted young liberal Protestants from around the world?

Hans and Therese did indeed do precisely that, founding an international college reportedly attracting young liberal Protestants supported by the very religious institutions (in touch with those same liberal Protestant groups) penetrated and manipulated by the Central Intelligence Agency both in Europe and the United States.[135]

## The Counterintelligence Clue

After the Kennedy assassination and the subsequent American espionage investigation of both Albert Schweitzer College and the missing Lee Harvey Oswald, the FBI's protection of the college's Bureau "source" for the seven Oswald documents sent to it from Albert Schweitzer College was a major counterintelligence clue.

If Albert Schweitzer College had been (in part or in whole) a creation of U.S. intelligence, its post-Oswald record was revelatory: the college began declining after the FBI/Swiss Federal Police inquiries concerning Lee Harvey Oswald: it never recovered, ultimately disappearing from history.

Only the files at the Harvard Divinity School Library in Cambridge and at the Unitarian/Universalist Service Committee in Boston have preserved fragments of the college's curious past.

# Essay Four

# Allen Dulles, Manipulating Religious Individuals and Groups, Destabilizing Eastern Europe, and the OSS/Unitarian Connection

For over forty years, Allen Dulles (an agent of the U.S. Foreign Service, the OSS, and the CIA) manipulated key religious individuals and groups (largely Protestant institutions in Europe and the United States) through two World Wars and the ensuing Cold War to achieve economic and political goals for U.S. intelligence and the American establishment. In particular, the American spymaster misused prominent Unitarians, American Unitarian Association officials, the Unitarian Service Committee, and board members of the Unitarian-supported Friends of Albert Schweitzer College to reach those goals.

In 1959, Lee Harvey Oswald failed to make an appearance at Albert Schweitzer College, reportedly defecting to the Soviet Union. Allen Dulles' history from 1917 through 1959 of opportunistic espionage involving faith-based groups established the frame for that dramatic defection.

CIA Director William Colby had argued that his Agency's use of religious institutions and clerics did not damage either their moral integrity or their religious mission.[1] With one word, Latin American historian Penny Lernoux responded: "Absurd."[2]

The roots of the collaboration between religious institutions, anti-Communist political movements, and American intelligence were planted and nourished early in the First World War, and the dark gardener was Allen Dulles, when Dulles began using dedicated religious groups, especially Quakers, Unitarians, and other liberal Christian sects, as sources of crucial intelligence information.[3]

The Central Intelligence Agency's long-time abuse of religious organizations in Central and South America has been well documented[4], but the record of both OSS and CIA manipulation of European religious connections and assets has been carefully cloaked.[5] Additionally, John Foster Dulles' misuse of religious groups for personal, corporate, and national political and economic ends has been an untold story, a manipulation closely paralleling his brother Allen's cynical intelligence activities.[6]

Provocatively, but only referring to the links between the Catholic Church in Latin America and the CIA, John D. Marks had reported that at least 30 percent of the clergy he interviewed during his investigation of American intelligence abuse of religious groups were aware of an Agency-Church "connection."[7] Hinting at a documentary record for OSS and CIA misuse of American religious organizations based in the United States but not offering such a record, Christopher Simpson cited the CIA's "penetration of the senior leadership of trade unions, corporations, religious groups, and even student organizations."[8] In a study of the CIA and culture, Frances Stoner Saunders ignored religion and religious institutions, though one of Saunders' chapters ("The Guardian Furies") seemed to promise an examination of the Agency's abuse of American church-related groups[9]: "The religious imperative motivated Cold Warriors such as Allen Dulles who, brought up in the Presbyterian tradition, was fond of quoting from the Bible for [the Israelites'] . . . use of spies . . . ."[10] Saunders pointed out that Reinhold Niebuhr, Henry Luce's favorite theologian, was the "honorary patron of the [CIA-sponsored and financed] Congress for Cultural Freedom . . ."[11] and that Niebuhr was not highly thought of by Martin Luther King; it was a promising beginning.[12] But after a few pages on Billy Graham, Joe McCarthy, Leslie Fiedler, Elia Kazan, and public confession, Saunders' otherwise splendid study offered nothing on the topic of religion and the Cold War.[13] One other Cold War and culture study by Stephen J. Whitfield[14] might have explored the topic but did not.[15]

## Allen Dulles, 1917: the Origins of U.S. Intelligence's Manipulation of Religious Groups and Individuals

Where did U.S. intelligence's manipulation of liberal religion begin? Early in 1917, Allen Dulles had joined the United States Foreign Service, the State Department's "career staff," sent first to Vienna, then to Bern, Switzerland, where he became "a junior intelligence officer."[16]

Dulles was posted as the associate of Hugh Wilson, a senior Department of State official; by the end of 1918, Dulles and Wilson had "built up a network of European refugees and American expatriates who [literally] functioned . . . as intelligence agents for the American embassy [in Switzerland.]"[17]

Bern was then a center of ethnic antagonists, "emigre' insurrectionists," and elite businessmen who knew no boundaries except the extent of their money's power.[18] Allen Dulles "was assigned responsibility for liaison with representatives of . . . Central European liberal/nationalist groups . . . rebelling against the disintegrating Austro-Hungarian Empire."[19]

A key contact in that Wilson/Dulles network was the eminent Herbert Haviland Field.[20] Dr. Herbert Field was a distinguished American scientist, the patriarch of the family of Fields of Boston; during World War One, he had resided in Zurich, Switzerland.[21] A practicing Quaker, "pacifist[,] and dedicated internationalist,"[22] Herbert Field impressed Dulles' associate Hugh Wilson as a gentle and candid man[23], "unsophisticated and lovable."[24] But that reportedly child-like Quaker was also the distinguished graduate of a German university and a zoology scholar who had come to Zurich "to run the Concilium Bibliographicum, an international institute . . . [dedicated to compiling] a full bibliography of [worldwide] scientific research . . . ."[25] Further, Field spoke the German language "flawlessly,"[26] and as a political liberal had "unique relationships" with both the European academic community and anti-fascist individuals and groups throughout Germany.[27] Field was, in fact, the reported source of a "mine of information" for the Wilson/Dulles intelligence operations.[28]

## The Lenin Link

Curiously, Herbert Field was later the target of an attack on his character and judgment involving Vladimir Ilich Lenin, Lenin's American Foreign Service connection in Switzerland, and Allen Dulles himself. Since the ultimate source of the story (recorded by Leonard Mosley and repeated a dozen times thereafter) was Allen Dulles himself, the shape of the narrative spoke directly to Dulles' willingness to sacrifice his closest intelligence collaborators for purely personal goals. In this instance, the sacrifice was Herbert Field, a well-known Quaker. Years later, it would be Noel Field, Herbert Field's son.[29]

Lenin, living in exile in Switzerland and "separated from his homeland by Germany and Austria,"[30] had been in periodic touch with James C. McNally, the American Consul General in Zurich[31], the "German" center of Switzerland and the neutral country's industrial and financial capital. The information sent from Lenin to McNally was of major intelligence value to the Allies: it came directly from Russia to Lenin and then to McNally.[32] However, according to Leonard Mosley (relying significantly on Allen Dulles), neither Bern nor Washington found the Lenin/McNally intelligence valuable.[33] It was a piece of espionage history not especially believable.

But Foreign Service Counsel McNally had another important source of intelligence information: his daughter was married to an officer in the German Navy "who had argued against the Berlin decision to wage unrestricted submarine warfare [in the Atlantic], because he correctly predicted [it] . . . would bring the United States into the war."[34] The couple was residing in Berlin and in touch with German refugees flowing into Switzerland.[35] Reportedly unhappy with his government's aggressive U-Boat decision, McNally's son-in-law alerted the American counsel to "at least two major German offensives."[36] Intelligence information on Germany therefore flowed from the McNallys through Switzerland into General Pershing's HQ in France.[37]

McNally, however, had too many suspect German connections, so Herbert Field, Dulles' trusted Quaker connection residing in Zurich, passed on his negative judgment[38]: Field accused McNally of "consorting with the enemy"[39], a charge that had some substance[40], especially given how Lenin got to the Finland Station in Petrograd.

According to Leonard Mosely, Dulles' biographer, on Easter Sunday, 1917, Allen Dulles was the duty officer at the Bern legation (apparently working alone).[41] The phone rang and Dulles answered. A man, reportedly speaking in German with a "heavy accent," said he was Vladimir Ilich Lenin, told his listener he would be in Bern later that day, and said he had to contact someone in authority at the American legation in Bern.[42] Further, "Lenin reportedly insisted on speaking to someone who should take an important message and negotiate with him."[43]

"The caller requested that the [subsequent] meeting be secret."[44]

Lenin at that moment was already "known to the Americans as the leader of . . . [Russian] revolutionaries . . . in Zurich."[45] But he was also a recognized intelligence source of the American counsel in Zurich[46], and, as one of the leaders of a revolutionary movement that had just overthrown the Imperial Russian government, Lenin would ultimately be able to place a halt on the entire Russian war effort.[47] Further, Lenin had made no secret of his opposition to Russia's role in the conflict[48], and the revolutionaries, now coming to power in Russia, would eventually be led by Lenin.[49]

The version of the Lenin story Dulles told to Mosley included the transmission of Russian intelligence material from vague "sources in Petrograd,"[50] some of which "Berne did not even bother to send on [to Washington]."[51] But could those "sources" have, indeed, sent their intelligence through Lenin and then to McNally or, even directly, to Allen Dulles?

The most authoritative version of the Lenin story is that given by Peter Grose[52], but it is also the most provocative; indeed, one of Grose's endnotes calls attention to "the fun of this [Lenin] investigation," strongly suggesting a darker, less "delightful romp" was involved.[53]

How dark? First, what was Allen Dulles doing in Bern, Switzerland? Dulles was the third secretary at the American Embassy in Vienna, Austria, in March, 1917 (and presumably in April), until he was posted to Bern. With Germany's submarine warfare catalyzing the imminent response, the United States Congress declared war on Germany, April 6th, 1917.[54] The American Embassy in the Austrian capital was virtually emptied; nearly the entire staff had gotten aboard an evacuation train bound for Switzerland.[55] According to his biographer Peter Grose, Allen Dulles had given up celebrating his birthday that week because of the chaos in Vienna and his last-minute support of Red Cross evacuees from Austria.[56]

Again, according to Grose, Dulles disembarked from the evacuation train[57] at Bern, Switzerland, and began "retrieving his uprooted personal affairs at the United States Legation . . ."[58], certainly a most inelegant and strange turn of phrase. But why did Allen Dulles have "uprooted personal affairs" in Bern when he was officially working in Vienna?

Is it possible that Austria-based Dulles was periodically operating out of Bern on certain secret intelligence operations? Grose observed that Dulles would not be officially "posted" to Bern until April 23rd[59], "but as we have seen, Allen was in Bern well before his official posting."[60] But, of course, Grose NEVER mentioned that Dulles was in Bern "well before" April 23rd. Had that piece of information been carefully edited out of Grose's book while the revealing footnote was overlooked?

Whatever Dulles would ultimately do in Bern supposedly on Easter weekend could have been prepared for in the embassy in Vienna and concluded at the Bern Legation offices on Sunday.

After the United States declared war on both Germany and Austro-Hungary on April 6th, 1917, "the U.S. Embassy packed up to leave Vienna, [but] Allen Dulles had already been posted [according to biographer Leonard Mosely] to the American Legation in Berne . . . ."[61] Could Peter Grose have misread his sources? Could the posting date, in fact, have been March 23rd rather than April 23rd when Dulles was sent from Vienna to Bern?

As distinct from a deserted Bern Legation office to which Dulles arrived after leaving Vienna in early April, the in-training spymaster joined the United States Legation in Bern, according to biographer Mosley, "at the end of March 1917" when the legation was "a humming hive of activity."[62]

Could both dates be correct? Could Dulles have been working in Bern as of March 23rd, 1917, but not have been officially posted to Bern until April 23rd? If so, what were the two different dates helping to keep hidden?

Dulles' official Bern Legation title was "political officer[63]," but Dulles had adopted the role of legation intelligence officer immediately upon his arrival because of the nearly total disorganization he reportedly found there. Not exactly the image of a beehive. The "harassed first secretary" Hugh Wilson told Dulles: "I guess the best thing for you to do is take charge of intelligence."[64]

But what was Dulles doing in Vienna, performing last-minute third-secretary duties and then boarding an evacuation train to Bern, when he was already IN Bern? Was Dulles, in fact, train-hopping between Vienna and Bern to accomplish an important but still undisclosed mission? Indeed, the available evidence suggests the answer is "Yes."

Early in 1917, Allen Dulles had constructed "a new transmittal route for the [Vienna] embassy's communications."[65] Newspapers, mail, and the all-important diplomatic pouches (holding sensitive communications, intelligence reports and coded messages to various political and military figures) had to go through Berlin and then transit a neutral Baltic port before being sent to Bern (where the messages could then be cabled to the United States). But the Germans held up communications in and out of Vienna for as much as one month.[66]

So Dulles assumed the role of on-hands communications officer, sometimes carrying "as many as two dozen of the bulky leather [diplomatic] pouches."[67] Every week in 1917 Dulles took the "arduous two-day train trek to Bern. The train journey . . . [itself finally ended in] Zurich before the traveler took a local trolley to Bern . . . ."[68]

A local trolley car to Bern.

Each week in 1917, Allen Dulles was absent from Vienna for at least two days, traveling first to Zurich and then Bern and then back again: Zurich, where Russian revolutionary exile Lenin lived; and Bern, where the German Legation made the final plans for Lenin's sealed train trip to Petrograd. And between Zurich and Bern, just a short Swiss trolley ride.

Peter Grose's discoveries in both U.S. and Soviet sources have been extremely relevant[69], in particular, Lenin's location in March and April, 1917: "Lenin spent his years of exile in Zurich, not Berne, but the Leninist archives in Moscow showed that . . . Lenin and his common-law wife . . . went to the Swiss capital [Bern] that [Easter] weekend to complete a still-unrevealed matter of intrigue."[70] Grose clearly indicates it was Easter weekend and no other.

Tantalizingly, Peter Grose did not reveal what he might have found about that specific "matter of intrigue," but he did add that on that "crucial" Easter Sunday, Lenin had nothing scheduled.[71] Might Lenin, Grose speculated, have decided "to compare notes with a representative [unnamed] of the United States government," to establish "common cause" against Germany?[72]

Grose's speculation, however interesting, lacks merit: Lenin, once in power, was clearly intending to break off Russian relations with the Western Allies and close down the Russian "Eastern" front against Germany, exactly why a far more important "matter of intrigue" was probably the issue in Bern.

Rather than a common cause against Germany, a common cause in support of closing the Eastern Front was much more likely.

According to Grose, because "no more senior officer at the [Bern] Legation was available," Allen Dulles was asked to take an incoming phone call[73] (despite Dulles not yet having been officially posted to the Bern Legation). It was from an "unknown foreigner" who (yet) was recognized by Dulles as "one of those Russian emigre agitators" in Swiss exile.[74] According to Grose, just at that moment in history "the tsar had abdicated, and the revolutionaries were maneuvering to go home [presumably from, for example, Switzerland] and take over."[75]

When the Lenin call came in, Dulles was about to leave on a date[76], a story in at least two extant versions. In one, Allen Dulles and his "closest friend in Bern . . . Robert Craigie, a second secretary at the British Embassy . . ."[77], had agreed to a "weekend rendezvous at a country inn" with Swiss twins of reputedly major mammorial dimensions.[78] In the other and more dignified version of the story, Dulles had a date with a "girlfriend" for tennis[79] who was, according to a knowledgeable source, "a young lady [of unreported breast dimension] named Helene Herzog."[80] Ms. Herzog was, in fact, "the daughter of a Swiss family he met in his school years."[81]

For Allen Dulles at that moment (if we are to believe any of the several versions of the Lenin story), sex, whether in singles or doubles, had reportedly trumped politics and intelligence, his two jobs at the Bern Legation (at least officially after April 23rd). He reportedly dismissed Lenin, telling him to call back at ten on Monday (the morning of the next day) when the Bern legation office officially opened.[82] Given the ensuing world-shaking events, Dulles (according to biographer Leonard Mosley) "had learned his lesson, and [he] never neglected an emigre again."[83]

On October 20th, 1963, Allen Dulles told a final and absurd version of the Lenin call to the Bern Legation: according to Dulles, he had "received an invitation to a reception hosted by an eccentric Russian exile in Zurich. Dulles declined the offer . . . in favor of a tennis match with a young lady."[84]

Why the odd story with its several odd variants?

Given Dulles' elaborate train travel between Vienna and Bern, with Zurich as a required changeover stop through March, 1917, and the still-to-be-explained "matter of intrigue" involving Lenin, Easter Sunday, and Bern, Allen Dulles may himself have sent Comrade Lenin to Russia. Or at the very least Allen Dulles colluded with German military intelligence in the Finland Station enterprise, afterward patsying his close friend and intelligence source Herbert Field, the gentle Quaker.

The Lenin story was simply unbelievable: a budding spymaster (who no later than April 23rd, 1917, was responsible for U.S. intelligence at Bern, the neutral capital of Switzerland) had passed up the opportunity to make direct contact with revolutionary leader Lenin at the moment of the Russian revolution. According to Mosley, Dulles had reportedly hypothesized: "[W]hat did it matter who was in power in Russia so long as they [the Russians] remained allies and went on fighting the Germans?"[85]

But Dulles would have been either stupid or obsessed with anticipated sex (or at least with tennis) to believe his own nonsense. Any powerful Red in exile who managed to get home would, in fact, help to "take Russia out of the war,"[86] precisely what the Germans wanted.[87] And if Dulles was, if only in part, instrumental in sending Lenin to Russia, the Bern intelligence officer's intention would have been to further destabilize Russia, thereby taking pressure off Germany's Eastern Front. After Lenin arrived in Moscow, the "winter of 1917-1918 brought to Bern [a] . . . set of diplomatic newcomers . . . , representatives of the Bolshevik government . . . who . . . demanded control of the old czarist embassy [in Bern]."[88] And those Bern arrivals spoke for a Lenin government that had strongly hinted it "might . . . take the Russians out of the war . . . ."[89] Lenin, in fact, having arrived in Russia, almost immediately directed that Russian-German peace discussions be initiated.

Intelligence officer Dulles should have known.

Lenin went to Russia in a German train[90] without reported Allied or American Foreign Service support, "in a [so-called] sealed railway coach [chosen] by the German intelligence chief Colonel Walther Nicolai . . . ."[91] Nicolai's intelligence group had secretly supported the Bolsheviks in their effort to take Czarist Russia out of the war[92], and Lenin accomplished exactly that goal.[93]

Lenin's negotiations with the German government for passage first through Switzerland then through Germany and the Scandinavian north were concluded the night of April 8th: "the German Legation in Bern [had] signaled final departure for the next morning."[94]

Within an incredibly short time, including the morning he spoke to Allen Dulles and was reportedly rebuffed, Lenin had transformed himself from a poverty-stricken "exiled head of a small extremist revolutionary party that had relatively little following even within Russia"[95] into the ruler of 160,000,000 people in greater Russia. Michael Pearson's research (published in 1975) in British, German, and Soviet sources established Lenin had been supported and financed by the Imperial German government, not only in his "sealed train" ride to the Finland Station of Petrograd but also in his successful takeover of the Russian revolution.[96] By supporting Lenin, the German military and German intelligence bought themselves an assured withdrawal of Russian forces from the Eastern Front.

The German Legation in Bern had been in cooperation with Lenin and his "sealed train" to Russia; at the same time, in Bern, Allen Dulles had monitored the desks and phones of the United States Legation.

Allen Dulles was certainly no friend of socialist or Communist reform and revolution whose major political and economic changes focused on his good friends in German industry and banking. A defeat of the Germans followed by a Communist Russian regime threatening (Eastern) Germany would have been seen as extremely dangerous to Dulles' associates in German manufacturing and commerce.

Consorting with the enemy?

Allen Dulles would have initiated the charge of consorting with the enemy against James C. McNally, the United States General Counsel in Zurich (where Lenin was in exile), and boosted the charge through Herbert Field (Allen Dulles' intelligence asset) precisely as a preemptive strike, deflecting the consorting charge away from himself. Then his ludicrous versions of the Lenin story and the defamation of Herbert Field would have completed his series of defensive moves.

Whether or not he had directly participated in Lenin's Finland Station operation[97], Allen Dulles made certain he would not be accused either of collaborating with the Bolsheviks or of aiding the German war effort. But both accusations were most probably true. Thirty years later during the Second World War when he again became "the American intelligence chief in Switzerland, Allen Dulles's assignment was . . . to consort with the enemy."[98] That consorting observation was made, in fact, by Peter Grose, Dulles' admiring biographer.

## Allen Dulles, Herbert Field, and the Quakers

Allen Dulles' negative commentary on Herbert Field was far from the truth. According to Dulles, the spymaster had made contact with Field because Dulles first viewed him as a "fertile source of intelligence."[99] But Dulles maintained he had been rebuffed by Field. In truth, Dulles was a frequent visitor to the Field's family home, making important contacts of intelligence value; for Dulles' spy operations, Field and his often powerful friends were intelligence "go-betweens."[100] Dulles had cultivated these active and influential people, "first in Vienna and then in Bern."[101] They were "individuals who happen[ed] to have access to different parties . . . [and were] willing to make their access available."[102] They were cut-outs, connections between persons or groups who, for whatever reason, wished to avoid "direct contact."[103]

And Herbert Field functioned as one of Dulles' major intelligence cut-outs, making available to the American espionage chief "a wide range of intellectual associates across Europe."[104] When the war first began, Field, reputedly an "ardent pacifist,"[105] became "the head of a lively Quaker relief organization which ran food relief programs for the starving populations of war-torn Europe."[106] But the Quaker program also serviced eminent émigrés with powerful political, economic, and intelligence links, and Dulles quickly learned how important it was to spend time "in the company of Czech, Slav, Moravian, Bothian, . . . Serbian [and other] groups operating on neutral Swiss ground . . . ."[107]

That Allen Dulles used the Quakers, of course, in no way detracts from the Friends' extraordinary program of care for the hungry, the naked, the sick, and the imprisoned from the post-World War One period through the political ascendancy of Hitler, World War Two, and after.[108] But Allen Dulles would not forget the pragmatic utility of a religious help organization (like the Quakers) as a cover for intelligence activity. And he would not forget the Field family, especially one of Herbert Field's young sons, Noel Field[109], whom he first met in Zurich in 1918. Herbert Field's Quaker-based network in World War One became the foundation for Allen Dulles' Second World War spy operations, and it was Henry's son Noel who helped run it for Allen Dulles.[110]

## Allen Dulles: American Agent

Just after World War One, Allen Dulles joined his brother John Foster Dulles at the Paris peace conference in 1919. Foster was an "an assistant to the chief U.S. negotiator, Norman Davis," and both Dulles and Davis concentrated on "German war reparations."[111] In essence, the Dulles brothers' job was financial intelligence. At the same conference, Allen Dulles was attached to the "Czech Boundary Commission"[112] as well as being "in charge of the U.S. delegation's political intelligence efforts in Central Europe."[113]

Just as John Foster Dulles was always close to the centers of industrial and financial power in both Germany and the United States, so also Allen Dulles was always available for American intelligence work, official or not.[114] "In 1926, after service in Berlin, Constantinople, and Washington, Dulles left the diplomatic service to join his brother [Foster] in the . . . firm of Sullivan and Cromwell, specialists in international law corporate practices."[115] Dulles then worked for two decades through his legal, economic, and political connections to supply significant data to the elite of the United States.[116]

Officially, Dulles rejoined American intelligence with the Office of the Coordinator of Information (COI).[117] In January, 1942, he was made the chief of the COI's office in New York[118] in Room 3663, International Building, Rockefeller Plaza.[119] Though Dulles' COI Manhattan staff had "projects" targeting the entire globe, Dulles, the ultimate espionage pragmatist, concentrated on Germany, including that nation's entire range of political entities.[120]

Led by Arthur Goldberg, Dulles' "Special Activities desk" in New York argued for the establishment of a German committee made up of anti-Hitler émigrés that "would act as a front for American [intelligence] support of a . . . resistance organization [in Germany]."[121] Right, middle, and left would, of course, be part of the operation[122], the plan closely anticipating Dulles' later OSS activities in Switzerland. Chosen to head the committee was Heinrich Bruening, a former Weimar Chancellor and a prominent "German Catholic."[123]

## Karl Frank, Alias Paul Hagen: Dulles' Special Operative

But the left was especially important: Dulles' operatives chose Austrian psychologist Dr. Karl Frank (alias "Paul Hagan," alias "Willi Mueller").[124]

Beginning in 1935, Frank had made several visits to the United States contacting leading socialists, including Reinhold Niebuhr, prominent Protestant minister, theologian, and active Socialist Party member.[125] By the time Frank immigrated to the United States in December, 1939, he had also cultivated key figures in U.S. intelligence.[126] Frank/Hagen held credentials that linked him to influential anti-Nazi Socialist and Communist circles[127], vitally important for any resistance movement. In New York, his close connection with Dulles' operative Arthur Goldberg was ultimately established "through mutual friends in the Jewish Labor Committee and the Emergency Rescue Committee."[128] Frank himself was one of founders of the Committee.

But charges based on Frank's "left-wing past" plagued Arthur Goldberg and his agent Karl Frank, threatening Dulles' All-Germany project.[129] Finally, the State Department, objecting to "Communists," reactionaries, and "Junkers" as members of Dulles' front committee in support of the German resistance, killed the program.[130]

Dulles, however, never gave up his basic principle: to work with "the devil himself" to achieve his goals[131], a covert philosophy he carried out in Switzerland after he left New York.

Dulles' allies in American intelligence remained busy with espionage activity. The American Friends of German Freedom organization was, for example, a U.S. intelligence operation founded by Methodist minister and University of Newark president Frank Kingdon[132], theologian Reinhold Niebuhr[133], Karl Frank, who became its research director[134], and David Seiferheld, an OSS counterintelligence officer who became secretary of the American Friends of German Freedom.[135] Seiferheld worked with Secret Intelligence (SI) in its "Censor unit," maintaining a close connection with Karl Frank and his Arthur Goldberg/Labor Department associates.[136] David Seiferheld was "an early recruit into the OSS and a confidant of its director, William Donovan."[137]

## Karl Frank, the OSS, and the CIA

Karl Frank worked closely with the American Friends of German Freedom and the OSS-supported[138] Emergency Rescue Committee, just as, later, he would work with the

CIA-supported International Rescue Committee.[139] With the help of Frank and his friends, key German refugees who had successfully entered the United States became employees of Shortwave Research, Inc., "a front organization for the COI Foreign Information Service . . . interlocked with both the Emergency Rescue Committee and the American Friends of German Freedom."[140] Eventually most of the outstanding anti-Nazi refugees were hired by the OSS, finding jobs with its Research Branch.[141]

In June, 1940, the Emergency Rescue Committee (ERC) was formed following the eloquent argument for its creation by Thomas Mann's daughter at a fund-raising luncheon just three days after France surrendered to Germany. American Friends Frank Kingdon became Chairman and David F. Seiferheld became Treasurer of the ERC. With support from Karl Frank, Frank Kingdon, and David Seiferheld, the ERC had major multiple links to U.S. intelligence and its political goals.

Sharing Karl Frank's friendship with Reinhold Niebuhr was Joseph Buttinger, an Austrian underground activist and associate of Frank.[142] Buttinger began as a social democrat but moved further and further to the right during his long association with the Emergency Rescue Committee and the later International Rescue Committee.[143] In the 1930s, Buttinger had been a member of die Funke, a small Leninist group with ties to the underground German organization New Beginnings.[144]

"Buttinger and Frank served as the 'moving spirits' of the ERC during its first days . . . . Frank[, for example,] could connect the new relief organization with New Beginning members in exile."[145] And it was New Beginnings that figured importantly in the rescue and intelligence work of Varian Fry.

## Varian Fry, Karl Frank Alias Paul Hagen, and the Fight Against Fascism

When Varian Fry met Karl Frank, then known as "Paul Hagen," an extraordinary continental rescue operation was ultimately conceived that involved covert intelligence, radical dedication to the survival of contemporary European culture, and a major religious cover identity for its primary operative.[146]

Varian Fry was a liberal American journalist who had spent enough time in Germany to know and understand the country's most brutal and anti-cultural dimensions under the Nazis.[147] As he had done when General Franco and his Italian and German allies attacked Spanish democracy, Fry volunteered his services in the fight against fascism.[148]

When Fry joined the American Friends of German Freedom[149], he began his close connection to Karl Frank. The American Friends had split into two camps, activist and isolationist; though the factions agreed on the basic principle of rescue, their agreement ended there.[150] Disturbed with the split, Fry and Hagen (Karl Frank) had held an "emergency meeting" on May 16th, 1940, at Child's restaurant in New York[151], and a plan developed that was carried over to a following fund-raising affair. The Emergency Rescue Committee was born with its distinguished roster of board members and their major U.S. intelligence links.

The new organization was ready to help save German intellectuals and artists from the Nazis[152], but though the Emergency Rescue Committee[153] had dedicated itself to saving European minds and talents, it also began collecting key intelligence data from its network of continental and stateside contacts and saved refugees.

Neither Fry nor Hagen held any office with the ERC, but Varian Fry has often been called a "founding father" of the Emergency Rescue Committee. And Fry had his own intelligence-linked relationship: when the Committee needed an office, "Fry offered his [Horizon Books space] . . . at the [American] Foreign Policy Association as a makeshift headquarters . . . ."[154] Three weeks later, the Committee had its 'permanent' office on East Forty-Second Street.[155]

Someone from the Committee had to go to France to begin the ERC's work of rescue, and Fry volunteered. Fry's associate Frank/Hagen initially said no to Fry. But when no one else seemed suitable or available, Hagen agreed that Fry should go.[156]

Why did Hagen assent? According to Hagen, Fry did not fit the Gestapo profile of someone who would be interested in spiriting away key cultural foes of the Nazi nation.[157]

But just as Hagen (Karl Frank) had controlled the domestic options of the rescue effort, Hagen now controlled the European option: ostensibly sending Fry to France.

In order to be effective in the Committee's planned rescue operations, Fry needed both a valid civilian passport and "some cover."[158] His trip was "in essence a secret mission . . . to appear transparent, innocent, and public."[159] What the Emergency Rescue Committee found was the "perfect cover."[160] The YMCA (Young Men's Christian Association) agreed to give Fry false documentation as the representative of that religious group.[161]

Equipped with a passport and papers identifying Fry as a member of the YMCA, "a religious, politically neutral organization . . ."[162], Varian Fry began an heroic operation that helped rescue, among others, Marcel Duchamp, Andre Masson, Marc Chagall, Max Ernst, Franz Werfel, Hans Habe, Victor Serge, Hannah Arendt, André Breton, and scores of scientists, intellectuals, and other artists, including Alma Mahler, herself an accomplished musician, who brought the precious musical scores of her first husband, Gustav Mahler, to America.[163]

It was "[Paul] Hagen [who] had decided Fry should head first to Marseille"[164] in his search for refugees, and it was Hagen who directed Fry in his work from the moment the decision was made to send Fry to France as the covert agent of the "OSS-supported"[165] Emergency Rescue Committee. But in August of 1940, just two days before Fry flew out of America on his way to France, a strange event occurred, pointing to an even deeper covert operation involving both Hagen and Fry.

Someone whom Fry knew quite well (but whom he never identified) visited him at his apartment.

His close friend pleaded to let him go to France in Fry's place[166]; he noted they had similar physiques and were about the same height.[167] He argued that he could get by Customs posing as Fry.[168] Then the clandestine visitor attempted instilling fear in his friend, telling Fry that he just did not know with whom he would be dealing. The shadowy visitor warned that Fry's adversaries were extremely dangerous.[169] Further, he argued, Fry had no experience whatsoever "in this kind of underground work, or what it really involved. He himself did . . . ; he could be far more effective."[170]

Fry declined his friend's offer. We are told by Fry's biographer that Varian was "astounded at the [visitor's] insane proposal"[171] and Fry "wouldn't break the laws of his country by this fraud."[172] But Fry had already committed "fraud" by his untruthful passport application statements, falsely asserting he was an official of the YMCA.

Fry's chronicler concluded: "Logical deduction points to Paul Hagen as Fry's doppelganger. Hagen had the [necessary] experience . . . ." Fry's biographer then supplied arguments for judging Hagen's offer as "rash and impractical."[173]

The late night double agent was, of course, Karl Frank/Paul Hagen, the anti-Nazi Austrian left-wing activist turned American intelligence agent working for Allen Dulles in New York. But his proposal was neither rash nor impractical. Resembling Fry, Hagen would have entered Europe with a valid passport identifying the bearer as an American religious official with legitimate papers supporting that false identity. Karl Frank/Paul Hagen would have been a convincing version of an American intelligence "illegal," a covert entity bearing the name of 'Varian Fry'. Everything that Fry's dark visitor said pointed to an operation much more secret and even more dangerous than the rescue of artists and intellectuals threatened by the Gestapo.

Varian Fry was always aware of his clandestine cloak, recording his debt to Hagen: "Paul Hagen and . . . others who've had experience with underground work told me you needed some sort of cover operations, something that would provide an innocent explanation for what you had to do on the surface."[174]

Whether Fry fulfilled any of the goals Hagen would have himself attempted as Fry's double, Fry's own subsequent actions in Europe have strongly suggested Fry or at least his American handler was aware of the connections between European relief/rescue work, dedicated religious groups, and productive intelligence sources. Those connections helped U.S. spymaster Allen Dulles with his grand plan for using both European and U.S. faith-based organizations.

## Varian Fry, the Unitarians, the OSS, and Covert Intelligence

Fry's intelligence history was dangerous: Fry was linked to President Roosevelt's private intelligence system through Frank Kingdon, the chief of the Emergency Rescue Committee, who, in turn, reported regularly to Adolph Berle, "assistant secretary of state and a key advisor to President Roosevelt on intelligence matters."[175] Berle had long and close relationships with the Emergency Rescue Committee, the International Rescue Committee, and U.S. covert operations.[176]

From Paul Hagen/Karl Frank, Varian Fry accepted a "list of New Beginning members in exile who would be a focus for the efforts of the Marseille office. Frank was already working closely with government agencies, and New Beginning members were placed in key positions throughout the intelligence community during World War II, undertaking activities ranging from 'black' propaganda to paramilitary operations."[177] Contacting names on that list meant that, whatever were his humanitarian and religious identities, Varian Fry was a spy.

Indeed, besides his double covert connection to U.S. intelligence through the Kingdon/Berle/Roosevelt and the Hagen/Frank Emergency Rescue Committee channels, Fry had a third and related clandestine link, established just after he arrived in France.

First, despite Fry's reported confusion in Lisbon, Portugal, where a Unitarian Service Committee office was established[178], he was able to make extraordinary contacts throughout the religious relief community with all the major groups, including, of course, the YMCA (to which he was ostensibly attached), the American Jewish Joint Distribution Committee, and the Quaker Mission.[179] Varian Fry had entered Lisbon and gone directly to the Hotel Metropole, where Dr. Charles Joy of the Unitarian Service Committee had an office.[180]

Fry was sometimes "mistakenly" identified as a "Quaker,"[181] but his pragmatic approach to problem-solving meant he was in frequent attendance at Quaker sites during his rescue work.[182] The Quakers in Marseilles had, in fact, provided Fry with desperately needed food.[183]

Rev. Waitstill Sharp, the director of the Unitarian Service Committee office in Lisbon, was asked by Varian Fry to be the representative of Fry's OSS-connected Emergency Rescue Committee in the Portuguese capital[184], and another link was forged uniting religious service groups with American intelligence. "Both organizations were interested in the rescue of . . . anti-Nazi political leaders, and the collaboration continued throughout the war . . . ."[185]

The Sharps were only able to reach Europe with the aid of Percival Flack Brundage, then a member of the governing Board of the American Unitarian Association (AUA): Brundage obtained air passage to Lisbon for the Sharps, though Brundage's motivation for getting the Sharp couple to Europe may have gone beyond his humanitarian interests, given the AUA's wartime links to the Office of Strategic Services.[186]

Just having arrived in France, Fry departed for a visit to Madrid, meeting the British ambassador to Spain and the embassy's military attaché[187] (almost always an intelligence officer). Fry presented his packet of letters of reference[188] that included "a letter of introduction from Sumner Welles, under secretary of state, who wrote it at Eleanor Roosevelt's behest."[189] The Roosevelt connection was an obvious "back channels" intelligence tie, though the president's wife was herself a devoted supporter of the Emergency Rescue Committee (and later the International Rescue Committee).

Fry and the British ambassador agreed on using the Emergency Rescue Committee to establish "escape routes for British soldiers trapped in occupied France, with the understanding that some of the political refugees [on the Hagen/Frank New Beginning underground list] stranded in Marseilles could exit by the same means."[190] The British promised Fry ten thousand dollars (in the early 1940s, an impressive sum) delivered to his Emergency Rescue Committee.[191] Fry also brought to British intelligence a map of Mediterranean Nazi mine fields, given to him by an Italian socialist sanctuaried in Marseilles.[192]

By accepting the British agreement that included funding the Emergency Rescue Committee, Fry became "a British secret agent."[193] But that dramatic designation was Varian Fry's own[194], most likely a personal deflection from his two more serious intelligence credentials (one, Kingdon/Berle/Roosevelt; the other, Frank/Hagen and the Emergency Rescue Committee). Throughout his writing, Fry carefully bypassed his extensive relations with the Quakers and the Unitarians[195]; he offered nearly nothing about his relations with the Marseille Corsicans[196]; and he never intimated that the Emergency Rescue Committee had Office of Strategic Services connections.[197]

In Marseille, Fry contacted Dr. Donald Lowrie, a one-time officer of the International YMCA, a dedicated relief official, and an excellent source of information for Fry.[198] Though Lowrie maintained connections to the YMCA, he was at the time Fry made contact "associated with the international student colony at the University of Paris."[199] With the help of the Lowrie contacts and others, Fry began a European Underground Railway for cultural refugees.[200]

At the same time, Varian Fry became an important part of a network of relief organizations directly tied to the OSS and Allen Dulles. Included in that network was Dr. Charles Joy of the Lisbon Unitarian mission. Arian Fry and Joy were clearly partners in covert refugee work: Fry worked out of Joy's Lisbon headquarters for the Unitarian Service Committee at the Hotel Metropole.[201] Joy, most probably an OSS asset[202], was in communication with Charles Dexter, the Unitarian Service Committee executive director who, no later than June 17th, 1942, was already an important Dulles OSS operative.[203] Five days earlier, on June 13th, 1942, the Office of Coordinator of Information (OCI) had been transformed into the Office of Strategic Services.[204] Elizabeth Dexter, Robert Dexter's wife, was also a member of the OSS-associated group[205], as was René Zimmer of the Marseille Unitarian medical program.[206] Apparently another part of the network was Robert Lowrie himself: he had accepted Varian Fry's false YMCA identity (created by U.S. intelligence in New York) and Lowrie would recommend Unitarian Noel Field (the future Dulles/OSS operative) to Dr. Charles Joy for a key Unitarian Service Committee position.[207]

Robert Dexter had met with Allen Dulles in June, 1942, accepting Dulles' commission of espionage, resulting in Dexter and other members of the Unitarian Service Committee delivering "large sums of money to resistance leaders in France."[208] Dexter and his intelligence Unitarians made contact with "OSS agents in Madrid and in Marseilles . . . [to gather] information."[209]

In Marseilles, Varian Fry was in close touch with Corsican "gangster families"[210], a pragmatic decision solving some of Fry's immediate refugee problems[211] but helping to initiate troubling links between American religious service organizations, American intelligence, and the European Mafia involved in narcotics traffic. Immediately after the war, American intelligence and Organized Crime in Marseille cooperately blocked "anti-Communist" workers and Socialist activists, exchanged vital information, and partnered in narcotics trafficking that financed their operations. Wartime links between religious relief groups, American intelligence, and the Marseille mob had dark consequences: CIA assets Jay Lovestone and Irving Brown "of the AFL (later AFL-CIO) Free Trade Union Committee had passed [Agency] funds . . . to French ["anti-Communist"] strong-arm gangs on the Marseille waterfront, which in turn worked with the Corsican heroin labs and traffickers integrated by Meyer Lansky into the Luciano-Coppola-Gentile drug-trafficking network."[212]

Varian Fry's clandestine bent was nowhere better illustrated than in his initial operations in Marseilles. Almost all of the twenty-eight refugees on Fry's initial rescue list made it to Lisbon[213], and he had been in the city only two weeks. Suspected of cutting some suspicious corners, Fry needed to assure local authority "that he would never countenance any illegality . . . ."[214] He therefore established "a proper office . . . under the name of the Centre American de Secours (The American Relief Center) . . . ."[215] According to Fry, if an undercover operation with acceptable cover were to succeed, that action had to appear totally innocent.[216]

Just as Allen Dulles and his operatives manipulated faith-based individuals and groups, Varian Fry also used people, including Unitarian minister Waitstill Sharp. Fry had already recruited Sharp to front for Fry's Emergency Rescue Committee in Lisbon) in a hair-raising rescue mission[217] exposing the already heroic Sharp to mortal danger.[218]

Ultimately, Varian Fry may have seriously upset his American intelligence handlers at the Emergency Rescue Committee. He certainly upset the State Department's Foreign Service that was following its own German agenda.[219] If Fry's daring cultural rescues became for him more important than the intelligence information he sent to the Emergency Rescue Committee (and therefore to U.S. intelligence), he would have become expendable.

In fact, Fry was indeed sent home in September, 1941.

He tried to reenter the exciting and productive war stream of things to which he had become accustomed. He applied to the Office of Strategic Services, "for which surely, of almost all Americans, he was uniquely qualified."[220] But he was refused (most probably because he had been compromised). All his efforts to rejoin the fight against Fascism were blocked by both the State Department and the FBI.[221]

On April 12th, 1967, Fry was awarded a major citation for his intelligence work by the French government, but both his rescue work and his intelligence operations remained unrecognized by the United States.[222] Before he died, Varian Fry was accused of being a Communist while he was being investigated by the FBI.[223] At the same time, he was an active member of several right-wing anti-Communist organizations closely tied to the CIA.[224] After Varian Fry died in 1967, Israel honored him as a "righteous man." Fry would not, of course, be the only dedicated religious service person used (and abused) by American intelligence.

Paul Hagen (aka Karl B. Frank), the man who would have been "Varian Fry" had the Emergency Rescue Committee representative agreed to Hagen's clandestine scheme, continued working with Allen Dulles' COI office in New York, and succeeded in persuading Dulles to support Hagen's plan for a collaboration between American intelligence and the anti-Nazi "Underground Movement" in Germany.[225] In a memorandum to Allen Dulles dated April 10th, 1942, Hagen argued for the establishment of a new "agency" that would link American intelligence with the German radical and labor underground, with technical and research staffs, with the "reorganization of contacts in Switzerland, Sweden, unoccupied France, maybe also Ankara [in Turkey] . . ."[226] and tapping the refugee flow into both the United States and also Central and South America.[227] On May 12th, 1942, Dulles forwarded the Hagen report to Arthur Goldberg, then in Washington, the chief of the OSS's Labor Section in London.[228]

## Allen Dulles' Spy System in Switzerland: Was He Guilty of Treason?

Coupled with the future work of Dulles operatives Emmy Rado and Noel Field in manipulating liberals, radicals, volunteer service and religious organizations, Paul Hagen's proposals had ably assisted Allen Dulles in structuring his Switzerland spy center.[229] For good or ill (or both), the American espionage system, fronted by faith-based groups, waited for the lightning to strike.

Six months after Pearl Harbor, the Office of the Coordinator of Information (COI) became the Office of Strategic Services—the OSS.[230] By presidential order on June 13th, 1942, the OSS was established "to collect and analyze strategic information" but also to "plan and operate . . . special services."[231] The president and a few core intelligence people knew what the phrase "special services" meant: the emerging agency would not simply gather information; "OSS was to have charge of resistance, intelligence, and sabotage . . . ."[232] The Office of Strategic Services was a potential spymaster's espionage dream come true.

And so, in the fall of 1942, about to be shipped from New York to London to occupy an unexciting OSS desk, Allen Dulles knew exactly where he really wanted to be. The center of war intelligence would be Bern, Switzerland[233], and he quickly petitioned for a transfer change. His petition accepted, he was off to Bern.[234] In early November, 1942, the man whose espionage machine had been responsible for sending Varian Fry to Europe left New York for Switzerland.[235]

Dulles had anticipated the Allied "penetration" of Nazi Germany[236], both in its short-term and long-term consequences: first was, of course, the defeat of the Axis enemy. But second (and possibly more important) was the political and financial stability of Germany (and, therefore, of Europe) and the post-war preservation of the German economy and industry.

"He arrived [in Switzerland] carrying letters of introduction to the prominent [powers] in every important area of Swiss life. He also knew the anti-Nazi German politicians, labor leaders, religious figures, scientists, professors, diplomats, and businessmen [from all over Europe] living in exile in Switzerland."[237]

Dulles came with both money and power backed by Sullivan and Cromwell, his (and his brother John Foster's) law firm, and the company's European officers who were viciously anti-Bolshevik.[238]

Allen Dulles had superior credentials for clandestine spying on Germany: "Dulles' chores with Sullivan and Cromwell [had] involved him intimately in the affairs of the elite among Germany's industry. He sat on the boards of directors of both the Schroeder Trust Company and the J. Henry Schroeder Corporation, American branches of Germany's great Schroeder international banking firm. The German firm was directed by Baron Kurt von Schroeder, at whose house in Cologne Adolf Hitler and von Papen negotiated their agreements for Hitler's rise to power."[239]

One of many possible treasonous actions by Allen Dulles was channeled through a Sullivan and Cromwell officer: the law firm's "correspondent" in Vienna met Dulles when he arrived in Bern[240], bringing with him "a list of sympathetic [German] financiers and industrialists throughout the Nazi hegemony."[241] But the Sullivan and Cromwell double agent asked for something in return from Allen Dulles, something perhaps, the Cromwell agent suggested, on U.S. "aircraft production figures."[242] Dulles gave his Sullivan and Cromwell contact U.S. production aircraft "projections" that were then turned over to Nazi intelligence.[243]

Whatever the alibi, by giving Sullivan and Cromwell officer Kurt Grimm out of Vienna[244] top-secret information on American aircraft, allegedly according to Dulles "to terrify the Luftwaffe,"[245] the spy chief had indeed consorted with the enemy.

Dulles' long-term plans for Germany meant he would have to court the leaders of the same middle and upper classes that had supported Hitler in his rise to power but who now saw Germany's potential defeat as a political and economic disaster. So Dulles received "a flood of high-placed, right wing Germans"[246] eager to help Dulles reconstruct post-war Germany.[247] Influential businessmen, bankers, and industrialists came to meet with Dulles[248], recognizing him as one of their own.[249] With the help of old Sullivan and Cromwell hands, Dulles made contact with "Vichy" French who were ready to collaborate with the American OSS[250] and the Gaullist resistance.[251]

Dulles' long-term goals were now in the hands of the German elite, German industrialists, and the anti-Nazis.[252]

Dulles and the OSS spent a significant amount of time intercepting bank communications, following German and Swiss money trails left by a "malevolent old boys' network [that] stretched across wartime Europe."[253] The interests of IG Farben, the Schroeder Bank, and Standard Oil of New Jersey were intimately linked, and Allen Dulles and John Foster Dulles were board members of Schroeder and IG Farben: those economic interests had to be protected through the end of the war.[254]

But first, Germany had to be defeated, and, for Dulles, as quickly and painlessly as possible. How would the American spymaster deal with the waves of anti-fascists breaking on his Swiss beach?

The number of left-wing/anti-Nazi refugees streaming into Switzerland was awesome: Spanish Loyalist veterans and anti-Franco groups; Free French; and liberal, social democratic, socialist, and Communist individuals and organizations from all over Europe streaming in through the first two years of the war. Dulles wanted a key contact.

## Allen Dulles and Noel Field: Quakers and Unitarians as Intelligence Sources

He found that person in Noel Field[255], Herbert Field's son.[256] After the Field patriarch died in 1921, the Field family, including Noel Field and his younger brother Hermann Field, returned to the United States and took up residence in Cambridge, Massachusetts.[257] Noel Field's earliest career history included working with the American State Department (where he met Allen Dulles for the second time[258]) and then at the League of Nations, including activities and associations that in 1938, before an American Congressional committee, prompted an undocumented accusation that Noel Field was a card-carrying Communist[259]; Field's Moscow adventure; and Field in Spain in 1938, when it became apparent the Republican Loyalist cause was all but lost. Noel Field worked in Spain representing a League of Nations commission attempting to evacuate the international brigades that had fought against Franco.[260] In Field's efforts to save the foreign nationals who had supported the Loyalists, the compassionate Quaker radical made contact with hundreds of anti-fascists from dozens of countries[261], managing "to meet scores of people whose names were destined to become symbols of power in [European] postwar communism."[262] When the League felt its mission in Spain was finished, the League of Nations left, but Field and his wife stayed on, working in refugee camps and performing what "relief work" they could with their limited resources.[263] Loyalist troops and Republican sympathizers streamed into France.

Noel Field was a living example of Hans A. Schmitt's "Quaker portrait": "a personal relation with the Creator free from scriptural or hierarchic mediation, the advocacy of peaceful conflict resolution, and a commitment to abate human suffering wherever it may be found."[264]

After Germany occupied Austria, the Nazi war machine moved into Poland. Noel Field resigned from the League, though he was paid by that declining international body for over a year after he departed, working first in Prague (on refugee relocation) and then in France with the organization *Comite' pour le Refugees Anti-Fascistes* linked to the U.S. Joint Anti-Fascist Refugee Committee. Later, in the United States, the latter committee was labeled a Communist "front."[265]

Noel Field's actual organizational connection was ambiguous: some thought he was working with the Quakers[266] as his father did in the First World War; others thought he was performing "some sort of survey" for the League of Nations.[267] But he had no official group backing.[268]

Around the city of Marseilles huddled thousands of dirty, hungry refugees. The Emergency Relief Committee, the Quakers, the YMCA, the Scouts, and a dozen other groups did what they could.[269] Prominent among these European relief organizations were the Unitarians who had "organized relief work in Czechoslovakia in 1938 and [then] in France . . . ."[270] Dr. Robert Dexter, in 1938 the Director of the American Unitarian Association's Department of Social Relations[271], had urged "Unitarians to organize relief for refugees from the Sudetenland . . . ."[272]

The Czechs held a special place in Unitarian consciousness: the taking of the territory by Germany "was a personal tragedy for the people whom we now regard as founders of the Unitarian Service Committee."[273] As early as 1921, both the American and British Unitarians urged establishing a permanent center for the faith in Prague.[274] Dr. Robert Dexter, who had been to Prague[275], joined other Unitarians in supporting the creation of a relief organization.[276]

On October 5th, 1938, the AUA Board of Directors announced the Unitarians would "explore the possibilities of a joint Unitarian-Quaker enterprise for the relief of refugees . . . ."[277] The Unitarian operation was, therefore, from its beginning associated with Quaker service activities. Robert Dexter, representing the Unitarians, and Richard Wood, the Quaker delegate, visited Europe on a fact-finding tour.[278]

Commissioned by the AUA after it received an especially grave report from Dr. Dexter, Unitarian Rev. Waitstill Sharp and his wife Martha arrived in London the first week of February, 1939, and began a series of meetings with Quakers, Unitarians, and British government groups that were bringing in "relief" to the Czechs and assisting some of them to get out the country.[279]

Dexter's Unitarian report has needed perspective. Dexter and other liberal, compassionate religious individuals saw the obvious problem: fascism, whether in Spain, Italy, or Germany, destroyed democratic institutions and placed thousands of innocent people at risk. Inevitably, if Dexter had not yet approached Allied intelligence (or been approached by those services), the potential connection between refugee service operations and anti-Nazi activities would have been obvious. Dexter's report to the Unitarians became the basis for Unitarian medical and humanitarian services for the war's émigrés and internees.[280]

The Sharps made contact with key people in Prague, including "Helen and Donald Lowrie, formerly with the International YMCA, . . . [who agreed] to be the Sharps' liaison in Paris."[281] The Sharps then began an extraordinary series of relief actions in cooperation with a dozen international organizations.[282]

But the Unitarian relief effort in Czechoslovakia came to an end, and the proposed project for Poland had to be abandoned.[283] With the Unitarians still committed to "continued relief and emigration work," the need for an independent Unitarian service group became obvious; among the influential Unitarians supporting a continued European effort was John Howland Lathrop.[284] Unitarian Frederick May Eliot and Boston businessman Seth Gano met to explore the founding of a Unitarian committee similar to the Quakers' American Friends Service Committee.[285]

The Dexters were again commissioned to go to Europe "to conduct a four-month fact-finding tour . . . ."[286]

In 1939, unhappy with the relatively conservative Quakers' program of relief, Noel Field met with Unitarian minister Stephen Fritchman, a radical political activist (who would become the pastor of the First Unitarian Church of Los Angeles in the 1950s). According to three well-placed Unitarian/Universalists, "Fritchman mobilized support for the idea of a separate Unitarian humanitarian relief agency, and succeeded a year later [in 1940] in persuading the General Assembly of the Unitarian Association to create a new agency . . . ."[287]

## The Unitarian Service Committee, Refugees, and U.S. Intelligence

Probably the combined efforts of the AUA Refugee Committee, the Dexters, Stephen Fritchman, and others were responsible for the founding of the Unitarian Service Committee in early May, 1940.[288] Robert Dexter was appointed executive director, and the Sharps were asked to return to Europe as the Committee's "ambassadors extraordinary."[289] From its beginning, then, the USC was directed by Robert Dexter, the man who no later than 1942 would be a key component in Allen Dulles' faith-based OSS intelligence operations.

In fact, the USC's "initial nature" was extremely close to that of the OSS-supported Emergency Rescue Committee: "the rescue of Europe's intellectual, academic and [anti-Nazi] political leaders . . . ."[290] The two groups collaborated, and the Unitarian Sharps in Lisbon took messages from New York sent by the Emergency Rescue Committee or acting on cables from the Committee's Marseilles "agent,"[291] Varian Fry.

In its beginning, the Unitarian Service Committee was funded by the American Unitarian Association; later, it was additionally financed by Unitarians, Quakers[292], "other [unidentified] organizations" and the American "government-backed National War Fund."[293] By November, 1945, the Unitarian Service Committee was 'registered' with the War Relief Control Board and 'endorsed' by the National War Fund [NDF] through "Refugee Relief Trustees, Inc."[294]

Was the support of the Unitarian refugee effort by a "government-backed" fund suspect? Recall that by 1942, Unitarian Robert Dexter, appointed executive director in Portugal of the Unitarian Service Committee[295], was a covert agent of the Office of Strategic Services, reporting directly to Allen Dulles, the OSS chief in Europe.[296]

Was the Unitarian Service Committee (USC) even more closely linked to government funding of covert operations?

In 1942, the Emergency Rescue Committee and the International Relief Association had merged, becoming the International Relief and Rescue Committee (IRRC), retaining both organizations' original radical orientation as well as their intelligence ties. Name changes later occurred: in 1949, the IRRC became International Rescue (Inc.), and it, in turn, became the International Rescue Committee (IRC).

In 1942, the U.S.'s War Relief Control Board began monitoring every relief agency, including the Unitarian Service Committee.[297] Then in January, 1943, the U.S. government centralized all refugee relief fund-raising: the National War Fund (NWF), with awesome economic clout[298], was the only group designated to raise funds for "global war" relief.[299] In that same month of 1943, an extraordinary fusion of humanitarian, religious and political powers occurred: the OSS-supported International Rescue and Relief Committee (successor to the OSS-backed Emergency Rescue Committee), the American Churches Committee for Refugees, and the OSS-connected Unitarian Service Committee joined to establish the "Refugees Relief Trustees."[300] This "coalition" then allocated funds to the International Rescue and Relief Committee (IRRC) and the Unitarian Service Committee.[301] Attending the National War Fund budget meetings and assisting in the Fund's financial affairs was the influential David Seiferheld, American Friends of German Freedom officer, recently an Emergency Rescue Committee official, and covert OSS operative.[302] Monitoring the Unitarian Service Committee/Refugees Relief Trustees linkage was Percival Flack Brundage, American Unitarian Association officer, later a Bureau of the Budget official, and a Cold War friend of both the Pentagon and the Central Intelligence Agency.[303]

On May 17th, 1944, Brundage sent a memorandum to fellow board members of the Refugee Relief Trustees, the memo distantly titled "Statement Regarding Relation of Unitarian Service Committee to War Refugee Board."[304] Brundage's "Statement" was, in fact, about OSS-connected Unitarians and their involvement in government-sponsored refugee activity and, therefore, intelligence-gathering. The elaborate maze of government and 'private' rescue and relief operations had become even more complex when the new and powerful War Refugee Board was established. Any doubt about the War Refugee Board's reach, including its major U.S. intelligence links, are effectively erased by consulting the Board's 1,522 files at the FDR Library and Museum.[305] Charles Joy, board member of both the Unitarian Service Committee and the Refugee Relief Trustees, responded to the new development by writing to John J. Pehle, Executive Director of the War Refugee Board, expressing the concern of the Unitarian Service Committee. Joy succeeded in meeting Pehle in both Washington and New York, resulting in the new Committee on Special Refugee Problems, a powerful group advisory to the War Refugees Board. One key Unitarian was voted to the chair of the new oversight committee, and Charles Joy was elected the new committee's secretary. In Lisbon, USC officer Dexter was designated the official representative of the War Refugee Board, and an IRRC member with intelligence links became the War Refugee Board's Swiss representative.[306]

The Refugee Relief Trustees and its intelligence-connected partners, the Unitarian Service Committee and the International Relief and Rescue Committee, had successfully moved to protect their government support through the War Refugee Board, and key Unitarians, including Reverend Charles Joy (most probably an OSS asset), had been placed on its advisory committee to insure that protection.

Earlier in 1940, Charles Joy, then the Unitarian Service Committee's Lisbon representative[307], enlisted the help of Donald Lowrie, who had been the director of the Young Man's Christian Association (YMCA) with headquarters in Geneva; Joy needed a Unitarian director for France, and Lowrie recommended Noel Field.[308] Joy met with Field, reportedly was immensely impressed, and hired both Field and his wife. The Fields moved to Marseilles in 1941.[309]

Led by Noel Field, the Unitarian Service Committee in France took on a giant task, adding refugee camp infirmaries to the committee's relief work.[310] The camps had held at least 29,000 people from forty-four countries.[311] When Field identified the camps he had examined as the responsibility of the Unitarian Service Committee, that body's Boston headquarters sent Reverend Mr. Howard Brooks to evaluate the European situation.[312] But Brooks himself was a double agent: representing the Unitarian Service Committee, he was also on an intelligence mission for the Free French.[313]

Still, Brooks fully supported Field[314]; Field's staff was much expanded; and Field's operation was heavily financed by a massive new American government fund that was intended "to enlarge the resources of the various private American relief groups working abroad."[315]

Noel Field was eventually appointed "European director of the Boston-based Unitarian Service Committee [entering] . . . into an intense refugee rescue mission in both Marseilles and Geneva during the early 1940s . . . ."[316]

Field had placed exiled German Communists on his help list; when one of his associates was questioned by Howard Brooks, she convinced the Reverend Brooks that the aid was humanely justified.[317] The German leftists made Field a major part of their support and rescue system, and "thousands of dollars, in Swiss francs, were given to Noel from communist funds in Switzerland for the use of the German [Communist] Party in France."[318] Utilizing a French "underground" established to effect unlawful crossings into Switzerland[319], Field sent German Communists from France into the country.[320] Eventually, Field had a network of anti-fascist contacts, including "Polish, Hungarian, Yugoslav and Bulgarian communists in Switzerland."[321]

The German Army swept through unoccupied ("Vichy") France in November, 1942, anticipating the Allied invasion of Europe, and Field and his wife avoided internment, barely escaping the German Gestapo and military border guards as they themselves crossed into Switzerland.[322]

Robert Dexter, Unitarian Service Committee's European Executive Director headquartered in Lisbon and key operative for Allen Dulles' Office of Strategic Services, recognized the unique quality and utility of the information Field was capable of collecting and the importance of the people with whom he was in contact. But Dexter reportedly did not know the extent of Field's Communist links.[323] So Robert Dexter brought Noel Field to Allen Dulles, who was now headquartered in Bern, and the old Field family connection to Dulles, the American spymaster, was re-established.[324]

Allen Dulles and the family of Field.

For Allen Dulles and the OSS, "Noel Field . . . [initially] presented opportunities for access to escapees from occupied France and to underground cells of the resistance working to obstruct the Nazi war effort."[325] Field began his service as the crucial contact between the German Communists and the OSS, both focusing on the defeat of Nazi Germany. William Casey (OSS operative and, later, President Ronald Reagan's CIA chief) was involved in developing false identity "Illegals" for the OSS during World War Two who were recruited from some of those same "German Communist refugees" in England.[326]

When Allen Dulles brought Field into his Swiss fold, Dulles did so with full awareness of Noel's impressive Communist connections. But was Field an actual OSS spy? He was certainly an agent of Allen Dulles and the OSS. "Dulles regularly gave him money for the communists" that Field passed on to the anti-fascist refugees, but he apparently was not paid a regular OSS stipend or salary.[327] "Dulles handed out $10,000 [an impressive sum for wartime Europe] to Communist paymasters through Field, and afterward insisted privately that he got back more than his money's worth."[328]

## Noel Field and Alger Hiss

Whether Field was a 'commissioned' agent of the OSS (or later of the CIA) was far less important to certain U.S. researchers and writers than establishing Field's alleged earlier covert identity as a home-grown Communist. Most especially, they were interested in Field's alleged attendance at a Communist "cell" in Washington and Alger Hiss's reported failure to recruit Field for Hiss's alleged spy group.[329]

These allegations were certainly intended to establish Alger Hiss had been a Communist traitor guilty of espionage; but Hiss was neither tried for nor found guilty of that charge.

From what innocent source might the story have originated of Alger Hiss and Noel Field attending a D.C. Communist "cell"? In the 1930s, Alger Hiss "had been a member of one of the study groups on foreign affairs . . . popular among Washington intellectuals, meeting once a month or so to talk about . . . Hitler[,] . . . Italian aggression . . . , and what could be done about them. There were . . . members of the Foreign Policy Association . . . and their wives . . . [and State Department people, including] Noel Field . . . and one or two others [attending]."[330] Ideas, of course, can sometimes have dire consequences.

The earliest single Eastern European origin for the repeated charges against Hiss was pushed by a Hungarian researcher and writer Maria Schmidt who "unearthed" the record of Noel Field's questioning in Hungary. According to Schmidt, she found the interrogation in "secret [Hungarian] police files in 1993."[331] However, these anti-Hiss conclusions were not reported by Schmidt herself but by Sam Tanenhaus, who was then writing a book on Whittaker Chambers.[332] Tanenhaus announced Schmidt's alleged discoveries on the Op Ed page of the *New York Times* on October 15th, 1993.[333]

Why would Schmidt entrust the publication of such a significant finding to another writer? And why in an op-ed version? Why? Apparently both Schmidt and Tanenhaus were members of a 'conservative' group of writers whose principle goal was arguing that Alger Hiss was guilty of espionage: "A little over a month later, [on] Nov. 18, 1993, Tanenhaus revealed in the *Wall Street Journal* that he had found significant documents regarding Alger Hiss . . . in the . . . National Archives."[334]

What had been found by the writers?

What Schmidt had reportedly discovered in the Hungarian archives that linked Hiss and Field was a single document ostensibly written by Noel Field charging Hiss with being a Soviet agent in 1935.[335] Given the obvious delight of several writers with Noel Field's reported statements concerning Alger Hiss, none of them pointed out the obvious problem they shared: if Field was correct about Hiss, then all his other statements (used dramatically in the Communist purge trials) might also be correct, despite their being coerced from him by his Communist jailers (and despite their being both outlandish and absurd). But if Field's statements were suspect because they had all been supplied by him under extreme stress, then his specific statements about Alger Hiss were also suspect.

A later use of the same questionable Schmidt materials surfaced in 1996. In this manifestation, Noel Field was accused of being an (earlier) NKVD and (later) KGB agent and identified as a personal friend and professional associate of Alger Hiss.[336] The sources, authors Breindel and Romerstein, reported they had found a summary of the questioning of Noel Field by the "Ministry of National Security" in the Czech "state archives."[337] The alleged summary repeated the charges against Hiss reportedly made by Noel Field, but the summary did not supply evidence as to why these specific charges (obviously made under duress by Field) should be taken any more seriously than all the others Field had made but had been rejected as political fictions.[338]

The anti-Hiss group continued to pound away. Allen Weinstein (the author of *Perjury: The Hiss-Chambers Case*[339]) and former Soviet KGB agent Alexander Vassiliev co-wrote *The Haunted Wood[:] Soviet Espionage in America—the Stalin Era*[340]. Basing their charges against Alger Hiss on KGB files in Moscow[341], Weinstein and Vassiliev asserted they had found extensive references to Noel Field (protected, they said, by a code name) and Hiss.[342] But these KGB-based revelations were, in fact, nothing more than Soviet reports of the communications of Hede Massing to Soviet intelligence. Therefore, Hede Massing's messages were the ONLY source Weinstein and Vassiliev had for their anti-Hiss information. Significantly, Weinstein and Vassiliev referred to Massing as "Hedda Gumperz," and in only one of their references was she identified indirectly as Hede Massing: "Hedda Gumperz rejoined her husband and fellow agent Paul Massing . . . ."[343] Though they listed Massing's book in their bibliography, the authors were careful not to cite it when they examined the alleged relationships between Field, Hiss, and Massing, since double agent Hede Massing was, in fact, their primary and ONLY source for the Hiss/Field charges.

The authors also ignored Noel Field's intelligence relationship to OSS spy chief Allen Dulles, Dulles' willingness to use Communists as agents and assets, and Alger Hiss's personal, familial, and professional relationship to John Foster Dulles. Additionally, Weinstein and Vassiliev omitted any mention of the crucial role Noel Field played in the Stalinist purge trials[344] as well as the widely-held suspicion that Frank Wisner and Allen Dulles manipulated Noel Field in their successful plan to destabilize Eastern Communist Europe.

Finally, an extensive review of the alleged evidence against Hiss (published in *The Nation*) concluded that charges of treason and espionage against Hiss could not be documented from any so-called "secret files."[345]

The best defense of Alger Hiss, honed with the Occam's Razor of a top-ranking KGB spymaster, was outlined by Pavel Sudoplatov. His narrative in 1994 anticipated later revelations about FDR's private presidential spy system. According to Sudoplatov, in the summer of 1941, President Roosevelt's trusted advisor Harry Hopkins, following FDR's orders, established "confidential relations" with the Soviet ambassador's office in Washington. D.C.[346] Sudoplatov and Soviet embassy officers connected productively with American Foreign Service and State Department officers, several of whom were part of President Roosevelt's personal intelligence operation.[347]

The Yalta meeting was crucial for Sudoplatov, who was responsible "for preparing the psychological profiles of all the . . . [members of the] American delegation to Yalta . . . and [whether] they were under our control as [KGB] agents."

So, was Alger Hiss a KGB agent, or was he a trusted member of FDR's covert intelligence corps?

The Soviet embassy in Washington had made crucial back channels connections with several Yalta attendees: one of them was Alger Hiss.[348] Sudoplatov evaluated Hiss's relationship to the Soviets as a commission from FDR himself, "acting under the instructions of [Harry] Hopkins."[349] "On our list of [Yalta] psychological profiles, Hiss was identified as highly sympathetic to the interests of the Soviet Union and a strong supporter of postwar collaboration between American and Soviet institutions."[350]

But was Alger Hiss a KGB agent? According to Sudoplatov: "[The KGB had] no indication that he was a paid or controlled [KGB] agent, [of] which I would have known or would have been marked."[351]

Sudoplatov, once a KGB spy chief, was in touch with an old Soviet intelligence friend who was a "retired GRU officer"[352] who told Sudoplatov that "Hiss was chosen by Hopkins and Roosevelt for confidential contacts with Soviet diplomats and intelligence officers, knowing that he had [such] contacts and was pro-Soviet."[353]

Allegedly Roosevelt's private intelligence network had reportedly been penetrated by the Soviets: "[Sudoplatov's] retired GRU officer remembers . . . a controlled agent source of information in Roosevelt's office. He was Roosevelt's assistant on intelligence affairs . . ."[354] and on unfriendly terms with both the FBI and the OSS. But this negative attitude may have reflected his own superiors' judgment: both FDR and Harry Hopkins "were ill disposed toward" the Office of Strategic Services and the Federal Bureau of Investigation.[355] Soviet "GRU files reflect[ed] that Roosevelt set up his own informal intelligence network during the war, used by him for sensitive [back channel] missions."[356] Former Soviet spy chief Sudoplatov reported that his old retired GRU friend was "certain that Alger Hiss, Harry Hopkins, and Averil Harriman were in this [back channels] trusted group."[357]

Though the statute of limitations had run out on Hiss's alleged espionage activity, Hiss was still charged with perjury. But at least for a time he was surrounded by high-level protection emanating from both the Dulles family and President Truman (who had been, of course, FDR's wartime Vice President). And Alger Hiss's confidential contacts for the State Department and the White House had crossed the paths of both Dulles brothers; for example, Foster Dulles so admired Alger Hiss that he had "recommended him to head the Carnegie Foundation after World War II."[358]

Alger Hiss stood trial twice, and finally was found guilty of perjury (not of espionage or treason). "The mild sentence he received, the incoherent accusations against him, and the neutral stand of the [Truman] administration . . . could [have] indicate[d] that he knew too much that was damaging to the prestige of both Roosevelt and Truman."[359] With Joseph McCarthy (and Richard Nixon, among others) bringing charges of Communism and even treason against New Dealers, liberals, and various State Department luminaries, those charges would have reached to the White House (both past and present) directly through Alger Hiss.

To use Hiss in that way may have been, in fact, part of the plan.

Sudoplatov's "old GRU veteran" surmised "the FBI had more material on Hiss than was revealed, and . . . perhaps there was a deal between Truman and Hoover . . . [to have] the charges [against Alger Hiss] be confined to perjury."[360] The Bureau's Hiss material need not have contained any direct evidence of espionage. The FBI's files on Alger Hiss need only have contained information on Hiss's long-time political interaction (back-channeling for FDR) with Soviet officials from 1941 through 1945, supported by evidence that both the State Department and the White House had commissioned those (now suspect) interactions.

Given the multiple mail-opening operations by U.S. intelligence in the 1940s and 1950s[361], Alger Hiss's postal communications probably were part of the Bureau's priority reading list; his phone conversations were certainly treasured trophies: "In 1948, William Marbury, one of Hiss's lawyers, was told by an [unidentified] FBI agent that Hiss's phone had been tapped for years, and the FBI had three cabinets full of [phone] transcripts, but [that] nothing [either] derogatory or incriminating had been found."[362]

"Some eighty percent of intelligence information on political matters comes not from agents but from confidential contacts."[363] The Bureau's Hiss files would, therefore, have been stuffed with back-channel evidence from World War II, not incriminating but now embarrassing to the Roosevelt-Truman administrations.

Later charges concerning "Hiss's connections to Soviet military intelligence" (that is, to the GRU) surfaced only in those dubious Hungarian secret police materials reputedly about Noel Field.[364]

Ironically, Alger Hiss was charged with Communism because of his lack of religiosity: according to Hiss' major accuser, Communists could not belong to a Christian denomination, so Alger Hiss "was [therefore] forbidden to go to church."[365] Hiss's response was that he and his wife regularly attended the nearby Episcopal Christ Church: "I have been a lifelong member of the Episcopal Church."[366]

Attempting to smear Alger Hiss through Noel Field had ultimately tracked back to the same liberal Protestantism that the Dulles brothers had manipulated to achieve their long-term economic, intelligence, and political goals.

## Noel Field, The Unitarians, and the OSS

After his recruitment by Allen Dulles, Noel Field worked simultaneously for the Unitarian Service Committee and the Office of Strategic Services (OSS) in Switzerland. During the latter part of the war, in the midst of cooperative anti-fascist and anti-German activity, Field carried out a number of important assignments, often at the same time for the Communists, the Unitarian Service Committee, and for Allen Dulles[367], but Noel's work with the OSS was never officially reported to the Unitarian Service Committee in the United States.[368]

Field's liberal and radical connections were treasured by Allen Dulles, who quickly accepted "an offer by Noel Field to put him in contact with Julius Leber, the German socialist leader, and other exiled union officials who kept open lines to potential saboteurs and spies in factories and on railroad lines."[369] Allen Dulles' two labor union assets, Gerhard Van Arkel and John Clark, had been linked by Noel Field to Field's radical union associates.[370] Erika Glaser, Field's foster-daughter, "became secretary-interpreter to Van Arkel while [she was] still a member of the Swiss Communist underground youth movement."[371] Van Arkel had been OSS officer Arthur Goldberg's delegate to anti-Nazi labor groups.[372]

By 1945, the covert labor connections Noel Field (and Erika Glaser) made available to Allen Dulles meant "few trains moved within the German Reich that were not reported to Dulles within hours; the Rhine River bargemen had been organized into a network, and even the water levels of the Rhine itself were radioed to Eisenhower's Paris headquarters, lest the Germans open the floodgates during an Allied crossing."[373]

The U.S. Congressional Medal of Honor has sometimes been bestowed for less.

Self-praise (even muted) and fellow OSS officers' support for Dulles' often heavily-advertised achievements cannot obscure the fact that the more material released from the OSS/CIA files, the less grand have become Allen Dulles' espionage "scoops": by January, 1944, Washington was cabling Dulles in Bern about his shortcomings and inadequacies, and internal OSS documents and other OSS sources further confirm that Dulles' intelligence was sometimes deficient.[374]

But for Dulles, his political and financial goals always remained primary, regardless of the quality of his espionage reports: to defeat Germany with the least possible damage to the country's banking system, its industry, and its economy; to preserve the German economic elite as future political partners; and to oppose Communism, even at the cost of crippling democratic movements.[375] His brother, John Foster Dulles, was in absolute agreement with these goals.

## Allen Dulles' Manipulation of Religious Groups and Individuals

To those ends, Allen Dulles used religious individuals and groups. "Dr. Stewart W. Herman [a Lutheran minister] had been pastor of the American [Church] community in Berlin from 1936 to 1941. After . . . December 1941 he was interned . . . before he could return to the United States. [I]n 1942 he was [reportedly] drafted for the OSS."[376] No later than 1943, Herman was an active OSS operative in London.[377] After the war, Allen Dulles supplied Herman with "travel orders, transportation, and accommodations . . ."[378] and deployed him to the World Council of Churches staff in Geneva where Herman "was given the responsibility for helping rebuild" the German Protestant churches.[379] Herman had become the "Deputy Head of the Reconstruction branch of the World Council of Churches."[380] By 1970, Herman was the President of the Chicago Lutheran School of Theology.[381]

Swiss-born Emmy Crisler Rado[382] was the wife of Sandor Rado, a psychiatrist who was an associate of Sigmund Freud.[383] In the fall of 1941, she began work in New York for the Oral Intelligence Group of the Office of Coordinator of Information.[384] Rado belonged to a COI "nuclear intelligence net"[385]; in a secret Manhattan office she interviewed refugee arrivals from eight European cities under siege or attack by the Nazis, culling valuable pieces of information from which she developed carefully wrought, insightful intelligence reports.[386] When COI was terminated, Emmy Rado joined the Office of Strategic Services, becoming an OSS German analyst. The information she began to accumulate suggested a productive pattern the OSS ought to pursue: "In mid-1943 Emmy Rado had started the co-called 'Biographical Records' project of the OSS."[387] Rado then "proposed [to Allen Dulles in October, 1944] that the [German] Catholic and Protestant churches . . . be used as a base for [what was delicately called] German political reconstruction."[388] "She felt OSS could work effectively through the World Council of Churches to aid [reputedly] anti-Nazi German clergy of the 'Christian Socialist' variety."[389] Approving of Rado's plan, Dulles designated her the OSS coordinator of the intelligence group's manipulation of the German religious community.[390] Dulles then "met with a group of leaders in the [German] religious field during a trip to New York."[391] When the German church leaders returned to Europe, a World Council of Churches staff member from Geneva "was appointed to work through OSS underground sources to contact pastors inside Germany."[392] Four months later, because Rado's work had been so successful, Dulles brought her to Switzerland, relying on Rado to draw up a list of the anticipated "Crown

Jewels" of post-war Germany[393] that included important religious figures "as clean of Nazi involvement as possible."[394] The OSS assets in the German churches were then linked to anti-Nazi religious groups outside of Germany.[395]

Speaking German, French, Italian, Danish, and English[396], Rado became a distinguished multi-purpose operative for Dulles. "She assembled a checklist of all German Confessional churches and pastors in Germany who could be relied upon to influence public opinion. The new German Reformation was mapped out by her [OSS] people in Switzerland . . . with substantial backing from the World Council of Churches."[397] Rado's OSS "German pastor-contacts within Germany . . . [then] sent out invaluable intelligence on conditions within the Reich."[398]

Rado was remembered by her fellow officers as a remarkable combination of intelligence and beauty who, for example, "loved to swim nude in the Danube."[399]

She remained active after the war; she personally met Wilhelm Hoegner, the Bavarian anti-Communist socialist, chauffeuring him from Switzerland to Germany[400], where he began his work for an OSS-directed rehabilitation of his country. Continuing to work for American intelligence, Emmy Rado was granted an early SHAEF pass for defeated Germany, where she met many of her liberal church "Crown Jewels" and received from them their promises to take part in the "spiritual rebirth of Germany."[401] Those same Rado religious individuals became key figures in supporting the anti-Communism agenda of John Foster Dulles, working through the same church groups exploited by Allen Dulles.[402]

Of the greatest importance after the Field and Rado connections were the wartime ties between Dutch Reformed churchman W.A.V. Hooft, who was General Secretary of the World Council of Churches (WCC) in Geneva, and OSS spy chief Allen Dulles.[403] Visser't Hooft was so valuable an intelligence connection that the church official was given "474" as his personal OSS code identification.[404]

Extensive OSS records and documents made available in the early 1990s contain "a series of reports on the [so-called] German church situation that . . . Hooft . . . forwarded to Allen W. Dulles on the latter's request."[405] One of those confidential Hooft reports to Dulles in December, 1943, extensively reviewed "The Situation of the Protestant Church in Germany."[406] The Hooft documents were important in Dulles' mobilizing of religious groups for anti-Nazi activities. "Like his brother John Foster Dulles, who was a leading member of the American Federal Council of the Churches of Christ, Allen was interested in strengthening the religious element in a post-war world, both as a stabilizing factor for . . . the German people, and as a stronghold against Bolshevism."[407] So commented the editors of the newly-available OSS documents; other goals, possibly as important, were left unexplored.[408]

Reverend Visser't Hooft was personally connected to the so-called 'Kreisau plotters' against Hitler, culminating in their allegedly participating in the failed assassination attempt against the German dictator.[409] Hooft had supplemented Dulles' alternate connection to the Kreisau Circle and its "reform program of Christian Socialism for postwar Germany."[410] But Reverend Hooft had also reportedly betrayed some of his anti-Hitler associates to Dulles when they attempted to reach Stalin to negotiate a Nazi/Soviet armistice[411]: Dulles and closing down the Eastern Front had an interesting echo. In at least one instance, Dulles transmitted a long report from Visser't Hooft with an appended note to the American State Department indicating that the intelligence being sent by him had only "psychological warfare" value[412], and that no "serious organization of the opposition group in Germany" existed.[413] In effect, Dulles had cut off the Kreisau group from any real U.S. intelligence or covert support.[414] That the "Kreisau Circle" was a party to the July 20th, 1944, anti-Nazi overthrow attempt was never completely proven, though the Circle's alleged complicity was dramatically argued by the Nazis.[415] The group, arraigned "before the Nazi people's court,"[416] "was comprised of men with deeply held Christian convictions . . . whose opposition to the Nazi regime was primarily based on moral aversion. Their concern was . . . with the fundamental problems that would confront Germany when the Nazi era was over."[417] Still, the Circle's "highly placed members . . . were [reportedly] committed to killing Adolf Hitler and toppling his regime before Germany was destroyed."[418]

Dulles's Swiss operatives who had connections with the anti-Hitler plots also reportedly communicated with Soviet intelligence. Using a false name for security reasons, Pavel Sudoplatov, who had held a series of significant Soviet intelligence positions from 1939 through 1946 (and who was responsible for plotting Trotsky's assassination in Mexico), met with Averell Harriman, then U.S. ambassador to the Soviet Union.[419] Harriman clearly indicated he was interested in emerging business and investment opportunities following the defeat of Germany.[420] Spymaster Sudoplatov apparently knew what Harriman wanted to hear: "I told him we [in Soviet intelligence] were impressed by the information provided to us by American agents in Switzerland who had contacts with the German underground [that is, Dulles' intelligence network], in particular with the Halder and General Ludwig Beck's group[s], who had tried . . . to overthrow Hitler."[421]

Less well known than the Kreisau Circle and its liberal Protestant supporters, those Halder and Beck groups had similar (if not identical) political, economic, and religious links as the better-known Dulles network (including his contacts with the Kreisau group).

Because Allen Dulles had long-standing ties, both business and personal, to important members of the Kreisau Circle[422], the group's post-war recovery commitment was enough to have it become part of the U.S.'s European intelligence-gathering operation. The Circle, well known to the Office of Strategic Services in Washington, had its own OSS intelligence code name: the "Breakers."[423]

No later than 1944, at the request of the U.S. War Department, the OSS's Research and Analysis Branch[424] closely examined the German churches for what intelligence, military, and political materials could be gained from them, and Research and Analysis prepared a confidential report, dated July 22nd, 1944.[425] OSS then tapped into the liberal German religious community.

But it was not only American espionage at work in the fields of the Lord: Soviet intelligence had penetrated and manipulated the Russian Orthodox Church[426] (always patriarchal, hierarchical, and patriotic), directing its powerful prelates to join and exercise influence from inside a number of international religious bodies.[427] And, like the OSS and later the CIA, the KGB infiltrated the World Council of Churches.[428]

Reciprocally, the CIA used the KGB-infiltrated Russian Orthodox Church.[429] The Dallas/Fort Worth White Russian community in the 1960s (where Lee Harvey Oswald and his wife Marina were unlikely participants) centered many of its (ostensibly) social activities in that same intelligence-penetrated Orthodox Church.[430] With KGB's control of the Russian Orthodox Church and the Dallas church receiving Central Intelligence Agency "philanthropy,"[431] the competitive reciprocity between American and Soviet intelligence was definitively illustrated by the Dallas-area Russian Orthodox Church.

Arrested in 1938 by the Nazis and imprisoned in Dachau until the end of the war, German theologian Martin Niemoeller had afterward related a disquieting story: from his post-war pulpit he had attempted to tell members of his congregation that "they bore a heavy responsibility for all that had happened [in Germany and Europe]."[432] Their response was, according to the pastor, to "whistle, stamp, and even get up and leave the church . . . ."[433]

Ironically, Reverend Niemoeller had related his discouraging experience to Mary Bancroft, the OSS agent and lover of spymaster Allen Dulles, just after Niemoeller had attended a 1945 international conference in Geneva of the World Council of Churches (WCC).[434] The WCC had been penetrated by the Soviet KGB and manipulated by Allen Dulles of the OSS while he resided in Switzerland promoting the interests of American foreign policy and international financial institutions.

By 1960, any religious-associated institution in Europe, especially if it were out of the liberal Protestant or Quaker/Unitarian social welfare traditions—for example, Albert Schweitzer College in Switzerland—was viewed with suspicion by both American and Soviet counterintelligence.

In the Cold War years, sharing "the CIA's fear that communism might be spreading, German church groups worked with . . . Christian and Social Democrats"[435] who in turn were supported by front organizations funded by the Central Intelligence Agency.

Every post-war version of U.S. intelligence opted for manipulation of religious institutions and individuals. Following the end of the war, the Office of Strategic Services was abolished on September 20th, 1945, by President Harry Truman.[436] Let loose by the OSS, Richard Helms and Frank Wisner opted for American military intelligence, with Wisner maintaining his European espionage network.[437]

## The Manipulators of Religious Groups and Individuals: First the OSS, Then the CIA

President Truman determined that the void left when OSS was disbanded had to be filled with a coordinating intelligence body, and on January 22nd, 1946, the president "issued his Directive on Coordination of Foreign Intelligence Activities to the secretaries of state, war, and navy."[438] Led by a "director of central intelligence" but subordinate to the National Intelligence Authority (NIA) was the Central Intelligence Group (CIG)[439], created by the NIA on February 8th, 1946.[440] Though operational, "the Central Intelligence Group remained essentially a transitional organization pending the creation of a permanent [operations and intelligence] organization through [Congressional] legislation . . . ."[441]

The CIG nevertheless quickly followed the examples of American intelligence in World War One and the OSS in World War Two by tapping religious individuals and groups: CIG Directive No. 15 (besides targeting business, scientific, and educational groups as sources) established "Exploitation of American . . . Religious Organizations with Connections Abroad . . . as Sources of Foreign Intelligence Information."[442] Cited as a victory for J. Edgar Hoover because the CIG had placated "the recalcitrant Hoover with promises to respect his domestic [intelligence and counterespionage] authority,"[443] Directive No. 15 was actually a coup for the CIG and for the future CIA (both directed by the same elite establishment) as the Agency inherited the Central Intelligence Group's prerogatives: "Under the directive the [DCI] . . . was . . . charged with coordinating the exploitation of such sources nationwide with other government agencies, particularly the armed services and the FBI."[444]

The unit of the Central Intelligence Group establishing Directive No. 15 connections to U.S. "Religious Organizations with Connections Abroad" was the CIG's "Domestic Contacts Service," a branch of intelligence the CIA absorbed in founding its own "program for domestic intelligence."[445] In the CIA, this unit with a major interest in using religious groups both at home and abroad became the Agency's Domestic Contacts Division whose Dallas office was headed by J. Walton Moore. Moore, of course, was an associate of Baron George de Mohrenschildt, Lee Harvey Oswald's odd friend when the Oswalds and de Mohrenschildt were members of the Fort Worth/Dallas circle of anti-Communist Russians who attended the CIA-funded St. Nicholas Orthodox Church in Dallas.

On September 18th, 1947, the Central Intelligence Agency was created[446], and twenty-four hours later, "[DCI] Hillenkoetter submitted a . . . memo, requesting that the NSC [National Security Council] approve the continuance . . . of all NIA and CIG directives [including Directive No. 15] . . . ."[447] With the CIA Act of 1949[448] and, later, the collusion of George Kennan (in 1948 the chief of the State Department's Policy Planning Staff) and Frank Wisner, NSC 10/2 was drafted, largely by Kennan. Following Kennan's recommendation, Wisner became director of the new Office of Policy Coordination (OPC); the Director of Central Intelligence would become the ultimate boss of the vastly-improved CIA.[449]

Directive No. 15 remained in operation, the Agency's *carte blanche* license to penetrate and exploit any religious organization it pleased (as the CIA subsequently did), skewing elections in Europe and controlling missionaries and Catholic service groups in Central and South America.

## Trouble in the OSS-Oriented Unitarian Service Committee

Earlier, a "bitter encounter" in 1944 had involved key figures in the Unitarian Boston and Lisbon offices[450], all three persons part of the Unitarian/OSS network. Elizabeth and Robert Dexter brought charges against Charles Joy of "incompetence and dishonesty."[451] What was the Dexters' "key issue"? Robert Dexter was both the Executive Director of the Unitarian Service Committee and its chief of European operations.[452] The USC Board investigated and then concluded the Dexter accusations against Charles Joy were without merit. But the Board also moved to split Dexter's jobs: Charles Joy would become Executive Director and Robert Dexter would be the European Director of the USC.[453]

The decision was unacceptable to the Dexters, both of whom resigned.[454] Charles Joy did accept the position of Executive Director in Boston[455], though more problems for Charles Joy with American intelligence and the Unitarian hierarchy were still to come.

## The OSS and Noel Field's Achievements

As the OSS's National Archives materials in Records Group 226 (and others) are further explored, Noel Field's wartime achievements and Allen Dulles' pragmatic and unethical manipulation of Field's religious (largely Unitarian) and radical contacts will be further proven. But a first set of documents have now been analyzed relating to the OSS's work with CALPO: the *Comite' Allemagne Libre Pour l'Ouest*, whose origin can be traced to August 3rd, 1943[456], when a "Committee of German Exiles" was established that ultimately became CALPO.[457] On August 1st, 1943, a group of influential German exiles met and drafted its approval of an earlier Moscow-supported Free Germany Committee and its goals.[458] The American committee requested that Thomas Mann be the leader of "a [new] provisional Free Germany group in the United States."[459] When Mann was warned off by the State Department (for whatever reason) and refused leadership[460], the New York group "invited Protestant theologian Paul Tillich to be their leader. Tillich accepted their offer."[461] The switch from Mann to Tillich looked very much like an Allen Dulles manipulation. First, the support for the new American-based committee had come from "the U.S. Communist Party and other anti-Nazi organizations, including the Joint Anti-Fascist Refugee Committee."[462] Second, American intelligence tampering was evident when the Luce media empire, probably through Allen Dulles' associate C.D. Jackson (at Time/Life/Fortune), first openly supported the committee[463] and then opposed it as "a Soviet attempt to lay the groundwork for a Communist government in postwar Germany."[464]

Regardless of the intelligence games being played in the United States by C.D. Jackson and Allen Dulles, by January 10th, 1945, in Europe, CALPO's successes were extraordinary in resistance, counterintelligence, penetration of the Wehrmacht, propaganda, and still other intelligence actions[465] running from 1943 through 1945.

CALPO and Noel Field were major sources of "secret intelligence" for Allen Dulles and the OSS.[466]

With the opening of the OSS's Record Group 226 files, a slanderous story concerning Noel Field and Allen Dulles (circulated through several published books without adequate response) can now be refuted. Allied armies were advancing into Germany, and Field argued to Allen Dulles that an "orderly" administrative structure be put in place in Germany for the moment when German field commanders realized it was politic to surrender their corps before the American and British troops entered Berlin.[467] The Germans could then capitulate to an already-established civil government.

"Field suggested that CALPO and its contacts be used for this task and that CALPO provide a steady stream of agents who could be parachuted or taken into Germany by some other means."[468] Dulles thought the Field plan excellent and sent his Unitarian agent to the OSS in Paris[469], where CALPO was headquartered.[470]

Young OSS officer Arthur Schlesinger, Jr., said he knew exactly who Noel Field really was: a "Quaker Communist" was Schlesinger's least offensive defining phrase.[471] But Schlesinger never explained what Field's mental acuity, religious convictions, or political beliefs had to do with the success of a covert Allied military operation. The Paris office of the OSS, reportedly following Schlesinger's judgment, disapproved of the parachute plan; but Allen Dulles supported Noel Field's infiltration scheme, "using people whom Field suggested."[472] Radicals chosen by Noel Field went into Yugoslavia, Hungary, Czechoslovakia, and Germany[473], helping to establish civil order where chaos could have prevailed. When the later Eastern European purge trials opened, these OSS-supported socialists and Communists linked to Noel Field were presented as evidence of American intelligence's corruption of Eastern Europe.

According to author Stewart Steven, Noel Field had duped Allen Dulles in the CALPO action, and Dulles, therefore, was eager for "revenge." But no other source has given so weak a motive for Dulles' betrayal of one of his key agents[474], especially since, according to actual OSS records, CALPO was clearly a major Allied triumph[475].

Noel Field had the reputation of knowing "almost everyone worth knowing in . . . Eastern Europe."[476] An undocumented source (obviously referring to CALPO) stated that Field "established leading Communists in Poland, Czechoslovakia and Hungary as representatives for the Unitarians. One condition for this aid was . . . to . . . send [intelligence] reports concerning economic conditions . . . for which the aid was destined . . . ."[477] Those reports, flowing through Unitarian officials Charles Joy and Seth Gano[478], were dispatched to Robert Dexter, Unitarian Service Committee executive and key OSS operative in Lisbon[479], and then on to Allen Dulles.

Documented in the OSS Records 226 files, all of CALPO's successful physical and intelligence operations supporting Allied efforts in Europe were dependent on "Communications . . . effected by two courier chains from within Germany, one reaching Paris via Switzerland and involving a Swiss representative of CALPO, the other controlled by the Swiss Free Germany Movement . . . in Germany."[480] A major figure "in this communication [network] was Noel H. Field, CALPO's representative in Marseilles . . . who kept wires [open] to Swiss Communists and members of the Free Germany Committee and . . . to OSS representative Allen W. Dulles in Bern."[481]

As more documents of the Records Group 226 on the OSS become available to historians, the negative and self-serving comments of former OSS worker Arthur Schlesinger (and others) will be further corrected.

## The Unitarians Investigate Noel Field

Immediately after the end of World War II, Noel Field continued his work in Europe as Director of the Unitarian Service Committee.[482] Eventually a group of New York Unitarians led by the Reverend Mr. Donald Harrington decided to investigate reports concerning the Paris office of the Unitarian Service Committee and its volatile director Herta ("Jo") Tempi.[483] But Tempi, though "deeply entangled . . . all her life in both underground and open communist organizations"[484] and a close associate of Noel Field, was able to conceal her left-wing life from the Unitarians who visited her.[485]

Tempi had been using the Unitarian Service Committee Paris office to rescue hundreds of threatened refugees who were both Christian and Jew, but she also allegedly promoted and supported Communists and Communism. Tempi's humanitarian and political balancing act was, in fact, supported by "an anonymous U.S. intelligence report dated October 5, 1945[:] . . . Jo Tempi was even-handed in her approach to clients."[486] The Agency report concluded: "all of Mrs. Tempi's efforts were bent in carrying out objectively the aims of the Unitarian [Service] Committee."[487]

But the rumors the Harrington group received ultimately meant Noel Field had to send Herta Tempi to the United States to repair her Unitarian fences.[488] The outcome was a murky disaster, quite possibly orchestrated by the hostile FBI. Tempi was accused of sexual intimacies with a Unitarian minister allegedly occurring on a train to New York; the 'couple' was also accused of registering at a New York hotel as husband and wife.[489] Apparently the Bureau had been monitoring Jo Tempi during her entire stay in the States.[490] A Unitarian inquiry board found its suspect minister guilty, stripping him of his "offices and duties."[491] Though the Unitarian official "steadfastly denied any impropriety between himself and Tempi, he was fired in August 1946 . . . ."[492] It did not help Unitarian matters that the Unitarian in question had earlier taken part in a serious quarrel with OSS agent Charles Dexter[493], and both internal Association politics and U.S. intelligence concerns might have been involved.

The Harrington Unitarian group helped send the Reverend Ray Bragg to Paris, and with the power of the Boston Unitarian home office behind him, Bragg fired Jo Tempi.[494] But Noel Field quite openly continued to support her.[495] Bragg confronted Field on his close link to Tempi and the stories concerning Field's own alleged Communist bias in distributing Unitarian relief.[496] Whether Bragg was aware of Herta Tempi's exemplary history of support for both Christians and Jews (among whom were

Socialists and Communists) [497], Bragg urged Field to get out of Europe and come home to Unitarian Boston. [498]

Herta Tempi indeed sheltered sometimes shattered veterans of the war and its aftermath, including anti-Nazi Helene Rado [499], the radical wife of Alexander Rado; sentenced in absentia in Geneva to a year in prison and "expulsion from Switzerland, . . . she escaped and came to France late in 1944." [500] The Soviets so valued her extraordinary work they "continued to pay her for past services [through the end of 1945]." [501] What the French called a "burned" Soviet espionage agent [502], Helene Rado "obtained a position with the American Unitarian Service Committee in France [run by Herta Tempi] . . . ." [503] But by 1950, Rado was "tired, disillusioned, and gravely ill." [504] Herta Tempi had done all she could for Ms. Rado.

Despite the charges brought against her, Herta (Jo) Tempi, the director of the Unitarian Service Committee's office in Paris from 1944 through 1947, was a wondrous service worker. Few relief officials in the last one hundred years have been more dedicated. [505]

Field's subsequent arguments mailed to the United States in support of Jo Tempi were judged to be inadequate [506], but Field still refused to return to Boston to deal with the charges against Tempi and himself. [507] Further, the Unitarian Association was seriously divided on the "issue" of Communist "influence" within the Unitarian Service Committee. [508]

## The Unitarians and the FBI

The Association's efforts to establish the truth about Noel Field "repeatedly led to Unitarian inquiries to the FBI, and the FBI [also repeatedly] refused to open its files [to the Unitarians]." [509] One of the key Bureau agents responsible for withholding information from the Unitarians was FBI Special Agent Robert J. Lamphere. [510] In 1941, Lamphere had "joined a squad in the New York [Bureau field] office working on Soviet espionage matters . . . [and] until 1955 . . . [was] a specialist in counterintelligence and . . . spy cases of the Cold War era." [511] Despite Lamphere being a part of the FBI team responsible for the Bureau's unconstitutional mail intercept program [512], the same FBI operation that intercepted Lee Harvey Oswald's postal communications, Lamphere wrote nothing in his own memoir about this significant and illegal N.Y. Bureau activity. His February 11, 2002, *New York Times* obituary also omitted this unconstitutional action. The obit did, however, mention that Lamphere "was not as well known as his friend James J. Angleton, who headed [the Central Intelligence Agency's] counterintelligence operations" [513] with whom Lamphere collaborated in counterespionage activities.

Lamphere's achievements in spy code decryption have been recorded in the history of the so-called Venona case: reportedly, the Army Signal Corps and Lamphere's Bureau team opened up and decoded "thousands of enciphered telegrams sent by Soviet spies in the United States to Moscow . . . ." [514] KGB Spy Chief Pavel Sudoplatov, however, suggested delicately that the Lamphere narrative was exaggerated: "former

FBI agent Robert Lamphere . . . presents a complicated story of how the FBI re-created our codebooks . . . . That may be true. I cannot absolutely exclude that code breaking might have played a role in exposing our agents . . . . But we have reason to believe that the FBI, wanting to hide its [double] agent source of information, invented the story of codebreaking."[515]

Lamphere was also close to Hede Massing, used by American intelligence to charge Noel Field with being an active Soviet agent whom Massing (as a Soviet agent herself) allegedly attempted to recruit. Massing failed in her recruitment attempt because, according to her, Alger Hiss told Massing that Noel Field was already his agent.[516] But this Massing story was obviously a strategy to defame Alger Hiss, and, except for Massing's personal assertions, has remained without documentation.[517] Lacking actual proof, the Unitarian Association decided it could not move against Noel Field[518], but the Unitarians also dodged the ethical issue by informing Field of a 'reported' reduction in its funding; his European Director's office, therefore, was no longer necessary.[519] In 1947, the year of the founding of the CIA, Noel Field, Allen Dulles' personal left-wing liaison, was out of his Unitarian job.

## Noel Field, Allen Dulles, Jozef Swiatlo, and Destabilizing Eastern Europe

On May 5th, 1949, and still without work, Noel Field disappeared.[520] Who was responsible? Why did Field vanish? And what did Field's disappearance and its consequences have to do with Allen Dulles and, finally, Lee Harvey Oswald?

Colonel Jozef Swiatlo was officially an officer of the Polish "Tenth Department, the secret section for important political matters in the [Polish] secret police . . . ."[521] He was, in fact, "the deputy director . . . at the time of his defection."[522] But Swiatlo may, in fact, have been an espionage "illegal" invented by the CIA, inserted into Poland, and then run by American intelligence after World War II.[523] Or he may have been an "illegal" created by the KGB for penetration of the West and then captured by the CIA and turned by the Agency.[524]

The smell of someone's "illegal" clung to Swiatlo, despite his official history.[525]

The Polish Cold War espionage story involved an astonishing range of characters and organizations that included the CIA, CBS, Solidarity and the Polish anti-Communist labor movement, CIA operative William King Harvey, Jr., the Vatican, and the Roman Catholic Church in Poland.[526] And Polish espionage Colonel Jozef Swiatlo bobbed to the top of that thick intelligence mix.

By 1948, the CIA had reportedly obtained control of Swiatlo, whatever his initial intelligence source: in Warsaw, Swiatlo had attempted to defect to the British in 1948[527], but the Brits, "for various [undefined] reasons,"[528] passed Swiatlo on to American intelligence.[529] Captain Michael Sullivan, chief of British Secret Intelligence Service (SIS) operations in Poland, made the initial connection to Swiatlo.[530] Sullivan then sent a coded report to SIS in London[531] that convincingly argued Swiatlo was an intelligence agent completely trusted by both the Poles and the Soviets and that his material was "not only explosive but totally up-to-date."[532]

British intelligence worried over the Swiatlo file until it was decided he was a "genuine defector."[533] But why, they asked, did he defect? Was it disenchantment with Communism, as Swiatlo had presented to SIS espionage agent Sullivan?[534] Michael Sullivan had another theory: Swiatlo was at odds with Jakub Berman, the second-most powerful man in Poland, "responsible for security and party ideology."[535] Berman had been a "United Press stringer in Warsaw" prior to World War Two[536], and his Western connections[537] would only darken his image for Swiatlo who "knew well that, because of the checkered history of Poland during the past few years, not everyone was who he seemed to be . . . ."[538] The comment, of course, applied to Swiatlo himself. But British SIS operative Sullivan argued that Swiatlo's offer to defect was impulsive, based principally on his antagonism to Berman[539], and Sullivan's argument was reportedly accepted.

But even if the Sullivan coded memorandum was accurate (and even if its contents as given to Steven were accurately presented), the suspicious nature of Swiatlo's defection story was still readily apparent. What followed did not lend credibility to the story.

Suddenly, without creative inventiveness, British SIS gave Swiatlo a "grade-two defector" status because he "had made a few innocuous remarks to Sullivan about the high standard of living in the West . . . ."[540] The SIS then sent his name (along with others) to "Foreign Secretary Bevin, the nominal head of SIS."[541] Bevin, reportedly scornful of British intelligence efforts in Eastern Europe, disapproved of the entire list[542], and Swiatlo, "an invaluable find—an intelligence man's dream," was lost to SIS.[543] If you believe the story.

SIS then decided Swiatlo would be given to the CIA; Sullivan informed Swiatlo; and in Washington, the SIS called Allen Dulles, a Sullivan & Cromwell senior partner, about Swiatlo.[544]

Without any official intelligence status, Dulles requested that Swiatlo hold his Polish intelligence job until Swiatlo was further contacted.[545] At the time, Allen Dulles was "a close consultant to the Agency"[546] but would not become the CIA's Deputy Director until 1951.[547]

The Dulles brothers had maintained their banking, business, intelligence and Protestant connections through the end of World War Two. "From 1946 until 1948 [Allen] Dulles ran private intelligence operations inside Eastern Europe with funds collected from wealthy friends and companies. Like his brother, John Foster, [Allen Dulles] . . . was involved with a number of religious and charitable institutions, many with international connections . . . [offering] a useful cover."[548]

In 1949, Dulles and his CIA allies had opened up a two-front assault on radical and Communist parties and governments in both Western and Eastern Europe. Dulles, George Kennan, DeWitt C. Poole, and the Council on Foreign Relations organized the attack's Western wing, run by the Committee for Free Europe.[549] Characterized as a "private sector anticommunist organization," the Committee had extraordinary establishment, government, and intelligence-connected luminaries as board members[550], including Poole, who had been chief of the Foreign Nationalities Branch of the OSS.[551] The Branch's official duty was keeping track of the "political activities of . . . anti-Axis exile and immigrant groups in the United States . . . ."[552] But Poole ultimately commanded his own covert intelligence operation, including "surveillance of exile leaders by OSS officers"[553] and the illegal opening of diplomatic mail pouches.[554] With Dulles' blessing, Poole "served as president of the CIA-funded National Committee for a Free Europe, 1949-1951."[555]

In 1949, the U.S. Congress established the Central Intelligence Agency Act that "exempted the CIA from all federal laws requiring the CIA" to disclose anything.[556] That same act allowed the Director of Central Intelligence to allocate funds for Agency projects "without regard to . . . law and regulations relating to the expenditures of government funds . . . ."[557] At least a portion of those covert funds were channeled through Dulles-approved organizations, secular and religious, in the war to destroy Eastern Europe.

The intended (and historically-realized) goal of the American intelligence attack initiated in 1949 was the destabilization of the European Left.[558] And Jozef Swiatlo played a major part in Dulles' brilliant political counterespionage process, though the American spymaster was still technically a CIA "consultant."

After Noel Field lost his Unitarian Service Committee directorship, he was reluctant to return to the United States: Joseph McCarthy was laying waste to the liberal establishment[559], the first Hiss trial was scheduled to start on May 31st, 1949[560], and Noel Field's early association with Hiss was sure to be aired. Field might even be called as a hostile witness.[561]

In 1949, Field applied for a Czech visa, an action that reportedly "triggered [Soviet] surveillance of him . . . ."[562] A year earlier, Field had indicated he wished "to report on developments in Eastern Europe as an independent journalist"[563], his research material subsequently to be developed as a book. But one source maintained that Noel Field went to Prague to visit a close friend of Jakub Berman, head of the Czech security services and the reported enemy of the CIA's alleged double agent Colonel Jozef Swiatlo[564]: further, Berman's secretary was Anna Duracz, who "had a distinguished record as a Communist activist before the war and had worked with [Noel] Field in Switzerland during the war."[565] Still another story related that Field went to Prague to inquire about a university teaching position: "in October, 1948[,] Field [had] asked for a Czech resident's permit . . . with the hope of getting a job as a lecturer at Charles University in Prague."[566]

### Was Quaker/Unitarian Noel Field Used by Dulles and Swiatlo to Destabilize Eastern Europe?

The most reliable evidence suggests that Noel Field was sent to Prague on May 5th, 1949, by Allen Dulles (or by Dulles' deputy Frank Wisner) so that Jozef Swiatlo, using Noel Field, could initiate Dulles' planned destabilization of Eastern European Communism.[567] Berton Hersh, relying on his extensive and knowledgeable intelligence sources, commented that "Colonel Swiatlo . . . perhaps [more than] any individual . . . helped break loose the anti-Communist tide that swamped Europe in 1956."[568]

And Swiatlo accomplished that purpose using Allen Dulles' Quaker/Unitarian asset Noel Field.

Earlier, Frank Wisner had quit the Department of Defense and moved into the State Department; then, with George Kennan's assistance, he had organized and run the Office of Policy Coordination (OPC), a largely-unsupervised covert intelligence operation[569] with its own secret budget.[570] Allen Dulles (then a key CIA consultant) recommended that OPC become an incorporated unit in the young Central Intelligence Agency, and Wisner was appointed the CIA's "deputy director of Plans."[571] Wisner had run anti-Communist political actions in Italy using Italian Catholics, ultimately destroying the democratic process in Italy. He also coordinated his anti-Communist counterespionage in Europe with General Gehlen's Nazi agents and military units in Germany[572], establishing "small private armies" of reactionaries and dissidents, Rumanian, Hungarian, Ukrainian, and Bulgarian[573], to be used in anticipated paramilitary "missions" in Europe.[574] General Gehlen, Wisner's chief German representative, gained his reputation for accurate first-hand intelligence information through "the torture, interrogation, and murder by starvation of some 4 million Soviet prisoners of war."[575]

Four million tortured and murdered prisoners of war.

In brief, Wisner's CIA within the CIA was the fastest growing, most powerful, totally immoral, and absolutely arrogant clandestine club in the Agency.[576] When Allen Dulles became the CIA's new "deputy director for Plans,"[577] he had the rabidly anti-Communist Frank Wisner and his OPC espionage network available for his own continuing dirty tricks and wet affairs.

Recall that Jozef Swiatlo reportedly attempted to defect to the British, but they (again reportedly) refused him their protection and sent him to U.S. intelligence.[578] British SIS supposedly alerted Frank Wisner to Noel Field's alleged long-time Communist Party membership[579] and Field's trip to Prague to work with the Czech Communists.[580] Finally, Soviet double agent Kim Philby (British intelligence's delegate to the CIA) and Frank Wisner had worked closely on several intelligence programs[581]; after Wisner had been the CIA's Chief of Office of Policy Coordination and its Deputy Director of Plans, he was sent to London as the CIA's station chief.[582]

Could one of the joint Wisner/Philby projects have been the patsying of Noel Field, a move benefiting both Philby's Soviet and Wisner's intelligence associates, including Allen Dulles?

Of course, Field needed no Party card (as reported by British intelligence) to collaborate with Communists. He had done so for years because of his political, ethical, and social convictions and because Allen Dulles had instructed him to do so. Field was the OSS spymaster's key link to the European anti-fascist organizations both during the Second World War and immediately after.

Further, Noel Field's stepdaughter Erika Glaser "remained convinced [apparently with good reason] that Noel Field had been deliberately set up by Allen Dulles, who [Erika believed] spooked him into making a break for Prague and then had him denounced through CIA channels [specifically through Polish Colonel Swiatlo] to his communist captors."[583]

Leonard Mosely (relying on his American and British intelligence sources) supported the Wisner elements of the Field story, commenting: "The Wisner operation to 'blow' Noel Field to the Soviets is one of the black secrets of the CIA . . . ."[584] Dulles, aware of Frank Wisner's plan (if not the actual progenitor of Wisner's espionage operation using Field), gave his counterintelligence chief the go-ahead signal.[585] Wisner controlled Colonel Swiatlo, who "was in close touch with the KGB in Moscow and the security services of the other east European satellites."[586] Wisner then reportedly instructed Swiatlo to contact all East European security and intelligence forces and inform them that Noel Field was actually a CIA agent on special assignment under the direct control of Allen Dulles.[587] Later, the suspicion that Field was, in fact, "a double agent"[588] for Dulles had not been limited to the Communists; in the West, speculation circulated that Noel Field, "while appearing to defect to communism . . . was still following CIA orders [from Allen Dulles]."[589]

Whether duped or doubled and witting or not, Noel Field fulfilled the destabilizing goal advanced by Wisner and Dulles.[590]

In the process, not only Noel Field but also Herta Field (Noel's wife), Hermann Field (Noel's brother), and Erica Glaser/Wallach (Noel Field's stepdaughter) were all arrested and imprisoned on espionage charges by the Communists.[591]

Noel Field was reportedly kidnapped in Prague by Communist Hungarian intelligence officers[592]; his arrest and subsequent detention "released all the pent-up paranoia that . . . began to surge through the corridors of Soviet power in eastern Europe."[593] The arrests throughout the Communist nations reached an estimated 200,000 with at least thousands executed. Noel Field and Allen Dulles were linked in hundreds of show trials[594], and, though Wisner commented with great satisfaction the Communists "were doing our dirty work for us"[595] in decimating the Eastern European Communist parties and governments, the Wisner/Dulles deception and its outcome actually did the dirty work for Soviet dictator Josef Stalin, who now had the satisfaction of eliminating nationalistic or reform Communists, "anyone in power in the new communist states"[596] whom he intensely disliked, and whom he "thought would not toe the Moscow hard line [against the West]."[597] The trials and political purges ground on for three years[598] until Stalin died.

## Operation X/Operation Splinter Factor:
## the Dulles/Swiatlo/Field Action

How would Allen Dulles validate the Field revelations? John Foster Dulles, Allen's brother, "in what appeared to be a monumental indiscretion, spoke of it in public—that Operation X had been mounted by the CIA."[599] Operation X was the Allen Dulles/Swiatlo/Field action: truth had become fiction, and fiction, truth. Allen Dulles, according to John Foster Dulles, was the author of Operation X, and Allen had created the code name for his own CIA action: "Operation Splinter Factor."[600]

Noel Field's stepdaughter considered the Communist political massacre "an enormous victory for Allen Dulles."[601] The purges "devastated those [Eastern] governments for years afterward."[602] Dulles had actually destroyed any chance of peaceful reformation in the Communist East: "no economic reform, no progress, and they never recovered from those purges, not ever."[603]

Noel Field's stepdaughter commented: "Would Allen Dulles do such a thing? Of course. It was his job. And it was easy enough to do. [The Central Intelligence Agency] had contacts everywhere in those governments."[604] The documentary evidence was abundantly available: during the Second World War, "Soviet and American agents in Germany [had] co-operated . . . against Hitler Germany."[605] CALPO was one such extraordinary action versus the Nazis, and two such "agents" were Noel Field and Allen Dulles. "The OSS had [indeed], through Field, subsidized and even relocated a number of Communist functionaries trapped in Western Europe by the eruption of war."[606]

Erika Glaser added: "Evidence was easy to come by. [Recall that] many of those early [Communist] party leaders had [operational] connections with the OSS during the war [through, for example, CALPO] . . . . But what made it all work was having Noel Field there, still loyal to communism and willing to denounce anybody for anything."[607]

Erika Glaser concluded that "Allen Dulles had a certain arrogance [:] . . . he believed . . . he could work with the Devil . . . [and, therefore, he] could work with Noel Field and [then] betray him . . . ."[608]

The Wisner/Dulles Operation Splinter Factor was "probably the foremost intelligence battle of the Cold War,"[609] and "set back the possibility of detente between East and West for a generation."[610] Eastern Europe never recovered from the Swiatlo charges and the Field revelations: the suspicion and fear of double agents lasted through the 1960s, a Communist bloc counterpart to the McCarthy period in the United States.[611] Wisner and Dulles had been extraordinarily successful.

Further, Dulles and Wisner helped run the National Committee for a Free Europe (NCFE), the archetypal model for all future CIA corporations and proprietaries.[612] What Swiatlo, Field, and the Eastern European show trials and purges did not accomplish, the NCFE successfully brought to Cold War closure.[613]

## Swiatlo in the United States and the JFK Assassination

In 1953, Swiatlo finally 'defected' to the United States, his CIA mission—to create political chaos in the Communist world—accomplished. A kind of inverted Agency "illegal," Swiatlo was given American citizenship and supplied with a new identity by the CIA.[614] In late September, 1954, after a brightly-lit press conference in Washington devoted to anti-Communist revelations, Swiatlo officially disappeared into some darker place in the United States.[615]

But that darkness was still another American intelligence operation: Swiatlo broadcast in Polish for Radio Free Europe/Radio Liberty (RFE/RL) between 1955 and 1983, a psychological warfare action run by Swiatlo's old handler, the CIA's Frank Wisner.[616] The overall psyopsmaster responsible for RFE/RL was C.D. Jackson. Ominously, of the four Polish defectors (including Swiatlo) who worked for RFE/RL, two redetected to Poland[617], most probably doubled or even tripled agents by the KGB and the CIA. And Swiatlo fed the paranoid fires: "Over Radio Free Europe, month after month, Swiatlo beamed into the East Bloc a smorgasbord of niceties about the apparatus he had served, every tidbit of corruption down to the identities of office snitches."[618]

Immediately following the Kennedy assassination and documented in a CIA memo buried in the National Archives, Jozef Swiatlo reportedly re-surfaced, identified (or misidentified) as a "Polish illegal" and, therefore, a suspected Communist espionage agent. The event apparently caused the CIA some anxiety, since the Agency might have recalled a radio broadcast in both Polish and English from Warsaw on October 25th, 1954, in which Polish security forces accused Swiatlo of being an "illegal" of the United States, "an agent provocateur . . . who, with the aid of forged identity papers and disguising himself and taking advantage of defects in the exercise of control, . . . managed to infiltrate . . . the [Polish counterintelligence] public security organization."[619]

Why had the key agent in the Noel Field/Allen Dulles Eastern European destabilization operation run by the CIA shown up in the Kennedy assassination investigation? Why had Swiatlo been identified as an "illegal"? Was the Agency, in fact, being haunted by the reappearance of its Oswald false identity problem?

No later than two months after the Communists declared Swiatlo was a Western intelligence illegal, the CIA was tracking Noel Field stories that implicated him, no matter how dubious the source, as "a convinced Communist and Soviet agent."[620]

Counterintelligence focused on Noel Field in both the FBI and CIA was energized with Swiatlo's surfacing; dated December 20th, 1954, the Agency's document from its Deputy Director of Plans that called attention to Field's Unitarian Service Committee "activity" and established the CIA and FBI both had a continuing "interest in the [Field] case" was routed (as had others) to the Bureau's Sam Papich, the associate of William Sullivan. Papich and Sullivan were the FBI's top counterespionage team concerned with both intelligence illegals and U.S. citizens who might be working for the Soviets.

Broader and possibly more terrible in their consequences than Operation Splinter Factor were the Wisner/Dulles counterespionage programs run by so-called diplomat George F. Kennan, who had a major planning, producing, and directing job "in the CIA-sponsored anti-Communist exile programs of the 1940s and 1950s, including those that employed Nazi collaborators."[621] For Kennan, Wisner, and Dulles, the Cold War "was the means for tens of thousands of Nazi criminals to avoid responsibility for the [atrocities and] murders they had committed."[622]

## Allen Dulles' Episcopalian Connection

Allen's brother Foster had close relations with both the American Presbyterian Church and the Anglican Church of England[623] (the spiritual base of the American Episcopal Church) throughout his political life. But what about Allen Dulles himself? An Internet search combining either "OSS" or "Central Intelligence Agency" with "Episcopal Church" yields scores of obituaries of agents and officers of both the Office of Strategic Services and the CIA who were faithful Episcopal parishioners, often holding important positions in their local vestries. The ranks of the OSS and the CIA were staffed with top-college graduates who were also active Episcopalians. Through two world wars and the subsequent "Cold War," these intelligence-connected Episcopalians remained on call, but to what extent they volunteered for service in their capacity as influential church members or were covertly used by American intelligence and Allen Dulles has not yet been documented.[624]

After President John F. Kennedy accepted Allen Dulles' resignation as CIA Director in 1962, the spymaster had no reported link to any center of Protestant power. But Dulles had generated a considerable hoard of documents ultimately preserved by his estate, and those materials covered all the historical periods of his tangos with liberal church individuals of many denominations in Europe and the United States.

Who could be knowledgeable enough about those intelligence records but also discreet enough as to their references to well-placed American Protestants, especially in the Episcopal Church, to organize, catalog, and if necessary sanitize the documents of Allen Dulles?

Dr. F. Garner Ranney had studied at London University, Cambridge University, and Harvard, earning an A.B. there in 1942.[625] During the Second World War, Ranney was "[the] Top Secret Officer on the staff of [the] Commander U.S. Naval Forces Europe."[626] After the war, Ranney was "a Desk Officer in the Department of State."[627] It would be noteworthy if Ranney had indeed been a Foreign Service Officer: "In the late 1950s . . . at least 75 percent of raw [intelligence] information came from people gathering intelligence around the world. At least two thirds of that [intelligence] came from foreign service officers engaged in overt [non-covert/non-spying] activities."[628]

Ranney's postwar professional record included unspecified "library work in Baltimore . . . at the Peabody Institute and . . . Maryland Historical Society."[629] But from 1962 on, Ranney was involved in a serious American intelligence task.[630]

After Allen Dulles left the CIA, Ranney "served [from 1962 through 1969] as [the personal] archivist to . . . Allen W. Dulles."[631] Therefore, as protector of the Allen Dulles archives, Ranney held that sensitive position throughout the former CIA director's stint as a member of the Warren Commission investigating the murder of John F. Kennedy.

And after Dulles died, Ranney "was for twenty years a member of the committee of three administering the Allen Welsh Dulles Papers at Princeton University."[632]

But beginning in 1960, F. Garner Ranney was also the chief archivist of the prestigious Maryland Episcopal Diocesan Center and the Diocesan historiographer from 1974 through 1995.[633]

Privy to Allen Dulles' documentary secrets and as a major gatekeeper for the Episcopal Church, Ranney effectively triangulated American intelligence (Ranney/ Dulles: 1962-1969); the Maryland Episcopal diocesan records, closely related to church activities in Washington, D.C. (Ranney: 1960-present); and Allen Dulles' political/intelligence documents (Dulles/Ranney: 1969-1989).

Allen Dulles, the Episcopal Church, and the CIA could not have asked for better support.

## U.S. Intelligence Protects Its Unitarian Assets

The American Unitarian Association established its wartime Unitarian Service Committee whose officers collaborated in covert intelligence-gathering with the Office of Strategic Services (World War Two's anticipation of the CIA), including its Swiss spymaster Allen Dulles. The American Unitarian Association also helped found the American Friends of Albert Schweitzer College, and the Association's officers actively supported the Swiss college. After the CIA took over the records of the OSS, the Unitarian Service Committee in 1978 attempted to discover its own wartime undercover history and applied to the CIA.

The Unitarian Service Committee found that the Agency was still protecting at least one of the OSS's intelligence sources.[634]

Who might have been that protected person?

In Frederick May Eliot, the liberal wing of the elite establishment of the United States, the American Unitarian Association, the Unitarian Service Committee, Albert Schweitzer College, the college's supporting American Friends of Albert Schweitzer College, and the Office of Strategic Services all met. While Eliot hoped to achieve a better world through participation in his religious, philosophical, and cultural organizations, the OSS and the CIA hoped to accomplish their own political ends using those same groups. Was Frederick May Eliot, in fact, manipulated by American intelligence?

In 1960, Judge Lawrence G. Brooks, then chair of the Board of Directors of the American Unitarian Association, celebrated the life and works of Frederick May Eliot (who died in 1958) in The Proceedings of the Unitarian Historical Society. The following analysis of Eliot's activities has drawn on the (abridged) version of Judge Brooks' Eliot celebration: "FREDERICK MAY ELIOT AS I KNEW HIM."[635]

Frederick May Eliot was one in a procession of prominent Unitarian ministers, educators, and poets belonging to several related and distinguished families. Eliot graduated from Harvard College in 1911 and from Harvard Divinity School in

1915, afterward being ordained a Unitarian minister. Most of America's liberal elite establishment counted Harvard as its leading educational institution. So did the Central Intelligence Agency: no later than 1986, at least one out of every four CIA officers held a Harvard degree.[636]

In 1934, seeking definitive answers to troubling questions about the decline of Unitarianism, the American Unitarian Association created a Commission of Appraisal and appointed Eliot as its chairperson. Challenged to effect a major change in American Unitarianism, Frederick May Eliot responded brilliantly. The Unitarian Church was revolutionized, with massive increases in its membership, scores of new churches, hundreds of fellowships, and the emergence of the American Unitarian Association as a leading humanitarian and cultural institution.

In 1938, significant Unitarian relief services had begun in Europe, with the Dexters, who ultimately made covert contact with Allen Dulles and the OSS, as key Unitarian operatives. The effort was fully realized when the Unitarian Service Committee (USC) was established with Frederick May Eliot as an influential member of the USC's Executive Committee. The European networks created by Noel Field in contact with Allen Dulles and the OSS through Robert Dexter were in action.

Eliot, fearful of repressive Christian orthodoxy in Europe and the United States, explored and found exciting "liberal religion," joining what became the International Association of Religious Freedom, one of the earliest and most enthusiastic supporters of Hans Casparis' Albert Schweitzer College.[637] When Casparis established the Swiss institution, Eliot became a highly visible backer, a founding member of the Board of Directors of the American Friends of Albert Schweitzer College. Eliot and Casparis exchanged letters through the first years of college on shared educational and cultural concerns.

As President of the American Unitarian Association, Eliot had to withstand charges of radicalism, especially brought against a Unitarian Service Committee led by Charles Joy, the Dexters, and Noel Field in Europe. The USC indeed supported socialist and Communist refugees streaming out of Spain and France. Further, Eliot's defense of Rev. Stephen H. Fritchman, radical editor of the *Christian Register*, brought Eliot criticism from anti-Communist liberals in the Unitarians ranks that included the highly vocal A. Powell Davies and Donald Harrington.

Eliot felt Humanism was an important component of his religious and philosophical viewpoint, making him a target of outspoken Unitarian conservatives. Yet throughout his life Frederick May Eliot moved within extremely powerful elitist circles dominating American publishing, education, business, banking, and government.

Those elitist links gave Eliot the leverage to perform humanitarian acts, but they also made him vulnerable to American intelligence abuse.

## The OSS/CIA Files on the Unitarians

With the wartime collaboration between the Unitarian Service Committee and the Office of Strategic Services (specifically through American spymaster Allen

Dulles) known at least to some Unitarians for several decades, the American Unitarian Universalist Association (AUUA) used the Freedom of Information Act in 1978 to obtain covert intelligence files on officers of the wartime American Unitarian Association and the Unitarian Service Committee. The OSS documents and files had been 'inherited' by the Central Intelligence Agency, and though the CIA sent 246 documents to the AUUA, most of the files were extensively sanitized by the Agency (rather than by the earlier OSS).[638]

The Unitarian Universalist Service Committee History Archives[639] contain a "Guide to CIA papers in the UUSC file" entitled "UUSC HISTORY PROJECT [:] CIA MATERIALS (in UUSC archives only)."[640] The UUSC Archives/Project retained the received CIA numbering system for the 246 "items" the Agency released to the UUSC, but the OSS material was reorganized chronologically by the UUSC into six file folders labeled (with Roman numerals) I through VI.[641]

Folder I holds the "Correspondence [of the USC] with Lisbon [USC headquarters], 1942-1943 and other Lisbon business [of interest to the Office of Strategic Services]."[642] The Folder I documents "include correspondence [sent] from Charles Joy and Seth Gano to the Dexters in Lisbon."[643] With the permission of Unitarian Service Committee officers in the field[644], the Office of Strategic Services had photocopied USC correspondence destined for the USC's European headquarters in Lisbon[645]; the OSS then transmitted the USC documents to Lisbon, using the State Department's "diplomatic pouch."[646]

The Dexters in Lisbon and, most probably, Charles Joy were aware of the OSS's use of the Unitarian Service Committee; but no available letters or memoirs record whether the USC fully recognized that exchanging the security of a diplomatic pouch for the integrity of the USC's humanitarian activity might have been an uneven and ultimately unethical trade.

In 1978, the Unitarian Universalist Service Committee established that the materials it entered in its Folder I contained "only a small percentage of the mail that passed through the OSS on its way to Lisbon . . . ."[647] Other material the Committee received it organized in its Folder III[648], documents proving the Office of Strategic Services had handled a significantly larger volume of Unitarian Service Committee mail than the actual copies of correspondence the CIA had released to the Unitarian Universalist Service Committee indicated.

The UUSC organized the most important collection of covert U.S. intelligence material it received from the CIA in Folder II: "Business Between USC and the OSS." Here was the actual evidence of extensive OSS/USC wartime collaboration: "These papers relate to [1.] meetings between [Unitarian] Service Committee personnel and OSS officers, [2.] financial dealings [between the two groups], [3.] requests [by the USC] for facilitation of passports and other [identity and travel] matters, and [4.] the mail service provided [to the USC] by the OSS through the [State Department/Foreign Service] diplomatic pouch."[649]

How did the Universalist Unitarian Service Committee know that the wartime cooperation between the OSS and the Unitarian Service Committee was much larger than the highly restricted number of actual communications the CIA allowed the UUSC to see? UUSC's Folder III: the "Record of Correspondence sent to Lisbon but not included in CIA papers." "These letters provide an extensive—perhaps a complete—record of the mail . . . sent from USC headquarters or from the office of Seth Gano to Lisbon between 1942 and 1944."[650]

The documentary evidence for American intelligence manipulating religious individuals and groups is substantial (despite the CIA's "redaction" of scores of documents), specifically for the operational links between the Office of Strategic Services and the Unitarian Service Committee. The Administrative Records of the Executive Director of the Unitarian Service Committee, at Andover-Harvard Theological Library (bMS 16007), are preserved in 27 boxes of 10x12 files (folders).[651]

These files were apparently 'sanitized' at some earlier time: records from 1946 through 1957 are missing—the period when American intelligence (both the OSS and the CIA) manipulated religious groups and individuals; records for the 1950s are missing—the early Cold War years; and files for 1960-1962 are missing. For the latter, since the OSS/CIA penetration of religious groups, especially the American Unitarian Association, bears directly upon the history of Albert Schweitzer College (heavily supported by its Unitarian-dominated American Friends of Albert Schweitzer College) from 1959 through 1964 (including the intervention of Lee Harvey Oswald), the nexus of AUA, OSS, Albert Schweitzer College and Oswald may easily account for the missing 1960-1962 records.

But combined with the OSS/CIA records now housed at the Unitarian Universalist Service Committee headquarters in Cambridge, the Andover—Harvard Theological Library bMS 16007 files represent substantial evidence for 1., the extensive relations between the OSS and the USC, 2., a subsequent Central Intelligence Agency cover-up (to protect still unidentified Unitarians), and 3., the 'redaction' of OSS documents sent by the CIA to the Unitarian Universalist Service Committee in 1978, despite the apparent sanitizing of the Harvard files.[652]

Beyond my suspicion that the CIA cleansed the OSS records in its possession and possibly the 27 boxes in the bMS 16007 files at the Harvard Library, boxes 23 and 24 remain crucial. In the library finding-tool for bMS 16007, 23 and 24 are listed as simply containing "Cables" and "Letters" to and from "Geneva, Switzerland" in 1945-1947. But 23 and 24 hold immense supportive evidence of the relations between Noel Field, Robert Dexter, Charles Joy, Herta Field and (implicitly) the OSS and Allen Dulles. Noel Field's hundreds of cables (and letters) are vital as substantive support for the OSS/USC intelligence collaboration (and as raw materials for a future history of Unitarian refugee work). Given the flow of information from Field and other onsite refugee workers through the OSS State Department pouch transmission line to Unitarian Service Committee headquarters in Lisbon, these communications define the significant intelligence value Allen Dulles and the OSS received from Unitarian Service Committee sources.

The CIA's deliberate intent to obscure the OSS/USC evidence and therefore withhold the truth from the Unitarian Universalist Service Committee in 1978 helps explain UUSC's awkward Folder III title[653]: "This [UUSC-organized] file consists of [USC] cover letters from various members of [the] USC enclosing letters to [USC's European headquarters in] Lisbon and, in some cases, responses from the OSS indicating that the [USC] mail had been forwarded or internal memos with instructions for forwarding the [USC] letters to Lisbon."[654] The CIA had withheld the bulk of wartime OSS/USC correspondence from the Unitarian Universalist Service Committee, apparently protecting OSS agents or assets who still had in 1978 some continuing (possibly important) relation to the Agency and/or whose revealed identity would compromise still-secret covert operations.

But the CIA might have had a more simple motive for sanitizing a USC/OSS record that tracked back to the origins of both the OSS and the CIA: the identity of a World War II OSS agent or asset inside the American Unitarian Association (or even a Cold War agent or asset of the CIA inside the Unitarian Church) whose exposure might have proved embarrassing to a prominent Unitarian family.

The UUSC's Folder IV included whatever the CIA had sent the Committee on Noel Field.[655] "We [the UUSC] must assume that much of the material that the CIA refused to send . . . pertained to Field."[656] UUSC Folder VI held "two sets of papers originating with the State Department that were sent in a separate mailing. They deal with the closing of the [Unitarian Service Committee's] Lisbon office in 1950 and the Noel Field trial."[657]

The Unitarian Universalist Service Committee "received only one copy of all undeleted materials . . ."[658], but it was sent two copies of the OSS documents subjected to CIA deletions.[659] The UUSC placed the second set of redacted OSS material in Folder V, "Expurgated Copies—2nd copy."

## CIA Protection of Unitarian Cooperation with the OSS

All of the relevant OSS documents were heavily sanitized by the CIA, clearly signaling that as late as 1978 the Central Intelligence Agency had a significant stake in withholding certain information about links between the Office of Strategic Services (and possibly the CIA), the Unitarian Service Committee, and the Unitarian Church. In her excellent historical study of the Unitarian Service Committee, Ghanda Di Figlia discreetly described the working partnership between the USC and the OSS. But in a personal communication to me, Ms. Di Figlia stated: "I have no doubt that there are intelligence files on those members of USC who were involved [in working with the Office of Strategic Services]: the Dexters, Charles Joy, possibly Howard Brooks, William Emerson . . . who was privy, I believe, to the OSS involvement . . . [and] possibly Frederick May Eliot, president of the American Unitarian Association."[660]

In fact, the close collaboration between the Dexters, Charles Joy, Noel Field and Allen Dulles (and the Office of Strategic Services) could not have existed except for the cooperation of Frederick May Eliot.

After Beacon Press came under attack and its editor Thomas Bledsoe was dismissed because of a series of controversial book contracts in 1958, Frederick May Eliot planned to meet Unitarian Secretary Walter Donald Kring in New York in a move to support the publishing house. Eliot was scheduled to preach at the Unitarian All Souls Church, and Kring and Eliot were to confer after Eliot's sermon. But a terrible snow storm held up Kring's train outside of New York, and Eliot, on his way to preach, suddenly fell dead at the gate of the garden of All Souls.[661]

*Whatever the CIA kept secret concerning Unitarian cooperation with the OSS (and the Agency for International Development[662]), the relationships between U.S. intelligence, the American Unitarian Association, the Unitarian Service Committee, and the Friends of Albert Schweitzer College (supported by key Unitarians), had met significantly in Frederick May Eliot.[663]*

## Appendix to Essay Four: The Catchpool Connection

Corder Catchpool, born in 1883, was a practicing Quaker throughout his life. In January, 1917, he was jailed for refusing to serve in the British armed forces, though he had volunteered in the Allied ambulance service in France for twenty months.[664] After three political trials and thirty-six months spent in prison, he was set free in April, 1919[665], still defiant, pledging to destroy "Prussianism the Quaker way."[666] Later that same year Catchpool became one of many Quakers in Berlin, working inside of "pacifist and ecumenical circles."[667] With other religious individuals and groups in Germany, Catchpool and his fellow Quakers helped clothe and feed the many victims of the recent terrible war.[668]

### Catchpool and the Quakers

In the early 1930s, Catchpool was part of the movement to enlist Quakers and others in support of the German people and their "objections to the [first World War] peace settlement."[669] By 1932, Catchpool was one of many Quakers (and others) supporting general disarmament.[670] But after the Nazi takeover, Catchpool moved "from spiritual messenger to activist defender of a new generation of victims."[671] He became a close observer of the Nazis and the German people's support for what Catchpool characterized as the Nazi "uprising."[672]

Accused by the Gestapo of being a Communist, consorting with suspicious "visiting foreigners," and of maintaining a file on mistreated anti-Nazis[673], Catchpool determined to be more even-handed; he joined those British citizens who viewed the Treaty of Versailles as the root cause of German mischief, advocating cooperation with Hitler's government to achieve peace and disarmament.[674] Catchpool's fellow Quakers, including several with impressive credentials, accused Catchpool of being "pro-Nazi" and an apologist for the dictator's suppression of German freedoms.[675] By 1935, Catchpool was viewed by no less than British Foreign Secretary Anthony Eden as a pawn of the Nazi propaganda. Catchpool, on the other hand, saw his own efforts as "bridge-building," necessary steps to be taken toward conciliation.[676] Still, that same year, Catchpool and his fellow Quakers in Berlin realized their "efforts on behalf of the politically persecuted . . . [had been] reduced to a kind of traffic control . . . ."[677]

Whatever the merits of Catchpool's work among the Germans, the Nazis churned out "Gestapo reports on [the] Friends for 1935 abound[ing] with speculations on Quaker conspiracies" that were never fully explained.[678] But at least the "political police in Bavaria . . . claimed that members of Socialist organizations were receiving money, food, and shelter" from the Quakers.[679] The Gestapo was apparently assured by Catchpool that Quaker "work for political prisoners was the exclusive responsibility of British and American Friends" and did not involve Quakers who were German citizens.[680] In turn, Nazi criticism of Quaker activities was muted by the Friends' "willingness to help people whose welfare concerned the German government."[681]

Tolerated by the Gestapo, the Quakers worked through the middle and late 1930s at "indiscriminate humanitarianism."[682] But in a few short years, Germany became an "occupied country" with the Nazis in complete control of the nation's economic, political, and social life.[683]

## Religious Groups and Individuals Against the Nazis

The religious life of Germany was deeply marked and often split by Nazi tyranny. The German Confessional/Confessing Church, for example, inspired by the Protestant theologian Karl Barth, "resisted Nazi interference in church affairs."[684] In opposition to the so-called "German Christian" movement, the Confessing Church attempted to preserve "the autonomy and integrity of the Christian church [in Germany]."[685] German Methodists, however, officially praised Hitler for his series of successful territorial acquisitions.[686] Other religious groups, including priests and ministers, opposed Hitler's dictatorship and paid dearly for their spiritual principles.[687] The ethical dilemma that faced the churches in Germany (and throughout Europe) elicited hundreds of heroic acts by Christian clerics.[688]

In 1936, Corder Catchpool and his wife returned to England, and the Berlin Quaker leadership posts were filled by Margaret B. Collyer (from Great Britain) and Albert and Anne Martin (from the United States).[689]

### Catchpool and the Quakers Once Again

Catchpool continued to belong to a select group of so-called "British appeasers"[690] of Nazi Germany, including "practicing Christians" who held high office in England.[691] "All of them believed that the Nazi revolution was the product of the inequities of the [World War I] peace settlement . . . and were confident that by lending an ear to German grievances they were performing a major service for the cause of peace and justice."[692] Members of the group traveled extensively, including the "peripatetic"

Corder Catchpool, often between England and Germany.[693] After leaving Berlin, Catchpool, for example, "continued to be involved in a variety of Quaker projects on the Continent and to pop in and out of the German capital until war actually broke out."[694]

Catchpool worked for several years to preserve what peace there was, opposing Britain's entry into the war, justifying German absorption of European territory and hoping always to appeal to the so-called "better elements" in Nazi Germany.[695] The ever-optimistic Quaker worked tirelessly with whatever friends of peace and conciliation he could contact in Germany, and all the while engaging in his favorite pastime: "mountain climbing in Switzerland."[696] Might Catchpool have visited Bern on one of his many pleasure trips to the Swiss mountains?

Catchpool's double character has been noted by his closest and most devoted friend: "During his last three years as the Quaker representative in Berlin[,] Corder had . . . to walk very delicately. Attacked from one side as a Communist, from another as a pro-Nazi, with the German Quakers dreading that he might bring them into trouble, and his colleagues in the International [Quaker] Secretariat doubting the wisdom of some of his activities, with the secret police watching all his movements, and with fugitives from the same police coming to him for help, Corder went quietly on with his immensely varied work."[697]

Curiously, Catchpool's public record in England was largely empty throughout the war, though at the end of the conflict Catchpool was again busy with "positive peace-making"[698] when the bulging "displaced-person camps" taxed the laboring Friends' "emotional resources."[699] Re-enlisting in Quaker humanitarian activity, Corder Catchpool and his wife then attempted "to get mutually hostile ethnic groups within camps to work with each other and with postwar German authorities whom inmates understandably resented . . . ."[700]

## Quaker Catchpool and Intelligence-Gathering

Hans A. Schmitt, one of Catchpool's chroniclers, confirmed the Quaker's early intelligence role: "Shocked by the terrifying consequences of Hitler's investiture as head of the German government, Corder Catchpool instituted a network of agents who fed him eyewitness accounts of [Nazi] terrorist acts that he [then] transmitted to Friends House in London."[701] London, of course, in addition to being the British headquarters for the Quakers ("Friends House"), was the home of Catchpool's highly-placed Nazi apologist friends, was the base of British intelligence friendly to American spymaster Frank Wisner (who ran an extensive espionage operation in Germany using Nazis), and was the locale of the offices of the American OSS, whose European intelligence chief, Allen Dulles, operated out of Bern, Switzerland.[702]

Catchpool's curiously changing public stance toward Nazi Germany, his association with prominent British apologists for the German dictatorship, the suspicion that somehow he was a Communist, his frequent trips to Switzerland, and his postwar work with refugees (who were most attractive to both American and British intelligence) all suggest that Corder Catchpool might well have lived the life of a dedicated intelligence agent.[703]

But, on the other hand, Corder Catchpool might just have been as complex and contradictory as all the rest of us.

# Essay Five

## Slow Dance with the Devil: John Foster Dulles, the American Elite Establishment, the Liberal Protestant Church Tradition, and American Foreign Policy Goals

"**D**uring Foster's postgraduate year in Paris he first affected the umbrella and the bowler hat which convinced decades of bystanders that he was associated in some capacity with the English clergy."[1]

John Foster Dulles' manipulation of the liberal Protestant tradition in support of Foreign Service and State Department policy goals (highly beneficial to the elite establishment and its economic allies) exactly paralleled Allen Dulles' manipulation of the same tradition in support of American espionage and intelligence goals (highly beneficial to the identical elite establishment and its economic allies).

In a fusion of family, class, and financial clout, the Dulles brothers had pursued both their political and personal goals and simultaneously gave major service to the key institutions of the National Security State.

### Elitist Religious Origins of the American Establishment

Despite the all-encompassing Presbyterian environment within which the Dulles brothers lived in the Foster/Dulles family, the American Establishment they so zealously served and supported, though not Presbyterian, had its origin in "a real religious establishment—the Unitarian church of Massachusetts."[2] Outlasting the Anglican establishments of New York and the South and the Congregationalist establishments of New England, the Unitarians and their Liberal Christianity ultimately triumphed.[3] Harvard College was early captured by the Unitarians and became the "command center of the Unitarian wing of the [ostensibly Calvinist Congregational] church and part of the official apparatus of the Commonwealth of Massachusetts."[4]

Contrary to the received folklore about the American Republic, though the First Amendment prohibited instituting an established church, it left untouched the already-established churches of the individual states.[5] In fact, not until 1940 did the United States Supreme Court finally ban established churches in all of the individual states.[6]

Powerfully supported by its Board of Overseers, including influential public officers, and richly supported by state-legislated tax revenues, Harvard became the training site of the Eastern Establishment Brahmins, both ministerial and secular.[7]

Unitarianism, realized in Liberal Christianity, promoted tolerance, anti-sectarianism, and a warm regard for New England economic power, resident in "the merchants and businessmen of Boston."[8]

Led by the "trinitarian Congregationalists" and other "nonestablished churchs," the legislature in 1833 finally stripped the Unitarian Church of its special status.[9] But the power of its ideas and "the ethos it had cultivated survived, passing from New England into the [national] Establishment . . . ."[10] And though secularized, that ethos was embodied in a social and political class, its generations made up of "lawyers, academics, businessmen,"[11] the sons and grandsons of the earlier Brahmins who had been educated at Harvard in that same liberal tradition.

Walter Lippmann a Harvard-educated New Yorker[12], shaped the ethic of the modern Establishment in his 1929 book *A Preface to Morals*, prescribing a vision for the elite that included "a disinterested world view" to be imposed on the ordinary people from above by a "new class of moralists,"[13] the American Establishment whose guiding principles were to be "disinterest and public morality—which is why . . . [that Establishment] resembles a state church."[14] Biographers of the American "establishment" have distinguished it from business whose "aim" was "profit" and from politics whose "aim" was "power."[15] But it was precisely the triangulation of business, politics, and the Establishment (the ultimate trinity of profit, power, and public morality) that was the basis of the cynical manipulation of morality, especially as it was embodied in Liberal Christianity: that is, in the liberal Protestant churches that were taken advantage of by both Allen Dulles and John Foster Dulles.

Ironically, the Silks, witty chroniclers of the "establishment" they defined as the "national force, outside government, dedicated to truth, liberty, and . . . the broad public interest,"[16] offered a definition of elitist behavior remarkably similar to the machinations of the Dulles brothers: "The Establishment is often vulnerable to the extremely serious charge of pursuing the private interests of its members behind a mask of disinterest."[17] Indeed. And the charge may be more serious: pursuing the power and profit of its class behind a mask of morality.[18] The Silks ignored, of course, the actual training center for the American Establishment from at least the 1870s through the 20th century: Skull & Bones, the senior-year society at Yale.[19] Yale Skull & Bones members who frequently moved to important Harvard positions simply verified that the Cambridge school, as the Silks observed, was the Establishment's 'official' higher educational institution.

## John Foster Dulles: How He Began

A child of the American establishment, John Foster Dulles ("Foster Dulles" as he preferred to be called) was named after his maternal grandfather, John Watson Foster, President Benjamin Harrison's Secretary of State during Harrison's last eight months in office.[20] Earlier, Grandfather Foster had seen service in the Civil War and afterward was appointed Minister to Mexico, Russia, and Spain.[21] Foster's Presbyterian ethic included "his moderate political liberalism"[22], and though certainly not the Liberal Christianity of the New England Unitarians, it fused with other major influences on John Foster Dulles.

Dulles' paternal grandfather was John Welsh Dulles, a zealous Presbyterian missionary.[23] In the next generation, Reverend Allen Macy Dulles, Dulles' father, was a "liberal" who urged his lawyer son "Foster" to enter the religious confrontation in the 1924 Presbyterian General Assembly where William Jennings Bryan (and the fundamentalists) opposed Dr. Henry Emerson Fosdick (leading the "modernists") on the theological question of the Virgin Birth.[24]

But that same "liberal" father required his children, including Foster, to attend all three of his Sunday preachings, take notes, later attend his Wednesday prayer meetings,[25] and memorize both hymns and biblical passages, recited while Dr. Dulles presided.[26]

If this mixed religious experience were not enough, Grandfather Foster made certain that grandson "Foster" was inundated each summer with grandfather's "talk about pioneering, war, diplomacy and the law."[27]

Establishing an undistinguished record at Princeton[28], Dulles was reportedly examining future possibilities: his father urged him to become a minister, while his mother supported his interests in "more worldly prospects."[29] But his maternal grandfather apparently was the major influence[30]: John Foster, a representative of the Chinese Imperial Government[31], took his grandson, a nineteen-year-old undergraduate student at Princeton, on the diplomatic trip to The Hague in 1907. John Foster Dulles was then made the Chinese delegation's secretary, apparently because of his alleged knowledge of the French language.[32] But later records clearly indicated he was "competent only in English."[33]

Yet barely one year after his strange French experience at the Hague conference, he received a Sorbonne scholarship[34], suggesting a remarkable improvement in his French language proficiency. Reportedly focusing on philosophy, Dulles still "elected to take some courses in international law, [including] . . . lectures on international fishing rights."[35]

Back from France, Dulles presented the revision he had made of his future to his parents at their new home in Auburn, New York, where Dulles' father was now a professor of apologetics at the Auburn Theological Seminary. Dulles argued for "a career that would combine the practice of law with dedicated lay service to the church."[36] How he came to this union of secular law and Christianity has not been recorded; his parents ultimately approved of his becoming "a Christian lawyer."[37]

## Foster Dulles in Support of Financial Power

But Dulles apparently made no attempt to find any such position, and Wall Street law firms (where he actually concentrated his work search) found his credentials without merit.[38] Foster's grandfather came to his grandson's rescue, and Dulles became a clerk at Sullivan and Cromwell where his career combining law, commerce, Latin American investment, and politically-motivated covert operations began.[39]

William Nelson Cromwell himself had been a key lobbyist in persuading America to build the Panama Canal[40], subsequently becoming the legal representative of the Panama Canal Company, the Panama Railway Company, and British, French, and German investors in Central and South America.[41]

With his limited ability to use the Spanish language, Dulles was still commissioned by Sullivan and Cromwell to handle the firm's Central American legal business.[42] He had his salary increased, he married[43], and after five years with the Sullivan and Cromwell, became a "respected associate."[44] In 1917, Dulles' first intelligence operation was "to gain assurances . . . Panama, Costa Rica, and Nicaragua would harmonize their policies toward Germany with that of the United States."[45] In fact, what Sullivan and Cromwell (and the United States) demanded was a simultaneous war declaration from the three Latin countries.[46] The Secretary of State was Robert Lansing, Dulles' uncle[47], and Dulles's law firm, Sullivan and Cromwell, would be able to dispatch a lawyer into Central America ostensibly on company business.[48] John Foster Dulles was the obvious choice for the action.

In 1918, Dulles received an Army captain's commission and was attached to the War Trade Board[49], where his operations were both military and economic, including his service "as liaison between the War Trade Board and the War and Navy Departments . . . ."[50] Promoted to the rank of major by the end of the war[51], Dulles was held in high opinion by Vance McCormick, his boss on the War Trade Board, who was also the chairperson of the Democratic National Committee[52], and by Bernard Baruch, chief of the War Industries Board.[53]

The complex wartime trade and shipping relations between the American government, the Netherlands, the Scandinavian nations, and Germany had been successfully negotiated by Foster Dulles and his associates.[54] The war ended, President Wilson sent McCormick and Baruch to Versailles.[55] Baruch, now on the "Reparations Commission," chose Dulles as his legal representative.[56]

The British and French demanded that Germany accept its "war costs"[57], but Foster Dulles and Baruch argued that Germany should not be pressed to pay "war damages" that would "sow bitter seeds of a new war."[58] For Sullivan and Cromwell and the firm's investors, Germany was saved[59]: Article 231 of the "treaty" accepted "Germany's finite capacity to pay war [damages and reparations] . . . ."[60]

Following his post-war service at Versailles[61], Dulles for twenty years "combined law with international finance and diplomacy"[62] at Sullivan and Cromwell, handling a series of legal and financial assignments that involved oil, coal, and other lucrative commodities.[63]

## Foster Dulles Joins the International Power Structure

But Germany's war debt occupied much of Dulles' attention through the 1920s[64] until an odd series of deaths "catapulted [him] to the top of . . . [his] large and famous law firm . . . ."[65] Dulles' pleasures could now be realized: his "special fondness for French wines, caviar, brandy and cigars, and . . . the diversions of European nightclubs."[66] But he was without any interest in art or music[67], according to at least one source "a plain, rugged and rather gauche figure . . . ."[68]

Despite his successes at Cromwell and Sullivan, Dulles was, according to a sympathetic biographer, a failure as a parent.[69] Still, his son Avery ultimately reversed his own personal downward spiral.[70] Though a Dulles biographer reported Avery Dulles renounced the family's Presbyterian faith in 1939[71], Avery asserted "There was nothing there really to reject [that is, renounce] . . . ."[72] Coming to spiritual consciousness while a Harvard Law student, Foster's son Avery finally chose to become a Roman Catholic. An officer of American Naval intelligence in World War II, he was hospitalized with a bout of polio; during his recovery period, he decided to become a Jesuit priest.[73] Avery was "brilliant, gentle, and obviously well suited to the calling . . . ."[74] At the age of 82, culminating his career as an eminent Roman Catholic theologian, Avery Dulles was named a cardinal of the Catholic Church[75], remaining an important source on Foster Dulles'dubious religiousity.

## Religion and Foster Dulles

If John Foster Dulles was to become a major manipulator of religious institutions for the sake of his own and his Establishment goals, where, in fact, was his religion? Where was his spirituality?

Thomas E. Dewey, who at one time was invited to join Cromwell and Sullivan, met Dulles in 1937[76], the year recognized by Dulles' biographers as the date of his apparent Damascus road experience.[77] Dewey's later comment about Dulles was perceptive: "I think he spent some years as an atheist."[78] Indeed, Dulles may never have been a practicing Christian at all (as distinct from reported public appearances at church services): "his theology [was] . . . a generalized faith in [some vague and completely undefined] . . . 'universal moral law' . . . [and] a belief [beginning no earlier than 1937] that the church . . . [had] a role to play in the political process . . . ."[79]

Despite the valiant attempts by a half-dozen Dulles biographers to argue for some kind of continuity between the Dulles family's Presbyterian origins and his Christian "rediscovery" in 1937, Dulles, according to his son Avery, was not a religious person. Interviewed about his family's religious activities, Cardinal Avery commented: "My family had [earlier] been very church-committed, but then we got a country house out on Long Island, and [our] . . . church practice [that is, physical attendance] fell off. My father [John Foster Dulles] found his religion rather irrelevant to his life. He didn't have any particular connection to a church."[80]

In February, 2001, the Dulles clan was characterized by a *New York Times Magazine* interviewer as "a family of agnostic Protestants."[81] Avery Dulles, a designated Roman Catholic cardinal, accepted the identifying phrase without comment.[82]

Despite the unconvincing attempts to spiritualize his moral opportunism, Foster Dulles was precisely defined: "Jim Hagerty said he was a Roundhead, a Puritan,"[83] clearly suggesting Foster Dulles was the Protestant equivalent of a Spanish Inquisitor. Writing to Avery in 1949 (after his son had entered the Jesuit priesthood), Dulles clearly defined his own amoral ethic: "I know that you have contempt for 'expediency,' but that is what in fact determines most of people's conduct . . . ."[84]

A 1962 "Reappraisal" of Dulles (in its last chapter) referred to Foster Dulles as a "Presbyterian elder"[85] with a "deep Presbyterian sense of morality"[86], but earlier the same author went to considerable lengths to characterize Dulles as "devious"[87], embodying "casuistry" and "ingenuity"[88], "ruthlessness"[89], "intransigence"[90], "righteousness"[91], and "inhumanity"[92], a portrait not especially spiritual.

Indeed, Foster Dulles was without any recognizable Christian convictions. In both Dulles' written and spoken works, "there was rarely any reference to sin, no admission . . . [that] ethical decisions are fraught with moral ambiguity, and no evidence of an understanding that the dimension of self-interest, self-preservation and self-righteousness is implicit in every exercise of power."[93]

Andrew H. Berding, who became Dulles' Assistant Secretary of State in March, 1937 (the crucial year of John Foster Dulles' spiritual epiphany), characterized his boss as "an intensely religious man."[94] Yet Berding gave no evidence in support of this alleged religious intensity; instead, Berding contradicted himself: "In my numerous conversations and meetings with him[,] I recall no instance where he made a point of religion."[95]

Still, according to several sources, Dulles acted as if he were either the right hand of God or the deity himself.[96]

## Did Foster Dulles Experience a Political Damascus Road Moment?

What happened in 1937? Despite Tom Dewey's observation about Dulles' apparent atheism and Avery's statement about his father's uninvolvement in any church, Dulles "had [reportedly] remained a prominent Presbyterian layman."[97] With his undocumented church attendance (unattested to by his son Avery who was a Jesuit priest), Dulles was supposed to have "taught a Sunday-school class at various [unidentified] periods."[98] But Dulles felt in that fateful year of 1937 he had not given "enough attention to the possibilities of public service."[99]

Were there political pressures in 1937 on John Foster Dulles that might have been a major factor in his alleged religious reconversion?

Powerful forces had indeed come together to enlist Dulles as a major player in the expected dark times. In 1938, John D. Rockefeller, Jr., had offered him the direction of a "task force" that would evaluate "missionary activities throughout the world."[100] Given the historical connections between the Rockefeller family's goals in investment, politics, intelligence, and evangelistic religion, the offer to John Foster Dulles was anticipatory.

The Rockefeller clan and its missionary intelligence network had emulated other powerful families, including the historic Medici. The Papacy (for over a thousand years) and later the Spanish Inquisition in both Europe and the Americas used the Church's missionaries for intelligence data collection. Their modern counterpart was the Rockefeller family operating in the American West and, later, in Central and South America.

As early as 1883, the Rockefellers had "used [Christian] missionaries to gather intelligence about [Native American] insurgences in the West or to discourage them."[101] In the United States and later throughout Central and South America, Family Rockefeller power was linked to Christian missionary work.[102] The growth of the Rockefellers' wealth was exactly matched by the family's collaboration with Christian Fundamentalist missionary action.[103]

By 1957, the Rockefellers had decided to support the Fundamentalist revivalism of Billy Graham[104], whose supporters included the ostensibly "liberal" Protestant Henry Pitney Van Dusen, a Rockefeller Foundation trustee[105] and editor of Foster Dulles' "spiritual legacy." The Establishment Protestant churches hoped to enlist converts if they supported Graham, but the Rockefellers' allies in Fundamentalism ultimately triumphed.[106]

Though Dulles was unable to join the Rockefeller missionary commission as its director, he did complete a part of his task, visiting Chinese General Chiang Kai-shek.[107] Dulles assessed the Asian leader as a stalwart anti-Communist and "sincere Chinese patriot"[108], the target of unfair Communist propaganda concerning the general's anti-democratic propensities.[109] For Foster, the visit was the beginning of his long involvement in Sino-American politics.[110] But Dulles' appraisal of Chiang Kai-shek was also an important illustration of the Rockefeller family's fusion of profit-seeking and Christian missionary work, paralleling Allen Dulles' manipulation of religious institutions for American intelligence purposes and Foster's religious fervor in support of both the Cromwell and Sullivan law firm and American political goals. Dulles would have a lengthy relationship with Rockefeller interests throughout the rest of his life, not the least of which was his chairmanship of the Rockefeller Foundation.[111]

In 1937, just before his trip to China, Dulles accepted two invitations significantly linked to a pair of major international gatherings later cited as catalysts for his religious "rediscovery." But it was more likely that Dulles (and his backers) decided to revive Foster's dormant relation to the Divinity as a perfect tool of foreign policy and intelligence. His brother Allen's earlier success during World War I using the same tactic may, in fact, have been Foster's model.

John Foster Dulles was invited to attend the "Conference on Intellectual Co-operation in Paris, under League of Nations auspices, . . . called to study the possibilities for peaceful change in a world . . . moving inexorably toward war."[112] Dulles' later negative response to this political meeting was suspicious, dovetailing too neatly with his next immediate "religious" experience.

The ensuing Conference on Church and State meeting in Oxford, England, had invited world-prominent clergy and secular leaders.[113] According to one of his biographers, Dulles was most impressed "by the scope and range of the ideas the churchmen had to offer."[114] Apparently aware of the economic and political importance of the world conflict that was to erupt, Dulles recognized the "moral dynamism potential"[115] of the liberal Protestant tradition.

## Was Foster Dulles' Experience More Political than Spiritual?

Dulles therefore reportedly experienced a religious revelation in July, 1937. Yet "some [commentators] thought . . . the more than casual effort to demonstrate a revival of his faith reflected an attempt to give himself a more appropriate 'image' for church work."[116] With Dulles' longtime commitment to German and Japanese economic and industrial development, his "reasons for moving deeply into church work at this time may . . . have been complex."[117] His "church work" after 1937 was, in fact, troubling to a number of observers.[118]

But why? Both the secular Paris conference and the religious Oxford conference in 1937 had been organized by the same international elite establishment, and undoubtedly for the same purpose: to support an alliance of Western "Christian" power in opposition to the anticipated strength of the Communist East, led by the Soviet Union. Dulles' son Avery summarized his father's intention succinctly: "He began to be interested in using the churches [beginning in 1937] as a means . . . to overcome . . . nationalism and promote world peace."[119] And, of course, to support a supranational capitalist world order maintaining its own peace but pitted against the Communist USSR.

Dulles' most intelligent and sympathetic critic could only conclude that he "experienced a limited and intellectual type of 'conversion' in the sense that he departed [the conference] with the impression that religion could serve as a significant social force" capable of supporting his political agenda.[120]

## Foster Dulles: the Liberal Protestant Church Manipulated

For ten years as the executive officer of Sullivan and Cromwell whose European and Asian clients were among the wealthiest and most powerful supporters of the German and Japanese war efforts, Dulles was concerned about the real possibility the United States would enter the war and hence tip the balance in favor of the anti-Axis nations, resulting in the disastrous defeat of Japan and Germany and the decimation of their industrial strength.

How to justify, therefore, the saving of essentially tyrannical governments and economies?

To argue his Establishment political goals through the media of the liberal Protestant churches was John Foster Dulles' brilliant pragmatic choice. In his exhortations to both religious and secular audiences in the late 1930s, Dulles most often referred to an "undefined 'spiritual element'"[121] that (earlier) was to bolster America's noninterventionist stance and, after Pearl Harbor, was to direct the West's wartime activity with "humility and repentance."[122] Neither humility nor repentance was defined in any Christian sense.

In 1924, Dulles had tested the religious waters with his political toe. Appointed to the Presbyterian General Assembly's Committee on War by the New York Presbytery[123], Dulles authored an essay embodying one of his earliest political programs: though "worthy of the followers of Christ . . . [it] did not necessarily proceed from a peculiarly Christian premise."[124] The 1924 essay anticipated all of Dulles' subsequent "spiritual" arguments: the content of those diplomatic, economic, or political arguments was always delivered in an empty rhetorical vehicle, whether the carrying cart was "Christian, "moral,' or "righteous."

Ultimately, whatever the ethical or even specifically Christian frame of Dulles's thesis, his major thematic concerns were always political: "the obsolescence of national sovereignty . . . [and] the need for long-range national objectives . . . ."[125] No matter that the two ideas contradicted each other; they became closely coupled with Dulles' Christian/anti-Communist "spiritual element."[126]

As a certified delegate of the American Federal Council of Churches, Dulles began in 1938 to travel, write, and speak (ostensibly) in support of the Council "[127]on the side of constructive efforts for peace."[128] Dulles filled five intense years "making speeches in all parts of the country and taking part in study groups and public discussions."[129] He reportedly felt this period of his life had been a part of a major "missionary movement."[130] "He kept [dozens of] . . . speaking engagements a year, talking [for example] to church [meetings], . . . business groups . . . [and] YMCA organizations . . . ."[131]

But those five years were not a seamless stretch of moral arguments. For example, the word "peace," with all of its feelingful connotations, was prominently displayed in Dulles' many presentations during the period. But before America's entry into the war, he clearly advocated non-intervention; afterward, he argued for a peace that included the "rational" acceptance of Japanese and German economic needs. None of his definitions of peace was ever either spiritual OR religious.

In the late 30s, Foster Dulles began to explore serious participation in international politics, and the World Council of Churches offered him a friendly forum at a number of WCC conferences.[132]

In July and August of 1939, Dulles was in Geneva attending the small[133] but grandly titled International Conference of Lay Experts and Ecumenical Leaders of the World Council of Churches[134] where he reportedly helped shape "three principles . . . [embodying] a Christian formula for world peace."[135] But that formula was generic Dulles.[136] It called for a "coextensive" exercise of world "political power and responsibility"[137]; it affirmed that "all human beings [were] . . . of equal worth in the eyes of [a presumably Christian] God; and it asserted that "[it was as] necessary to effect changes [in the world order] in the interest of justice as to secure the protection of the *status quo.*"[138]

Aside from an apparent vote for the American Declaration of Independence (and, by extension, its European ethical origins), Dulles had argued for a political world order that would support Japanese and German economic challenges ("to effect changes in the interest of justice") while strongly suggesting the Western powers were guilty of self-interest in preserving the world's *status quo* at the expense of both justice and necessary change.

Further, Dulles accused the United States, Britain, and France of post-war "blunders so colossal . . . they must be paid for."[139] Witting or not, Dulles used the word "paid" as it carried both its religious and economic meanings. He condemned the three governments of "policies" that "spawned forth" the "evil creatures" then running Japan and Germany.[140]

Dulles was "much impressed . . . by the effectiveness of the World Council as a platform for international pronouncements . . . . From that time onward his interest in and participation in the council's work never flagged."[141]

On October 28th, 1939, in Detroit, before the National Council of the Young Men's Christian Association, Dulles made his position absolutely clear: the United States ought not to enter the European war: "I see neither in the underlying causes of the war, nor in its long range objectives, any reason for the United States becoming a participant in the war. Were we now to act, it would be to affirm an international order which by its very nature is self-destructive and a breeder of violent revolt."[142]

When Dulles wrote for the Council on Foreign Relations' *Foreign Affairs* and the journal of his suddenly renewed religiosity, *Presbyterian Life*[143], his focus was always political rather than spiritual.[144] The engines of the Council on Foreign Relations and the Federal Council of Churches were running on identical fuel: Dulles' "Can We Be Neutral" that was written for the Council on Foreign Relations[145] was identical both in spirit and idea to his speaking and writing on behalf of the Federal Council of Churches.[146] Because Dulles was the intellectual leader of both organizations, his work was for both interchangeable: it was always political and never spiritual.[147] Since the Council on Foreign Relations was the creature of the American Establishment, particularly the Rockefeller family[148] with whom Dulles was closely allied, the Council consistently anticipated or echoed the Federal Council of Churches.

In 1940, Dulles accepted the chairmanship of "the committee of direction" for the Federal Council of Churches' Commission on a Just and Durable Peace[149], an organization he had, in fact, helped to create. The Commission had "over a hundred representatives from all the Protestant communities making up the Federal Council of Churches, and thus [it] directly represented about twenty-five million people."[150]

Probably the Commission's "best known achievement"[151] was more political than religious: it published a booklet in 1941 embodying Dulles' critique of the Roosevelt/Churchill Atlantic Charter[152] in which Dulles prophesied that the "end of the present war" would "find an overwhelming concentration of power in one or two nations."[153]

But Dulles did not call for justice to be exercised at the conclusion of the conflict for the millions who were dying and would die because of fascist tyranny. Rather, he asked for "a beneficent reality."[154] Dulles argued for a European human services operation that supplied "medicine, food, and clothing"[155] to alleviate the anticipated post-war chaos; for a "federated commonwealth" in Europe[156]; for "assurance to Japan of access to markets and raw materials . . . ,"[157] given the Japanese record of war crimes in Asia, a shocking political/economic proposal; and for the continuing control of "all nonself-governing colonies" to be placed under European "international mandate."[158]

Dulles' proposals presented neither support for democracy nor elimination of exploitation, bigotry, racism, and genocide. In fact, his Charter revisions looked remarkably like an argument for sheltering Western and Japanese state-protected capitalist economies. Further, Dulles was now in direct conflict with dedicated Protestant church figures led by Henry Sloane Coffin, then president of Union theological Seminary, arguing that the European war indeed presented a "major moral issue"[159] supporters of Dulles were ignoring. The division between a Coffin-led ethical argument for joining the war against Germany and Foster Dulles' Federal Council of Churches advocating a post-war reconciliation was clear: Dulles had rejected any Christian church support for the anti-Nazi forces. He wrote to Henry Sloane Coffin that he "was distressed by the tendency to bestow a church sanction on the Allied war effort."[160]

## Friedrich Wilhelm Sollmann: A True Liberal Christian

John Foster Dulles' self-serving 'Christian' morality can be most fully appreciated in contrast to the authentic spirituality in the service of peace practiced by Friedrich Wilhelm Sollmann. Born in Germany, Sollmann was a Christian journalist and editor targeted by the Kaiser as an enemy of the state during World War One, and he was one of the founders of the Weimar German Republic, subsequently becoming a member of its General Assembly.[161] In 1933, Sollmann was "the first member of [the German] parliament attacked by Nazi stormtroopers . . . ."[162] Severely wounded, Sollmann escaped to edit a Saar territory daily, then left the Saar when the Nazis entered, and eventually resided in Woodbrooke, Birmingham, England, where he made his first contact with Quakers.[163] In 1937, the year of Foster Dulles' conversion, Sollmann became a resident of the United States, lecturing throughout the country.[164] In America, he addressed almost one thousand audiences, and became a resident of the Quakers' Pendle Hill[165], from where he made manifest his argument for "modern Christian democracy": "1. Work for all. 2. The highest development of useful production. 3. Just distribution of the wealth produced. 4. No economic monopolies by private corporations or governments. 5. Insurance for all needy citizens against private emergencies. 6. Mediation and arbitration between social groups in the nation. 7. Mediation and arbitration between nations. 8. A regional federation of free nations with the ultimate aim of a world federation of all nations. 9. Progressive limitation of armaments as gradual steps to disarmament. An international police force. 10. Education leading to voluntary national and international cooperation. 11. Emphasis on the supreme importance of liberty for the growth of the individual. 12. Fusion of individual liberty with a powerful leadership responsible to the people. 13. A new concept of the moral character of statecraft. 14. Strengthening of national and international solidarity. 15. Stress on the universal character of Christianity.[166]

Sollman's "Christian democracy" put Dulles' self-serving righteousness to shame.

## Foster Dulles Manipulates the Protestant Churches

One month after Pearl Harbor, Dr. William Temple, the Archbishop of Canterbury, hosted an international Church of England conference at Oxford, England, reportedly "to define the spiritual bases of peace."[167] Dulles and Dr. Walter Van Kirk, an officer of the Federal Council of Churches, flew the Atlantic Ocean to attend the interfaith meeting. But it was a curious trip, suggesting that the British and American governments, now wartime allies, had co-sponsored the religious conference. Van Kirk and Dulles were passengers on a United States military aircraft that brought them to a blacked-out Limerick Airport in Ireland.[168] From there, the two Americans were placed aboard a British military plane landing at Bristol, from where an official car transported them to London and then to Oxford.[169]

Anticipating a much later concern of the Establishment, Dulles addressed the Oxford conference on the benefits of international economic agencies that transcended national boundaries. In effect, he called for globalization administered by a "supranational executive organ."[170] Astonishingly, an unidentified "churchman" who attended the conference approved of Dulles' call to move beyond "abstract principles" (principles found, for example, in the Sermon on the Mount?) and to "get down into the gutter of international politics."[171]

John Foster Dulles' priorities could not have been more clearly defined.

Left unexamined by Dulles (as distinct from his advocacy of a global administrative power) was the Oxford conference's call (in its "Malvern Report") for European unity in a cooperative "commonwealth,"[172] its critical look at capitalism, and its support of "social security."[173]

As a key officer, representative or delegate at more than a dozen national and international religious conferences and organizational meetings from 1937 through 1953[174] (when he became Secretary of State), Dulles authored over "fifty addresses and articles concerned . . . [according to Henry P. Van Dusen] with the moral and spiritual foundations of world order, the significance of religion, and the role of the [Western Christian] churches."[175] By collecting twenty-two of those Dulles pieces,

Van Dusen supplied a representative sampling of Dulles' "spiritual" work from 1937 through 1958.[176] In his introduction, Van Dusen summed up certain recurring themes and ideas embodied in Dulles' "Christian convictions": "moral law"; "human beings as children of God . . . with certain inalienable rights"; the "teachings" of Jesus having "authority and practicability"; "faith" as necessary for a righteous life; and political "action" required to fulfill a Christian's commitment.[177] But Dulles' citations of moral law and inalienable political rights in his works were not, in fact, specifically Christian; and though he was correct that Jesus' Gospel teachings apparently embodied "ethical principles"[178], Dulles omitted any references to the Christian belief in Christ's divinity (save in passing, as in: "The church, being a creation of God in Jesus Christ . . ."[179]); in Jesus' death and resurrection; or in Jesus' defining act of sacrificial redemption.

Certainly these three convictions, central to Christianity, ought to have been part of the "faith" in "action" Dulles was so fond of featuring in his writing and speaking for twenty-one years. But they were not. Dulles did refer to Christians dedicating themselves to pursuing a "just and durable peace"[180] and "seeking forgiveness for their sins"[181], though the latter reference appeared in a conclusion to a proposal for the adoption of a "moral law" embodying "God's purpose for the world made known in Jesus Christ"[182], a "law," Dulles argued that both "Christians and non-Christians [could] . . . accept."[183] In 1939, however, Dulles defined Christian "sins" as political and economic, committed exclusively against Japan and Germany.[184]

One year after the United States entered World War II, Dulles set forth his "guiding [political] principles" in an address adopted by the Federal Council of the Churches as the Council's own statement in December, 1942. It would be the last time Dulles was so "Christian," despite his "spiritual legacy."[185]

## Foster Dulles as Hypocritical Opportunist

Even Reinhold Niebuhr, the favorite theologian of the governing American Establishment, had characterized Dulles' ostensible Christian ethic as "Self-righteousness . . . [:] the inevitable fruit of simple moral judgments."[186] Another source not especially *friendly* to Dulles reported the Presbyterian elder had commented to French Foreign Minister Christian Pineau: "For us[,] there are two sorts of people in the world: . . . those who are Christians and support free enterprise and . . . the others." Succinctly, Dulles had united capitalism and Christianity against all "the others."[187]

In 1948, I.F. Stone brilliantly summarized Foster Dulles's hypocritical ethics, pinpointing an early "Dulles conversion" occurring during World War II, "when the fortunes of war had turned definitely against the Axis[:] . . . Dulles [then] raised the slogan of 'a Christian peace.' He who had never risen to plead for the victims asked mercy in defeat for the oppressors."[188]

Stone cited Dulles' speech at the meeting of the World Council of Churches in Amsterdam: Dulles had presented Jesus as "a symbol to be drafted in the Cold War."[189] For Stone, "The man who keeps Mammon for a client shouldn't talk so much about

God."[190] To evaluate the "Christian" Dulles, Stone recommended reading Matthew 7:15-16.[191] "Beware of false prophets who come to you in sheep's clothing but who are, inside, ravening wolves."[192]

By 1950, Dulles saw the United States as a moral enclave in a "predominantly hostile world"[193] destined to be destroyed if it did not take action against the Communists: for Dulles, "A United States which could be an inactive spectator while the barbarians overran and desecrated the cradle of our Christian civilization would not be the kind of a United States which could defend itself."[194] Though President Eisenhower agreed that the United States was broadly "a product and representative of the Judaic-Christian civilization"[195], he always chose "economic rather than moral considerations."[196]

Dulles' Cold War anti-Communism generated his thesis supporting Western/ Christian exploitation of the Third World; he cited the "wise statesmanship" and "moderation" of the Western world that resulted in the "withering away of political rule by the West . . . ."[197] But Dulles' entire argument was bereft of evidence, suggesting, at best, self-deception: "We . . . should not forget those spiritual leaders who in the past implanted in Western colonial policies the basic concept of human liberty so that, from the beginning, Western colonialism had a liberating quality."[198]

In 1954, appearing before the Council on Foreign Relations, Dulles proposed his major foreign policy goal: "a maximum deterrent at a bearable cost"[199], what the media dubbed "massive retaliation."[200] Rather than ethical or moral, the policy looked like an amoral response to a perceived provocation, implying "that the [Eisenhower] administration would risk the incineration of tens of millions, Americans included, to prevent peripheral ["Communist"] aggression . . . ."[201]

In 1956, Dulles spoke in Ames, Iowa, condemning "neutrality" as obsolete and almost always "immoral."[202] Dulles arrived at this conclusion by contrasting the nonaligned "third world" with the United States in its epic battle with Communism: American foreign policy was dictated by what Dulles called "moral law."[203] But the Secretary of State did not elaborate: what moral law? The Torah? The Gospels? Paul's letters?

Dulles' "moral" arguments have most recently been characterized by a friendly commentator as "excessive," "gratuitous," and full of "ethical posturing": a "smoke screen of . . . provocative rhetoric."[204] "Dulles' critics . . . [have] pronounced him a hypocrite."[205] Dulles' pragmatic diplomacy coupled with his self-serving moralistic language strongly suggested that Eisenhower's Secretary of State had his own psychological warfare agenda. A recent full and even-handed analysis of Dulles' political and religious proclamations characterized them as shallow, pretentious, and weak in vision[206] with, at best, "a heavy dollop of religiosity."[207]

## Foster Dulles and the Rhetoric of Prophetic Dualism

Though Foster Dulles did not invent U.S. foreign policy that trumpeted its moral superiority, he certainly helped perfect it: comparing American rhetoric with American behavior "through the 1950s," communications expert Justin Lewis concluded that "U.S. foreign policy . . . [had] little to do with moral or ethical imperatives, despite widespread assumptions to the contrary."[208]

Aristotelian logic (in its simplest and most powerful manifestation, that something must either be A or null-A) has been critiqued by a dozen major logicians, philosophers, and semanticists, but no more effectively than Alfred Korzybski, Kenneth Burke, Anatol Rapaport, and Wayne Brockriede, who have influenced communications theorists and rhetorical analysts closely examining the fusion of symbolic act and persuasive rhetoric. With communicationist Martin Medhurst, a group of these academics have focused largely on American Cold War language.[209]

Philip Wander (a member of that group) has been interested in both foreign policy language and domestic political speech.[210] In particular, he has concentrated on the linguistic strategies of the Eisenhower/Dulles administration, calling those strategies "prophetic dualism."[211] For Wander, in Foster Dulles' rhetoric (after 1937), the world was a battlefield where two opponents were in absolute and irreconcilable conflict, one "act[ing] in accord with all that is good, decent and at one with God's will, the other act[ing] in direct opposition."[212] For Foster Dulles, one side embodied the Divine Spirit, the other Evil Incarnate. No nation, no group, and no individual could stand outside this conflict: "neutrality [was] . . . a delusion, compromise [was] appeasement, and negotiation a call for surrender."[213]

Prophetic dualism operated from the beginning of American history, more specifically in the 1950s, finally embodied in that period by individuals who successfully utilized the strategy.[214] Beginning with the landing of the Puritans at the fabled rock, religion became a major part of American "public discourse"[215], ultimately melding the sacred and the patriotic in the argument (through two World Wars) for the American "mission."[216] If prophetic dualism defined American political use of the sacred, then "patriotism virtually became law, criticism of government policies grounds for censorship, [and] public protest evidence if not of treason then [of] some lesser form of Un-Americanism."[217]

The archetypal practitioners of prophetic dualism (absolute good versus absolute evil) in the American government of the 1950s were, of course, Dwight David Eisenhower and John Foster Dulles.[218]

Though Wander does not speculate on who might have influenced Eisenhower to adopt "prophetic dualism" as a rhetorical strategy from the time that Eisenhower was World War II's Allied commander through his successful campaign for the presidency[219], that individual (assuming his existence) certainly must have been deeply versed in psychological warfare: someone with a way with words to sway a whole nation.[220]

Though the argument of an absolute split between Good and Evil in American political life did not originate with either Eisenhower or Dulles[221], Foster Dulles went far beyond Eisenhower's largely traditional morality, in the 1950s calling down Divine wrath on his Godless opponents; and he did so both in support of his own economic and political ends and American international hegemony. "One advantage of [Dulles'] prophetic dualism . . . [was] that it stifle[d] . . . debate; another . . . that it posit[ed] a life-and-death struggle . . . [and therefore] encourage[d] . . . a heightened dependence on the established order. Conflict [was] inevitable between Good and Evil."[222] Both of these advantages were embodied in Foster Dulles' pragmatic morality, an ethic largely empty of real spirituality.

## Foster Dulles and His EndTimes Dualism

Nearing his death, Dulles had apparently come to believe in the rhetorical split he had made between West and East, capitalism and Communism, Good and Evil[223], and God and the Devil[224], manifested throughout the Eisenhower administration and dominating the closing acts of Dulles' life and career.[225] Dying of cancer, Dulles addressed the National Council of Churches (NCC) in Cleveland on November 18th, 1958.[226] For several years, in press conferences, interviews, and addresses, Dulles had attacked the Godless Communists of the Soviet Union and the People's Republic of China. Though he now stressed the value of change and adapting to it[227], he still argued in his "morally righteous" mode for the continued exclusion of China from the United Nations.[228] Friends and former allies who had worked with Dulles on the Federal Council of Churches' Commission for a Just and Durable Peace (from 1940 through 1948) were in his National Council of Churches' audience as he railed against the Reds.[229] But a majority attending were no longer moved by Dulles' "moral" arguments: "within a few hours of his talk they voted a resolution that put the National Council of Churches on record"[230] backing China's bid for United Nations' membership and calling for the United States to recognize China.[231] Ironically, Allen Dulles' CIA had secretly funded the National Council of Churches.[232]

For Foster Dulles, the NCC vote was a "personal blow and repudiation."[233] On December 4th, 1958, before he died, he would give one more major address that again condemned Communist China[234]; and though Berlin, his last major crisis, would challenge his now-questionable moral authority, Dulles and his political agenda lost the support of the liberal Protestant churches; his manipulation of those churches ceased.[235]

It was 1959.

# Essay Six

# The Oswald Psyops Enigma

John Foster Dulles had been dead but two months[1] when in the summer of 1959 the president made a startling change: he personally took over the diplomacy of the United States[2], despite Christian Herter, John Foster Dulles' designated choice, now held the office of the Secretary of State. Eisenhower later refused (on many occasions) attributing his fresh approach to American/Soviet relations to a rejection of Foster Dulles' "rigid negatives [that] . . . had progressively isolated the United States from the sympathies and the aspirations of most of mankind."[3]

But freed from the deadly Foster Dulles domination of state affairs that had closed down communication between the American government and the Soviets[4], the president began examining his remaining time in office, asking himself what could be done to advance the cause of his country.[5] His response was to reopen that blocked channel of communication.[6]

## Eisenhower Without Dulles

Together with his White House advisor James Hagerty[7], Eisenhower constructed four major political trips: to Europe, to eleven allies on three continents, to Latin America, and to the Far East.[8] In September, 1959, Nikita Khrushchev visited the United States.[9] "In effect, [Eisenhower] . . . and Khrushchev tacitly agreed to work toward general detente."[10] Despite setbacks in Latin America, Eisenhower's tour was supportive of his new peace effort.[11] By May, 1960, international peace was a strong possibility[12], and the president was the world's best hope for that peace.

Earlier in 1955 when the president was seriously ill, I. F. Stone published an essay on October 3rd, 1955, titled "The President's Illness."[13] Identifying Eisenhower's backers as "the Eastern Seaboard moneyed interests standing in opposition to the Pentagon, to "swollen military expenditures," to "the aviation lobby," and to the Democrats as "the cold war party"[14], Stone characterized Eisenhower as a genuine "man of peace," someone willing to sit down with the Soviet leadership and negotiate.[15]

Therefore, the most economical means of discrediting the president (genuine peacemaker or not) was to destroy the scheduled US/Soviet talks, using a provocative

U-2 flight over the Soviet Union, precisely what had happened in May, 1960, two weeks prior to the summit meeting between Eisenhower and Khrushchev in Paris.[16]

## Using Lee Harvey Oswald

What about Lee Harvey Oswald? Why had an apparently defecting Marxist Marine been dropped into an unholy Cold War cauldron? What purposes did Lee Harvey Oswald serve, whether or not it was he who actually went to Europe?

Oswald's first-class mail had been monitored by both the FBI and the CIA from 1959 through 1964.[17] In that major unconstitutional process, both agencies were alerted to a strange and faulty version of the traditional intelligence "illegal" or "legend" (or a version of someone who intended to take part in the creation of an illegal or legend), when Inactive Reserve Marine Lee Harvey Oswald departed for Europe. Once Oswald had defected to the Soviet Union, his resume then looked remarkedly like that of a "dangle" or "false defector."

But whose "illegal"? Whose "false defector"? Was Oswald a creature of the CIA, the FBI, the GRU, the KGB? Or was Oswald the "illegal" agent of an alliance of FBI and CIA officers who had run the pre-assassination Mexico City action involving a fake Oswald?[18] Attorney Bud Fensterwald once observed to me that all clandestine operations have at least two purposes. What purposes could there have been in sending Oswald to Moscow?

One goal (suggested by earlier analysts) was to use Oswald in a plot to mangle President Dwight David Eisenhower's credibility and sabotage the developing Soviet-American peace process. What evidence supports that goal?

Near the end of his Marine career, Oswald had apparently been prepped through a series of military adventures and defense secrets: "Lee Harvey Oswald's movements in the Far East . . . dovetail[ed] with the salient points of the U-2's contribution to the [ongoing] strategic debate [on the so-called Soviet threat] in Washington."[19] Oswald was at Atsugi from September through November, 1957, and both Sputnik and early Soviet ICBM tests occurred[20]; he was with Operation Strongback maneuvers from November 1957 through March 1958[21]; he was at Cubi Point in the beginning of 1958, tracking U-2 "overflights of China"[22] that helped to give the United States significant information about Chinese military movements, China's relations with the Soviet Union, and other important intelligence information.[23] Oswald was in Taiwan in the fall of 1958, privy to American military intentions in the Taiwan Straits.[24] From March through August, 1958, when Oswald was back at Atsugi, the Soviets halted their testing of ballistic missiles[25], and the U-2 flights at Atsugi verified this information.[26] Again Oswald had knowledge of vital military information. After Taiwan, when Oswald was at Atsugi in October and November of 1958, the Atsugi U-2 flights he was monitoring confirmed that the Soviets still had not restarted their ballistic missile testing.[27]

At the very least, Oswald was loaded with U-2 information collected on both China and the Soviet Union, and the KGB would have been extremely interested in what the United States knew about Soviet strengths and weaknesses.[28] Yet when the CIA opened its Oswald 201 file, it failed to "mention . . . his [stated] threat to give up military secrets [to the Soviets]."[29] This failure, historian John Newman remarked, was "extraordinary"[30]: Newman concluded that "circumstantial evidence [indicated] . . . Oswald gave away something the Soviets used [to bring down Gary Powers' U-2 flight]."[31] For Newman, the CIA's so-called molehunters had failed to open a 201 file on Oswald in 1959 "when they knew . . . Oswald had defected and offered to give up radar [and other] secrets . . . [,] a conspicuous breakdown of the Agency's security and counterintelligence functions."[32]

But for this theoretical construction, no breakdown in Agency security need have occurred. Lee Harvey Oswald was deliberately stuffed with military secrets and sent to the Soviets and the KGB by elements of American intelligence, possibly with the collusion of Richard Bissell, the Agency man who authorized the fateful U-2 flight, contravening the President's explicit ban on any further flights. Bissell's mission would have been to destroy the American/Soviet effort at coming to some kind of peaceful terms. This mission might, in fact, have been run by a treasonous cabal of hard-line American and Soviet intelligence agents whose masters were above Cold War differences.

## Complicating the Original Oswald Operation:
## Was Eisenhower the Target?

Either the CIA's Office of Security or its Counterintelligence (or both) apparently piggy-backed a KGB molehunt onto the original Lee Harvey Oswald operation, probably delighting those who had originally planned the Oswald action that sent him to the Soviet Union to be found missing from Switzerland. But the same CIA officers running the Agency's illegal HT/LINGUAL program had made their mail intercept program vulnerable to discovery by attaching an operation to the Red Marine who was himself an HT/LINGUAL mail intercept target.

The Oswald overload may have been effected, however, by a far darker espionage source, intent on ridding itself of an upstart president and compromising the operations of those intelligence agents it had chosen as fall guys. If the National Security State decided President Eisenhower was expendable sooner than the next scheduled national election, and, after having emptied the highest office, had decided to back Richard Nixon in 1960, what better false sponsor than Allen Dulles could the Power Structure have chosen for the elimination—possibly even the murder—of President Eisenhower? And was Oswald (or one of the several defectors who would become redefectors) originally intended as the designated patsy in an attempt on Eisenhower?

No known assassination attempt, however, was run against Eisenhower, and the leaders of the U.S. establishment apparently decided to let American politics take its course, with Richard Nixon running against John F. Kennedy.

At the same time Oswald was picking up his intelligence credits throughout the Far East and simultaneously developing still further his persona as the Red Marine, someone inside the military/Marine/intelligence complex was preparing him to apply for an early discharge, a new passport, and a suspicious tour of Europe that included an application to a progressive Protestant, Unitarian-linked Swiss college whose very name ("Albert Schweitzer") suggested liberal religiosity, the very kind of Christianity that had allied itself idealistically with American intelligence during the First World War, the Second World War, and the Cold War, operations run by the master spy himself, Allen Dulles. Yet that same espionage activity had significant links to reputed Communist agents and assets like Noel Field with his major Quaker and Unitarian connections.

## Oswald as the Perfect Illegal: But with Defects

Oswald had been equipped with what was absolutely necessary to create a perfect espionage illegal, what could have been an authentic intelligence legend. He reportedly brought with him to Europe a real birth certificate and a real passport; according to one author with excellent intelligence connections, Oswald even had his Marine "discharge papers" in his possession when he was in the Soviet Union.[33] Yet everything he was before and after his defection signaled a spy disaster, an inverted illegal who may have been created by American intelligence, was courted by Soviet intelligence, and mistrusted by everyone. Was he, in fact, a false defector being dangled before the suspicious Soviets? His curiously faulted pedigree moved both American and Soviet intelligence to keep him under careful watch (especially through his first class mail) without closing him down.[34] Almost immediately following his reported defection, Oswald was suspected by the FBI as part of an intelligence illegals operation. But whose operation? And why?

Was anyone aware of the bizarre legend being built out of Oswald's Marine history and his trip to Europe, specifically with a new passport?

At least one person was. He was Lee Harvey Oswald (or someone who had designed the false identity dangle acting in his name). On March 19th, 1962, the Office of Naval Intelligence (ONI) prophetically reopened Oswald's file because "Oswald might seek updating of his discharge in the near future."[35] And Oswald indeed made precisely that request in a letter from Minsk that was postmarked March 21st (but dated March 22nd)[36], just three days between the ONI prophecy and its Oswald fulfillment.

As Robert Sam Anson noted, Warren Commission critics assumed Oswald was presenting an argument concerning his defection, wondering where in Minsk he had found a copy of the U.S. Code to support his pleas.[37] That in itself clearly signaled Oswald was being assisted either by the American State Department, American intelligence, or some Soviet entity friendly to Oswald.

But Anson's correction of those critics focused on forged passports as intelligence artifacts and the possibility of an Oswald imposter in the Soviet Union. Though that correction was relevant, the Oswald citation of the U.S. Code had another major intention. The former Marine had argued that the Marine Corps did not have the right to change his discharge to "undesirable" because he was not guilty of violating Title 18, section 1544 of the Code.

What did that section of Code state? That "whoever willfully and knowingly uses or attempts to use any [VALID] passport designed for the use of another" has broken the law.[38] Oswald (or someone prompting Oswald) was specifically denying his passport had been misused in the making of an espionage illegal.

That specific postal act constituted Oswald's smoking letter, proving to anyone who checked the U.S. Code that Lee Harvey Oswald (or his Intelligence handler) was denying knowledge of a false identity/"illegals" action for which he had never been charged. The signal had been sent.

## Was Oswald Used by a KGB/CIA Collaboration?

Barely hinted at in surviving documents and illustrated by non-assassination incidents, the KGB and the CIA (that is, cooperating elements of the ostensibly competing agencies) may have run a 'joint operation' using Oswald, Marina Oswald, or both.[39] Both the CIA and KGB had institutional value invested in the Cold War. But other potential origins for the Oswald Game were the CIA's Office of Security, the Office of Naval Intelligence, or a still undiscovered American business organization supplying cover for Department of Defense "civilian" operatives.

## Was Lee Harvey Oswald a False Defector?

Closely associated with the False Identity/Illegals programs of U.S. intelligence was its False Defectors operation.[40] One American company that certainly qualified as a cover for U.S. false defectors to the Soviet Union was the Rand Development Corporation (RDC).[41]

Sometime between 1973 and 1975, two JFK assassination researchers, Michael Canfield and Alan J. Weberman, attempted to locate the New York headquarters of Rand Development Corporation.[42] Finding RDC's listed Manhattan phone number, they called the number and, instead of RDC, reached the megacorporation Martin-Marietta, listed with the same number.[43] Though the researchers had discovered that Rand Development Corporation was the "crushed foam" division of the conglomerate, Martin-Marietta's response (at the identical number for RDC) was "no one at Martin-Marietta [had] ever heard of Rand [Development Corporation]."[44] Queried at its main office in Rockville, Maryland, Martin-Marietta (with a "large aerospace division"[45]) responded that "Martin-Marietta has a lot of things going on but Rand Development isn't one of them."[46]

The curious ambivalences continued: Canfield and Weberman visited the address given in the New York phone book and found Rand Development was not listed in the building's register.[47] A doorman at the address told them he had worked his post for thirty-four years, but, he said, "there's never been a Rand Development corporation in this building . . . ."[48] The doorman added: "[M]aybe you want the Rand Corporation—it's right across the street at 405 Lexington Avenue."[49]

The RAND Corporation's name has often been spelled "Rand."

The two researchers discovered that Rand Development Corporation was first listed in the Manhattan telephone book in 1958[50], the year the False Defector/False Identity/Illegals programs of U.S. intelligence were revving up their engines. Oddly enough, the RAND Corporation was not listed until 1960, after which (except when the Rand Development Corporation disappeared in 1971-1972 from the phone book) the two companies were both represented.[51]

Though RDC was reportedly established by the Rand family[52] and "RAND" in RAND Corporation was reportedly a acronymic contraction of "Research and Development" (R+AND+D)[53], propinquity may have been all for the two Rand companies.

Physical closeness of the two companies was matched by their U.S. intelligence connections. The RAND Corporation was a well-known think tank with excellent elitist connections[54] and first established for the U.S. Air Force and financed by the Central Intelligence Agency[55]; Daniel Ellsberg had copied the so-called Pentagon Papers while employed at RAND.[56] In the 1950s and 60s, Allan Dulles counted on "former" CIA agents and officers who went into businesses associated with U.S. intelligence and defense, including RAND.[57] RAND was so closely tied to the Agency that crucial CIA documents were often circulated "through other governmental organizations and extra-governmental organizations such as the Rand Corporation . . . ."[58] Rand Development also had close ties to U.S. intelligence: RDC worked on a number of Central Intelligence Agency contracts[59]; its president, Dr. Henry J. Rand, and George Bookbinder, another officer of the company[60], were veterans of the Office of Strategic Services[61]; and, in the late 1950s, "CIA agent Christopher Bird was Rand Development's Washington representative."[62]

The RAND Corporation and Rand Development were not only linked (at least indirectly) by their CIA contracts and contacts; they were also connected through their aerospace programs and the U.S. Air Force. One of the divisions of Martin-Marietta, the parent company of Rand Development Corporation (despite Martin-Marietta's denials[63]) was a leader in aerospace research and development. RAND, "formed by the Air Force,"[64] was ostensibly a creature of the Pentagon, but was most probably a black budget CIA operation. A Pentagon/CIA insider described how the CIA used the U.S. government's offer of aircraft (and afterward, of course, a necessary airfield and base) to eager second and third world nations in order to establish a CIA base.[65] RAND gave important briefings to the CIA and the Pentagon in advanced military technology, including a major presentation on ballistic missiles.[66] As early as April, 1959, RAND was reporting on the development of camera lenses that would ultimately be used in the CIA's U-2 program.[67]

RAND, organized by the Air Force and ultimately funded by the CIA, was, according to one source, initially financed by Sperry-Rand, an aerospace corporation "working closely with the United States Air Force."[68] The vice-chairman of the Sperry-Rand Corporation (the "Rand" in "Sperry-Rand") was the father of the president of the Rand Development Corporation.[69] But this connection between the two "Rands" was, at best, indirect. RAND and Rand Development were directly linked through their Air Force/aerospace interests, but Sperry-Rand (with its provocative Rand family connection) did not midwife the Rand Development Corporation: RDC's actual initial sponsor was Douglas Aircraft.[70]

Still, links between RAND, aerospace companies, and intelligence were relevant: for example, two former officers from RAND moved to Northrop Corporation and, in 1961, hired Bill Savy, "a French lawyer in Paris . . . who ran several [informational] agencies . . . . [Savey] had been an intelligence officer, used for several [unidentified] investigations into the US aerospace industry."[71]

Both RAND and Rand Development Corporation had been part of an intelligence/ military matrix especially attractive to the U.S. False Defector program.

## Robert Edward Webster

Robert Edward Webster, a Navy veteran, was employed by the Rand Development Corporation as a "plastics technician."[72] Webster took part in an RDC "trade exhibition" in Moscow and chose to stay in the Soviet Union rather than return to the United States with the rest of Rand Development's exhibition group.[73] Why was RDC in Moscow? It had been among the earliest U.S. corporations "to negotiate with the Soviet Union for the purchase of [U.S.] technical products and information."[74]

After announcing his decision to remain in the Soviet Union, Webster met with Rand Development Corporation officers Henry Rand and George Bookbinder and the U.S. Embassy's Second Secretary Richard Edward Snyder[75], a Foreign Service officer (characterized in the Warren Report as a former Department of State intelligence official).[76] Snyder had admitted to being a CIA agent for eleven months in 1949 and 1950; the evidence on Snyder's career (collected and analyzed by Philip H. Melanson) supports the suspicion that Foreign Service Officer Snyder was, in fact, a CIA agent under diplomatic cover from 1959 through 1961, the time he was stationed at the U.S. Embassy in Moscow. Relying apparently on James Jesus Angleton, his major CIA source, Edward Epstein stated that Snyder was a CIA agent when he interacted with both Lee Harvey Oswald and Robert Webster. [77]

The House Select Committee on Assassinations (HSCA) was more than curious about Snyder's CIA connections. The committee had discovered that Snyder worked for the CIA as a university campus "spotter" in 1956 and 1957[78], assigned to gain "access to others [unidentified and unexplained] who might be going to the Soviet Union."[79] The HSCA apparently had not realized that U.S. students may have been recruited by the

Agency's campus "spotters" to attend certain overseas educational institutions targeted by the CIA for penetration or observation, including Albert Schweitzer College.

Not many U.S. students would have been planning to go the Soviet Union at the height of the Cold War. Could CIA spotters have been operating at California's El Toro Naval Base or at the First Unitarian Church in Los Angeles in 1958 and 1959, looking for likely recruits?

Whatever Snyder, Rand, and Bookbinder (the attending trio of "former" U.S. intelligence agents who met with Robert Webster) said to Rand Development Corporation's Webster about his defection has not been made available. Declaring he would not come home to the U.S., Webster obtained a technician's job in the Soviet Union, lived with his "Soviet common-law wife" (probably a KGB agent) despite his having an American spouse, and (like Oswald) eventually registered his disappointment with the Soviet Union, asking for repatriation.[80] Robert Edward Webster and Lee Harvey Oswald were on the same timeline: less than two weeks before Oswald announced his defection, Webster had announced his[81]; and Webster left the Soviet Union two weeks before Oswald.[82] A handful of apparent U.S. defectors with suspicious credentials were in the Soviet Union at the same time as Webster and Oswald.[83] The pattern of defection was provocative.

## Richard Edward Snyder: CIA Operative

The temporal confluence of Snyder, Webster, and Oswald in the Soviet Union strongly suggested Richard Edward Snyder, ostensibly a State Department Foreign Service officer, had been assigned by the CIA to monitor an experiment in U.S. intelligence 'dangles' and double agents that included Webster, Oswald, and at least one other U.S. defector, his identity still protected, who wound up in Oswald's Minsk.[84] All of the reputed defectors with whom Snyder had been in touch seemed to display a curious fusion of False Identity, False Defector, and Illegals indicators. And though Snyder was the most important Oswald-as-Defector witness of record, Snyder listed his monitoring of the U-2/Powell episode in the Soviet Union as his one post-graduate accomplishment.[85]

Curious.

Webster and Oswald had a few strange post-Soviet connections. After the Oswald family had returned to Texas, Lee's wife Marina told a Russian friend that her husband had worked at a U.S. "exhibition" in Moscow[86] and had then defected to the Soviet Union.[87] Marina Oswald was, of course, speaking about another former Navy man and defector, Robert Webster, whose Leningrad apartment building address (without his name) had been entered into Marina Oswald's address book.[88]

Could Marina have been mistaken about who her Soviet husband was?

Lee Harvey Oswald, Marina's husband of record, also had an interest in fellow-defector Webster: in 1961, while making arrangements for his family to return to the U.S. from the Soviet Union, Oswald had "asked about the fate of . . . [Robert] Webster who had come to the Soviet Union shortly before he did . . . ."[89]

Webster's re-defection was much more dramatic than Oswald's: Webster was "debriefed in great depth by CIA staff working in conjunction with Air Force representatives."[90] Recall the weave of military (including the Air Force) and intelligence (including the CIA) between RAND and Rand Development (the employer of Robert Webster).

Robert Webster was then "brought to Washington and interrogated for two weeks."[91]

No record of any U.S. intelligence debriefing of Lee Harvey Oswald has ever been made available, though tantalizingly circumstantial evidence has pointed to such an event.[92] Certainly Oswald was as important a defector (and redefector) as Webster.

Were Robert Webster and Lee Harvey Oswald ever mistaken for each other? "[In fact,] Robert Webster . . . looked rather like Oswald," and a CIA psychiatrist who had run a debriefing of a "young American just back from Russia" thought he recognized photos of Lee Harvey Oswald as that "young American."[93]

Or was it the other way around?

If the intention of the Oswald Game was to deter a full examination of and yet heighten anxiety about Lee Harvey Oswald, the bizarre histories of Oswald and his wife Marina and the Webster/Oswald interface were completely successful.

## Oswald's Missions

What might have been Oswald's intelligence role beyond being offered up to the Soviets in the U-2 incident? Realistically, he looked like the point person in a dual secret mission: first, assisting in the search for Soviet intelligence Illegals, including their mail drops and accommodation addresses; and second, helping to trace the double-agent "mole" links between the CIA and the KGB through religious and educational institutions in the United States, Switzerland, and the Soviet Union. Hence his application to the liberal Protestant Albert Schweitzer College with its largely Unitarian background that resonated with the history of Allen Dulles' Swiss intelligence activities and the spymaster's misuse of European churches, clergy, and religious service groups.

That double covert intention would explain why a deliberately faulty False-Identity (and False-Defector) operation was carried out by American counterintelligence utilizing Lee Harvey Oswald. Whoever directed the Oswald Game was thoroughly knowledgeable about both the OSS's and the CIA's counterintelligence manipulation of Quakers, Unitarians, Lutherans, Dutch Reformed clerics, and World Council of Churches' officials as intelligence and espionage contacts, assets, and informants. And those directors were also aware of the FBI's responsibility in tracking down and identifying Soviet illegals and double agents.

Therefore, from the moment Oswald registered to attend Unitarian-sponsored Albert Schweitzer College and without ever setting foot in Switzerland, he moved (or was moved) to the center of a complex and dangerous double-agent operation.

With so many suspicious flaws and so many obvious connections to American intelligence, Oswald was a "legend" begging to be exposed. Yet he was allowed to go largely unchallenged by American intelligence, compromising both the FBI and the CIA as apparent pre-assassination accessories.[94]

Oswald was the perfect patsy to be used in any way his creators saw fit. In the deadliest of all games, Lee Harvey Oswald was framed[95] as the designated assassin in the murder of John F. Kennedy on November 22nd, 1963.

The Illegals and False Defectors projects of Soviet and American intelligence were mutual reciprocals of each other. The U.S. intelligence Illegals operation was a covert psychological warfare (psyops) program, and Oswald's suspicious Marine severance, his passport application, his Albert Schweitzer College application, his projected European trip, and his Soviet defection all looked like a deliberately defective and therefore provocative psyops Illegals action. The U.S. Intelligence False Defectors program was also a covert psyops program, and again Oswald's resume was a perfect fit: a deliberately defective and therefore provocative False Defectors action.

What psyops genius could have created this "Oswald"?

## The American Psychological Warfare Master

C.D. Jackson[96] was the archetypal American establishment operator, yet he was nearly invisible as he stood at the elbow of political power: "although one of the most significant figures in U.S. Cold War history, [he] has remained strangely unknown, his activities largely unrecognized."[97] Thoroughly upper class, Jackson was a member of the board of directors of the Boston Symphony[98], the Lincoln Center for the Performing Arts, the Metropolitan Opera Association, and Project HOPE[99]; he was one of fourteen trustees of the Carnegie Corporation (among the oldest and most powerful of philanthropic organizations)[100]; and he was, of course, a top executive of the Luce publishing empire (Time, Life, and Fortune).

Even before attending Princeton, Jackson had traveled extensively, had been educated in Switzerland, and spoke both Italian and French with great fluency.[101] In the fall of 1931, C.D. Jackson visited "his good friend"[102] Henry R. Luce (then Time's editor-in-chief) and, despite lacking any media experience, Jackson reportedly persuaded Luce to hire him, becoming Luce's "assistant to the president."[103] When Luce introduced Life magazine six years later, Jackson was appointed its general manager.[104] By 1940, Luce was the acknowledged master of American popular media, in touch with his enormous reading audience and, at the same time, shaping that audience's consciousness[105]; and his chief associate in that operation was C.D. Jackson.

In 1940, C.D. Jackson's ability to read attitude and ideology was already firmly established, and Jackson was appointed an administrative vice president of Time, Inc., a position emphasizing "trouble-shooting and public relations."[106]

Whether in advertising or propaganda, Jackson had become the master of the word.[107]

That same year, Luce and Jackson decided to support the British war effort and overcome any remaining American isolationism, preparing Time/Life audiences for entry into the European conflict.[108] Jackson and Luce established the Council for Democracy, characterized by an admiring biographer as "a committee of liberal and moderate journalists and academicians . . . to promote democracy in American society."[109] The Council was one of Jackson's earliest public explorations of psychological warfare activity, opposing all groups, "nazi, fascist, communist, [and] pacific"[110] committed to keeping the U.S. out of the war.[111]

The Council's greatest success was "to highlight Jackson's talents as a propagandist."[112]

Certainly more striking in its psyops dimension was another Jackson formulation in 1941: promoting the establishment of an American "institute for democratic leadership."[113] Speaking at Princeton University, Jackson argued that the proposal was "not in slavish imitation of the Nazi idea"[114]: though, in fact, it was a version of the Reich's "Fuehrer Schule."[115] Young Americans would be trained for two years as "pro-Consuls of democracy" in a program that sounded remarkably like behavior modification.[116] Jackson (with Christian Herter, later to become Foster Dulles' successor as Secretary of State) sponsored the Foreign Service Education Foundation, just such a leadership institute ultimately folded into Johns Hopkins University's School for Advanced International Studies.[117]

C. D. Jackson was a major organizer of Freedom House in 1942, dedicated "to mobilize public opinion" against America's wartime ally, the Soviet Union[118]; in a propaganda pamphlet, Freedom House president Herbert Ager characterized the Soviet Union as a "slave system."[119] The argument was, of course, C.D. Jackson's. Jackson had helped plant psyops seeds in 1940-1942 blossoming three years later into Cold War flora.[120]

In 1942, Jackson was called upon by the U.S. State Department's Bureau of Economic Warfare to run a "mission to Turkey."[121] At risk was a British/U.S. contract to mine and buy precious Turkish chrome; the West's contract was vulnerable, and German agents were moving in.[122] Jackson used his linguistic, public relations (read "psyops"), and covert operations skills (an early fusion of his several political tricks) to defeat the German attempt at co-opting the Allies' chrome source.[123]

The people who helped run the Cold War's psychological warfare operations gained their training and experience as agents of the Office of Strategic Services (OSS) in the OSS's branch called "Morale Operations" (MO)[124]; those OSS/MO veterans subsequently taught psyops students in the CIA. The work of the "Morale Operations" branch was "disinformation" and "black" propaganda: "subversive, its sources [were] disguised and its products disowned by . . . [the U.S.] government if an operation backfired."[125] Among the OSS's MO officers was the influential Edmund Taylor, a former CBS newsperson who had composed "the basic book on psychological warfare, *The Strategy of Terror.[126]* Much of what C.D. Jackson practiced was apparently absorbed from Taylor's published record of his own experience of German psychological warfare and, as an OSS officer, his subsequent psyops theory.[127]

In Washington, representatives of the State Department, the Office of War Information, the Army and Navy, and the "Morale Operations" Branch of the OSS had met weekly as members of the Psychological Warfare Board coordinating information and disinformation as propaganda instruments.[128]

## C.D. Jackson and SHAEF

But it was in London at Supreme Headquarters Allied Expeditionary Forces (SHAEF) commanded by General Dwight David Eisenhower[129] (and in the field) that the blackest psyops propaganda campaign of World War II was successfully run in 1944-1945. Though it often appeared as if the OSS operated independently of U.S./Allied military command, the Office of Strategic Services, created in June, 1942, was (as defined within the wartime chain of command) a service of the American Joint Chiefs of Staff.[130] On October 27th, 1943, the JCS commissioned "Morale Operations" (created on January 3rd, 1943[131]) to perform "all forms of morale subversion."[132] The "psychological operations" against Germany, run out of Eisenhower's SHAEF, were driven by his Psychological Warfare Division controlling and directing the OSS's Morale Operations Branch[133] using "dirty," fictional, and deceptive materials, including faked documents, radio transmissions, newspapers (real and fraudulent), and other media and communication devices to achieve the Division's psyops goals.[134]

The director of the Office of War Information (OWI) was Elmer Davis who had rejected several attempts to convert the OWI to psyops.[135] Bill Donovan argued for an American "black" propaganda intelligence capability, but Davis had successfully kept OWI out of the field.[136] Donovan, however, held on, and with the birth of the OSS followed by the jousting in early 1942 for influence over the OSS through the "Joint Psychological War Committee," the end of 1942 saw the OSS safely under the protection of the Joint Chiefs of Staff, its psyops license issued by the JCS.[137]

Yet when the (non-combat) psyops program in London at Supreme Headquarters, Allied Expeditionary Forces, was fully operational, the psyops expert who organized and ran General Dwight David Eisenhower's Psychological Warfare Division at SHAEF was an official of the Office of War Information (OWI): C.D. Jackson, a veteran of the North African campaign.

## C.D. Jackson in North Africa

What had happened in North Africa?

The United States had rejected Charles De Gaulle as the leader of its French anti-German allies; instead, President Roosevelt and General Dwight David Eisenhower supported the representatives of the Vichy French government in North Africa[138] headed by Admiral Darlan, "a notorious Nazi collaborator."[139] Public opinion in Great Britain and the United States fulminated against Eisenhower's apparent collaboration with his Nazi allies; the entire "anti-Fascist" world was upset.[140] But

Eisenhower stubbornly maintained that all political problems were secondary to military decisions.[141]

Why?

As early as February, 1941, President Roosevelt had used an "undercover emissary" to find an alternative to de Gaulle and to close an important economic accord.[142] He succeeded; North Africa, controlled by Nazi collaborators, was freed of an Allied blockade and was opened to American "economic penetration."[143] Oil was on the mind of the United States.[144]

But Great Britain, supporting De Gaulle and his commitment to maintaining the French colonial empire (and implicitly backing British imperialism), found American pragmatic conduct in North Africa intolerable.[145] So did the U.S. Office of War Information in North Africa.[146] The situation was "untenable."[147]

President Roosevelt sent Milton Eisenhower[148], the general's brother and the associate director of the Office of War Information (OWI), to North Africa with four "specific assignments" in December, 1942.[149] Most important for C.D. Jackson and the future of American psyops, the OWI associate director was "to study the work of the OWI in psychological warfare and make changes if they were needed."[150]

Milton Eisenhower, a convinced psyops advocate, found that "drastic action" was necessary; he began a systematic exclusion of Gaullist sympathizers, replaced by OWI agents who arrived with Patton in North Africa.[151] But the transformation was not complete.[152] In the spring of 1943, C.D. Jackson was called from his *Time* magazine post to serve the American government, having already established his major psyops credentials. As an OWI officer, Jackson was deployed to North Africa to be in "full charge of OWI operations"[153]; he became "deputy chief" of the Psychological Warfare Branch (PWB) in General Dwight David Eisenhower's North African Allied Force Headquarters (AFHQ)[154]. He was the civilian director of the PWB[155], given a challenging task: "to integrate psychological warfare into America's overall military policy."[156]

Arriving in North Africa, Jackson met and ultimately bonded with General Robert Alexis McClure[157], who would become his psyops associate and close friend.

## General Robert Alexis McClure:
## American Military Psyops and C.D. Jackson

McClure had spent time in the Philippines and "in a variety of infantry and service-school assignments . . . ."[158] In 1941, he was sent to London, a lieutenant colonel, as an assistant military attaché.[159] McClure's previous military career (from 1915 through 1941) had qualified him for special intelligence duties: he became a brigadier general, then the American Embassy's military attaché in London, with special duty as the "military attaché to nine European governments in exile."[160]

In September, 1942, General Eisenhower designated McClure as his "[military] chief of intelligence for the European theater of operations."[161] Then in December, 1942, McClure was given a new assignment: he was designated the chief of the (North

African) Allied Headquarters Information and Censorship Section (INC), fusing "public relations, censorship, and psychological warfare."[162] McClure drew a number of separate Army functions into a single military command.[163] With C.D. Jackson controlling the "civilian" side of psyops in the North African operation, Eisenhower had his psychological warfare team in place.

In the spring of 1943, Milton Eisenhower made an address, "Psychological Warfare"[164], to the Kansas Bankers' Association in Topeka, stressing the war was not simply physical but "a struggle for men's minds."[165] "Truth," the OWI associate director had asserted, was on the side of the Allies[166], or at least C.D. Jackson's version of the truth.

OWI official Milton Eisenhower put his seal of approval on Jackson's reorganizational job[167], and by October, 1943, C.D. Jackson had General Eisenhower's complete "acceptance of the Psychological Warfare Board as a regular part of Allied Headquarters."[168] It was "one of the earliest [headquarters] units to achieve a truly allied organization."[169]

Despite a common perception that General Eisenhower thought psyops a tactical war weapon rather than strategic, the North African invasion—Operation Torch—and subsequent events dictated that "psychological warfare" would ultimately take precedence over "conventional military tactics," first in North Africa, then in Sicily and Italy, and, finally, especially after the war, in Germany.[170]

When Eisenhower established his Psychological Warfare Division at Supreme Headquarters, Allied Expeditionary Force (PWD/SHAEF) in London, General McClure became its military director, again complementing C.D. Jackson as PWD's civilian director. McClure, "commander of all U.S. Army psychological warfare activities during World War II and much of the cold war, called C.D. Jackson and William Paley (of CBS) his "right and left hands" during World War II, crediting the pair with a profound grasp of psyops policy and practice.[171]

All the techniques of behavior modification, false identity, deep deception, and fictional event-staging[172] that became key elements of American espionage legends, illegals, and false defectors were developed and practiced successfully under C.D. Jackson in SHAEF's Psychological Warfare Division.

Jackson as psyopsmaster had shuffled easily from an operation ostensibly dedicated to straight media communication (Elmer Davis' Office of War Information) to "black" psyops (SHAEF's Psychological Warfare Division), and he would dance from information to disinformation and back again throughout his relatively short but intense career.

In July, 1946, McClure wrote to Jackson (who had already returned to Time-Life, Inc., as its Vice President); he summarized for Jackson what it really meant to be the military director of the Psychological Warfare Division: "We now control 37 newspapers, 6 radio stations, 314 theatres, 642 movies, 101 magazines, 237 book publishers, 7,384 book dealers and printers, and conduct about 15 public opinion surveys a month, as well as publish one newspaper with 1,500,000 circulation, 3 magazines, run the Associated Press of Germany (DANA), and operate 20 library centers . . . ."[173]

Just one year after the end of World War II, the American Army was running the largest psychological warfare operation in history, with C D. Jackson's friend and psyops associate in charge.

Though Jackson had returned to the Luce publishing empire, he continued his propaganda work: Henry Luce designated Jackson the developer of the new international editions of both Time and Life, and Jackson pushed "capitalism and its bourgeois values by disseminating as many copies of his [Time, Inc.] magazines as possible [into Eastern Europe] . . . before the Iron Curtain slammed down."[174]

Psychological warfare in the immediate postwar period and during the Truman years[175] remained on the shadowy edges of intelligence gathering and covert operations, the term "psychological warfare" itself characterized as "an almost elastic perversion of language designed to prevent acceptance and responsibility for its implications."[176]

Beginning in 1946 (and through four subsequent years), Robert McClure argued for a regular place in the Army's instructional and in-the-field plans for psyops training and strategy, writing to both influential military personnel and civilian government figures, including C.D. Jackson.[177]

In early 1946, McClure wrote the War Department, arguing that America's "military psychological warfare capability" was absolutely indispensable and should be rebuilt.[178] On December 12th, 1946, the U.S. National Intelligence Authority was sent a psychological warfare report from the Coordinating Committee of the State Department, War Department, and the Navy (the Committee to be replaced ultimately by the National Security Council) establishing psyops as central to American "national aims and military objectives."[179]

McClure's persistence paid off: he was sent from Germany to the United States in the summer of 1948 as "Chief, New York Field Office, Civil Affairs Division, [reporting to Chief of Civil Affairs, the Pentagon,] . . . responsible for supporting U.S. reorientation and re-education efforts in the occupied countries of Germany, Austria, Japan, and Korea."[180]

McClure used his German organizational structure in the New York Field Office, with "sections for press, periodicals, motion pictures, radio, theatre, music, arts, exhibits, libraries and book rights."[181] Now the pair of psyops masters who had shared psychological warfare duties during the North African and European campaigns were working in New York, in charge of the two largest producers of white, grey, and black pro-America propaganda: on the civilian side, C.D. Jackson at Time, Inc.; on the military side, Robert McClure.

In May, 1948, George Kennan, the State Department's chief of the new Policy Planning Staff, signed on to pysops[182], and with NSC 10/2, drafted by Kennan, a CIA within the CIA was created: the Office of Special Projects that later became the Agency's Office of Policy Coordination.[183] One year earlier, the CIA's General Counsel had raised concerns about the legality of running psyops, "morale operations" and "black propaganda" without obtaining Congressional approval.[184] But Kennan[185], his associate Frank Wisner[186] (a close friend of C.D. Jackson), and Jackson himself had no scruples about avoiding legalisms in the service of psyops (nor about U.S. intelligence collaborating with "Nazi criminals"[187]).

Just as the OSS and later the CIA used religious groups and individuals through two World Wars and the Cold War, the Agency by 1948 was using the "Non-Communist Left," including intellectuals, artists, and former Party members in the fight against Communism, often knowingly, sometimes not.[188] One of the Agency's leaders in its anti-Communist pysops action enlisted the help of a psyops hero, C.D. Jackson, who gave the Agency enthusiastic support and advice.[189]

## C.D. Jackson: America's Psyops Chief

C.D. Jackson was an archetypal anti-Communist; just a few years before he became Eisenhower's "Psychological Warfare Director," Jackson planted his forward flag: "The ingredient that is going to make us win [this psychological war] is fanaticism. Not only must we be fanatics ourselves, but, we have to instill fanaticism for our cause in a lot of doubtful friends and even more doubtful on-the-fencers."[190]

In May, 1949, Jackson joined Allen Dulles in the founding of the National Committee for a Free Europe and, despite a clause in the Committee's "founding statute" to the contrary, dedicated to Cold War propaganda.[191] The group (most often designated as the "Free Europe Committee"[192]) became the mother of all psyops, with its founding fathers including Dulles, Jackson, Lucius Clay, Francis Spellman, John C. Hughes, and Dwight David Eisenhower[193], a veritable Who's Who of CIA psychological warfare innovators and supporters.

The initial idea for the committee has been attributed to Allen Dulles, who in turn went to Frank Wisner and his backlist of hundreds, possibly thousands, of "dispossessed Eastern European notables fidgeting throughout the West . . . ."[194] Dulles then took Wisner to Columbia University president Dwight David Eisenhower, who was always a dedicated psychological warrior; with "Eisenhower's prestige, Dulles picked up backers from everywhere in the Establishment."[195]

In 1949, as if to celebrate his preeminence among Establishment Cold Warriors, C.D. Jackson became the publisher of Time, Inc.'s *Fortune* magazine.[196]

## C.D. Jackson Spreads His Psyops Wings Across America

Psychological manipulation of individuals and groups, whatever the procedure may have been called in the 18th and 19th centuries, drew upon discoveries in anatomy, mesmerism, hypnotism, counseling, studies in "hysteria," rhetorical theory, psychoanalysis, advertising, behavior modification, and psychiatry. In the same periods the literary forms of irony, satire, and comedy and the less reputable verbal arts of slander, libel, and manufactured lies were applied. Most of these genres, forms, and strategies were enlisted in the service of social class and political power, though counterattacks by alternative and adversarial outlets were still available But by the time the U.S. establishment had declared a pysops war against Communism, the American establishment media had been overtaken almost completely by the crusade against perceived revolutionary movements, and that mainstream media was led by the Jackson/Luce *Time* machine: "The ninety-eight boxes of [Jackson's] ... correspondence in the Eisenhower Library ... reveal that the starting points for many of his views on foreign policy and international business were the conferences in Time offices with Luce and his associates. In the hierarchy of American Centurions, CDJ and Luce directed the hydra-headed media team."[197]

The National Committee for a Free Europe expected "the voluntary silence of powerful media personalities ... to cloak its true operations in secrecy."[198] In fact, influential popular media officers were some of the earliest members of the NCFE: DeWitt Wallace of Readers' Digest, Henry Luce of Time and Life, and, most importantly, the 1951 entry to the NCFE who would run Radio Free Europe, C.D. Jackson, chief editor of Fortune magazine.

Key members of the NCFE admitted that the organization's American intelligence links, government funding, and fundamental overt political and covert intentions would never surface as they were protected by the union of psyops, media, and money dedicated to U.S. Cold War goals.[199]

The corporate-propaganda complex developed still further. Enlisting key elements of the American business/government collaboration, C.D. Jackson established "Enterprise America," an open psyops conspiracy of large dimensions: "Enterprise America was [intended] to transform private domestic business ... into a cooperative effort involving international expansion, government support, and interchangeable business-government personnel practices."[200] What had been an ad hoc crossover of commercial and government people for at least one hundred years was now to become public policy: Jackson had patented D.C.'s revolving door.

At an open and non-conspiratorial level, C. D. Jackson's plan for an American government/corporate fusion was an exact match for his in-place psyops conspiracy: "Through ECA, the Point Four Program, and participation at all levels of the Washington bureaucracy, business would merge with the State, and [C.D. Jackson's] Enterprise America would be affirmed."[201] "As publisher of the Fortune, CDJ was in the unique position of being able to promote a new partnership between business and government among the very people who had opposed all New Deal policies and ... continued to oppose ... [the] reconstruction program for devastated Europe."[202]

Cromwell and Sullivan, John Foster Dulles at State, and Allen Dulles (always helping to run one covert operation or another) found Jackson's business/government/culture combination extremely appealing.[203]

Jackson promoted Enterprise America in a series of appearances and writings in 1949 and 1950, melding "free enterprise," anti-Communism, and advertising in a simmering psyops soup.[204] And Jackson left no doubt as to who would lead this revolutionary American transformation: its hero was General Dwight David Eisenhower.[205]

## Jackson and McClure in Psyops Control

Enterprise America scored its first important victory in 1950: Jackson (as America's top psyops expert) was called upon to present "a list of psychological warfare personnel suitable for employment in sensitive posts . . . submitted to the Office of the Secretary of the Army . . . ."[206] The Jackson list complemented an earlier memorandum of June, 1947, that General Robert McClure had sent to then Army Chief of Staff Dwight David Eisenhower, giving "a list of former PWD/SHAEF members . . . [McClure] recommended for forming a [military] psychological warfare reserve."[207] Following Jackson's recommendations, Eisenhower, Bedell Smith, Lucius Clay, and C.D. Jackson began in 1950 developing "America's political-warfare strategies"[208]: though three of the four had held generalships and Jackson had worked directly for General Eisenhower, the four became the earliest directors the United States' civilian presence on the "experimental battlegrounds" of psychological warfare.[209]

Concurrently, almost immediately after hostilities broke out between South and North Korea[210], Robert McClure was asked to report to Major General Charles Bolte, Army Staff G3, in order to assist in preparing certain "organizational steps" to implement using psychological warfare in "the Korean situation or . . . a general war."[211] First a psychological warfare division was established in G3 with McClure as its director, then a "special staff office reporting directly to the Army Chief of Staff," and finally, on January 15th, 1951, the Office of the Chief Psychological Warfare (OCPW), with Robert McClure holding the Office title.[212] McClure was certain that "unconventional warfare" was the natural partner of psyops, and argued for its complementary development within his "Office."[213]

The Pentagon accepted McClure's argument, and he established three divisions for the OCPW: "Psychological Warfare, Requirements, and Special Operations."[214] Prototype psyops field units out of Fort Riley were developed and dispatched to Korea and Europe "in the event of war with the Soviet Union."[215] Hence, whatever positive motives McClure had for serving his nation and the American military, his OCPW became a part of the escalating Cold War.

## C.D. Jackson, Dulles, and the CIA

By 1951, C.D. Jackson had unfurled the flag of the "American Crusade"[216] to be led by the Crusade for Freedom, a CIA front[217], ostensibly a private and independent agency, with Jackson's associate (former general) Lucius Clay as chairperson[218]. Behind the Crusade for Freedom, organized to appear to be a "spontaneous movement" lauding freedom and, more importantly, to support and raise funds for Radio Free

Europe, was the National Committee for a Free Europe (NCFE).[219] In February, 1951, C.D. Jackson became the president of the National Committee.[220]

The entire NCFE structure had "CIA officers in [all its] key positions"[221], placed there by Jackson's partner, Allen Dulles.[222] In Germany, Theodore Shackley, the CIA Station Chief in Berlin, "coordinated [his Agency] activities with [Jackson's] Radio Free Europe . . . ."[223]

The Crusade for Freedom sported the actor Ronald Reagan, "a leading spokesman and publicist"[224], and laundered funds for an operation, "the International Refugee Committee" in New York, run by ex-OSS agent and future CIA director Bill Casey; the IRC "allegedly coordinated the exfiltration of Nazis from Germany to the States"[225] where they then joined Jackson's anti-Communist psyops campaign.[226]

Jackson's NCFE became a major educational psyops force, using European exiles recruited by American intelligence for anti-Soviet research and lectures.[227] The NCFE created the Free University in Exile, based in Strasbourg and incorporated in 1951 as an educational institution under New York State law.[228]

The entire NCFE operation was a psychological warfare triumph for C.D. Jackson as he lied to the world and, in particular, to the American people, running both open and covert "bizarre activities," all of them provocations designed to free the Central European countries under the control of the Soviet Union.[229] And the crown jewel of Jackson's NCFE was Radio Free Europe.[230] Both RFE and Radio Liberty continued to operate with full CIA direction and support through June 30th, 1971.[231]

Double agents like Josef Swiatlo, the Polish defector used by Allen Dulles against Noel Field, worked for C.D. Jackson at Radio Free Europe, and Swiatlo surfaced alarmingly (for the CIA) in the JFK assassination inquiry.[232]

"[Most of] America's cultural Cold Warriors found themselves caught in a dangerous paradox," arguing for "art and politics" to be totally distinct when the Nazi connections of certain artists and writers were examined, but happily fusing the political and the artistic in support of anti-Communism.[233] But paradox never bothered Jackson; in the name of psyops he manipulated American artists and writers; European émigrés; assorted poets, novelists, and literary critics; movie producers, directors, writers, and actors; whole orchestras.[234] "In the early 1950s, one man alone did more than any other to set the agenda for American cultural warfare. As president of National Committee for a Free Europe, and later, special advisor to Eisenhower on psychological warfare, C.D. Jackson was one of the most influential covert strategists in America.[235]

Propaganda techniques developed during World War II were tested and perfected in early Cold War newsreels and documentaries made for the United States Information Agency (USIA) and probably American intelligence by Hearst-Metrotone News in New York, recorded in dozens of languages for worldwide distribution.[236] C.D. Jackson was active in cinema psyops[237]: directing the National Security Agency's Operations Coordinating Board, he was able to "oversee the activities of [both] the CIA . . . [and] the USIA . . . ."[238]

George Michael Evica

In May, 1952, C.D. Jackson was burning brightly in a sky of psyops stars. Since he had first been called to North Africa during the war to transform Eisenhower's psyops program, Jackson had worked to integrate all of the American civilian efforts in psychological warfare.[239] An important Jackson moment came at the historic Princeton meeting, in May, 1952.[240] Representatives congregated from the State Department, the CIA, the Psychological Strategy Board, the CIA's Center for International Studies (officially housed at M.I.T.), and the National Committee for a Free Europe and Radio Free Europe (RFE).[241] Jackson's super psyops conference was to make a major statement on policy, a "blueprint" for anti-Soviet action[242]: Jackson, his NCFE, and his RFE pushed for crucial psychological warfare goals.[243]

In that same May of 1952, Robert McClure convinced General J. Lawton Collins, Army Chief of Staff, to fuse "the training activities for psychological warfare and Special Forces."[244] The Psychological Warfare [and Special Forces] Center at Fort Bragg, North Carolina, was initiated as the Psychological Warfare School with "two instructional divisions," one for psyops, the other for Special Forces.[245]

C. D. Jackson participated as an idea generator and speech writer in Eisenhower's successful run for the presidency, with his salary and that of Emmet Hughes paid for by the Luce media empire. After Eisenhower was victorious, important work had to be done fine-tuning the intelligence/psyops engine.

## C.D. Jackson, Eisenhower, and the Control of Psyops in America

Both the National Security Council and the CIA had been established during Truman's presidency, but C.D. Jackson's Enterprise America president was Dwight David Eisenhower.[246] The transformations of both the State Department and CIA anticipating an Eisenhower era were executed with the approval of a powerful American establishment that controlled American spycraft: "The choice of John Foster Dulles [as Eisenhower's Secretary of State] was looked upon as a double plus by the intelligence community leaders . . . [:] Dulles . . . [had] ties to military intelligence [that] went back to before World War I . . . [as] an active member of the intelligence subculture fraternity, aiding an operation here and there with his legal and business connections as well as being himself a producer and consumer of intelligence information."[247] John Foster Dulles' duplicity certainly did not impede the development of a strong psyops component in American espionage activities.

The development of a major psychological warfare dimension of American Intelligence, the designation of Allen Dulles as Director of the CIA, the reorganization of Eisenhower's National Security Council, and, finally, the actual control of the Central Intelligence Agency were all placed in the hands of Robert Cutler, whose American establishment resume included a Harvard College degree, service in the American Expeditionary Force, 1917-1919, a Harvard Law School degree, a prestigious Massachusetts law practice, World War II military experience (he exited as a brigadier general) with significant "procurement" duties, executive experience in broadcasting,

Truman's secretary of the Army, Atomic Energy Commission chairperson (including overseeing the hydrogen bomb project), the Psychological Strategy Board's initial director, and president and director of Boston's prestigious Old Colony Trust Company Bank[248]; Cutler left Old Colony only when Dwight David Eisenhower called him to presidential service.

Robert Cutler became Ike's "special assistant for National Security Affairs"[249]: prior to ever taking office, Eisenhower as president-elect informed the executive secretary of the National Security Council (NSC) that "Robert Cutler would be his administrative assistant with special responsibilities for the NSC."[250] Cutler had become, in fact, the president-elect's NSC representative and reorganizer.

Cutler exhaustively reviewed the history and performance of the National Security Council and carefully codified the NSC's structure and operation, making sure that Council practice from 1947 through 1953 and the National Security Act of 1947 became the fused frame of future NSC actions and operations.[251] Only a few but important modifications were necessary to make C.D. Jackson, who was already Eisenhower's Cold War/psyops chief officer, a key facilitator of major CIA covert operations.[252] Cutler's carefully-prepared NSC reforms allowed C.D. Jackson to move in and out of crucial advisory capacities and roles in the State Department, the National Security Council, the CIA, and the White House while simultaneously monitoring the power structure's disinformation and propaganda media operations, specifically at Time, Inc.[253]

On March 17th, 1953, Eisenhower accepted Cutler's report on the National Security Council and the CIA.[254]

Cutler (and most probably Jackson) had anticipated the problem of controlling American psyops espionage activity. Cutler recommended that the director of the Psychological Strategy Board be dropped as an "observer" to the National Security Council[255] and "the special assistant to the president for Cold War Planning . . . [become] an advisor to the council . . . ."[256] The accepted recommendation seemed to eliminate psyops representation on the NCS, but it actually elevated C.D. Jackson, already Eisenhower's "Cold War" designate to the NSC, to be the White House's ad hoc director of national psychological warfare.

Almost immediately after taking over as Eisenhower's special assistant for National Security Affairs, Cutler perceived still more 'problems' of National Security Council coordination.[257] Relying on Cutler's judgment, Eisenhower established on January 24th, 1953, the President's Committee on International Information Activities: its commission was (take a deep breath) "to make a survey and evaluation of the international information policies and activities of the executive branch and the policies and activities related thereto, with particular reference to the international relations and national security of the United States."[258]

The key word was, of course, "information." What kind of information (and disinformation)? And who would monitor and produce that information?

The chairman of the committee was William H. Jackson (former deputy chief of the CIA); as many committees and commissions were designated by their chairperson's name, the committee was identified as the "Jackson Committee." Its seven members were all dedicated supporters of American intelligence[259], especially covert operations and psychological warfare, and the inclusion of Robert Cutler, Gordon Gray, and C.D. Jackson made its recommendations predictable. In fact, Jackson's psyops influence during the group's deliberations resulted in the "Jackson Committee" often being attributed to C.D. Jackson.[260]

C.D. Jackson frequently wore several symbolic identification badges at Cold War intelligence gatherings, a technique he developed that blurred his actual representative role. At Jackson Committee meetings, for example, he "officially . . . represented the State Department . . . while informally he represented the president."[261] John Foster Dulles would have been surprised, at least, that Jackson represented any part of the Secretary of State's Cold War strategy.

The Committee recommended that the National Security Council's Psychological Strategy Board (an offspring of C.D. Jackson's associate, Gordon Gray) be eliminated.[262] Yet C.D. Jackson gained more psyops power because of that excision: how could less become more?

The earlier April, 1951, National Security Council modifications established an important subcommittee, the Psychological Strategy Board (PSB).[263] The specific revision, as it recognized the close fit between covert actions and psychological warfare operations, charged the PSB with examining all existing and proposed NSC/CIA covert projects and establishing their "desirability and feasibility."[264] Why, then, would Gordon Gray, the very progenitor of the Psychological Strategy Board, vote for its abolition? The "staff," "board," or "panel" that made the covert machinery run for the National Security Council, placed between the NSC and the Psychological Strategy Board, rendered the effective control and direction of psyops cumbersome[265]; further, the Jackson Committee had a crucial argument for eliminating the Psychological Strategy Board; according to the panel (led by Gordon Gray, Robert Cutler, and C.D. Jackson), "there is a 'psychological' aspect or implication to every diplomatic, economic, or military policy and action."[266] EVERY policy decision AND every overt or covert operation had a psyops "aspect or implication." Therefore, in place of the PSB, the Jackson panel recommended that an "Operations Coordinating Board" (OCB) be established "to coordinate the detailed implementation of detailed operational plans developed . . . to carry out [so-called] approved NSC policies."[267] Note the important redundancy: "detailed."

The OCB had only five members: the undersecretary of state (the OCB's chair); the deputy secretary of defense; the director of the Foreign Operations Administration; the Director of the CIA; and "a representative of the president to be designated by the president."[268]

Only two of those OCB participants had any real American intelligence power, and both were dedicated psyops supporters: Allen Dulles, the Director of the Central Intelligence Agency, and the president's "representative," C.D. Jackson.[269]

When the OCB was established, "the president designated his special assistant for Cold War Planning [who was C.D. Jackson] to serve as . . . [Eisenhower's] representative on the OCB."[270] Therefore, critical covert intelligence operations (all by definition having a psyops dimension) AND psychological warfare operations were under the direct influence of C.D. Jackson for the first two (or more) years of the Eisenhower administration.

Even before the Jackson Committee report was presented to the president, C.D. Jackson was running "psychological warfare operations" for the White House, according to Jackson himself, "constantly informing and persuading the members of the Government as to their Cold War responsibilities."[271]

When the Jackson Committee finally submitted its report to Eisenhower, the president was disturbed: what about the crucial "psychological factor"?[272] Jackson gave the president his assurance that inside the Operations Coordinatingl Board (the OCB) was now a smaller "think tank" monitoring the "psychological dynamics" of ALL covert actions.[273] This "think tank" was, in fact, the "Planning Board" (later called by a series of names and number combinations) inside the OCB, and dominated, of course, by the president's designate, C.D. Jackson.

## C.D. Jackson and the Korean Brainwashing Problem

As Eisenhower's pysops chief, Jackson also had to deal with the other and even darker side of psychological warfare. During the "Korean Conflict," captured American servicemen had been ill-prepared for hostile interrogation and sometimes successful behavior modification: "Government officials had long known of the deplorable behavior of American POWS, but had worked fastidiously to conceal the facts from a wider audience."[274] On orders from C.D. Jackson, "indoctrinated Korean prisoners" (that is, returned U.S. POWs who had reportedly been "brainwashed") were to be "kept in one place"[275], segregated and under guard, until Jackson (or his designated psychological warfare spokesperson) could manufacture a cover "story."[276] What else was done with those segregated veterans may be an even more important story. Many of the Korean vets who were not sequestered by Jackson were strongly suspected by the CIA of having been subjected to "mind control."[277]

Jackson was everywhere that psyops was a necessity: he "attended meetings of the Cabinet, the National Security Council, the Council on Foreign Economic Policy, and the . . . Operations Coordinating Board . . . to administer political and economic warfare . . . and oversee the activities of the CIA, the USIA, and all Cabinet departments."[278]

## C. D. Jackson and the Cold War Psyops Fronts

When tensions mounted in the Cold War, President Eisenhower would call together a small, inner "circle" of psyops advisors: Allen Dulles, John Foster Dulles, and C.D. Jackson.[279]

Throughout his career, Jackson was supremely opportunistic, a function of his creative/situational responses to immediate political stimuli.[280] Significantly, C.D.

Jackson played a major part in the Eisenhower administration's response to Stalin's death in March, 1953, developing it into a media-wide propaganda action[281] that included Eisenhower's "Chance for Peace" speech on April 16th, 1953.[282]

In that same year, one of Jackson's OPC psyops consultants James Burnham estimated that more than one billion dollars a year was being allocated to "a wide variety of [unidentified] psychological warfare projects . . . ."[283]

Having been given control of U.S. covert operations, the National Security Council's 54/12 committee, the "inner circle" of power in the OCB (its five members including Allen Dulles and C.D. Jackson) made the decision in early August, 1953, to overthrow the legal government of Guatemala.[284] On September 4th, 1953, the Eisenhower administration's in-house covert operations experts combined with the president's top psyops advisors led by C.D. Jackson to plan and execute the destruction of the Arbenz government of Guatemala.[285] Assembling material from Army G-2 files and the FBI, CIA, and State Department, C.D. Jackson's Special Staff at the OCB prepared a plan deliberately and falsely blackening President Arbenz' character and reputation; the material was then sent "to appropriate individuals throughout the Americas."[286] A series of propaganda and terrorist actions followed, targeting Arbenz and Guatemala[287], including unprecedented "search and seizure" of ships bound for Guatemala.[288] "According to all U.S. conventions, the policy represented terrorism, illegal and belligerent action [that] . . . was historically considered an act of war."[289]

The United States, with the president in full agreement, had decided to run a "secret" war against Guatemala, using black propaganda, bombers flown out of Honduras and Nicaragua dropping explosives on defenseless Guatemalan towns, fighter planes that strafed passenger trains and villages, and weapons delivered by airlift that armed the CIA-backed anti-Arbenz military forces.[290]

"The invasion of Guatemala was political warfare at its most detailed."[291] Running the Guatemala operations was the U.S. government's "Guatemalan Group" consisting of representatives from the Defense Department, the USIA, and the CIA; characterized as Eisenhower's "psychwar committee," the group enlisted the major talents of David Atlee Phillips and E. Howard Hunt.[292] Phillips "had learned black propaganda techniques from a CIA specialist who had been in the Morale Operations branch of the OSS."[293] Phillips and Hunt were both assigned as psyops teachers of anti-Arbenz recruits trained in Miami.[294] Both were cited as key psychological warfare agents by CIA Deputy Director Richard Bissell in his in-house review of the "Cuban Operation" (including the Bay of Pigs invasion).[295] Phillips had at least an indirect link to C.D. Jackson through PBSUCCESS, the Agency's code name for covert psyops action[296] monitored by C.D. Jackson's anti-Arbenz "Guatemalan group," but E. Howard Hunt's association was direct, working as a writer and war correspondent for C.D. Jackson's *Life* magazine in 1943, the same year he joined the Office of Strategic Services, ultimately becoming a close friend and working associate of Allen Dulles[297]; again in that same year, C.D. Jackson left Life magazine to join OWI and, eventually, Eisenhower in North Africa, running the General's psychological warfare program.

With C.D. Jackson an early and continuing major force in the psyops dimensions of the plot against Arbenz[298], the ugly enterprise eventually succeeded, figuring prominently in apparent false expectations[299] of a similar defeat of Fidel Castro. The Bay of Pigs fiasco would eventually follow.

In 1953, Robert McClure was sent to Iran to head the U.S. Military Mission there, working closely with the Shah and "Iranian senior military"; it was McClure's last intelligence assignment.[300] Promoted to major general, McClure retired. Four years later, on his way to San Clemente, California, accompanied by his wife, McClure became very sick, finally succumbing to a fatal heart attack at Fort Huachuca, Arizona, on January 1st, 1957.[301]

## C.D. Jackson and the Control of Nuclear War

While McClure was in Iran, his friend C.D. Jackson was inventing one psyops action after another for his president. On December 8th, 1953, Eisenhower presented his historic Atoms for Peace speech to the General Assembly of the United Nations.[302] The address has been almost universally accepted as a well-meant attempt (whatever its outcome) to separate peaceful from military applications of nuclear energy; virtually all discussions of the speech's development (some in great detail), have argued for the speech's basic positive thrust.[303] But only after the history of American nuclear policy during the Eisenhower administration was examined did the truth emerge, and Martin J. Medhurst (the most reliable analyst of both the speech and its subsequent psyops campaign) summarized that truth: "Dwight Eisenhower's Atoms for Peace program, far from being idealistic, propaganda for the sake of propaganda, or an inconsistent and contradictory part of arms control policy, was, instead, a carefully designed—and highly successful—component of the basic defense and foreign policy stance of the Eisenhower administration. As part of a coordinated campaign to achieve national security goals, Atoms for Peace can be seen as the rhetorical counterpart to the New Look doctrine. By diverting audience attention, paving the way for the nucleurization of NATO forces, and serving as the rationale for export of nuclear technologies, Atoms for Peace was a central component of the administration's national security strategy."[304]

The strategist who conceived that policy and wrote the substance of Eisenhower's speech was, of course, C.D. Jackson.[305] Jackson had the "central role" in and was the "chief propagandist" and coordinator of Eisenhower's international nuclear action.[306]

President Eisenhower's address, according to rhetorical analyst Medhurst, "marked the public commencement of a persuasive campaign the dimensions of which stagger the imagination."[307] Though Medhurst earlier promised a detailed examination of the psyops action[308] that was inaugurated by the presidential speech, he already persuasively analyzed its rhetorical content[309] and matched it to the resulting political and propaganda history of the Eisenhower administration: "Planned at the highest levels of government, shrouded in secrecy, aided by the military-industrial complex, and executed over the course of two decades . . ."[310], the speech was fashioned, written, and delivered in order to strike a psyops Cold War blow intended to cripple the Soviet Union, not as a legitimate disarmament proposal.[311]

The entire campaign was chalk-boarded and successfully coached by C.D. Jackson in his capacity as a key media psyops agent. He supplied advance copies of the Eisenhower speech to Newsweek, the New York Herald Tribune, and, of course, Time.[312] It was C.D. Jackson in his capacity as a key intelligence psyops agent who directed the Operations Coordinating Board, the Voice of America, Radio Free Europe, the Central Intelligence Agency, and other covert/cover venues in promoting his rhetorical and psychological "Atoms for Peace" strategy—as if the speech were "a serious peace proposal."[313] Two world leaders had, in fact, been perceived as serious challenges to Eisenhower's nuclear policies, and both, as we have seen, became dark targets of American intelligence actions: Albert Schweitzer in Gabon and Patrice Lumumba of the Congo.

In January, 1954, Jackson left his government psyops machinery in place and returned to the Luce media empire.[314] But several close friends of American covert operations and psychological warfare followed C.D. as presidential representatives, including Jackson's immediate replacement, Nelson Rockefeller.[315] Regardless of who held the position as White House psyops chief, C.D. Jackson had his hand on the throttle of American psychological warfare from 1954 through 1959, "so frequently" shuttling between his positions with Luce and Eisenhower's administration that Jackson's staff at Time created a party game out of his "send-offs and welcomes."[316]

## C.D. Jackson and the Elite Establishment's Psyops Programs

In 1954, Jackson staying in touch with key psychological warfare operations, wrote in support of Robert A. McClure, his associate and influential military psyops professional, commander of the American Military Mission in Iran after the CIA coup.[317] Analysts for the Agency regularly sent their reports to both the CIA and C.D. Jackson.[318]

Jackson was able to bring his psychological warfare perspective to the United Nations in 1954 as the American delegate to the UN's Trusteeship Committee, but it was a troubling time as he tried to make political sense of the "United States' ambiguous attitude toward colonialism . . . ."[319] Jackson felt "the Western World," outnumbered by "the swirling mess of emotionally super-charged Africans and Asians and Arabs," would discover that this "much-needed world forum" would finally be witness to "putting white prestige on the skids."[320] Notably absent from Jackson's concern for "white prestige" was any sense of either color-free justice or the truth.

Jackson was a key member of the World Trade Foundation that "intensified the movement to globalize America's international business interests."[321] In 1953, C.D. Jackson had become the acknowledged founder of the Bilderberg group in the United States, with President Eisenhower an enthusiastic working partner of the new political and economic establishment.[322] Jackson himself attended every Bilderberg meeting anywhere in the world until he died in 1964.[323]

With the American branch of the Bilderberg Conference established[324], Jackson moved to develop an "economic expansion" project fusing potent symbols with powerful trade and commerce plans: images and actions were to be combined to "counter the lure of communism."[325]

That project was established at the Princeton Conference for a World Economic Plan[326], held on May 15th and 16th, 1954; Jackson shared his global vision with Allen Dulles.[327] Jackson's careful selection of images and words, embodied in the Princeton Conference recommendations, "became the basis for . . . a new world economic policy for the United States."[328] Both the appropriate language and action of the transnational corporations were initiated by the master of American psyops.[329]

Despite C.D. Jackson's "crisis-mongering,"[330] President Eisenhower realized how important propaganda was to the success of his "Foreign Economic Policy Battle Plan"[331]: the Advertising Council of America was enlisted[332], a "private" Committee on Foreign Trade, Inc. was established, and through that front group Time,Inc., again commanded by Henry Luce and C.D. Jackson, "contributed expansively to [Eisenhower's] . . . success."[333]

By 1956, Eisenhower had captured significant support with his vigorous and creative word choice; Paul Hoffman praised the president, noting that "Semantics are important . . . ."[334] C.D. Jackson must have beamed. If a Third World War were to happen, President Eisenhower had reportedly confided to C.D. Jackson that it would be won by American psychological operations.[335]

Jackson continued to be called on by the president to brainstorm new intelligence ideas and operations. But those operations were frequently corrupt and corrupting.[336] As a key agent of the U.S. power elite, C.D. Jackson was deeply involved in manipulating American social, educational, and cultural institutions. Just before Eisenhower had called on him again to serve as the president's Cold War/psyops expert, Jackson attended a crucial academic meeting whose agenda was damage control from seven years of CIA collaboration. Initiated in 1950, Project Troy (the name probably alluding to the penetration of Troy's fortifications by Odysseus' hollow horse) had collected a group of top-drawer Harvard faculty, the project ultimately morphing into the Center for International Studies (CENIS)[337], responsible for key analyses of the Soviet Union, China, and nuclear weapons.[338] Because Harvard banned on-campus classified research, Troy/CENIS had to meet at the Massachusetts Institute of Technology.[339]

The original Cambridge group had been given a typical C.D. Jackson psyops directive to solve a "specific [apparently technical] problem"[340]: how could the Central Intelligence Agency overcome "Soviet jamming" of the CIA's propaganda broadcasts to Eastern Europe?[341] Within one year, the Agency spent $300,000 so that CENIS could "research worldwide political, economic and social change . . . in the interest of the entire intelligence community."[342]

Seven years after Troy/CENIS tackled its initial problem, a CENIS review 'board' met to examine the difficult question of "academic integrity."[343] Despite a fundamental reality, that the Cambridge faculty had been bought by the CIA, the reviewers worried over "corrosion" of the academic "channel," as if individual faculty members were somehow like metal tributaries through which classified analysis flowed into the main Agency pipe.[344] McGeorge Bundy, an intimate friend of the CIA who chaired the CENIS review, immediately saw the value of the metaphor: as he put it, "The channel is more important than that a lot of water should be running though it."[345]

There could be no doubt as to whose imagery had captured the flawed ethic of the Cambridge operation. Attendee C. D. Jackson observed that American intelligence "work has got to be done . . . ."[346] And, he added, "I have not noticed any visible corrosion."[347]

So much for the integrity of Harvard Yard's academic plumbing.

The program continued, and the initial intrusion of the CIA was almost immediately matched by the Agency corrupting Harvard's Center for International Affairs through (at least) 1957.[348]

In the summer of 1955, Nelson Rockefeller called a conference on "the psychological aspects of U.S. strategy" with key psyops stars from the Operations Research Office, Johns Hopkins University, including it School of Advanced International studies; the U.S. Military Academy; the director of CENIS, housed at M.I.T.; the director of the Council on Foreign Relations' "studies"; American air intelligence; the New England Electric System; and others, including Henry Kissinger, at the time hanging his hat at Harvard.[349] The top U.S. psychological warfare veteran in attendance was, of course, C.D. Jackson.[350]

Whatever moral rant John Foster Dulles was directing at that moment against Russia and China, Jackson and associates were running the American psyops show.

On May 7th, 1956, Jackson again met a powerhouse of "psychwar" people, including DeWitt C. Poole, A.A. Berle, Tom Braden, and Nelson Rockefeller, who were attempting to reenergize the OCB as Eisenhower was at the same time applying a brake to the government's psychological warfare engine.[351] Whenever possible, psyops agents had been active outside the White House and the State Department.

Through 1955 and 1956, Allen Dulles, Frank Wisner, the CIA, C.D. Jackson and his Radio Free Europe/Radio Liberty had cooperatively stirred the bubbling European pot of anti-Soviet revolution[352], hoping for American establishment and intelligence support. But President Eisenhower distanced himself from the more ferocious of the Cold War/psyops crusaders; the worst of a dangerous Cold War period was coming to a close, and C.D. Jackson apparently lost some power and influence.[353]

Yet Jackson still remained a key figure in the administration's "rollback" programs, commanding the Operations Coordinating Board.[354] American covert actions had supported "fifty surviving garrisons of Eastern European paramilitaries [including old hands of the notorious General Gehlan] hanging on in Germany . . . ."[355] The "Hotspur" Colonel Philip Corso[356], C.D. Jackson's OCB agent, was given the job of "salvaging" and "reactivating" the rollback battalions.[357]

But C.D. Jackson was called to a meeting with the Secretary of Defense and the Secretary of State: Jackson's provocation that might have led to either a major Soviet retreat or the opening of World War III never went beyond the Wisner/Jackson planning stage.[358]

Eisenhower now had serious doubts about Foster Dulles' excessive anti-Communist denunciations[359], a rhetoric that was increasingly out of step with Eisenhower's enthusiasm for more subtle psychological warfare. The president met with the peripatetic Secretary of State in 1957, asking him about bringing in C.D. Jackson as Eisenhower's "advisor on Cold War matters."[360] Dulles responded with an immediate and absolute "No": he saw clearly how much a policy rival Jackson would be if he sat at a desk in the White House.[361]

But the president was still searching for a breakthrough, an alternative to Cold War confrontation. For Eisenhower, one man could offer the president such a breakthrough: C.D. Jackson. In January 1958, Eisenhower contacted Jackson, asking him to meet with Foster Dulles and propose that Dulles become "Special Assistant and Advisor to the President" (a title conferring on its holder no foreign policy power), while Jackson, replacing Dulles, would become Secretary of State.[362]

## C.D. Jackson's Waning Power

After the Jackson-Dulles meeting, the psyops master wrote to the president, apparently hoping that his positive spin on the discussion with Dulles might move Eisenhower to effect what the meeting had not brought about.[363] But Eisenhower's response was to offer Jackson the position of Under Secretary of State running the nation's "Cold War effort."[364] Though it may have appeared that Jackson did not wish to serve under Dulles and therefore be frustrated in his endeavors[365], it is more likely the sticking point was Eisenhower wanting Jackson's psyops genius in support of "total" disarmament.[366] For Jackson, that was completely unacceptable: a president who rejected "liberation," "intervention," and "political warfare" was someone for whom C.D. Jackson could not work.[367]

One month later, in February, 1958, Eisenhower, most likely borrowing a psyops idea from Jackson[368], proposed that ten thousand young Russians be invited to study in the United States on one-year government scholarships.[369] The president's primary intent (Eisenhower was always a student of C.D. Jackson) was to score a propaganda coup, though the president was also "a great believer in promoting international understanding through [the] exchange of students . . . ."[370] But both Foster Dulles and the State Department argued vigorously against the idea, and Eisenhower eventually let the proposal pass.[371]

Still, some Soviet students did arrive in 1958, including Soviet Fulbright scholar (and KGB agent) Oleg Kalugin, who ultimately became a master psyops warrior for Soviet intelligence.

## C.D. Jackson and the Student Exchanges and Programs

Reciprocally, C.D. Jackson was a prime mover in psyops actions targeting students visiting Europe in the late 1950s.[372] Major student/youth festivals had been held in the Soviet Union and Eastern Europe perceived by the CIA as significant Communist propaganda successes.[373] The Soviets had funded, for example, the World Federation of Democratic Youth. For 1959, a World Youth Festival was planned for Vienna, the first time such an event would be held in the West.[374] C.D. Jackson conferred with CIA officer Cord Meyer and U.S. establishment leader John J. McCloy[375], and the three organized a covertly-funded "alternative" youth delegation to represent the United States.[376] Jackson and Meyer hired young Gloria Steinem as their Vienna Festival agent, who then established a CIA front in Cambridge, Massachusetts, named (eventually) the Independent Research Service.[377] Steinem was able to get tax-exempt status for her group, and C.D. Jackson placed her in touch with several U.S. companies that provided her with some funding. Most of the operational cash, however, came from the Agency through Jackson, tucked inside a "special account."[378]

The Free Europe Committee (earlier called the Committee for a Free Europe) assisted the McCloy/Jackson/Steinem operation[379], setting up a CIA-financed front operation called the Publications Development Corporation with Samuel S. Walker, Jr., as its president.[380] Walker, vice-president of the Free Europe Committee and a close associate of C.D. Jackson, functioned as Gloria Steinem's control in the CIA's psyops action in Vienna: "Steinem ended up working closely with Samuel S. Walker, Jr."[381]

Steinem remained with the Independent Research Service, receiving CIA funds through 1962. Though she insisted the CIA never asked her to report on the students whom she encountered, she voluntarily wrote at least one extended political analysis of students, a report submitted to C.D. Jackson.[382]

C.D. Jackson had actively planned and supported CIA penetration of youth and student groups traveling to Europe, including Finland, from 1959 through 1962. CIA funding also supported the World Assembly of Youth.[383] The CIA/psyops involvement in student and youth organizations, especially those with religious affiliation, may be one of U.S. intelligence's last important secrets. Though the Agency's success in controlling "the senior leadership of . . . religious groups and even student organizations"[384] has been recognized, the documentation is tantalizing but thin.[385] Because C.D. Jackson's papers have been carefully sanitized, it may be some time before his complete psyops record in the manipulation of educational institutions is exposed.

Foster Dulles, seriously ill, went on leave in late February, 1959[386]; in mid-April, 1959, the dying Dulles resigned as Secretary of State.[387] With the waning of Dulles' power, the president had begun making pacific moves in the face of Cold War antagonism generated by Time, Inc., whose consortium was headed by Luce and Jackson[388]: in March, 1959, the Berlin Crisis had energized C.D. Jackson at Time headquarters, who found his war drum and begun to thump it.[389] But the president rejected the belligerent hysteria supported by America's conservative media, led by the Luce publishing empire.[390]

In 1958, Jackson left Eisenhower's administration and returned to Time, Inc., where Luce and company "shifted allegiance and began to promote John F. Kennedy for the presidency . . . ."[391] At Time, Inc., Jackson and Luce now imaged Eisenhower as a "do-nothing president" who was worse than no president at all.[392]

After John Foster Dulles died on May 24th, 1959, C.D. Jackson was one of Foster's pall bearers[393], certainly a heavy burden for the psyops master to have carried.

## C.D. Jackson Fades

Two months later, in July, 1959, C.D. Jackson made his final attempt to reverse the Eisenhower administration's declining interest in psyops; Jackson convinced the White House staff to hold a so-called "stag party" for him attended by establishment and government luminaries. But the administration remained "profoundly hostile" to reenergizing psyops.[394] On September 11th, 1959, Jackson wrote to the one party attendee in sympathy with his psychological warfare argument: Vice President Richard Nixon.[395] The wordmaster, always alert to a psyops opportunity and mindful of America's probable political future, wrote to Nixon: "It is no exaggeration . . . that with the possible exception of Allen Dulles, you [Richard Nixon] have a more experienced 'feel' for these [psyops] matters than any [other person] in the Government . . . ."[396]

While Eisenhower made fresh overt moves toward peace in 1959 and 1960, C.D. Jackson burned with anti-Communist fever, deeply disturbed that the president was apparently taking no aggressive actions in crucial hotspots that included Africa and Cuba.[397] The President appointed a propaganda committee on February 17th, 1960, including C.D. Jackson, but the psychological warfare master was now most often out of the White House loop, and Luce and Jackson were apparently not privy to the actual increase in the CIA's covert operations in 1960.[398]

Still, as Eisenhower moved to lessen international tension, the entire Time/Life/Fortune media empire, with Jackson and Luce in charge, persistently (and sometimes) viciously attacked the president, characterizing him as "tired" and "absurd."[399]

On April 24th, 1960, Jackson was appointed Life magazine publisher.

On May 14th, 1960, President Eisenhower called upon C.D. Jackson and his psyops magic for the last time in support of a government program. Faced with budget cut proposals that the president was certain would cripple American foreign policy and trade, Eisenhower urged Jackson to "suggest [again] a crusade for our country."[400]

But the engine of psychological warfare had, at least for a while, run out of fuel.

On January 17th, 1961, Dwight David Eisenhower delivered his Farewell Address.[401] Certainly the president's suspicion of the "military-industrial complex"[402] was relevant, but even as he spoke, the Central Intelligence Agency and its allies, the nation's psychological warfare agents, cast shadows across his lectern. Still, one dimension of his warning would have disturbed Allen Dulles (the surviving spymaster) and C.D. Jackson. Calling attention to the contemporary "conjunction of an immense military establishment and a large arms industry" in America, Eisenhower characterized that fusion as having a "total influence—economic, political, even spiritual" that was being felt at every level of American society[403]: an influence "even spiritual."

According to Drew Pearson, "Life magazine [was] always pulling chestnuts out of the fire for the CIA," citing C.D. Jackson has a key Agency chestnut savior.[404]

Though Jackson has not always been named when 20th century propaganda, public relations, public opinion manipulation, and psychological warfare have been analyzed, his major role in the creation of a rhetorical "reality," what has been called the "myth in media and public discourse" regarding the essential goodness of American foreign policy and the retailing of the Cold War fiction, is overwhelmingly evident.[405]

## C.D. Jackson and Lee Harvey Oswald: Degrees of Separation

One major link between the worlds of C.D. Jackson and Lee Harvey Oswald reflecting on their roles in the murky world of psychological warfare has waited to be explored. An American military defector, Oswald reportedly wished to redefect to the United States with his new Russian wife. Both at home and overseas, Oswald was a prolific letter writer.[406] In January, 1962, extremely impatient with the slow pace of his anticipated exit from the Soviet Union, Oswald reportedly wrote two letters to the International Rescue Committee (IRC) "explaining his situation and requesting that it contact the American Embassy in Moscow in order to contribute financial assistance for his trip home [to the United States]."[407] The earlier version of the IRC, the Emergency Rescue Committee, was an OSS-supported operation.[408] The International Rescue Committee (IRC) in 1947 was CIA-funded, engaging in, for example, exfiltrating Nazis out of Europe and into the United States.[409]

A dozen documents relating to the International Rescue Committee are in the Warren Commission's records: one document has immediate relevance. Dated May 1st, 1964, a letter from the program director of the IRC to J. Lee Rankin, Warren Commission Special Council, described the Committee as "strongly anti-Communist"[410] and gave details of the IRC's interaction with Lee Harvey Oswald.

The International Rescue Committee/Oswald story began in the Soviet Union. In early January, 1962, Lee Harvey Oswald was attempting to leave the Soviet Union. Someone had given Lee information about the International Rescue Committee and its supportive functions[411]; Lee had even been supplied with the committee's Manhattan address on Park Avenue.

Oswald then sent a letter to his mother, dated January 2nd, 1962, urging she contact the Red Cross in Vernon, Texas, so that it might intercede with (in Oswald's words) "a organization called 'International rescue committee' or any organizations which aids persons from abroad get settled." Given the single-mindedness of Oswald's mother, the International Rescue Committee became Mrs. Oswald's sole target.

Marguerite Oswald contacted the State Department and asked for the address of the International Rescue Committee. A telegram from Allyn Donaldson at State on January 12, 1962, immediately responded: "Address [of] International Rescue Committee is 251 Park Avenue South, New York City." Lee's mother was now armed.

Marguerite called on Helen Harwell, Executive Secretary of the Vernon, Texas, Red Cross, as Lee had directed. According to Oswald's mother, the contact was not a happy one. Harwell would not open the Red Cross office until Mrs. Oswald thoroughly badgered her. Then, when Harwell and Marguerite were finally in the Vernon office, the Red Cross officer proceeded to argue from a determined anti-Soviet position against assisting Lee Harvey Oswald.

Marguerite would have none of that argument: Harwell and the Red Cross were there, she said, to help people in need. Especially her son and his family.

In the second week of January, 1962, the Special Consular Service of the U.S. State Department telephoned the International Rescue Committee and recommended the IRC assist Oswald and his family in leaving the Soviet Union.[412] Given the International Rescue Committee's long history of close cooperation with the Central Intelligence Agency, the Consular Service call must have sounded like a marching order.

Less than two weeks later, the International Rescue Committee received a letter dated January 14th, 1962, from Mrs. Helen Harwell of the Wilberger County Red Cross Chapter in Vernon, Texas.[413] According to the IRC, two letters were attached. The first was from Consul Norbury in the American Embassy in Moscow[414], apparently a version of the State Department's telephoned pressure on the International Rescue Committee to assist Lee Harvey Oswald; the second attached letter was "addressed to the International Rescue Committee . . . and ostensibly written by Oswald . . . ."[415] The U.S. Embassy letter included a handwritten note: "Mrs. Helen Harwell, Executive Secretary, American Red Cross."[416]

The International Rescue Committee officer was apparently quit skittish: he had compared the reputed Oswald letter with the Embassy letter and concluded that "To a layman's eye it would appear that both copies [of the letters] were typed on the same typewriter."[417] Sylvia Meagher asked: "Was it possible that the [American] Embassy and the State Department, in their ardor to repatriate Oswald, had gone so far as to write letters [or at least one letter] in his name?"[418]

How did Lee Harvey Oswald discover the International Rescue Committee while in the Soviet Union? One piece of curious evidence is suggestive. In his so-called "Address Book"[419], Oswald wrote in Cyrillic letters the equivalent of "INDEREDKO." Either the FBI or the Warren Commission staff had annotated this entry in the Warren Commission's records, suggesting Oswald's scribble might stand for an acronym of the International Rescue Committee. The IRC's two "acronyms" have been "IRC" and "INTRECOM." Charles Drago has commented that "Given the tendency of LHO (and/or his amanuensis) to misspell and mistranscribe," the notation as a Cyrillic version of INTRECOM "makes sense."[420]

Though inconclusive, Oswald's "INDEREDKO" note strongly suggests someone in the Soviet Union, possibly an official of the U.S. Embassy in Moscow or a cooperative CIA asset (or someone who was both) prompted Oswald to query the CIA-connected International Rescue Committee for exit support. And that query could only have rung more False Identity/Illegal alarm bells.

The International Rescue Committee was a major part of a Cold War network of religious and secular relief agencies and intelligence operators. In its earlier Emergency Rescue Committee/OSS manifestation, it included Varian Fry working with the

Unitarian Service Committee and Paul Hagen/Karl Frank and his OSS/Dulles links[421]; in the committee's Cold War period, the IRC was directed by Leo Cherne. Throughout his life, Cherne was a major U.S. intelligence player, cooperating with Richard Nixon, Gerald Ford, George Bush, and William Casey.[422] After serving as a "consultant" to General Douglas MacArthur, Leo Cherne became an IRC Board member in 1946; in 1951, Cherne was elected Chairman of the International Rescue Committee and held that office for forty years.

When Lee Harvey Oswald reportedly applied to the International Rescue Committee, the Committee and its Chairman Leo Cherne were so deeply in the mix of refugee and intelligence operations that IRC was widely considered to be an extension of the Central Intelligence Agency.[423] Unitarian Percival Flack Brundage, close friend of both the U.S. military and the CIA and a major founder of the American Friends of Albert Schweitzer College, was a dedicated worker for the Unitarian Service Committee laboring precisely in the same refugee fields as, and often in cooperation with, the International Rescue Committee.

Lee Harvey Oswald had discovered a way to send at least one letter of appeal for financial support to the CIA-supported International Rescue Committee while he was in the Soviet Union; yet Oswald (or someone) simultaneously raised a serious question about the authenticity of his application to that same CIA-funded organization.

The International Rescue Committee, to whom Lee Harvey Oswald had applied for help while residing in the Soviet Union, was a major part of the refugee/religious/ intelligence operations run by Allen Dulles through two World Wars and the ensuing Cold War; but it was also a major component of the international psyops network of C.D. Jackson. The IRC's officers and board members, including Leo Cherne and William Casey, had State Department, military, U.S. intelligence and, in particular, psychological warfare links as they were officers and board members of USIA, Radio Free Europe/Radio Liberty, the Research Institute of America, the National Endowment for Democracy (NED), Freedom House, and the Center For Strategic and International Studies (CSIS), the latter founded and run initially by Ray Cline, former deputy director of the CIA.

The International Rescue Committee board members and officers were, in fact, perfect examples of the fusing of intelligence-gathering and C.D. Jackson's psyops techniques.

## C.D. Jackson and Dallas

But the connection between C.D. Jackson and Lee Harvey Oswald did not end with Oswald's curious application for help to the International Rescue Committee. Time, Inc., C.D. Jackson, and his psychological warfare operations were present immediately after the presidential execution in Dallas.

On November 22nd, 1963, Patsy Swank[424] whispered into a closely-held phone; around her, Dallas Police Headquarters was chaos and total noise. Someone named

"Zapruder," she said, who was a local clothing maker, had reportedly taken a film of the JFK assassination. Swank, a Life Magazine part-time asset, was speaking to Richard Stolley, the Pacific Bureau Chief of *Life,* who had flown in to Dallas with Tommy Thompson and two photographers. Immediately upon hearing the terrible news from Texas. Listening carefully to Swank as he sat in his hotel room, Stolley was very interested. He finally contacted Zapruder and, on November 23rd, reportedly viewed the film.[125]

Stolley then reached C.D. Jackson in New York, and, according to the West Coast bureau chief, Stolley followed Jackson's orders and bought the "original" film[126] and one copy[127] (or several copies, according to conflicting reports) from Zapruder. Stolley recalled that the footage was delivered to Jackson, and after the psychological warfare chief looked at the film, Jackson "proposed the [Time, Inc.] company obtain all rights to the film and withhold it from public viewing at least until emotions had calmed."[128]

Among the many plots against Fidel Castro, "Operation Redcross" had a direct *Life*/C.D. Jackson connection. Supported by William Pawley (a powerful China Lobbyist and friend of the CIA) and by Julien Sourwine, influential counsel for the Senate Internal Security Subcommittee[429], the operation had enlisted at least four important participants: Johnny Martino and Eddie Bayo, both Organized Crime figures; a representative of the CIA; and journalist Richard Billings, commissioned to write about and photograph the "rescue" raid on Cuba for *Life.*[430] C. D. Jackson, who was, according to reporter/writer Carl Bernstein, "Henry Luce's personal emissary to the CIA"[431] , had reportedly allowed CIA assets and agents to carry Time, Inc., identification as cover[432], and the anti-Cuban Bayo/Martino/Pawley action had most probably been funded (as were other anti-Castro attempted hits) by Henry Luce through C.D. Jackson.[433] Richard Billings, the *Life* journalist accompanying Operation Redcross, was, at that moment, an in-law of C.D. Jackson.

Richard Billings' connections to the Kennedy assassination story also included his authorship of a key article on the JFK murder for *Life* (for which he was an editor); after the assassination, he was Editorial Director for the House Select Committee on Assassinations that examined the Kennedy killing; and he co-authored (with G. Robert Blakey, the committee's chief counsel) a study of the assassination based largely on the Select Committee's materials.

Being directly connected to an anti-Castro operation whose members included Organized Crime, the CIA, and Time, Inc., and gaining full and exclusive possession of the original Zapruder film (and then suppressing it for over ten years) were not the only links C.D. Jackson had to the Kennedy assassination story. James Herbert Martin, former manager of Seven Flags in Arlington, Texas, the Wynne-Murchison-Rockefeller Great Southwest Corporation motel, had been Marina Oswald's business manager for a time; he had arranged a sizeable amount of money to be paid to himself, to his lawyer, to Lee's brother Robert Oswald, and an advance of $25,000[434] to Marina (Lee's wife) from Meredith Press through Thomas Thompson or *Life* editor Edward K. Thompson[435], Isaac Don Levine, *Life*'s representative in Dallas (called "the dean of American anticommunist writers")[436], and C.D. Jackson.[437] According to television newsperson Bob Schieffer (at the time of the Dealey Plaza murder, a *Fort Worth Star-Telegram* police reporter), a "New York-based *Life* magazine reporter named Thomas Thompson, also . . . from Fort Worth, . . . managed to put the Oswald women [that is, both Lee's wife and mother] under exclusive contract to his magazine and . . . secreted them away in a Dallas motel." Time, Inc. was well-represented in the aftermath of the JFK assassination.

C.D. Jackson (for *Life*) had directed the taping of Marina Oswald's personal story, scheduled to be transcribed by Ilya Mamantov.[438] Mamantov was a close friend and associate of Peter Gregory, who had apparently controlled Marina's police testimony on the alleged JFK murder rifle.[439] Earlier, Gregory and Mamantov helped organize a CIA-funded/anti-Communist Orthodox parish for the White Russians of the Dallas/Ft. Worth area supported by the CIA-financed Tolstoy Foundation.[440] The Oswalds had been befriended by Paul M. Raigorodsky, a member of the "White Russian Emigré community" in the area[441]; Raigorodsky was a member of the Board of Directors of the Tolstoy Foundation.[442]

A Tolstoy family member had been a World War II OSS officer, and, later, "members of the [CIA-funded] Tolstoy family were in regular contact with . . . [C.D. Jackson's] Psychological Strategy Board in the early 1950s . . . ."[443] By 1953, Jackson was directly involved in obtaining funding for the Agency-supported Tolstoy Foundation.[444]

Isaac Don Levine, who at the time of the JFK assassination was a member of the Liberation Committee of the CIA[445], had been scheduled to ghost the Marina Oswald story[446]; Levine was "a veteran China Lobbyist [like C.D. Jackson's friend William Pawley] who had previously collaborated on anti-Soviet projects with the CIA and the CIA-subsidized Tolstoy Foundation."[447] Levine reportedly spent a full week with Marina Oswald before her February 3rd, 1964, testimony to the Warren Commission, a period that has been characterized by one informed source as witness coaching.[448]

In 1953, Allen Dulles, Isaac Don Levine, and C.D. Jackson had collaborated on the CIA/Eisenhower administration's major psyops response to Stalin's death.[449]

James Martin, part of the *Life*/Meredith Press 'publishing' deal, had a relationship with Jack Ruby, Oswald's killer, dating back to Martin working for the Statler-Hilton and, afterward, managing a Dallas "bottle club" similar to Ruby's Carousel.[450] In addition to his involvement in the Time, Inc./Marina Oswald publishing scheme, Martin was responsible for the sale of the so-called "backyard rifle photo," allegedly of Lee Harvey Oswald, to *Life* magazine.[451] For *Life*, C.D. Jackson made much of that same rifle photograph, an odd and tilted image that nevertheless helped to convince many Americans of Oswald's guilt. *Life*'s cover of February 21st, 1964, featuring the photo was an apt illustration of C.D. Jackson's psyops abilities, introducing Jackson's commissioned 'psychoanalytic' review of Oswald carried inside the magazine.[452]

But Jackson and the photo editors of *Life* did have a major problem: the rifle being held by the man in the picture, presumed to be Oswald, did NOT match the Mannlicher-Carcano allegedly recovered at the Texas School Book Depository after the

JFK assassination. The weapon's stock in the photo was altered[453] and the telescopic site was retouched, both transformations by *Life*'s photo experts, so that the rifle in the photograph (scheduled for nationwide distribution on the cover of *Life*, the Luce/Jackson media powerhouse) looked more like the alleged murder weapon.[454]

Jackson was reportedly responsible for selecting only thirty-one frames (in black and white) of the Zapruder film for the November 29th, 1963, edition of *Life*; nine in color for *Life*'s December, 1963, edition; and (just before C.D. Jackson's death on September 18th, 1964) selecting a limited number of frames for the *Life* edition of October 2nd, 1964, anticipating the first anniversary of November 22nd, 1963.[455]

The several versions of the Zapruder film that have circulated for almost thirty years (including, most recently, marketed copies of the alleged "original") have been subjected to close and critical analyses, raising serious questions about the film's authenticity.[456] Those questions carry even greater weight given C.D. Jackson's lifelong history of using both words and images to manipulate and disinform public reality.

Acting as *Life*'s publisher, Jackson not only suppressed the Zapruder film; he also converted it to a propaganda instrument supporting the government's dubious Lone Assassin theory. Jackson apparently allowed *Life* writer Paul Mandel to view an alleged copy of the film, then commissioned Mandel to describe what he saw: as Robert Sam Anson commented, Mandel's take on the film, published in the December, 1963, edition of *Life*, was "totally fictitious."[457]

Early in 1964, C.D. Jackson helped found the private International Executive Service Corps, becoming its board chairman.[458] And on February 25th, 1964, Jackson apparently allowed the members of the Warren Commission, the FBI, and the Secret Service to view a version of the Zapruder film in the possession of Time/Life/Fortune. On July 8th, 1964, C.D. Jackson was appointed Senior Vice President of Time, Inc.

On September 18th, 1964, less than one year after gaining control of the Zapruder assassination film, C.D. Jackson was declared dead, reportedly the victim of cancer.[459]

Writer Gerald Posner asserted that C.D. Jackson, whom Posner stated died of a heart attack, had only one link to the Kennedy assassination. According to Posner, Jackson "was the *Life* magazine executive who decided to purchase the Zapruder film."[460]

So much for a would-be Pulitzer Prize winner.

## Who Manipulated Lee Harvey Oswald?

From 1959 through his death in 1963 (and even beyond), Lee Harvey Oswald was a classic psychological warfare principal; the U.S. intelligence programs in Illegals, False Identities, and False Defectors were psyops; the Dulles brothers' manipulations of religious individuals and groups were psychological warfare operations. C.D. Jackson's entire career in publishing, advertising, fund-raising, public-opinion shaping, wartime propaganda, black intelligence operations[461], political campaigns, and economic global planning was a lifetime in pure psyops.

Only someone with extraordinary psychological warfare abilities[462] could have created the psyops Red Marine: Lee Harvey Oswald, mortally wounded by Jack Ruby on November 24th, 1963, after the accused assassin had protested his innocence in the assassination of President John F. Kennedy on November 22nd, 1963.

# Essay Seven

# Percival Brundage, The Bureau of the Budget, James R. Killian, Jr., Lyndon Baines Johnson, and the Unitarian Matrix

Working in less than mysterious ways, the U.S. National Security State in its earliest manifestations controlled the White House, its legislative and budgetary operations, and its military and intelligence activities. Chief among those controls were the Bureau of the Budget, Percival Flack Brundage, James R. Killian, Jr., Lyndon Baines Johnson, and key Unitarians and their partners in U.S. covert intelligence. Among the most important of those budgetary and religious assets was Percy Brundage.

## Percival Flack Brundage

Percival Flack Brundage was born on April 2nd, 1892, the son of Charlotte Flack Brundage and William Brundage[1], a Methodist cleric who became a Unitarian minister.[2]

Receiving his Harvard undergraduate degree ("cum laude") in 1914[3], Percival Brundage joined the New York accounting firm of Patterson & Ridgeway and rose from "office boy" to "senior accountant" in two years.[4] Brundage resigned in 1916 to take a wartime "civilian" position with the Material Accounting Section of the War Department's Quartermaster Depot Office in New York[5], a job combining extensive and confidential record-keeping with major military procurement operations. Brundage held that crucial position through the Armistice of 1918.[6]

In just five years, Percival Brundage had distinguished himself as a major American accounting mind.

From 1919 (when he became a Certified Public Accountant in New Jersey) through 1954, Brundage reportedly established an unequaled record in accounting, business, business law, and commerce, holding national offices in the AICPA, the National Conference of Lawyers and CPAS, the Massachusetts Society of CPAS, the New York State Society of CPAS, the New York Chamber of Commerce, the Society of Business Advisory Professions, the National Bureau of Economic Research, and lectureships at both Oxford and Harvard.[7]

When he was not a major public service official or a fulltime National Security Council or Cabinet member of the U.S. government, Brundage was a senior partner at Price Waterhouse (not unlike his friends at Sullivan and Cromwell, Allen Dulles and John Foster Dulles). Percival Brundage's global concerns were, in fact, identical to those of the Dulles brothers: Brundage was the director (1940-1954) and chair (1951-1954) of the Federal Union that argued for "federation of the [so-called] Atlantic democracies"[8]; he was the treasurer of the International Movement for Atlantic Union, an affiliation of the Federal Union[9], and the treasurer and director of the Atlantic Council of the United States.[10]

In 1954, at the height of his global activity and while an active member of the Council on Foreign Relations, Percival Brundage accepted the position of Deputy Director of the Bureau of the Budget (later the Bureau of Management and the Budget) in Eisenhower's first presidential administration.

In 1956, the master accountant of America became the Director of the Bureau of the Budget[11], monitoring the debits and credits of the Eisenhower government, an office he held until 1958. After his official retirement from government service, he signed on with the Bureau of the Budget for two more years as the Bureau's key "consultant."

From 1954 through 1960, Percival Brundage kept close watch on the national budget of the United States; and for those six years, Percival Brundage was obviously aware that the Department of Defense and the CIA (and therefore the "black budget" operations hidden in the accounts of the Pentagon, the Central Intelligence Agency, and the rest of the departments and divisions of the U.S. government) would not be critically reviewed by his own Bureau of the Budget. Neither the CIA nor the Department of Defense was subject to the ordinary government-wide funding and spending survey performed by Brundage's Bureau of the Budget. The Bureau, in fact, had acted as a participant in promoting and maintaining both intelligence and military budgets.[12]

## How Did Percival Brundage and His Bureau of the Budget Achieve Power?

Mandated by the Constitution of the United States, every chief officer of every division and department of the U.S. government was required to submit a "budget" to the executive branch of U.S. government, and after 1920, to the Director of the Bureau of the Budget, for close analysis.

Profiteering by "war contractors" in World War One had reached so gluttonous a level "a public cry of outrage against them . . . reverberated for two decades."[13] But despite that rush of citizens' anger, the U.S. government's 1916-1918 accommodation to the suppliers for the War Department (when Percival Brundage was working as a civilian procurement officer in New York) was institutionalized in 1921, when the Bureau of the Budget was created[14], a signal agency "in increasing the power of the [sitting] President."[15]

The Budget and Accounting Act of June 10th, 1921, established that the new Bureau of the Budget function "under a Director appointed by and accountable to the President [alone], . . . created . . . to carry out the task of budget preparation."[16] But with the recognition of "fiscal responsibility" also came recognition of the president's further "responsibility" to "initiate legislation," therefore the necessity to create "machinery [within the executive branch] for central clearance of legislative proposals from the executive branch."[17] The Bureau was, in fact, that legislative "machinery." The double power of initiating legislation and monitoring expenditures meant that the Bureau of the Budget would effectively control the distribution of key military and intelligence funds.[18]

## The Bureau of the Budget, U.S. Intelligence, and the American Military

President Franklin Delano Roosevelt expanded his legislative/budgetary powers, and afterward Truman and Eisenhower further enhanced those powers.[19] Congress did little to check this growth of executive clout, and though the Department of Defense and the U.S. intelligence community eventually freed themselves of any Bureau of the Budget control, the Bureau remained through the 1960s a powerful executive instrument, called upon for support by Congressional leaders like Lyndon Baines Johnson and power players like James Killian, Jr.

The strength of the Bureau of the Budget and the secret funding of covert operations had an almost identical history. When, for example, the earlier version of the Office of Strategic Services was inaugurated as the office of the Coordinator of Information (COI), President Roosevelt sent a note (on June 18th, 1941) "to officials of the Bureau of the Budget to set up the [COI] office . . . and to fund it initially out of the $100 million in secret, unvouchered funds that Congress had [previously] appropriated . . . ."[20] Presidents both before and after Roosevelt had called on the Bureau to develop new agencies, prepare the initiating legislation, fund their operations, and on occasion direct the dismantling of existing offices. The Bureau of the Budget was, in fact, instrumental in setting up the COI and later decommissioning its later manifestation, the OSS, to prepare the way for the CIA.

Roosevelt operated his Bureau of the Budget "as a presidential 'secretariat' for monitoring the activities of the entire executive establishment."[21] On September 8, 1939, President Roosevelt had declared a "Limited Emergency" following Nazi Germany's successful penetration of Poland.[22] His Reorganization Act then reconstructed the Executive Office of the President: its key provision transferred the Bureau of the Budget from the Treasury Department to Roosevelt's Executive Office[23], insuring that the massive military procurements resulting from the U.S.'s participation in World War II would be monitored by friendly bookkeepers in the Bureau of the Budget.

But that "reorganization" also insured that Roosevelt's private intelligence operations would be protected on both the domestic and foreign fronts. For his international connections, the president's agents included Averell Harriman and

Harry Hopkins.[24] The Bureau became a powerful wing of FDR's personal intelligence apparatus, in control of the budget but also commissioned by the president to make major evaluations of the nation's intelligence agencies throughout World War II, each year, 1941 through 1945.[25]

To insure his domestic information was unfiltered and completely trustworthy, Roosevelt sent his Bureau of the Budget agents "into every branch of the government, and their reports came directly back to the President."[26]

Later, in 1953, when the Eisenhower administration was interested in paring down its national debit column, it suddenly discovered what the government spent was largely protected as "built-in costs." President Eisenhower (reportedly with reluctance) therefore opposed any significant reductions in the only areas where cuts could have been made: budget items for the military and "other national security needs."[27] A budgetary fiction developing at least since the military procurement days of the First World War had a Cold War update.

Ultimately the most sensitive, illegal, and unconstitutional military, intelligence, and psyops programs, costing billions of dollars, were not only freed of Bureau of the Budget oversight but were actively promoted by the Bureau. The BOB either ignored buried expenditures or supported those outlays, approving or overlooking fund transfers from other cooperating government departments and agencies.[28] In available Bureau of the Budget documents, those funding transfers were most often called "arrangements." In fact, the Central Intelligence Act of 1949 authorized the Agency to "transfer to and receive from other government agencies such sums . . . approved by . . . [the Bureau of Budget] for the performance of any functions or activities authorized . . . without regard to any provisions of law limiting or prohibiting transfers between appropriations."[29]

From Roosevelt through Eisenhower, the budget machinery developed by the Bureau of the Budget transferred actual spending power from Congress to the Executive Office of the President (from where military and covert operations funding was ultimately handed over to the National Security Council, the Department of Defense, and the CIA). That transformation was "the result of struggle, usurpation, delegation, abandonment, abduction, and atrophy."[30] Howard E. Shuman succinctly summarized the context of that transference: "Each act and each transfer of power [over the budget] was preceded by economic problems, panics, wars, depression, or constitutional crisis."[31] At every instance of that budgetary transference, powerful individuals and groups associated with the Federal Reserve, the Treasury, the American banking industry, and the Bureau of the Budget were present as midwives.[32] Shuman correctly diagnosed the unconstitutional takeover of the budgeting function from Congress by agents and assets of a series of presidents[33], but he did not fully appreciate how the Bureau of the Budget created a military budget "review" of a joint meeting of the Bureau, Defense, and the sitting president over a period of years from 1947 through 1960 and then assisted in transforming the military-industrial and intelligence-establishment complexes into para-federal operations.[34]

Walter L. Pforzheimer[35] helped direct the U.S. intelligence community through World War II and the Cold War that followed as the CIA achieved maximum power, and his abiding concern was concealing the funding for the covert operations of both the OSS and the CIA.[36] Appropriately, Pforzheimer was the CIA's liaison to the U.S. Congress when the Agency operated without any "legislative charter . . . running covert operations around the world before it had the slightest legal authority to do so."[37] He recalled that in 1949 the U.S. Congress "passed legislation authorizing the agency's secret [and, therefore, unmonitored] budget . . . ."[38]

## The William T. Golden Operation for the Bureau of the Budget

In the fall of 1950, during the Korean "police action," a major step was taken in the nexus of Bureau of the Budget and U.S. intelligence interests. The director of the BOB and his senior staff were apparently alerted by their military and intelligence friends that crucial policy options bearing on spending for "defense" and covert operations ought to be anticipated. Senior members of Budget Director Frederick J. Lawton's staff, without prior presidential direction, contacted William T. Golden about exploring certain important policy issues and then writing a report for the president under the auspices of the Bureau of the Budget.

Golden was then a Manhattan investment banker, but earlier he had been with the U.S. Navy in World War II, probably in technological intelligence, and in 1946 helped establish the Atomic Energy Commission. Golden "knew, or had access to, most of the principal civilian and military officials in the government, as well as many of the [U.S.'s] most influential scientists . . . ."[39] Golden's resume was powerful.

Without either presidential direction or authority, Bureau of the Budget consultant Golden[40] proceeded to meet with key American scientific individuals possessing high academic, military, and Congressional connections.[41] On October 20th, one day AFTER the Bureau of the Budget had submitted a memorandum to President Truman proposing what Golden was already deeply engaged in for the Bureau of the Budget, Golden met with Herman A. Spoehr, the new science advisor to Undersecretary of State James Webb.[42] Both Spoehr and Webb were quite comfortable with State Department intelligence and the CIA.

Golden had begun his scientific intelligence survey early in September, 1950; after a short series of meetings with scientific and political people, the key conversation with Webb's science advisor took place. Less than eight months later, Golden had completed his remarkable tour of the community of military/intelligence/technology experts thought relevant to the Bureau of the Budget's "detailed investigation."[43]

Golden's Bureau of the Budget records and memoranda are available at the American Association for the Advancement of Science Internet site.[44] His key Bureau of the Budget memoranda[45], covering most of his Bureau's field work from September, 1950, through April, 1961, outline an extraordinary exploration of possible covert technological operations, with the Bureau of the Budget, the State Department, and the CIA closely consulted.

Of the three "non-physicists" most interviewed by Golden, two were part of the larger BOB/intelligence context: Don K. Price, a political scientist, who had predictably been with the Bureau of the Budget; the other, James Killian the president of MIT.

Over an eight-month period, Killian, in fact, was an important conversation topic in fifty phone calls from Killian to Golden, Golden to Killian, and Golden to a series of military, academic, and intelligence figures.[46] As the Bureau of the Budget's field investigator, Golden was very interested in the management of "scientific intelligence," and Killian looked like the person for the job; ultimately the MIT president, for several years running the "science" side of the White House's intelligence policy options, indeed later became President Eisenhower's Science Advisor.

Through Golden's information-gathering of eight months, crucial areas were examined helping to shape how American science took part in the Cold War, especially as it was a working ally of American intelligence.[47]

October 27th, 1950, signaled the beginning of the Bureau of the Budget/U.S. scientific intelligence "review." It quickly became apparent that key issues besides satellites and super-sonar were being explored.[48] James E. Webb, Undersecretary of State, introduced as conversation topics with Golden the "U.S. Information Service and the Voice of America," "CIA intelligence activities in [undefined] scientific matters," a reference to the Troy Report (concerning Killian's Troy/Cenis operation at MIT), and the State Department's "Special Assistant-Intelligence": W. Park Armstrong, who was in fact the chief of the State Department's intelligence operations. The implicit Webb interest was, of course, psychological warfare: psyops. Bureau of the Budget master scout Golden would have his attention called to this crucial area of "technological intelligence" throughout the entire eight months of his BOB review.

Webb directed Golden to W. Park Armstrong at State, who then fed Golden material in certain "scientific matters," recommended Golden consult the Director of Scientific Intelligence for the CIA, and observed that Webb's scientific assistant at State would be doing "scientific intelligence" work for the Agency.[49]

## James R. Killian Enters

On December 19, 1950, Golden had an important telephone conversation with James R. Killian[50]; the MIT president was running an "ad hoc group" examining the entire area of scientific advice to the president. Clearly Killian wished to convey to Golden that the topic of a scientific advisor (and an associated supporting committee) for the president had not been fully explored, a tactic promoting Killian as the soundest source for such an exploration rather than any diverse group that had not been able to define its discourse (as Killian had implied). At one point, Killian obligingly described his ideal candidate for the presidential scientific advisor slot, a description remarkably like a profile of Killian himself. Golden could not have missed the implication.

Finally, Killian asserted that his group had "a definite feeling that representation [on the president's scientific advisory committee] should not be of the physical sciences exclusively; that is, there was a genuine recognition of the growing importance of the social sciences, particularly . . . the interrelationship [of the two] . . . ." Killian then cited "the Troy Report now under way . . . at MIT."

Killian could not have been clearer: scientific technology in the 1950s had to include what C.D. Jackson had introduced to Troy/Cenis: psychological warfare.

On December 21, 1950[51], Golden met with Lloyd Berkner, "a good friend of James Webb, Undersecretary of State," who was devoting half of his work time to the Troy Report under the "direction" of the MIT "Dean of Humanities," who answered, of course, to James Killian. By now Killian's man Berkner was being pushed as one of the leading candidates for the scientific advisor post.

That office finally went to Dr. Herman Spoehr, James Webb's scientific advisor, and the BOB/intelligence grip on "technological intelligence" seemed secure. Spoehr, however, left the office early, and Golden conferred with Dr. Lawrence Hafstad on February 6th, 1951.[52] The ideal person for the job (Lloyd Berkner, Killian's Troy man was no longer available) sounded, again, remarkably like James Killian: "a younger, more enterprising, vigorous and idea full man was necessary, and particularly one who knew his way around in the Government and especially in Washington."[53]

Lawrence Hafsted, on cue, informed Golden he was "much interested in [Golden's] . . . intelligence and overall studies of the Troy type . . . ." Psyops was the major topic again.

On February 20th, 1951[54], Golden met with the CIA's Assistant Head of the Agency's Scientific Section: the Company delivered to Golden its "critical comments" on Killian's Research and Development Board, nothing less than a confirmation of the CIA's "technological" intentions.

On March 6th, 1951[55], near the end of Golden's review of scientific intelligence sponsored by the Bureau of the Budget, Golden had a crucial conversation with James R. Killian at Golden's home in New York. Killian let Golden believe he was in full agreement with whatever the BOB's agent had discovered and concluded. But, Golden recorded in his memorandum, "as we were walking to his train at Grand Central, he spoke of his interest [in] . . . unorthodox warfare matters, and we talked briefly about this [topic] with reference to the Troy report . . . ."

Killian had again established the priority of psyops, and the Bureau of the Budget and U.S. intelligence had established their agenda for the 1950s.

The relations between Percival Brundage and his associates fused intelligence and budget control issues that further defined the sources of U.S. power and profit. Brundage had a select circle of powerful elitist friends, and chief among them was fellow Unitarian[56] James R. Killian, Jr.

Because of the OSS/CIA links to the Unitarians, Killian's religious connections have remained relevant.[57] At a local 'parish' level, Killian was the chair of the Standing Committee of the Unitarian Church in Wellesley, Massachusetts; more importantly, he had been a member of the Board of Directors and the Moderator of the national American Unitarian Association. What the Unitarians did both nationally and internationally would be of interest to Killian, whose personal and professional links were both.

## Killian and MIT: Technology and Intelligence

James Killian, MIT, and the exploitation of technology for intelligence purposes were united, beginning with World War II: MIT had cooperated with the U.S. military in "communications" and "navigation" research and development; the Cold War introduced the government-sponsored "Project Lincoln" that spawned MIT's Lincoln Laboratory.[58] One of the laboratory's project, in turn, became "SAGE," the Semi-Automated Ground Environment tracking program.[59] Finally, Mitre (a derivative of the Lincoln Lab) and SAGE both were developed into prototype military and civilian space control systems.[60] Throughout his tenure at the academic tech center, James Killian had directed MIT's union with U.S. technological intelligence.

Killian's managerial expertise began when he earned a degree in "management" at MIT, serving as the editor of *The Tech*, MIT's undergraduate newspaper in his senior year. Invited to write a sometime column on MIT undergraduate education for *Technology Review*, Killian became the assistant managing editor and, afterward, the managing editor of the magazine from 1930 through 1939. Killian also reportedly helped to establish MIT's "Technology Press."

In 1939, Killian became executive assistant to MIT's president Karl Taylor Compton, and when the National Defense Research Committee called on MIT President Compton to join in the war effort, Killian became the MIT president's "surrogate" in running the Cambridge technological center at precisely the same time MIT was deeply involved in development and research for the U.S. government. Killian had made himself so indispensable that on June 8th, 1942, Compton wrote to Killian's draft board, requesting that his executive assistant receive a 3B deferment so that Killian could continue to direct MIT's collaboration with the War Department.[61] James Killian was certainly responsible for enlarging MIT's role as the "largest of the university military contractors."[62]

By 1943, Killian had become executive vice president of MIT, and by 1945, he was vice president of MIT and an MIT Corporation member.

In 1949, Killian accepted the presidency of the Massachusetts Institute of Technology (MIT) beginning his career in the development of science, technology, and the arts at MIT, his service to the U.S. government, and his direct involvement in American covert intelligence. It was an unprecedented rise to academic/technological power: "Killian had spent his entire adult life at MIT—an undergraduate in business and engineering, editor of the Technology Review and then while climbing the bureaucratic ladder until he became [MIT] president in 1949."[63]

Killian reportedly registered his support for academic freedom immediately after his inauguration as MIT president.[64] But within a year of his becoming the leader of the Cambridge institution, Killian accommodated Harvard's Project Troy (later CENIS, the Center for International Studies) for meetings on his MIT campus. Project Troy/CENIS became a think tank dedicated to intelligence analyses of China, the Soviet Union, to nuclear weapons and their delivery systems.[65]

Troy/CENIS's fusion of intellectual exploration, psychological warfare (sparked by C.D. Jackson), and practical defense application must have been the exact mix that excited James R. Killian, Jr., whose "vision . . . gave a humanistic sensitivity to [MIT's] . . . role as a foremost institution of science and technology."[66]

"The Center for International Studies [CENIS] at MIT . . . was at its founding financed . . . by the Central Intelligence Agency."[67] James Killian's MIT programs, receiving CIA "secret funds," were, in fact, being monitored by James Killian himself, whose "board" was "designed to provide . . . surveillance of the CIA . . . ."[68] The comment from a close friend of U.S. intelligence was exact: "It could be argued that MIT was . . . providing 'cover' for [the] CIA."[69] In fact, MIT provided "cover" for both American military and intelligence for fifty years.[70]

In 1951, Killian's intelligence links were further developed when MIT's Lincoln Laboratory was established, where the U.S. SAGE "air defense system" was researched and developed.[71] In turn, Lincoln Lab was founded on the work of Edwin Land (Killian's associate) and a series of government-sponsored Cold War investigations; Land had, in fact, a major "secret career as a military advisor" to President Eisenhower.[72]

The year 1954 was a key moment in the lives and careers of both Percival Brundage and James Killian. Topping three years of dedicated work for U.S. technical intelligence while still at the helm of MIT, Killian accepted the chair of President Eisenhower's Technological Capabilities Panel, commissioned to measure the nation's "security and intelligence capabilities following the Soviet Union's announcement in August of 1953 . . . it had successfully tested a hydrogen bomb."[73] From that moment on, Eisenhower relied heavily on Killian-approved scientists and technicians for advice on "arms control" and military questions.

The new Killian panel was authorized to study both military and intelligence applications of (what was then called) "high-flight reconnaissance," in effect technological snoopery that involved people in applied science and covert operations like Edwin H. Land (of Polaroid) and Richard Bissell and, of course, the magical "U-2."[74] Aerospace espionage was the top and bottom lines.[75]

Land had been appointed by James Killian as the chief of the top-secret intelligence section of the Air Force Technological Capabilities Panel, giving Land theoretical control of all high-flight reconnaissance operations and establishing a research and development line that led to the U-2 and major U.S. "satellite technology."[76] Further, Land was responsible for Eisenhower's decision to give the U-2 program to the CIA.[77]

Predictably, the Killian Panel recommended increased reliance on science and technology in the collection of aerospace military intelligence[78], followed by a continuing close cooperation between Killian, Land, Bissell, and Eisenhower's close White House associate, General Andrew Goodpaster.[79]

In 1957, following his three-year technical intelligence work for the government, Killian was appointed President Eisenhower's Special Assistant for Science and Technology, holding a cabinet-level portfolio in everything except name. Killian's assignment from 1957 through 1959 was "evaluating national technological and intelligence capabilities."[80]

Like Percival Brundage, Killian was a full-fledged member of the American elite, the "advisor, trustee, or director for . . . organizations such as the Alfred P. Sloan Foundation, . . . the Boston Museum of Fine Arts, AT&T, Cabot Corporation, General Motors, IBM, Ingersoll-Rand, and Polaroid."[81]

Obviously, Killian's organizational expertise was especially valued in the corporate sector of defense and aerospace.

While Killian served as a remarkable and productive number of years as MIT President and then Chairman of the MIT Corporation from 1948 through 1971, he remained in intimate touch with U.S. intelligence activities. Immediately after he concluded his chairing of the national Technological Capabilities Panel, Killian, newly designated Eisenhower's Special Assistant for Science and Technology, was appointed by the president in 1956 as first chairman of the U.S. Board of Consultants on Foreign Intelligence Activities, an oversight committee created by Eisenhower on January 13th, 1956 (and later reconstituted under John F. Kennedy as the President's Foreign Intelligence Advisory Board).[82]

In establishing his Board of Consultants, President Eisenhower had closely followed the advice of the Hoover Commission on White House/intelligence re-organization[83], heavily supported by the Bureau of the Budget's Percival Brundage.[84] The Board, led by James R. Killian, Jr., eventually served as an effective cover for foreign covert intelligence programs, including the historic U-2 flights. Among the members of the Board in its first six months was Joseph Kennedy, the father of (then) Senator John F. Kennedy; but Ambassador Kennedy resigned when his son began his unsuccessful campaign to become the Democratic Party's Vice Presidential candidate in 1956.[85] Led by James Killian, Eisenhower's Board of Consultants was to oversee and "report to him [the president] periodically on the work of the [U.S.] intelligence organizations . . . , particularly the CIA . . . ."[86]

As the chair of the president's Board of Consultants, Killian asked David Bruce, an experienced U.S. foreign diplomat and former OSS officer, and attorney Robert Lovett to examine the CIA's clandestine operations and report to the president: the "Bruce/Lovett" report is still secret. But enough of it has been leaked to researchers and writers to establish that the report attacked the intimate relationship between Allen Dulles and John Foster Dulles, a relationship repeatedly resulting in foreign policy most friendly to the Dulles' own interests.[87]

Killian's 1956 strategy had insured he would be called upon to instruct the president concerning crucial intelligence decisions in the future; further, his support of a finding critical of the Dulles brothers' collaboration did not mean Killian could not be an intelligence team player, including controlling the U-2 program.

## U-2, Allen Dulles, and the CIA

A history of the monitoring of U.S. intelligence could rightly be called "The Hen House: Enlisting the Available Fox." When it became clear that the U-2 would revolutionize aerospace and high-flight intelligence surveillance, a dozen information-gathering units of both civilian and military intelligence put in their bids for operational control. Following the advice of his Board of Consultants led, of course, by James Killian and Edwin Land, Eisenhower called on CIA Director Allen Dulles to organize and oversee the U.S. manned high-flight surveillance program; in turn, Dulles delegated the work to his deputy Richard Bissell. According to Bissell, the program was funded from the CIA's "contingency reserve."[88] The reserve was dedicated to covert operations, and was "replenished periodically" by the U.S. Congress without being reviewed with the same rigor as rest of the Executive Branch's budget.[89] This special Agency budget exemption was based on a control fiction: any outlay of funds "had to be authorized by the director of the Budget of the Bureau and approved by the president."[90]

Reportedly no record was demanded detailing the cost of the clandestine operation, insuring "quickness and flexibility" as well as "greater secrecy," but the procedure "also created opportunities for misuse that the CIA would exploit in future years for [at best] questionable programs . . . ."[91]

Supported by the ever-present Bureau of the Budget, the project was "code-named Aquatone."[92]

Bissell enlisted an all-star supportive intelligence team that included Robert Lovett, veteran of the Departments of Defense and State and American intelligence; James Baker of Harvard; Edwin Land (of Polaroid); Kelly Johnson (of Lockheed); Trevor Gardner (formally Assistant to the Secretary of the Air Force for Research and Development); and Bissell's brightest star, James Killian of MIT.[93] Killian ran the high-flight operation until 1958, when other intelligence concerns reportedly had higher priorities.[94]

In the midst of developing the White House's argument for what would become "NASA," on February 7th, 1958, Edwin Land, the ever-present James Killian, and Andrew Goodpaster, Eisenhower's close aide and CIA contact, met with President Eisenhower to argue that the Air Force was, in effect, a failure at developing "a photographic reconnaissance satellite."[95] The Air Force program, first designated SENTRY and then SAMOS, was then turned over to the Central Intelligence Agency, with Kelly Johnson and Richard Bissell appointed as the leaders of the program, renamed CORONA.[96]

Killian's small circle of elitists continued to control the U.S.'s most advanced intelligence technology.

When Killian resigned from the president's intelligence Board of Consultants, leaving for Boston, the Board "went into hibernation and . . . ceased to be a functioning body . . . ."[97] No official document has established why such an important presidential intelligence group would stop functioning. Later, apparently responding to a signal from Eisenhower's staff or from an unidentified high-ranking official of the U.S. intelligence community, Eisenhower's slumbering Board of Consultants awoke for just a moment and, just two weeks before John F. Kennedy was inaugurated[98], officially "disbanded on January 7, 1961, when the entire membership [including Chairman James R. Killian, Jr.,] resigned [ostensibly] in anticipation of the new [JFK] administration."[99] Contrary to the often inaccurate "history" of the Kennedy administration, JFK did NOT disband the Eisenhower/Killian intelligence board; the group cancelled itself BEFORE Kennedy ever took presidential office. After the Bay of Pigs disaster, JFK moved quickly to re-establish the White House's connection to foreign intelligence monitoring, and, following the advice of close associates, Kennedy offered the chair of his new President's Foreign Intelligence Advisory Board (PFIAB)[100] to a trusted friend of U.S. intelligence operations: James R. Killian, Jr.[101]

Killian's technological and intelligence credentials, especially in high-flight surveillance and aerospace, had impressed the new president, aware of the MIT president's continuing involvement in the U.S. space program. When Killian welcomed Project Troy to his Cambridge campus and then, in 1951, established Lincoln Laboratory, he had signaled he was already a major player in the national aerospace/intelligence game.

From the moment in 1947 when the National Security Council and the Central Intelligence Agency were created, the control of the government's "space policy" dictated major civilian and military involvement in aerospace and, therefore, the path to immense power and profit. When the smoke cleared, that policy was "molded chiefly by the National Aeronautics and Space Administration (NASA), the nation's [ostensibly] civilian space agency, and the Department of Defense (DOD), especially the US Air Force."[102]

## Who Had Structured the Control of U.S. Space Policy?

After World War II, the "American military had decided to concentrate on the [U.S.] existing manned aircraft fleet to deliver its nuclear might and not actively pursue the development of an intercontinental ballistic missile (ICBM)."[103] The Soviets, without "air power" and behind the U.S. in "nuclear warhead technology," opted for developing "the enormous rocket boosters required to carry their heavy nuclear bombs over intercontinental ranges."[104] The so-called "missile gap" had been born.

Edwin Land (according to MIT scholar Victor McElhney) was a secret military advisor to President Eisenhower on "photoreconnaissance technology."[105] Land participated in a series of "advisory committees and study panels, including Project Charles and Project Beacon Hill."[106] And it was "Project Charles," focusing on the U.S. "air defense measures,"[107] that "provided a justification for . . . MIT's Lincoln Laboratory . . . ."[108] For James Killian, the ultimate chief of Lincoln Lab, Land was a key intelligence asset.

In 1951, Killian's MIT Lincoln Laboratory analyses on "U.S. air defense" had been initiated[109], and in January of 1951 the U.S. Air Force gave its first "funded ICBM study contract to Convair . . . ."[110] The American ICBM program was inaugurated. Four years later, despite both the Army and the Navy being deeply involved in "missile development," the U.S. Air Force and associated aerospace companies such as General Dynamics (having taken over the Convair ICBM operations), Martin Marietta, and Douglas received the Eisenhower administration's official blessing.[111] Friends in very high places, including James Killian, Percival Brundage, and Lyndon Baines Johnson, helped.[112]

In the fall of 1955, the American government had three possibilities for launching satellites; two were tested vehicles closely associated with the Pentagon.[113] The third was "an entirely new launch vehicle based on the Viking sounding rocket technology."[114] Despite the new and largely untested launcher having both military and intelligence support, and despite its primary advocate being Bureau of the Budget officer Percival Brundage who was a long-time advocate of the dominant military/intelligence/corporate mix, President Eisenhower apparently accepted the argument that Brundage's launcher was a scientific/civilian operation, and, given the strong psyops orientation of the White House, that it would help "to present an image to the world of the United States fostering the peaceful uses of space . . . ."[115] That image was, of course, a fiction: Project Vanguard had always been about satellite military surveillance.[116]

For the next two years, despite Percy Brundage's support, the Vanguard was a total multi-million dollar failure.[117] By the fall of 1957, aerospace/Air Force advocate Senator Stuart Symington was calling for "a full investigation," and Senator Lyndon Johnson announced he planned an immediate inquiry into the missile/satellite "Gap."[118] Too little money, too little expertise[119]: the U.S. space program, both civilian and military, needed an immediate hero.

On November 7th, 1957, only forty-eight hours after the second successful Soviet "Sputnik" launching, President Eisenhower announced that Dr. James R. Killian, the president of MIT, a powerful member of the Unitarian community, had accepted the position of his Science Advisor. When Eisenhower established the "President's Science Advisory Committee" (PSAC), he handed Killian still another technological baton, with the MIT leader clearly the PSAC's chief honcho. It was no coincidence that Edwin Land, a key Killian associate, immediately became a powerful member of the PSAC, co-authoring a policy paper that helped establish the National Reconnaissance Office (NRO), one of the most secret of U.S. secret intelligence programs.[120] Killian coordinated Department of Defense and Central Intelligence Agency agreements organizing the NRO. Killian's deputy Edwin Land and his PSAC continued to review "proposals and provide technical oversight for spy-plane and spy-satellite projects" through the Cold War period until President Nixon closed down the group.[121]

Edwin Land, Killian's close associate, ultimately served five U.S. presidents and an equal number of CIA directors, steering a technological ship that was manned by Killian and Land's military, intelligence, corporate, and academic allies.

It seemed inevitable that Killian would gain control of the U.S. space program, but the institutional distribution of power, privilege and profit within that program was a major concern of the establishment, the Pentagon, American intelligence, and, of course, the aerospace corporate community. "NASA" and the Pentagon's missile and high-flight surveillance operations were about to become airborne.[122]

## The Space Program as Psyops

Space historian Homer Newell (who was also a major participant in the development of U.S. aerospace) did not name C.D. Jackson as the chief source of Eisenhower's space psyops program, but the president was clearly following Jackson's recommendations on presenting the "appearance"[123] of U.S. aerospace leadership, whatever the Soviets were achieving: beginning in the "formative months of late 1957 and the first half of 1958"[124], the various U.S. "academic, industrial, and political forces [reportedly] merged in a common conviction that the country must put its space house in order."[125] Next came a campaign to prove that American space leadership (read 'dominance') would be "open"[126], a psyops theme common both to Percival Brundage's "Open Skies"/Vanguard promotion and C.D. Jackson's campaign in support of Eisenhower's "Open Skies" argument. Brundage and Jackson were quite well aware that the satellite program was, in fact, intended to give the United States unparalleled overflight surveillance intelligence.

"It was [therefore] an important thesis for the U.S. public to continue to believe and to sell to the rest of the world and, therefore, in a matter as portentous as space seemed to be, special efforts were needed to present the proper image."[127] The "proper image" of the U.S. space endeavor (whatever its reality) was to be "open, "unclassified," "visibly peaceful," and "conducted . . . to benefit, not harm, the peoples of the world."[128]

C.D. Jackson would have enthusiastically agreed with what was undoubtedly his own "thesis," and whether or not James Killian was fully aware of the major psyops dimension of Eisenhower's space proposal, Percival Brundage, in his advocacy of the Vanguard, certainly was.

The solution to the organizational control of U.S. aerospace development, both civilian and military, would have been to establish an independent agency with two sub-divisions, one clearly scientific and research-oriented, the other clearly and powerfully Pentagon, combining the efforts of the Army, Navy, Air Force and any of the defensive/offensive on-going or planned aerospace programs.

But one big problem was the absence of the Thirteenth Fairy who was not invited to Aerospace Beauty's birthday party. Where was U.S. intelligence? Where was the CIA, the NSC, the NCO, the Pentagon, the DIA, the ONI, and all the rest?

The cover story continued to be that, though the military (and intelligence, its covert partner) had the major aerospace experience, "the program should be set up under civilian auspices."[129] Newell's official history of the period simply falsifies several key factors, including Eisenhower being "distressed over the enormous power and unmanageability of . . . the military-industrial complex . . ."[130] and the president's concern about "adding still another very costly enterprise to the Pentagon's responsibilities."[131] The "complex" simply was not a public issue until the end of Eisenhower's administration, and nothing in the Bureau of the Budget's documents even hints at any Eisenhower worry about a growing debit column for the Department of Defense.

What was really relevant was a reconstruction within the Eisenhower administration, including replacing the Secretary of Defense, establishing the Advanced Research Projects Agency, and passing the Defense Reorganization Act with its Office of the Director of Defense and Research Engineering.[132] These changes (and still others) helped create a maze of defense and research appointments in space operations, allowing the real national players to take control of U.S. aerospace, including James Killian.

As Eisenhower's top gun for science and technology, James Killian led his associates on the President's Science Advisory Committee, the Rocket and Satellite Research Panel, the National Academy of Sciences, the Space Science Board, the American Rocket Society, and still other organizations and groups of concerned scientists and researchers in "pressing for a space program under civilian management with a strong scientific flavor."[133]

Despite this heavy support for a "program under civilian auspices," a "deluge of proposals descended upon various congressional committees" that guaranteed the final decision would be made by a small group of powerful people.[134]

## The Killian/Brundage/Bissell/Rockefeller Space Program

Killian's solution was, therefore, both bizarre and yet absolutely perfect for the man who would ultimately control the development of both civilian and military aerospace: Killian organized his argument in favor of NACA, the National Committee for Aeronautics, the least likely candidate to run the American Space program.[135] "NACA would not have been the choice of most scientists. As a highly ingrown activity, the agency did not enjoy a particularly great esteem in scientific circles, being thought of more as an applied research activity serving primarily industry and the military."[136] By the time Killian chose NACA, "many scientists . . . as well as aircraft manufacturers and military officers . . . [felt] that NACA had withered into a timid bureaucracy . . . ."[137]

At best, beginning with its creation in March, 1915, NACA had pursued "solid, aerodynamic research," first for the War Department and then the Department of Defense and the successive department's collaborating corporations.[138]

But NACA had at least one significant and authentic intelligence link that compromised all its future scientific goals, a link initiated by the Brundage/Killian/Bissell network: "In early 1956, [Richard] Bissell paid [a] . . . call on Hugh Dryden, . . . head of the National Advisory Committee on Aeronautics [that was then] purely a domestic operation, furnishing information on air turbulence and other problems to military and commercial aircraft makers."[139] Bissell informed Dryden about the U-2 and enlisted NACA and its chief in the high-flying spy story: "NACA would announce the existence of a plane called the U-2 to be used for a NACA weather program."[140] Despite NACA's "nervous" response[141], Dryden signed up NACA as the CIA's espionage cover, announcing that the Lockheed U-2s were on loan from the Air Force, their civilian pilots on loan from Lockheed itself.[142]

Killian prepared his NACA proposal plan in close cooperation with Percival Brundage, the friend of military and intelligence spending and his Bureau of the Budget.[143]

A mini-committee of three: Nelson Rockefeller, another admirer and supporter of U.S. intelligence and the chair of the President's Advisory Committee on Government Organization; Director Percival Brundage of the Bureau of the Budget; and Eisenhower's Special Assistant James Killian "jointly delivered" to the president on March 5th, 1958, their memorandum nominating NACA as the "civilian" wing of the U.S. space program; though they admitted to a "number of liabilities" in promoting NACA, the triumvirate assured Eisenhower these problems would be "overcome by enacting appropriate legislation."[144]

Rockefeller, Killian, and Brundage had, in fact, 'structured' a shell labeled "NACA," renamed it the "National Aeronautical and Space Agency," argued for retaining NACA's seventeen-member "governing committee," and assured the president that NACA's committee "membership would be changed and its power reduced."[145]

But though a shell, NACA ultimately turned over considerable assets to NASA, including eight thousand employees, three laboratories (renamed "research centers"), a flight station, a rocket facility, and a $100 million budget.[146]

The president accepted the Rockefeller/Killian/Brundage "civilian space agency" proposal (as described in their memorandum) on the same day he received it.[147] The White House immediately commissioned Percival Brundage and his Bureau of the Budget to "draft [Congressional] legislation."[148] Preparing to submit his enabling bill to Congress, Brundage received "assistance" from NACA, now a powerless agency, and, most significantly, from the office of Eisenhower's special assistant for science and technology, James Killian.[149] Thus Killian and Brundage, the allies of the aerospace corporations, the Pentagon, and U.S. intelligence, controlled the administration's legislative proposal for a "civilian" space program.[150]

On April 2nd, the president offered his Brundage/Killian "NASA" legislation to Congress.[151] Now Percival Brundage argued for "a single responsible head for the new [space] agency" who would not be hampered by any "board of experts."[152] The critical arguments piled up against the administration's legislative proposal, for example, that its "provisions" lacked key "congressional oversight" or "international cooperation" and that it was missing a score of fundamental elements crucial to defining the distinction between civilian and military aerospace controls and goals[153], but Congress still adopted the administration's Brundage/Killian legislation.[154] How could it have happened?

## LBJ, the Bureau of the Budget, American Intelligence, and the Space Program

Aerospace, U.S. intelligence, and the Bureau of the Budget had a close friend in Congress. Beside his multiple legislative identities insuring control of any aerospace bill about to come before the Senate, on February 13th, 1958, Majority Leader Lyndon Johnson had been elected the chair of the Senate's Special Committee on Space and Astronautics, and with LBJ as its chief, the body soon became a permanent committee overseeing the crucial U.S. space budget.[155] LBJ's potent cooperation was vital to moving the Brundage/Killian legislation through the Senate, despite the bill's obvious defects.[156]

On April 14th, 1958, the Eisenhower administration's space bill was introduced in Congress. "NACA" was to become "NASA," and U.S. aerospace operations would be administered in some undefined relationship between "NASA" and the Pentagon, "with no formal coordination dictated in the legislation."[157] Some critics of the (less than specific) empowering Congressional legislation had questioned who, in fact, would be in charge of the American aerospace effort, but James Killian and his Scientific Advisory Committee sternly "advised that to [set up a joint civilian-military space program] would violate President Eisenhower's personal philosophy and jeopardize the US initiative to reserve space for scientific and peaceful purposes."[158]

The Killian advice sounded remarkably like what Percival Brundage at the Bureau of the Budget had already offered the Eisenhower administration.[159]

Though the Senate version of the Eisenhower space bill differentiated between "NASA" and the Department of Defense (the two entities designated to cooperate in organizing the U.S. aerospace program), the Congressional "conference committee" opted for the House version that only established a "military liaison committee . . . of personnel from the DOD."[160] This "liaison committee" was then given the absolute power to coordinate NASA (a still non-existent entity) and Pentagon operations.[161]

Ongoing Army and Navy space "capabilities" were folded into "NASA," while the U.S. Air Force and the operations of the Advanced Research Projects Agency (ARPA) became major components of the Department of Defense's aerospace endeavors.[162]

Following Senator Johnson's impressive lead, Congress had not defined "the specific content of the space program with which the NASA Act was concerned."[163] The entire organization of the U.S. aerospace operation, including its research, military, and "civilian" dimensions, was left undefined.[164]

As Percival Brundage intended, the "lack of a specifically prescribed [aerospace] program gave the first administrator of NASA a wide degree of latitude . . . , a freedom of choice . . . little curtailed by [whatever] guidance . . . James Killian supplied in the summer of 1958 . . . ."[165] That lack of "guidance" by Killian as the president's science advisor meant that only the proper people in both 'civilian' space research and the more highly developed intelligence programs of the Department of Defense would wield actual aerospace power.

Theoretically, "an administration for space was established, including [1.] a mechanism for adjudicating possible conflicts between NASA and DOD [the Pentagon] via the Civilian-Military Liaison Committee and [2.] a method for forming total space policy via the National Aeronautics and Space Council with the President [of the United States] as the [Council's] first Administrator."[166]

By law, Eisenhower had indeed become both a working member of the Council and its chair. But the "Council" was a cumbersome organization based, though not by law, in the White House's Executive Office of the President, its membership made up of the Director of NASA, the Chair of the Atomic Energy Commission, the Secretaries of Defense and State, and three presidentially-appointed members.[167]

The president "made little use of the Aeronautics and Space Council,"[168] the legislated governing body of NASA. Killian, Brundage, and Senator Johnson had fashioned a "civilian" aerospace control mechanism that was unworkable. Crucially, the president (impatient with the Council's complexity) had not provided the Council with its own permanent Executive Office staff[169], "so it was left to NASA [in charge of aerospace "field" operations] and the Bureau of the Budget to do the [Council's] staff work."[170]

The Bureau of the Budget was now in charge of the administrative side of U.S. aeronautics.

By September, 1960, NASA and the Pentagon had established an "Aeronautics and Astronautics Coordinating Board" that effectively "took over the functions of the [so-called] Civilian-Military Liaison Committee."[171] Whatever non-military brake on the U.S. aerospace intelligence program that had been (at least theoretically) in place was now gone.

But NASA registered a series of launch failures; the Bureau of the Budget and LBJ's Senate committees broadcast NASA's ineptitude; and in the 1960 presidential campaign, John F. Kennedy, following the advice of his partner LBJ, pressed the argument of both missile and space "gaps."[172]

## John F. Kennedy, LBJ, and the Space Program

After defeating Richard Nixon, John F. Kennedy immediately began to plan America's major entry into space, to eliminate the reported "missile gap," and to advance his vision of a U.S. lunar landing. Responding to Lyndon Johnson's urgent request to command U.S. aerospace, Kennedy "decided in January 1961 that . . . Johnson would have special responsibilities for coordinating and overseeing US space efforts."[173] The National Aeronautics and Space Council (NASC) was placed officially in the Executive Office of the President, the Vice President (replacing the President) was by law designated its chair, the Council was decreased in size, and, with LBJ as its chief, the NASC was now commissioned to coordinate cooperation "among all departments and agencies of the United States engaged in aeronautical and space activities."[174]

LBJ had become the head of Kennedy's entire aerospace program.

Johnson's first assignment was to find a new chief for NASA.[175] Though LBJ had several candidates available who were considered "outstanding" and whose experience in space technology was considerably greater than his ultimate choice[176], the Vice President immediately selected James E. Webb.

Recall that Webb was closely associated with a Bureau of the Budget search that touched on psyops, the Troy project, James R. Killian, Jr., and the CIA. His earliest credentials were in education and law[177]; beginning in 1932, Webb worked in politics and public service. Between 1936 and 1944, he moved from personnel director to vice president at Sperry Gyroscope, leaving the company to serve as a Marine officer in World War II. After the war, Webb returned to Washington and joined the staff of an old friend, O. Max Gardner, then Under Secretary of the Treasury. A consummate Beltway insider, Webb was perceived to be a wizard of bureaucratic manipulation.

From 1946 through 1949, when the Bureau of the Budget capped its deconstruction of the Office of Special Services (OSS) by supporting the establishment of the National Security Agency and the Central Intelligence Agency, James E. Webb was the Director of the Bureau of the Budget.[178]

The Bureau had surfaced again.

Nominated on LBJ's recommendation, Webb was "endorsed" by LBJ's old "Space Committee" and then gained the enthusiastic confirmation of the U.S. Senate.[179] To hire his "NASA" chief, Vice President Johnson had gone directly to the administrative unit historically supportive of U.S. space intelligence: the Bureau of the Budget.[180]

The National Aeronautics and Space Council, reactivated by President Kennedy, was also turned over to the vice president[181] , making Lyndon Baines Johnson, earlier the key Senate supporter of the Bureau of the Budget during Percival Brundage's years at the Bureau, JFK's most powerful aerospace officer. LBJ would now control the contracts and connections that made Texas the mega-productive center of military and intelligence aerospace.

Whatever scientific or purely non-military goals the U.S. space program might have had, Percival Brundage, James Killian, and Lyndon Baines Johnson insured that the matrix of aerospace/corporate/intelligence would benefit from the U.S. reach beyond the Earth.

The fiction that NASA was ever the "civilian" side of U.S. space programs has become threadbare: from NASA's inception, led by James R. Killian and Percival Flack Brundage, it was conceived as an intelligence and military operation. William E. Burrows, America's foremost historian of the Space Age, concluded in 1998: "Where international politics and the balance of power were concerned, the military and civilian space programs were not only interchangeable, they were fundamentally inseparable."[182]

Alan Shepard's successful flight into space was followed by JFK's commission to his aerospace commander: LBJ was "to study the matter in hand" and then bring a bold proposal to enter the race against the Soviets in space. Johnson assigned McNamara and James E. Webb (the perfect union of corporate power, Pentagon, Bureau of the Budget, and intelligence) to write the proposal that would define NASA's next major goal, the Moon, as "part of the battle along the fluid front of the cold war."[183]

Given the identity of the team LBJ put together (including Johnson himself) and their military-intelligence interests, President Kennedy must have known that his inspired Moon goal was being supported by people with less exalted aspirations. For Lyndon Baines Johnson and his close military, intelligence, and corporate friends, the lunar landscape was covered with gold.

To his presidential partner, LBJ left JFK a dream of stars. From John F. Kennedy's inaugural address through the end of his administration in a killing Dallas crossfire, JFK's "personal and decisive participation in [aerospace] policymaking . . . gave the nation a clear space policy with management by a strong civilian agency, with a firm goal, and with strong direction expected to continue [after his murder] from the top of the Government."[184]

However romantic that assessment, it was close to the truth.

## The Budget Monitoring Fiction: The Bureau of the Budget and the CIA

Throughout the Truman/Eisenhower/Kennedy/Johnson administrations, budget monitoring was a successful fiction. Contrary to accepted but faulty information, the so-called "budget" of the Department of Defense was seldom (if ever) independently monitored and analyzed by the Bureau of the Budget[185] (or after 1969 by the Office of Management and Budget).[186] Most often, during the Eisenhower and later presidential administrations, the chief representative of the Joint Chiefs of Staff conferred with the Director of the Budget (or his designate, the Deputy Director of the Budget), usually prior to a joint meeting between the Secretary of Defense, the Director or Deputy Director of the Bureau of the Budget, and the current president. No matter what the apparent Defense arguments and Bureau of the Budget counter-arguments, the padded Pentagon shopping list would finally be approved, minus some of its stuffing.[187]

If we realize this special handling of defense appropriations outside of the budget/ auditing process, we then understand comments like: "During the Eisenhower years, the Bureau of the Budget (BOB) . . . played a . . . relatively minor role in defense budgeting. [Later] . . . BOB had virtually no independent role in the formulation of the defense budget . . . ."[188] Put plainly, the Joint Chiefs of Staff, the Pentagon bureaucracy, and their friends the military contractors had no need to fear being slashed by the Bureau of the Budget's blunted quills.

In the 1950s, this outside-the-accounting "process" insured that what Eisenhower called the "military-industrial complex" would be well-served with weapons, support systems, and intelligence black budget items (both military and "civilian") hidden in the Pentagon's so-called budget.[189]

After the National Security Council and the Central Intelligence Agency were established in 1947, the Bureau of the Budget was, in fact, a working partner of the CIA and at worst "a minor irritant" to the Agency.[190] As late as 1974, the "International Affairs Division's intelligence branch" of the Office of Management and Budget (the later manifestation of the Bureau of the Budget) had a staff of only five persons to oversee the CIA, the National Security Agency, the National Reconnaissance Office, the Defense Intelligence Agency, and all "the rest of military intelligence."[191] Given even the best of budgetary intentions by the Bureau of the Budget, its job in the earlier 1950s was overwhelming.[192]

When the National Security Council (NSC) mapped out its military and intelligence goals and established its range of necessary funding, the NSC then released the Bureau of the Budget from any further responsibility for monitoring the CIA's spending, allowing the Agency to deal directly with the Congress's various oversight committees and subcommittees, especially the CIA's longtime Senate and House supporters.

What was true in the late 1940s and 1950s was still true in the late 60s: "the CIA has been granted certain privileges uncommon to government agencies. It is not required to publish personnel data in the *Federal Register*; it is exempted from certain congressional and Bureau of the Budget oversight requirements; and it can bring up to 100 aliens into the country annually outside the normal immigration channels. Finally, very few public officials even know what the CIA's budget is[,] since it is effectively concealed within the budgets of a number of other agencies."[193]

Almost everyone simply has had to guess at the Agency's 'actual' spending power: "It was not until 1997 that the CIA finally disclosed the annual intelligence budget: $26.6 billion."[194] But that figure was still not accurate: though it included all "intelligence" outside of the Pentagon, it did not add the value of and income from various properties and proprietaries (including, most probably, banks) the CIA either owned or operated.

When Bureau accountants in the 1950s cut social and human expenditures (but not military funding), President Eisenhower was "understandably reluctant [as were the presidents before and after him] to overrule his own budgetary watchdog."[195] So budget cutting by the Bureau was supported by the White House: the Director of the Bureau of the Budget was all powerful, except, of course, for the double clout of the Department of Defense and the Central Intelligence Agency. The 1958 fiscal budget was the largest "ever drawn up in peacetime"[196] and dominated by defense and foreign aid, the latter two areas "accounting for close to 60 percent of all federal expenditures."[197] Eisenhower apparently had wished for some reductions in funding projections; but the Joint Chiefs of Staff, unhampered by the Bureau of Budget, appeared before Congressional appropriations hearings and not only opposed any suggested expenditure cuts but begged for still more money.[198] In the 1950s, with no real control exerted by Percival Flack Brundage's Bureau of the Budget and Congress eager to support ongoing or new defense programs located in their home states, the Pentagon got what it wanted.

Despite the 1947 enabling act that placed the CIA outside the legal and constitutional monitoring process, the fiction of Bureau of the Budget overview was thinly maintained; yet even then the CIA flaunted its extra-budgetary strength. For example, the Agency refused to allow the Bureau of Budget 'examiner' to enter its headquarters until his questionable identity was checked.[199] But the Central Intelligence Agency finally eliminated even that minor annoyance by placing "former" CIA operatives as auditors in the Bureau of the Budget who were then assigned to examine the Agency's books for the Bureau.[200]

Yet, even then, every incident of accounting challenge to the CIA was met with Agency "attitude": its actions were regularly announced as "above normal bureaucratic restraints."[201] From 1947 through the 1960s, the Bureau of the Budget[202] absolutely failed "to exercise any degree of meaningful control over the CIA."[203] That crucial period included the six-year tenure of Percival Brundage as Deputy Director, Director, and key "consultant" of the Bureau of Budget.[204]

## Eisenhower, Brundage, the Bureau of the Budget and Defense Spending

President Eisenhower had worked closely with Percival Brundage and the Bureau on the difficult 1958 fiscal budget, but he knew that control of defense spending was, in fact, a two-step dance performed by the hungry Joint Chiefs of Staff and a compliant Congress.[205] Despite Brundage's national auditing record, the Eisenhower time in office was one long accounting disaster[206] for the federal government: "Lax and sloppy enforcement of government regulations and contractual provisions, preferential treatment of the giant [defense] contractors, unconcern with the economic consequences of military [and black budget operations] spending . . . became the order of the day . . . ."[207] All the supposedly responsible divisions of the U.S. government, especially the Bureau of the Budget (theoretically the president's funding watchdog), so lost national accounting control that military and covert intelligence spending was simply set free from civilian (and constitutional) oversight.

The Joint Chiefs and Brundage's Bureau of the Budget played the same self-serving game throughout the Eisenhower years; the Joint Chiefs of Staff regularly complained "that the Bureau of the Budget's conservative approach to government expenditures was impairing new [military] programs such as those for intercontinental ballistic missiles, nuclear aircraft carriers, the B-70 bomber and the nuclear-powered airplane."[208]

But the Bureau of the Budget never blocked such programs except in support of some other equally or more important division of the same intelligence-corporate-military complex.

When Senator Lyndon B. Johnson became chair of the Committee on Aeronautical and Space Science, the Texas powerbroker had been able to wear two significant military/intelligence hats, chairing both the Senate Preparedness Subcommittee and Aeronautical and Space Science.[209] In 1959 and then in 1960 during Senate hearings called "Missiles, Space, and Other Major Defense Matters"[210], Johnson gave a splendid "I'm shocked" response to testimony from the Bureau of the Budget, the Joint Chiefs, and from a raft of "military experts."[211] Even Eisenhower's Secretary of Defense cooperated with Senator Johnson in establishing the fictional but crucial "missile gap."[212] A typical LBJ topic—how big was his "missile" opposed to any one else's—had been established (despite its military fiction), and, given LBJ's enthusiastic support, it became a major political argument in the JFK/LBJ presidential campaign[213], an issue often mistakenly attributed to John F. Kennedy himself.

## LBJ, the Bureau of the Budget, and Funding the CIA and the Pentagon

Having for several years tanked in every encounter with the Pentagon, the Bureau of the Budget took another dive during the 1960 LBJ Senate hearings as the Bureau wore the somber colors of Eisenhower's "administrative failures."[214] Senator Johnson was able to generate "a litany of military requests" that became, in fact, a Defense Department "shopping list."[215] Throughout the Eisenhower administration, Senator Johnson was the crucial ally of the military/intelligence coalition as it collected its funding from inside the Pentagon budget, especially after the heavily publicized threats of Soviet space and missile programs.[216] The softest entry for U.S. intelligence's black budget operations then became the hot areas of "air" and "space," specifically through the U.S. Air Force's programs in research and development, and then through NASA[217]: hence Johnson's 1959-1960 Senatorial pressure on the Eisenhower White House that was topped by his 1960 Senate hearings.[218]

What followed were the "research and analysis" contracts (with their significant intelligence dimensions) for aircraft and space companies and think tank/development corporations funded by the Pentagon, all of them ostensibly working for the Air Force and the U.S. "aerospace" program. For LBJ and Texas, following his collaboration with the USAF, aerospace research and development (both in the government and business), the Budget Bureau, and with covert intelligence operations hidden inside persistent Pentagon funding appeals, the payoff was staggering: "As President, [LBJ] . . . helped engineer the greatest Pentagon raid on the [U.S.] treasury since World War II. Among other results was a gigantic defense-industry boom for his home state, Texas."[219]

Johnson had elected to join the Budget Bureau/Pentagon/black budget intelligence team in the early 1950s, collecting Senatorial power and privilege; then as Vice-President he acquired more potency for U.S. space and missile programs, the only areas that really mattered to him and Texas, until he "rode the tiger of military [and covert intelligence] spending into the White House . . . [and] it rode him out."[220]

When Defense Secretary Robert McNamara had been commissioned by President John F. Kennedy to business manage the Pentagon, the Bureau of the Budget had reportedly "lost whatever influence it once had over military spending to the National Security Council [NSC] . . . ."[221] But the Budget Bureau's most crucial job was over; the transfer of budgeting power to that same National Security Council had been completed. The NSC had effectively taken control of both defense spending AND intelligence funding.

Did the Bureau of the Budget ever actually collude with the Central Intelligence Agency? Indeed, the Bureau not only protected the CIA for decades; it actively conspired with the Agency. In the mid-1960s, for example, the Bureau 'discovered' that the "CIA budget for Vietnam provided for dollar expenditures at the legal ['piasters'] exchange rate."[222] But the Bureau of the Budget also knew that the CIA was using the Vietnamese "black market" to buy "piasters" so that the Agency had "two to three times" more buying power than the Agency's official "budget" indicated[223]: in brief, the CIA was making a monetary killing.

The Bureau of the Budget moved in, flashing its financial fangs, demanding "all [CIA budget] figures [for Vietnam] be listed at the actual black-market rate."[224] But the Bureau of the Budget also requested that the CIA purchase black-market Vietnamese piasters for the REST of U.S. government operations in Vietnam[225], a cost-cutting though (obviously) illegal action. The CIA "managed to avoid" this Bureau of the Budget's money-saving request, arguing that the Company did not want "the secrecy of its money-exchange operations disturbed."[226] Obligingly, the Bureau of the Budget backed off.

"The budget of the fiscal year 1959 [prepared in 1958] was almost entirely the work of the [reputed] old-fashioned budget-balancer, Percival Brundage . . . ."[227] At least on paper, Brundage's national accounting ledger "called for expenditure of a smaller percentage of the estimated . . . gross national product than the budget of the previous year."[228] Brundage the "budget-balancer" had reportedly struck again: except that "spending for [any program] other than [for] defense purposes [now] had . . . a smaller [percentage] slice of what was available."[229]

In brief, Percival Brundage had performed an accounting sleight-of-hand: defense spending in his 1959 budget had RISEN, not diminished.

In the 1959 Senate hearings on "Major Defense Matters" (referred to earlier) and while former top Budget officer Percival Brundage was still operating as the Bureau's key "consultant," two full days of Senatorial sessions were dedicated to "The Role of the Bureau of the Budget in Formulation and Execution of [the] Defense Budget."[230] Senator Lyndon B. Johnson, then chair of the powerful Senate Preparedness Committee[231], interrogated Bureau of the Budget Director Maurice H. Stans (Bureau consultant Brundage's chief) on the BOB's national funding "straightjacket" and the Bureau's "arbitrary limitations" on military preparedness.[232]

But Budget boss Stans assured Senator Johnson and his committee that the Bureau of the Budget "did not even review the Pentagon's budget requests the way it did those of other agencies."[233] According to Stans, the Bureau of the Budget only did a "joint" review of military funding proposals and NEVER attempted to "eliminate" Pentagon monetary requests.[234] Stans further testified to Senator Lyndon B. Johnson and his watchdog committee that, for the Department of Defense, the Bureau of the Budget did not "make [any] eliminations or [even] determine a budget figure."[235]

According to official Senate Preparedness Committee records, Johnson, the powerful master of the U.S. Senate, seemed more than curious about how the Pentagon could overrule what Constitutional budgetary control the Bureau of the Budget allegedly possessed.[236] Budget Director Stans assured LBJ and his fellow senators that several definitive reasons excluded the Budget watchdogs from prying into Defense Department matters.[237] Though Director Stans' "explanations" lacked common sense[238], Senator Johnson and his associates apparently accepted the Bureau of the Budget's dubious assurances.[239]

After John F. Kennedy was assassinated, President Johnson's Defense Secretary Robert McNamara gave testimony before the House Armed Services Committee on U.S. military funding[240]; the Committee's chair asked McNamara whether the Bureau of the Budget exercised any significant control over the Pentagon budget.[241] McNamara confidently replied: "The Bureau of the Budget has absolutely no authority to determine in any way the budget of the Defense Department."[242]

Challenges to the administration's military budget were, in fact, rebuffed regardless of who sat in the Oval Office, and the Bureau of the Budget was always there to fend off any attempt to breach the White House walls. Senator William Proxmire once attempted "to press [Bureau of the] Budget Director Robert May, asking questions about items in the defense requests . . . ."[243] Mayo "loftily replied" that "the president's flexibility is better served by not getting into a debate on what is and what is not in the Defense budget."

But how could the White House (and, afterward, Congress) have lost control not only of Pentagon funding but also of U.S. intelligence? An official paper trail of executive decisions had to be laid down that stripped U.S. presidents of any real authority over American intelligence operations, a trail that was left by a joint effort of the Bureau of the Budget and American intelligence, both ultimately the creatures of the U.S. establishment. Just as the Bureau of the Budget had cooperated with the profit-engorged coalition of American military and U.S. defense industries, the Bureau had manipulated U.S. covert operations in support of U.S. governing class goals.

Following World War II, the elitist officials of the Bureau of the Budget (operating under President Harry Truman) had dissolved the wartime Office of Special Services, an organization too independent for establishment tastes, and promoted a series of bureaucratic acts culminating in the creation of the National Security Council and the Central Intelligence Agency.[244]

Because President Eisenhower had lived with intelligence operations from his World War II North African campaign through the surrender of Nazi Germany, Ike had "paid considerable attention to [intelligence] . . . during his tenure in the

White House."[245] His major intelligence briefings came from his meetings with Foster Dulles, his Secretary of State, and Allan Dulles, his Central Intelligence Director[246]; his intermediate source may have been the most relevant: the president "had [the bulk of] his intelligence information channeled primarily through his [so-called] staff assistant Colonel . . . Andrew Goodpaster."[247]

Though the president might not have fully realized it, Goodpaster was the White House's direct line to the operational side of the CIA: listed with a variety of titles, Goodpaster (who by 1961 would be a brigadier general), was both Eisenhower's White House staff secretary and the president's Pentagon liaison. Colonel Goodpaster, wearing several of his White House hats, also collaborated with the Bureau of the Budget and Percival Brundage in 1957 on the funding of the technological spy Project Vanguard[248], "the result of NSC 5520 and . . . intended to establish [the high-sounding] 'Freedom of Space'—[but actually] the [U.S.] right to overfly foreign territory for future intelligence satellites."[249]

Goodpaster was the perfect link between the Bureau of the Budget, Percival Brundage, [250]the President, including a program that united the National Academy of Science, NASA, the Department of Defense, and budgetary decisions effecting serious intelligence collection.[251] When Gary Powers' U-2 spy plane was brought down, Allan Dulles convened a "CIA" task force to evaluate the event, and Goodpaster was in attendance, ostensibly representing the White House.[252]

In 1959, Eisenhower needed vital intelligence information, especially about Berlin.[253] Brundage and Eisenhower had worked on several successive national budgets, a process actually constituting a review of viable covert intelligence actions, and Eisenhower was energized: "As a result of the President's [heightened] interest, the Bureau of the Budget increased its review of the size and scope of the United States intelligence effort."[254] The president apparently wanted to direct a major overhaul of U.S. intelligence machinery. But the Bureau of the Budget inundated Eisenhower with eighteen proposed budget surveys, and only two of them "concerned the work of the intelligence agencies."[255] Robert Macy, the chief of the Bureau's International Division, had taken an intensely "active interest in the work of the intelligence agencies . . ."[256]: Macy, in fact, was crucial as the Bureau's intelligence expert.[257] Despite all the memoranda smoke generated, "the Bureau's proposal for . . . intelligence studies could not seem to get moving. All discussions resulted in such complete disagreement that nothing happened."[258] The friends of U.S. intelligence in the Bureau of the Budget, including Robert Macy, had accomplished their purpose.

Despite Eisenhower's farewell address cautioning America about the marriage of Pentagon and corporate power, the Bureau of the Budget had acted in the Eisenhower years as a facilitating institution to develop the "military-industrial complex" and its intelligence allies[259]; and once the Bureau had helped build that profit-making project, it assisted in turning over the "complex" to the Pentagon and the Central Intelligence Agency, freeing both of those big spenders from any effective administrative restraints.[260]

## Percival Brundage and the American Power Structure

Following a long line of establishment money managers in the Treasury and the Bureau of the Budget from World War I through the Cold War, Budget Director Percival Flack Brundage (a valued participant in official Cabinet meetings) sat with the power mongers of defense and intelligence as a regular member of Eisenhower's National Security Council, his presence reverently noted by *U.S. News and World Report* of April, 1956.[261]

The Director of the Bureau of the Budget continued to attend National Security Council sessions: for example, while Brundage was still at the Bureau of the Budget, the NSC met in April, 1960, to examine C.D. Jackson's anti-Castro psyops programs in radio broadcasting.[262]

And while Brundage was still a consultant at the Bureau of the Budget in May, 1960, just after the U-2 disaster closed off the scheduled U.S./Soviet peace talks[263], the Bureau again "initiated a study of all U.S. intelligence activities."[264] Not officially a National Security Council operation, it was sponsored by the Bureau of the Budget and staffed by "a special task force headed by the Director of Central Intelligence and . . . representatives from State, Defense, the White House, the Budget Bureau, and CIA . . ."; the task force had been "charged with the responsibility of preparing a comprehensive report to outgoing President Eisenhower prior to the end of 1960."[265] Those two final phrases were awkwardly symptomatic: the force, made up of close and influential friends of the Pentagon (whose intent was to build a unified military intelligence operation), had been handed its commission: organize and consolidate the Department of Defense's covert operations before John F. Kennedy, the probable incoming president, took office.

Officially, of course, the "motivating force behind the desire of the [outgoing] President and the Budget Bureau . . . was the need for consolidating various Pentagon intelligence activities."[266] But note the triangulation: the White House, the Pentagon, and the Bureau of the Budget.

The recommendations of the Bureau of the Budget's intelligence task force of May, 1960, have never been open to public scrutiny, but the outcome of that BOP operation was readily apparent: the "creation of the Defense Intelligence Agency . . . and a corresponding reorganization of the U.S. Intelligence Board."[267] In brief, the individual military services lost their voting rights on the Board while the new Defense Intelligence Agency gained significant leverage, displacing Army, Navy, and Air Force intelligence units that were now reduced to non-voting Board observers.[268]

The Bureau of the Budget had once again assisted in giving major support to the Pentagon and its intelligence apparatus.

Despite his retirement from Bureau business, Brundage was apparently still operating as an asset of the BOB in 1962. Serious anxieties about funding for U.S. covert operations, including several "much-criticized public media projects," were aired at a meeting organized by a "former budget official" who had brought together officers of "the Bureau of the Budget, CIA, FIAB, and relevant Undersecretaries in consideration of budgetary modifications."[269] This conference in the early 1960s, organized by this "former budget officer" (unnamed but obviously Percival Brundage), was described and cited in the minutes recorded (on January 8th, 1968) at the Council on Foreign Relations' third meeting of the CFR's "Discussion Group on Intelligence and Foreign Policy."[270] According to the almost cryptic record of that 1968 meeting, the "problem" faced by the earlier Bureau of the Budget conferees was two-fold: retaining successful intelligence "programs" and cutting away failed actions in hidden budget items, black ops, and psychological warfare, the latter delicately designated "public media projects."[271] Though the psyops programs had accomplished their black budget goals, they had also received heavy criticism.[272]

That early 1960s Bureau of the Budget meeting (cited at length by former CIA Deputy Director Richard Bissell in 1968) had faced a watershed moment: how could the Bureau and the U.S. intelligence community cooperatively open up the budget to explore new programs replacing old, less successful, programs, without reducing the entire budget?[273] Crucially, the Bureau of the Budget, in cooperation with the Central Intelligence Agency and its allies, needed to keep the national budget at its reported spending levels yet still support new and more productive covert operations in reaching U.S. foreign policy objectives.

The Central Intelligence Agency stalled, not wanting to lose covert funding for an (unnamed) allied "foundation"; precious time was lost; and though the Agency's distress was ultimately reduced, before any significant operational backing could be achieved for both old and new CIA programs, the "next [scheduled] big review" of the combined Bureau of the Budget, CIA, and allied departments (where both the old and the new could have received budgetary support) was trumped "as a consequence of the Cuban missile crisis."[274]

So much for national priorities.

Richard Bissell's 1968 secular parable of an earlier Budget/intelligence/foreign policy "problem" illustrated how difficult it was in 1968 to achieve an agreement on funding new covert actions without cutting old (and treasured) operations and institutions.

One other attendee at the Dillon/Bissell Council on Foreign Relations meeting in 1968 who had worked with both U.S. intelligence and "private industry" and had actively supported (what he called) the "combined cryptologic budget"[275] seconded Bissell's argument.[276] But Douglas Dillon moved to close off this apparently sensitive area of concern.[277]

The two "budget" meetings (one most probably in 1962, the other in 1968), clearly documented the long-time cooperation between the Bureau of the Budget and the CIA and the top officers of both federal agencies.

## The Bureau of the Budget, the CIA, the Military, and Percival Brundage

Though U.S. military and covert intelligence establishments knew the truth for some time, the average American citizen might have had some difficulty understanding that an historic transfer of "budgetary power" to the Executive Office of the President occurred after 1939, controlled "for the most part by the powerful Bureau of the Budget . . . ."[278] In turn, the Bureau was staffed at the top by solid business and banking figures out of the national establishment, including Percival Flack Brundage. The Appropriations committees in the House and the Senate (constitutionally responsible for national funding and spending) might trim a program here or there (especially in domestic social programs and foreign aid), but the Bureau, the mighty fiscal partner of U.S. military and intelligence, would triumph, working under the guise of "budget proposals from the President."[279] An unnamed "candid member of the [Senate] Appropriations Committee" during the Eisenhower years admitted that for Congress, the defense "budget" was, in fact, a large political pork barrel.[280]

The partnerships between the Bureau of the Budget, U.S. intelligence, and the American military lasted through Robert McNamara's assumption of Defense Department command in 1961, when (what Seymour Melman called) "Pentagon capitalism" was put in place, and the Bureau of the Budget was no longer needed as a convenient cover (out of the Executive Office of the President) for the direct management of America's permanent war economy.[281]

Percival Flack Brundage had left the Bureau of the Budget in 1960 precisely when it became unnecessary to have his accounting genius operate as the military/intelligence gatekeeper of the national budget.

The most comprehensive and even-handed examination of the Bureau of the Budget was authored, in fact, by Percival Flack Brundage.[282]

The "foreword"[283] to Brundage's volume by Robert P. Mayo, the Director of the Bureau of the Budget in 1970, established two major truths about Percival Brundage. The first was personal: "[Brundage was] remembered fondly by his many friends at the Bureau as a gentleman of great courtliness and generosity, . . . wise in the ways of raising the esprit of the staff to new heights."[284] The second was political, involving the recommendations of the so-called "second Hoover Commission" in reconstructing the accounting procedures of the U.S. government: Percival Brundage "was not only deeply involved in the effort to pass appropriate legislation [to effect that reconstruction], he was also responsible for establishing the Office of Accounting within the Bureau of the Budget to take the lead in an accelerated program for improving the accounting function throughout the government."[285]

That is, of course, except for defense and intelligence funding.

Brundage's historical examination of the spending procedures of the federal government from 1780 through 1970 was supported by seven charts and seventeen tables, clearly demonstrating his absolute and confident control of the business of national budgeting.

But despite Brundage's Chapter VIII devoted to the Bureau and the Department of Defense, Brundage did not confess to any collaboration between himself, his Bureau, and the military establishment. Instead, he quietly commented that, long after he left the Bureau, "former Budget Director Schultze and Director Mayo in June, 1969 [in their testimony to the Joint Economic Committee of Congress] . . . indicated that for several years the Bureau had not been questioning military priorities to the same extent that it had those of the civilian programs."[286]

Yes: "for several [Brundage] years."

Since Brundage had nothing in his book on the budgeting of the intelligence community, his chapter on "Social, Economic, and Other Civilian Agency Programs" might have had some comment on the Central Intelligence Agency and its protected budget. But except for two inconsequential references, Brundage provided NOTHING.[287] Further, except for one irrelevant FBI reference, Brundage did not cover ANY of the other intelligence-gathering or secret and covert operations of the federal government.[288]

Brundage did establish (with a few scattered citations) that he regularly sat representing the Bureau of the Budget at meetings of both the National Security Council and the president's Cabinet meetings and that the Eisenhower administration relied on the National Security Council to establish all the goals and expenditures of both the Defense Department and the Central Intelligence Agency.[289] And Brundage registered some minor fragments of his inside knowledge of the OCB (developed by psyops expert C.D. Jackson), the committee inside the National Security Council that ran the nation's most delicate covert operations.[290]

## The Percival Brundage Story:
## Refugee Work, American Intelligence, and the Unitarians

William Mifton Brundage, Percival's father, had given up his Methodist ministry and become a Unitarian. Percival Brundage absorbed his father's liberal Protestant consciousness and became an active and influential Unitarian, deeply involved in international youth movements and European refugee needs.

As early as 1938, with both religious relief organizations and American intelligence strongly interested in the flow of refugees out of Spain and into Portugal and France, Percival Brundage directed the American Christian Committee for Refugees. In 1942, Brundage was appointed director of the American Unitarian Association (AUA), holding that position through 1948, a time when the AUA was committed to humanitarian refugee work and U.S. intelligence was hungry for information being generated from those same refugees. Brundage was active throughout the war years with European refugee relief, the National War Fund, the International Rescue and Relief Committee, the Joint Anti-Fascist Refugee Committee, the War Refugee Board, and the Refugee Relief Trustees, a knowing participant in that government-supported and intelligence-linked tangle; Brundage held key meetings with Joy Gano, the Dexters, and others closely associated with collaboration between the Office of Strategic Services and the Unitarian Service Committee.[291]

On February 4th, 1942, Brundage met with Howard Brooks[292] and Varian Fry, a signal association of refugee work officials with clandestine connections; Brundage described the meeting in a letter to Robert C. Dexter, Allan Dulles' intelligence asset on the Unitarian Service Committee. Brooks and Fry urged that the Unitarians financially support what Brundage called Fry's "project." Though Brundage did not discourage Brooks and Fry, he pointed out the USC was short of funds "without tapping new sources of contributions." Brundage assumed Fry would contact other offices of the USC.

Earlier, in September, 1941, at the exact time Varian Fry was sent back to the United States, the Unitarian Service Committee met on financing projects in France and to hear certain "confidential reports" from Joy and Brooks, both of whom had intelligence connections in Europe.

As an officer of the Unitarian Service Committee (USC) primarily interested in refugee relief and USC funding, Brundage had been in a unique position to collect European intelligence information.

In 1949, Percival Brundage became the director of the USC, an office he occupied through 1954, marked by the USC's apparent continuing cooperation with U.S. intelligence, principally with the CIA. From 1952 though 1955, Brundage was the president of the International Association for Liberal Christianity and Religious Freedom (later the International Association for Religious Freedom: the IARF), with key American Unitarians, including Percival Brundage, holding influential offices in its world-wide liberal Protestant communion.[293] From 1959 through 1962, Brundage chaired the Unitarian Development Fund Campaign supporting key Unitarian domestic and international programs.

Percival Flack Brundage held pivotal offices in the Unitarian Church movement both at home and abroad from at least 1942 through 1954, the twelve years that saw the Unitarian Service Committee and officers of its parent organization working closely with the Office of Special Services (OSS) in World War II and, later, with Allen Dulles' CIA. In turn, the Agency protected its Unitarian assets, heavily censoring OSS/USC records in the Agency's possession before turning them over to the Unitarian Service Committee.

## Percival Brundage, the CIA, Paul Helliwell, and Southern Air Transport

After leaving the Bureau of the Budget, Percival Flack Brundage and a Brundage associate, E Perkins McGuire, a former Assistant Secretary of Defense, were asked in 1960 to hold the majority of a new airline's stock "in name only"; agreeing to do so, the two former federal officials assisted in establishing a major wing of the Central Intelligence Agency's vast air transport system that included the legendary Air America.[294] In specific, with Pentagon-friendly Perkins McGuire, Percival Flack Brundage became a registered stockholder of Southern Air Transport (SAT), incorporated in Miami to fly major missions in both the Caribbean and Southeast Asia for the Central Intelligence Agency.[295]

In World War II and the ensuing Cold War, E. Perkins McGuire was the right man to call on for coordinating the massive efforts of U.S. business and the nation's military machine. McGuire's dedication to meeting the material needs of America's fighting forces and their intelligence-collecting and covert-operations allies was coupled with his willingness to channel that dedication in the service of the U.S. power structure. By 1945, already familiar with the loci of critical decision-making, McGuire had become a member of Naval Secretary James Forrestal's Executive Office. Appropriately, McGuire was the Deputy Assistant Chief in charge of Industrial Readjustment

In 1952, the Pentagon's Army/Navy/Air Force Support Center was the key to the Defense's united supply and logistics strategies. With his end-of-the-war transitional experience, Perkins, now the Assistant Secretary of Defense for Supply and Logistics, became the crucial link between defense contractors, the national shippers of military common supplies, and the Armed Forces.

By 1955, Perkins had drawn close to the Joint Chiefs of Staff, testifying in the hearings of the Senate Committee on Foreign Relations on American support of Batista's Cuba and colonial control of Cambodia. His identity badge now read "Deputy Assistant Secretary of Defense for Mutual Assistance."

McGuire's Pentagon associates in the '50s, including Deputy Undersecretary of Defense Robert B. Anderson, Deputy Secretary of Defense Donald Quarles, and Deputy Secretary of Defense Thomas S. Gates, for example, were all at one time or another members of the select Operations Coordinating Board (by July 1, 1957, a part of the National Security Council staff). And, of course, for several critical years the inner directorial circle of the OCB (tasked with monitoring U.S. intelligence's covert operations) was made up of CIA Director Allen Dulles, C.D. Jackson, Special Assistant to the President in Psychological Warfare, and McGuire's close friend from the Bureau of the Budget, Percival Flack Brundage.

When not a formal government employee, Perkins McGuire remained close to military and intelligence activities dependent on profitable industrial and business support. Listed as a "corporate executive," McGuire was chair of the U.S. Commission on Government Procurement from 1969 through December, 1972, exhaustively examining and making recommendations on "legal remedies," "negotiation and subcontracting," "research and development," and "precontract planning." In 1985-1986, McGuire was the Chair of the "President's [temporary] Blue Ribbon Commission on Defense Management."

With Percy Brundage, E. Perkins McGuire was a perfect fit as one of the two stockholders of the CIA's Southern Air Transport.

The history of McGuire's and Brundage's Southern Air Transport began with Paul Helliwell, "the CIA's original overseas paymaster and Mister Black Bag."[296] Throughout World War II, Helliwell headed U.S. special intelligence in China for the OSS[297], afterward creating a maze of banking operations that handled funding of major CIA clandestine actions in East Asia and the Pacific.[298]

Helliwell bridged the gap between the demise of the OSS and the creation of the CIA as the "chief of the Far East Division of the War Department's Strategic Service Unit."[299]

In 1950, while an officer of Wisner's Office of Policy Coordination, Helliwell began the Air America/Southern Air Transport saga by helping to "negotiate the sale of General Claire Chennault's airline, Civil Air Transport, to the CIA."[300] By 1959, Air America and its "parent" company, the Pacific Corporation, were CIA owned and operated, devolving from the breakdown of the original Civil Air Transport into small operational units (including Southern Air Transport).

Helliwell established Sea Supply and Air America using "the Philippines and Thailand as staging bases for secret operations throughout Southeast Asia."[301] For example, Helliwell's "black money" supported the Lansdale/Kaplan CIA/Catherwood psyops and covert operations in the Philippines.[302] Helliwell's Sea Supply "ran guns and dope for the CIA in Thailand"[303]; his Castle Bank and Trust "was involved in fraud and political money movement in the Bahamas."[304]

Castle Bank's reach was extensive: "One client company of Castle Bank was tied . . . to the laundering of $5 million for the CIA's use . . . . The client company was run by Wallace Groves . . ."[305] Groves was an Agency asset, a convicted stock swindler, and a close partner of Organized Crime leader Meyer Lansky.[306]

Helliwell's OSS/CIA sponsoring of narcotics trafficking and his "series of banks through which both CIA funds and [covert operations and Organized Crime] drug profits were laundered"[307] resulted in "a nationally protected drug traffic."[308]

Helliwell was anointed by the upper reaches of the CIA's clandestine command as an unqualified success in the Pacific and Asia. Richard Bissell, the Agency's director of dirty tricks, "brought Helliwell back from the Far East to set up a Western Hemisphere version of Sea Supply and Air America out of Miami called Southern Air Transport, [together with] a new chain of black-money banks to pay for the Bay of Pigs operation that Bissell was planning."[309]

Southern Air Transport, therefore, had Caribbean duties and connections, carrying with it all of Helliwell's dark baggage of drugs and guns; further, as a CIA-controlled proprietary, SAT was directly linked to the support of the Bay of Pigs invasion, channeled through the Double-Chek Corporation.

Double-Chek, a CIA front founded in Miami on May 14th, 1959[310], recruited U.S. pilots for the Bay of Pigs.[311] When Double-Chek was lining up aviators for the U.S. attack on Cuba, its principle Florida attorney and officially-listed president was Alex E. Carlson.[312] In 1962, Carlson was also the registered legal representative "for [the] CIA proprietary, Southern Air Transport."[313] Under Carlson, SAT's chief operating officer, Southern Air Transport was described by the Pentagon as "a civilian operation holding a $3.7 million [Air Force] contract to move mixed [unidentified] cargo and [unidentified] passenger loads on Far Eastern routes."[314]

Military, weapons, shipments of heavy supplies, and narcotics were carried by SAT (with Percival Brundage listed as one of the airline's two owners and operators) in support of Pentagon and CIA covert operations in Vietnam, in Laos, and in Cambodia.[315]

The CIA's Southern Air Transport reportedly "operated out of offices in [both] Miami and Taiwan."[316] SAT's primary Asian address was "a post office box [PO Box 12124] in

Taipei, Formosa [Taiwan] . . . ."[317] Given its two stockholding operators (Brundage, a long-time Bureau of the Budget officer, the other, a former Department of Defense assistant secretary[318]), it was understandable that "Southern's role in the Far East was . . . flying profitable routes for the Defense Department."[319] As late as 1972, Brundage's Southern Air Transport company was financed (in part) by a "$2 million AID contract to fly [unidentified] relief supplies to . . . Bangladesh."[320] The intentionally-tangled CIA airline financial controls meant, for example, that one of the Agency's key operations, CAT, leased a Southern Air Transport jet in 1968 that would later crash on Taiwan.[321] In 1968 (and again in 1972), the Central Intelligence Agency supported Southern Air Transport (SAT), hoping to assist SAT in obtaining jet aircraft to continue to "live its [clandestine] cover."[322] In 1968, the Agency was still exploring "Southern [Air Transport]'s capabilities for future [covert] interventions in Latin America . . . ."[323]

As a knowledgeable high-level officer of the Bureau of the Budget from 1954 through 1960 and a long-time advocate of funding for black-budget military and clandestine operations bypassing Constitutional controls, Percival Brundage allowed his name to be used in support of CIA covert air operations in both Southeast Asia and Latin America that were organized by the CIA's paymaster Paul Helliwell. Following the revelations of several national investigations, Percival Brundage was identified in 1975 by the *Washington Post* and *Newsweek* as a knowing collaborator with the CIA in the Agency's covert air commerce carried by Southern Air Transport.

Even Brundage's apparently selfless acts of support for humanitarian causes had a shadowy side. Brundage served as the treasurer and director of Project HOPE, "the People-to-People Health Foundation," a medical ship program touring the ports of poverty and disease in the Pacific and Southeast Asia for many years.[324] But the biggest booster of the humanitarian project was psychological warfare expert C. D. Jackson, a close friend and advocate of the Central Intelligence Agency, who gloried only in Project HOPE's psyops payoff.[325] And Project HOPE extended its healing largesse over both land and sea by shipping its materials aboard Southern Air Transport[326], the CIA proprietary airline to which Percival Brundage had lent his good name.

During and after his service for the Bureau of the Budget, Percival Brundage was well aware of the special status of the Department of Defense (with its several branches of covert operations and intelligence gathering) and the Central Intelligence Agency. Brundage was also knowledgeable about the Bureau of the Budget's collaboration with U.S. military and intelligence clout.

## Hans Casparis, Percival Brundage, and the Establishment of Albert Schweitzer College

From 1950 through 1954, with Percival Brundage at the height of his power in both the Bureau of the Budget and the Unitarian Church, Swiss cleric Hans Casparis, together with Casparis' English wife and (reportedly) a group of liberal Protestant ministers, developed Albert Schweitzer College, a Swiss educational institution that could not have existed except for the untiring efforts of the inspired Unitarian movement in the United States. The American Friends of Albert Schweitzer College[327] gave the institution significant moral, spiritual, and monetary support from the middle 1950s through the 1960s. But the College's curious history, the dubious academic record of it major founder Hans Casparis, and the anxieties of FBI chief J. Edgar Hoover when he directed the investigation of Albert Schweitzer College after the non-appearance of its very special registree, Lee Harvey Oswald, all have demanded the closest look at the college's supporters and their backgrounds.

Percival Flack Brundage was the cooperative friend of the Pentagon and the Central Intelligence Agency while he worked at the Bureau of the Budget from 1954 through 1960 as the Bureau's Deputy Director, its Director, and then its key consultant; he was the signatory to the incorporation papers of Southern Air Transport, a notorious CIA proprietary; he was a major Unitarian Church officer from 1942 through 1954 when the Unitarian Church was actively cooperating with the OSS and the CIA; he was President of the IARF from 1952 through 1955 when Albert Schweitzer College was developed and then proudly supported by the IARF as its "crown jewel."

On April 17th, 1953, the Certificate of Incorporation of Friends of Albert Schweitzer College, Inc., was filed by the Law Offices of Francis T. Christy, 30 Rockefeller Plaza, New York, with the New York State Secretary of State.[328] Though the direction, energy, and monetary support for the college would come from Boston and Cambridge, the "principal office of the Corporation [was] . . . to be located in the Borough of Manhattan, City, County and State of New York."[329]

"The number of its Directors shall be not less than three and not more than fifty."[330] The minimum number of directors were listed: John H. Lathrop, John Ritzenthaler, and Percival Flack Brundage.[331] Ritzenthaler was a close friend of Percival Brundage, both residing in Monclair, New Jersey. John Howland Lathrop[332] was a great moment in the history of humanity's good works, a perfect director for the Friends of Albert Schweitzer College. Lathrop was listed as one of the "subscribers" to the college's New York State incorporation along with Ritzenthaler, Brundage, Edward A. Cahill and Frederick May Eliot.[333]

In 1938, John H. Lathrop worked with the Dexters (Allan Dulles' OSS connection to the Unitarians) and with Frederick Eliot and Seth Gano (who were both linked to the OSS). But Lathrop, of course, may not have been aware of his associates' U.S. intelligence operations.

That connection was, of course, through Percival Flack Brundage. The support for the strange Swiss educational institution received from the United States flowed through the organization established by its three directors, including Percival Flack Brundage with his American intelligence connections.

## Lee Harvey Oswald and Albert Schweitzer College: the Providence Connection

On December 5th, 1963, less than two weeks after the assassination of John F. Kennedy, Dr. Robert Schacht, pastor of the historic First Unitarian Church in

Providence and the U.S. Director of Admissions for Albert Schweitzer College, was interviewed by FBI agents. Schacht had called the Bureau immediately following the murder of the president in Dealey Plaza, having recognized Oswald's name. He remembered that "Oswald had filled out an application . . . in the spring of 1959 while still in the Marine Corps . . . . Because the Oswald application was approved, I [Dr. Schacht] am sure that he must have given three references[,] and their reports must have appeared satisfactory. But I cannot recall now who they were."[334]

Schacht's information (as I have earlier indicated) has called for careful examination. Did Oswald ever write a letter of inquiry to Schacht? The Unitarian pastor only referred to Oswald's March, 1959, college application itself. Did Schacht receive the shorter or the longer application form from Oswald? Only the longer form would have had the necessary three references listed (all of which, as we have seen, were fictions). Did Schacht, in fact, ever receive supporting letters from those non-existent references? If so, where are those letters? Schacht reported that Oswald's "application was approved . . . ."[335] How did Schacht receive this information? Did he get it from the Swiss college? From the FBI? From his own Benevolent Street file that was appropriated by the FBI agents who had interviewed him?

When the Albert Schweitzer College board of directors met in Switzerland just after the assassination, the chief concern it raised about Oswald was precisely the nature of Oswald's references. That body could not account for Oswald having been accepted by the American branch of the college's screening process run by Robert Schacht in Providence. To the FBI, Schacht had used the protective passive voice: "the Oswald application was approved."[336] Who, then, had "approved" the Oswald application?

For Pastor Schacht, December 5th, 1963, was, at the very least, stressful. In Providence, Schacht had been interviewed by FBI agents about the assassination of the President John F. Kennedy whose accused killer had been accepted as a student at Schacht's Albert Schweitzer College in Switzerland. Schacht had given up his Benevolent Street file on Oswald to the Bureau agents. And now he had to deal with a serious economic issue: literally, the continued life of the American Friends of Albert Schweitzer College, Inc.

## From Providence: An Urgent Message for Percival Brundage

Ernest Cassara from the College in Switzerland had contacted the members of the American Friends of Albert Schweitzer College on November 20th and again in the first week of December: the college's American "Committee" was in economic trouble, so Robert Schacht wrote to the one person in the Unitarian community most qualified to help the Friends and the college.[337] On the morning of December 5th, before the FBI had visited him about Lee Harvey Oswald, Schacht had already called Washington, hoping to make contact, had failed, and had then called his associate at his "home in [Pompano Beach,] Florida but could obtain no answer."[338] Schacht needed expert opinion on the relation between the American Friends of Albert Schweitzer College and the "Bureau of Internal Revenue."[339] Schacht's last paragraph closed a long loop of relationships:

"Perhaps you have learned the bizarre news that Lee Oswald actually registered in the spring of 1959 for study in the third term of '60 at A.S.C. His application was processed and references sent to the College in Switzerland. However, he never showed up. What a strange world!"[340]

Again the telling use by Schacht of the passive voice: Oswald's "application was processed and references [were] sent to the College in Switzerland."[341] Who else but Schacht would have "processed" and then sent the Oswald application to Switzerland? Who else but Schacht would have sent those references?

A "strange world" of "bizarre news" indeed: Robert Schacht had somehow allowed the future accused assassin of President John F. Kennedy to attach himself to Albert Schweitzer College. On the same day as the FBI interviewed Schacht about Oswald's relationship to the college, the Providence Unitarian minister had written to one of the closest friends of the U.S. military and intelligence communities. He had written to Percival Flack Brundage at his home in Florida, where Brundage had signed incorporation papers for the CIA's Southern Air Transport. Schacht had sent the letter to his Unitarian associate Percy Brundage who had been President of the American Friends of Albert Schweitzer College[342] from 1953 through 1958, crucial developmental years of the Swiss institution when it attracted students from the United States and around the world, most especially U.S. Marine Lee Harvey Oswald.

In 1958, Percival Flack Brundage, a close friend of U.S. military and U.S. intelligence, was Director of the Bureau of the Budget; he was one of the three incorporating officers of the Friends of Albert Schweitzer College[343]; and he was President of the American Friends of Albert Schweitzer College. In 1958, Lee Harvey Oswald had discovered the relatively unknown Albert Schweitzer College operating in Churwalden, Switzerland and, applying to it, had been accepted by Percy Brundage's Unitarian-supported educational center.

Less than one year later, Lee Harvey Oswald was listed as missing from Switzerland.

# Essay Eight

# The Oil/Intelligence/Unitarian Universe
# of Lee Harvey Oswald

"[Allen Dulles] joked in private that the [JFK] conspiracy buffs would have had a field day if they had known . . . he had actually been in Dallas three weeks before the murder . . . ; that one of Mary Bancroft's childhood friends had turned out to be a landlady for Marina Oswald . . . ; and that [the] landlady was a well-known leftist with distant ties to the family of Alger Hiss."[1]

Allen Dulles' post-assassination jocularity was seriously flawed. Mary Bancroft's so-called "childhood" attachment was to the mother-in-law of Marina Oswald's Ruth Paine, and Dulles had inaccurately identified Ruth Paine as Marina's "landlady": in fact, Marina Oswald and her children lived with Ruth Paine rent-free. The alleged Alger Hiss relationship to Ruth Paine's family, however, suggested how sensitive Allen Dulles was to the dangerously reticulate context of the John F. Kennedy murder.

## Lee Harvey Oswald and the Intelligence-Monitored Unitarians

From 1958 through 1963 and beyond, Lee Harvey Oswald's life and death were embedded in the Unitarian Church movement and its liberal religious associations[2]; in turn, that same Unitarian network was infused with major domestic and foreign intelligence connections, a Unitarian/intelligence matrix that defined the JFK assassination. U.S. intelligence's misuse of religious institutions could not have been better illustrated.

Albert Schweitzer College, Oswald's higher education choice, had been cooperatively created by European and American Unitarians and their liberal religious allies. Frederick May Eliot and Percival Flack Brundage, two powerful American Unitarians closely linked to U.S. intelligence, were significant leaders of the Unitarian coalition establishing and then supporting Albert Schweitzer College. As a counterintelligence False Identity candidate, Lee Harvey Oswald looked like an asset of OSS/CIA officers who had been led by Allen Dulles in manipulating religious individuals and groups, including Quakers and Unitarians, through two hot wars and the ensuing Cold War.

230

John Foster Dulles, with his own history of misusing liberal religious groups, had been a longtime ally of his master spy brother.

Following the JFK assassination and Oswald's death, Unitarian minister Robert Schacht in Providence, Rhode Island, program chairperson for U.S. citizens applying to Albert Schweitzer College, was visited by FBI agents who confiscated his Oswald file, never returning it. Later, the Warren Commission examined Lee Harvey Oswald's visit (or visits) to Los Angeles and his possible attendance at the First Unitarian Church of L.A. where he may have received information (directly or indirectly) about Unitarian-supported Albert Schweitzer College from Stephen Fritchman, a radical Los Angeles Unitarian minister whose activities were investigated by an American intelligence officer tracking both the L.A. minister and Lee Harvey Oswald.

Oswald had been enmeshed in U.S. intelligence-monitored Unitarianism in Europe and the U.S. But did Oswald have an even closer and more personal Unitarian connection in Texas?

## Lee Harvey Oswald and the Quaker/Unitarian Paines

When Marina and Lee Harvey Oswald settled in Dallas, Michael Paine and his wife Ruth Hyde Paine ("the kindly Quaker woman"[3]) were already residents of the area. After the Kennedy assassination, no other household in the United States supplied the Dallas Police, FBI, and Warren Commission with more "evidence" of Lee Harvey Oswald's alleged guilt than the Paines: the Paine garage in Irving, Texas, was an incriminating storehouse.[4] According to Galeton Fonzi, a Congressional investigator, "One glaring [negative] example of the quality of the [House Select] Committee's [assassination] investigation was . . . Ruth Paine was never called as a witness."[5]

Who, then, were Ruth Paine and Michael Paine?[6]

Ruth Paine's father and mother, William Avery Hyde and Carol Hyde, were prominent Unitarians in Ohio. The Unitarian Service Committee, a significant support for Oswald's Albert Schweitzer College, had collaborated with the OSS in World War Two and, later, with the CIA-penetrated Agency for International Development. During World War II, William Avery Hyde, Ruth's father, had been an agent of the Office of Strategic Services (OSS)[7] whose program (run by Allen Dulles) included manipulating religious individuals and groups. Later, Hyde worked for the Agency for International Development (AID) when it cooperated closely with the CIA; in addition, Ruth's brother-in-law John Hoke worked for the Communications Resource Division of AID.[8] According to John Gilligan, President Jimmy Carter's AID director, many offices of the AID were populated "from top to bottom" by CIA agents or assets.[9] "The idea [according to Gilligan] was to plant operatives in every kind of activity we had overseas—government, volunteer, religious, every kind." In an area marked by a confluence of volunteer, humanitarian, religious and intelligence operations, Gilligan's observation is precisely to the point.

Ruth Hyde Paine's familial intelligence connections were close. Ruth's sister, Sylvia Hyde Hoke, worked for the Air Force, the CIA, or both.[10] In 1957, William Avery Hyde (Ruth's father) was evaluated for a CIA assignment in Vietnam but (at least officially) was not used by the Agency.[11] Hyde toured Latin America from October, 1964 to August, 1967, covering Peru, Bolivia, Ecuador, and Panama, afterward composing a report sent to both the State Department and the CIA. William Avery Hyde and George De Mohrenschildt had both worked for the International Cooperative Alliance (ICA).[12] A post-assassination intelligence report on Ruth Paine and her father recorded that William Avery Hyde and his wife Carol had closely associated with known CIA operatives, but the report contained an additional and important notation: "Sam Papich" had been given the Paine/Hyde information. Papich was, of course, the partner of William Sullivan in the FBI's counterintelligence operations, cooperating with James Jesus Angleton of the CIA's corresponding unit; Papich was the Bureau's CIA counterintelligence contact reporting directly to Angleton; and both Papich and Sullivan were longtime Bureau investigators of False Identity and Illegals espionage cases.

One such case concerned Lee Harvey Oswald.[13]

## Ruth Paine's William Avery Hyde

Baron George De Mohrenschildt[14], Oswald's closest friend in the Russian-speaking community of Dallas/Fort Worth and a world traveler with close links to at least four information-gathering spy agencies[15], had a working relationship with J. Walton Moore[16], the chief of the CIA's Domestic Contacts Division in Dallas. When Joseph Dryer, an asset of the CIA, a friend of de Mohrenschild[17], and a witness for the House Select Committee on Assassinations was supplied with a list for possible identification "of names of a number of people who may have had some connection or association with George de Mohrenschildt."[18] Asked to respond, Dryer recognized two names: one was "Dorothe Matlack."[19] Ms. Matlack was the U.S. Army's Assistant Director of the Office of Intelligence and the Office's contact with the CIA. In effect, Dorothe Matlack was the Pentagon's liaison to the Agency. In turn, Director Matlack and the peripatetic De Mohrenschildt met on May 7th, 1963, just prior to the Baron and his wife leaving for Haiti on an intelligence-related mission. The meeting between Army intelligence (linked directly to the Agency) and Oswald's reputed "sitter" was, in fact, a reticulate thicket: it involved Clemard Charles, a Haitian banker who dealt in arms sales, acting as a CIA funding conduit, functioning as a top advisor to the president of Haiti; Army intelligence officer Sam Kail, close associate of anti-Castro Cubans at the Miami JM/WAVE station and responsible for key elements of the Army/Agency plots against Fidel; CIA officer Tony Czaikowski, an Agency staff officer representing the CIA's interest in Haiti as a launching platform for another invasion of Cuba; pleas from Clemard Charles to overthrow President Duvalier (at least one plot reportedly including de Mohrenschildt) as the Haitian banker who toted apparently large sums of money around Washington for investment and (according to some sources) for gifts to D.C. politicos just short of bribery; and at least two cover stories for the Baron: a Haitian-approved "geological survey" and a contemplated exploration of sisal and hemp plantation purchases or leases.[20]

The second name House Select Committee on Assassinations witness Joseph Dryer recognized was "William Avery Hyde."[21] Ruth Paine's William Avery Hyde.

Everything about Hyde and De Mohrenschildt (and, indeed, Lee Harvey Oswald) suggested their foreign travels would have been valuable to the CIA's Domestic Contacts Division both in Washington and in Dallas. Certainly William Avery Hyde's OSS/CIA links, given Hyde's closeness to his daughter Ruth Paine, ought to have troubled any government investigator of the JFK assassination.

Ruth Hyde Paine's family was apparently dysfunctional. William Avery Hyde consigned his wife of over thirty years to an Ohio mental institution before he and Carol Hyde divorced in 1961.[22] Carol was "treated for paranoia and delusions," but her daughter Ruth was reportedly doubtful about the grounds for her mother's commitment[23], feeling Ruth herself may have been partly responsible (no matter how "accidentally") for her mother's behavior.[24]

After the divorce, Carol Hyde was released from the Ohio sanitarium, entered Oberlin College and pursued "ministerial studies"[25] to become a "hospital chaplain."[26] Ruth mother's Carol Hyde would, in fact, be ordained a Unitarian minister.[27]

## Michael Paine's George Lyman Paine

Michael Paine's father was George Lyman Paine, called Lyman Paine by his son and those who knew him well. Lyman Paine was a Harvard graduate, a New York architect, and, after the Great Depression, a serious explorer of Marxist alternatives.[28] Moving to Los Angeles, Lyman Paine married Freddie Drake and joined a "socialist splinter group,"[29] becoming a key figure in the anti-Stalinist Trotskyite movement in the United States.[30] The Socialist Workers' Party, chief organ of the Trotskyites in the United States, was closely monitored and even infiltrated by U.S. intelligence, becoming a path for American counterintelligence to run operations against the Communist Party and keep a close watch on the Fair Play for Cuba Committee, heavily supported by Trotskyites. Lyman Paine was suspected (by some) of being a double agent tasked to penetrate and permanently cripple Trotskyism as an independent Socialist entity. Oddly enough, Michael Paine, apparently knowledgeable about nuances of Marxist/Leninist anti-Stalinism, once characterized his friend Lee Harvey Oswald as Trotskyite[31], and FBI Agent Hosty testified to the Warren Commission that on November 5th, less than two weeks before the murder in Dealey Plaza, Ruth Paine told Hosty that Oswald "admitted to her being a Trotskyite Communist." (4 H 472) According to a Dallas FBI agent, "George Lyman Paine, Jr., had telephoned [his son Michael] . . . the night of the assassination. A long-distance operator . . . illegally listened in on the conversation [why?] and later reported what she had heard to the FBI."[32] The Paines' telephone lines were obviously being monitored by U.S. intelligence. According to that same Bureau agent, "George Paine was a well-known Trotskyite, and during his telephone call to his son . . . said, 'We all know who did this . . . . '"[33] The FBI had, in fact, been monitoring George Lyman Paine for some time as a Bureau "security-index subject."[34] From no later than 1953 through as late as October 2, 1963, the FBI submitted regular reports on Lyman Paine: one in 1953, another in 1955, three in 1956, two in 1957, one in 1958, three in 1959, three in 1960, and the last in 1963, just before the assassination, all the Bureau's reports preserved in the Warren Commission's documents (CD 600-615). Apparently the FBI found the coincidence not at all remarkable: that the Paines, with their liberal/anti-Communist orientation and with a major anti-Communist/Trotskyite link in their family, should befriend the family of an admitted Trotskyite (who had redefected from the Soviet Union), at least according to Michael and Ruth Paine.

Despite the clear contradictions in Oswald's left-wing resume, including his closeness to the son of a major anti-Stalinist socialist being tracked by the FBI, the Bureau apparently took no further notice after November 22, 1963. But the Warren Commission did pay some attention to the odd confluence, closely questioning Michael Paine about his father, about Lyman Paine's political interests, and whether Michael was aware that his father had used at least two pseudonyms: "Thomas L. Brown" and "Lyman Pierce," the latter probably a pun on that which caused pain, a pierce; or the surname of Charles Pierce, a philosopher Lyman Paine admired; or both.

## Michael Paine's Mother: Ruth Forbes Paine Young

Michael Paine's mother was Ruth Forbes (for a time known as Ruth Forbes Paine) who had an important intelligence connection: she and Mary Bancroft, Allen Dulles' OSS lover and fellow agent, were lifelong friends. In Mary Bancroft's careful rendition of her life as an Office of Strategic Services spy[35], she identified George Lyman Paine and Ruth Forbes Paine as her close friends both in Boston and New York; but they disappeared from Bancroft's OSS narrative after 1933[36], though Ruth Forbes Paine remained a part of Bancroft's life.

Following the divorce of George Lyman Paine and his wife Ruth Paine, Ruth married Arthur Young, and she was thereafter variously known as Ruth Young, Ruth Forbes Young, and Ruth Forbes Paine Young. Ruth and Arthur Young, her second husband, were intimates of Allen Dulles' OSS lover Mary Bancroft (despite their absence from Bancroft's "autobiography" after 1933).

Ruth Forbes Paine Young became a World Federalist, founded the International Peace Academy, and, together with her husband Arthur Young, created the Institute for the Study of Consciousness, Berkeley, California. Arthur Young, Michael Paine's stepfather (the second husband of Michael's divorced mother), was an inventor, deeply interested in (what would later be called) general systems theory, including its parapsychological and spiritual dimensions; he reportedly "had a serious interest in both extrasensory perception and astrology,"[37] though the latter comment was an oversimplified tag for Young's belief in a pervading cosmic synergy. Young was (at least) one of the creators of the Bell Helicopter[38] and was responsible for obtaining a high-tech/high security clearance job for his stepson Michael Paine at the Bell Helicopter operations near Dallas. Michael had earlier worked for the Franklin Institute, a CIA "conduit."[39]

Oswald-family intimate Ruth Hyde Paine apparently considered Arthur Young (her husband's stepfather) and Ruth Forbes Paine Young (her husband's mother) important elder mentors: she periodically consulted the Philadelphia-area Youngs about undisclosed topics, especially in the summer of 1963.

Michael and Ruth Paine were originally from the Philadelphia area, where they were reportedly[40] active Quakers. How had it all begun?

## Ruth Avery Hyde: the Beginning

Ruth Avery Hyde (Michael Paine's future wife) established her earliest liberal, philosophical, and political credentials at Antioch College[41] in Yellow Springs, Ohio. By 1951, she had become a member of the Quakers, the Society of Friends.[42] Ruth instructed senior Russian Jews at the Y in Philadelphia and taught physical education to young schoolchildren in a Friends program[43], her post-graduation years lived in "Quakerism's great American stronghold, southeastern Pennsylvania . . . ."[44]

Ruth Avery Hyde and Michael Paine met in 1955, attended Quaker services together, initiated their mutual madrigals experience, and were married in December, 1957.[45] For a short time Ruth and Michael lived in a "barn" on the estate of Arthur Young, Michael's stepfather.[46] It was here, reportedly working with Arthur Young on "aeronautical designs," that Michael picked up sufficient expertise to get his engineering job at Bell Helicopter in Fort Worth.[47] But Arthur Young may have had even more to do with Michael landing his Texas position, since it was Young's patent, sold to Larry Bell in 1941, that made the Bell Helicopter possible.[48]

The Paines moved to Irving, Texas; by 1958, given Ruth Paine's professed Russophilia, the Paine couple became active in the Dallas/Fort Worth area's expatriate Russian community. But that community was demonstrably conservative, anti-Soviet, and Orthodox Christian, with a parish church whose hierarchy was reportedly infiltrated by both the CIA and the KGB. Prominent among the White Russians was Paul M. Raigorodsky, at one time employed by the NATO Special Representative to Europe[49], probably an intelligence-related office. In 1963, Raigorodsky was a member of the Board of Directors of the CIA-supported Tolstoy Foundation.[50]

Though Ruth Paine was apparently attracted to the Dallas/Fort Worth Russians, a fit between the Philadelphia Paine couple (ostensibly liberal and Quaker) and the Russian expatriates (reactionary in both domestic and foreign orientation) was curious.

## The Oswalds Meet Ruth Paine

In February, 1963, Lee and Marina Oswald were brought by George De Mohrenschildt and his wife to a social gathering of a military/industrial/intelligence group in the Dallas/Fort Worth area.[51] There the Oswalds met Quaker/Unitarian Ruth Paine, and an intimate and significant relationship between Ruth Paine and Marina Oswald began. Ruth and Michael Paine had recently separated, yet the couple remained close enough to allow Marina Oswald and her first child to live with Ruth while Michael Paine and Lee Harvey Oswald, each living elsewhere, periodically visited the Paine residence.

The circumstances surrounding that initial Ruth Paine/Oswald meeting[52] resonate with special intelligence dimension, suggesting Lee Harvey Oswald was being evaluated (or was even being prepared) as a possible patsy in a right-wing JFK assassination "conspiracy."[53]

## Oswald and Volkmar Schmidt

In the 1950s, both George de Mohrenschildt and his wife had major connections to the CIA; and though the Baron played with a variety of political ideas, he was ultimately an anti-Communist elitist involved in petrochemical intelligence.[54] Among de Mohrenschildt's many conservative and reactionary friends (with oil interests and suspected intelligence links) was a young man named Volkmar Schmidt. An emigré from Germany, Schmidt had resided in the United States for less than two years, becoming a research chemist at the Mobile (Socony-Vacuum) Magnolia[55] Research Laboratories in Duncanville, Texas.[56] The Baron reportedly decided that Schmidt (the German reactionary) and Oswald (the anti-Soviet Marxist) should meet and converse.[57]

But Lee Harvey Oswald began his relations with the Russian emigré circle before de Mohrenschildt made his Oswald/Schmidt decision: according to Gaeton Fonzi (a researcher for the House Select Committee on Assassinations), Oswald had contacted Peter Gregory, "a petroleum engineer teaching Russian language courses at the Fort Worth library" no later than June 20, 1962.[58] In turn, Gregory was in touch with George de Mohrenschildt and all the other members of the Russian-speaking conservative group in the Dallas/Fort Worth area. Finally, the Baron was meeting with the CIA's Domestic Contact Division in Dallas, specifically about Lee Harvey Oswald.

Ms. de Mohrenschildt prepared a buffet-style dinner, planned to bring together Volkmar Schmidt and Lee Harvey Oswald. The de Mohrenschildts and the Oswalds then awaited the arrival of Schmidt.[59] When Volkmar Schmidt made his appearance, Marina and the de Mohrenschildts withdrew and sat together in one part of the house, conversing in Russian, leaving Lee and Schmidt in the kitchen, where the pair talked for over three hours.[60]

According to Edward Epstein, Schmidt found Oswald "articulate" but "emotionally detached" in his impressive political commentary that contrasted the Soviet Union and the United States.[61]

But Oswald must have intended to provoke Schmidt (who reportedly did not rise to Oswald's baiting) or Schmidt deliberately falsified his experience of the conversation. According to Schmidt (as reported by Epstein), Oswald violently attacked President Kennedy's foreign policy, specifically pinpointing the Bay of Pigs and the Cuban Missile Crisis[62], citing them as instances of U.S. "interventions" and "imperialism."[63] But every assassination witness who knew anything of Oswald's political feelings testified Lee admired John F. Kennedy.[64] The alleged Oswald outburst against JFK should therefore be considered either an Oswald provocation or a Schmidt (or Epstein) fabrication.

Schmidt feigned sympathy for Oswald's positions, reportedly employing a psychological strategy he learned in Germany.[65] Schmidt baited Oswald with a negative analysis of right-wing General Edwin A. Walker and an impending American fascism. According to Schmidt (again as reported to Epstein), Oswald became increasingly agitated.[66]

After the Oswald/Schmidt encounter, the Oswalds and George and Jeanne drove home in the Baron's car. Their talk turned to Volkmar Schmidt, characterized in the conversation as a neo-Nazi fascist whose ideas were embodied in the John Birch Society. But Lee was silent.[67]

Musing over his new acquaintance, Schmidt decided he had closely read Oswald's distorted psyche, concluding that Oswald was completely alienated, self-destructive, and suicidal.[68] And Schmidt decided to do something positive about Lee's problems: he would organize a party for this character out of Dostoevsky[69] so that (as Epstein phrased it) Lee "could meet and talk to other people interested in political ideas."[70]

## The Magnolia Party

Volkmar Schmidt shared his living space with three other men: Everett Glover of the house[71] and a research chemist at Magnolia Research Laboratories[72] who apparently worked in Dallas[73]; geologist Richard Pierce[74], also at Magnolia, and Michael Paine (separated from his wife Ruth Hyde Paine), a "research engineer" at the Bell Helicopter operations located between Fort Worth and Dallas.[75] Glover had met Lee and Marina earlier at the de Mohrenschildts[76], and he thought it would be entertaining to have Oswald air his views on the Soviet Union.[77] But after joining Glover in planning the Oswald party and sharing in its costs, Volkmar Schmidt left for Germany "on business"[78] and reportedly never saw the Oswalds again.[79]

Both Michael Paine (a member of the Glover all-male household) and his wife Ruth Paine were invited to the Schmidt/Glover party, but, oddly enough, Michael did not attend, despite Volkmar Schmidt's reported intention to link Oswald and Paine because they shared an interest in politics.[80] Invited and attending were Betty

MacDonald[81] (NOT "Betty Mooney MacDonald," the onetime Jack Ruby employee) who was the Magnolia Laboratories librarian and the "girlfriend" of Magnolia employee Richard Pierce[82]; also attending was another Magnolia research employee, Norman Fredricksen, with his wife Elke.[83]

On February 22, 1963, the separation of Lee and Marina Oswald by Ruth Paine and the Russian émigrés (assisted by the Magnolia employee group) began at the Glover party. Seated in the kitchen were Ruth Paine, Marina Oswald, and the de Mohrenschildts.[84] Though Ruth Paine was a student of the Russian language, she spoke in English, the de Mohrenschildts translating her questions and comments into Russian for Marina.[85]

Marina's isolation had begun.

In the living room, Elke Fredricksen, Norman Fredricksen, Betty MacDonald, Richard Pierce, and Everett Glover, the entire Magnolia party group, "pulled their chairs . . . in a circle around Oswald and began asking [him] questions about what life was like in the Soviet Union."[86]

## The Sun Oil Company Context

The most inclusive frame of reference for that Magnolia party was not Mobile Oil, Socony/Vacuum Oil, or even the Magnolia Research Labs, but rather Ilya Mamantov's Dallas employment by the Sun Oil Company (Sunoco). Sun Oil was owned and operated by multi-millionaire J. Howard Pew and his family[87], among the richest and most powerful financial supporters of the Republican Party in the 1950s and 1960s, major funders for extreme right-wing political groups in the United States, and enthusiastic backers of key anti-Communist Christian revivalists.[88] Though the Pew Memorial Fund was one of the thirteen most heavily-endowed of U.S. philanthropies[89], its operations were carefully cloaked: Texas Congressman Wright Patman, for example, complained about the Pew Fund's "defiance" of his Congressional investigation.[90] Like Arthur Young, Ruth Forbes Paine Young, and the Catherwood family, the Sun Oil Pews (despite their Dallas connection) were a prominent part of the Philadelphia elite: twenty-one Pew family members were listed in the Philadelphia Social Register.[91]

Among the many Sun Oil/Pew Memorial Trust activities linked to both political and petroleum intelligence was the Pew/Rockefeller operation supporting Wycliffe Bible/Summer Institute of Linguistics evangelism in Brazil's Amazon forests, a part of the Rockefellers' long history of using religion for the family's political and economic ends. The fusion of bible-thumping and oil exploring in the dense Brazilian rain forest called for a futuristic sky vehicle capable of taking off from postage-stamp airstrips, able to make fast getaways under fire, and yet capable of hovering at very slow speeds over an area targeted for religious pamphlet bombings or the collection of intelligence on hostile Amazon natives. Or (take a breath) both.

The Helio Courier was precisely that kind of aircraft.

A Miami Cuban-American, reportedly a CIA contact, had a Helio Courier plane available, purchased from him and presented to the Wycliff Bible/Pew/Rockefeller operations in Brazil. The Cuban-American received a payment split between Sam Milbank, a Rockefeller agent, and the Pew Memorial Fund.[92]

The Helio in the Amazon concretely illustrated the manipulation of religion by invasive oil companies (Pew/Sun Oil and Rockefeller) and the CIA.

In the 1960s, Pew/Sun Oil operative Ilya Mamantov was a solid indication that reactionary oil operations had serious U.S. intelligence connections in Dallas. His influence in the area was pervasive: in the conservative and intelligence-connected Russian-speaking Dallas/Fort Worth community; in establishing that community's Catherwood/CIA-supported Russian Orthodox Church parish; in his teaching of scientific Russian to Magnolia technology experts; and in his intelligence-based translating of Marina Oswald's first post-assassination statements.

After the JFK murder, neither the Dallas Police, the Dallas County Sheriff's Office, the Secret Service, nor the FBI initially gained control of Marina Oswald's earliest statements on key evidence: Jack Alston Crichton, a "petroleum independent operator," a member of the Army Reserve's Intelligence Service[93], the chief of "a local [Dallas] Army Intelligence Unit"[94] was quickly at Marina Oswald's side when she needed interpretation. Crichton, the oil/intelligence officer, then called Sun Oil agent Ilya Mamantov to assist in interpreting Marina.[95]

Mamantov and Crichton shared a right-wing orientation centered in the Republican Party: Ilya Mamantov was a precinct boss for the GOP, and Jack Crichton became the party's candidate for governor in 1964.[96]

Beginning in 1955, Mamantov was a Dallas Sun Oil research geologist; in 1960 he taught technical Russian "in the Dallas area" to "scientific personnel" pursuing "scientific research"[97] at the Magnolia Research Lab in Duncanville, Texas.[98] Mary Ferrell recalled that the majority of research people at Magnolia Labs, including French and Russian technicians, held "doctorates."[99]

Why, after all the corporate decisions that transformed Vacuum Oil, Socony Oil, Socony-Vacuum, and Mobile, did Magnolia (though primarily its laboratories) remain Magnolia? The Mobile/Socony-Vacuum decision was obvious: it would keep its oil exploration, research, and intelligence focus in the Magnolia Labs as a single Cold War entity, opening it to expatriate French, German, and Russian oil experts.

Among those experts was Ilya Mamantov.

Mamantov was well-known in Dallas; James Herbert Martin, local lawyer with connections to Jack Ruby (and, after the JFK assassination, to Marina Oswald and *Time*, Inc.) was asked during his Warren Commission testimony about Mamantov; Martin replied: "I think he works for Sun Oil Company . . . ."[100]

But Ilya Mamantov was not only well-known; he knew, in turn, everyone who came to the Magnolia Party for Lee Harvey Oswald.

## The Magnolia Party's Connections

Magnolia Labs chemist Everett Glover[101], working with Volkmar Schmidt[102], was a member of the madrigal singing ensemble that included both his housemate Michael Paine and Ruth Paine[103]; Glover's Magnolia group (professionally interested in petrochemical research and intelligence) had studied Russian with Ilya Mamantov, one of the two Russian expatriates who helped establish the Dallas-area St. Nicholas parish of the Russian Orthodox Church[104], a denomination receiving CIA funds through both the Tolstoy Foundation and Catherwood Foundation. Peter Gregory, a Dallas-area "consulting petroleum engineer"[105], and Sun Oil Ilya Mamantov were involved in translating, interpreting, and finally manipulating Marina Oswald's statements and testimony after the JFK assassination.[106] Volkmar Schmidt and Norman Frederickson had psychological warfare connections: Schmidt admitted to being "fascinated with the techniques of hypnosis"[107], and, in Germany, "Fredricksen's father had been director of Radio Free Europe"[108], a communication program utilizing pysops methods. The chief of Radio Free Europe was C.D. Jackson, the major innovator of psychological warfare in the 1950s.[109]

The Magnolia party for Lee Harvey Oswald had included people with CIA-supported and ultra-conservative religious affiliations, psyops and right-wing links[110], petrochemical intelligence and military/industrial connections, and at least one significant Quaker/Unitarian presence: Ruth Hyde Paine.

## Ruth Paine Inserts Herself

Two months after Ruth Paine and Marina Oswald met, Lee announced he was moving to New Orleans to seek employment, and Ruth asked Marina to bring her infant daughter and live with Ruth in her home. In May, 1963, Oswald informed Marina and Ruth he had found work in the southern city, and Ruth Paine then drove Marina and her child to New Orleans.

On September 23rd, 1963, Marina, pregnant with her second child, was once more transported by Ruth Paine, this time from New Orleans to Irving, Texas; once more Marina was to live with Ruth, with whom Marina and (now) the two Oswald children resided until just after the JFK assassination. Prior to their leaving New Orleans, Oswald had told Ruth and Marina he would be looking for work in Houston or Philadelphia. Houston of course, made sense, since Dallas/Fort Worth, Houston, and New Orleans constituted a kind of triangular job area. What about Philadelphia? Both Michael and Ruth Paine had been residents of the area; Michael's parents were still in the area; Ruth herself may have suggested the city to Oswald.

Even this possible beneficence on Ruth's part had a somber side: the Russian-speaking community of the Dallas area's Russian-speaking St. Nicholas Parish had received substantial support from an important source of CIA money, the

Catherwood Foundation, founded in Bryn Mahr, Pennsylvania, ten miles outside of Philadelphia.[111]

After Oswald returned to the Dallas area, he lived away from Marina and the children, but he visited them on the weekends at the Paines' home.

Ruth Paine, for whatever humanitarian or personal reasons, had kept the Oswalds apart during a crucial period before the Dealey Plaza assassination; she had been successful in getting Oswald a job at the Texas School Book Depository in October, 1963, effectively preparing Lee as the patsy-on-the-spot in the Dallas killing; and her garage, her household, and her later Warren Commission testimony combined to make up the bulk of the so-called evidence against Lee Harvey Oswald. Only Lee's wife Marina constituted a worse witness against the accused assassin.

In both Ruth's and her husband's family background were humanitarian, religious, and government-related/intelligence activity.

## Quaker Ruth Paine and the U.S./Soviet East-West Exchanges

Beginning in 1957, Ruth Paine began an intensive study of the Russian language: Berlitz, records, University of Pennsylvania and Middlebury College courses, the latter program as late as the summer of 1959[112], just before the Paines moved to Irving, almost as if Ruth were preparing for an important Russian experience in Texas.

In Philadelphia in 1958, Ruth was an active member of the (Quaker) Young Friends Committee of North America, acting, according to the testimonies of both Ruth and Michael Paine to the Warren Commission, as the primary liaison between its East-West Contacts Committee and the U.S. State Department. Earlier, Ruth and her Friends had promoted correspondence between young Americans and Soviet citizens; later they planned a visit by young Soviets to the United States.[113] Paine's Quaker committee eventually brought three Russians to America, "a journalist, a factory worker, and an economics student,"[114] with Ruth assisting in "preparations for their tour" and later meeting the Soviets at a Philadelphia party.[115]

But this apparent good-will gesture had a particularly dark, multi-layered dimension.

In January, 1958, Ambassador William Sterling Byrd Lacy (for the United States) and Ambassador Georgi N. Zaroubin (for the Soviet Union) signed an agreement to establish technical, cultural, and educational exchanges between the two Cold War combatants. On February 21, 1958, the U.S. Council on Student Travel in New York and the Soviet Youth Committee in Moscow jointly announced that the exchange program signed by Ambassadors Zaroubin and Lacy would become a reality. With Lacy's official signature, Ruth Paine's Philadelphia Quaker plan could move forward.

## William S. B. Lacy

Born in Grand Junction, Colorado, in 1910, Lacy attended the elitist Morey Preparatory School in Denver; he received his bachelor's degree from the University of Colorado in 1932. In World War II, Lacy was appointed chief of the division of controls and analysis in the Foreign Economic Administration (FEA); its mission was overseeing America's "foreign economic affairs." Created on September 25, 1943, by presidential decree, the FEA incorporated six already-existing relief and rehabilitation organizations and operations, including the Office of Economic Warfare. In addition, the FEA became the political/economic cover for the Export-Import Bank of Washington, the Petroleum Reserves Corporation, the Rubber Development Corporation, and the U.S. Commercial Company.

William S. B. Lacy brought with him his Foreign Economic Administration experience in political and economic intelligence when he moved to the United Nations Relief and Rehabilitation Administration (UNRRA). UNRRA was actually a function of the U.S. government, its "United Nations" label adopted before the U.N. was established. Lacy was appointed assistant deputy director of UNRRA handling major supplies and procurement for the "liberated areas" and "planning for the control of occupied territories."

A flood of political, military, economic, industrial, and displaced persons/refugees information flowed through the Foreign Economic Administration and UNRRA while William S.B. Lacy held key positions in both wartime institutions. Much of the actions and decisions of the two agencies were strongly influenced by the U.S. Department of State, and in 1945 Lacy joined the Department and was assigned to its Division of Philippines and Southeast Asian Affairs, headquartered in Washington, D.C.

## William Lacy, the Philippines, Southeast Asia and Ed Lansdale

The Division's federal archives, the "Confidential U.S. State Department Special Files" on Southeast Asia (1944-1966), contain a huge body of information and intelligence on "Indochina," "Thailand," "China and Taiwan," Hong Kong, "Indonesia," Japan, Macao, Malaya, South Vietnam, Laos, Cambodia, the Republic of Korea (South Korea), "North Korea," and the Philippines. The largest mega-file in this collection is the "Records of the Philippine and Southwest Asian Division, 1944-1952." In this archive are the available papers and documents on "the plans and overall policies of the State Department for the Philippines" as well as plans and policies for the occupied islands of the Pacific Ocean and the "European colonies in Southeast Asia." The mega-file holds documents covering U. S. policies that governed the "political, economic, commercial, and military matters" of the entire Pacific/Southeast Asian areas, including the Philippines.

In Washington from 1945 through 1950, William S.B. Lacy helped to create and maintain these State Department records, laboring at the Office of the Philippine and Southeast Asian Affairs. In 1950, he was appointed Director of the crucial division.

John F. Melby was a State Department associate of Director Lacy in the Office of the Philippine and Southeast Asian Affairs. A career U.S. Foreign Service Officer from 1937 through 1955, Melby gave an "Oral Interview" for the Truman Presidential Museum and Library in November, 1986. He was questioned by Robert Accinelli about William S.B. Lacy and the activities of the division.

During his tenure at the division, Melby was in close contact with the CIA's Ed Lansdale in the Philippines. Melby believed Lansdale's anti-Huk operations had nothing to do with "Communist groups outside the Philippines"; rather, the Huk group was a populist "radical movement . . . [that] came out of the rice situation in Luzon."

In 1950, William S.B. Lacy became Melby's "immediate supervisor." Melby described his director as flamboyant, dressed in funereal black with bright red hair and a theatrically-curled "guardsman" mustache. According to his division associate, Lacy was a "great poseur," desperately interested in establishing a Lacy family link to British nobility, "a sort of Louis XIV reactionary"; Melby, however, may have been deflecting any real examination of Lacy's serious side.

Melby noted that Lacy had "strange people" with French Indochinese and OSS backgrounds occupying critical division desks. Strange people, that is, with relevant intelligence experience.

Melby was obviously the most knowledgeable person about the Philippines at the division; he was, in fact, "in charge of the Philippines" who had headed a "Melby Mission" out of the Pentagon to the Pacific in late 1950. The mission's tour had included Indochina and the Philippines assessing anti-Communist military needs and checking crucial arms traffic for the Defense Department. The Philippines and Thailand, in fact, were the only "Asian" allies of the U.S. that sent troops to Korea in 1950. Melby, a Foreign Service officer, united major intelligence and military concerns of the U.S. government.

William Lacy had predicted that "we" would eliminate all the "Commies," and then, "by God," all "the goddamn liberals." He was moved to the Philippines in 1952 to join a crucial military/intelligence operation.

Lacy followed a flood of U.S. military, intelligence, and economic missions that began in 1950. From 1952 through 1955, Lacy, "a brilliant and aggressive diplomat," was Counselor and Deputy Chief of Mission at the U.S. Embassy in Manila, first working with the Philippine military and with Ed Lansdale's anti-Huk CIA program of psychological warfare in support of Ramon Magsaysay, the Agency's choice of Filipino defense minister/general. Magsaysay was ultimately elected president of the Philippines in 1953, a psyops-driven victory. Lacy and Lansdale, representing the U.S. State Department, the U.S. military, and the CIA, effectively ran President Magsaysay and his government. Lansdale, Magsaysay's closest advisor, linked the Central Intelligence Agency, the Joint

U.S. Military Advisory Group (in control of military and intelligence), and the U.S. Embassy through William S.B. Lacy. *Time* magazine (November 23, 1953) took note of the American pair, citing Lansdale's crucial roles in Magsaysay's anti-Huk campaign, presidential victory, and subsequent elevation to anti-Communist sainthood. *Time* also noted that "Polished, precise William Lacy, Councillor of the U.S. Embassy, became the man to whom Magsaysay turned daily for counsel."

Flushed with counterinsurgency success in the Philippines, Lansdale left in 1953 to supervise two Southeast Asian narcotics investigations before he was deployed to Vietnam. William Lacy was awarded the fifth-highest "military and security" decoration of the Philippines, the Legion of Honor (established in 1947), carrying its highest rank: "commander."

Yearning to be a full-fledged ambassador, Lacy was posted in 1955 to the Republic of Korea as an "envoy," a "minister-counselor." But after less than a year, Lacy was booted out of Korea. His antipathy to races other than Caucasian (and his other abrasive qualities) resulted in President Syngman Rhee declaring Lacy persona non grata. Lacy's official State Department obituary listed him as "Ambassador (Ret.)."

Lacy died on December 11, 1978, the victim of a ravaged stomach already three-quarters removed. He had been a member of the Board of Examiners for the Foreign Service and, for a time, the Deputy Commandant of the National War College, whose curriculum always emphasized "the politico-military aspects of Defense policies and programs," a perfect focus for politico-military Lacy.

## William S.B. Lacy: Foster Dulles' Special Assistant

But before retiring in 1961, William Sterling Byrd Lacy, a frustrated illiberal racist, was appointed by Secretary of State John Foster Dulles as Dulles' Special Assistant for East-West Exchanges. The year was 1956. Lacy would oversee the key State Department program of student exchange between the Soviet Union and the United States following a formal agreement. In early October, 1957, Frederick T. Merrill, Director of the East-West Contacts Staff at the State Department and, through William Lacy, separated by one degree from Secretary Foster Dulles, announced that State was "making plans to actively facilitate such exchange." By November, 1957, the Office of East-West Contacts was focusing on Soviet/U.S. youth group exchanges. The compact between the two nations that would enable Ruth Paine and her fellow Quakers to bring Soviet citizens to the United States was formalized in January, 1958, between Soviet Ambassador Zaroubin and Ambassador William S. B. Lacy, the State Department's Special Assistant for East-West Exchanges, his resumé stuffed with political, economic, and military intelligence.

For the Warren Commission, both Michael and Ruth Paine reportedly could not recall the State Department official with whom Ruth Paine had communicated to effect her Soviet/U.S. student exchange, but that person was most likely the Director of the East-West Contacts Staff who worked under William S. B. Lacy :"The entire [student-exchange] project had the official encouragement of the U.S. Department of State and received approbation from Frederick T. Merrill."

## Who Was Frederick T. Merrill?

In the late 1920s, Merrill was already participating in a national behavior modification program focusing on the negative effects of illegal substances. Merrill and his associates argued available narcotics were traceable (with questionable evidence) to the Far East. Merrill published papers in 1927, 1928, 1938, and 1950 supporting this Fu Manchu narcotics argument. With Harry J. Anslinger, Commissioner of the Bureau of Narcotics, Merrill co-wrote articles on drugs and appeared as a presenter on panels organized and chaired by Anslinger. At a Marijuana Conference on December 12, 1938, for example, Merrill presented a paper at the gathering under the auspices of the Bureau of Internal Revenue and the Treasury's Bureau of Narcotics.

Frederick Merrill was identified at that 1938 conference as a member of the Foreign Policy Association, the Establishment's middle-octave equivalent to its Council on Foreign Relations. FPA member Frederick T. Merrill joined the U.S. Foreign Service in 1940 in the midst of his intense anti-drug activities A participant in the FPA's persuasion programs targeting the educated U.S. middle-class, Merrill was active on the FPA's Narcotics Committee. In turn, Bureau of Narcotics Director Harry Anslinger had a long history of interest in drugs capable of inducing behavior modification and had cooperated closely with the Central Intelligence Agency in its search for the key to mind control. Before retiring in 1965, Anslinger's long-time associate Frederick Merrill was a member of the U.N. Office on Drugs and Crime team that visited Thailand in 1964 investigating Thai narcotics production. Merrill was listed as a "specialist in opium problems in the Far East."

C.D. Jackson's Free Europe Committee (ultimately the Committee for a Free Europe) distributed covert CIA funding to a series of anti-Communist exile groups, especially the Assembly of Captive European Nations (ACEN). Frederick Merrill, Foreign Policy Association member, State Department Foreign Service officer, and anti-Communist narcotics expert, helped transfer the Free Europe Committee's CIA funds to the ACEN in 1955-1957.When Ruth Paine's Quakers were organizing their East-West exchange, Ruth was in touch with Frederick Thayer Merrill, the Director of the East-West Contacts Staff of the Department of State.

## Ruth Paine's Exchange: The KGB Component

Ruth Paine's East-West exchange program had another dark layer. On August 2nd, 1957, Eugeni Alekseevich Zaostrovtsev [116]became Cultural Attaché for Cinema and Education at the Soviet Embassy in Washington, D.C.[117] Five months later the major cultural/educational agreement was signed between the Soviet Union and the United States. In April, 1958, the Quaker East-West Contacts Committee (including Ruth

Paine) met to plan a U.S. trip for the three reputedly 'young' Soviets, all between 26 and 32 years old; that same spring, Soviet Cultural Attaché Zaostrovtsev assisted Ruth Paine's Friends Committee to bring those three Soviets to the United States.[118] Any of the three Soviets, of course, could have been a KGB asset or agent.

Zaostrovtsev, in fact, had a major clandestine link. After assisting Ruth Paine's American Friends Committee, Zaostrovtsev continued to pursue his Quaker connection that ultimately resulted in a double-agent spy sting run against Zaostrovtsev that was directed by the FBI.[119] On May 15th, 1959, Eugeni Zaostrovtsev, Second Secretary of the Soviet Embassy, the cultural attaché who had made Ruth Paine's Quaker/Soviet exchange possible, was expelled from the United States. According to the FBI, he was a KGB agent.[120]

Ruth Paine's Quakerism had involved the U.S. State Department, State's East-West Contacts Staff run by two Foreign Service officers with extensive ties to American intelligence, the Soviet KGB, and the FBI.

## The Quaker Paines Join the Unitarians

Ruth and her husband Michael were Quakers when they settled in Irving, Texas. Testifying under oath before the Warren Commission, Ruth Paine affirmed that she was indeed a Quaker; but, according to her husband Michael, when the Paines came to Texas, they found no substantial Quaker group in the Dallas area.[121] So Michael joined the local Unitarians, later worrying about not meeting his pledge promise to the Dallas Unitarian Church[122]; then Michael and Ruth (reportedly still a Quaker) sang in the madrigal group of the local Unitarian congregation[123]; and Ruth was perceived to be a member of that same Unitarian congregation, though she did not attend with any regularity.[124] During Ruth Paine's Warren Commission testimony, the staff was curious about Ruth's religious practices and her Soviet friendship activities[125]: the Warren Commission had discovered that, beyond Ruth's Quaker connections, Unitarianism was, for her, familial: Carol Hyde, Ruth's mother, was a recently ordained Unitarian minister.[126] But though the Commission established Ruth Paine's questionable Soviet interests and her odd Unitarian/Quaker orientation, it finally backed off from any further exploration of these important leads.

After the Kennedy assassination, the FBI asked Quaker questions about Ruth Paine, but the Bureau asked them only timidly. Ruth Paine had delivered Marina Oswald to New Orleans and contacted Ruth Kloepfer, a Quaker who was the clerk of the Orleans area Friends Meeting; Ruth Paine had informed Kloepfer that Lee Harvey Oswald was now in New Orleans, asking Quaker Kloepfer to assist the Oswald family. Responding, Kloepfer and her two daughters, both just happening to be studying Russian, visited Lee and Marina.[127] What assistance they offered to the Oswalds has not been recorded.

The Bureau did take SOME note, however: it was concerned that a possible connection had been made between Oswald and the New Orleans Council for Peaceful Alternatives[128], a Friends organization embodying Ruth Paine's reported pacifist outlook. The FBI Bureau had begun exploring the murky links between Ruth Paine, the Quakers, Mexico City, and Lee Harvey Oswald.

## The "Oswald" in Mexico Quaker Connection

Though it was highly unlikely Lee Harvey Oswald actually visited Mexico City and the Soviet and Cuban embassies there prior to the JFK assassination, someone certainly did show up in Mexico who represented himself as Oswald and who displayed convincing identity documents. For the FBI and the CIA, this series of events conjured up unpleasant possibilities of a Soviet KGB or Communist Cuban involvement with Oswald.[129] Real or fake, an Oswald in Mexico City who had contacted Soviet or Cuban intelligence was ominous.

For the FBI, a Quaker/intelligence connection to Oswald with a Mexico City locale was one more unwanted complication, primarily because of Ruth Paine[130] and her closeness to the Oswald family.

The locus of that Quaker complication was the Friends House, the Casa del Los Amigos[131], in Mexico City. In September, 1963, Homobono Amo Alcaraz[132], himself a Quaker, had reportedly met an "Oswald" in the company of several Quakers at Sanborn's Restaurant located (according to researcher Mary Ferrell) next to the American Embassy in Mexico City. All the Quakers were either staying at the Casa del Los Amigos or were connected to it. Alcaraz asserted that "Oswald," riding on the back of the motorbike of an unidentified U.S. citizen, had left the restaurant for a trip to the Cuban Embassy, ostensibly in an attempt to get "Oswald" (or both of them) a Cuban visa.

Interviewed by the FBI, Von Peacock, the Acting Director of the Quaker's Casa del Los Amigos, suggested the motor biking American could have been Robert Kaffke, a San Francisco Quaker who, along with fifty-seven other students, visited Cuba illegally in the summer of 1963[133]: but the Kaffke story sounded too much like a botched attempt to implicate "Oswald" in a Cuban-sponsored murder of JFK. This "Oswald" had left the Quaker House before Kaffke registered; Kaffke reported that Casa residents "were still talking about Oswald's visit."[134] He also stated that "Oswald" was in possession of a sizable amount of money and the Casa residents "were really scared when the name of Oswald [was] mentioned"[135], the latter presumably after November 22nd, 1963.

Beyond the confused calendar, what made the Kaffke revelations suspicious was his intelligence link: he was an undercover informant for the FBI's San Francisco office.[136] Helpfully, the FBI reported it did not believe Kaffke was the motorbike companion of "Oswald."

Ms. Barrie Milliman, a Berkeley undergraduate, visited Homobono Amo Alcaraz in Mexico City and heard about Oswald's alleged Quaker connections there. Milliman then reportedly told another student, Judith Gordon, and on January 15th, 1964, Gordon notified the FBI office in San Francisco: like Robert Kaffke of San Francisco, Gordon was also an undercover Bureau informant.[137]

The Quaker Good Samaritan who wanted to go to Cuba with "Oswald" was later reportedly identified as Steve (or Larry) Kennan.[138] Homobono Alcaraz, interviewed in 1994 by researcher/writer Tony Summers, stated that the Quaker on a motorbike in Mexico City was from Philadelphia[139]: he was, indeed, Steve/Larry Kennan, and Kennan was most probably "LICOZY-3," a double (if not a triple) agent run by the CIA operating in Mexico City. Kennan was a Quaker from Philadelphia "recruited [earlier] by the Soviets while a student in Mexico City . . . [who then] reported [his] . . . recruitment [to the CIA] and [afterward] worked for the [Agency's] Mexico City station."[140] And when he returned to the United States, double-agent Kennan became, of course, an FBI undercover informant.[141]

The Oswald-among-the-Quakers in Mexico City story was obviously rich with CIA/FBI ramifications, not the least of which was the Philadelphia/Quaker identity of the motor biking friend of "Oswald."

Ruth Paine's influential in-laws, Ruth Forbes Paine Young and Arthur Young, were powerful Quakers in the Philadelphia area. Philadelphia was the international center of the Quakers; the American Friends Service Committee (AFSC) was headquartered in Philadelphia and was responsible for that same Casa De Los Amigos, the Mexico City Friends' hostel/camp for U.S. students. Like its Unitarian (USC) counterpart, the Quakers' service operation had cooperated with U.S. intelligence through two wars and after.

## The CIA, the Catherwood Foundation, the Young Family, the Philippines, and Ed Lansdale

Both the CIA and the Catherwood Foundation had been established in 1947; both supported the Russian Orthodox Church in the United States, including St. Nicholas Parish in the Dallas/Fort Worth area.[142] And Ruth and Michael Paine were part of that curious Texas community of Russians. Throughout the Cold War, the Catherwood Foundation operated as a CIA front and conduit for funding covert Agency operations, its offices in Bryn Mawr, Pennsylvania, just ten miles outside of Philadelphia where Ruth Forbes Paine Young and her husband Arthur Young lived. Cummins Catherwood, born in Philadelphia, was the founder of the Catherwood Foundation and "a financier, philanthropist, banker, oilman, patron of the arts, [and] avid yachtsman . . . , a pillar of the Philadelphia establishment."[143] The Catherwood Foundation had been a major presence in the Philippines in the 1950s, the period when Colonel (later General) Edward Lansdale[144] ran the country for the CIA, using psychological warfare techniques[145] remarkably similar to C.D. Jackson and CIA agents E. Howard Hunt and David Phillips.[146] "Lansdale had found a niche in psychological warfare with the OSS during World War II as an intelligence officer on MacArthur's staff, working for General Willoughby. By the war's end, he was their chief of intelligence in the Philippines."[147]

Lansdale's "alter ego" was "Gabe Kaplan, New York lawyer, politician, and public relations man . . . [whose] first operational cover [as a CIA agent] was the Asia Foundation, later the Committee for Free Asia, and then the Catherwood Foundation . . . ."[148]

The Catherwood family and the Youngs (Ruth Paine's in-laws) were members of the same Philadelphia elitist circle, and both had significant ties to the Central Intelligence Agency; further, Ruth Paine considered the Youngs her mentors, visiting them frequently in Philadelphia.

## Were Ruth Paine's Quaker/Unitarian Identities Other Than Spiritual?

Could Ruth Paine have been a Quaker of convenience[149], given the Quaker/Soviet spy incident involving her American Friends and the "Philadelphia" Quaker incidents in Mexico City? Did Ruth bend the truth in her Warren Commission testimony concerning her Texas switch from Quakerism to Unitarianism?[150] The Dallas/Fort Worth area had, in fact, a strong Quaker presence; Ruth and Michael Paine could have easily resumed their American Friends identity immediately after arriving in Texas.

Why, then, would Ruth return to her family's Unitarian orientation, rich with intelligence intrigue, after moving to the Dallas area? Were Ruth and Michael Paine willing participants in the patsying of Lee Harvey Oswald, or were they, like Oswald, manipulated?

## Michael Paine: Another "Oswald"?

Michael Paine, a physical double of Lee Harvey Oswald in 1963, extended his interests in Oswald's contradictory politics by participating in a questionable action that mimed Lee Harvey Oswald's often provocative posturing. In the Spring of 1963 at the edge of Dallas's Southern Methodist University[151], Michael Paine lounged at Luby's, eating lunch and holding "conversations or debates" with SMU students who dropped in for a Sunday afternoon lunch.[152] According to the FBI, Paine argued for "peaceful coexistence" in Eastern Europe and supported Castro's Cuba against ongoing U.S. policy, maintaining Fidel Castro had only responded to major American provocations.[153] Both opinions were consonant with positions held by the Socialist Workers Party, the Fair Play for Cuba Committee, and Lee Harvey Oswald.

Michael Paine had set up these SMU political confrontations after being a Sunday communicant at a "nearby" Unitarian Church.[154]

## Lee Harvey Oswald, The Unitarian Church, and the FBI Investigation

From 1958 through 1963, Lee Harvey Oswald's extensive Unitarian connections were focused on and made local in Ruth and Michael Paine who had defined Oswald's fate.

For more than fifty years, Mary Ferrell[155], the matriarchal presence in JFK research, lived just blocks away from Dallas' First Unitarian Church on Preston Road. After the JFK murder, Mary learned that Ruth and Michael Paine had attended that same First Unitarian Church[156]; she asked a young friend of her first son if he knew anyone from the church to whom she might be introduced.

Mary Ferrell met Reverend Byrd Helligas, the assistant pastor of the First Unitarian Church, who told Mary "the government" had visited his Dallas church and examined its records, looking for anything about Lee Harvey Oswald.

Byrd Helligas also recalled that federal agents "didn't just do that in Dallas . . . [;] they went all over the country picking up [Unitarian] records." What had happened in Providence and in Dallas, according to Reverend Helligas, occurred throughout the United States: the "government" had, in fact, searched for any relationship between Lee Harvey Oswald and the Unitarian Church.

Unitarian individuals and groups connected to the accused assassin were linked to significant U.S. intelligence actions throughout the Cold War. After the JFK murder, a persistent and honest inquiry by the FBI, the CIA, the Warren Commission, and subsequent investigations would have discovered all of them. But an honest inquiry would also have exposed U.S. intelligence's manipulation (through two hot wars and the subsequent Cold War) of religious individuals and groups, including the Quakers, the Unitarians, and especially Albert Schweitzer College, with its Board of Directors and its American Friends of Albert Schweitzer College.

An honest inquiry would also have asked whether Lee Harvey Oswald was deliberately sent to a Swiss college that had such significant U.S. intelligence ties. And that honest inquiry would have asked why. But no honest government inquiry was ever initiated in the assassination of John F. Kennedy.

## Character Witnesses for Ruth and Michael Paine: From the Dark Side

If an electronic search is made with the word "Unitarian" in the NARA online database covering all the official investigations of the JFK assassinations, only ONE (apparently irrelevant) document will be found. A search of the name "Ruth Paine" will produce a mountain of material, but none of it will be about Unitarianism. Since the Unitarian churches of Providence, Los Angeles, and Dallas (at least) were investigated by federal officers before and after November 22, 1963, the absence of official JFK assassination documents relating to Unitarianism is, at least, profoundly disturbing.

Beyond the FBI checks of Ruth and Michael Paine's several families, the Bureau apparently needed character references for the Paines, given their closeness to Lee Harvey Oswald and his wife Marina. Support for Michael and Ruth was offered by their friends Nancy Osborn and Frederick Osborn, Jr., recorded by the Bureau.[157] But the FBI did not explore (at least not recorded in its available documents) why members of the internationally prominent Osborn family should feel the Paines needed their personal support.

What the Bureau found but suppressed or what it declined to explore was a history of elitist/right-wing social and political positions held by the Osborn family that tracked back to 1902. Those often extremist positions were consonant with political and social values espoused by Allen Dulles and John Foster Dulles, by Caucasian/Protestant eugenics activists, by CIA-supported psychological war enthusiasts (including C.D. Jackson), and by U.S. military behavior modification ("mind-control") researchers.

## Henry Fairfield Osborn

In 1902, Professor Henry Fairfield Osborn, director of the New York Zoological Society and the American Museum of Natural History, joined a growing eugenics movement that already included leading eugenics researchers and scientists, the Carnegie Institution, the Brooklyn Institute of Arts and Science (with its Long Island Cold Harbor laboratory), and enthusiastic eugenics supporters throughout Europe.[158] For twelve years, Osborn was a key figure in establishing and directing a series of organizations sponsoring national and international meetings on eugenics.[159] Though war in 1914 halted international eugenics cooperation (at least in Europe), "America continued its domestic eugenic program and held its place as the world leader in eugenic research, theory and activism."[160]

After the war, the United States commanded the world's eugenics troops, with Henry Fairfield Osborn as the president of the Second International Congress of Eugenics, scheduled for 1921 in New York.[161] "The second congress was rich with typical raceological dogma and dominated by American biological [race] precepts."[162] In his speech opening the congress, Osborn left no doubt that the most intellectual of eugenicists could also be a racist.[163]

The International Committee on Eugenics, the governing body supported by Osborn and his associates, became the Permanent International Commission on eugenics, again dominated by the United States.[164] That American dominance insured that the most racist aspects of the world-wide eugenics movement were enforced for over fifty years. Through World War II (and even after), "hundreds of thousands of Americans and untold numbers of others [throughout the world] were not permitted to continue their families by reproducing. Selected because of their ancestry, national origin, race or religion, they were forcibly sterilized, wrongly committed to mental institutions where they died in great numbers, prohibited from marrying, and sometimes even unmarried by state bureaucrats."[165]

The entire process was intended to "create a superior Nordic race"[166], whatever the careful, high-minded pronouncements of its elitist collaborators. In fact, "this pernicious white-gloved war was prosecuted by esteemed professors, elite universities, wealthy industrialists and government officials colluding in a racist, pseudoscientific movement called eugenics."[167]

Before Henry Fairfield Osborn died on November 6, 1935, he lived to see Nazi Germany take the lead in its pursuit of an "Aryan master race," heavily influenced by the work of Osborn and his fellow American eugenics advocates.[168] The racial purification programs both in the United States and in Europe always contained key elements of propaganda, persuasion, and coercion, psychological warfare against the weak[169], behavior modification in support of a better life through biochemistry.

## Frederick Henry Osborn, Sr.

By 1937, the leadership of the American push for racial purity passed to the Pioneer Fund and its secretary, Frederick Henry Osborn, Sr.,, the nephew of Henry Fairfield Osborn and the father of the character witness for Michael and Ruth Paine: Osborn was a "leading proponent of racial eugenics."[170] "Although virtually unknown to the American public, Osborn was one of the most influential men of his generation."[171] Osborn numbered the Roosevelts and the Rockefellers among his elitist friends, was a trustee of Princeton University, and held influential positions with the Carnegie Corporation, the Population Association of America, the American Society of Human Genetics, and was "a founder and the first administrator of a key Rockefeller enterprise, the Population Council."[172]

## The Pioneer Fund

The Pioneer fund, created in 1937, was funded by "a group of wealthy Northeastern conservatives"[173] led by Frederick Osborn and Wickliffe Preston Draper, "heir to a Massachusetts [textile] manufacturing fortune"[174] and well-known for his "support of southern segregationists."[175] Draper asked Osborn and Harry Laughlin, who contributed to Nazi Germany's race purification programs, to "organize research projects and distribute pro-eugenic propaganda."[176]

Osborn's partner Harry Laughlin was Director of Carnegie Institute's Eugenics Record Office[177]; one year before Draper tapped both Laughlin and Osborn as the Pioneer Fund's chief research contributors, Laughlin had received a signal honor from Germany for his "contributions to Nazi eugenics."[178] His acceptance statement noted that America and the German nation had a "common understanding" regarding the future of "racial health."[179] In 1937, Frederick Henry Osborn announced that the racial sterilization program adopted by Nazi Germany could be "the most important social program which has ever been tried."[180]

The Laughlin/Osborn Pioneer Fund had just begun in 1937 when its directors developed a plan to improve the breeding stock of America, focusing on the U.S. Army Air Corps. For many, the Corps was a company of heroic aviators following in the slipstreams of the brave wingmen of World War I.[181] Frederick Osborn held at least two meetings with Harry H. Woodring, President Roosevelt's Secretary of War, pitching the Pioneer Fund's eugenics proposal.[182] Impressed with the Pioneer project, Woodring connected Draper, Laughlin, and Osborn with "top military leaders," including Air Corps General "Hap" Arnold[183]; in the late summer of 1937, Arnold gave his approval.[184]

The Pioneer Fund had organized a "pilot procreation plan," singling out top U.S. (all-Caucasian) airmen who had sired at least three children but who were reluctant to have more.[185] The Fund offered the Air Corps families the contemporary equivalent of $60,000 for the education of any child born in 1940. A behavioral psychologist, John C. Flanagan, ran the project[186], an especially telling choice, since the project involved behavior modification bolstered by a monetary reward.

The children chosen by the Pioneer Fund ultimately became decent but ordinary U.S. citizens.[187] The racial strengthening experiment of Laughlin, Draper, and Frederick Henry Osborn was a failure, but its underlying dark intention spoke to the fears and prejudices of elitists who saw little to disapprove of in Nazi Germany's eugenic experiments.[188]

Frederick Henry Osborn had begun to move away from some of the more obvious racist arguments and intentions of the eugenics movement as early as 1933.[189] Though he remained a dedicated eugenicist until his death, the behavior modification aspects of the Pioneer Fund's airmen experiment now loomed large in Osborn's mind. With the United States moving closer to actual participation in the war in Europe, "Osborn eased into government service, chairing a joint Army-Navy committee on potential morale issues in wartime."[190]

## Frederick Osborn and Behavior Modification

Soon after, bolstered by his "boyhood" friendship with President Franklin Delano Roosevelt[191], Frederick Osborn was offered a general's rank and the command of "a new branch of the [U.S. Army's] service focused on issues of morale, training, and education."[192] Osborn enlisted Army Chief of Staff George Marshall in his plan, "bringing social science techniques to bear on the analysis of morale."[193] Given a green light, Osborn and his social scientists tested, evaluated, and stored data on tens of thousands of U.S. military personnel that resulted in a massive behavior modification program utilizing "tools of social manipulation"[194] not yet fully analyzed.[195]

Frederick Henry Osborn's wartime pysops program began in October, 1941, as the Army's "Morale Branch"; it then became its "Morale Services Branch" in June of 1942, its "Special Services Branch" in November, 1942, and its "Information and Education Division" in February, 1944.[196] Osborn's Army "morale" program extended through 1947, but the records of his psychological warfare operation (including its application to later Korean, Vietnamese, and Cold War conflicts), have remained unexplored.

Frederick Henry Osborn was the key rescuer of the post-war eugenics movement.[197] Operating under a new rubric, "genetics," but largely embodying older elitist and racial goals, the eugenics advocates pursued their same purificationist agenda while Osborn argued for a more enlightened approach to bolstering the human gene pool.[198]

But eugenics was not Osborn's only elitist interest. Graduating from Princeton in 1910 between John Foster Dulles (1909) and Allen Dulles (1911), Osborn had maintained a friendly and productive letter exchange with the Dulles brothers. In 1949, still attempting to reorganize American eugenics by applying a more acceptable social scientific movement, Osborn joined his associates Allen Dulles and Arthur W. Page as organizing founders of the National Committee for a Free Europe (NCFE)[199], incorporated on May 11, 1949.

## The National Committee for a Free Europe

George Kennan, the creator of the State/Defense Office of Policy Coordination, had made the first suggestion to gather together elite U.S. citizens in a major Cold War/anti-Communist effort. The idea was taken up by Allen Dulles (acting as a "consultant" to the Central Intelligence Agency) and Frank Wisner, Dulles' nominee to run the Office of Policy Coordination (OPC), the newly-created intelligence group theoretically reporting to both State and Defense. Dulles and his intelligence-connected associates established the National Committee for a Free Europe in 1949, assigning its undercover direction to Wisner's OPC. When the OPC was absorbed by the CIA (in 1950) as its International Organizations Division (IOD), the IOD took over as the Agency office responsible for the National Committee for a Free Europe (NCFE).

In 1949, the NCFE had created the Crusade for Freedom (CFF); by the early 1950s, the Crusade was the NCFE's "highly visible [public] presence."[200] Three long-time CFF supporters, often sitting together at CFF fund-raising dinners, were high-ranking spiritual warriors in Allen Dulles' campaign against the Reds[201]: Cardinal Spellman, Bishop Henry Knox Sherrill, and Rabbi David de Sola Pool. Spellman had been long-time enthusiastic collaborator with the CIA. Bishop Sherrill was elitist, liberal, and anti-Communist, the leader of the Episcopal Church in the United States and later the head of the World Council of Churches (WCC): Dulles and his OSS had counted on the Council's information-gathering during World War II. Orthodox Rabbi David de Sola Pool was the spiritual director of the Sephardic Shearith Israel in New York (the rabbi's wife was a passionate Zionist).

The triad more than adequately illustrated Allen Dulles' post-war manipulation of religious groups and individuals for elitist political and intelligence purposes.

The Crusade quickly developing Radio Free Europe (RFE) and Radio Liberty (RL). NCFE, CFF, RFE, and RL were, in fact, all covert psychological warfare operations of the CIA, and all were sponsored, organized, directed, and funded by the Central Intelligence Agency.[202]

But where was the operational funding to come from?

Funding was obviously vital for the NCFE's covert operations (including the CFF, RFE, and RL), but open financing of any CIA politically-motivated action was illegal. So the Crusade for Freedom functioned as the NCFE's major money-laundering operation. Publicly it created the fiction of U.S. citizens enthusiastically supporting the NCFE's anti-Soviet actions; covertly, directed by the CIA, it funneled Agency funds into the CIA's psychological warfare and other covert operations.

## Osborn, Dulles, and Arthur W. Page

Frederick Henry Osborn, Sr., Allen Dulles, and Arthur W. Page had helped establish the National Committee for a Free Europe, Inc.[203], its massive committee list stuffed with elitist power, including Dulles, Osborn, and Page.[204] In turn, the CIA's allies had appointed Frederick Osborn the Chairman of the Crusade for Freedom (CFF), establishing its headquarters in New York City and enlisting Mayor Vincent R. Impellitteri as its honorary chairman.[205]

On October 4, 1950, one week before the Agency initiated its major domestic propaganda operation that finally covered twenty-six states (the "Bell" would be installed in Berlin on October 24, 1950), Crusade for Freedom Chairman Frederick Osborn wrote a careful letter to CIA consultant Allen Dulles. It concerned the funding of the Crusade, its "Freedom Bell," and implicitly its support of the rest of the CIA's covert operations agenda, including Radio Free Europe and Radio Liberty.[206] Indeed, the Hoover Institution's RFE/RL site has recently announced the Crusade "was incorporated to raise funds [for] and promote Radio Free Europe."[207]

Osborn pointed out the obvious: that the Manhattan-based Crusade campaign was intended "on getting [as many] signatures to the [Freedom Bell] Scrolls and as many small subscriptions as possible,"[208] since the overt campaign was, in fact, pure psyops. Osborn continued: "The whole setup is directed to this end and we are not in a position to go out for large subscriptions. The reasons are quite obvious in our organization . . . ."[209]

Osborn wrote that the actual funding for the National Committee for a Free Europe (and therefore its overt operations) would have to come from "another group."[210] Osborn knew what he was saying: despite the massive nation-wide psyops campaign, the CFF actually raised only $1,317,000 in "small subscriptions" in its first year[211], totally inadequate for financing the anticipated covert actions of the NCFE/CIA.[212]

So, Osborn recorded, "if you [Allen Dulles] and Arthur [Page] can do anything towards getting large subscriptions . . . , there is more likelihood of success . . . ."[213] Osborn's last line was telling: "I am writing a similar letter to Arthur."[214]

Two letters from Frederick Osborn, one to Allen Dulles, the other to Arthur Page, both on funding the National Committee for a Free Europe through "large subscriptions" developed by "Allen" and "Arthur."

Allen Dulles' source for "large subscriptions" was, of course, Frank Wisner and the Office of Policy Coordination in the CIA.

## Arthur W. Page: Power Player and Psyops Master

What about Arthur W. Page, who was the recipient of Osborn's second letter? Page had lived an exemplary elitist life: AT&T, Chase Bank, Westinghouse, Kennecott Copper, a trustee of both Bennington College and Columbia University's Teachers College, the Carnegie Corporation, the Metropolitan Museum of Art, the Morgan Library, a member of the overseers of Harvard University, and consultant to presidents (Roosevelt through Eisenhower), cabinet secretaries, and the powerful military/intelligence community.[215]

Page began his covert career in World War I on General John "Black Jack" Pershing's AEF G-2-D staff, a propaganda/psyops intelligence unit.[216] His influence in the American power structure can be traced through the Coolidge, Taft, Hoover, Roosevelt, and Truman administrations, but especially as he was a close friend and political associate of the legendary Henry L. Stimson from no later than 1930.[217]

An early and enthusiastic student of psychological warfare, Arthur Page exchanged letters with Frederick Osborn on military morale while Osborn was the chair of the Joint Army Navy Committee on Welfare and Recreation (JANC) in 1941; after Frederick Osborn left the Committee to take on other psyops duties, Page joined the JANC and headed a subcommittee on radio communication and propaganda targeting the U.S. military.[218] Page was named "a special consultant to the Secretary of War, a title he held for the duration [of World War II]."[219]

A key Page wartime job was to craft the statement presented to American troops chosen to invade Nazi-held Europe. Page finally became the major psyops consultant for the U.S. Army's public relations program in World War II[220]. In that capacity, Page worked as a troubleshooter for General Frederick Osborn in 1945 when Osborn was the chief of the U.S. Army's Information and Education Division.[221] In that same year, Page was a key participant in controlling the guarded information about the so-called Manhattan Project[222], and just before the Japanese surrender, Page prepared President Truman's announcement admitting the American use of an atomic weapon against Japan.

In 1949, Page was a key founder of the National Committee for a Free Europe that in turn "created" Radio Free Europe.[223] As early as 1951, C.D. Jackson joined Osborn, Arthur Page, and Allen Dulles on the Committee. By 1953, Page had become chairman of the Executive Committee of the "Free Europe Committee," the major Cold War manifestation of the National Committee for a Free Europe run by the Central Intelligence Agency.

Arthur Page, Frederick Osborn, C.D. Jackson, and the Dulles brothers all worked vigorously to elect Dwight David Eisenhower president; after Eisenhower's victory, the president invited twenty-two leading government and business celebrities to a special thank-you dinner: among the twenty-two were John J. McCloy, Arthur Page, Abbott Washburn, and C. D. Jackson.[224] Osborn, Page, and Jackson played key roles in the psyops justifications for America's atomic weapons and atomic energy policies.

Clearly, when Frederick Osborn wrote to Arthur Page as well as Allen Dulles about major financial support for the NCFFE, Arthur Page's "large subscriptions" would be exactly the same as those of Allen Dulles and the only source of so-called "large subscriptions" for the National Committee for a Free Europe: the Central Intelligence

Agency. Abbott Washburn, a former OSS agent, managed the fund-laundering for Page's Crusade for Freedom, funneling CIA money into the Page/Dulles/Osborn psyops programs.[225] Washburn's secretary made regular trips to the Wall Street offices of Henry Sears & Co., where a member of the investment firm, World War II veteran (General) Charles Saltzman, former N.Y. Stock Exchange officer, former Assistant Secretary of State, confidante of General George C. Marshall, later an active supporter of Dwight David Eisenhower for the U.S. presidency, would pass on the CIA's laundered beneficence.[226]

Arthur Page worked with psychological warfare expert C. D. Jackson; he often cooperated directly with the CIA, including key Agency officers involved in psyops, especially Cord Meyer, and was in constant communication with Allen Dulles.

Page, a close associate of John Foster Dulles, Allen Dulles, and Frederick Osborn throughout his career, was the father of corporate public relations and a consummate psyopsmaster for U.S. intelligence.

Arthur Page died in New York on September 5th, 1960, but the psychological warfare infrastructures he helped shape for the military, intelligence, and business in the interests of behavior modification, interests he shared with Frederick Osborn, continued without pause beyond his death.

## The Osborn Matrix and the Paines

*Any* reference to Frederick Henry Osborn (the father of the Paines' character witness) after the assassination of John F. Kennedy ought to have elicited a flood of material linking the Osborn family to sixty years of elitist (sometimes racist), military, intelligence, and behavior modification records. Yet key references to these leads, especially to Frederick Henry Osborn fronting for a crucial CIA proprietary, the National Committee for a Free Europe, were apparently edited out of Osborn's several biographies and obituaries sometime after the JFK assassination.

Only through Arthur W. Page can Osborn's complete intelligence operations and connections now be discovered. Immediately following the killing in Dealey Plaza, the appropriate references linking Frederick Osborn, Arthur Page, Allen Dulles, and the Central Intelligence Agency must still have been available. In 1956, Nancy Osborn and her husband Frederick Osborn, Jr. (the son of Frederick Henry Osborn, the Page/Dulles friend and associate), were still members of the leading American "genetics" organization supporting the senior Frederick H. Osborn's eugenics orientation. Just eight years later, the same Nancy and Frederick Osborn were the FBI's character witnesses for Michael and Ruth Paine in the assassination of John F. Kennedy.

The Federal Bureau of Investigation and the Warren Commission were both silent about the Osborn family's extraordinary connections, just as the Bureau and the Commission were silent about Ruth and Michael Paine and the Paines' Unitarian/U.S. intelligence links.

## "Don't Go There"

But the patterns of elitist and intelligence power in the Osborn and Paine families should now tell us where we will discover the real killers of JFK. The Osborns were enmeshed in a National Security State complex devoted to anti-Communism, including the powerful Stimson Committee on the Marshall Plan, the Council on Foreign Relations, an Ivy League complex of Harvard, Columbia, Yale, and Princeton, U.S. intelligence, the Committee for a Free Europe, and the Crusade for Freedom (with its sub-proprietaries, Radio Free Europe and Radio Liberty).[227]

The oil/intelligence/Unitarian universe of Lee Harvey Oswald was a perfect multiple nexus. The petroleum-intelligence side of the context into which the Oswalds were imbedded would allow Oswald to be routed in any of several directions: either left or right; either CIA or KGB; either domestic or foreign (the Soviet Union, in particular). The Unitarian-intelligence side of the context into which the Oswalds were imbedded (especially with the participation of the Paines) would allow Oswald to be routed in any of those same several directions. But the added Osborn family 'character references' for Ruth and Michael Paine insured that a major signal was being sent to any post-assassination federal investigator who ventured into the Osborn family's rich elitist past: "Don't go there."

# Epilogue

# A Summary and Some Conclusions

A *Certain Arrogance* is a reticulation[1] of eight essays on the history of international intelligence (primarily U.S. espionage), on Allen Dulles and John Foster Dulles and their manipulation of religious groups and individuals to achieve U.S. elitist goals, on the development of U.S. psychological warfare operations, and on the sacrificing of Lee Harvey Oswald in the assassination of John F. Kennedy.

## The Dulles Brothers

American Spymaster Allen Dulles, based in Switzerland, had abused religious (largely Protestant) individuals and institutions for U.S. intelligence through two World Wars and the subsequent "Cold War."[2] His brother John Foster Dulles also used major religious groups (again, largely Protestant) from 1937 through 1959 to further both his own and the American establishment's political and economic goals.[3]

## Noel Field

One religious individual, Noel Field (American Quaker, Unitarian, and Marxist) was used by Allen Dulles to manipulate religious relief organizations in World War II and in the post-war period.[4] Dulles finally utilized Field to help destabilize Communist Eastern Europe. Dulles apparently collaborated in this plan with Jozef Swiatlo, a Communist/CIA double agent, who later surfaced in the Warren Commission's Kennedy assassination investigation of Lee Harvey Oswald.[5]

## Albert Schweitzer College, the Unitarians, and U.S. Intelligence

Swiss-based Albert Schweitzer College had major religious origins that were both social and political.[6] Post-war liberal Protestant movements in Europe, including the International Association for Religious Freedom, helped to create the college in Switzerland, the country at the center of Allen Dulles' fifty-year spy program.[7] In the United States, the college was supported by a powerful coalition of American religious liberalism, primarily the Unitarian Church, the Unitarian Service Committee, and the American Friends of Albert Schweitzer College.[8]

Albert Schweitzer College's history strongly suggests that American espionage assets helped establish the college and then used it, possibly with the knowledge and even cooperation of some of its religious supporters in the Unitarian Church movement and those who worked for the college in Switzerland.[9] One leading Unitarian who worked closely with both U.S. intelligence and the military in the '40s and '50s was President of the American Friends of Albert Schweitzer College, exactly when Lee Harvey Oswald applied.[10] That same intelligence-connected Unitarian worked with a second influential Unitarian to help control U.S. space programs, including the U-2 overflights[11], and in the '60s, that intelligence-connected Unitarian fronted for a major CIA proprietary.[12] Those who set policy for Albert Schweitzer College were, therefore, elite members of the establishment and allies of the Central Intelligence Agency. In 1959, Lee Harvey Oswald registered to attend Albert Schweitzer College and therefore became a direct link between the college and American intelligence.

Whoever masterminded the Oswald college action was knowledgeable about both the OSS's and the CIA's use of Quakers, officials of the World Council of Churches, and Unitarians as contacts, assets, and informants (often as double agents) AND about the FBI's responsibility in tracking down and identifying Soviet illegals and double agents.[13] Oswald was, therefore, a creature of someone in American counterintelligence who possessed precisely that double body of knowledge.

## Oswald: the Imperfect Prospect

At the same time that Albert Schweitzer College was extending its international recruiting effort, both the Soviet and American Illegals and False Identity programs were operating.[14] For those espionage groups, Lee Harvey Oswald initially looked like a candidate for their intelligence operations. But Oswald was a stunningly imperfect False Identity/Illegals prospect. A faulty False Identity operation had apparently been carried out using Lee Harvey Oswald and run by a branch of American intelligence.[15]

Oswald's imperfections were certain to trip counterespionage alarm wires.[16] The context of the Oswald "legend" game was Switzerland, earlier the center of massive spy operations run by Allen Dulles in two World Wars and the following Cold War.[17]

Oswald had called maximum attention to his strange exit from the Marines, his dubious trip to Europe, his suspicious registration at Albert Schweitzer College, his failure to arrive at the college, and his so-called defection to the Soviet Union. In a very short time, Oswald piled up obviously faulty documents and suspect postal communications. What followed was a major FBI inquiry in 1959 and 1960 that apparently attempted to find the missing Oswald. Oswald's Marine Corps record, including his Pacific duty experience and U-2 service, made him a prime candidate for Soviet civilian and military intelligence, and both American and Soviet intelligence groups were aware of his candidacy.[18]

Oswald's espionage activities most probably included information he gave the Soviets concerning U-2 flights, leading to the collapse of imminent Soviet/American peace talks. He was also apparently scheduled to play a part in exposing Soviet intelligence moles in activist student movements and liberal Protestant institutions like Albert Schweitzer College in both Europe and the United States.[19]

From the moment Oswald registered to attend Unitarian-sponsored Albert Schweitzer College, and without ever setting foot in Switzerland, Oswald moved (or was moved) to the center of a complex and dangerous double-agent operation.[20]

Lee Harvey Oswald looked—possibly too obviously—like a false defector. When he returned to the United States as a redefector from the Soviet Union, he was suspect: at least five intelligence agencies (the GRU, KGB, CIA, FBI and ONI) found his curious false-identity profile highly suspicious. But that same profile was extremely well-suited to those who ultimately planned to murder President John F. Kennedy. Oswald could be manipulated, like the religious institutions that American intelligence had used through almost fifty years, in a half-dozen ways and in a half-dozen ongoing espionage games.[21]

## Oswald: Perfect Patsy

Why had Lee Harvey Oswald become the designated lone assassin patsy in the JFK murder?[22]

Six years (or more) of complex and questionable U.S. intelligence and espionage activities with their initiators, sponsors, and handlers were threatened if a full investigation of Oswald were held after the assassination of John F. Kennedy.[23]

The threat ran from the very top of the American establishment to the grunt levels of the American military and intelligence.

After the JFK murder, a real investigation of Lee Harvey Oswald would have closely covered, for example, his probable "Marine" intelligence activity, his Cuban contacts, his mail coverage by the CIA's HTLINGUAL program, the Agency's multiple "mole" inquiries, the real origins of Albert Schweitzer College, Oswald's Fair Play For Cuba Committee connections, and the plots against President Eisenhower. A real investigation would have closely examined the persuasive but circumstantial evidence of his employment (after his return to the United States from the Soviet Union) by a yet-to-be-discovered "private investigative agency doing industrial-security work"[24] and funded by either U.S. intelligence or the U.S. military.[25] Peter Dale Scott has called attention to the "numerous signs that Oswald's [post-defection] employment recurrently coincided with opportunities for surveillance of FBI subversive targets."[26] But Oswald apparently was the field asset of "other investigative agencies as well, . . . [including] the Alcohol, Tobacco, and Firearms unit . . . of the U.S. Treasury."[27] Though Oswald's targets were or seemed to be those of the FBI, he was more likely to have been "an employee not of the FBI but of a private agency with contracts to more than one federal government agency."[28] Therefore, any examination Oswald's real work history after returning from the Soviet Union would have been a disaster, not only for government intelligence but also for private "intelligence" in the "industrial-security" area.

Each node of any real post-assassination investigation would have registered multiple extensions; each of those nodes would have been recognized, for example, as a psychological warfare operation. Examining HTLINGUAL in depth would have required a close look at U.S. Illegals and False Identity programs; examining the CIA's mole investigation would have led to HTLINGUAL, to U.S. counterintelligence's Illegals and False Identities operations, to U.S. intelligence's misuse of domestic and foreign postal systems, to the abuse of liberal Protestant institutions in the U.S. and in Europe, and to the grey history of Albert Schweitzer College.[29] And examining the oil/intelligence/Unitarian complex in Dallas would have meant exposing the Osborn family, character witnesses for Ruth and Michael Paine, as intimate associates of the U.S. elite establishment, the U.S. military, U.S. intelligence, the government's psychological warfare and behavior modification programs, and its key Cold War covert operations.

At the end of each of those potential investigative extensions was the enigmatic Oswald.[30] Lee Harvey Oswald became, therefore, the perfect patsy, manipulated finally in the deadliest game of all: in Dallas, on November 22nd, 1963.[31]

# ENDNOTES

## Notes: Prologue

[1] An extended and revised version of an earlier essay published in *The Kennedy Assassination Chronicles*, Volume 1, Summer, 1995, #2.

[2] The basic government sources on the JFK assassination are:

1. U.S. Warren Commission, *Report of the President's Commission on the Assassination of John F. Kennedy* (Washington: Government Printing Office, 1964. Hereafter cited as R, with appropriate page number or numbers, as in R 12;

2. U.S. Warren Commission, *Hearings Before the President's Commission on the Assassination of President Kennedy* (Washington Printing Office, 1964). Hereafter cited as H, with appropriate volume number preceding and page numbers following, as in 12 H 21; sometimes with appropriate Commission Exhibit added, hereafter cited as CE, as in 17 H (CE 737) 511.

   Here, the text reference "fifth volume" is to 5 H, hereafter so cited.

3. U.S., National Archives, Warren Commission Documents, cited hereafter as CD, as in CD 1052.

   To help demystify the "Warren Commission" and its materials, please consult George Michael Evica, "Researching in and Writing on the JFK Assassination and Related Topics" in *The Assassination Chronicles*, Volume 2, Issue 1, March, 1996, published by JFK Lancer Productions and Publications, Grand Prairie, Texas.

[3] 5 H 1-32.

[4] 5 H 3.

[5] 5 H 4.

[6] 5 H 5-6.

[7] 5 H 6.

[8] 5 H 11.

[9] 5 H 6.

[10] 17 H (CE 834) 804-813.

[11] 17 H (CE 833) 787-803.

[12] 5 H 4.

[13] 5 H 6.

[14] 5 H 6,7.

[15] 5 H 7.

[16] 5 H 7.

[17] 5 H 7.

[18] 5 H 8.

[19] 5 H 9.

[20] In 17 H 804-813.

[21] 5 H 11.

[22] 5 H 11.

[23] 5 H 11.

[24] 5 H 11.

[25] 5 H 11.

[26] 5 H 11.

[27] 5 H 11.

[28] 5 H 11.

[29] 5 H 11.

[30] 5 H 11.

[31] 5 H 11: emphasis added.

[32] 5 H 11: emphasis added.

[33] 5 H 11.

[34] 5 H 11.

[35] 5 H 11.

[36] 5 H 11.

[37] 5 H 11.

[38] 5 H 12.

[39] 5 H 12.

[40] 5 H 12.

[41] 5 H 12.

[42] 5 H 12.

[43] 5 H 12.

[44] 5 H 12.

[45] 5 H 13.

[46] 5 H 13.

[47] 5 H 13.

[48] 5 H 13.

[49] 5 H 13.

[50] 5 H 14.

[51] CE 834 in 17 H 804-813.

[52] 5 H 14.

[53] 5 H 14.

[54] 5 H 14-18 and 29.

[55] 5 H 16-32.

# Notes: Essay One

[1] John Newman, *Oswald and the CIA* (New York: Carroll and Graff, 1995) 135-136, hereafter cited as Newman. John Newman is the only author (other than I) calling attention to what he dubs 'Mr. "Fannan": FBI Mystery Man' 134). Newman points out "confusing" and "curious" aspects of the "Fannan" story (134, 135) originally a small part of a lengthy interview conducted by a U.S. Secret Service agent on 12/25/63. Newman found the interview in the NARA JFK records, RIF 124-10062-10049 (551 note # 2). The interview has always been available in the Warren Commission's documents, though buried at 16 H CE 270 721-748, hereafter cited as CE 270. Though the Marguerite Oswald interview was the second recorded on the Secret Service interview tape, the first with Robert Oswald, the two interview reports are printed in reverse in 16 H CE 270: Mrs. Oswald 721-748, then Robert Oswald 749-761.

    The Secret Service interviewer recorded "Fannan (phonetic)" twice during his questioning of Mrs. Oswald. I have made an extensive and thorough internet search for three versions of the alleged FBI man's name: Fannan, Fannen, and Fannin. Fannan and Fannen elicited nothing; Fannin yielded up two individuals: one a former FEMA official, John Fannin, the other Walter C. Fannin, Captain, Burglary and Theft Bureau, Dallas Police, who was involved in the JFK Dallas investigation.

[2] Jean Stafford, A *Mother in History* (New York: Farrar, Straus and Giroux, 1966) 65, hereafter cited as Stafford.

[3] Stafford 6.

[4] Stafford 18.

[5] CE 270 728. Also, see later.

[6] Stafford 13.

[7] See later.

[8] Stafford 13.

[9] Stafford 13.

[10] Stafford 13.

[11] See later.

[12] See later.

[13] See later.

[14] See later.

[15] See later.

[16] Stafford 5.

[17]  See later.

[18]  CE 270 729. Also, see later.

[19]  CE 270 729. Also, see later.

[20]  See later.

[21]  Mrs. Oswald voiced that disturbing possibility several times in her letters and statements.

    My portrait (above) of Lee's mother was developed within a framework assuming her innocence. But what if Mrs. Oswald was not at all innocent? For example: 1. Why did she agree to what can only be called a fake workplace accident? 2. What about her extraordinary series of address changes? Changes of address were an important way for a peripatetic agent to maintain contact with American intelligence: see Lee Harvey Oswald's own record of residence changes. 3. What about the stream of apparently confused information she supplied official government and police agencies both before and after the assassination? 4. What about the "agent" noise ("Fannan" and "Fain") she injected into her son's disappearance? Were there, in fact, two FBI agents (Fannan and Fain) or only one? Was she interviewed twice or only once? If once, by whom? 5. What about all her curious omissions, hesitations, and lapses?

[22]  See later.

[23]  How to lose a college: to search for Albert Schweitzer College both at NARA and on the Web, enter the correct spelling; but also enter: Schweitzr; Sechweitzer; Schweitzer; Scweizer; Schwetzer; Scweitzer; and Switzer.

    Also, try "Albert College."

[24]  See later.

[25]  John Ranelagh, *The Agency[:] The Rise and Decline of the CIA* (New York: Simon and Schuster, 1986) 271, hereafter cited as Ranelagh.

[26]  Ranelagh 271.

[27]  Lyman B. Kirkpatrick, *The Real CIA* (New York: Macmillan Company, 1968) 61, hereafter cited as Kirkpatrick.

[28]  Christopher Simpson, *Blowback* (New York: Weidenfeld & Nicolson, 1988) throughout, hereafter cited as Simpson; Leonard Mosely, *Dulles[:] A Biography of Eleanor, Allen, and John Foster Dulles and Their Family Network* (The Dial Press/James Wade: New York, 1978): "Switzerland" is not in Mosely's index, but see 126, 129, 136, 147, and 155, hereafter cited as Mosely; Robin W. Winks, *Cloak & Gown* (William Morrow and Company: New York, 1987) 102, 122-123, hereafter cited as Winks; Nigel West, *Games of Intelligence* (Crown Publishers, Inc.: New York, 1989) 107-108, hereafter cited as West; William R. Corson, *Armies of Ignorance* (Dial Pres: New York, 1977) 9, 198, hereafter cited as Corson *Armies*; and Kirkpatrick 61.

[29]  Rhodri Jeffrey-Jones, *The CIA and American Democracy* (New Haven: Yale University Press, 1989) 178, hereafter cited as Jeffrey-Jones. Dulles "ran a one-man espionage ring about which many yarns have been spun," in Barry M. Katz, *Foreign Intelligence[:] Research and Analysis in the Office of Strategic Services[,] 1942-1945* (Cambridge, Massachusetts: 1989) 23, cited hereafter as Katz. In *Switzerland Under Siege* ed. Leo Schelbert (Rockport, Maine: Picton Press), Dulles is barely present (38, 46, 158); intelligence and counterintelligence are totally absent from the book, despite the text dedicating one-half of its essays to "Challenges of Neutrality." Dulles does

make an appearance in an Appendix, "Switzerland's 'Benevolent Neutrality,'" excerpted from his book *The Secret Surrender* (New York: Harper & Row, 1966) 25-27. But Dulles himself does not hint at his own massive challenge to Switzerland's neutrality.

[30]   See later.

[31]   22 H (CE 1114) 77.

[32]   22 H (CE 1114) 77.

[33]   Ray and Mary La Fontaine, *Oswald Talked[:] The New Evidence in the JFK Assassination* (Gretna, La: Pelican Publishing Company, 1996) 66, hereafter cited as La Fontaine.

[34]   La Fontaine 66.

[35]   La Fontaine 66.

[36]   La Fontaine 76.

[37]   La Fontaine 76-77.

[38]   22 H (CE 1114) 77. For an analysis that ultimately supports the above argument see Jerry D. Rose, "On Getting Too Excited," *The Fourth Decade*, September, 2000, Volume 7, Number 6, 3-6, hereafter cited as Rose. Rose concluded that the entire passport application was a forgery: Rose 4.

[39]   La Fontaine 78.

[40]   CE 2892, cited in La Fontaine 78.

[41]   La Fontaine 78.

[42]   La Fontaine 79.

[43]   La Fontaine 66-67.

[44]   La Fontaine 67.

[45]   La Fontaine 70.

[46]   See La Fountaine 188-189.

[47]   La Fontaine 69.

[48]   La Fontaine 69.

[49]   Edward Jay Epstein, *Legend: The Secret World of Lee Harvey Oswald* (New York: Reader's Digest Press, McGraw-Hill Book Company, 1978) 90-91, hereafter cited as Epstein.

[50]   La Fontaine 69.

[51]   LaFontaine 69.

[52]   La Fontaine 70.

[53]   22 H (CE 1114) 77.

[54]   La Fontaine 89-70.

[55]   22 H (CE 1114) 77.

[56]   La Fontaine 84-85.

[57]   Epstein 338 and 69, 71-72, 74, 77-78.

[58]   See Rose: Doug Horne was incorrect asserting Oswald "enlisted his buddy Stout to sign the required affidavit." Rose 4.

[59]   22 H CE 1114 77; see also R 699 and 796.

[60]   22 H (CE 1114) 77.

[61]   16 H (CE 228) 621.

[62]   16 H (CE 228) 622.

63  22 H (CE 1114) 77.

64  National Archives Record (NAR) # 124-10023-10236, hereafter cited as NAR # 124-10023-10236; FBI file # 105-82555-10.

65  Same. This Swiss Federal Police report summarized in the first of four communications from the Legat to Director J. Edgar Hoover is subsequently contradicted, without explanation, by the fourth and last Legat communication that suspiciously anticipated the Warren Commission's conclusions about Oswald's Albert Schweitzer College intentions: see later.

66  R 688.

67  22 H (CE 1114) 78.

68  Same.

69  R 689.

70  R 580.

71  Epstein 86-87.

72  Epstein 86.

73  Epstein 86.

74  Epstein 86.

75  Jim Garrison, *On the Trail of the Assassins* (New York: Warner Books, 1988) 51-53, hereafter cited as Garrison *Trail*.

76  Garrison 53.

77  See, for example, Epstein 86, 88.

78  Given the mail-opening program then operating at Fort Holabird, Oswald's Marine postal record should have been available to government assassination investigators, but it was not: see a work in progress by the author, hereafter cited as *INTERCEPT*.

79  1 H 214.

80  Paul L. Hoch, "CIA Activities and the Warren Commission Investigation," unpublished manuscript, 1975, in *The Assassinations[:] Dallas and Beyond—A Guide to Coverups and Investigations*, Peter Dale Scott, Paul L. Hoch, and Russell Stetler, editors (New York: Vintage Books, 1976) 400-495, specifically 479-480, hereafter cited as *The Assassinations*. 479.

81  *The Assassinations* 479.

82  *The Assassinations* 479.

83  *The Assassinations* 480.

84  16 H (CE 228) 621-625.

85  See below.

86  Jerry D. Rose, "Double Agent Unmasked: A Reconstruction," *The Third Decade*, Volume 3, #6, September, 1987, 3, speculates on "the probable existence of such a defectors program[, for which there are a number of circumstantial pieces of evidence] . . . ." Rose "Double" endnote # 5, page 10.

87  See, for example, 8 H 323, 8 H 147, 11 H 103, and 11 H 116.

88  R 689.

89  R 689.

90  Epstein 91.

[91] 22 H 77-78. According to the Warren Report, Oswald had earlier worked in the import/export field: R 688.

[92] Quoted in Epstein 91.

[93] R 689.

[94] R 689.

[95] Epstein 91.

[96] R 869.

[97] R 689.

[98] R 689.

[99] R 689.

[100] 22 H (CE 1114) 78.

[101] R 690.

[102] R 690.

[103] Jim Marrs, *Crossfire* (New York: Carroll and Graff, 1989) 118, hereafter cited as Marrs. Marrs probably relied on Epstein (94), but Epstein, relying on Angleton, had reported that Oswald apparently consulted "the Soviet Embassy." (Epstein 94)

[104] R 690.

[105] R 690.

[106] R 690.

[107] R 690.

[108] R 690.

[109] See, for example, Newman 3-4.

[110] Same.

[111] NAR # 124-10023-10237.

[112] Same.

[113] 16 H (CE 72) 234.

[114] Barron *KGB* 323.

[115] Cited in Barron 323.

[116] Following the developing but tangled history of Soviet intelligence and espionage agencies can be daunting. To simplify: the NKVD operated from 1922 through 1946—that is, through World War One and the early "Cold War"; the NKGB operated only in 1946; the MGB operated from 1946 through 1953 (and, in that same period, the KI operated from 1947 through 1951); in 1953, Beria's MVD operated; and from 1953/1954 through the demise of the Soviet Union, the KGB was the Soviet's major intelligence/espionage operator: see Barron 457-465.

The Soviets' military intelligence operation, the GRU, ran from the spring of 1920 on, including it Illegals operations through World War II, but it was infiltrated by both British MI-6 and the CIA. (Barron 464-465) To block this significant penetration, the Soviet's military espionage wing was put under the control of the KGB no later than the early 1970s. (Barron 465)

[117] Barron *KGB* 323.

[118] Barron *KGB* 323.

[119]   Barron *KGB* 323.

[120]   Barron KGB 323.

[121]   Gordon Thomas, *Journey into Madness* (New York: Bantam Books, 1989), 31-32, 43, 68-69, 73, 223, 225, 231, hereafter cited as Thomas, Journey.

[122]   Epstein 111.

[123]   Epstein 299 note 19.

[124]   Epstein 111.

[125]   16 H CE 71 234.

[126]   Epstein 111. See also Joseph J. Trento, *The Secret History of the CIA* (New York: Carroll & Graf {Publishers, 2005): "While he was being processed out of the Marines in Los Angeles, the FBI photographed him meeting with Lieutenant Colonel Pavel T. Voloshin, a top KGB recruiter who was in LA with a Soviet dance troupe. The FBI placed the picture in a counterintelligence file on KGB 'watchers' of cultural organizations visiting the United States. The FBI also took another picture of Oswald . . . visiting the Cuban consulate in Los Angeles." (219) Trento's personal sources were the files and persons of James Jesus Angleton and William R. Corson. According to Trento, the FBI did not know who Oswald was or why he was visiting with Voloshin and the Cubans.(219) Since FBI counterintelligence, run by Branigan, Sullivan, and Papich, was always in close touch with Angleton and his Agency counterintelligence group, it seems highly unlikely some exchange did not occur between the FBI and the CIA on these alleged Oswald visits. And why has Trento now been able to reveal this "Oswald" KGB/Cuban material so long after all of it was withheld from the Warren Commission? Trento(and therefore Angleton and Corson?) missed the Albert Schweitzer College (ASC) connection. Or did they? Epstein, whose source was Angleton himself (you will recall), reported the Voloshin ASC link.

[127]   Epstein 87.

[128]   Epstein 87).

[129]   Epstein 286 note #3.

[130]   Epstein 286: also, see the questions Epstein raised about Oswald's reported shadowy visitor: 286 note # 3.

[131]   Epstein 88.

[132]   Meagher 321-322, 325, 326.

[133]   Meagher 325.

[134]   Stephen Fritchman deserves a sympathetic biography. For material on Fritchman relevant to this inquiry, see Essay Four. Fritchman files and collections are at the Harvard Divinity School Library, found just after Albert Schweitzer, 1945-1953, at BMS 204 28 (and on) and at two Los Angeles sites: 1. the First Unitarian Church of Los Angeles itself and 2. the Southern California Library of Social Studies and Research, Selected Collections on Los Angeles: First Unitarian Church Collection, 1938-1981 (archives @socallib.org).

[135]   The following Pauling material is based on the Unitarian/Universalist Association's website biography of Linus Pauling (www.uua.org), hereafter cited as Pauling.

[136]   Pauling.

[137]   Pauling.

[138]   Pauling.

[139]   Pauling.

[140]   11 H 110.

[141]   11 H 110.

[142]   11 H 110.

[143]   Record Number 124-10063-10127; Record Series DL; no date recorded.

[144]   Beyond Nelson Delgado, Kerry Thornley was probably the chief source of the "Red Marine" image created for Oswald; Thornley could very well have been an important source of disinformation concerning Oswald.

[145]   I have queried the present pastor of the First Unitarian Church of Los Angeles, but she has been unable to sort through the materials Stephen Fritchman left behind. Therefore, among the unorganized Fritchman documents and papers in L.A. may well be valuable Albert Schweitzer College materials.

[146]   10 H 54.

[147]   Dick Russell, *The Man Who Knew Too Much* (New York: Carrol & Graf, 1992) 346, hereafter cited as Russell.

[148]   Russell 347.

[149]   Russell 347-348.

[150]   Russell 346.

[151]   Russell 348.

[152]   Russell 356.

[153]   Russell 348.

[154]   Russell 349.

[155]   See *INTERCEPT*.

[156]   Nagell's intelligence records may bring some light to the darkest part of the JFK assassination conspiracy. See Garrison, *Trail* 212-216, 263, 267; *Probe*, November-December, 1995, Volume 3 No. 1, "The Life and Death of Richard Case Nagell"; and the CIA files on Nagell: see nara.gov/research/jfk/arrb.html. See also the JFKLANCER web site for the Nagell CIA file (over 200 pages). Though the Warren Commission apparently never interviewed Nagell, the Assassinations Records Review Board did mail a letter dated October 31st, 1995, to Nagell, inquiring about his possible possession of JFK assassination records. Nagell then promptly died of "heart disease" the next day, November 1st, 1995 (see previous Probe citations).

[157]   See Dave Reitzes' Website for several effective arguments against Nagell's assertions. But the early military/intelligence interest in Thornley, Fritchman, and the Los Angeles Unitarian Church remains unexplained except as part of an investigation of the Oswald/Unitarian/Albert Schweitzer College complex.

[158]   Stephen Fritchman's earlier association with Noel Field and the establishing of the Unitarian Service Committee with its significant OSS/Allen Dulles links cannot be ignored: see Essay Four.

[159]   For Stephen Fritchman and Nagell, see Russell 356.

[160]   See, for example, Russell 356.

[161]   Russell 356: Nagell's notebook was "filled with their names."

[162] For the Warren Commission's interest, see Paul Gregory on the "Russian University" and "Peace University," both references to Lumumba University, 9 H 147; George J. Church's testimony, 11 H 116; and the "University of People's Friendship," again a reference to Lumumba University, 1 H 107 and CD 72; see also Thorney on Schweitzer College, 11 H 103.

[163] Did Soviet and American hawks in civilian, financial, military, and intelligence institutions, motivated by the will to power and greed, collaborate after World War II to create the so-called Cold War? The history of that collaboration would, of course, include Lee Harvey Oswald and John F. Kennedy.

[164] The following discussion of Patrice Lumumba is based on eight sources: 1., John Henrik Clarke, "The Passing of Patrice Lumumba," originally written in 1961 by Clarke, then the U.N. Correspondent on African Affairs, World Mutual Exchange, and International New Features, an article (with a page of documentation, 11 pages long) available at www.nbufront. org/html/Masters Museum/JHClarke: hereafter cited as Clarke; 2., Linda Slattery, "The Congo: How and why the West organized Lumumba's assassination[:] Review of two BBC documentaries: *Who Killed Lumumba?* and *Mobuto*, World Socialist Web Site (www.wsws.org), dated "10 January 2001," hereafter cited as Slattery; 3., Alex Duval Smith, "Eisenhower ordered Congo killing," posted on *The Independent*'s www.independent.co.uk/story site, hereafter cited as Smith; 4., Brian Carnell, "Did Eisenhower Order Lumumba Killing?" posted on www. leftwatch.com/articles, hereafter cited as Carnell; 5., Ludo de Witte, *The Murder of Lumumba* (Verso Books, 2001), hereafter cited as de Witte; 6., Richard D. Mahoney, *JFK: Ordeal in Africa* (New York: Oxford University Press, 1983), hereafter cited as Mahoney; 7., U.S. Congress, Senate, Select Committee to Study Governmental Operations with Respect to Intelligence Activities, Book Two, Intelligence Activities and the Rights of Americans, 94th Congress, 2nd Session, Senate Report No. 94-755 (Washington: Government Printing Office, 1976, hereafter cited as Church Report; and 8., *Lumumba*, a film by director Raul Peck, hereafter cited as *Lumumba*.

[165] See for example, Craig Roberts, *The Medusa File* (Tulsa: Consolidated Press International, 1997) 234, hereafter cited as Roberts: "Lumumba, a pro-Marxist trained in Moscow . . . ." Despite this overstatement, Roberts has expertly described and cogently analyzed the "Secret Crimes and Coverups of the U.S. Government": the latter phrase is the subtitle of *The Medusa File*.

[166] Cited in William Blum, *The CIA: A Forgotten History* (London and New Jersey: Zed Books Ltd., 1986) 175, hereafter cited as Blum.

[167] See Andrew Tully, *CIA[:] The Inside Story* (New York: William Morrow and Company, 1962) 220-222 for some important details of the Lumumba story, but from a largely negative and CIA-oriented position, hereafter cited as Tully.

[168] Adam Hochschild, *King Leopold's Ghost* (Boston, New York: 1998) 301, hereafter cited as Hochschild.

[169] Hochschild 301; see also Roger Anstey, *King Leopold's Legacy* (London: Oxford University Press, 1966) 39-45 for details on Congo mining activities, hereafter cited as Anstey.

[170] Hochshield 301.

171  According to Dmitiry Bilibin, the chancellor of the People's Friendship University of Russia (the institutional successor to Lumumba University), Nikita Khrushchev had visited Indonesia in February, 1960; informed that Indonesia intended to establish a university for foreign students, Khrushchev responded that the Soviet Union already had one in existence; within twenty-four hours, "Patrice Lumumba University" had been organized and was operational: from the website of *The Russian Journal* (published in English from Moscow).

172  Anstey 39-45 and 144.

173  Blum 175.

174  Roberts 235.

175  Blum 175.

176  Quoted in Blum 175.

177  Roberts 235.

178  Blum 175.

179  Roberts 235-236.

180  Cited and quoted in Blum 175; see also Roberts 236.

181  Roberts 236-237.

182  Hochschild 278-279 (and 301). Though highly praised, the Hochschild text has no references to pitchblende, uranium, nuclear weapons, or, in fact, to Katanga.

183  Robert B. Edgerton, *The Troubled Heart of Africa[:]  A History of the Congo* (New York: St. Martin's Press, 2002/2003) 168, hereafter cited as Edgerton.

184  J. Ellsworth Weaver III, "A Brief Chronology of Radiation and Protection" website: contact JEW1@pge.com.

185  See previous note.

186  The sum of $350,000,000 is impossible to convert to a 21st century equivalent, but a reasonable estimate would be $2,000,000,000.

187  See, for example, Anstey 144.

188  African Unification Front, at africanfront.com, hereafter cited as AUF.

189  AUF.

190  AUF.

191  Slattery.

192  Slattery.

193  Slattery.

194  Smith.

195  Smith.

196  Slattery and De Witte.

197  Slattery.

198  Slattery.

199  Almost no event is inevitable. See Edgerton for a different though not totally opposite reading of the Congo/Lumumba narrative, especially on Lumumba's personal history (embedded in the Belgian Congo's culture), Belgian Congo racism, Lumumba's opportunism, the terrible events of 1960 in the Congo, Lumumba's visit to the U.S, and the State Department, Mobuto

and Belgian Intelligence, the Lumumba assassination and its aftermath: 166, 168, 180-193, 196-197, 200.

[200]  Roberts 234.

[201]  See Essay Six for an analysis of those connections. See Madeleine G. Gelb, *The Congo Cables*, 1982, (128-133), for the Lumumba-Castro links, still more evidence for Oswald's opportunistic application to Lumumba University.

[202]  Dennis Bartholomew, "LHO on Campus," *The Fourth Decade*, Volume 4, # 3, March, 1997, pp. 3-10; see also "Albert Schweitzer College Revisited," *The Fourth Decade*, Volume 6, #1, November 1998, pp. 15-23, hereafter cited as Bartholomew. Bartholomew's "LHO on Campus" explores major mysteries surrounding Oswald's connection to Albert Schweitzer College (ASC), very often the same mysteries I examine at greater length in this Essay (and later). See especially Bartholomew's ASC summary (6); the Oswald/ASC/Weibel correspondence puzzle (5); Oswald's "cleared" ASC application (5); the Metropole problem (7); Marguerite's two letters (8); the problem of the ASC exhibits: what was their source? (8); and the entire "nothing to hide" oddity (9).But Bartholomew apparently confuses the records of ASC and the Unitarian Service Committee and the sources of those records in Boston and Cambridge: see his note 6, page 10. However, anyone pursuing the Oswald/ASC complexity must take note of Bartholomew's excellent articles (see above).

[203]  A particularly potent context for these espionage collaborations was Cold War Berlin: a special source of tantalizing hints can be found in Murphy, Kondrashev, and Bailey, *Battleground Berlin[:] CIA vs KGB in the Cold War* (New Haven: Yale University Press, 1997), rich with exhausting detail but ultimately a major venting vehicle for former Soviet and American intelligence officers: see especially 267-281 and 440-446. Note the off-handed definition of illegals as "intelligence officers [rather than assets or agents] documented as foreign citizens and sent abroad . . . ." 267; see also 440.

[204]  See in this essay and in Essay Three.

[205]  See in this essay and in Essay Three.

[206]  16 H (CE 228) 622-625. On the Oswald application being a fabrication, see later.

[207]  8 H 323.

[208]  See Essay Three.

[209]  See Essay Six.

[210]  1 H 214.

[211]  See Mrs. Oswald's testimony, 1 H 213.

[212]  16 H (CE 228) 624 (copy of original), 625 (transcript of facing page of original).

[213]  See earlier.

[214]  See, for example, Oleg Kalugin, *The First Directorate* (New York: St. Martin's Press, 1994), cited hereafter as Kalugin, who commented that "Helsinki . . . nearly rivaled Vienna as a stomping ground for Soviet spies." (164) Kalugin was meeting an American intelligence agent who was either a "genuine" espionage recruit or "a CIA plant." (164)

[215]  See Essay Three for the extraordinary connection between Albert Schweitzer and Patrice Lumumba that most probably accounted for both of Oswald's college applications.

[216]  1 H 6; Newman 16-19.

[217]  April 6th, 1964 FBI report titled "Lee Harvey Oswald," 17 H CE 833 p. 789.

[218]  Same.

[219]  R 494-495; 16 H (CE 294) 814.

[220]  16 H (CE 206) 594; Herter was a long-time political and social associate of OSS/CIA masterspy Allen Dulles: the FBI agent's suggestion might have been intended as a provocation.

[221]  R 697.

[222]  Oswald's spelling and punctuation, his grammar and sentence structure, his rhetoric, and his logic varied so considerably throughout his reported communications and writing as to raise serious questions about what he might have personally written, what was dictated to him or copied by him verbatim, and what was fabricated, imitating either closely or very broadly his handwriting and 'style.' Anything relatively well-written and largely free from error might therefore be suspect as an intelligence invention, unless, of course, its very literacy was intended to raise questions about a fictionalized Oswald.

[223]  16 H (CE 295) 815-822.

[224]  American intelligence interception of this letter was confirmed by Edward Epstein, who received his information from James Angleton, the CIA chief of the Agency's mail interception game. (Epstein 103) "This letter appeared in Washington, D.C., among the letters from Moscow routinely turned over to a CIA operations sector working under Angleton in counterintelligence." (Epstein 103) The "CIA operations sector" (an odd phrase) was, in fact, the Agency's HTLINGUAL mail interception program: see *INTERCEPT*.

[225]  R 697 and 16 H (CE 297) 825.

[226]  R 697; 16 H (CE 206) 3994; 22 H (CE 101) 704, CD 8 p. 7.

[227]  Same.

[228]  R 594.

[229]  16 H (CE 206) 594.

[230]  R 697; see CE 202, CE 206, and 1 H 204.

[231]  16 H (CE 206) 594.

[232]  Newman 152.

[233]  See later.

[234]  See below.

[235]  Newman 152.

[236]  Newman 152.

[237]  See later, and *INTERCEPT*.

[238]  See Essay Three. Kirkpatrick states that "the FBI's domestic intelligence unit devotes . . . part of its effort against intelligence personnel of the Soviet Union operating . . . through 'illegal' networks established by agents under deep cover . . . ." (141) Kirkpatrick, a World War Two intelligence agent and a CIA officer from 1947 to 1965, held two major offices in the Agency.

[239]  See later; see also *INTERCEPT*.

[240]  See later; see also *INTERCEPT*.

[241]  Newman 150.

[242]  16 H (CE 206) 594).

[243] Same.

[244] FBI report of April 6th, 1964, "Lee Harvey Oswald," in CE 833, 17 H 789-790.

[245] Newman 152.

[246] Newman 155.

[247] Newman 152.

[248] Newman 155.

[249] Newman 152: this office, you will recall, was responsible for the Bureau's Z Coverage mail intercept program.

[250] Newman 152.

[251] Newman 152.

[252] Newman 152.

[253] Newman 153.

[254] Newman 153.

[255] Newman 153.

[256] Newman 135-136; and, see earlier.

[257] 16 H (CE 206) 594-595.

[258] 16 H (CE 206-277) 594-620.

[259] 16 H (CE 311) 600.

[260] Newman 136.

[261] Newman 136.

[262] Robert Sam Anson, *They've Killed the President!"[:] The Search for the Murderers of John F. Kennedy* (New York: Bantam Books, 1975) 167, hereafter cited as Anson.

[263] Anson 166-167.

[264] Anson 167.

[265] Anson 168.

[266] Anson 168.

[267] Anson 168.

[268] Newman 137-139.

[269] Newman 139.

[270] Newman 139.

[271] Newman 139.

[272] Newman 139.

[273] 16 H (CE 213) 602).

[274] Newman 140.

[275] 16 H (CE 230) 628.

[276] Personal communications.

[277] 16 H (CE 228) 621.

[278] 16 H (CE 230) 628.

[279] 16 H (CE 228) 621-622.

[280] 16 H (CE 228) 621.

[281] 16 (CE 230) 628; see below.

[282] 16 H (CE 228) 621.

[283] The form was most probably duplicated by mimeographing, though some early photocopying was not impossible.

[284] See above: 16 H (CE 228) 621.

[285] Same.

[286] Same.

[287] 16 H (CE 230) 628.

[288] Same.

[289] 16 H (CE 230) 628.

[290] 16 H (CE 228) 622-623.

[291] Same.

[292] 16 H (CE 228) 622-625.

[293] 16 H (CE 230) 628.

[294] 16 H (CE 228) 622-623.

[295] Same.

[296] The author's several research trips to Providence in 2000.

[297] See below.

[298] 16 H (CE 228) 624.

[299] Bartholomew 15-16.

[300] 16 H (CE 228) 624.

[301] Epstein 286 note #5 and 338.

[302] Epstein 338.

[303] Epstein: for Oswald's close friends, see 53-124, throughout. Neither the 'actual' Botelho nor Calore qualifies.

[304] 16 H (CE 228) 624.

[305] Same.

[306] 16 H (CE 230) 628.

[307] Same.

[308] Same.

[309] Bartholomew 15; see also 22 note #9.

[310] Same.

[311] 16 H (CE 230) 628.

[312] 16 H (CE 230) 828.

[313] 16 H (CE 235) 634.

[314] 16 H (CE 230) 628.

[315] 16 H (CE 235) 634.

[316] Epstein 287 #6.

[317] Epstein 287 #6.

[318] 16 H (CE 231) 629.

[319] Epstein 90.

[320] Epstein 287 #7.

[321] 16 H (CE 231) 629.

[322] Epstein 90.

[323] Epstein 90.

[324] Epstein 90.

[325] 16 H (CE 235) 634.

[326] When searching for Hans Casparis at NARA and on the Web, enter both Casparis and Gasparis.

[327] Bartholomew 17.

[328] Bartholomew 19.

[329] 16 H (CE 229) 627.

[330] 16 H (CE 228) 621-622.

[331] 16 H (CE 229) 626. Did the series "Ana" misspelled as "Anna" replaced by the incorrect "Barbara" anticipate the subtle 'mistake' in Oswald's mailing addresses once he came home to Texas and New Orleans?

[332] Same.

[333] Bartholomew 21.

[334] Bartholomew 18.

[335] 16 H (CE 229) 626.

[336] Same.

[337] Same.

[338] 16 H (CE 228) 621.

[339] Same.

[340] 16 H (CE 229) 626-627.

[341] Same.

[342] Same.

[343] Bartholomew 19.

[344] Bartholomew 18.

[345] Bartholomew 18.

[346] Same.

[347] See later.

[348] Bartholomew 18.

[349] 16 H (CE 231) 629-630 and (CE 236) 637.

[350] 16 H (CE 231) 629.

[351] Same.

[352] 16 H (CE 235) 634.

[353] 16 H (CE 234) 633.

[354] Same.

[355] 16 H (CE 231) 629.

[356] 22 H 101 (CD 8 p. 7).

[357] 17 H (CE 833) 789-790.

[358] Newman 155-156.

[359] 7 H 6.

[360] Newman 156.

[361] Newman 157.

362  Newman 157.

363  Newman 156.

364  Newman 156.

365  Newman 156.

366  Quoted in Newman 156.

367  Newmam 156.

368  Newman 156.

369  Newman 156.

370  Newman 156.

371  Newman 159.

372  Newman 158-159.

373  Flora Lewis,

*Pawn[:] The Story of Noel Field* (Garden City, New York: Doubleday & Company, Inc., 1965), hereafter cited as Lewis. Her "red pawn" metaphor may derive from her pro-US/anti-Communist orientation: see Edward S. Herman, *The Real Terror Network* (Boston: South End Press, 1982 [Second Printing, 1983]) 173-177 and 194.

374  Epstein 140.

375  As I have named it. The gaming aspects of intelligence and espionage have been explored most extensively in so-called "spy" fiction, primarily in the United Kingdom and the United States. Gaming phenomena can be observed in detectival fiction, in popular romance, in the history of "comic books," in the development of action cinema, including the "serials" of the 1930s and 1940s, and in the confluence of these popular culture strands in video games.

376  Some well-known JFK assassination figures are also available as game pieces, but others, including Noel Field (discussed later), obviously qualify.

377  Newman 422.

378  Same.

379  Fain report quoted in Newman 141.

380  Same.

381  16 H (CE 206) 594-596.

382  Same.

383  Same: as she had reportedly informed the Ft. Worth agent.

384  Newman 143.

385  See *INTERCEPT*.

386  Newman 157.

387  Newman 157.

388  Newman 422.

389  My experience has suggested that both the FBI and CIA are uninterested in supporting historical research in the JFK assassination. Arguing that a number of non-government archives, files, and documents be designated "JFK Assassination Records," to be preserved at NARA, might be more productive.

390  New York Field Office air telegram quoted in Newman 143.

[391] Same.

[392] Newman 143.

[393] Newman 143.

[394] Hoover letter quoted in Newman 144.

[395] 16 H (CE 233) 632.

[396] Same.

# Essay Two: Notes

[1] See Melissa B. Robinson's Associated Press summary, hereafter cited as Robinson.

[2] Robinson; see also Bartholomew 20.

[3] Bartholomew 20. December 28th, 1995: ARRB documents 124-10023-10234 through 10238, all officially released to the ARRB by the Swiss government.

[4] Robinson.

[5] See above, *New York Times*, February 23rd, 1975, and Anson 199-200, especially Anson's note on 200.

[6] FBI File #105-82555, CD 1114, cited in Anson 200.

[7] Anson 200.

[8] Anson 200.

[9] Anson 200.

[10] Robinson.

[11] Bartholomew 20.

[12] See later.

[13] Peter Dale Scott, *Deep Politics and the Death of JFK* (Berkeley: University of California Press, 1993).

[14] See Scott 38-74.

[15] Scott 55-56. The "public relations" dimensions of Oswald's story and the JFK assassination are explored further in Essay Six.

[16] Scott 57.

[17] Scott 38-47.

[18] Scott 64.

[19] Scott 66-67.

[20] See *INTERCEPT*.

[21] Epstein 16.

[22] Epstein 16.

[23] Epstein 16.

[24] Epstein 16.

[25] See Epstein 16-17.

[26] Epstein 253-254.

[27] See the CIA Inspector General's Report on Cubela. In fact, the Kostikov-Cubela connection might have been dangerous for the Bureau to pursue vigorously: if the FBI knew of Cubela

and knew that the CIA was running Cubela, Cubela then constituted a potential conspiratorial link between the CIA and the FBI. A distorted version of this hypothesis may be seen in FBI agent James Hosty's "bombshell" story about the suppressed evidence reportedly not available to the Warren Commission about an alleged meeting between Oswald and Kostikov in Mexico City: see James P. Hosty, Jr., *Assignment: Oswald* (New York: Arcade Publishing, 1996) 139-140 and 215; on Oswald and his alleged contacts with Cubans and the Soviets, see Hosty throughout; especially, see Hosty's index on 324: "Mexico City," hereafter cited as Hosty.

[28]  Duffy 139-140.

[29]  Hugh Thomas, *The Cuban Revolution* (New York: Harper & Row, Publishers, 1977) 103, hereafter cited as Thomas.

[30]  Thomas 103-104.

[31]  Thomas 103-104.

[32]  Fidel's response may have been his first public expression of ambivalence toward Cubela; but, on the other hand, he may have known exactly with whom he was dealing.

[33]  Tad Szulc, *Fidel[:] A Critical Portrait* (New York: William Morrow & Co., 1986) 56, hereafter cited as Szulc *Fidel*.

[34]  Evica 122-123, 138, 148, 167, 198, 245, 277, 282, 288, 290-291, and 328.

[35]  Hinkle and Turner 191.

[36]  Hinkle and Turner 191.

[37]  Szulc 56.

[38]  The Inspector General's Report.

[39]  Inspector General's Report 34; see 34 through 49 for detailed examination of CIA/AMLASH/Cubela relations, despite heavy "redacting."

[40]  George Michael Evica, *Bringing Down Batista [For Fidel: the CIA Support of Castro]*, a work in progress, hereafter cited as *Bringing*.

[41]  *Bringing*; see also Szulc *Fidel* 55-56 and 427-430, for example.

[42]  Inspector General's Report, editor's footnote 49. See also the "Comment," apparently of the Inspector General's CIA authors, 49.

[43]  Summers 351.

[44]  See Summers 423-426 and 436.

[45]  Summers 353.

[46]  Evica 286: see endnote documentary support; see also 221, 284, 287-288, 290-291, 304, 311, 327 and endnote documentary support. See also Inspector General Report 35, especially Peter Dale Scott's footnote linking Cubela to Santo Trafficante, the Organized Crime boss out of Havana and Tampa.

[47]  Tad Szulc, "Cuba on Our Mind," Esquire, 1974, reprinted in *The Assassinations[:] Dallas and Beyond*, Peter Dale Scott, Paul L. Hoch, and Russell Stetler eds. (New York: Vintage Books, 1976) 384, hereafter cited as Szulc "Cuba."

[48]  Anson 256.

[49]  Anson 256 footnote and Inspector General's Report, Peter Dale Scott's footnote 43.

[50]  I G Report, Peter Dale Scott's footnote 43.

51   Anson 256 footnote.

52   All FBI Legat communications on Oswald and Cubela available at NARA, with significant
     continuing "redactions."

53   Scott 324 note # 26.

54   American intelligence, the Warren Commission, and all subsequent investigations ignored
     the direct links between Cubela's patron, Carlos Prio, and Jack Ruby, the killer of Lee Harvey
     Oswald: see Evica 148, 167, 277, 282, 289, 305, 319.

55   The CIA continued to nudge forward if not actively push the Cubela/Kostikov 'connection':
     Epstein, relying on Angleton, pressed the Cubela question, suggesting that Cubela's contacts
     with Kostikov were, in fact, a Cuban (Castro) "provocation" (Epstein 254). But a provocation
     for what? To provoke a counterattack on Castro? To establish a motive for attacking JFK (or
     someone else)? And what did the Agency really make of the Cubela/Kostikov connection,
     unless it was, in fact, one CIA asset (Cubela) contacting another CIA asset (Kostikov)? But
     were they, then, both suspect? As part of the ongoing larger espionage game, this possibility
     is, at least, intriguing.

56   See the [CIA's] *Inspector General's Report on Plots to Assassinate Fidel Castro, 1967*, published by
     Prevailing Winds Research, August 4th, 1994, pp. 0-61 (the Prevailing Winds edition has
     "Memorandum For the Record" preceding the Report's covering memo that is not paginated,
     hence, "0": the specific Cubela material 34-49, hereafter cited as IG Report. See also, in the
     same publication placed before the reproduced IG Report, Peter Dale Scott, "The Inspector
     General's Report: An Introduction, with its own pagination, pp. 1-11, hereafter cited as Scott
     IG Report. Scott's commentary is extremely valuable throughout, but his specific Cubela
     material is a Scott IG Report 6-8 and in "Editor's note" commentary throughout the Cubela
     section of the IG Report. To simplify, Scott perceives the "The CIA AMLASH 1963 Project
     as a CIA Revolt against [JFK] Presidential Policy," Scott IG Report 6 (6-8).

57   Peter Dale Scott: see earlier. "Phase One" was the Communist conspiracy theory of the JFK
     assassination; "Phase Two," the Lone Assassin theory.

58   See earlier cable sources.

59   See earlier cable sources.

60   See earlier cable sources.

61   FBI memorandum cited in Robinson.

62   Excerpt from FBI memo quoted in Robinson.

63   Bartholomew 21.

64   Bartholomew 21.

65   Robinson; see also Bartholomew 21.

66   Robinson.

67   Bartholomew 21.

68   Robinson.

69   Personal communication.

70   "As liberal religion affirmed and refined theological ideas about God's universal love, the
     perfectibility of humankind, the applicability of reason to religious questions and freedom
     of conscience, it inevitably applied those ideas to the social order." Di Figlia 2-3. In that

sense, given the life of Albert Schweitzer who belonged to that liberal religious tradition, the establishing of Albert Schweitzer College in Switzerland was all but inevitable. As early as 1917, the Unitarian Fellowship of Social Justice moved "to institutionalize Unitarian social activism . . . ." Di Figlia 6.

71 Sensitive personal correspondence.

72 Boake, "Personal Memories of the IARF," found at the website IARF-religiousfreedom.net.

73 Robinson.

74 Robinson.

75 FBI memorandum quoted in Bartholomew 21.

76 Personal correspondence.

77 Bartholomew 20-21.

78 Commentary on document at ARRB web site.

79 Same.

80 Same.

81 Document duplicated at ARRB web site.

82 Same.

83 Epstein 07: he does not identity his source.

84 Bartholomew 21.

85 Bartholomew 21.

86 Bartholomew 21.

87 Newman 213.

88 CD 1294J.

89 Robinson.

90 Bartholomew 16: NAR # 124-10086-1003.

91 Quoted in Bartholomew 16.

92 NAR #124-10170-10010.

93 NAR #124-10086-10003.

94 Bartholomew 17.

95 Bartholomew 17.

96 Bartholomew 17.

97 Bartholomew 17.

98 See Essay Four.

99 See Essay Four.

100 See Essay Three and, earlier, Essay One.

101 David Wise and Thomas B. Ross, *The Espionage Establishment* (New York: Random House, 1967) 18, hereafter cited as Wise and Ross.

102 Wise and Ross 18; see also 19-23.

103 Wise and Ross 18.

104 Wise and Ross 23.

105 William Corso, Susan B. Trento, and Joseph J. Trento, *Widows* (New York: Crown Publishers, Inc., 1979) 221, hereafter cited as Corson *Widows*.

106 Corson *Widows*.

[107]  Wise and Ross 23; see also Bittman 152.

[108]  Mangold 209.

[109]  Corson *Widows*; see also Bittman 152-153 and Mangold 209-210.

[110]  See Epstein, throughout, relying on two top counterespionage officers, James Angleton of the CIA and William Sullivan of the FBI.

[111]  See Mangold on Nosenko 160-207, and on Oswald 173-175, 191, 198, and 204.

[112]  Wise and Ross 23 and Bittman 151, and see also 152-153.

[113]  Wise and Ross 24: see also 38-39, and Ronald Kessler, *Spy vs. Spy* (New York: Charles Scribner's Sons, 1988) 295, for a formal definition of "illegal" as a covert intelligence agent, hereafter cited as Kessler.

[114]  Wise and Ross 31-32.

[115]  Wise and Ross 32.

[116]  Wise and Ross 32; see also 31-32, especially the footnote on 32-33 for commentary on real as opposed to altered or forged passports.

[117]  Christopher Andrew and Vasili Mitrohhin, *The Sword and the Shield* (New York: Basic Books, 1999), 165, hereafter cited as Andrew.

[118]  Andrew 165.

[119]  Andrew 605 note # 14.

[120]  Andrew 605 note # 15.

[121]  Wise and Ross 32.

[122]  See, for example, the "Prikhodko Lecture," part of a 1960-1961 series of GRU lectures, in Appendix I in Penkovsky, specifically on agent communications in the United States, so-called "accommodation" addresses, and various delivery systems, including mail "to a post office box rented by the agent . . . ." (294; see also 300-301) According to Prikhodko, Soviet illegals had to be aware of the FBI's "severe counterintelligence" program and the Bureau's "constant surveillance." (268)

[123]  Wise and Ross 32.

[124]  Sanford J. Ungar, *FBI* (Boston: Little Brown and Company, 1976) 473, hereafter cited as Ungar.

[125]  See, for example, Kessler 248.

[126]  Corson *Widows* 221.

[127]  David Wise, *Molehunt* (New York: Random House, 1992) 100, hereafter cited as Wise.

[128]  Wise 22-23.

[129]  Wise and Ross 263.

[130]  Wise and Ross 263. For a fuller and different, though not more accurate, rendering of the Abel/Powers story, see Michael R. Beschloss, *May-Day* (New York: Harper & Row, Publishers, 1986) 345-354 and sources, 466, last paragraph: these citations do not inspire confidence in Beschloss's research aspirations, hereafter cited as Beschloss, *May-Day*.

[131]  Corson *Widows* 384.

[132]  Corson *Widows* 384.

[133]  West 33.

[134]  West 33.

[135] Wise and Ross, 33.

[136] Wise and Ross 35.

[137] On KGB illegals (in general), see Barron 28-29.

[138] Walter Laqueur, A *World of Secrets[:]The Uses and Limits of Intelligence* (New York: Basic Books, Inc., Publishers, 1985), 240, hereafter cited as Laqueur.

[139] Peter Deriabin and Frank Gibney, *The Secret World* (New York: Ballantine Books, original copyright 1959, Ballantine Books "Fourth Printing" 1987) 107, hereafter cited as Deriabin.

[140] Deriabin 107.

[141] West 85.

[142] West 85.

[143] Barron 106-107; see also 111.

[144] Barron 106.

[145] The following discussion is based on two articles by Steven Lee Myers out of Moscow, "In Treason Trial, Echoes of Soviet Past and K.G.B. Secrets," *New York Times*, June 11, 2002, hereafter cited as Myers 1, and "Russia Convicts a Former K.G.B. General Now Living in U.S.," *New York Times*, June 27, 2002, hereafter cited as Myers 2.

[146] David Stout, "Once a Top Russian Spy, Now a Proud American," *New York Times*, August 24, 2003: Kalugin reported he was then a "KGB trainee" recognized by "Communist officials" for "his skill with languages," hereafter cited as Stout.

[147] Meyers 1.

[148] Meyers 1.

[149] Meyers 1.

[150] Stout.

[151] Kalugin 36.

[152] Kalugin 36.

[153] Kalugin 102.

[154] Kalugin 192-193.

[155] Kalugin 57, 58.

[156] Meyers 1.

[157] Andrew 204.

[158] Obviously I suspect Oleg Kalugin of running an operation for the Central Intelligence Agency inside the KGB and collecting agents both double and doubled.

[159] Kalugin 48, 75, 101-102, 116-118.

[160] Meyers 1.

[161] Meyers 1.

[162] Meyers 2.

[163] Myers 2.

[164] Andrew 209.

[165] Andrew 209. In 1994, Kalugin implicitly minimized the RFK link, most probably because the back channels stories were then circulating: see Kalugin 75.

[166] Ladislav Bittman, *The KGB and Soviet Disinformation* (Washington [etc.]: Pergamon-Brasseys' International Defense Publishers, 1985) 68, hereafter cited as Bittman.

[167] Bittman 68.

[168] Kalugin 178-186, 206-207, 249.

[169] Wise and Ross 10-11; 63-67; 204-209. See also Barron 464-465.

[170] Penkovsky 316.

[171] Penkovsky 68-69.

[172] Penkovsky 69.

[173] Penkovsky 70.

[174] Penkovsky 70.

[175] Penkovsky 72.

[176] Wise and Ross 65.

[177] Penkovsky 72.

[178] Penkovsky 73.

[179] Penkovsky 71. A major Soviet (GRU) illegals network operated in Switzerland during World War II (Wise 65-67) that included an extraordinary false identity agent, Alexander Foote, who may have been a British Communist (Wise 67), was a Spanish Civil War veteran, and was finally a Soviet spy-ring radio operator. (Wise 67) After the collapse of the GRU's Swiss espionage network, Moscow blamed Foote (Wise 67); in 1947, apparently fearing for his life, he defected to the British. (Wise 67) Unless Alex Foote simply went home to his actual handlers.

[180] Wise 207-208; see also 202-236 throughout, and Wise, *Molehunt* 166.

[181] Wise 208.

[182] Barron 464-465.

[183] Barron 465.

[184] Wise and Ross 212: see also 211-223 and 232-236; Wise 109; and West 21-22 and 48-49.

[185] See, for example, Wise 166.

[186] Wise 171.

[187] Wise 171, 172.

[188] Wise 214-217 and 231, note.

[189] Wise 231 and 258.

[190] Wise 232.

[191] Corson *Widows* 221.

[192] Newman.

[193] Epstein throughout.

[194] Epstein 164.

[195] James Srodes, *Allen Dulles[:] Master of Spies* (Washington, D.C.: Regnery Publishing, Inc., 1999) 73, hereafter cited as Srodes.

[196] John H. Waller, *The Unseen War in Europe* (New York: Random House, 1996) 7, hereafter cited as Waller.

[197] Srodes 73-74.

[198] Srodes 73.

[199] Joseph E. Persico, *Piercing the Third Reich* (New York: Viking, 1979) 37-38 and 153, hereafter cited as Persico *Piercing*. According to retired Agency operative Tom Gilligan *CIA Life*

Guilford, CT.: Foreign intelligence Press, 1991), he had been on "an extended tour of duty under deep cover, or 'nonofficial cover' as it is known in CIA. Known as NOCs, nonofficial cover officers operate overseas outside official installations, usually posing as businessmen or scholars . . . without] diplomatic immunity . . . ." (67: see also 69)

# Essay Three: Notes

[1]  Summarizing extensive personal correspondence and Internet investigation.

[2]  From Section IV of Gaebler's IARF presentation.

[3]  Same.

[4]  Richard Boeke's recorded statement defining IARF's history at IARF's web site, hereafter cited as Boeke.

[5]  Boeke.

[6]  From "A Summary of IARF History" at the IARF web site, posted as of May, 1999.

[7]  Personal e-mail message from a former Albert Schweitzer student.

[8]  Harvard Divinity School, Andover-Harvard Theological Library, bMS 1223-1, correspondence and memoranda of the officers of the Friends of Albert Schweitzer College in the United States, 1953-1972. But: the records for 1959-1960 are missing except for one key class list (see later). The documents, bMS 1223-1, have been preserved in one (stuffed) box. Both here and in other Unitarian, Universalist, and Albert Schweitzer College document files (see later), the letters and memos are typically carbon (or other) copies of a communication from person "A" to person "B" but apparently from the files of person "C" who was often not identified. Since it was the INTERNAL evidence preserved in the communications that was most important to my inquiry, I have avoided excessive or irrelevant 'citation' information: my main text carries the primary citation. Here and throughout, when using the Harvard materials, I will use a minimalist referential system. If future historians need to consult the records, the Harvard librarians are guarding the gates against the barbarians. All documents from bMS 1223-1 (a single box of records) will hereafter be referred to and cited as bMS 1223-1.

[9]  In bMS 1223-1, from a document of seventeen pages, probably composed in 1965 or 1966.

[10]  bMS 1223-1.

[11]  bMS 1223-1.

[12]  See later.

[13]  bMS 1223-1.

[14]  bMS 1223-1.

[15]  See Essay Four: Jeremy Taylor's website has recorded that Noel Field met with his Unitarian minister friend, Steve Fritchman, who then helped establish the Unitarian Service Committee: see jeremytaylor.com.

[16]  See Essays One and Three.

17  My search for religious liberal youth files at the headquarters of the Unitarian/Univeralist Service Committee in Cambridge elicited nothing about Albert Schweitzer College.

18  Friends.

19  bMS 1223-1.

20  bMS 1223-1.

21  bMS 1223-1.

22  bMS 1223-1.

23  See Essays Three and Six.

24  See later.

25  A summary of the author's personal communications with John Casparis, Hans Casparis' son.

26  bMS 1233-1 See also bMS 1223-1 on early teaching at the college: "Most of the instruction was provided by the director of the school . . . Casparis, the principal founder, . . . first director . . . and a resident tutor."

27  bMS 1223-1.

28  Personal email correspondence with "Albert Schweitzer" institutions that communicated no knowledge of Albert Schweitzer College, Churwalden, Switzerland.

29  bMS 1223-1.

30  bMS 1223-1.

31  bMS 1223-1.

32  bMS 1223-1.

33  See earlier and *INTERCEPT*.

34  bMS 1223-1.

35  Who knows?

36  bMS 1223-1.

37  Albert Schweitzer's personal mail was being intercepted in 1956 by the Central Intelligence Agency: see below.

38  See earlier.

39  The following commentary on Albert Schweitzer and the Eisenhower administration draws heavily on Lawrence S. Wittner, "Blacklisting Schweitzer," *The Bulletin of the Atomic Scientists*, May/June 1995, Vol. 51, No. 3, reproduced on the Bulletin's web site, hereafter cited as Wittner.

40  Wittner.

41  Wittner.

42  Wittner.

43  Wittner.

44  Wittner.

45  Wittner.

46  Wittner.

47  Wittner.

48  Wittner.

49   The Central Intelligence Agency refused to declassify the purloined Schweitzer letters; "Schweitzer believed that people . . . were tampering with his personal mail at the Lambarene post office." (Wittner)

50   Wittner.

51   Wittner.

52   Wittner.

53   Wittner.

54   Wittner.

55   Wittner.

56   Wittner.

57   See Essay Six.

58   In bMS 1223-1.

59   In bMS 1223-1.

60   In bMS 1223-1.

61   In bMS 1223-1.

62   In bMS 1223-1.

63   In bMS 1223-1.

64   In bMS 1223-1.

65   I assume that #4, if it ever existed, was taken out of the Harvard records (for some unknown reason), though logically it should NOT have existed.

66   In bMS 1223-1.

67   In bMS 1223-1.

68   Albert Schweitzer College student Bjorn Ahlstedt may be contacted at his website: bjorn. ahlstedt@telia.com, hereafter cited as Ahlstedt.

69   bMS 1223-1.

70   bMS 1223-1.

71   bMS 1223-1.

72   bMS 1223-1.

73   bMS 1223-1.

74   See Essay One.

75   bMS 1223-1.

76   bMS 1223-1.

77   My associate Charles Drago believes the FBI agents were from Providence rather than Boston: logically, they should have been.

78   See Essay One.

79   Spelling in original.

80   bMS 1223-1.

81   bMS 1223-1.

82   bMS 1223-1.

83   bMS 1223-1.

84   Personal email communication from Ernest Cassara.

85   bMS 1223-1.
86   bMS 1223-1.
87   bMS 1223-1.
88   bMS 1223-1.
89   bMS 1223-1.
90   bMS 1223-1.
91   bMS 1223-1.
92   bMS 1223-1.
93   bMS 1223-1.
94   Email communication from Swiss Casparis genealogy expert, hereafter cited as "Casparis expert."
95   bMS 1223-1.
96   bMS 1223-1.
97   bMS 1223-1.
98   bMS 1223-1.
99   bMS 1223-1.
100  bMS 1223-1.
101  bMS 1223-1.
102  bMS 1223-1.
103  For example, from Zurich: an email to me dated 9/04/2001: "I inform you that Hans Casparis did not receive a degree at Zurich University and that he was not a student at this university 1919-1934." Universitaet Zuerich, Archiv, Dr. Heinzpeter Stucki.

     I received personal communications by email from all the universities confirming Casparis did not receive degrees or diplomas from any of them: see following endnotes.
104  Personal email communication from the University of Chicago.
105  Personal email communication from the University of Chicago.
106  Personal email communications from the universities.
107  Personal email communication from the university.
108  Personal email communication from the university.
109  The biographical commentary in the text is drawn principally from two posted articles: http://www.harvardsquarelibrary.org/unitarians/douglas_p.html, in the "Notable American Unitarians" biographical archive: "Paul H. Douglas: United States Senator" adapted from "an article in the *Illinois Historical Journal* (Volume 83, Summer 1990) written by Edward L. Schapsmeier, Distinguished Professor of History at Illinois State University," and "Congressional Bio: Douglas, Paul Howard, 1892-1976."
110  Eric Thomas Chester, *Covert Network* (Armonk, New York: M.E. Sharpe, 1995) 154, hereafter cited as Chester.
111  Chester 153.
112  Chester 153.
113  Chester 153.
114  Chester 153.
115  Chester 153.

[116]  Chester 154.

[117]  Chester 179-182.

[118]  Chester 182.

[119]  Chester 182.

[120]  The following biographical commentary is based on "James Luther Adams" in the Dictionary of Unitarian and Universalist Biography at http://www.uua.org/uuhs/duub/articles, written by Van Eric Fox and Alice Blair Wesley.

[121]  Louis Budenz, *The Techniques of Communism* (1954), Chapter 10.

[122]  This paragraph and the following based on an article on Adams by George W. Pickering, *American Journal of Theology and Philosophy*, May, 2000, Volume 21, No. 2.

[123]  Translated from German.

[124]  Unfortunately, over 1200 pages of Adams' autobiographical materials (located in the Andover-Harvard Theological Library, Harvard Divinity School Archives) have been reduced to 425 printed pages (not entirely successfully) including additional materials from other (important) Adams' autobiographical sources, in James Luther Adams, *Not Without Dust and Heat [:] A Memoir* (Chicago: Exploration Press, 1995): "An Introduction to a Memoir" by Max L. Stackhouse, xi-xii. Adams' essays and materials themselves as they are represented do not clarify key issues associated with Adams; the pages still at Harvard Divinity may do so. In *Not Without Dust or Heat*, for University of Chicago, 223-282 and 417-418; for Meadville 223-245 and 258-266; for Unitarians 415-416 (inadequate); for Paul Douglas and the Independent Voters of Illinois 221, 245, and 271 (inadequate); for Germany 168, 169, 173-177, 179-187, 189, 194-196, 198: see also 204-205; on Albert Schweitzer 68, 165-167, 212 (mixed response) and 421 (a single positive response). Note that absolutely no hint is given in the published materials of Adams' close working relationship to the Friends of Albert Schweitzer College and the Admissions Committee of the college. On Adams as a socialist, see a few scattered comments: 225 and 227, for example. For the best single review of Adams as a liberal and global thinker, see David Little, "Liberalism and World Order: The Thought of James Luther Adams," *Harvard Divinity Bulletin*, Volume 31, Number 3, Summer 2003, 7-9.

[125]  Casparis expert.

[126]  Casparis expert.

[127]  Casparis expert.

[128]  Personal email communications: for example, "The name Callie is . . . not to be found in the students' records of the University of Heidelberg." The latter email received from Dr. Hans Ewald Kessler (wiss. Angesteller) at Heidelberg.

[129]  Email communication from Ali Burdon.

[130]  Casparis expert.

[131]  Same.

[132]  Same.

[133]  Same.

[134]  Extensive Swiss military records on Hans Casparis received by the author.

[135]  See earlier.

# Essay Four: Notes

[1]   Penny Lernoux, *Cry of the People* (New York: Penguin Books, 1982) 286, hereafter cited as Lernoux.

[2]   Lernoux 286.

[3]   Owen Chadwick, *The Christian Church in the Cold War* (London: Allan Lane, The Penguin Press, 1992) though in several ways a valuable study, offers nothing about American intelligence and foreign service manipulation of religious individuals and organizations.

[4]   Most importantly, Lernoux throughout.

[5]   See, for example, Anthony Cave Brown, ed., *The Secret War Report of the OSS* (New York: Berkley Medallion Books, 1976), with NO references to any religious individual or group in touch with or working with the OSS: the intelligence links between religious organizations and the OSS (and, later, the CIA) have obviously been carefully concealed.

[6]   See Essay Five for John Foster Dulles' misuse of religious organizations to further his economic, policy, and political goals.

[7]   John D. Marks, "The CIA's Church Connection: Missionaries as Informants," *National Catholic News Service*, July 18, 1975, cited in Lernoux 285 and 502 note # 12.

[8]   Simpson 284. Simpson gave documentation for all his categories EXCEPT "religious groups." He did cite Cardinal Spellman as the Roman Catholic link to the CIA (91), but that was all.

[9]   The Cultural Cold War (New York: New York Press, 1999) 278-130, hereafter cited as Saunders.

[10]  Saunders 280.

[11]  Saunders 281.

[12]  Saunders 281. Yet Niebuhr still saw Dulles for what he was, though almost near the end: see Reinhold Niebuhr, "The Moral World of Foster Dulles," *The New Republic* CXXXIX, December 1, 1958.

[13]  See also Hilton Kramer, *The Twilight of the Intellectuals[:] Culture and Politics in the Era of the Cold War* (Chicago: Ivan R. Dee, 1999) that purports to be a full intellectual history of the Cold War as it helped shape American culture and politics. But Kramer has offered nothing on the relevant subject of religion and politics. He did align himself clearly with the "Hiss was guilty" group (see 27-31, for example), and was at best uncharitable attacking the administration of President John F. Kennedy (19) and the Kennedys' support of the arts: "Only in a capital as intellectually provincial as Washington could a president like John Kennedy earn a reputation as a supporter of the arts simply by inviting Andre' Malraux and Igor Stravinsky to dinner." (328)

[14] *The Culture of the Cold War* (Baltimore: The Johns Hopkins University Press, 1991), hereafter cited as Whitfield.

[15] Whitfield did list a relevant text in his bibliography: Mark Silk, *Spiritual Politics: Religion and America since World War II* (New York: Simon & Schuster, 1988): 240.

[16] Christopher Simpson, *The Splendid Blond Beast* (Monroe, Maine: Common Courage Press, 1995) 21, hereafter cited as Simpson *Blond*.

[17] Smith 205.

[18] Simpson *Blond* 21.

[19] Simpson *Blond* 22.

[20] Smith 205. Borrowing material from each other, Dulles biographers have repeated an interesting error: designating Herbert Field as "Henry" Field (possibly because Henry Hyde was also an important Dulles operative in Europe). Srodes correctly names Field (81) but then defames the dedicated Quaker and patriot (81) whom Allen Dulles manipulated in World War One.

[21] Smith 205.

[22] Hermann Field and Kate Field, *Trapped in the Cold War* (Stanford, California: Stanford University Press, 1999) 2, hereafter cited as Field *Trapped*.

[23] Smith 205.

[24] Smith 205.

[25] Mosely 49.

[26] Smith 205.

[27] Smith 205.

[28] Smith 205: Smith's evaluation of Herbert Field was ultimately based on Wilson's own commentary: see Smith 403 #2.

[29] An important source for the negative Herbert Field story was Robert Murphy, a powerful Foreign Service officer. (Robert Murphy, *Diplomat Among Warriors* (Garden City, New York: Doubleday & Company, 1964 7-8, hereafter cited as Murphy. But Murphy's account was carefully edited: Allen Dulles as a spymaster played no part in Murphy's account of both World Wars, though Switzerland was an important Murphy site. Further, the Lenin role in the McNally/Field narrative was altogether missing. How knowledgeable (or deliberately unwitting) Murphy was of intelligence activities can be gained through one important paragraph of commentary, its OSS/CIA spin quite apparent:

"Incidentally, I have followed with interest the career of Herbert Field's son, Noel, who entered the foreign service after World War I and eventually defected to the Communists. He was last heard from in Budapest, but defectors live in danger and apparently the Communists suspected Noel Field of being a double agent. At any rate, he vanished. Perhaps some day we may learn what happened to this too-bright young man who worked secretly for the Communist side in the Spanish Civil War, using a League of Nations job as cover for his activities." (Murphy 8)

[30] Mosely 46.

[31] Mosely 46.

[32] Mosely 46.

[33]   Mosely 46.

[34]   Murphy 7.

[35]   Mosely 46.

[36]   Murphy 7.

[37]   Mosely 46.

[38]   Mosely 46-47.

[39]   Murphy 7.

[40]   But see Murphy 7: here, Herbert Field is identified only as "a retired clergyman," the source of an "ignorant accusation."

[41]   Mosely 47.

[42]   Mosely 47.

[43]   Srodes 81.

[44]   Waller 7.

[45]   Srodes 80.

[46]   Srodes 72.

[47]   Mosley 46-47.

[48]   Rex A. Wade, *The Bolshevik Revolution and Russian Civil War* (Westport, Connecticut: Greenwood Press, 2001), 122, hereafter cited as Wade: "Lenin became one of the most extreme antiwar spokesmen, calling for transformation of the world war into [worldwide] civil war and arguing that Russia's defeat was the lesser evil." (Wade 122)

[49]   See Srodes: "Lenin was heading off to take control of the Russian Revolution . . . ." (80)

[50]   Mosely 46.

[51]   Mosely 46.

[52]   *Gentleman Spy* (Boston: Houghton Mifflin, 1994) 26-27, hereafter cited as Grose.

[53]   Grose 578 note #4.

[54]   Grose 26.

[55]   Grose 26.

[56]   Grose 26.

[57]   Was there ever an "evacuation train" from Vienna to Bern? Certainly such a train could have run from Vienna to Zurich (the residence of both Herbert Field and Lenin), but apparently only local transportation existed between Zurich and Bern: see later.

[58]   Grose 26.

[59]   Grose 26, footnote.

[60]   Grose 26-27, footnote.

[61]   Mosley 39.

[62]   Mosely 45.

[63]   Grose 27.

[64]   Mosely 39 and 39-40; see also Srodes 71.

[65]   Srodes 69.

[66]   Srodes 69.

[67]   Srodes 69.

[68]   Srodes 69.

[69]   See especially Grose's CIA 1995 material, 575.

[70]   Grose 26, footnote.

[71]   Grose 27, footnote.

[72]   See previous note.

[73]   Grose 26.

[74]   Grose 26.

[75]   Grose 26.

[76]   Mosely 47.

[77]   Srodes 78.

[78]   Srodes 80. But this version of the story is hopeless: it includes a call from Lenin on "a Friday afternoon" (80) and Dulles instructing Lenin to "call back the next day" 80). That "Friday" was, of course, Good Friday, Easter weekend.

       This version, however, is not the most noteworthy. On June 21st, 2004, James L. Pavitt reported the following version, possibly heard from Dulles but more likely a variant transmitted to Pavitt in a faulty oral tradition. "Indeed, some of our best officers have learned from their mistakes. In the previous century, a junior intelligence officer in Switzerland received word on Sunday evening that a disturbed Russian sought to speak to an American official. Not wanting to spoil his weekend tennis outing, our officer told the duty officer to direct the disturbed Russian to return the next day—Monday—during duty hours. Unfortunately, Vladimir Lenin chose not to return to the mission. Allen Dulles . . . was the junior intelligence officer. He recovered admirably from this early stumble and learned a lesson he imparted to future generations of operations officers." This version adds the fascinating possibility that Lenin had actually visited the "mission" in person. The address to the Foreign Policy Association was delivered by James L. Pavitt, in 2004 the Deputy Director for Operations, Central Intelligence Agency (http://www.fas.org/irp/cia/product/ddo_speech062404.html).

[79]   Srodes 80.

[80]   Waller 7.

[81]   Grose 26.

[82]   Mosely 47; see also Srodes 81.

[83]   Mosely 48.

[84]   H. W. Brands, Jr., *Cold Warriors* (New York: Columbia University Press, 1988) 50, hereafter cited as Brands.

[85]   Mosely 47.

[86]   Mosley 47.

[87]   Mosely 47.

[88]   Srodes 79.

[89]   Srodes 79.

[90]   Waller 8.

[91]   Waller 8.

[92]   Waller 8.

[93]   The Lenin story can be more than adequately reviewed in a Greenwood Press Guide to Historic Events of the Twentieth Century: Wade 20-24; 7-19; 97; 123-124; and 159-161.

[94]   Grose 27.

[95]   Michael Pearson, *The Sealed Train* (New York: G. P. Putnam's Sons, 1975) vii, hereafter cited as Pearson. Pearson's research, especially in Soviet materials (and the apparent assistance he received from British sources) is of primary importance in the Lenin story. But the book is poorly indexed: for example, neither Berne nor Bern appears in the index.

[96]   Pearson 112, 144, 150, 152, 193, 289-290, 291-292, 292-293, and 294. See Alexander Helphand named "Parvas" (throughout), the Marxist/capitalist double-agent conduit of German funds for Lenin.

[97]   Lenin had a long connection to Finland, including a stay in the country after arriving back in Russia: see Wade 19, 70, 88, 97, 123-124, 159-161.

[98]   Grose 168. For more on this questionable behavior, see below.

[99]   Mosely 48.

[100]  Grose 32.

[101]  Grose 32.

[102]  Grose 32.

[103]  Grose 32.

[104]  Grose 32.

[105]  Mosely 49.

[106]  Mosely 49.

[107]  Mosely 48.

[108]  See especially the excellent study, Hans A. Schmitt, *Quakers and Nazis[:] Inner Light in Outer Darkness* (Columbia, Missouri and London: University of Missouri Press, 1997, hereafter cited as Schmitt. See also Roger C. Wilson, *Quaker Relief* (London: George Allen & Unwen Ltd., 1952): "An account of the relief work of the [British] Society of Friends [,] 1940-1948," from the title page; see especially "France," 127-167, and "Germany," 223-275.

[109]  Mosely 49.

[110]  Smith 209.

[111]  Simpson 22.

[112]  Simpson 22.

[113]  Simpson 22.

[114]  Simpson, throughout.

[115]  Stephen E. Ambrose, *Ike's Spies[:] Eisenhower and the Espionage Establishment* (Garden City, New York: Doubleday & Company, Inc., 1981) 172, hereafter cited as Ambrose.

[116]  Ambrose 172. Ambrose had a remarkable opportunity to explore the dark infrastructure of the international elite network that used and supported Allen Dulles, the OSS, and the CIA and, when that network could, manipulated Eisenhower, but Ambrose opted out. The book promised much (see, for example, the back flyleaf): "It is an account of the transformation of the wartime OSS into the CIA . . . ." But Ambrose's *Ike's Spies* is no such thing, ignoring, for example, the important story of Arbenz in Switzerland, giving the reader only a photograph of the exiled couple; ignoring the Atsugi U-2 Air Base except for a single reference (290); ignoring Allen Dulles in "Berne" except for a single reference (173); ignoring the FBI except for three pages (162-163). Its fullest and most relevant discussion—on the U-2 (265-293)—was

apparently controlled by CIA agents and assets: see 272, 279-280, 282-283, and 288. See also Richard H. Immerman, Ambrose's "Research Associate," and his background, connections, and interviews: 347-349; 350-351; 356-357.

[117] Mosely 113.

[118] Smith 208.

[119] Mosley 113-114.

[120] Smith 208-209; see also Mosley 114.

[121] Smith 208.

[122] Smith 208.

[123] Smith208.

[124] Smith 208.

[125] Chester 13.

[126] *American Intelligence and the German Resistance to Hitler[:]* A *Documentary History*, Jurgen Heideking & Christof Mauch, eds. (Boulder Colorado: Westview Press, 1996) 17, hereafter cited as Heideking. "The majority of documents printed in this volume are part of the National Archives collection of OSS records (Record Group 226 [RG226])." (Heideking 425) Consult in particular Heideking, Bibliography, Note on Sources, 425.

[127] Smith 208.

[128] Smith 208.

[129] Smith 208-209.

[130] Smith 209.

[131] Smith 209. See, later, on the decision to work with anyone to defeat Nazi Germany: Persico 167. The immoral decision to accomplish good ends through evil means was also made by Allen Dulles' brother, John Foster Dulles, and again that decision included the manipulation of religious individuals and institutions for personal and political goals: see later, Essay Five. Political decisions fundamentally immoral, unethical, and evil have been at the heart of American intelligence's misuse of religious individuals and institutions. But Robert N. Bellah has concluded that evil, in fact, was central to the American ethos, planted on American soil by exclusionist Puritan Protestants and becoming a significant part of the American Establishment's deep structure: Robert N. Bellah, "Evil and the American Ethos," hereafter cited as Bellah, in Nevitt Sanford, Craig Comstock, & Associates, *Sanctions for Evil* (Boston: Beacon Press, 1971) 177-191, hereafter cited as *Sanctions*: see especially Bellah, *Sanctions* 184.

[132] Chester 14.

[133] See Chester 245.

[134] Smith 217.

[135] Smith 217-218.

[136] Winks 256-257.

[137] Chester 18.

[138] Smith 404 note #10.

[139] Smith 404 note # 10.

[140] Smith 405 note #33.

[141] Smith 217.

[142]  Chester 12.

[143]  Chester 11-13, 15, 143, 163-173.

[144]  Chester 12.

[145]  Chester 13.

[146]  See Varian Fry, *Surrender on Demand* (Boulder, Colorado: Johnson Books, 1997). Fry's own account of his astounding rescue work is heavily sanitized (possibly by Fry himself). A most important example follows: Fry's "Paul Hagen" (10, 14, 27, 32, 238, 252, and 257) who appears in Fry's dedication, "For Anna Caples and Paul Hagen, who began it . . . ," is never identified by Fry as OSS intelligence agent Karl Frank. In a long and fairly informative "Afterward" (245-260) attributed to the "United States Holocaust Memorial Museum" (260), Paul Hagen is identified as "Karl Frank" (247), but the index simply gives "Frank, Karl, see Hagen, Paul" (indexed at 247). The "Afterward" is apparently a careful instance of damage control, possibly with the assistance of Israeli intelligence in cooperation with the CIA. And Fry's close connections to religious organizations, specifically the Quakers and the Unitarians, are also cloaked: see 37, 73, 106, 251, and 254. The links between the religious humanitarian groups and American intelligence would be reasons enough for Fry's editorial care.

[147]  Andy Marino, A *Quiet American[:] The Secret War of Varian Fry* (New York: St. Martin's Press, 1999) 3-32, hereafter cited as Marino.

[148]  Marino 35-36.

[149]  Marino 36.

[150]  Marino 36.

[151]  Marino 36-37.

[152]  Marino 35-45.

[153]  Marino 44-45.

[154]  Marino 45.

[155]  Marino 47.

[156]  Marino 48-49. According to Chester, "Karl Frank was instrumental in recruiting Fry for the post of European representative of the Emergency Rescue Committee." (15)

[157]  Marino 49.

[158]  Marino 49.

[159]  Marino 49.

[160]  Marino 49.

[161]  Marino 49; see also Fry on "cover," 254.

[162]  Marino 49.

[163]  Marino throughout, but see especially the "lists": 53-55. Alma Mahler was also married to Walter Gropius and Franz Werfel.

[164]  Marino 53.

[165]  Smith 404 note #10.

[166]  Marino 56. Marino apparently did not know of Hagen's close links to American intelligence, citing only his political activism (33-34) and "idealism" (34).

[167]  Marino 56.

168 Marino 56.

169 Marino 56.

170 Marino 56.

171 Marino 56.

172 Marino 56.

173 Marino 56-57.

174 Fry 10.

175 Chester 15-16.

176 Chester 15-16, 61, 69, 78, 106-107, 113,

177 Chester 16.

178 Marino 180.

179 Marino 90.

180 Fry 73.

181 Marino 49.

182 Marino 90, 119, 150.

183 Fry 37.

184 Di Figlia 20.

185 Di Figlia 20.

186 Brundage most probably worked directly with the OSS: see Essay Seven.

187 Chester 17.

188 Chester 17.

189 Chester 15.

190 Chester 17. "These same escape routes were later used by OSS agents to maintain contact with French resistance fighters." Chester 17)

191 Chester 17.

192 Chester 17.

193 Chester 17.

194 Chester 17.

195 Fry 37, 73, 106, 251, and 254.

196 Fry 46.

197 Fry 77, 220, 2464, 249, 250, and 252.

198 Marino 119.

199 Di Figlia 15.

200 Marino 122-130.

201 See Marino 148; for Fry and Joy, see Marino 180.

202 Ghanda Di Figlia's e-mail to me on 5/17/2001.

203 Di Figlia 29.

204 Mosley 121.

205 Di Figlia 29.

206 Di Figlia 29.

207 See later.

[208]  Roger Fritts, "The Unitarian Service Committee," sermon at Cedar Lane Unitarian Universalist Church, Bethesda, Maryland, hereafter cited as Fritts. Fritts, the knowledgeable rector of a key Unitarian parish, cited Di Figlia but also used other non-cited sources.

[209]  Fritts.

[210]  Fry 45-52.

[211]  Marino 127-129 and 149.

[212]  For links between U.S. intelligence and Organized Crime in Marseilles, see Scott 165, 176, 178, and 194-195.

[213]  Marino 138.

[214]  Marino 138.

[215]  Marino 138.

[216]  Marino 138. Fry assistant Miriam Davenport accidentally met Dr. Burns Chalmers, the chaplain at Smith College where she had studied, who was now at the local American Friends Service Committee office: Fry had found another religious service link (Marino 139).

[217]  Marino 185-186.

[218]  The Unitarian Service Committee worked closely with Varian Fry: for example, at least once, Joy brought important information to Fry: Fry 106.

[219]  Marino: see 279-280.

[220]  Marino 320.

[221]  Marino 320.

[222]  Marino 348-349. For a splendid summary of the importance of Fry's work to humanity and especially to American culture, see Marino 337-338; see also Fry 259.

[223]  Marino 320: see note on 373: "Fry's FBI file is a matter of fact."

[224]  Marino 339, 342-344.

[225]  Heideking 17.

[226]  "Memorandum by Paul Hagen: How to Collaborate with the Anti-Nazi Underground in Germany" (NA, RG 226, Entry 106, Box 12, Folder 88) in Heideking 17-19.

[227]  Heideking 19.

[228]  Editors' comments in Heideking, footnote, 17.

[229]  For how extensive was the success of the COI and then the OSS in recruiting and organizing anti-Nazi liberal and radical circles, see the "Memorandum by Willy Brandt ([from] Stockholm): Opposition Movements in Germany" (NA, RG226, Entry 100, FNB-INT-13 GE-928), in Heideking 97-115. Brandt named Paul Hagen as a key leader of one of the "oppositional socialistic groups . . . based upon democratic principles." (Heideking 112)

[230]  Smith 2.

[231]  Presidential Order quoted in Stewart Alsop and Thomas Braden, *Sub Rosa[:] The OSS and American Espionage* (New York: Harcourt Brace & World, Inc., 1946, 1964) 13, hereafter cited as Alsop.

[232]  Alsop 13.

[233]  Smith 209.

[234]  Smith 209. Despite several negative comments circulated about Dulles and his Swiss intelligence-gathering, some knowledgeable sources have verified the value of Dulles'

work; for example: "An exceedingly small staff of agents . . . produced some of the best OSS intelligence of the war." (McIntosh 175) That information included "early intelligence on atomic and bacteriological research, location of the V-1 and V-2 development and testing sites, the . . . attempt on Hitler's life, and negotiations . . . for the surrender of Axis forces in northern Italy . . . ." (McIntosh 175)

235   Smith 209.

236   Persico 46.

237   Persico 46. For Allen Dulles and the OSS' "penetration" of Nazi Germany, see Persico 45-72, 91-97, 147-154, 225-226, 271-276, 313-314, and 326-329.

238   Burton Hersh, *The Old Boys* (New York: Charles Scribner's Sons, 1992) 93-95, hereafter cited as Hersh.

239   Tully 38-39. Von Schroeder later held an SS rank equivalent to a general; he was also the leader of a secret operation that pressed funding from Ruhr business leaders to support Heinrich Himmler (89).

240   Hersh 93-94.

241   Hersh 94.

242   Hersh 94.

243   Hersh 94.

244   Hersh 93.

245   Hersh 94.

246   Charles Whiting, *The Spymasters* (New York: E.P. Dutton & Co., 1976) 116, hereafter cited as Whiting.

247   Whiting 116-117.

248   Whiting 117.

249   Whiting 117; see also 168-169.

250   Grose 168.

251   Grose 168.

252   Former OSS and CIA hands (as well as faithful biographers) have praised Dulles' Second World War espionage activities in Switzerland, but many British intelligence sources have minimized and even trivialized Dulles' trumpeted accomplishments. One relatively disinterested, well-informed, and conservative commentator on Dulles has been Angelo M. Cordevilla in his *Between the Alps and a Hard Place [:] Switzerland in World War II and Moral Blackmail Today* (Washington, D.C.: Regnery Publishing, Inc., 2000), hereafter cited as Codevilla. Codevilla served as a U.S. Naval Officer, a Foreign Service officer, a senior staff member of the Senate Select Committee on Intelligence, and a Stanford University Hoover Institution senior research fellow. He concluded that "Swiss intelligence enjoys a mythic [that is, a largely fictional] reputation, as does the role of intelligence gathered [in World War II] in Switzerland." (68) On American intelligence, he added that "the information and intrigue that flowed through . . . [Switzerland] played [little] more than a marginal role in the outcome of World War II." (68) Codevilla did note that "America's Office of Strategic Services (OSS) began as an extension of Colonel William Donovan's private contacts." (71) But the reality was that Dulles' Swiss OSS operations were also based on major "private

contacts" with American/German industrial and financial individuals and groups, religious institutions and human service activists, and with liberal/radical resistance organizations. Allen Dulles' two overarching goals were 1. to defeat Germany and 2. save German industrial power. Codevilla ignored the overwhelming evidence, relegating the output of Allan Dulles to a dependent clause: "The pressure of events—rather than anything that Swiss intelligence or America's spymaster in Switzerland, Allen Dulles, did—was what increased the flow of intelligence [leaked from German sources into Allied operations]. (73)

[253] Adam LeBor, *Hitler's Secret Bankers* (Secaucus, N.J.: Birch Lane Press Book, Published by Carol Publishing Group, 1997) 135, hereafter cited as LeBor.

[254] LeBor 134-135.

[255] Grose 168-169.

[256] Field's adventures and complexities deserve a tragic epic; see, for example, Hede Massing, *This Deception* (New York: Duel, Sloan and Pearce, 1951), on Field and Marxism, and on Field as an intellectual, 165, 167, and 171, on psychoanalysis 169, and on Field at the Lincoln Memorial 171; hereafter cited as Massing. For a physical description that was valid until his arrest in Prague, see Massing 168; see also Lewis 129.

[257] Field *Trapped* 12.

[258] Waller 359.

[259] Lewis 121-122; the House Un-American Activities Committee, in Massing 164. Waller (359) asserted that Field was " . . . a member of the Communist party" and an avowed " . . . Communist and Soviet apologist . . ." but offered no evidence or proof for the party membership except to cite the standard anti-Hiss sources: see Waller 360 and 433 notes #4 and 5.

[260] Field *Trapped* 81.

[261] Lewis 107.

[262] Lewis 108.

[263] Lewis 112.

[264] Schmitt 9.

[265] Lewis 120.

[266] Lewis 121.

[267] Lewis 121.

[268] Lewis 121.

[269] Lewis 126-127.

[270] Lewis 127.

[271] Di Figlia 1.

[272] Di Figlia 1.

[273] Di Figlia 13.

[274] Di Figlia 13.

[275] Di Figlia 13.

[276] Di Figlia 13-14.

[277] Di Figlia 14.

[278] Di Figlia 14.

279 Di Figlia 15.

280 Di Figlia 14.

281 Di Figlia 15.

282 Di Figlia 15-17. See Fritts. The Cedar Lane pastor cited Ghanda Di Figlia as his "Primary Source," and his discussion of the Sharps is succinct and useful, but he deviated from Di Figlia significantly: for example, though he covered Jo Tempi, he eliminated Noel Field from the Unitarian/OSS story.

283 Di Figlia 17.

284 Lathrop was involved in recruiting young progressives for the Unitarians.

285 Di Figlia 17-18.

286 Di Figlia 18.

287 Jeremy Taylor, "UU Roots—The Founding of the Unitarian Service Committee," at jeremytaylor.com for the three knowledgeable UUs from whom Reverend Taylor received the Noel/Fritchman story.

288 Di Figlia 18.

289 Di Figlia 19.

290 Di Figlia 18.

291 Di Figlia 20.

292 Taylor 1.

293 Lewis 127.

294 In bMS 10007-9.

295 Lewis 141.

296 Lewis 133-134 and 141.

297 Chester 18.

298 Chester 19.

299 Chester 18-19.

300 Chester 19.

301 Chester 19.

302 Chester 19.

303 See later.

304 See later.

305 War Refugee Board records include, for example, the Bureau of the Budget; National War Fund budgets; Stephen H. Fritchman; IRRC; USC licenses (4 boxes); USC (2 boxes); Dr. Donald Lowrie, key contact between Dexter, Joy, and Noel Field; National War Fund; Refugee Relief Trustees; War Relief Control Board; and three files on the Office of Strategic Services, the last of three listed as "Strategic Services, Office of," and, as of May, 2003, still CLASSIFIED.

306 See earlier, Brundage's "Statement."

307 Personal e-mail communication from Di Figlia.

308 Lewis 127.

309 Lewis 127; see also Whiting 117. The best summary of the Field's relief work is Di Figlia 22-26.

[310] Lewis 128.

[311] Lewis 128.

[312] Lewis 128.

[313] Lewis 129.

[314] Lewis 129.

[315] Lewis 129.

[316] Field *Trapped* 81.

[317] Lewis 137.

[318] Lewis 139; "communist" spelling found in original.

[319] Lewis 139.

[320] Lewis 139.

[321] Lewis 140.

[322] Lewis 147-148.

[323] Lewis 141.

[324] Lewis 141-142; see also Hersh 109.

[325] Grose 168.

[326] Joseph E. Persico, *CASEY[:] From the OSS to the CIA* (New York: Viking Penguin, 1990) 70-73, 73-75, and 77-78, hereafter cited as Persico *Casey*. Allen Dulles appeared as an important but yet minor character in Persico's Casey story, and Dulles is given no credit for developing an illegals program. Neither Herbert Field nor Noel Field is mentioned in Persico's Casey biography.

[327] Lewis 143.

[328] Hersh 109.

[329] See, for example, Massing 180.

[330] John Chabot Smith, *Alger Hiss [:] The True Story* (New York: Penguin Books, 1977) 101, hereafter cited as Smith *Hiss*.

[331] Grose 589 note # 8.

[332] Herbert Romerstein, "Soviet Archives Confirm Hiss' Guilt," *Human Events* 1/21/94, Vol. 50 Issue 2, hereafter cited as Romerstein "Soviet." Tanenhaus eventually published his book: *Whittaker Chambers: A Biography* (New York: Random House, 1997).

[333] Romerstein "Soviet."

[334] Romerstein "Soviet."

[335] Romerstein "Soviet." The alleged Hungarian document repeated the charges of Hede Massing about Hiss and Field, but no evidence was offered to support the original Massing statements.

[336] Eric Breindel and Herbert Romerstein, "Hiss: Still Guilty," *New Republic* 12/30/96, Vol. 215, Issue 53, hereafter cited as Breindel.

[337] Breindel.

[338] Breindel: "Shipped from Czechoslovakia to Hungary, the hapless Field . . . was used as a 'witness' in the show trial of Hungarian Foreign Minister Lazlo Rajk. Subsequently, Field . . . also provided a 'confession' that served as evidence in the 1952 Slansky trial, an ugly anti-Semitic affair that sent Rudolf Slansky, the General Secretary of the Czechoslovakia

Communist Party, to the gallows." Given all the trumpted-up charges based on Field's dubious testimony, why should his specific statements about Alger Hiss be accepted as truthful?

[339] (New York: Random House, 1997).

[340] (New York: Random House, 1999), hereafter cited as Weinstein *Haunted*.

[341] Weinstein *Haunted*: "[Random House president] Alberto Vitale . . . negotiated an agreement with the KGB's retired agents' group, as a result of which the Russian Foreign Intelligence Service, a KGB successor agency, allowed a small group of Western and Russian scholars . . . access to previously unavailable Soviet intelligence files." (xi) Weinstein and Vassilie also were supported by the Central Intelligence Agency and the National Security Agency. (xii) Left unexplored by at least the American co-author Allen Weinstein, with a distinguished professional resume (403) was to what extent he was manipulated by both former Soviet and present Russian intelligence agents as well as cooperating American intelligence.

[342] Weinstein *Haunted* 4-11, 34-35.

[343] Weinstein *Haunted* 8.

[344] Weinstein *Haunted* on "purges": 89, 153-154, 189, 223.

[345] Later I suggest a motive for John Foster Dulles(Allen's brother)patsying Noel Field as a double agent. See also the website of Alger Hiss's son, Tony: homepages.nyu.edu/~th15.

[346] Sudoplatov 226.

[347] Sudoplatov 227.

[348] Sudoplatov 227.

[349] Sudoplatov 227.

[350] Sudoplatov 227.

[351] Sudoplatov 227.

[352] Sudoplatov 229.

[353] Sudoplatov 229.

[354] Sudoplatov 229.

[355] Sudoplatov 229.

[356] Sudoplatov 229.

[357] Sudoplatov 229; see also 230.

[358] Mosley 311.

[359] Sudoplatov 229.

[360] Sudoplatov 229.

[361] See *INTERCEPT*.

[362] John Chabot Smith, *Alger Hiss[:] The True Story* (New York: Holt, Rinehart and Winston, 1976)143, hereafter cited as Chabot Smith.

[363] Sudoplatov 230.

[364] Sudoplatov 228 footnote #6.

[365] Alger Hiss, *In the Court of Public Opinion* (New York: Alfred A. Knopf, 1997) 52, hereafter cited as Hiss.

[366] Hiss 52.

[367] Lewis 168-180.

[368] Lewis 173.

[369]   Srodes 330.

[370]   Smith 227.

[371]   Smith 227: see also 237: Erika Glaser, Noel Field's adopted daughter, worked at the center of Allen Dulles' manipulation of radical German unions. And see McIntosh 184 and McIntosh's discussion of Glaser's later life and death: 184-187.

[372]   See, for example, Smith 12; see also Srodes for Van Arkel, Goldberg, Erica Glaser, and Emmy Rado: 212 and 310.

[373]   Srodes 330. Not every OSS intelligence agent appreciated Noel Field: see Srodes 360-361. For the same OSS stories, see McIntosh 184.

[374]   Simpson 218, footnote.

[375]   Simpson, see Chapter 4, "Bankers, Lawyers, and Linkage Groups" 43-57, especially Sullivan and Cromwell 46-51, footnote on 56, and 273-274; John Foster Dulles' legal work 48-50; Dulles, United Fruit, and Germany 56 and 329 note #48. See also Simpson 190, beginning "Allen Dulles understood . . . ."

[376]   Heideking 296, the editors' comments.

[377]   Smith 236.

[378]   Smith 236.

[379]   Smith 236.

[380]   Heideking 296: the editors' comment.

[381]   Smith 236.

[382]   Elizabeth P. McIntosh, *Sisterhood of Spies* (Annapolis, Maryland: Naval Institute Press, 1998) 78, hereafter cited as McIntosh.

[383]   Srodes 212.

[384]   Elizabeth P. MacDonald, *Undercover Girl* (New York: The Macmillan Company, 1947) 248, hereafter cited as McDonald.

[385]   MacDonald 249.

[386]   MacDonald 249; see also McIntosh 79-80.

[387]   Heideking 312: editors' comment.

[388]   R. Harris Smith, *OSS* (Berkeley: University of California Press, 1972) 223, hereafter cited as Smith. See also MacDonald 250.

[389]   Smith 223; see also Hersh, 95 and 158: Rado eventually worked with Frank Wisner (158).

[390]   Smith 223.

[391]   MacDonald 251.

[392]   MacDonald 251.

[393]   The Rado action had been called, in fact, "the top-secret 'Crown Jewels' operation . . . ." (Macdonald 251).

[394]   Srodes 310.

[395]   MacDonald 251.

[396]   MacDonald 248.

[397]   MacDonald 251.

[398]   MacDonald 251; see also McIntosh 82-83.

[399]   McIntosh 83.

[400]   Smith 236.

[401]   MacDonald 251.

[402]   See later.

[403]   See, for example, Srodes 258-259.

[404]   Grose 260.

[405]   Heideking 162.

[406]   Heideking 162-171.

[407]   Heideking 162: the editors' comment.

[408]   Though Katz in *Foreign Intelligence* gave no indication OSS Research and Analysis had any interest in examining and exploiting religious and church contacts, the available OSS documents indicate, in fact, extensive contacts and manipulation. See Heideking 97 153, 154-155, 172-176, 237; and for a specific OSS Research and Analysis document on contact with the churches, see 296, 299, 300, 301, 312, and in general 300-317.

[409]   Srodes 258, 259.

[410]   Smith 213. For Dulles' connection to the circle, see Waller 278, for example.

[411]   Srodes 259.

[412]   Srodes 260. The irony of having "only" psyops intelligence value must be remembered when the reader reviews the psychological warfare actions of Allen Dulles, John Foster Dulles, Dwight David Eisenhower, and C. D. Jackson: see Essays Four, Five, and Six.

[413]   Srodes 260.

[414]   Srodes 260.

[415]   J[ohn]. S. Conway, *The Nazi Persecution of the Churches* (New York: Basic Books, Inc., Publishers, 1968) 289, hereafter cited as Conway. See also Conway 289: "it was never proved that any of this circle of high-minded men were actually engaged in the plot . . . ."

[416]   Conway 289.

[417]   Conway 289.

[418]   Srodes 247-248.

[419]   Sudoplatov 223.

[420]   Sudoplatov 225.

[421]   Sudoplatov 225.

[422]   Srodes 248.

[423]   Srodes 248. For Dulles' further involvement with the Circle see Srodes 247-248. For its original inspiration see Waller 72 and 176, and for the Circle's connections, 244. For the Circle's greatest activity, see Waller 280—281, with an extensive list of Kreisau Circle participants, including several German Protestant pastors, on 281, footnote. Two of the seven Circle members charged with plotting Hitler's assassination were hanged: Father Augustin Rosch and Dr. Theodor Haubach: Waller 281, footnote. For the most recently released OSS documents on the "Breakers," see Heideking, Documents # 34, 35, 36. 48. 51, and 61, pp. 191-193, 232, 235, and 273.

[424]   See Katz, throughout: despite the breadth and depth of Katz's well-written history, nothing of the OSS's involvement with religious institutions was examined or even mentioned. For key documents indicating R and A's work in the area, see later.

[425] NA, RG 59, R&A 1655.22 in Heideking 237-240. See also NA, RG 59 R&A No. 2189 in Heideking 323-328.

[426] Barron 117-118; see also Andrew 497-498, and, in general, Chapter 28: "The Penetration and Persecution of the Soviet Churches," 486-507.

[427] Andrew, Chapter 28, 487-507.

[428] See, for example, Andrew 488-489, and personal correspondence with a WCC officer.

[429] See Peter Dale Scott, *The Dallas Conspiracy*, cited in Anson 381 note # 155.

[430] Anson 176; see, for example, 9 H 5.

[431] Philip H. Melanson, *Spy Saga* (New York: Praeger, 1990) 79 (citing Peter Dale Scott, *Dallas Conspiracy*, Chapter 3, page 9), hereafter cited as Melanson.

[432] Mary Bancroft, *Autobiography of a Spy* (New York: William Morrow and Company, 1983) 256, hereafter cited as Bancroft.

[433] Bancroft 256. Niemoeller was much more negative about the post-war future of the "German church" than the OSS, primarily because American intelligence (and the Dulles brothers) viewed the institution as a social and political instrument, while the German theologian thought it should have been measured by the (less pragmatic) canons of religious morality: "He was pessimistic about the revival of the German church and personally thought that 'the spirit of the Nazis' had never been stronger in Germany [AFTER the war], meaning not just the Nazis' political concepts but the whole evil, totalitarian, godless attitude that oversimplified everything and chose violence to achieve its ends."(Bancroft 256)

[434] Bancroft 255.

[435] Lernoux 304.

[436] Grose 255.

[437] Grose 255.

[438] David F. Rudgers, *Creating the Secret State[:] The Origins of the Central Intelligence Agency, 1943-1947* (Lawrence, Kansas: University Press of Kansas, 2000) 90, hereafter cited as Rudgers.

[439] Rudgers 90.

[440] Rudgers 110. For the organization and functioning of the CIG, see Rudgers 110-129.

[441] Rudgers 129.

[442] Rudgers 126.

[443] Rudgers 126.

[444] Rudgers 127.

[445] Corson 281.

[446] Rudgers 149.

[447] Rudgers 150.

[448] Rudgers 166-168.

[449] Rudgers 171-173.

[450] Di Figlia 28.

[451] Di Figlia 28.

[452] Di Figlia 28.

[453] Di Figlia 28.

[454] Di Figlia 28.

455  Di Figlia 28.

456  NA, RG 226, Entry 144, Box 15, Folder P[lanning] G[roup] # 41, "Memorandum . . . to Hugh R. Wilson (OSS Planning Group) . . . . ," dated August 3rd, 1943.

457  Same.

458  Soley 209.

459  Soley 210.

460  Soley 210.

461  Soley 210.

462  Soley 210.

463  Soley 210-211.

464  Soley 211.

465  "Minutes of OSS Inter-Branch Meeting[:] OSS Relations with the CALPO Resistance Group," dated January 10th, 1945, in Heideking 354-360.

466  Editors' comment in Heideking 354.

467  Steven 85.

468  Steven 85.

469  Steven 85.

470  Steven 85.

471  Smith 228. The entire ugly condemnation of Field was repeated in Steven 85.

472  Steven 86.

473  Steven 86; See also Hersh 138-140: though Hersh repeated Schlesinger's anti-Field comments, he reported Dulles' actual use of "Field's people," placing them "ahead of the [Allied] troops . . . in Germany[,] . . . Yugoslavia, Hungary, and Czechoslovakia." (Hersh 139)

474  Steven has reported that Dulles was ready to "settle accounts" with Field (97), but the personal motivation he suggested lacked any real authority. Regardless of Dulles' pride," the spymaster perceived that the "Swiatlo-Field link could be so twisted . . . that through it the Soviet Empire could be torn apart." (Steven 97)

475  See earlier.

476  Steven 89.

477  Steven 89-90.

478  "UUSC [Unitarian Universalist] HISTORY PROJECT]: CIA MATERIALS (in UUSC archives only)" at the files of the Unitarian Universalist Association, 130 Prospect, Cambridge, MA: see four page finding outline developed by Ghanda Di Figlia (at the same address), hereafter cited as UUSC CIA.

479  UUSC CIA.

480  "Minutes of the OSS Inter-Branch Meeting . . ." in Heideking 355.

481  Editors' comment in Heideking 355. A recent study by Patrick K. O'Donnell, Operative, Spies and Saboteurs [:] The Unknown Story of the Men and Women of World War II's OSS (New York: Free Press, 2004), either deliberately or ignorantly attributes the Noel Field operation to "Lieutenant William Casey" of the OSS: "Plan Faust," obviously Field's own successful infiltration plan: see 246 and 262.

482  Field *Trapped* 14-15.

[483] Lewis 174.

[484] Lewis 173.

[485] Lewis 173.

[486] CIA report cited in Di Figlia 51.

[487] Quoted in Di Figlia 51.

[488] Lewis 174-175.

[489] Lewis 175.

[490] Lewis 175.

[491] Lewis 175. "Jo Tempi came to the United States on a speaking tour, and because of her previous membership in the German Communist Party, the FBI followed her." (Fritts 4) The Bureau claimed Tempi was "sexually involved with . . . Dr. Charles Joy." Denying all accusations, Joy was still fired by the Unitarian board in August, 1946. (Fritts 4)

[492] Di Figlia 50.

[493] Di Figlia 28.

[494] Lewis 176.

[495] Lewis 177.

[496] Lewis 178.

[497] Lewis 178.

[498] Lewis 178.

[499] Alexander and Helene Rado are, of course, not Allen Dulles' Emmy Rado and her husband: on Emmy Rado, see earlier. "Rado" is a not-uncommon Hungarian family name, and the husbands may have been related.

[500] David J. Dallin, *Soviet Espionage* (New Haven: Yale University Press, 1955 ("Third Printing, March, 1964") 314, hereafter cited as Dallin.

[501] Dallin 314.

[502] Dallin 314.

[503] Dallin 314.

[504] Dallin 314: see Dallin 314-315 for the latter part of Helene Rado's story.

[505] Di Figlia 35-37.

[506] Lewis 178-179.

[507] Lewis 179-180.

[508] Lewis 180.

[509] Lewis 180.

[510] Robert J. Lamphere and Tom Shachtman, *The FBI-KGB War* (New York: Random House, 1987) 57, cited hereafter as Lamphere.

[511] From "About the Authors" in Lamphere 321.

[512] See *INTERCEPT*.

[513] *New York Times* obituary, February 11, 2002, by Douglas Martin.

[514] Srodes 436. Srodes added some dubious commentary on Lamphere's reputed success, including, for example, identifying Alger Hiss as a spy, "confirmed by subsequent probes." (436) Lamphere's *New York Times* obituary of February 11, 2002, devoted most of its memorial

to Lamphere's reported Venona achievements but omitted any mention of Lamphere's illegal mail interception program.

515 Sudoplatov 218.

516 See, for example, Lamphere 53.

517 Massing repeated her charges in a Canadian *KGB Connection* video without offering any documentary support for her accusations.

518 Lewis 180.

519 Lewis 180.

520 Lewis 197.

521 Lewis 201; see also 238.

522 Field *Trapped* 366.

523 See later.

524 See later.

525 Stewart Steven, *Operation Splinter Factor* (Philadelphia and New York: J.B. Lippincott Company, 1974), for Swiatlo's official early biography 40-46, hereafter cited as Steven.

Steven is the primary and most reliable source for "Operation Splinter Factor." Though he has cited Flora Lewis (Steven 227) as his initial "springboard," it is more likely he was first alerted to the Field/Swiatlo story by at least one member of British intelligence. Though referred to throughout his text, British/English intelligence and its Secret Intelligence Service (SIS) are NOT indexed; SIS Captain Michael Sullivan IS indexed (249): see 34-39 and 49-56. Steven identified "four distinct categories of sources" (229) for his Operation Splinter Factor history: former CIA members (229-230); former operatives of East European security and military services who defected (230); East European government officials (230); and "Current employees of government and governmental organizations in the West." (230) This last "source" is curious, because it is made up mainly of British intelligence, as a close reading of Steven throughout verifies.

Because of its British intelligence sources, Steven's account is accurate but also marked by disinformation. For the disinformation side: British intelligence's negative attitude toward Allen Dulles; for accuracy, Frank Wisner's (and possibly Kim Philby's) connection to the Field/Swialto story (see later).

Jozef Swiatlo, who initially established a British counterintelligence link but was sent to American intelligence by British SIS (see later), was contacted by Steven (230) and apparently agreed (at least initially) with Steven's Operation Splinter Factor analysis. (230) But Swiatlo "corrected my original information—that this [Splinter Factor operation] was a British rather than an American operation." (230) Though Steven apparently accepted Swiatlo's statement, the story still strongly suggested that a British/American counterintelligence cabal was responsible. Steven gave one extremely significant clue, admitting that "the [British SIS officer] Sullivan material [actually] came from a former employee of the CIA who was on the inside track of Operation Splinter Factor from its very beginnings and who personally knew Sullivan." (234)

Jozef Swiatlo's biography, reasonably detailed in Steven (40-46), might by absolutely accurate (that is, well recounted from Steven's sources) and still be a work of "illegal" fiction, constructed on the early record of a Jozef Swiatlo who died and whose identity was then constructed and given to an intelligence agent (American or Soviet) who became "Swialto."

[526] See George Michael Evica, A *Cold Solidarity*, a work in progress.

[527] Blum 59.

[528] Blum 59.

[529] Blum 59.

[530] Steven 35 and 46.

[531] Steven 49.

[532] Steven 51.

[533] Steven 51.

[534] Steven 51-52.

[535] Steven 52.

[536] Steven 52.

[537] Berman was also a friend of Quaker/Unitarian/OSS operative Noel Field (see later).

[538] Steven 53.

[539] Steven 52-53.

[540] Steven 54.

[541] Steven 54.

[542] Steven 54-55.

[543] Steven 55.

[544] Steven 56.

[545] Blum 59.

[546] Blum 59.

[547] Blum 59.

[548] Steven 65.

[549] Srodes 417.

[550] Srodes 417; see also 416-417.

[551] Smith 25.

[552] Smith 25.

[553] Smith 26.

[554] Smith 26.

[555] Smith 25, footnote.

[556] Ambrose *Spies* 168.

[557] Ambrose *Spies* 168.

[558] Srodes 416-417.

[559] Field *Trapped* 417.

[560] Field *Trapped* 106.

[561] Field *Trapped* 106.

[562] Field *Trapped* 417.

[563] Field *Trapped* 417.

564  One murky source reported that Anna Duracz, Berman's secretary, who coincidentally had been Field's secretary in Switzerland, "agreed to transmit a letter from Field to Berman asking him to facilitate contacts with Russians . . . ." Swiatlo gained possession of a copy of the letter, and was able to compromise both Berman and Field. In Wifred Burchett, *At the Barricades* (New York: Times Books, 1981) 149, hereafter cited as Burchett. The letter may have been an intelligence invention: Duracz was probably working for either Dulles, Swiatlo, or both.

565  Steven 91.

566  Steven 103-104.

567  Blum 60: the extraordinary, infrastructered complications of the Swiatlo/Dulles/Field story are summarized in Blum 60-61. See especially "Operation Splinter Factor" in Blum 354-355 note # 2.

568  Hersh 390-391.

569  Saunders 40.

570  Mosely 272.

571  Mosely 272.

572  Mosely 273-275 and Simpson 92-94. For a softer version of Wisner's relationship to Gehlen but still informative, see Smith 240.

573  Mosely 275.

574  Mosely 275.

575  Simpson 44.

576  Saunders 41.

577  Mosely 273.

578  Blum 59.

579  Mosely 276 and 510; see also Saunders 167-168.

580  Mosley 276.

581  Saunders 167.

582  Smith 126, footnote.

583  Srodes 413. Dulles' biographers have attempted to minimize the spymaster's counterintelligence and political duplicity, but Allen was agreeable to Glaser working with the OSS's labor movement operatives in Germany, despite the high probability that he learned from Field about Erika's Swiss Communist connections; see, for example, Mosely 172. See also Burchett 148-149.

584  Mosely 510: Mosley's British intelligence source for the Wisner/Field story did not wish to be identified (510).

585  Mosely 275-276.

586  Mosely 276.

587  Mosley 276.

588  Grose 303.

589  Grose 303.

590  Compare Grose 303.

[591] Field *Trapped*: on Erica 144; on Swiatlo'a arrest of Hermann 364; on Herta's arrest, etc. 142, 363, 366, and 369; on Swiatlo's interviews of both Noel Field and Herta Field 366. Before Herta Field herself went to Europe to find her husband Noel, she had asked his brother Hermann to investigate Noel's disappearance (4 and 19), citing "complexities" and the Hiss trial for not going to American authorities for assistance. (19) Though scattered throughout the book, Kate and Hermann's commentary on their own work, their disbelief in Noel's substantive spying for Dulles, and their minimization of Hermann's curious history all suggested the strong possibility Hermann Field was also involved, no matter how minimal, in intelligence activity. Kate Field had been working in British refugee work in 1938 (122) when she met Hermann. Though he had no experience in refugee service, he agreed to become involved at Kate's request (122-123) and was remarkably successful (123), assisting displaced and threatened people to enter Great Britain. (418) Hermann's possible intelligence connections can be reviewed on 4, 167-169, 69-72, and 157, for example. Though Herman asserted he did not believe Noel's intelligence links to the OSS (109), he allowed that Noel could very well have been a spy. (171) Kate and Hermann Field dismissed Operation Splinter Factor (that is, the plot using Swiatlo and Noel Field to destabilize Communist Eastern Europe), but their conclusion concerning the functions of the purge trials is precisely the same as mine. (See 415-417) The curious "Afterward" written by Stanford professor Norman M. Naimark (who was apparently responsible for getting Stanford University Press to publish the book) cited Flora Lewis's *Red Pawn* and *The Haunted Wood* for information on Noel Field, but nothing else, yet Naimark went beyond Kate and Hermann Field in examining Hermann's refugee work (420) and the "similarities" between Hermann and Noel. (420) Professor Naimark descended into absurdity by asserting that Noel Field used Allen Dulles. (421) While rejecting the Swiatlo story (423-424) and Field's involvement in a plot to destabilize Eastern Europe, the professor did at least admit that Noel Field "was friendly with the likes of Allen Dulles . . ." (423), a considerable understatement.

[592] Hungarian intelligence had intercepted and reviewed Allen Dulles' radio communications that probably included reports on his meetings with Max Egon von Hohenlohe in an attempt to establish a peace separate from the Soviets; since the Soviets had penetrated Allied intelligence and were aware of Dulles negotiating with the Nazis (Simpson 122-124, 124-125, and 347-348 note #23), the Hungarians and Soviets may indeed have believed Dulles was a traitor to the Allied/Soviet war effort. It was no secret among international cognoscenti that Allen and John Foster Dulles were "two of the more influential advocates of separate peace tactics in elite U.S. circles." (Simpson 121)

[593] Mosely 276.

[594] See, for example, Grose 302.

[595] Mosely 277.

[596] Whiting 228.

[597] Whiting 228. Hermann and Kate Field (Noel Field's brother and sister-in-law) did not accept the argument that the CIA, through Swiatlo and Noel Field, catalyzed the Eastern Europe purges, but their conclusions as to the trials' intent and outcome were identical to those here presented: see Field *Trapped* 110-111.

598  Grose 302.

599  Steven 104.

600  Steven 106.

601  Srodes 414.

602  Srodes 414.

603  Srodes 414.

604  Srodes 414.

605  Massing 180.

606  Hersh 387.

607  Srodes 414.

608  Srodes 415.

609  Steven 9.

610  Steven 9.

611  Lewis 206-258.

612  Saunders 130.

613  Saunders 130-134.

614  Mosley 276.

615  Mosely 276.

616  Simpson 264. See Essay Six for C.D. Jackson's key role in the Radio Free Europe/Radio Liberty psyops program.

617  RFE/RL, Polish Unit, Files Concerning Polish Defectors and Redefectors, 1955-1983, Preliminary Inventory of Ponds 300, Records of the Radio Free Europe/Radio Liberty Research Institute, Series 7. In the Open Society Archives at Central European University: see website.

618  Hersh 391.

619  Field *Trapped*.

620  Letter from Deputy Director of Plans, CIA, to Director J. Edgar Hoover, FBI, "Attention: Mr. S. J. Papich," "SUBJECT: Noel FIELD," the date: December 20th, 1954. The letter reported that Jules Humbert-Droz, a "prominent Social Democrat," had "enrolled Field in the Swiss Communist Party." Humbert-Droz was less than a reliable source, "described [in the letter's report] as the President of the illegal Swiss Communist Party during the War." Because several passages in this letter have been censored, Swiatlo may very well have been referred to.

621  Simpson 290.

622  Simpson 288.

623  See Essay Five.

624  I have been advised by several American clergy that the Episcopal/OSS/CIA nexus was "well-known."

625  Maryland Diocesan Archives site, "About the Archivist," hereafter cited as Ranney.

626  Ranney.

627  Ranney.

628  Bobby R. Inman, "Spying for a Long, Hot War, *New York Times*, October 9, 2001.

629  Ranney.

[630] Ranney.

[631] Ranney.

[632] Ranney.

[633] Ranney.

[634] The CIA could have been protecting any number of Unitarians, but chiefly among them would have been Eliot, Percival Flack Brundage, and James Luther Adams.

[635] Hereafter cited as Brooks.

[636] Jeffrey-Jones 71.

[637] See earlier.

[638] UUSC History Archives, DRAWER THREE, Row 1, [Topic] "6. UNITARIAN SERVICE COMMITTEE—CHARGES AGAINST": [Subtopic Two:] "Central Intelligence Agency Papers: retrieved by UUSC in 1978 through Freedom of Information Act[.]" This subtopic is then organized into eight files: A, B, and 1. through 6. File A is [UUSC] "Correspondence with CIA, 1978, 1983"; File B is "Guide to CIA." Hereafter cited as UUSC History Archives.

[639] UUSC History Archives.

[640] UUSC History Archives.

[641] UUSC History Archives.

[642] UUSC History Archives.

[643] UUSC History Archives.

[644] UUSC History Archives.

[645] UUSC History Archives.

[646] UUSC History Archives.

[647] UUSC History Archives.

[648] Discussed below.

[649] UUSC History Archives.

[650] UUSC History Archives.

[651] In 27 boxes, the bMS 16007 files are reasonably organized. In the following brief review of those boxes, when I indicate I found nothing of relevance or value, I refer only to my research topic, including American intelligence's misuse of religious groups and individuals. I do not intend to minimize the great value these documents have for a future history of the heroic refugee efforts of the Unitarians and Universalists.

The file folders in the 27 boxes are organized from "A" through "Z," but each letter does not have its own box.

Box 1: nothing.

Box 2: most interesting are the folders of files of/on the American Friends Service Committee ("Quakers"), 1942-1945, covering Jews and seven European nations; 1945 American Unitarian Association files, including Frederick May Eliot and Stephen Fritchman; and the American Unitarian Youth.

Box 3: most interesting are the American Unitarian Association/New York Regional Headquarters files for 1945.

Boxes 4 and 5: nothing.

Boxes 6 and 7: most interesting in both boxes is Unitarian correspondence, 1941-1945. The correspondence in Box 7 is carefully organized by letter, A though Z, but key sets of correspondence for several letters appear later under their own letters (given the alphabetical order running through the 27 boxes): Dexter correspondence, for example, appears separately in Box 8. Box 7 also has two interesting files, both titled "Cuba, Visas, 1941-1945."

Box 8: most interesting is Robert Dexter's correspondence, 1942-1945. Box 8 is devoted to letters "D" and "E," but Frederick May Eliot's correspondence and memos are absent.

Box 9: most interesting and extremely important are the Noel Field folders, filled with correspondence, cables, notes, diary materials, etc. Though not identified by the finding document for bMS 16007, Robert Dexter is also represented in Box 9.

Boxes 10 through 22: nothing.

Boxes 23 and 24: In the finding file, apparently communications to and from Geneva, Switzerland, 1945-1947. But these boxes are extremely important, preserving in immense supportive detail the relations between Noel Field, Robert Dexter, Charles Joy, Herta Field, and (implicitly) the OSS and Allen Dulles. Noel Field's hundreds of cables (and letters) are vital both for a future history of Unitarian refugee work and as substantive support for the OSS/USC intelligence collaboration. Given the flow of information from Field and other onsite refugee workers through the OSS pouch transmission line to Unitarian Service Committee headquarters in Lisbon, these cables (and letters) definitively verify the substantial intelligence value Allen Dulles and the OSS received.

Boxes 24, 25, and 26: nothing.

Box 27: most interesting is a 1945 World Council of Churches file.

The contents of bMS 16007 hold The Unitarian Service Committee's Executive Director's Central Administrative Subject Files called "Box 1." But it is, in fact, only one box of eighteen files. The finding document lists "Box 1" as "-A-": but it is the only letter of the alphabet given and it is without referential value.

Eight of the 18 folders are of potential value, but none contain relevant material on Albert Schweitzer College, the Unitarian Service Committee, or American Intelligence.

[652] Thirteen Unitarian Service Committee documents (a total of 98 single-spaced pages) preserved in bMS 16007 covering 1942 through 1946 clearly illustrate the value of Unitarian Service Committee material to the Office of Strategic Services. The documents detail the field work of Robert Dexter, Charles Joy, and Noel and Herta Field. Dexter and the Fields (and most probably Joy) worked directly with the Office of Strategic Services and Allen Dulles. With permission, they have been copied and are in the possession of the author.

[653] UUSC History Archives.

[654] UUSC History Archives.

[655] UUSC History Archives.

[656] UUSC History Archives. See earlier extensive discussion of Noel Field.

[657] UUSC History Archives.

[658] UUSC History Archive.

[659] UUSC History Archive.

660  Email to the author dated 5/17/2001.

661  Walter Donald Kring edited the papers of Frederick May Eliot, bMS 00378, Andover-Harvard
     Divinity School Library. The last paragraph has drawn heavily on Kring's "A Few Comments
     on the Contents of the . . . Eliot A.U.A. Presidential Papers" preceding the listing of the Eliot
     correspondence helping document.

662  The United States Agency for International Development (AID) has been widely suspected of
     collusion with the CIA; see, for example, A. J. Langguth, *Hidden Terrors* (New York: Pantheon
     Books, 1978), 120, 138, 232, and AID's "police advisory program," suspected of having close
     ties to the Agency: 35, 120, 125, 138, and 300.
     "In the late 60 s the U.S. Agency for International Development [AID] contracted with the
     UUSC [the Unitarian Universalist Service Committee] to run a social work education project
     in Vietnam. Reports that the Central Intelligence Agency was infiltrating private agencies
     working in Vietnam on AID contracts alarmed opponents. In May 1969 a group of divinity
     students staged a sit-in at UUSC for five days, protesting . . . . When the contract with AID
     ended in 1971[,] the UUSC withdrew from the controversial project." Roger Fritts, sermon
     on February 9, 1997, on website.

663  Eliot is one of two most likely candidates for the protected OSS/CIA asset or agent among
     the Unitarians; Essay Eight (below), reviews the second. It is not impossible, of course, that
     both candidates were, in fact, being protected: one dead, one still alive at the time of the
     transmission of the sanitized OSS records.

664  Hans A. Schmitt, *Quakers and Nazis[:] Inner Light and Outer Darkness* (Columbia, Missouri and
     London: University of Missouri Press, 1997) 4; hereafter cited as Schmitt.

665  Schmitt 4.

666  Schmitt 4.

667  Schmitt 17.

668  Schmitt 32-33.

669  Schmitt 33.

670  Schmitt 23.

671  Schmitt 61.

672  Schmitt 61.

673  Schmitt 62. See also William R. Hughes, *Indomitable Friend[:] The Life of Corder Catchpool*
     (London: Housmans, 1964) 85 and 91, hereafter cited as Hughes.

674  Schmitt 63; see also Hughes 91-92.

675  Schmitt 64. See also Hughes 93: Catchpool spent more than two years attempting to book
     a lecture tour for Colin Ross, a German writer and traveler and the brother of a German
     Quaker whom Catchpool had aided. (Hughes 93) But Ross was also "an ardent Nazi . . . who
     believed that Sir Oswald Mosley was destined to be the British Fuhrer . . . ." (Hughes 93) As
     Hughes dryly commented: "a series of lectures given by him in England would certainly not
     have served the [Catchpool] cause of reconciliation." (Hughes 93)

676  Schmitt 66.

677  Schmitt 69.

678  Schmitt 71.

[679]  Schmitt 71.

[680]  Schmitt 73.

[681]  Schmitt 89.

[682]  Schmitt 89; see 89-94.

[683]  Schmitt 95.

[684]  David Chidester, *Christianity[:] A Global History* (San Francisco: HarperSan Francisco, 2000) 502, hereafter cited as Chidester.

[685]  Chidester 502. See also the splendid historical and analytical study, J[ohn]. S. Conway, *The Nazi Persecution of the Churches* (New York: Basic Books, Inc., Publishers, 1968): for the "Confessing Church," see the Index 466; for "German Christians," see the Index 467; and see "Concordat," Index 466. Though beyond the focus of my own study, Conway's work is both precise and moving; anyone interested in the complexity of the terrible time in Germany must see Conway on the following topics: documents xi; Nazi subversion of the German churches xiii; the struggle of the churches xiii-xviii; the destruction of the churches 328; faith and conspiracy 329; the fatal weakening 329; the stressful mixed record of the Nazis and the Germans 329-332; the "four factors" helping to explain the German Christian failure to oppose Hitler 332-337; the reawakening (as of 1968) 337; and the Christian anti-Nazi heroes 338. I realize this full citation repeats an earlier full citation: the Conway text deserves the duplication.

[686]  Schmitt 96.

[687]  Schmitt 96; see also Chidester 501-506.

[688]  Jonathan Glover, *Humanity[:] A Moral History of the Twentieth Century* (New Haven and London: Yale University Press, 2000) 381-390, hereafter cited as Glover.

[689]  Schmitt 111. "Just how and why Albert and Anne Martin . . . were chosen, remains a mystery." (Schmitt 111) But Albert Martin himself is a special mystery, suggesting he may have been involved in Allied intelligence activities: see Schmitt 111-114.

[690]  Schmitt 165.

[691]  Schmitt 165; see also Hughes 93.

[692]  Schmitt 165-166; see also Hughes 79-80, for example.

[693]  Schmitt 165.

[694]  Schmitt 113.

[695]  Schmitt 168-169.

[696]  Schmitt 172.

[697]  Hughes 95.

[698]  Hughes 185. This Catchpool peace-making, however, had its bizarre aspect; with the world about to discover the breadth and depth of the crimes against humanity committed by the Nazis, Catchpool wrote and spoke "to remind people of the 'forgotten Germany,' the Germany of romantic idealism, love of nature, simple piety, philosophy, poetry and music." (Hughes 185) All of this nostalgia for an earlier Germany was, like John Foster Dulles' concern for moral righteousness and German industry, "to show how inconsistent with the Christian way a retributive peace would be." (Hughes 185)

[699]  Schmitt 207.

700   Schmitt 207.
701   Schmitt 216; see also Hughes 79 and 85.
702   According to Schmitt (216), Catchpool had a change of heart, realizing he ought not to take sides in what was essentially a German "civil war." (Schmitt 216) Of course, Catchpool's apparent reversal might well have been dictated by a branch of Allied intelligence.
703   Catchpool's humanitarian dedication, his persistence in peace-making, his Quaker spirituality, have all been movingly attested to by William R. Hughes, his close friend. (Hughes 187-233)

# Notes: Essay Five

1 Hersh 24.

2 Silk 11.

3 Silk 12.

4 Silk 12.

5 Silk 11.

6 Silk 11.

7 Silk 12.

8 Silk 13, 14.

9 Silk 14.

10 Silk 15.

11 Silk 15.

12 Though Lippman was Jewish, he was perfectly attuned to the Protestant/Establishment consciousness of Harvard.

13 Silk 17.

14 Silk 19.

15 Silk 19.

16 Silk 20.

17 Silk 20.

18 The Silks ignored Yale's incredible national and international influence; see 18, for example, where Yale is listed as the first of a number of cultural institutions not covered by the Silks. See Yale, throughout, but especially McGeorge Bundy [Yale]) 49, where no CIA connections are given, and William Bundy 205-206, where no relevant Yale connections are given.

19 See Antony C. Sutton, *America's Secret Establishment* (Billings, Montana: Liberty House Press, 1986), hereafter cited as Sutton. Though occasionally marked by conservative bias, Sutton's work is more relevant to an extended close study of the American Establishment and the National Security State than the Silks. See especially Sutton 36-46, where Sutton places the Council on Foreign Relations, the Trilateral Commission, and several other important Establishment organizations in their proper relationship to what Sutton has called "The Order." See also Sutton's excellent summary of the major influence of the Bundy family (Yale and Skull & Bones) 47-52, and contrast it with the Silks deliberately minimizing both McGeorge and William Bundy's Yale connections: Silks 49 and 205-206.

[20]   Townsend Hoopes, *The Devil and John Foster Dulles* (Boston: Little, Brown and Company, 1973) 9, cited hereafter as Hoopes.

[21]   Hoopes 10.

[22]   Hoopes 10.

[23]   Hoopes 9.

[24]   Hoopes 9-10.

[25]   Hoopes 10.

[26]   Hoopes 10. See also Ronald W. Pruesson, *John Foster Dulles* (New York: The Free Press, 1982) 3-4 and 8 for a relatively sympathetic commentary on these early religious experiences, hereafter cited as Pruessen.

[27]   Hoopes 11. The best examination Dulles' character and actions (with an excellent bibliography) is Michael A. Gulin, *John Foster Dulles[:] A Statesman and His Times* (New York: Columbia University Press, 1972), hereafter cited as Gulin. Gulin intelligently reviews the "religious" influences on Dulles, 12-15, including the 1924 Presbyterian conflict, 14-15, and Dulles' involvement, 15.

[28]   Hoopes 17-21.

[29]   Hoopes 21.

[30]   Hoopes 21.

[31]   Hoopes 21.

[32]   Hoopes 21.

[33]   Hoopes 22.

[34]   Hoopes 22-23.

[35]   Hoopes 23.

[36]   Hoopes 24.

[37]   Hoopes 24.

[38]   Hoopes 25.

[39]   Hoopes 25-28.

[40]   Hoopes 25.

[41]   Hoopes 26.

[42]   Hoopes 26.

[43]   Hoopes 26.

[44]   Hoopes 26.

[45]   Hoopes 26.

[46]   Hoopes 26.

[47]   Hoopes 27-28.

[48]   Hoopes 28.

[49]   Hoopes 28.

[50]   Hoopes 28.

[51]   Hoopes 28.

[52]   Hoopes 28.

[53]   Hoopes 28.

[54]   Hoopes 28.

55    Hoopes 28.

56    Hoopes 28.

57    Hoopes 29.

58    Hoopes 29.

59    Hoopes 28-32.

60    Hoopes 31.

61    Hoopes 28-32.

62    Hoopes 33.

63    Hoopes 33-34.

64    Hoopes 34.

65    Hoopes 34; for the deaths, see Hoopes 33-34 and James Goold-Adams, *John Foster Dulles: A Reappraisal* (Westport, CT: Greenwood Press, Publishers, 23-24, hereafter cited as Goold-Adams.

66    Hoopes 40.

67    Hoopes 40.

68    Hoopes 40.

69    Hoopes 43-45.

70    On Avery's "rebellion," see Hoopes 44-45.

71    Hoopes 44.

72    Lorenzo Albacete, "Divine Promotion," *New York Times Magazine* February 11, 2001, 27, hereafter cited as Albacete.

73    Hoopes 44.

74    Hoopes 44-45.

75    Albacete.

76    Hoopes 35.

77    See, for example, Hoopes 50.

78    Hoopes 35.

79    Hoopes 35.

80    Albacete.

81    Albacete.

82    Albacete.

83    Herbert S. Parmet, *Eisenhower and the American Crusades* (New York: The Macmillan Company, 1972) 186, hereafter cited as Parmet *Eisenhower*.

84    Parmet *Eisenhower* 186.

85    Goold-Adams 300.

86    Goold-Adams 287; see also Parmet *Eisenhower*: "Dulles was a strong Presbyterian" (186). Presbyterians ought to register a strong objection to being associated with so un-Christian a character as John Foster Dulles.

87    Goold-Adams 4.

88    Goold-Adams 4.

89    Goold-Adams 5.

90    Goold-Adams 5.

[91]   Goold-Adams 5.

[92]   Goold-Adams 6.

[93]   Hoopes 35.

[94]   Andrew H. Berding, *Dulles on Diplomacy* (Princeton, New Jersey: D. Van Nostrand Company, Inc., 1965) 161, hereafter cited as Berding.

[95]   Berding 161.

[96]   Hoopes 35.

[97]   John Robinson Beal, *John Foster Dulles* (New York: Harper & Brothers, 1957) 87, hereafter cited as Beal.

[98]   Beal 87.

[99]   Beal 87.

[100]  Beal 87.

[101]  Gerard Colby with Charlotte Dennett, *Thy Will Be Done[:] The Conquest of the Amazon: Nelson Rockefeller and Evangelism in the Age of Oil* (New York: HarperCollins Publishers, 1995) 13, hereafter cited as Colby.

[102]  Colby 15; see also 20-22.

[103]  Colby 45; 109; 122-123; 126; and throughout. See also Myer Kutz, *Rockefeller Power* (New York: Simon and Schuster, 1974) 22-26, 39-41, hereafter cited as Kutz.

[104]  Colby 291-292.

[105]  Colby 293.

[106]  Colby 293-294.

[107]  Beal 87.

[108]  Beal 88.

[109]  Beal 88.

[110]  See Hoopes, index, "China," 543.

[111]  See, for example, the ties between Standard Oil, Sullivan and Cromwell, the CIA, and Chase Manhattan Bank: Blum 75.

[112]  Beal 89.

[113]  Beal 89.

[114]  Beal 89.

[115]  Beal 89.

[116]  Hoopes 50.

[117]  Hoopes 51.

[118]  Hoopes 50-53.

[119]  Albacete.

[120]  Gulin 117; see also 120-121, 121-122, and 124.

[121]  Hoopes 51.

[122]  Louis L. Gerson, *John Foster Dulles* (New York: Cooper Square Publishers, Inc, 1967) 18-19, hereafter cited as Gerson.

[123]  Gulin 39.

[124]  Gulin 39.

[125]  Hoopes 51.

[126] Hoopes 51.

[127] Hoopes 51.

[128] Beal 89.

[129] Beal 89.

[130] Beal 89.

[131] Hoopes 51.

[132] Mosely 96.

[133] Pruessen 188.

[134] *The Spiritual Legacy of John Foster Dulles*, ed. Henry Van Dusen (Philadelphia: The Westminster Press, 1960) 89, hereafter cited as Van Dusen; see also Gerson 18.

[135] Gerson 18.

[136] Van Dusen 145.

[137] Gerson 18.

[138] Gerson 18.

[139] Gerson 18.

[140] Gerson 18.

[141] Mosely 97.

[142] Gerson 19; see also I. F. Stone, *The Haunted Fifties* (New York: Random House, 1963), "John Foster Dulles: Portrait of a Liberator," 12-16, especially 12-13 and 13-15.

[143] Hoopes 51.

[144] Hoopes 51-52.

[145] Silk 195.

[146] Hoopes 51; Beal 89.

[147] See especially Silk 195-199.

[148] Ferdinand Lundberg, *The Rockefeller Syndrome* (Secaucus, New Jersey: Lyle Stuart Inc., 1975) 297-305, hereafter cited as Lundberg.

[149] Gulin 48; Beal 90.

[150] Goold-Adams 31.

[151] Goold-Adams 31.

[152] Beal 90.

[153] Beal 90.

[154] Beal 91.

[155] Beal 91.

[156] Beal 91.

[157] Beal 91.

[158] Beal 91.

[159] Pruessen 188.

[160] Pruessen 188. The Coffin argument for ethical and moral support of the Allies is summarized in Pruessen 188-189.

[161] Introduction [no given author], in F. W. Sollmann, *Religion and Politics* (Wallingford, Pennsylvania: Pendle Hill Pamphlets, 1941 [not given in the publication] 3, body of text hereafter cited as Sollman.

[162]  Sollman 4.

[163]  Sollman 4.

[164]  Sollman 4.

[165]  Sollman 4.

[166]  Sollman 59-60. See also Sollman on the "moral force in politics," 61, "Christianity," 62 and 8, and what it meant to become a "revolutionist": "To become wiser." 24.

[167]  Beal 92.

[168]  Beal 92.

[169]  Beal 92.

[170]  Beal 93.

[171]  Beal 93.

[172]  Editors' comment, in Heideking 168.

[173]  Hooft memorandum to Allen Dulles, December, 1943, in Heideking 168: see earlier documentation.

[174]  Van Dusen 231-232.

[175]  Van Dusen ix.

[176]  Van Dusen 5-228.

[177]  Van Dusen xviii-xx.

[178]  Van Dusen xix.

[179]  Van Dusen 106.

[180]  Van Dusen 106.

[181]  Van Dusen 106.

[182]  Van Dusen 101.

[183]  Van Dusen 101.

[184]  Gerson 18-19. Dulles was the U.S.'s major negotiator of a 1951 treaty that "sought to eliminate any possibility of [Japanese] war reparations." Steven C. Clemons, "recovering Japan's Wartime Past—and Ours," *New York Times*, September 4, 2001, A23: Dulles was able to establish "a deliberate forgetfulness whose consequences haunt us today."

[185]  Ronald W. Pruessen sympathetically charted Dulles' Christian/moral/ethical positions and principles (187-191, 192-193, 199, 205-206, 261, 303, 324, 350, 389-390) but could not discover more than Christian generalizations and clichés.

[186]  Hoopes 37. Walter LaFeber, *America, Russia, and the Cold War[,]1945-1990* (New York: McGraw-Hill, Inc., 1991) traced Neibuhr's shifting political positions that were always in support of the dominant establishment morality: see 46-48, 62, 63, 78, 122, 130-134, 190, and 334-336.

[187]  Blum 5: see Blum 345 note #12.

[188]  I.F. Stone, *The Truman Era* (New York: Monthly Review Press, 1953) 124: the essay itself, 124-125, hereafter cited as Stone *Truman*.

[189]  Stone *Truman* 124.

[190]  Stone *Truman* 125.

[191]  Stone *Truman* 125.

[192]  Edited by the author from the King James Version of the New Testament.

[193]  John Lewis Gaddis, *Strategies of Containment* (Oxford and New York: Oxford University Press, 1982) 131, hereafter cited as Gaddis *Strategies*.

[194]  Gaddis *Strategies* 131.

[195]  Gaddis *Strategies* 133.

[196]  Gaddis *Strategies* 132.

[197]  John Foster Dulles, *War Or Peace* (New York: The Macmillan Company, 1950) 87, hereafter cited as Dulles *War*.

[198]  Dulles *War* 87: the entire chapter, 74-87, but especially 87, must be examined closely for clear evidence of Dulles' incredible use of Christianity as a "liberating" force.

[199]  Brands 15.

[200]  Brands 16.

[201]  Brands 16.

[202]  Brands 17.

[203]  Brands 17.

[204]  Brands 18.

[205]  Brands 8.

[206]  Pruesson 500, 502-503, 504, and 505.

[207]  Pruessen 506. For a brilliant commentary and analysis on Foster Dulles' "religiosity," consult Joel Kovel, *Red Hunting in the Promised Land* (New York: BasicBooks, 1994). Kovel's judgment of Foster Dulles' ranting (65), moralizing (65), clamor (65), "madness" (66), "cunning" (66), "craft" (66), "bombast" (66), "threat" (66), "compromise" (66), and "nuance" (66), is accurate. See Kovel's sharp and cogent examination of Dulles' Old Testament posture, his argument for Christianity and Western imperialism, his so-called morality, his Aristotelian/ Augustinian splitting of absolute good and evil, and Dulles' Revelations/Apocalyptic view of the world (76, 85).

[208]  Justin Lewis, Constructing Public Opinion (New York: Columbia University Press, 2001) 153: see Lewis' extended commentary 153 154, hereafter cited as Lewis.

[209]  *Cold War Rhetoric[:] Strategy, Metaphor, and Ideology*, eds. Martin J. Medhurst, Robert L. Ivie, Philip Wander, and Robert L. Scott (New York/Westport, CT/London: Greenwood Press, 1990, hereafter cited as *Cold War*.

[210]  *Cold War*: see Philip Wander, "Political Rhetoric and the Un-American Tradition" 185-200 and "The Rhetoric of American Foreign Policy" 153-184, hereafter cited as Wander.

[211]  Wander 157.

[212]  Wander 157.

[213]  Wander 157.

[214]  Wander 157-158.

[215]  Wander 158.

[216]  Wander 158.

[217]  Wander 158.

[218]  Wander 158-160.

[219]  See Essay Six for an extended examination of the most probable candidate having such a major influence on Eisenhower.

[220] See Essay Six.

[221] Wander 162.

[222] Wander 161.

[223] Hoopes 491.

[224] Hoopes 488.

[225] Hoopes 487-491. The American nation finally united with John Foster Dulles in his pragmatic and spiritually-empty religiosity: see, for example, Charles C. Alexander, *Holding the Line [:] The Eisenhower Era[,] 1952-1961* (Bloomington, Indiana: Indiana University Press, 1975) 135-137. But Alexander also pointed out the parallel and directly-related explosion of "radical sectarianism" (137), an evangelistic expansion that by 1958 counted more than six million converts in the United States alone. (137) Ironically, the collector of Dulles' moral musings, Henry Van Dusen, commented that "Peter and Barnabas and Paul might find themselves more at home in a Holiness service or a Pentecostal revival than in the formalized and sophisticated worship of other churches, Catholic or Protestant." (137)

And, indeed, so might have Jesus.

[226] Hoopes 458.

[227] Hoopes 458.

[228] Hoopes 458.

[229] Hoopes 458.

[230] Hoopes 458.

[231] Hoopes 458.

[232] *Ramparts* magazine discovered the Agency/NCC connection: see James Munves, *The FBI and the CIA[:] Secret Agents and American Democracy* (New York: Harcourt Brace Jovanovich, 1975) 145.

[233] Hoopes 458.

[234] Hoopes 458-459.

[235] Given that the manipulators of the so-called Cold War had operated in bad faith, revisionist historical examinations have rightly called our attention to "the strategy of deterrence [that] prolonged rather than ended the [Cold War] conflict." Richard Ned Lebow and Janice Gross Stein, *We All Lost the Cold War* (Princeton, New Jersey: Princeton University Press, 1994) front flyleaf summary. However, that excellent analysis of Cold War fictions ignored Allen Dulles and John Foster Dulles as the major creative collaborators in the monstrous political deception called the Cold War.

# Essay Six: Notes

[1] Hoopes 492.

[2] Hoopes 492.

[3] Hoopes 492.

[4] Hoopes 492.

[5] Hoopes 492.

[6] Hoopes 492.

[7] Hoopes 492-493.

[8] Hoopes 494.

[9] Hoopes 495-496.

[10] Hoopes 496.

[11] Hoopes 498-499.

[12] Hoopes 498-499.

[13] Stone 104-106.

[14] Stone 106-107.

[15] Stone 105.

[16] Hoopes 499-500.

[17] See *INTERCEPT*.

[18] See *INTERCEPT*.

[19] Newman 47.

[20] Newman 42.

[21] Newman 42.

[22] Newman 42.

[23] Newman 42.

[24] Newman 42.

[25] Newman 42.

[26] Newman 42.

[27] Newman 42.

[28] Newman 43.

[29] Newman 50.

[30] Newman 50.

[31] Newman 43.

[32] Newman 50.

[33]   Epstein 49, 59, 107.

[34]   Though intelligence agent Richard Case Nagell argued persuasively that his Soviet handlers directed him to kill Oswald as they suspected the redefector of being a major player in a JFK assassination plot, Nagell did not (of course) complete his assignment, and Nagell was, at the same time, allegedly in touch with or taking orders from American intelligence. If Nagell was indeed a legitimate double or doubled (or even tripled) agent, who, then, wished Oswald dead and who wished him alive?

[35]   Anson 202.

[36]   Anson 202.

[37]   Anson 202.

[38]   Code quoted in Anson 202.

[39]   Anson 213.

[40]   See Summers Chapter 9, 152-181, and in particular 176-181.

[41]   The RAND/Rand Development story is tangled: see Epstein *Legend* 312; HR 207-209; 12 HH 463-465; and, ultimately, Peter Dale Scott, *Dallas Conspiracy*, Chapter Two, p.2.

[42]   Michael Canfield and Alan J. Weberman, *Coup d'etat in America* (New York: The Third Press, 1975) 23-24, hereafter cited as Canfield.

[43]   Canfield 24.

[44]   Canfield 24.

[45]   Canfield 23.

[46]   Canfield 24.

[47]   Canfield 24.

[48]   Canfield 24.

[49]   Canfield 24.

[50]   Canfield 24.

[51]   Canfield 24.

[52]   Summers 177 footnote.

[53]   Summers 177 footnote.

[54]   G.William Domhoff, *Who Rules America?* (Englewood Cliffs, New Jersey: Prentice-Hall, Inc., 1967) 65, hereafter cited as Domhoff.

[55]   Canfield 24.

[56]   Summers 177.

[57]   L. Fletcher Prouty, *The Secret Team* (Englewood Cliffs, New Jersey: Prentice-Hall, Inc.) 270, hereafter cited as Prouty.

[58]   Prouty 86.

[59]   Summers 177.

[60]   George Bookbinder worked with Frank Wisner, OSS/CIA officer and spymaster.

[61]   Summers 177-178.

[62]   Canfield 25.

[63]   Canfield 23.

[64]   Canfield 24.

[65]   Prouty 86.

66   Prouty 152.

67   David Wise and Thomas B. Ross, *The Invisible Government* (New York: Vintage Books, 1964) 306, hereafter cited as Wise *Invisible*.

68   Canfield 24.

69   Canfield 24.

70   Internet histories.

71   Anthony Samson, *The Arms Bazaar* (New York: The Viking Press, 1977) 141-143, hereafter cited as Samson.

72   Canfield 23, based on Scott.

73   Canfield 23.

74   Summers 177.

75   Summers 178.

76   R 618, cited by Robert Sam Anson 161.

77   Philip H. Melanson, *Spy Saga* (New York: Praeger Publishers, 1990) 15-16, 19-20, and especially 134-136, hereafter cited as Melanson.

78   Melanson 135.

79   Cited by Melanson 135.

80   Summers 178.

81   Summers 178.

82   Summers 178.

83   See Summers 178-179 for information about a most provocative defector from 1958-1959 who spent months in Oswald's Minsk but whose identity was protected by the CIA.

84   At least three other so-called defectors seemed to have been the responsibility of Foreign Officer Snyder.

85   Snyder's entry.

86   Summers 178.

87   Summers 178.

88   Michael Benson, *Who's Who in the JFK Assassination* (New York: Citadel Press Book, 1993) 473 (citing two sources), hereafter cited as Benson.

89   Cited in Summers 178.

90   Summers 220: see sources.

91   Summers 220. Gary Hill, "Webster and MKULTRA: the Smoking Gun," *The Fourth Decade*, Volume 5, Number 6, September, 1998, has been the most productive researcher in enlarging our understanding of William Webster. According to Hill, Dick Russell reported Webster had told him he knew Marina in the Soviet Union (13). Hill has concluded that Oswald and Webster were both "part of the same 'false defector' program." (13) Hill also concluded that both "were also subjects in the MKULTRA project which may have been used to create dual personalities . . . ." (13) Hill has made an excellent case for Webster being monitored and maintained by the CIA's MKULTRA program and then abandoned, left in a vegetative state. (14) See also Joseph J. Trento, *The Secret History of the CIA* (New York: Carroll & Graf Publishers: 2005), 217, for the Snyder/CIA confirmation, hereafter cited as Trento *Secret*.

92   Summers 221-222, for example.

[93]   Summers 561: "221 Note 60."

[94]   For American intelligence, either Oswald was the JFK assassin or he was not. For the CIA, the FBI, the Office of Naval Intelligence (and the rest of American military intelligence) if, in fact, Oswald was the lone shooter, then all the agencies still have to answer a fundamental question: why was so suspect an individual allowed the kind of freedom Oswald obviously enjoyed both before his trip to the Soviet Union and especially after? But if, for the agencies, he was NOT the lone assassin, why did they not acknowledge that fact?
Or is the answer too obvious?

[95]   See Evica, Introduction.

[96]   Charles Douglas Jackson preferred "C.D."; he died on September 18th, 1964, at the age of 62: see "C.D. Jackson Dies; Time, Inc., Official," *New York Times*, September 20th, 1964, hereafter cited as CDJ Times obit. The Times story on Jackson, like much else that can be found (with some difficulty) about him is both incomplete and inaccurate. For example, the obituary identifies Jackson as an official of the "Allied Air Force Headquarters" in North Africa, 1943. Actually, he was an official at General Dwight David Eisenhower's Allied Force Headquarters (AFHQ) in Algiers. Both the error and omission are significant, since the 1943 North African collaboration between Jackson and Eisenhower probably marked at least one of the earliest between Eisenhower and "the confidant of [the] former President . . . ." (CDJ Times obit) Jackson has also been misidentified in some sources as "Charles David."

[97]   Blanche Wiesen Cook, *The Declassified Eisenhower* (Garden City, New York: Doubleday & Company, Inc., 1981) 122, hereafter cited as Cook. Burton Hersh, *The Old Boys[:] The American Elite and the Origins of the CIA* (New York: Charles Scribners' Sons, 1992) missed the entire point on Jackson, calling him, after two hundred and fifty-eight pages of history and commentary, "a big armchair psychological warrior." (259) Hersh, either deliberately or ignorantly, trivializes Jackson's historic psyops role (259, 341, 347, 377, and 411). Finally, so excellent an analysis as that of Justin Lewis, *Constructing Public Opinion* (New York: Columbia University Press, 2001) does not have a word about Jackson, though Lewis discusses the Eisenhower administration's propaganda operations against Guatemala: 130-132; 143; 153.

[98]   Domhoff 21.

[99]   CDJ Times obit.

[100]  Domhoff 69.

[101]  Rhodri Jeffreys-Jones 86.

[102]  Blanche Wiesen Cook, "First Comes the Lie: C.D. Jackson and Political Warfare," *Radical History Review* 31 (1984): 45, hereafter cited as Cook "First." I discovered Ms. Cook's article after completing my work on C.D. Jackson, and the *Radical History Review* editor graciously sent me a reprint of Ms. Cook's article. Cook and I have similar intent and strategy in covering C.D. Jackson, and I have only the highest regard for Cook's earlier and excellent pioneering effort in *The Declassified Eisenhower*.

[103]  Times CDJ obit.

[104]  Times CDJ obit.

[105]  James L. Baughman, *Henry R. Luce and the Rise of the American News Media* (Boston: Twayne Publishers, 1987) 1-2, hereafter cited as Baughman. Baughman's study must be used with

caution, if only because the author has no sense of C.D. Jackson's extraordinary importance at Time, Inc., his prominence in the Eisenhower administration, and Jackson's unique role in the creation and development of psyops for American intelligence. Baughman dismisses the irreplaceable scholarship and insight of author Blanche Wilson Cook *(The Declassified Eisenhower)* with the following: "the half-baked plans of Time Inc. executive C.D. Jackson to 'roll back' communism during his brief period in the [Eisenhower] administration are given great play [by Cook]." (Baughman 250-251)

[106] Times CDJ obit.

[107] Jackson's extraordinary bulk of correspondence with key political, economic, and intelligence figures for four decades is excellently illustrated in Cook's endnotes 347-400.

[108] Baughman 112; Cook 122.

[109] Baughman 112.

[110] Cook 122.

[111] Cook 122.

[112] Cook 122.

[113] Cook 122.

[114] Cook 123.

[115] Cook 123.

[116] Cook 123.

[117] Cook 123.

[118] Cook 29.

[119] Cook 29.

[120] Cook 30.

[121] Times CDJ obit.

[122] Times CDJ obit.

[123] Times CDJ obit.

[124] Elizabeth P. McIntosh, *Sisterhood of Spies: The Women of the OSS* (Annapolis, Maryland: Naval Institute Press, 1998) 12, hereafter cited as McIntosh. For a more detailed description of the MO Branch, see *The Secret War Report of the OSS*, ed. Anthony Cave Brown (New York: Berkley Medallion Books, 1976) 106-110 and 525-540, hereafter cited as Brown.

[125] McIntosh 12-13. See also 56: the "charge" of the Joint Chiefs of Staff to the Morale Operations branch of the OSS.

[126] McIntosh 55.

[127] Stoley 12-13.

[128] McIntosh 57.

[129] Brown 525 and 570.

[130] Brown 46, 48.

[131] Stoley 69.

[132] Brown 106.

[133] Brown 525.

[134] Brown 525-526.

[135] Corson 9 and 183.

[136]   Corson 184-185.

[137]   For the complex history of the development of pysops through Donovan, Hugh Dalton, Robert Sherwood, and Elmer Davis, see Lawrence C. Stoley, *Radio Warfare* (New York: Praeger, 1989) 31-102.

[138]   Cook 9.

[139]   Cook 9.

[140]   Cook 10.

[141]   Cook 10.

[142]   Cook 10.

[143]   Cook 10.

[144]   Cook 10.

[145]   Cook 10-11.

[146]   Cook 12-13.

[147]   Cook 11.

[148]   For Milton Eisenhower's political and psychological warfare record when he worked for both FDR and his brother Dwight David, see Brands 27-47.

[149]   Cook 11.

[150]   Cook 11-12. For the earlier history of Eisenhower's careful development of military psyops capacity, including the roles of Army officers Charles Hazaltine and Heber Blankenhorn, see Stoley 83-86, 93-98, and 105: see also all Stoley's endnotes.

[151]   Cook 12.

[152]   See Brands 27-29.

[153]   Cook 13.

[154]   Times CDJ obit (note, of course, the "Air Force" error and the Eisenhower omission in the obit).

[155]   Soley 222.

[156]   Cook 13.

[157]   Colonel Alfred H. Paddock, Jr. (USA Retired), "Major General Robert Alexis McClure[:] Forgotten Father of US Army Special Warfare," at hhtp://www.psywarrior.com/mcclure.html, hereafter cited as Paddock. Printed off its internet site, Paddock's ten-page mini-biography of McClure (including "Author's note" and "About the Author") is a perfect model of what a short biography ought to be. While Paddock was doing National Archives research for his doctoral dissertation "on the origins of the Army's special warfare capability . . ."(Paddock, Author's note), Paddock discovered McClure's seminal and nurturing roles in the development of the American Army's psychological warfare capability. (Paddock, "Author's note") The online article is based on Paddock's Duke University history dissertation, on Paddock's book on the American Army's Special Warfare origins, and on his later research in McClure's "personal papers," authorized by McClure's wife, Betty Ann McClure. Paddock himself is an important part of the history of American psyops, serving combat tours with American Special Forces in Southeast Asia; as instructor of strategic studies at the U.S. Army Command and General Staff College; in the Polito-Military Division of the Army Staff in Washington; as commander of the 6th PSYOP Battalion and the 4th PSYOP Group, Fort

Bragg; as "military member" of the Secretary of State's Policy Planning Staff; and, at the end of his Army career, as the Director of PSYOP, in the office of the Secretary of Defense. (Paddock, "About the Author")

Paddock has a distinguished educational and military record. (see Paddock, "About the Author")

158 Paddock.

159 Paddock.

160 Paddock.

161 Paddock.

162 Paddock.

163 Paddock.

164 Cook 349 note #16.

165 Cook 15.

166 Cook 15.

167 Cook 13.

168 Cook 13.

169 Cook 14. See Jackson's revealing summary of his total reorganization: Cook 14. See also Paddock: McClure's September, 1943, letter to his wife on (what Paddock calls) the "ungainly organization" of INC, with "military and civilian personnel" sounding very much like C.D. Jackson's "civilian" and "military" North African Psychological Warfare Board roster. Just as McClure indicated his military work crossed over into "civilian" areas, so Jackson noted that his civilian work included "military" components.

170 Soley 82.

171 Simpson, *Blowback* note #3 292-293.

172 Brown 525-526.

173 Quoted in Paddock.

174 Brands 118.

175 Corson 221-329.

176 Corson 200. note.

177 Paddock.

178 Paddock.

179 Rudgers 168. Rudgers, a former staff archivist for the National Archives and a senior intelligence analyst with the CIA, focuses on the years 1943-1947 in developing a history of the CIA's "origins." His coverage of "Psychological operations" on pp. 38 and 168-171 is helpful, but it is odd that the wartime Psychological Warfare Board, Eisenhower's Psychological Warfare Divisions in North Africa and at SHAEF, and C.D. Jackson (who ran both those operations) are absent.

180 Paddock.

181 Paddock.

182 Rudgers 170.

183 Rudgers 171.

184 Rudgers 172.

[185] Rudgers 171-172.

[186] Rudgers 173-174, 179.

[187] Simpson 290; see also 280-290.

[188] Saunders 57-72.

[189] Saunders 64.

[190] Quoted in Eliot Harris, *The "un-American" Weapon*
[*:Psychological Warfare*] (New York: M.W. Lads Publishing Company, 1967) 2, hereafter cited as Harris. Harris covers World War I in Chapter 4; World War II also in Chapter 4; the Korean war in Chapter 3; the Vietnam war in Chapter 2; and China in Chapter 5. With the above cited exception, C.D. Jackson is ignored as well as Dwight Eisenhower in their North African and European campaign use of psyops; the OSS and Allen Dulles are also ignored. The text has no index, and the most important part of the bibliography, "The Cold War," 208-209, promises much but offers little.

[191] Saunders 130.

[192] Saunders 131.

[193] Saunders 130-131.

[194] Hersh 256.

[195] Hersh 257.

[196] Cook 123.

[197] Cook "First," 45.

[198] Christopher Simpson, *Blowback* (New York: Weidenfeld & Nicollson, 1988) 126-127, hereafter cited as Simpson.

[199] Simpson 126-127.

[200] Cook 124.

[201] Cook 125.

[202] Cook "First," 46-47.

[203] See Saunders, throughout.

[204] See, for example, Cook 357 note # 16.

[205] Cook 126.

[206] Saunders 152.

[207] Paddock.

[208] Cook 121.

[209] Cook 121.

[210] Despite the largely unexamined premise that North Korea invaded South Korea, the opposite is most probably true: see I.F. Stone, *The Hidden History of the Korean War* (New York: Monthly Review Press, 1952. The Stone book is precisely (as the author indicates) a study of "war propaganda" (xvi): that is, psyops.

[211] Paddock.

[212] Paddock.

[213] Paddock.

[214] Paddock.

[215] Paddock.

[216] Cook 126.

[217] Cook 126.

[218] Cook 126.

[219] Cook 126.

[220] Cook 126.

[221] Saunders 132.

[222] Saunders 132.

[223] Soley 223.

[224] Saunders 132.

[225] Saunders 132.

[226] Saunders 132.

[227] Cook "First," 50.

[228] Cook, "First," 50.

[229] Cook 127.

[230] Cook 129-130. For Radio Free Europe's earliest successes according to C.D. Jackson, see Cook 357 note 21.

[231] Cook 373 note # 11.

[232] See earlier.

[233] Saunders 227.

[234] Saunders throughout; see especially 213-278.

[235] Saunders 146.

[236] The author was Music Editor, Sound Effects Editor, and Story Recording Director at Hearst-Metrotone News in New York in the 1950s with no control over content: the subtle yet clearly anti-Soviet scripting for the news and documentary programs produced for the U.S. government. Ironically, most of the script voice-over readers (in dozens of languages and dialects) were political liberals and radicals, passionately committed to democratic reforms in their home countries and suspicious of what they perceived were American neo-colonialist goals.

[237] Saunders 288 passim; see also, for United States Information Agency: Saunders, 193-194, 197, 292, 336, 339.

[238] Cook, "First," 53.

[239] Cook 177.

[240] Cook 177.

[241] Cook 177.

[242] Cook 177.

[243] Cook 177-178.

[244] Paddock.

[245] Paddock.

[246] Corson 332.

[247] Corson 334-335.

[248] Jeffrey-Jones 92 and Corson 336.

[249] Corson 336.

250 Corson 336-337.

251 Corson 337.

252 Corson 337-344.

253 For an elegant and focused summary of how C.D. Jackson became the key coordinator of U.S. psyops in the early 1950s, see Kalb 337-343.

254 Corson 340.

255 Corson 337.

256 Corson 337.

257 Corson 340-341.

258 Corson 341. See Cook 364 note # 52 for a detailed discussion of the committee.

259 Corson 341.

260 For a detailed discussion and documentation of the committee, its members, and its relations to the National Security Council, CENIS, and the Rockefeller Quantico meeting, see Cook 364-365 note # 52.

261 Brands 120-121.

262 Corson 341.

263 Corson 341.

264 Corson 341.

265 Corson 341.

266 Corson 342; see 341-342. See also Robert Bowie and Richard H. Immerman, *Waging Peace* (New York: Oxford University Press, 1998) 94, hereafter cited as Bowie.

267 Corson 342.

268 Corson 342.

269 Corson 342.

270 Corson 343.

271 Brands 121.

272 Bowie 95. For an excellent discussion of Robert Cutler's overhaul of Eisenhower's security and intelligence operations, see Bowie 83-95; unfortunately, Bowie and Immerman miss C.D. Jackson's importance during and after the Cutler revisions.

273 Bowie 95.

274 Saunders 462 note 20.

275 Saunders 462 note 20.

276 Saunders 462 #20.

277 Thomas, *Journey* 94-95.

278 Cook, "First," 53.

279 Grose 352.

280 See, for example, Brands 122-123.

281 Cook, "First," 55. Possibly no other speech had spearheaded so intense and widespread a world-wide psyops campaign: see Robert J. Donovan, *Eisenhower* (New York: Harper & Brothers, 1956) 75-76.

282 Cook 178-181.

283 Simpson 127.

284 Stephen Schlesinger and Stephen Kinzer, *Bitter Fruit* (Garden City, New York: Doubleday & Company, Inc., 1982) 108, hereafter cited as Kinzer.

285 Hersh 335-354.

286 Cook 264.

287 Cook 264-269.

288 Cook 268.

289 Cook 268-269.

290 Cook 270-280; see also, especially, 229.

291 Cook 271.

292 Soley 223.

293 Soley 223.

294 Soley 223.

295 *Psywar on Cuba[:] The Declassified History of U.S. Anti-Castro Propaganda*, Jon Elliston, editor and commentator (Melbourne and New York: Ocean Press, 1999) 20-21, hereafter cited as Elliston.

296 Elliston 20.

297 Benson 206-207.

298 Cook 227, 229, 264, 266. On July 6th, 2003, In the *New York Times*, Stephen Kinzer introduced eleven "previously classified" State Department documents illustrating in detail the CIA's role in PBSUCCESS. All of them, but especially "Memorandum for the record, Oct. 29, 1953," "Memorandum from PBSUCCESS headquarters to C.I.A. station in Guatemala, Apr.28, 1954," and "Dispatch from PBSUCCESS headquarters to all PBSUCCESS stations, June 13, 1954," could have been written by C.D. Jackson, and probably were.

299 Given the change of administrations with Kennedy's victory, a major modification in CIA plans intending the Bay of Pigs operation to fail may have occurred: several historians, including this author, have called the BOP a "perfect failure."

300 Paddock.

301 Paddock.

302 McGeorge Bundy, *Danger and Survival* (New York: Random House, 1988) 287.

303 See, for example, Ambrose *President* 147-151, 153, 310-311; Bundy 244, 287-295, 328, 350; and Bowie 204, 225-227, 230-235, 239, 248.

304 Martin J. Medhurst, summary of "Atoms for Peace and Nuclear Hegemony: The Rhetorical Structure of a Cold War Campaign," *Armed Forces & Society*, Summer 1997. Medhurst had apparently promised a new publication on the subject: "Eisenhower and the Atoms for Peace Campaign, 1953-1961," originally scheduled for 2002. See also an earlier version of Medhurst argument in Medhurst et al, "Eisenhower's 'Atoms for Peace' Speech: A Case Study in the Strategic Use of Language" 29-50, hereafter cited as Medhurst "Study."

305 Ambrose *President* 132-134 and Bundy 290-292.

306 Brands 129-130.

307 Medhurst "Study" 29.

308 Medhurst "Study" 29.

309 Medhurst "Study" 34-39 and 41-44.

[310]   Medhurst "Study" 29.

[311]   Medhurst "Study" 30, 31-33, 44-45: see throughout, especially, C.D. Jackson's primary psyops actions: 46-47. See also the notes on 48-50 for further documentation of Jackson's psyops intentions.

[312]   Medhurst "Study" 44-45.

[313]   Medhurst "Study" 44-45.

[314]   Stephen E. Ambrose, *Eisenhower, Volume Two, The President* (New York: Simon and Schuster) 1984, hereafter cited as Ambrose *President*. Michael Beschloss in *May-Day* made his first reference (of only two references) to C.D. Jackson, quoting (at length) from Jackson's personal records on John Foster Dulles' concerns about Eisenhower's "Vienna" conference vulnerability (97). The Dulles message to Jackson was delivered in December, 1954, when the Secretary of State might still have felt it was politic to call C.D. Jackson a "friend": but Beschloss should certainly have known better. Beschloss wrote that Jackson had been on "the [Eisenhower] White House staff" (95) before he returned to his Life/Time/Fortune position, certainly a major understatement.

[315]   Throughout 1954 and 1955, Jackson kept in close touch with Rockefeller; see, for example, Saunders 458 note 42: in a letter to Rockefeller, April 14th, 1955, Jackson issues several cautions to his Intelligence associates in the psyops area.

[316]   Time CDJ obit.

[317]   Cook 187.

[318]   Cook 159.

[319]   Cook 366 note # 66.

[320]   Cook 366 note # 366.

[321]   Cook "First," 46.

[322]   Cook 342.

[323]   Cook 342.

[324]   For the fullest account of the Bilderbergers, see Cook 398-399 note # 75; see especially the Jackson source for 1954-1964, 399.

[325]   Cook 304.

[326]   Brands 130-131.

[327]   Cook 304.

[328]   Cook 307.

[329]   Cook 307-313. The multinational/transnational connection is not a stretch: see Cook 300-301, 342, 344, and 399 note # 76.

[330]   Brands 131,

[331]   Cook 312.

[332]   Cook 313.

[333]   Cook 313.

[334]   Cook 314.

[335]   Eisenhower's absolute faith in psychological warfare has been 'reported' so many times without definitive documentation that it itself reads like a psyops action.

[336]   Kai Bird, *The Color of Truth* (New York: Simon & Schuster, 1998) 139, hereafter cited as Bird *Color*.

337 See Cook 364-365 note # 52 for a detailed discussion of CENIS.

338 Bird *Color* 139.

339 Bird *Color* 139.

340 Bird *Color* 138-139.

341 Bird *Color* 139.

342 Bird *Color* 139.

343 Bird *Color* 139.

344 Bird *Color* 140.

345 Bird *Color* 140.

346 Bird *Color* 140.

347 Bird *Color* 140.

348 Bird *Color* 140.

349 Cook 364-365 note # 52.

350 Cook 364 note # 52.

351 Cook 365 note # 52.

352 Cook 200-204.

353 Cook 204-205; see also Brands 132-136.

354 Hersh 411.

355 Hersh 411.

356 Hersh 411.

357 Hersh 411.

358 Hersh 411.

359 Ambrose *President* 444.

360 Ambrose *President* 444.

361 Ambrose *President* 444. But Foster Dulles' aide Roderic O'Connor reported that when Jackson was at the State Department, "Jackson fitted in perfectly." (Brands 231 note # 32). Whatever Foster Dulles' suspicion of C.D. Jackson, the psyopsmaster ingratiated himself with Dulles' staff.

362 Ambrose *President* 444.

363 Ambrose *President* 444.

364 Ambrose *President* 444. See also Cook 205.

365 Ambrose *President* 444.

366 Cook 205.

367 Cook 205-206.

368 Jackson was an innovator in using youth and student exchanges and visits for psyops goals.

369 Ambrose *President* 445.

370 Ambrose *President* 445.

371 Ambrose *President* 445-446.

372 The following discussion is based on 1., "C.I.A. Subsidized Festival Trips," *New York Times*, February 21st, 1967 and 2., Kai Bird, *The Chairman* (New York: Simon & Schuster, 1992) 483-485 and 727, hereafter cited as Bird *Chairman*, also posted at http://www.cia-on-campus.org/surveil/steinem.html.

[373] Bird *Chairman*, 483.

[374] Bird *Chairman* 483-484.

[375] Kai Bird is absolutely correct in identifying John J. McCloy as the elite establishment's "chairman": Bird *Chairman* 11. Though the McCloy family was originally Philadelphian working-class and shared the area's Quaker values, John J. McCloy became a Episcopalian (like many of the Philadelphian Quakers) operating within the highest elitist circle of Episcopal power rather than as a devout church member. See Bird *Chairman* 23-36, 57-58, 190.

[376] Bird *Chairman* 483-484.

[377] Bird *Chairman* 484.

[378] Bird *Chairman* 484.

[379] Bird *Chairman* 484; for the Jackson/Meyer/Walker/Steinem collaboration, see their correspondence: Bird *Chairman* 727 note # 142.

[380] Bird *Chairman* 484.

[381] Bird *Chairman* 484; see also 731 note 145.

[382] Steinem's communications to C.D. Jackson can be found in the C.D. Jackson papers at the Eisenhower Presidential Library in Abilene, Kansas. Steinem wrote to Jackson, for example, on March 19th, 1959: see Bird *Chairman* 727 note # 145. Years later, Steinem approved of the covert funding she received from the Central Intelligence Agency: Bird 727 note # 143.

[383] Saunders 142.

[384] Simpson *Blowback* 284.

[385] Simpson 353-354 note # 41.

[386] Ambrose *President* 508.

[387] Cook 211.

[388] Cook 210-211.

[389] Ambrose *President* 516-517.

[390] Ambrose *President* 517-519.

[391] Cook, "First," 65.

[392] Cook, "First," 65.

[393] Grose 460-461.

[394] Cook 373 note 111.

[395] Cook 373 note # 111.

[396] Cook 374 note # 111. In August, 1972, two Jackson psyops enthusiasts touched base: "President Nixon appointed Milton Eisenhower to chair a Presidential Study Commission on International Broadcasting to decide the future of RFE and Radio Liberty." (Cook 373 # note 107)

[397] Cook 205-206.

[398] Cook 206.

[399] Cook 210.

[400] Cook 339.

[401] Ambrose *President* 612.

[402] Sampson ascribed the address to Eisenhower's speech writer Malcolm Moos. (102) See Sampson's commentary (102).

[403]  Ambrose *President* 612.

[404]  Hinckle 165.

[405]  Lewis 130: see Lewis for an extensive analysis, 129-137, and "selling" the Cold War, 142.

[406]  Oswald's postal story is told in *INTERCEPT.*

[407]  Epstein 147-148.

[408]  Smith 208 and 404 note #10.

[409]  Saunders 132 and Simpson 200n, 203, and 205.

[410]  In CE 2766, cited by Meagher 333.

[411]  See Oswald's "Address Book," CE 18, 43: "Inderedko (Inter. Rescue Committee?)"

[412]  CE 2766, cited in Meagher 333.

[413]  CE 2766, cited in Meagher 333.

[414]  CE 2766, cited in Meagher 333.

[415]  CE 2766, cited in Meagher 333.

[416]  CE 2766, cited in Meagher 333.

[417]  CE 2766, cited by Meagher 333.

[418]  Meagher 333.

[419]  CE 18.

[420]  Personal e-mail on 4/9/2003, responding to the author's hypothesis.

[421]  See Essay Four.

[422]  Webster Griffin Tarpley and Anton Chaitkin, *George Bush* (Washington, D.C.: Executive Intelligence Review, 1992) 80, 301-302, 309, 321, 323, 325 (President Carter fires Cherne), 349, 389, 390, hereafter cited as Tarpley.

[423]  Simpson 200 footnote; 203; 205; 219; 269;, 339 note # 13.

[424]  The following discussion is based on a story in *Entertainment Weekly*, the edition of January 17, 1992, summarized in Benson 431-432.

[425]  Benson 431.

[426]  Anson 83.

[427]  One print, according to the Zapruder Film Chronology posted at the Sixth Floor Museum (Dealey Plaza, Dallas) website.

[428]  Robert Sam Anson, *"They've Killed the President!"* (New York: Bantam Books, 1975) 131, quoting Stoley, hereafter cited as Anson.

[429]  Scott 116.

[430]  Evica 278-279. For Pawley's extraordinary career, see Evica 219, 272-273, 278-280, 300, and 305. For a full discussion of the "mission," see Scott 113-116.

[431]  Scott 55.

[432]  Scott 55.

[433]  Scott 55.

[434]  Warren Hinckle and William W. Turner, *The Fish is Red* (New York: Harper & Row, Publishers, 1981) 165, hereafter cited as Hinckle.

[435]  Edward K. Thompson was the *Life* magazine editor who accepted responsibility for altering the shape of the rifle in the "Oswald" backyard photos: see 21 H 450-453 and Lane 358-359.

[436]  Hinckle 165.

[437]  Evica 166.

[438]  2 H 22.

[439]  Scott 268.

[440]  Scott 268.

[441]  Canfield 27.

[442]  Canfield 27.

[443]  Saunders 331.

[444]  Saunders 332.

[445]  Hinckle 165.

[446]  Scott 55.

[447]  Scott 288-289.

[448]  Benson 251.

[449]  Scott 55.

[450]  Evica 166-167.

[451]  1 H 496 and 2 H 23.

[452]  Anson 133.

[453]  See Evica 1-62: my work on the alleged murder weapon has remained the fullest discussion of its history and physical appearance.

[454]  Anson 134.

[455]  Anson 131.

[456]  James H. Fetzer, ed., *Assassination Science* (Chicago: Catfeet Press, 1998) 207-344.

[457]  Anson 131.

[458]  Times CDJ obit.

[459]  Times CDJ obit.

[460]  *Case Closed* 485.

[461]  Jackson significantly influenced Dulles, Wisner, Phillips, Kennan, Hunt, Harvey, and Angleton.

[462]  To be perfectly clear: I am NOT accusing C.D. Jackson of plotting the assassination of John F. Kennedy. But the individual or individuals who designed the suspicious false identity/defector/redefector called "Oswald" must have had extensive psyops experience. For example, C.D. Jackson practiced psyops in publishing, advertising, fund-raising, public opinion shaping, and propaganda and political pysops in magazine editing and publishing; in military black propaganda and covert intelligence operations for OWI, OSS, and PSB; in political campaigns and administrative propaganda operations; in economic/global and elitist/establishment actions; and working with or influencing psyops experts Allen Dulles, Frank Wisner, David Atlee Phillips, E. H. Hunt, and possibly James Jesus Angleton. Summarizing the information on C.D. Jackson in Essay Six:

C.D. Jackson was:

*     The organizer of General Eisenhower's wartime Psychological Strategy Board in North Africa and Europe.

*     A major manipulator of U.S. World War II "public opinion."

* The first "Cold War" advisor and director of national psyops for Eisenhower; the model for all future holders of that appointive office (under a variety of titles).

* Directed President Eisenhower's nuclear weapons/atomic energy initiative threatened by Albert Schweitzer and Patrice Lumumba.

* Ran major U.S. psyops through the NSC and the CIA in the 1950s.

* Directed psychological warfare for the CIA, its fronts, and CIA-supported propaganda/public relations organizations, 1951-1959.

* Joined with Henry Luce and Time, Inc., to sponsor and support American psyops programs and to protect the CIA.

* Worked with American intelligence psyops experts, including David Atlee Phillips, to destabilize foreign governments and in CIA assassination attempts on foreign leaders.

* Recommended, helped organize, and supported U.S. government and CIA psyops funding of student/youth organizations and individuals to attend European youth programs in Europe, 1959-1962, whose American intelligence goals were always anti-Communist and anti-Soviet.

* Organized and established the U.S. branch of the international Bilderberg Conference; was an active and influential member of the Council on Foreign Relations; and was a regular, enthusiastic attendee at all Bohemian Grove events.

* Assisted major corporations and the government, working together to create a new economic order, anticipating globalization.

* Worked for the CIA and the Luce media empire in Dallas immediately after the JFK assassination; isolated and manipulated Marina Oswald; used an "Oswald" backyard rifle photo for major media propaganda; withheld the Zapruder film from public viewing.

In addition, C.D. Jackson:

* May have teamed with Allen Dulles after World War II to run anti-Soviet psyops (including illegals and false defectors).

* May have worked with Allen Dulles and John Foster Dulles manipulating religious individuals and groups through World War II and the Cold War in pursuit of political and economic goals.

# Essay Seven: Notes

[1] Percival Brundage's available biography at http://cob.ohio-state.edu/acctmis/hof/brundage/html, hereafter cited as Brundage. The events of Percival Brundage's life are difficult to discover.

[2] Brundage.

[3] Brundage.

[4] Brundage.

[5] Brundage.

[6] See Brundage.

[7] Brundage.

[8] Brundage.

[9] Brundage.

[10] Brundage.

[11] Dwight David Eisenhower, *Mandate for Change [:] 1953-1956* (Garden City, New York: Doubleday & Company, Inc., 1963) footnote on 383, hereafter cited as Eisenhower *Mandate*. *See* the line of Budget Directors from January 21st, 1953 through January 20th, 1961. Percival Flack Brundage had a major presence in the Bureau of the Budget ending only in the earliest days of the Kennedy administration.

[12] See Percival Flack Brundage, *The Bureau of the Budget* (New York: Praeger Publishers, 1970), the only major contemporary source on the Bureau of the Budget. See also Francis E. Rourke, *Bureaucracy, Politics, and Public Policy* (New York: HarperCollinsPublishers, 1984, Third Edition, paperback), 28, 75, 140-141: the Bureau of the Budget as a major filtering/control agency for the presidency through Eisenhower; the Bureau's closeness to Congress; and its power through the Nixon presidency. See also David M. Barrett, *The CIA and Congress* (Lawrence, Kansas: University Press of Kansas, 2005), for the crucial role of the Bureau of the Budget from 1948/1949 through the Kennedy administration: 118, 49-50; 45, 121, 123, 146, 153-154, 159, 172, 221, 317, 333, hereafter cited as Barrett. See also Barrett's Index for CIA budget discussions. Despite awareness of the BOB's cooperative role in protecting the Agency's budgets, particularly its covert operations funding, Barrett regrettably shows no understanding of Percival Flack Brundage's major role in CIA covert financing and, by extension, Brundage's crucial actions in supporting other military and intelligence funding. Hence, Barrett's detailed history and analysis both lack the necessary coverage of critical Agency-friendly figures, including Cutler, Killian, Land, and Lovett, and,

again by extension, Lyndon Baines Johnson's massive legislative/budgetary presence in the BOB/CIA/Pentagon/Congress complex. See for example, Barrett's LBJ's Index listing that does not offer a topic breakdown.

13   Richard F. Kaufman, *The War Profiteers* (Indianapolis and New York: The Bobbs-Merrill Company, Inc., 1970): see especially 10-11.

14   Kaufman 143.

15   Kaufman 143.

16   Joseph E. Kallenbach, *The American Chief Executive* (New York: Harper & Row, Publishers, 1966) 341, hereafter cited as Kallenbach. Kallenbach's description and analysis of the power of "central clearance of legislative proposals" resident in the executive branch and, therefore, through the president in the Bureau of the Budget (341-342) are the best available.

17   Kallenbach 341.

18   Kaufman 150-151.

19   Kallenbach 342.

20   Srodes 204.

21   Rudgers 37.

22   William Stevenson, *A Man Called Intrepid* (New York: Ballantine Books, 1977) 177, hereafter cited as Stevenson.

23   Peter Woll, *American Bureaucracy* (New York: Norton & Company, Inc., 1963) 166, hereafter cited as Woll.

24   See, for example, Stevenson 177.

25   Rudgers: 1941-1945, 38 and 74; 1941, 75; 1942, 38; 1943, 38 and 75, 76-77; 1944, 38; in 1945, under Truman, 80, 88, 89, 90.

26   Stevenson 177.

27   Alexander 36. See also Donovan on 1953 budget concerns (55-57): on April 17th, 1953, at a Cabinet meeting, "[Bureau of the Budget Director] Dodge lamented the difficulty of putting through budget cuts . . . , particularly when these cuts affected social welfare, veterans benefits and public works." (57) But not altogether impossible: "[Defense Secretary] Wilson said that he interpreted [the prior discussion] to mean that nearly $10,000,000,000 more would have to be cut from the Defense Department budget. With the Korean Was continuing, . . . this would be next to impossible." (58)

28   See Louis Fisher, *Presidential Spending Power* (Princeton, New Jersey: Princeton University Press, 1975), for the best examination of the history, development, power, and ultimate diminution of the Bureau of the Budget, hereafter cited as Fisher. See especially Chapter 9 on covert financing, including "confidential funds" (203 and 207-208); "special projects" in 1955 (211); confidential/overt funding (211-213); secret/covert funding (213); and funding the CIA (214-223) and "padding" for the CIA 321.

29   The Agency Act cited and quoted in Prouty 383.

30   Howard E. Shuman, *Politics and the Budget [:] the Struggle between the President and the Congress* (Englewood Cliffs, New Jersey: Prentice-Hall, Inc., 1984) 16, hereafter cited as Shuman.

31   Shuman 20.

32   Shuman 209.

33  Shuman 16-21 and throughout.

34  Shuman is not unaware of the power (or former power) of the Bureau of the Budget and
    its Director: 16, 18, 20-21, 23, 25, and 31, but he does not realize the Bureau had redefined
    federal budgeting, first assisting in stripping Congress of its budgeting prerogatives, second
    transferring them to the President, and then all but exempting the Pentagon and the CIA
    from any budgeting oversight.

35  Tim Weiner, "[obituary of] W.L. Pforzheimer, 88, Dies; Helped to Shape the C.I.A.," *New
    York Times*, February 16, 2003, February 16, 2003, hereafter cited as Weiner.

36  Weiner.

37  Weiner.

38  Weiner.

39  American Association for the Advancement of Science site, http://archives.aaas.org/golden,
    "Memoranda of William T. Golden," hereafter cited as Memoranda, a collection more
    general and less intelligence-oriented: here, from the Introduction, and hereafter cited
    as Memoranda, Introduction; also, at the same site but reached effectively at http://aaas.
    org/spp/cstc/golden, "Impacts of the Early Cold War on the Formulation of U.S. Science
    Policy [:] Selected Memoranda of William T. Golden: October 1950-April 1951, hereafter
    cited as Selected, a collection heavily intelligence-oriented.

40  Golden's "consultancy" and its major influence on U.S. intelligence/technology should be
    used as a measure of the probable meaning of Percival Brundage's Bureau of the Budget
    "consultancy" in the 1960-1962 period, given Brundage's important military and intelligence
    connections.

41  Memoranda, Introduction.

42  Memoranda, Introduction.

43  Memoranda, Introduction.

44  Memoranda.

45  October 19, 1950:actually the memorandum from Bureau of the Budget Director F. J.
    Lawton to President Truman, in effect informing the president that the Bureau was already
    running what it called an "informal review" through William T. Golden for which it had not
    yet gotten presidential approval; Truman "approved" the Lawton memo on October 20,
    1950), in Selected; October 27, 1950, in Memoranda; November 1, 1950, in Memoranda;
    December 19, 1950, in Selected; December 21, 1950, in Memoranda; February 6, 1951, in
    Selected; February 20, 1951, in Selected; and March 6, 1951, in Selected.

46  Selected: the result of a "Killian" search.

47  Just as Killian was an important recurring topic in Golden's conversations, so also the
    Central Intelligence Agency appeared as a major topic of conversation in thirty-six Golden
    memoranda: the result of a search for "Central Intelligence Agency," in Memoranda.

48  Memoranda: Golden's conversation with James E. Webb, then Undersecretary of State.

49  Memoranda: November 1, 1950.

50  Selected: December 19, 1950.

51  Memoranda: December 21, 1950.

52  Memoranda: February 6, 1951.

[53]  The descriptive "ideafull" was perfect for Killian himself.

[54]  Memoranda: February 20, 1951.

[55]  Memoranda: March 6, 1951.

[56]  Killian was listed among "Notable American Unitarians": see hhtp://www.harvardsquarelibrary. org/unitarians/killian.html, hereafter cited as Killian.

[57]  According to Killian: "I find in Unitarianism the freedom and stimulus to seek a lofty sense of the meaning of life. The important thing is to build a faith in a divine power or principle larger and beyond oneself. For me, Unitarianism contributes most effectively toward this objective." Recorded at www.harvardsquarelibrary./org/unitarains/killian.html, the statement, with its defective syntax, cliché, and ethical dodges, effectively defines James Killian.

[58]  Mitretek Systems, www.mitretek.org/home.nsf/AboutUs/History, hereafter cited as MITRE.

[59]  MITRE.

[60]  MITRE: see Mitretek Systems, previous citation.

[61]  From "MIT: Still Collaborating with the Pentagon?" at http://cndyorks.gn.apc.org/news/ articles/mit.htm:. MIT has had a continuous relationship to the U.S. military since February 5th, 1917.

[62]  Richard F. Kaufman, *The War Profiteers* (Indianapolis/New York: The Bobbs-Merrill Company, 1970) 187, hereafter cited as Kaufman.

[63]  Beschloss *May-Day* 74.

[64]  Killian.

[65]  See Essay Six on Troy/Cenis.

[66]  Killian.

[67]  Henry Howe Ransom, *The Intelligence Establishment* (Cambridge, Massachusetts: Harvard University Press, 1970) 244, hereafter cited as Ransom.

[68]  Ransom 244.

[69]  Ransom 244.

[70]  MIT cooperated with the U.S. military and more secretly with the Central Intelligence Agency from the years following World War II through the Clinton Administration: American military and intelligence received immeasurable benefits and the MIT administration and faculty reaped superior rewards. See, for example, the excellent analysis, Bob Feldman, "MIT: Still Collaborating with the Pentagon?" posted as of March 25th, 2001, at cndyorks. gn.apc.org/news/articles/mit.htm.

[71]  Killian.

[72]  Asner.

[73]  MIT Tech Talk, web site, "Deutch to be named on Board Killian Once Chaired," hereafter cited as "Deutch."

[74]  Burrows 157-160.

[75]  Beschloss *May-Day* 67-84.

[76]  Asner.

[77]  Asner.

[78]  Burrows: see 157-160.

[79]   Beschloss *May-Day* 67-84, 87, and 119. See also Barrett for Goodpaster's constant presence at crucial Eisenhower administration decision-making moments: 212, 244, 249-250, 315-316, 322-324, 330, 367-368, 272-382, 385, 431. Barrett misses Goodpaster's multiple roles as confidante and secretary to, and Pentagon/CIA/Bureau of the Budget/legislative link, for Eisenhower.

[80]   Deutch.

[81]   Killian.

[82]   Killian.

[83]   Wise and Ross, *Invisible* 187.

[84]   Brundage had sent his analysis and recommendations to President Eisenhower on April 23rd, 1956; Eisenhower took note and approved of Brundage's "plans to have the Bureau of the Budget give greater emphasis in its work to the evaluation and advancement of administration in the executive agencies, as a means of more rapidly bringing about improvement in organization and management . . . throughout the executive branch." (Eisenhower's response to Brundage, April 29th, 1956) Brundage's analysis was reviewed by the Subcommittee of the Committee on Appropriations, House of Representatives, where the Hoover/Brundage proposals began their successful march through the existing Federal budget controls.

[85]   Wise and Ross, *Invisible* 186; see also Kirkpatrick 147.

[86]   Kirkpatrick 147.

[87]   Commentary on the so-called Bruce-Lovett Report of 1956 from several private sources.

[88]   Philip Taubman, *Secret Empire* (New York: Simon & Schuster, 2003) 109, hereafter cited as Taubman.

[89]   Taubman 109.

[90]   Taubman 109.

[91]   Taubman 109.

[92]   Taubman 109.

[93]   Kirkpatrick 147. When Allen Dulles left as the Director of the CIA, JFK again accepted expert advice and appointed "engineer and former chairman of the AEC" John Alex McCone: Kirkpatrick 243. The friends of the CIA then pressed McCone to develop "the scientific and technological aspects of intelligence" (Kirkpatrick 243), led by Edwin Land of Polaroid, William Baker of Bell Laboratories, and, of course, James Killian of MIT. All were members of the "President's Foreign Intelligence Advisory Board." (Kirkpatrick 243)

[94]   Andrew Tully, *CIA [:] the inside Story* (New York: William Morrow and Company, 162) 13, hereafter cited as Tully.

[95]   NRO CORONA-ARGON-LANYARD Collection:1/A/0001, "CIA, Project CORONA, April 25, 1958, 6 pp., hereafter cited as CORONA. See also Jeffrey T. Richelson, *The Wizards of Langley* (Boulder, Colorado: Westview Press, 2001) 22-23, hereafter cited as Richelson *Wizards*.

[96]   CORONA; see also Richelson, *Wizards* 23.

[97]   Tully 13.

[98]   Another crucial spy/space decision was made just days before JFK became president: in March, 1960, the Secretary of Defense recommended to President Eisenhower that the U.S.'s "huge conglomerate" of covert intelligence be closely reviewed; on May 6th, 1960, after the U-2

shootdown, a meeting of Killian's Board of Consultants, Thomas Gates, the DOD Secretary, Gordon Gray, Allen Dulles, Maurice Stans and the president met, resulting in a Joint Study Group being tasked to examine closely the U.S.'s "foreign intelligence effort"; the board's recommendations and three subsequent United States Intelligence Board meetings led to a National Security Council debate on January 12, 1961: Allen Dulles argued that the National Photographic Interpretation Center, whose program was already being run by the CIA, should continue to be administered by the Agency, since the material generated had "tremendous political significance" beyond its military intelligence value (Richelson *Wizards* 30-31). Allen Dulles won the argument for the CIA (Richelson *Wizards* 31): but with Killian, Gray, the Bureau of the Budget, and Dulles all on the same team, how could the outcome have been otherwise?

Given Richelson's deep interest in high-flight spy operations and the Langley "wizards," it is more than surprising that, except for a handful of passing references to NASA, neither the wizards' major responsibility for NASA nor NASA'a connection to military and civilian intelligence goals was examined by Richelson.

[99]   Wise and Ross, *Invisible* 187.

[100]   Though the received history of the Board is that President Kennedy "reorganized the panel" (Deutch), the Eisenhower "Consultants" board had voluntarily ended its existence on January 7, 1961. (Wise and Ross, *Invisible* 187)

[101]   Given Kennedy's interest in getting the very best people regardless of party or privilege for key positions in his new government, and knowing that he took advice from key members of the U.S. elite community, identifying the specific person who recommended Killian would be instructive.

[102]   Colonel Cass Schichtle, *The National Space Program [:] from the Fifties into the Eighties* (Fort Lesley J. McNair, Washington, DC: National Security Affairs Monograph Series 83-6, National Defense University Press, 1983) 2, hereafter cited as Schichtle.

[103]   Schichtle 40-41.

[104]   Schichtle 41.

[105]   Glen Asner, "Edwin Land and Restraint by Reconnaissance," February 12th, 1999, a review of Victor McElheney's presentation based on his Edwin Land biography, at wwww.cmu.edu/coldwar/mcelheny.html, hereafter cited as Asner.

[106]   Asner.

[107]   Asner.

[108]   Asner.

[109]   Schichtle 41.

[110]   Schichtle 41.

[111]   Schichtle 42-43.

[112]   Naming the three most important actors, of course, simplifies a series of complicated historical actions. From 1947 through 1961, the three sides of the powerful and profitable triangle were 1. Killian and Brundage, 2. Killian (with his associates) and LBJ, and 3. Brundage/the Bureau of the Budget and LBJ.

[113]   Schichtle 44.

[114]  Schichtle 44-45.

[115]  Schichtle 45.

[116]  See Brundage's memorandum to Eisenhower.

[117]  Schichtle 45-47.

[118]  Schichtle 47.

[119]  Schichtle 46-47.

[120]  Asner 2; see also Burrows 238-239.

[121]  Asner 2.

[122]  Homer E. Newell, Jr., *Beyond the Atmosphere: Early Years of Space Science*, at www.hq.nasa.gov/ office/pao/History/SP-4211, hereafter cited as Newell: Chapter 7, "Response to Sputnik: The Creation of NASA," is sixteen pages (1-16); see also pages 1-3. Newell's credentials both as a participant as an historian in and commentator on the development of U.S. "space science" and the origins of NASA are irreproachable. What Newell has to record concerning Percival Brundage, James Killian, LBJ, U.S. intelligence, and the aerospace industry is extremely relevant.

[123]  Newell 2.

[124]  Newell 2.

[125]  Newell 2.

[126]  Newell 3.

[127]  Newell 3.

[128]  Newell 3.

[129]  Newell 4.

[130]  Newell 4.

[131]  Newell 4.

[132]  Newell 4.

[133]  Newell 5.

[134]  Schichtle.

[135]  Schichtle 50-51.

[136]  Newell 5. Newell devotes three pages to the case against Killian's choice: 5-7.

[137]  Burrows 218.

[138]  Burrows 218.

[139]  Beschloss *May-Day* 110.

[140]  Beschloss *May-Day* 110.

[141]  Beschloss *May-Day* 110-111. Beschloss expanded on NACA nervousness, raising an interesting but unexplored issue: "In 1956, Congress was by no means resolved to spend vast sums to send men into space. If something went wrong with the U-2 and NACA was exposed as the CIA's servant, the space program might never get off the ground." (111) But why would Dryden worry about the space program: it was highly unlikely that NACA (dedicated to terrestrial "weather problems") anticipated being involved with space. Unless, of course, Bissell had already suggested just that future for NACA as a payment for its clandestine cover of U-2 spying.

[142]   Beschloss 110-111.

[143]   Schichtle 50.

[144]   Newell 7.

[145]   Newell 7.

[146]   Burrows 259.

[147]   Newell 7.

[148]   Newell 7.

[149]   Newell 7.

[150]   Newell 7.

[151]   Newell 7.

[152]   Newell 7-8.

[153]   Newell 8.

[154]   Newell 8. An irreplaceable source for the critical historical origins of NASA is Arthur L. Levine, "United States Aeronautical Research Policy, 1915-1958," doctoral dissertation, Columbia University, 1963: see throughout and especially 155.

[155]   Schichtle 49; see also Newell 9.

[156]   Newell 8-10.

[157]   Schichtle 51.

[158]   Schichtle 51.`

[159]   Schichtle 50-51.

[160]   Schichtle 53.

[161]   Schichtle 53.

[162]   Schichtle 55.

[163]   Newell 10.

[164]   Newell 10.

[165]   Newell 1.

[166]   Schichtle 52.

[167]   Schichtle 52.

[168]   Newell 14.

[169]   Newell 14.

[170]   Newell 14.

[171]   Newell 14.

[172]   Schichtle 58.

[173]   Schichtle 58.

[174]   See amended NASA ACT, cited in Newell 14.

[175]   Schichtle 58.

[176]   Schichtle 58.

[177]   Schichtle 58.

[178]   Schichtle 58. During the Truman administration, Webb was also Under Secretary of State (with apparent intelligence duties); from 1953 through early 1961 he was an important official of the Kerr-McGee Oil Corporation in Oklahoma.

[179]   Schichtle 58.

[180]   The official postings on James E. Webb have trumpeted his praises, giving him full credit for completing JFK's lunar initiative. But President Kennedy announced his space vision on May 25th, 1961, and Webb did not achieve JFK's goal until 1968, when the lunar landing operated as an heroic diversion from LBJ's failed domestic and foreign policy programs.

[181]   Schichtle 58-59.

[182]   Burrows 329; see also 216-218, 271, and, in general, 219-273.

[183]   The McNamara/Webb document cited in Burrows 329.

[184]   Schichtle 65.

[185]   Richard J. Barnet, *The Economy of Death* (New York: Atheneum, 1972) 136, hereafter cited as Barnet *Economy*.

[186]   See later.

[187]   See later.

[188]   Arnold Kanter, *Defense Politics* (Chicago: The University of Chicago Press, 1979) 126 note # 5, hereafter cited as Kanter. A slender but valuable study, including a useful bibliography, Kanter's work simply does not take note of the loss of spending control on the part of both the Office of the President and Congress with the invention, development, manipulation, and circumvention of the Bureau of the Budget in effectively monitoring "defense" (and intelligence) funding.

[189]   See, for example, Ransom 87, 161, 242, and, in general, Chapter VII, 159-179.

[190]   Victor Marchetti and John D. Marks, *The CIA and the Cult of Intelligence* (New York: Dell Publishing Co., Inc.,1975) 317, hereafter cited as Marchetti.

[191]   Marchetti 317.

[192]   Marchetti 317.

[193]   Charles E. Jacobs, *Policy and Bureaucracy* (Princeton, New Jersey: D. Van Nostrand Company, Inc.,1966) 172, hereafter cited as Jacobs.

[194]   "For the First Time, U.S. Discloses Spying Budget," *The New York Times*, October 16, 1997, cited in William E. Burrows, *The New Ocean* (New York: Random House, 1998) 528, hereafter cited as Burrows.

[195]   Marchetti 317.

[196]   Alexander 191.

[197]   Alexander 192.

[198]   Alexander 192.

[199]   Marchetti 317-318.

[200]   Marchetti 318.

[201]   Marchetti 318.

[202]   Obviously through the present moment in U.S. history: as late as 1971, CIA Director Richard Helms lied to the American Society of Newspaper Editors when he implied that the CIA budget was AUDITED "line for line by the Office of Management and Budget." (Marchetti 320) Anyone can READ a so-called budget "line for line."

[203]   Marchetti 320.

[204]  See, for example, Herbert S. Parmet, *Eisenhower and the American Crusades* (New York: The Macmillan Company, 1972) 497-498, hereafter cited as Parmet.

[205]  Alexander 192-194. Alexander, throughout, seemed unaware of the U.S. military's real spending power, the CIA's unlimited but secret funding, and the black budget items distributed through the materials Eisenhower and his Bureau of the Budget officers perused. Robert A. Caro, *Master of the Senate* (New York: Alfred A. Knopf, 2002) apparently believes that powerful senators control all federal funding through their committee positions and chairing of a few important committees, primarily Appropriations in the Senate: hence, Lyndon Johnson as, in Caro's phrase, the "master of the Senate." But Caro does not cover the powerful Bureau of the Budget through Johnson's senatorial years, does not outline the real funding operations of the Department of Defense and U.S. intelligence, and does not even index "budget, "budgeting," the "Bureau of the Budget," or "Appropriations Committee." The few relevant pages in Caro are: 65-66, 90, 133, 175, 176, and 385. Of course a powerful Senator Johnson or a powerful Senator Dodd could make Texas and Connecticut defense industries rich. But the real budgetary power has been and has remained in the hands of the war/defense industries, their administrative allies, and the establishment-run operations of intelligence.

[206]  Percival Brundage's probable involvement in a series of Eisenhower era budget crises and scandals has only been hinted at, and then only obliquely; see, for example, Chester J. Pach, Jr., and Elmo Richardson, *The Presidency of Dwight D. Eisenhower* (Lawrence, Kansas: University Press of Kansas, 1991): 167, 57-58, 107-108, and 213.

[207]  Kaufman xxvi.

[208]  Kaufman 30.

[209]  Kaufman 30-31.

[210]  Jaufman 30.

[211]  See Kaufman 30-31, for example.

[212]  Kaufman 31: see footnote # 7.

[213]  Kaufman 31.

[214]  Kaufman 30-31.

[215]  Kaufman 31.

[216]  Kaufman 31.

[217]  "Every year [through the 1970s] the budget of the National Aeronautics and Space Administration had some CIA money hidden within it." John Ehrlichman, *Washington [:] behind Closed Doors* [the paperback edition of the novel *The Company*] (New York: Kangaroo Book/Pocket Books) 52, hereafter cited as Ehrlichman. The former key Nixon aide displays a wealth of first-hand information on how the U.S. government operated in the 1960s and 1970s.

[218]  Kaufman 30.

[219]  Kaufman 31.

[220]  Kaufman 31.

[221]  Kaufman 156.

222  Marchetti 238.

223  Marchetti 218.

224  Marchetti 238.

225  Marchetti 238-239.

226  Marchetti 239.

227  Marquis Childs, *Eisenhower: Captive Hero* (New York: Harcourt, Brace and Company, 1958) 271, hereafter cited as Childs.

228  Childs 271.

229  Marquis 271.

230  Kaufman 151.

231  This crucial budgetary story is not in the highly-praised *Master of the Senate* study of Johnson's senatorial powers.

232  Kaufman 151.

233  Kaufman 151.

234  Kaufman 151.

235  Kaufman 151.

236  Kaufman 151.

237  Kaufman 151-152.

238  Kaufman 152.

239  Kaufman 152.

240  Kaufman 152.

241  Kaufman 152.

242  Kaufman 152.

243  Mark Green, James M. Fallows, and David R. Zwick, *Who Rules Congress* (New York: Bantam Books, 1972) 110, hereafter cited as Green.

244  Any future book on the Bureau of the Budget and its major influence on U.S. intelligence will be written based initially on the following leads: William Corson, *The Armies of Ignorance* (New York: The Dial Press/James Wade, 1977) 45-46 184-185, 202, 219, 228-230, 236, 239, 240-242-244, 244-246, 248-249, 250-267, 268-270, 274-275, and 277 ff.; and Michael Warner, "The Creation of the Central Intelligence Group," an article that was expanded from an earlier piece with the same title in *Studies in Intelligence*, Fall, 1995: on http://www.cia.gov. search?NS-search-page=document&NS-rel-dc . . . 6/19/2002.

245  Lyman B. Kirkpatrick, Jr., *The Real CIA* (New York: The Macmillan Company, 1968) 205, hereafter cited as Kirkpatrick.

246  Kirkpatrick 205.

247  Kirkpatrick 205.

248  Percival Brundage, Director, Bureau of the Budget, to the President, [on] "Project Vanguard," April 30, 1957, from Bureau of the Budget Files, Dwight D. Eisenhower Library, Abilene, Kansas, hereafter cited as "Vanguard."

249  Vanguard: introductory material to the Brundage memo. For detail on Project Vanguard, see Burrows 170-173, 181, 184, 187-188, 202. 205, 212-213, 216, 219, 226, 259-260, 268.

250 The sensitive links between Goodpaster and Brundage are not easy to locate, but a typical and important document is "Memorandum [from Goodpaster] for Director of the Budget [Percival Brundage]" n.d. [most probably late 1955 or early 1956] EPL. Department of the Navy (1), Office [White House] Staff Secretary [Goodpaster]: Paul T. Carroll, Subject Series, Alpha Subseries, box 20. The memo was sent in the middle of the controversy, and concerned the still not developed nuclear-powered aircraft then being promoted by the Navy.

251 See Vanguard, introductory comment.

252 Beschloss *May-Day* 243-244.

253 Kirkpatrick 206.

254 Kirkpatrick 206.

255 Kirkpatrick 206.

256 Kirkpatrick 206.

257 Kirkpatrick 206-207.

258 Kirkpatrick 207.

259 In the softbound edition of the earlier *Passion of the Hawks*, Tristram Coffin, *The Armed Society* (Baltimore: Penguin Books, 1964) passed up an excellent opportunity to examine the institutional collaboration between the Pentagon, American intelligence, and the Bureau of the Budget, especially at 19-20, hereafter cited as Coffin.

260 See, for example, Kirkpatrick 216 and the elaborate transfer of "a study on all foreign intelligence activities of all concerned United States departments . . ." from the Bureau of the Budget to a "special task force" headed by the Director of Central Intelligence (Kirkpatrick 216).

261 Cited in G. William Domhoff, *The Higher Circles* (New York: Vintage Books Edition, 1971) 131.

262 Elliston 29: April 14th, 1960 memorandum on "Discussion . . . of the National Security Council . . . ."

263 If the flight of the U-2 that came down, either because of malfunction or because the Soviets shot it down, was a deliberate move to sabotage the upcoming Soviet/U.S. talks, then the American officials directly responsible for sending it may have been the same people with interests in dooming the up-coming U.S./Soviet talks. In fact, Richard Bissell, the CIA's director of dirty tricks, sent Powers and his U-2 into Soviet skies with the approval of Colonel Goodpaster, Eisenhower's Pentagon/CIA liaison: Bleschloss *May-Day* 131.

264 Ransom 229.

265 Ransom 230.

266 Ransom 230.

267 Ransom 230.

268 Ransom 230.

269 Marchetti 371.

270 Marchetti, Appendix[:] The Bissell Philosophy. Minutes of the 1968 "Bissell Meeting" at the Council on Foreign Relations as reprinted by the Africa Research Group, in Marchetti (357-376), hereafter cited as Marchetti, Appendix.

271 Marchetti, Appendix 371.

272 Marchetti Appendix 371.

[273] Marchetti, Appendix 371.

[274] Marchetti Appendix 371.

[275] The phrase "combined cryptologic budget" is the first time I believe the entire "combined" budget of the United States intelligence/espionage/counterintelligence/psyops programs was so designated. The term "cryptologic" is more actually rendered as acronymic: for example, OSS, CIA, DOD, ONI, etc.

[276] Marchetti Appendix 371.

[277] Marchetti, Appendix, 371. Researchers into the history of the JFK administration should note that John F. Kennedy's Treasury secretary (and cabinet level boss of the Secret Service) Douglas Dillon had a long and productive relationship with U.S. intelligence.

[278] Woll 126.

[279] Woll 126: see also 123-129, and 129-130 on Congressional appropriations.

[280] Coffin 163.

[281] Seymour Melman, *Pentagon Capitalism* (New York: McGraw-Hill Book Company, 1970), see throughout, especially 17-18, 29-30, 38, 43 ff., and 181.

[282] Percival Flack Brundage, *The Bureau of the Budget* (New York: Praeger Publishers, 1970), hereafter cited as Brundage.

[283] In Brundage, Robert P. Mayo, "Forward" vii-viii, hereafter cited as Mayo.

[284] Mayo vii.

[285] Mayo viii.

[286] Brundage 144.

[287] Brundage 223 and 224.

[288] The Department of Justice and the FBI are included in a single paragraph: 218.

[289] Brundage: on the NSC: 132, 136, 137, 138, 212, and 223.

[290] Brundage: on the OCB, 223 and 234. For the actual power in establishing the Defense budget, see 134 and 136-137.

[291] Unitarian Service Committee records, bMS 16024.

[292] See Essay Four on Howard Brooks and French Intelligence.

[293] IARF was both an initiating organization and a supporting energy for Hans Casparis and his summer programs starting in 1950 and for his Albert Schweitzer College starting in 1955: see Essay One and Essay Three.

[294] David Alpern with Anthony Marro, Evert Clark, and Henry McGee in Washington, "How the CIA Does 'Business'," *Newsweek*, May 19, 1975, 27.

[295] The incorporation documents and other records of Southern Air Transport are available in Richardson, Texas.

[296] Seagrave 361.

[297] Jonathan Kwitny, *The Crimes of Patriots* (New York: A Touchstone Book, Simon & Schuster Inc.,1987, hereafter cited as Kwitny.

[298] Seagrave 361.

[299] Scott *Deep* 351 note # 10.

[300] Scott *Deep* 351 note 10.

[301] Seagrave 361.

[302] Seagrave 363.

[303] Kwitny 294.

[304] Kwitny 294-295.

[305] Kwitny 164.

[306] Kwitny 164. See also Penny Lernoux, *In Banks We Trust* New York: Viking Penguin Books, 1986) 77, hereafter cited as Lernoux *Banks*.

[307] Scott *Deep* 166.

[308] Scott *Deep* 166.

[309] Seagrave 364.

[310] Wise and Ross, *Invisible* 148.

[311] Marchetti 148.

[312] Marchetti 150-151.

[313] Marchetti 150-151.

[314] Darrell Garwood, *Undercover: The Thirty-Five Years of CIA Deception* (New York: Grove Press, 1985) 172, hereafter cited as Garwood. The Southern Air Transport/Air Force link: in Wise *Invisible* 146.

[315] Southern Air Transport's operations are difficult to separate from Air America's narcotics programs: see Alfred W. McCoy, *The Politics of Heroin in Southeast Asia* (New York: Harper Colophon Books, 1972), 247, 263-264, 267, 269-271, 274-283, 288, 290, 292-293, 307.

[316] Marchetti 154.

[317] Garwood 172; SAT's Formosa postal address: Wise *Invisible* 146.

[318] The titles "Assistant Secretary of Defense" and "Deputy Secretary of Defense" have been frequently confused in popular sources. If Brundage's associate in underwriting Southern Air Transport for the CIA was (rather than an "assistant secretary") a former "Deputy Secretary of Defense," then both he and Brundage would have served together with C.D. Jackson and Allan Dulles on the five-member OCB committee monitoring U.S. intelligence's covert operations, an even closer fit for the CIA's Southern Air Transport.

[319] Marchetti 154.

[320] Marchetti 154.

[321] Marchetti 161.

[322] Marchetti 162.

[323] Marchetti 163; see also 229.

[324] Project Hope at http:// americanhistory.si.edu/hope/07hope.htm

[325] C.D. Jackson was, in fact, a founding board member of Project Hope.

[326] Southern Air Transport was reportedly founded by arch-conservative Fred Bachelor.

Among SAT's notable officers has been Hugh Fred Grundy, who worked in Africa with Pan American Airlines (a military/intelligence partner inside the U.S. economic establishment) to build a supply route for the Allies in World War II. After serving in the Army Air Corps (most probably in an intelligence capacity), Grundy signed on with the China National Corporation (CNAC) in Shanghai, becoming CNAC's Chief Engineer, where he helped develop General Chennault's Civil Air Transport(CAT). For twenty years, Grundy was president of CAT, managing the CIA's Air America operations in Greater Asia directing the Pacific actions of Southern Air Transport. Grundy eventually commanded over 10,000 employees and operatives (open and covert) in Southeast Asia, Thailand, Japan, and Korea for U.S. intelligence. He retired from his Asian duties in 1976 and became senior vice president and then director of Southern Air Transport.

Southern Air Transport had a long history of association with the members of the "retired" U.S. intelligence community that congregated in Southern Florida. Among SAT's Miami Dade County operatives who served as the airline's legal counsel was attorney Thomas R. Spencer, Jr., who was General Counsel in the Department of Defense during the Nixon and Ford administrations. Though his various biographical sources do not specifically identify Spencer as a former agent of the CIA (or as a retired member of any other intelligence group), he has proudly announced himself a longtime working associate of Theodore Shackley, the notorious Agency operator who commanded assassination hitmen and death squads out of JMWAVE in Florida and in Vietnam, who was an active participant in the Bay of Pigs operation and the CIA's multiple assassination attempts against Fidel Castro, who worked closely with psyopsmaster David Phillips, and who directed such dark CIA figures as the admitted assassin David Sanchez Morales. When Ted Shackley died, Spencer delivered the funeral oration celebrating Shackley's covert intelligence career. Shackley's close associate Thomas Spencer has been a member of the Board of Directors of the powerful Miami-Dade chapter of the Association of Former Intelligence Officers (AFIO), serving there, for example, with the grandson of the CIA's James Jesus Angleton. Spencer remains a life-time member of AFIO and has been an active member of the AFIO's national board of directors (2003), directing programs and forums for the national ex-spooks' conventions and symposia. Spencer's intelligence links include the American Security Council Foundation Intelligence Officers; the National Business Intelligence Symposium (as chair for several years); the Overseas Security Advisory Council, U.S. Department of State, Bureau of Diplomatic Security; Infragard, Federal Bureau of Investigations (civilian status); and (but not limited to) Operation On Guard, Department of Homeland Security, U.S. Coast Guard Auxiliary, District 7, Miami Station 1. Finally,Spencer's resume includes his extensive and impressive Florida Republican Party connections, including his role as the Republican Party Executive Committee's chief poll watcher and recount witness after the disputed Florida vote in the 2000 national election.

[327] Sometimes indicated as the American Friends of Albert Schweitzer College.

[328] I requested the incorporation papers in late January, 2003, and subsequently received them from New York State in early February, 2003. These incorporation papers are hereafter cited as College Incorporation.

[329] College Incorporation.

[330] College Incorporation.

[331] College Incorporation.

[332] Lathrop biography.

[333] College Incorporation.

[334] Bartholomew 15; see also 22 note # 19.

[335] Same.

336 Same.

337 Letter dated December 5, 1963, from Robert H. Schacht to "Mr. Percival F. Brundage," in bMS 1223-1, Harvard Divinity School Library.

338 Same.

339 Same.

340 Same.

341 Same.

342 In 1955, the listed directors of the Friends of Albert Schweitzer College, Inc. (a non-profit organization registered in the state of New York) included director Frederick May Eliot (one of ten directors) and director Percival Flack Brundage, President of the Friends of Albert Schweitzer College, Inc.

343 College Incorporation.

# Essay Eight: Notes

1   Srodes 554-555.

2   That Unitarian reality was infused with a second religious reality, the Quaker connection: see later.

3   Hosty 28.

4   At least for the government's anti-Oswald argument: Ruth Paine had successfully muddied the government's thesis. (See Anson 76)

5   Gaeton Fonzi, *The Last Investigation* (New York: Thunder's Mouth Press: 1993) 10, hereafter cited as Fonzi.

6   What has been called the "Paine Project" led by researchers and writers Carol Hewett, Steven Jones, Barbara LaMonica, and William Kelly has meticulously documented the extraordinary participation of Ruth Paine and Michael Paine in the lives of Lee Harvey Oswald and Marina Oswald. Material in Essay Eight is based in part on presentations the four have made at several JFK research conferences (in Fredonia, New York, and in Dallas, for example).

7   CIA memorandum dated 12/5/63; his Agency file number: 157435, cited in Barbara LaMonica, Steve Jones, and Carol Hewett, "The Paines," *The Fourth Decade*, Volume 3, Number 4, 25-29, note # 28 (29), hereafter cited as LaMonica. The career of William Avery Hyde is extensively reviewed and analyzed in Barbara LaMonica, "William Avery Hyde," *The Fourth Decade*, Volume 5, Number 1, 8-12, and is drawn on in my discussion of William Avery Hyde.

The Paine/Hyde/Hoke familial network to which Michael and Ruth Paine belonged exhibited a complexity of U.S. intelligence connections either withheld from or ignored by the Warren Commission. The following discussion is adapted from A.J. Weberman's *http://www.weberman.com/nodules/nodule9.htm*) where the Paine/Hyde/Hoke infrastructure is heavily documented from FBI and CIA sources. The following outline recapitulates some of the material found in the main text, but it is presented with a different (and broader) emphasis.

William Avery Hyde, Ruth Paine's father, was the subject of several CIA file documents that referred to his family's support of Norman Thomas' anti-Communist Socialist Party when Thomas was being funded by the Central Intelligence Agency. Hyde and his wife Carol were associated with Talbot Bielfeldt, an agent of the Foreign Documents Division of the CIA; yet Carol Hyde (Ruth Paine's mother) was characterized as a "radical" by U.S. double-agent Herbert Philbrick, who cited as evidence Carol Hyde's activity in the Woman's International League for Peace and Justice, a Communist "front," according to Philbrick.

364

Sylvia Ludlow Hyde, Ruth (Hyde) Paine's sister, also called both Sylvia Hyde Hoke and Sylvia Hoke (after marrying John Hoke), was employed by the U.S. Labor Department from 1949 through 1953. During World War II and the Cold War, the OSS and the CIA (the OSS's successor) recruited anti-Nazi and then anti-Communist labor activists and union leaders. The U.S. Labor Department was, therefore, a long-time center of U.S. intelligence/anti-Communist activity and the site of U.S. covert penetration of both the domestic and foreign labor movements.

Sylvia Hyde was employed by the CIA as early as 1954; her "cover" was as a Personnel Research Technician, Placement and Employee Relations Division, Director of Civilian Personnel, HQ, Department of the Air Force, Washington, D.C. The Air Force had, in fact, provided sanctuary for both intelligence "black" budget items and covert intelligence personnel in the 1950s and '60s. Sylvia Hoke's Security File 348 201 was inside the CIA's Office of Security, Security Analysis Group. Sylvia's contacts included her mother-in-law, Mrs. Helen Hoke, who had a close relationship with Dorothy Wilson, allegedly a member of the Communist Party, North Beach Branch, California, in the early 1940s. Sylvia Hoke also worked at Time Magazine when she gave Gerritt E. Fielstra as a reference, reputedly a Communist sympathizer and labor organizer. But Fielstra may have himself been a U.S. double agent. On April 17, 1956, Sylvia Hoke was granted a Top Secret security clearance by the Agency for International Development (USAID), a long-time agency collaborating with the CIA. Because of her labor and left-wing associations (and those of her mother-in-law's), Sylvia Hoke's clearance was questioned by the FBI. Yet her clearance with USAID was revalidated on January 17, 1962. As late as November 11, 1963, the CIA's Office of Security was queried internally about Sylvia Hoke. The 1961 Falls Church, Virginia Directory listed Sylvia Hoke as an "emp CIA": that is, employed by the Central Intelligence Agency. Evidence also indicated that Sylvia Hoke either worked for Naval Intelligence at the same time or had an active file maintained by Naval Intelligence because of her husband's intelligence-related activity.

Sylvia Hoke's husband was John Lindsey Hoke (Ruth Paine's brother-in-law). On February 4, 1956, John Hoke was appointed an audio-visual consultant with the International Cooperation Administration (predecessor of USAID, the CIA-partnering Agency for International Development), U.S. Operations Mission, Panama City, Panama. John Hoke admitted to the Deputy Director of Communications, ICA, that he did "intelligence type work for the American Embassy." In Surinam and later in Washington, D.C., John Hoke worked for ICA and then USIAD, but ran into trouble with the House Subcommittee on Government Operations when it was discovered his solar-powered boat project in Surinam was also intended to generate "personal profit." On June 30, 1963, John Hoke left USAID, yet on August 22, 1963, the CIA granted a second and indefinite "Approval for Liaison" with John Hoke. Hoke remained in the good graces of both the U.S. military and U.S. intelligence through at least 1965, employed by the military-industrial partner Atlantic Research where he was the subject of a positive U.S. Naval Intelligence check.

The Hyde/Paine/Hoke network of intelligence and intelligence-related activities strongly suggests a liberal familial complex whose members were willing double-agents in support of anti-Communist goals. Ruth Hyde Paine was at the center of that Hyde/Paine/ Hoke counterintelligence complexity.

8   Ruth Paine's Jim Garrison Grand Jury Testimony, cited in LaMonica 28.

9   Quoted in George Cotter, "Spies, Strings, and Missionaries," (Chicago), March 25, 1981, *The Christian Century*, cited in Jim Garrison, *On the Trail of the Assassins* (New York: Warner Books, 1988) note on 370, hereafter cited as Garrison, *Trail*.

10  FBI 105-126128-29, 12/16/63 and CIA memorandum dated 11/29/63, cited in LaMonica, notes #34 and #35 (29).

11  FBI 105-126128-5, 12/12/63, cited in LaMonica, note # 29 (29).

12  LaMonica 28.

13  See Essays One through Four.

14  See Evica 291-300 for the most coherent outline available of the "White Baron."

15  Epstein xiv: according to Epstein, the Baron was the target of a seven-year FBI probe, including one initiated in April, 1963 (xiv).

16  Evica 294: Moore's name is misspelled twice (not "Dalton" but "Walton").

17  LaMonica 28.

18  12 HH 61.

19  12 HH 61.

20  See 12 HH 56-57; 60-61; and Summers 248-249; Russell 318-319; Fonzi 312-313; La Fontaine 197-198.

21  See 12 HH 60-61, cited in LaMonica, note 32 (29).

22  Thomas Mallon, *Mrs. Paine's Garage* (New York: Pantheon Books, 2002) 21, hereafter cited (with great reservation) as Mallon. Thomas Mallon is mean-spirited (disguised as irony, satire, and comedy): see his uncalled-for remarks about writer/researcher Carol Hewitt: 197.

23  Mallon 21.

24  Mallon 21.

25  Mallon 21.

26  Mallon 21.

27  See below.

28  Nancy Wertz, "Michael Paine—A Life of Unanswered Paradoxes," *Kennedy Assassination Chronicles*, Vol. 4, Issue 4, Winter 1998, 19, hereafter cited as Wertz.

29  Wertz 19.

30  Mallon 16.

31  3 H 104 (in Ruth Paine's testimony).

32  Hosty 39.

33  Hosty 39.

34  Mallon 16.

35  Mary Bancroft, *Autobiography of a Spy* (New York: William Morrow and Company, Inc., 1983, hereafter cited as Bancroft.

36  Bancroft's apparent reticence about Ruth Forbes Paine and Ruth's later marriage to Arthur Young echo her descriptions of her early marriage to Sherwin Badger; Badger worked for United Fruit when it had a heavy intelligence and organized crime connection; ultimately, he was at United Fruit's head office; he worked in a sugar operation in Cuba; later, he was with the Boston News Bureau, the *Wall Street Journal*, and Barron's (26, 36, 36-44, 45, 48).

Badger's career while Mary and he were married was suspiciously like that of an intelligence stringer gathering economic and financial information. Mary and Sherman were divorced in 1947, coincidentally the year the CIA was established.

37 Mallon 12.

38 Mallon 12.

39 FBI 105-126128 1st NR 26 and, on the internet, CIABASE, Ralph McGehee, Herdon, VA., 1992, cited in LaMonica, note #25 (29).

40 Specific records of Ruth and Michael Paine as Quaker activists in or around Philadelphia are presently not available.

41 Mallon 10-11.

42 Mallon 11.

43 Mallon 11.

44 Mallon 11.

45 Mallon 11-12.

46 Mallon 14.

47 Mallon 14.

48 Mallon 14.

49 Canfield and Weberman 27.

50 Canfield and Weberman 27.

51 Because this "Magnolia" party was so rich in military, industrial, intelligence, psyops, and liberal religious dimensions, a full examination has been delayed until later in this essay.

52 Edward Epstein, the confidante of both the CIA's James Jesus Angleton and FBI's William Sullivan and their counterintelligence associates, interviewed six (or more) people present at the Oswald/Ruth Paine party meeting (see Epstein 317, end note for Chapter XII: the party is covered on 203-206). Epstein apparently considered the party's ambiance a necessary factor in Oswald's motives for allegedly shooting at General Edwin Walker and, subsequently, John F. Kennedy. The reader must therefore keep Epstein's major anti-Oswald intelligence connections in mind when evaluating statements ostensibly made by the party's participants and subsequently 'reported' by Epstein.

53 That is, rather than a "Communist" conspiracy.

54 Evica 291-300.

55 The maze of oil company names associated with the Magnolia Research Labs can be mystifying and maddening. Texas oil explorations, oil company foundings, oil company mergers, and oil company name changes are Byzantine, but the ones associated with Magnolia Labs can be sorted out. In 1866, the Vacuum Oil Company (Texas) was incorporated. In 1879, John D. Rockefeller's Standard Oil Company of Ohio purchased a 75% interest in Vacuum Oil. In 1882, Rockefeller consolidated his oil holdings in the Standard Oil Trust, which was established and headquartered in New York. In 1911, with the breakup of the Standard Oil Trust, Socony (that is, Standard Oil Company of New York) was founded. That same year, Magnolia Petroleum Company (Texas) was organized, its pre-consolidation history dating back to 1898. Though Vacuum Oil was originally a Texas operation, it was controlled by Yankee Rockefellers; Magnolia Oil was perceived to be authentic Texas oil and, in particular, Dallas oil. In 1922,

the Magnolia Oil Building in Dallas was opened, crowned by the rotating, neon-bright Flying Red Horse symbolizing Magnolia Oil. Dallas proudly pointed out the Magnolia Building at 1401 Commerce Street as the tallest man-made structure west of the Mississippi River. But Magnolia gained in importance in Texas and the Southwest, and Standard Oil (Socony) took a special interest, purchasing Magnolia stock. Late in 1925, all Magnolia stock was exchanged for Standard Oil of New York stock, with Magnolia Oil properties consolidated and Socony the actual financial entity. In 1931, Socony Oil and Vacuum Oil were consolidated, becoming the Socony-Vacuum Oil Company; Magnolia became an "affiliate." By 1949, Magnolia was, in effect, owned by Socony-Vacuum. In 1955, Socony-Vacuum became the Socony Mobil Oil Company. In 1959-1960, the Socony Mobil Petroleum Company and its Magnolia affiliates were separated, at least on paper, and the Magnolia Building in downtown Dallas became the Mobile Building. The Magnolia Labs, still part of the mega-corporate structure of Mobile/Socony-Vacuum, were designated the home of the company's oil research (and Russian language instruction). Through the 1960s, Mobil Oil, Mobile Chemical, Mobile Petroleum, and Socony Mobil were titles of the company's various operations. Possibly because of its "affiliate" designation or because the Magnolia Labs had a special corporate objective (or both), "Magnolia" was therefore reserved for the research side of the mega-corporation.

[56] Epstein 203.

[57] Epstein 203.

[58] Fonzi 417.

[59] Epstein 203.

[60] Epstein 204.

[61] Epstein 204.

[62] Epstein 204.

[63] Epstein 204.

[64] See Meagher 234 and 245: the evidence is all but conclusive.

[65] Epstein 204: Schmidt had "studied and lived with Dr. Willhelm Keutemeyer, professor of psychosomatic medicine and religious philosophy at . . . Heidelberg." (204) According to Schmidt as reported by Epstein, "Kuetemeyer had been experimenting . . . on a group of schizoids during World War II. The experiments had been interrupted in 1944, when Kuetemeyer had become involved in the plot to assassinate Hitler and had been forced into hiding from the Nazis." (353) The network of double-agent intelligence activity surrounding the family and relatives of Ruth Hyde Paine was, therefore, enriched by this same plot against Adolph Hitler (July 2[0th], 1944), involving Dr. Keutemeyer, Dr. Hans Gisevius, Mary Bancroft (a close friend and companion of Ruth Paine's mother, an OSS spy, and the lover of Allan Dulles), and Allan Dulles himself (never examined by the Warren Commission). Dr. Keutemeyer's son was a close friend of the doctor's psychology student Volkmar Schmidt. Keutemeyer was also reputedly a colleague of Carl Jung, who had his own close associations with Mary Bancroft, Allan Dulles, David Bruce, OSS officer and future distinguished U.S. diplomat, and the psychological intelligence activities directed against Adolph Hitler: see Diedre Bair, *Jung* (Little, Brown and Company, Boston: 2003, 482-492.

[66] Epstein 205.

[67]  McMillan 259.

[68]  Epstein 205.

[69]  Epstein 205.

[70]  Epstein 205.

[71]  Epstein 205.

[72]  Epstein 205.

[73]  McMillan 276.

[74]  Epstein 205.

[75]  McMillan 277.

[76]  Epstein 205.

[77]  Epstein 205-206.

[78]  Epstein 206.

[79]  Epstein 206.

[80]  Epstein 205.

[81]  9 H 258.

[82]  Epstein 206.

[83]  Epstein 206 and 317.

[84]  Epstein 206-207.

[85]  Epstein 206-207.

[86]  Epstein 206.

[87]  Walter C. Pew, the grandson of Sun Oil Joseph Newton Pew, was listed in 1979 as the ninth-richest Philadelphian: E. Digby Baltzell, *Puritan Boston and Quaker Philadelphia* (New York: 1979) 210, hereafter cited as Baltzell. Joseph Newton Pew, always given credit for building the Pew Sun Oil fortune, in fact married into oil through Mary Anderson, "whose family had been pioneers in the oil business." (Baltzell 229)

[88]  Arnold Forster and Benjamin Epstein, *Danger on the Right* (New York: Random House, 1964) 182, 189, 191, 214, 217, 267-268.

[89]  G. William Domhoff 64-70.

[90]  Domhoff 70.

[91]  Domhoff 70.

[92]  Based on private communications.

[93]  9 H 103 and 106.

[94]  Warren Commission Document 386 and Secret Service Document 1058, both cited by Scott *Deep* 276.

[95]  9 H 103.

[96]  Scott *Deep* 276.

[97]  9 H 103.

[98]  9 H 129.

[99]  Personal communication.

[101]  2 H 23.

[101]  Glover was, according to the Warren Commission testimony, a chemist with the geology group exploration section of the Socony Mobile Field Research Lab in Dallas: 10 H 3; see

also 9 H 256: therefore, Glover worked for the Magnolia Laboratories of the Standard Oil of New York Research Laboratories: that is, Magnolia of Socony.

[102]  9 H 256.

[103]  McMillan 276.

[104]  Scott *Deep*: see 268-270, 272, 279, 284, 286-290.

[105]  Benson 290.

[106]  Scott *Deep* 268-269.

[107]  Benson 410.

[108]  Epstein 206.

[109]  See Essay Six.

[110]  Larrie Schmidt was one of the instigators of the anti-JFK advertisement that appeared in the *Dallas Morning News* on November 22nd, 1963; Larrie's brother Bob was the driver for General Edwin Walker; and Walker later suspected the Schmidt brothers, with Lee Harvey Oswald, were complicit in the alleged assassination attempt against him on April 10, 1963: Benson 410. No familial relation between the Schmidt brothers (both right-wingers) and Volkmar Schmidt has so far been discovered. Despite Ruth and Michael Paine's apparent liberal (if not left-wing) orientation, Peter Dale Scott characterized Michael Paine as "an extreme right-winger." (Scott Deep 277) Though Scott offered no supporting evidence for Michael's Paine's rightist orientation, the label is provocative given Paine's Trotskyist family background, his Bell Helicopter employment, and his living with the Magnolia men's association.

[111]  Evica 296.

[112]  Mallon 24.

[113]  3 H 134 and 9 H 274 and see *http://www.pendlehill.org/pamphlets/Lacey.html*, the Quaker Pendle Hill Pamphlets web site for *Experiment in understanding: A report by the East-West Contacts Committee of the Young Friends Committee of North America* by: Paul Lacey (editor), Wilmer and Rebecca Stratton, Richard Taylor, and Robert Osborn. Washington: Young Friends Committee of North America, 1959.

On January 9, 1964, the FBI questioned Wilmer Stratton and Paul Lacey concerning Ruth Paine, but NOT about the East-West Exchange program thick with intelligence meanings. Rather, both Quakers were queried about Ruth's initial relationship with Marina Oswald: both of Ruth's Friends associates had specific information about Ruth and Marina: see FBI interview IP 105-3441 Pettijohn/McDonald (1/15/64). The "105" prefix on the Bureau document indicates the interviews were part of a counterintelligence investigation.

See also the brilliant work of Greg Parker, a young Australian assassination researcher and writer, who has posted highly significant materials on *http://educationforum.* Parker has written important summaries on Ruth Paine and the US/USSR exchange program; the Council on International Educational Exchange (CIEE); the "Friends Journal" story on Ruth Paine and her Quaker exchange group (drawing on the FBI's Supplemental Report); the East-West Contacts Staff; Frederick T. Merrill; Merrill and Free Europe Committee; and on the "space race" "dominated at government committee levels by . . . Lyndon Johnson, James Killian, Nelson Rockefeller, and Percival Brundage." I have paraphrased or quoted Parker's work, here happily acknowledged. If I held any doubt about the large lateral significance of the Oswald story I was researching and writing as I followed it through Albert Schweitzer College, its Unitarian dimensions, Brundage and his elitist associates, and the Paines with their incredible connections, Greg Parker's independent discoveries in these same areas offered premium support for my work.

The Lacey, Lansdale, Merrill, and Anslinger materials that follow in the body of the text are based on a dozen sources, including Prouty, Chester, Valentine, Domhoff, and Scott, and the internet records of the Assembly of Captive Nations, the CIEE, the UNODC Bulletin on Narcotics, 1968, Issue 3, the internet site of the Foreign Policy Association, and Ms. Jennifer Walele, Office of the Historian, U.S. Department of State, who supplied obituaries for William Lacy and Frederick Merrill. Again, see the Greg Parker sources, given above. For Lansdale, the Embassy and Lacy, see Carlos P. Romulo and Marvin M. Gray, *The Magsaysay Story* (New York: the John Day Company, 1956), 125, 163, 210, 213, 286, hereafter cited as Romulo. For the Joint U.S. Military Advisory Group 23; the several missions, including the Melby Mission, see William J. Pomeroy, *An American Made Tragedy* (New York: International Publishers, 1974), 24-25; for Magsaysay and Lansdale: 25; for the Philippines and Thailand: 29.

114   Mallon 24.

115   Mallon 24.

116   George Carpozi, Jr., *Red Spies in Washington* (New York: Trident Press, 1968) 80, hereafter cited as Carpozi; the Zaostrovtsev story is given by Carpozi in detail on 79-87: "A Washington Spy Courts the Quakers." Carpozi's espionage revelations had a short but important run in the late 60s, based primarily on his access to FBI files and documents (Carpozi: see throughout). Reasonably objective, moderately liberal and rational, Carpozi pointed out that Elizabeth Bentley and her friends had brought dubious testimony and charges against innocent U.S. career government workers who MAY have cooperated with representatives of the government of the Soviet Union; but that alleged cooperation was never documented by Carpozi. Included in Carpozi's photo album (after 96) is a picture (according to Carpozi) of President Truman greeting Alger Hiss at the San Francisco United Nations meeting: but Alger Hiss would have needed a very long right arm with its hand reversed (at birth). Obviously, Truman's right hand is about to be grasped by an unidentified person at the meeting who was NOT Hiss.

Carpozi gave a fanciful 'description' of "illegals" who were being trained at the Soviet Marx-Engels Institute in Gorki (12-13), strongly suggesting his primary source was the FBI. See also Carpozi's commentary on "illegals" and "legals," again suggesting Carpozi's source and ultimately all his "spy" sources were J. Edgar Hoover, the Director of the FBI.

117   Carpozi 81.

118   Carpozi 83: Carpozi, of course, never named Ruth Paine; but see CD 435 page 8.

119   The Bureau sting did not reportedly involve Ruth Paine.

120   Carpozi 87. The East-West Exchange history is apparently still being protected by U.S. intelligence. One of the few documents covering that history: Guy E. Coriden, "The Intelligence Hand in East-West Exchange Visits," written sometime in the late 1950s for the IAC Ad Hoc Committee on Exchanges, is a bland 'review' of "the possibilities of a gain to the United States from a technical and intelligence point of view." The IAC was dissolved

on September 15, 1958. Coriden's paper, as late as "2 July 96" still heavily "sanitized" after a "CIA Historical Review Program Release," can be recovered at http://cia.gov/csi/docs/v02i3a09p_0001.htm.

[121] 2 H 385-386.

[122] 9 H 470.

[123] Posner 101.

[124] 10 H 24.

[125] The Warren Commission at least began an inquiry; the House Select Committee on Assassinations never called either Ruth Paine or her husband to testify. Before the HSCA had finished its deliberations, a set of important questions to be put to Ruth Paine had been delivered to the committee: see Evica 299-300.

[126] 2 H 431.

[127] R 726.

[128] Jerry Rose, *Fourth Decade*, Volume 5 #4, May 1998, cited in Bill Kelly, "Philadelphia Quakers with Oswald in Mexico City," in *Fairplay Magazine* on line at http://www.acorn.net/jfkplace, hereafter cited as Kelly, "Philadelphia."

[129] See Essay One and Essay Two, and *INTERCEPT*.

[130] See later: both Ruth Paine's family (the Hydes) and her husband's families (the Paines and Youngs) had significant government, military, and intelligence links (see earlier).

[131] The Friends House was sometimes identified as a "camp" or "haven."

[132] The Alcaraz allegations are based on FBI reports, sifted through Bill Kelly, "Philadelphia," and Anthony Summers, *Not in Your Lifetime* (New York: Marlowe & Co., 1998) 441, hereafter cited as Summers *Not*.

[133] Kelly "Philadelphia."

[134] Kelly "Philadelphia."

[135] Kelly "Philadelphia."

[136] Kelly "Philadelphia."

[137] Jerry Rose, sifted through Kelly "Philadelphia."

[138] Kelly "Philadelphia."

[139] Kelly "Philadelphia."

[140] Phillip Agee, *Inside the Company* (New York: Stonehill, 1975) 530, hereafter cited as Agee.

[141] Agee 530.

[142] "With the Quaker connection, there seems to be an underlying thread of detached financial and administrative assistance from a number of 'non-profit' religious oriented charity organizations" in the Oswald story: Kelly "Philadelphia."

[143] David Wise, *Nightmover* (New York: HarperCollins Publishers, 1995) 42, hereafter cited as Wise *Nightmover*.

[144] Lansdale's career ran from the Philippines to Vietnam and, some, believe, to Dealey Plaza: for a beginning look at Lansdale, see Blum, 40-43 and 137-139; Prouty, 11, 59-61, 107, 134-135, 174, 193-197, 199, 269-270, 288, 290, 374, 389, 406-407, 411-412, 414, 443; Newman JFK, 3-7, 20, 24-26, 34, 36-39, 41, 48-49, 56, 59, 72-73, 85, 130-136, 145, 146, and 318-319; and Scott *Deep*, 31, 275, 377-378: Scott affirmed Lansdale, of course, as the boss of Mongoose, but he

was careful not to subscribe to the Oliver Stone/Prouty charges against Lansdale: see 377-378. Also, for Lansdale, see earlier.

[145] Blum 37-43.

[146] See Essay Six.

[147] Sterling Seagrave, *The Marcos Dynasty* (New York: Harper & Row, Publishers, 1988) 143, hereafter cited as Seagrave: see 142 and 144-145.

[148] Seagrave 147; see also 147-154.

[149] Sylvia Meagher, for example, called attention to Ruth's "loftiness" (217), her contradictions (217), and her very un-Quaker behavior toward Lee Harvey Oswald (217-219).

[150] Ruth Paine had still another religious connection with possible intelligence connections: as a Quaker, she "taught Russian at St. Mark's School for Boys, a local Episcopal prep school." Wertz 21.

[152] FBI reports of June, 1964, summarized in Wertz 21.

[153] Wertz 21.

[154] Wertz 21.

[155] The following account is based on a personal communication from Mary Hughes Ferrell.

[156] Pricilla Johnson McMillan reported (without elaboration) that Ruth and Michael Paine "belonged to a Unitarian congregation . . . ." (386) As did other Warren Report supporters, McMillan ignored relevant and readily available Paine/Unitarian/Oswald materials. For example, Raymond Krystinik, a Bell Helicopter research engineer, met his friend and Bell co-worker Michael Paine at an American Civil Liberties Union meeting on the campus of Southern Methodist University, held the night of October 25'h, 1963. Paine had invited Lee Harvey Oswald to the meeting and introduced him to Krystinik; Michael Paine had an earlier conversation with Krystinik concerning Michael's fear he would not be able to fulfill his Unitarian tithe pledge; and just before the ACLU meeting, Michael Paine briefed his friend Krystinik on Oswald's politics. Rev. Byrd Helligas, the assistant pastor at Michael and Ruth Paines' First Unitarian Church in Dallas, was in charge of monitoring the ACLU's coffee supply and running the slide projector at the meeting. Krystinik, Paine, Oswald, and Helligas were involved in at least one reported conversation during the ACLU meeting. On December 1, 1963, ten days after the JFK assassination, a national newspaper quoted Helligas concerning that conversation with Oswald: the Unitarian cleric characterized Lee as "erudite" and "an intellectual." Rev. Helligas elaborated: "He had a good vocabulary. No dangling participles or split infinitives." But by December 19, 1963, when interrogated by the FBI, Helligas maintained he could supply nothing about either Oswald or the other ACLU meeting attendees at SMU. A Bureau sweep of Unitarian sites in search of Oswald connections had apparently taken place between December 1 and December 19. Sources: 9 H 461 and 464; Washington Post, December 1, 1963; CE 1388 (CD 206); and Helligas' statement to Mary Ferrell (below).

[157] Jones 18

[158] Edwin Black, *War against the Weak* (New York: Four Walls Eight Windows, 2003)

[159] Black: see, for example, 236-237.

[160] Black 236.

[161] Black 236.

[162] Black 237.

[163] Black 237.

[164] Black 238.

[165] Black xv.

[166] Black xv.

[167] Black xv.

[168] Black xvi-xvii.

[169] Black throughout.

[170] Douglas A. Blackmon, "A Breed Apart . . .": *Wall Street Journal*, August 17, 1999, reprinted at http://alex constantine.50 megs.com/ws_journal_on.html (6 pages at site), 3, hereafter cited as Blackmon.

[171] Meehan Reports: Mary Meehan, "Eugenics and the Power Elite," first appeared in *Social Justice Review*, November-December, 1997 and revised, July, 2001, posted at Meehan Reports: http://members.verizon.net/~meehan4/elite.html, cited hereafter as Meehan.

[172] Meehan.

[173] Blackmon 1.

[174] Blackmon 3. Frederick Henry Osborn, Sr., whose son was a character witness for Michael and Ruth Paine, was Wickliffe Preston Draper's ideological and financial partner in establishing the eugenics-driven Pioneer Fund in 1937. The web of Osborn/Draper family associations included William Draper, Jr., a cousin of Wickliffe Draper, who shared the military/industrial/eugenics mix of the Osborn/Draper right-wing alliance. The following summary is based on Christopher Simpson, *The Splendid Blond Beast* (New York: Grove Press, 1993) with page numbers, and Beth Hurd, "William H. Draper," Rigenweb-L Archives, RootsWeb.com

In the late 1920s and early 1930s, the investment house of Dillon, Read included James Forrestal, Paul Nitze, C. Douglas Dillon (who would run the Treasury Department and the Secret Service under President John F. Kennedy), Ferdinand Eberstadt (who would become a "central figure in the creation of the CIA"), and William Draper, Jr. With Sullivan & Cromwell (including Foster Dulles) acting as investment agent for American companies in Europe, especially in Germany, the money transfers through the banks and investment houses of the U.S. establishment were phenomenal; Draper, Dillon, Read, and the Dulles' brothers cooperated in generating enormous wealth for the elite establishment. Dillon, Read's V.P. William Draper "emerged as one of the most prosperous traders in these markets."(64)

Wickliffe Draper's wealth was based on his immediate family's ownership of "textile mills, patents on textile equipment, and a substantial share of the international trade in fibers."(249) His cousin, William Henry Draper, Jr., had similar textile origins. Noah Draper, an early 19th-century textile worker in England, had five sons; each of them went into textiles. One of those sons established the Massachusetts Draper line that included Wickliffe Draper. Another of the sons, Noah Draper (Jr.) had one son, William H. Draper (Sr.), who was five years old when his father moved to the United States. William's father first worked in textiles in Hebronville, Mass., but began to accumulate real estate, and in 1883 moved to Pawtucket, Rhode Island, now a relatively wealthy Republican and Methodist Episcopalian.

William H. Draper (Sr.) was first a mill worker, later a traveling jewelry salesman, then a retail jewelry store owner on North Main St. in Providence, and, finally following his father's lead, a real estate investment figure. His wealth grew appreciably, and he became one of the leaders of Rhode Island society: in 1913-14, for example, he was the "Commodore" of the Edgewood Yacht Club, Cranston, R.I., on Narragansett Bay.

His son, William H. Draper, Jr. would achieve prestige and power in the upper divisions of the National Security State, sharing conservative and even reactionary interests with his Draper cousin's family and the Osborn family.

In 1932, William H. Draper, Jr. had already financed the International Eugenics Congress, a longstanding Draper/Osborn interest. At the end of World War II, associates of Draper in the War Department and the Navy (Secretary Forrestal, former president of Draper's old firm Dillon, Reed) "engineered Draper's appointment as chief of the economic division of the joint Allied Control Council for Germany (the central occupation government at the time) and as director of economic policy for the German territories administered by the U.S." (248) In brief, Draper became the most powerful individual determining both the future financial and industrial power of Germany and the director of "denazification programs aimed at German bankers and businessmen." (248) Loyal to his class and financial interests, William H. Draper, Jr. destroyed the denazification programs and turned back Germany to the very banking and investment leaders who had supported Adolph Hitler.(249-253; 262-263) After Draper, of course, came John J. McCloy.

General William H. Draper, Jr. became a member of the Army's General Staff, 1945-1947; Under Secretary of War, 1947; and Undersecretary of the Army, 1947-1949. Draper was also called upon to cooperate with the Bureau of the Budget in shaping President Truman's 1947-1948 budgets.

Draper was a key figure in the population control/eugenics movement in the United States (joining the Draper/Osborn family fusion in behavior modification), holding leading positions in a half-dozen highly-influential population control organizations. At the direction of President Eisenhower in 1958, Draper, a four-star general and Chair of the U.S. Committee on Foreign, Military, and Economic Aid, produced the "Draper Report," advocating eugenics for the poorer nations of the world, an obvious population (and nation) control strategy.(Tobin)

[175] Blackmon.

[176] Barry Mehler, "In Genes We Trust: When Science Bows to Racism," posted at http://www. sntp.net/eugenics/genetics_1.htm, pp. 1-9 at site, 3-4, cited hereafter as Mehler.

[177] Mehler 4.

[178] Mehler 4.

[179] Mehler 4.

[180] Mehler 4.

[181] Blackmon 3-4.

[182] Blackmon 3.

[183] Blackmon 3.

[184] Blackmon 3.

[185] Blackmon 1, 3, 4.

[186] Blackman 3.

[187] Blackmon 5-6.

[188] Mehler 4; see also Black, throughout, especially summaries on xv-xxii.

[189] "Constructing a Postwar World: Background and Context," in "Constructing a Postwar World [:] The G.I. Roundtable Series in Context," at http://www.theha.org/Projects/GIroundtable/Analysis/Analysis1 . . . seven pages, 2, cited hereafter as Constructing.

[190] Constructing 2.

[191] Constructing 2.

[192] Constructing 2.

[193] Constructing 2.

[194] Constructing 2.

[195] Constructing 1, 2-3, 4.

[196] Constructing 4-5.

[197] Black 422.

[198] Black 422-423.

[199] Barbara LaMonica and Stephen Jones, two leading Paine researchers, discovered an important Frederick Osborn, Sr., document in Philadelphia. The letter illuminates both the Dulles/Page/Osborn and NCFE/CFF reticulations. Barbara LaMonica has graciously shared a copy of that document with me, hereafter cited as Osborn.

[200] Chester 249.

[201] Larry Collins, *The Free Europe Committee: American Weapon of the Cold War* (Carlton University [doctoral thesis on microfiche], 1975) 277, 302, 320, hereafter cited as Collins.

[202] Chester 248-249 and 179 and 209 on relations between the National Committee for a Free Europe and the Crusade for Freedom.

[203] Osborn.

[204] Osborn.

[205] Osborn.

[206] Osborn.

[207] Hoover Institution Archives: RFE/RL Records . . . at http://171.66.113.76/exhibit1/exhibits1_3.php, hereafter cited as Hoover.

[208] Osborn.

[209] Osborn.

[210] Osborn.

[211] Hoover.

[212] The Hoover site noted without comment that "the Crusade for Freedom never raised enough money to actually fund RFE—the CIA subsidized both radios [RFE and RL] until 1972 . . . ."

[213] Osborn.

[214] Osborn.

[215] Noel L. Griese, *Arthur W. Page[:] Publisher, Public Relations Pioneer, Patriot* (Atlanta: Anvil Publishers, Inc., 2001) throughout, hereafter cited as Griese.

[216] Griese 49, 60, 64.

217 Griese throughout.

218 Griese 233. See also the Arthur W. Page Society site at http://awpagessociety.com/public/about/block.html, hereafter cited as Page.

219 Griese 233.

220 Griese 254-256.

221 Griese 246.

222 Griese 248, 250-251.

223 Page.

224 Collins 322-323.

225 Griese 360-361.

226 Michael Nelson, *War of the Black Heavens* (Syracuse, New York: Syracuse University Press, 1997) 47-48, hereafter cited as Nelson.

227 To sort out the major elements of this mix of the elite establishment primarily from the perspective of Arthur Page's several careers with reference to both Allen Dulles and Frederick Osborn, see Griese, 344-347, 258-260, 355-366, 372-374, 384, 386, 401-402 note # 141, and throughout. For a splendid study of psyops experience, theory, and practice, see Christopher Simpson, *Science of Coercion* (New York: Oxford University Press, 1994), where a single reference to Frederick Osborn (60) is imbedded in discussions of Osborn's Morale Research Branch, 26-29, 34-35, and 58-60; General McClure 26, 35-36; the Army's Psychological Warfare Division, 25-27, 29, and 35; the Carnegie Corporation, 58, 59-60, 102, 112; the OPC and Wisner, 39-40, 45, 49; the Philippines and Lansdale 74-75; C.D. Jackson, 27, 75; the OSS and the OWI, 24-29, 32-34; DeWitte Poole, 25-26, 50, 131; and the National Committee for a Free Europe, Radio Free Europe, and Radio Liberty, 50, 126, 131. See also Simpson's irreplaceable "Bibliographic Essay." Finally, with a shift in focus, see Simpson, *Blowback*, for the reticulate complexities of the NCFE, CFF, RFE, RL, CIA funding and control, the International Rescue Committee, and the employment of Nazis, 125, 126, 127, 128, 128-129, 200, 205, 217, 219, 227, 228-229, 293 note #3, 317 note #1.

# Epilogue: Notes

[1]  Reticulaton: a three-dimensional structure. The eight essays may be read in any order, anticipating a future hypertext for the given information and accompanying analysis. Throughout this Epilogue, the specific essays relevant to the points being made are cited in the endnotes.

[2]  Essay Four.

[3]  Essay Five.

[4]  Essay Four.

[5]  Essay Four.

[6]  Essay One and Essay Seven.

[7]  Essay Three.

[8]  Essay Three and Essay Seven.

[9]  Essay One, Essay Three, and Essay Severn.

[10]  Essay Seven.

[11]  Essay Seven.

[12]  Essay Seven.

[13]  Essay Three.

[14]  Essay Two.

[15]  Essay One and Essay Three.

[16]  Essay One.

[17]  Essay Four.

[18]  Essay One, Essay Three, and Essay Six.

[19]  Essay Six.

[20]  Essay One, Essay Three, and Essay Six.

[21]  Essay One, Essay Three, and Essay Six. Throughout the histories of the OSS and CIA, Allen Dulles and John Foster Dulles, the manipulation of religious individuals and groups, Albert Schweitzer College, and Lee Harvey Oswald a strong, recognizable stream of psychological warfare activities (psyops) is discernible.

[22]  Essay Six. Since 1975, I have published one book, ten articles and given thirty major presentations at national conferences on the career and the death of John F. Kennedy. The long article "Perfect Cover" (see note 31, below) is the best summary source of my research and analysis. "Perfect Cover" is now being extensively revised.

[23]  Essay Six.

378

24 Scott *Deep* 246. See Scott 242-246 for his analysis of Robert C. Ronstadt, an employee of investigators who were industrial security consultants (Scott 244).

25 See Essay Six on a possible similar cover for Oswald when he went to Europe following his exit from the Marines.

26 Scott *Deep* 246.

27 Scott *Deep* 246.

28 Scott *Deep* 246.

29 Essay Six and Essay Seven.

30 Essay Six.

31 See George Michael Evica, "Perfect Cover," the original version published in *The Assassination Chronicles* Volume 1, Issue 4, December, 1995.

# Index

## A

Adams, James Luther  79,80
Advertising Council of America  181
Africa  71,72
Agency for International Development
 231
AID.  *See* Agency for International
 Development
Albert Schweitzer College  iii,2,6,8,12,
 15,16,20,26,27,32,35,50,65,66,73,8
 1,83,161,226,259. *See also* Oswald,
 Lee Harvey; U.S. Intelligence *under*
 United States
  and Lee Harvey Oswald  64
  curriculum information  15
  documents  26
  Oswald application  26
  scholarship  70
  student list  73
  student recruitment  68
  summer programs  67,68
Alcaraz, Homobono Amo  247
America  142,252
Americans  50,152
  racism  251
  young  165
American Admissions Committee  81
American Churches Committee for
  Refugees  106
American Embassy Paris  13,44
American Episcopal Church  129
American Establishment
  139,140,148,151

American Federal Council of Churches.
  *See* American Federal Council of the
  Churches of Christ
American Federal Council of the
  Churches of Christ  114,147
American Friends of Albert Schweitzer
  College  68,75,85,93,130,133,136,13
  7,227. *See also* American Friends of
  Albert Schweitzer College, Inc
American Friends of Albert Schweitzer
  College, Inc.  67,228. *See also*
  American Friends of Albert
  Schweitzer College
American Friends of German Freedom
  94,95
American Friends Service Committee
  105,248
American Jewish Joint Distribution
  Committee  98
American Presbyterian Church  129
American Relief Center, The  100.
  *See also* Centre American de Secours
American Unitarian Association
  66,68,81,98,104,222
  Department of World Churches  69
AMLASH  46,48
AMLASH-1  46. *See also* under Cubela,
  Rolando
Amman, Reverend  76
Angleton, James Jesus  12,18,20,29,45
Anglican Church of England  129
Ankara  101